DATE DUE

SEP 2 8 '95			
DE 1 4 '96			
Jan 23 97			

The Thirty-Fifth State

A DOCUMENTARY HISTORY
OF WEST VIRGINIA

Edited by

Elizabeth Cometti and Festus P. Summers

WEST VIRGINIA UNIVERSITY LIBRARY
MORGANTOWN
1966

"View of mountain region (the seat of war) in Western Virginia, from the summit of Limestone Mountain." *Harper's Weekly,* Nov. 23, 1861.

THIRD PRINTING 1970

McCLAIN PRINTING COMPANY
PARSONS, WEST VIRGINIA

The publication of this book was
made possible by a grant from the

WEST VIRGINIA UNIVERSITY
FOUNDATION

The sun does not always shine in West Virginia, but the people always do.—PRESIDENT JOHN F. KENNEDY at Charleston, June 20, 1963.

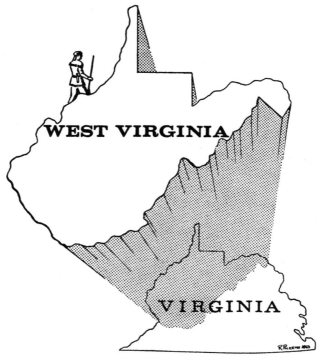

—West Virginia Centennial Commission

Acknowledgments

The selections here printed have been drawn from a variety of sources, chiefly from manuscript collections, official documents, newspapers, periodicals, and journals. Silent corrections of the texts have been held to a minimum.

The editors take pleasure in expressing their gratitude to those who have so generously aided them in the preparation of this work:

Anita C. Hutcherson and Frances Krauskopf for editorial assistance.

Otis K. Rice for special co-operation.

Edward V. McMichael for helpful suggestions.

William C. Blizzard, Ruth Woods Dayton, James G. Jones, Huntington Galleries for supplying materials.

Millard K. Bushong, Edwin P. Cubby, John C. Harlan, Ambrose E. McCaskey, George F. Moore, Robert L. Morris, Otis K. Rice, William P. Turner, James C. Welden, Isaiah Woodward, John A. Young for deletions and corrections.

J. William Bonner, Harry W. Ernst, Samuel Rosenman, Boyd B. Stutler, Roul Tunley, American Heritage Publishing Company, Inc., *The Atlantic Monthly, Broadcasting,* The Estate of Franklin D. Roosevelt, Harper & Row, The Historical Society of Pennsylvania, The Macmillan Company, The Mount Vernon Ladies' Association of the Union, Ohio State Museum, Princeton University Press, Rutgers University, *The Saturday Evening Post,* University of Minnesota Press, University of North Carolina Press for permission to use copyrighted materials.

The Library of Bethany College, Marshall University Library, West Virginia Department of Archives and History, West Virginia University Library for assistance in locating materials.

Claude Worthington Benedum Foundation, Student Government of Marshall University for financial assistance.

March 17, 1966   E. C.

                                                           F. P. S.

Introduction

West Virginia became the thirty-fifth state of the Union on June 20, 1863, nearly two weeks before the battle of Gettysburg. The creation of the mountain state was the culmination of more than a half century of sectional conflict which had kept eastern and western Virginia divided almost as unalterably as had the physical barrier of the mountains between them. Like most of its streams, the Trans-Allegheny was socially and economically, though not historically and politically, oriented toward the west. An adequate system of internal improvements linking east and west might have counterbalanced divisions stemming from geography, but such improvements the Virginia government with obstinate short-sightedness failed to provide despite repeated urging on the part of the west. Yet in 1861 when Virginians had to decide between loyalty to the state or to the nation, at least 19,000 votes were cast in present West Virginia for the Ordinance of Secession as opposed to 34,000 against; and at the outbreak of hostilities most of the men in the southwestern counties of Virginia and impressive minorities in the northwestern were ready to take up arms in defense of the Commonwealth. Even after the final break with the parent state, West Virginia retained many marks of the Virginia heritage—subtle ones of accent, cuisine, and social attitudes, along with the stronger ones of family connections and common political experience. It was not by accident that the new state maintained segregated public schools until the 1950's and that its constitution drafted by Bourbon Democrats in 1872 contained provisions inspired by the Virginia constitution of 1851.

Geographically and historically West Virginia defies easy classification. It is not wholly Southern, for its northern panhandle juts northward almost sixty-four miles from the Mason-Dixon line. Nor is it entirely in the Ohio River basin. The Potomac River rises in West Virginia and flows eastward between West Virginia and Maryland until it meets the Shenandoah at Harpers Ferry. Both in size—24,282 square miles—and in population—1,860,421, according to the 1960 census—West Virginia is a small state. The mean altitude is 1,500 feet, the highest of any state east of the Mississippi River.

West Virginia has an abundance of mineral resources, chief among which is bituminous coal. Coal has been king of the state's economy, indicator of its prosperity, and the object of its most intensive scientific research. The state also has oil and gas, as well as extensive deposits of salt brine, sandstone, limestone, sand, gravel, and nonrefractory clays. The extractive and related industries have dotted the steep slopes and narrow valleys with tipples, derricks, and industrial plants of ever increasing size and complexity; they have also left ghost towns and deep gashes from strip mining operations on the once verdant hillsides.

Despite the physical challenge which western Virginia presented to early travelers, they could still exclaim over its spectacular vistas. "The passage of the Potomac through the Blue Ridge is, perhaps, one of the most stupendous scenes in nature," quite "worth a voyage across the Atlantic", wrote Thomas Jefferson. He might have listed other sights of equal grandeur: the canyons of the Cheat, the New, and the Blackwater Rivers, and the narrow gorge of the South Branch called the Trough; Pinnacle Rock and Seneca Rocks; Blackwater Falls; Canaan Valley and Germany Valley; the vast panorama from the summit of East River Mountain; indeed, many parts of the state untouched by the ravaging hand of industrialization.

Although the recorded history of West Virginia opens in the seventeenth century with the advent of the Europeans, the Paleo-Indians, hunters of mammals long since extinct, roamed over this area about ten millennia ago. Their successors, the Archaic peoples, depended largely upon river mussel for their food supply, as is evidenced by the various shell middens found along the river bottoms. The most impressive remains of the West Virginia aborigines belong to the Adena period of c. 1,000 B.C. to 1 A.D. Commonly known as the Moundbuilders because of the tumuli in which they buried their ochre-painted dead, the Adenas left many artifacts such as projectile points, scrapers, gorgets, pipes, celts, shell and copper beads, rare fragments of textiles, plates of mica, and cord-marked sherds, in addition to the earthworks containing these evidences of their culture. The

XII

two largest mounds are at Moundsville, near the mouth of Grave Creek, and at South Charleston in the Kanawha Valley.

Equally significant, if less conspicuous, are the post-Adena sites, especially those of the Fort Ancient culture of which there are some along the New and the Kanawha Rivers and down the Ohio from the mouth of the Little Kanawha. One such site at Mount Carbon in Fayette County, once a palisaded village, has yielded artifacts of bone and stone and pottery from at least three cultural series—the Armstrong, Buck Garden, and Fort Ancient. Another fortified village in the Kanawha Valley, near Buffalo, probably had a population of at least five hundred and covered an area of from ten to fifteen acres.

Although the aborigines of this area never developed a written language, they left intriguing marks of man's eternal desire for self-expression. Among the most curious found thus far are the petroglyphs on the Guyandotte River in Cabell County and those at the Hamilton Farm site in Monongalia County. Pioneer archeologists of the nineteenth century noted and made sketches of these "sculptured rocks," as they called them, on which the Indians had engraved the outlines of human figures, birds, fish, and animals, and tracks of deer, bear, wolf, turkey, and other wild creatures.

Whatever the cause—disease, intertribal strife, emigration, but certainly not the lack of game—there were not many Indians living in the Trans-Allegheny at the coming of the white men. The Mohetan Indians of the upper New River Valley, mentioned by Robert Fallam in 1671, were probably the Monetons whom Gabriel Arthur met during his sojourn with the Cherokees in 1673-74. At some time or other and for varying periods the Cherokee, the Conoy—from whom the name Kanawha is probably derived, the Honniasont, the Susquehanna, the Delaware, and the Shawnee also lived in present West Virginia. When explorers began to penetrate this rugged area they found a vast wilderness broken here and there by "old fields" that the Indians had once cultivated, and by towns that they would soon abandon.

XIII

Table of Contents

Acknowledgments _____ IX
Introduction _____ XI

PART ONE: WEST VIRGINIA IN THE OLD DOMINION

I. Claims and Exploration

1. The Second Charter of Virginia, 1609_____ 3
2. The Expedition of Batts and Fallam_____ 5
3. John Fontaine's Journal of the Spotswood Expedition_____ 11
4. The Fairfax Line—Thomas Lewis's Journal of 1746_____ 16
5. Western Counties_____ 22
6. Expedition of Celoron_____ 24
7. Instructions to Christopher Gist and Second Journey of Gist_____ 26

II. Two Wars: The French and Indian and Dunmore's

8. Report on the Present State of Virginia_____ 35
9. Advertisements _____ 40
10. Preston's Journal of the Sandy Creek Expedition_____ 41
11. Washington's Proposals for Frontier Defense_____ 47
12. Preston's Register_____ 51
13. William Fleming to Governor Fauquier_____ 56
14. The Royal Proclamation of 1763_____ 58
15. Proclamation of Governor Fauquier_____ 62
16. Dunmore's War—Letter of Devereux Smith_____ 63
17. Lord Dunmore's Proclamation, April 25, 1774_____ 67
18. Answer of the Shawnees to the Virginians_____ 68
19. Dunmore Takes the Offensive—Letter to Andrew Lewis_____ 69
20. Colonel William Fleming's Journal of the Expedition Led by
    Colonel Andrew Lewis Against the Ohio Indians_____ 70
21. Logan's Speech _____ 76
22. Fort Gower Address and Resolutions, November 5, 1774_____ 78
23. Dunmore's Report to Lord Dartmouth, Secretary of State
    for the Colonies, December 24, 1774_____ 80

III. The Revolution

24. Letter from Fort Blair (Point Pleasant), June 12, 1775_____ 87
25. Addresses at the Conference Held in Pittsburgh, September,
    October, 1775_____ 90

26. New State Movements—Proposed State of Westsylvania_____ 94
27. The Murder of Chief Cornstalk _____ 96
28. Defense of Virginia—Letter of Patrick Henry to William Fleming__ 99
29. Attack on Fort Donnally, May 29, 1778_____102
30. Military Grants_____ _____106
31. Loyalism in Western Virginia—Garret Van Meter to Jefferson,
        April 14, 1781_____107
32. The Second Siege of Fort Henry—Report of Colonel Ebenezer
        Zane and Exploit of Elizabeth Zane_____109

IV. From Frontier to Towns and an Occasional Mansion

33. *Notes on the Settlements and Indian Wars*_____115
34. "Laws," from *Notes on the State of Virginia*_____123
35. An Act for Establishing a Town at Warm Springs_____ 130
36. An Act to Regulate the Inoculation of Smallpox _____133
37. Washington's Journey, 1784 _____135
38. An Act in Behalf of James Rumsey_____141
39. The Virginia-Pennsylvania Boundary Dispute—Report of the
        Commissioners _____143
40. Adam Stephen on the Ratification of the Federal Constitution____145
41. Journal of Col. John May of Boston, 1789_____147
42. Daniel Boone's List_____153
43. The Whiskey Rebellion_____154
44. Blennerhassett Island_____156

V. Education and Religion

45. Education in Western Virginia—Kanawha County_____161
46. Abstract of School Commissioners' Reports _____167
47. An Act Incorporating the Trustees of Bethany College _____168
48. Religion in Western Virginia—Philip Vickers Fithian: Journal____172
49. The Journal of the Reverend Francis Asbury_____175
50. Camp Meetings_____183
51. Constitution and Covenant of Simpson Creek Baptist Church____185

VI. Economic Developments and Tourist Attractions

52. John Marshall in West Virginia_____191
53. The Kanawha Salt Industry_____197
54. Report of Claudius Crozet_____204
55. The National Arsenal at Harpers Ferry_____207
56. Wheeling City c. 1830_____209
57. Formal Opening of the Wheeling Bridge, 1849_____213
58. Public Improvements in the Trans-Allegheny_____215
59. Opening of the Baltimore and Ohio Railroad at Wheeling_____217
60. Extension of Railway Facilities _____221
61. Charles Ellet, Jr., Proposes Meadow River Reservoir_____223
62. The Springs of Virginia_____227

VII. Sectionalism and Slavery—From Argument to Violence

63. The Constitutional Convention of 1829-30 _____237
64. The Ruffner Pamphlet (1847) _____246
65. Speech of George W. Summers at the Convention of 1850-51____251
66. Taxation and Finance—Constitution of 1851_____261
67. Reverend Campbell on the Fugitive Slave Law_____262
68. An Affair of Honor—The Clemens-Wise Duello_____265
69. John Brown's Raid _____269
70. John Brown's Death and Last Words as Reported by
    Porte Crayon_____275

PART TWO: WEST VIRGINIA

VIII. A House Divided—Secession and Reorganization

71. The Presidential Election of 1860 in West Virginia_____285
72. The Virginia Ordinance of Secession _____286
73. How West Virginia Delegates Voted on the Ordinance
    of Secession_____288
74. Last Train From Richmond_____290
75. Mayor Sweeney's Proclamations_____293
76. The Clarksburg Convention, April 22, 1861_____295
77. The Southern Rights Convention, April 26, 1861_____297
78. The Baltimore and Ohio in a Dilemma_____299
79. Judge George W. Thompson's Instructions to the Ohio County
    Grand Jury, May 10, 1861_____300
80. Resolutions Adopted by the First Wheeling Convention,
    May 15, 1861_____304
81. John S. Carlile and Waitman T. Willey Find Common Ground___308
82. Keynote Address at the Second Wheeling Convention,
    June 11, 1861_____310
83. Dennis B. Dorsey, Jr., Urges Immediate Statehood _____312
84. Chester D. Hubbard Supports Restoration of Virginia
    Government _____315
85. Governor John Letcher's Proclamation to the People of
    Northwestern Virginia, June 14, 1861_____316
86. West Virginia's Declaration of Independence, June 17, 1861_____319
87. John S. Carlile Supports Reorganization of the Virginia
    Government _____321
88. The Reorganization Ordinance Adopted June 19, 1861_____323
89. Francis H. Pierpont's Inaugural Address, June 20, 1861_____325

IX. West Virginia: The Thirty-Fifth State

90. The Edward Bates Letter _____331
91. An Ordinance Establishing the State of Kanawha _____333
92. Naming West Virginia _____337

93. Gordon Battelle's Plea for a Free State _____341
94. The Baltimore and Ohio Makes a Panhandle_____343
95. Restored Virginia Gives Consent _____345
96. Senator Willey Presents West Virginia's Application for
        Statehood _____347
97. Senator John S. Carlile and the Willey Amendment_____349
98. The House Debate on West Virginia Statehood_____353
99. The Cabinet Divides: The Case For and Against_____358
100. Final Pleas for the Statehood Bill _____364
101. President Lincoln on the Admission of West Virginia_____369
102. The West Virginia Statehood Law_____371
103. The Issue of Compensated Emancipation_____373
104. President Lincoln's Statehood Proclamation, April 20, 1863_____376
105. Governor Arthur I. Boreman's Inaugural Address, June 20, 1863__378
106. The West Virginia State Seal, Coat of Arms and Motto_____383

X. Four Years of Civil War

107. Charles J. Faulkner and the Bill of Rights, 1861_____389
108. Pinkertons Spy on General Wise, 1861_____392
109. The Union Advance and General George B. McClellan's
        Proclamations _____395
110. General Robert E. Lee's Report on the Battle of Philippi_____397
111. General McClellan Faces a New Confederate Challenge_____401
112. Governor Francis H. Pierpont Requests Federal Military
        Assistance _____402
113. General George B. McClellan: "Napoleon of the West"_____403
114. War Upon the Rails_____405
115. Secessionist Sentiment in the Kanawha Valley, 1861_____407
116. The Battle of Carnifex Ferry, September 10, 1861_____408
117. Harpers Ferry in Wartime, 1862_____412
118. Twisting the Rails, 1862_____415
119. The Jenkins Raid, 1862 _____416
120. Confederate Occupation of the Kanawha Valley, 1862_____418
121. Oil and Troubled Waters_____420
122. The Jones-Imboden Raid, 1863_____422
123. The Great Skedaddle: Hunter's Retreat, 1864 _____425
124. Rutherford B. Hayes in West Virginia, 1861-1864_____428
125. Those Who Served_____434

XI. The Ordeal of Reconstruction, 1865-1872

126. A Trip to Charles Town in 1865_____441
127. The Test Oath and Proscription Amendment_____443
128. The Continuing Strife_____444
129. Peter G. Van Winkle Defends President Andrew Johnson_____449
130. The Liberal Republican Movement_____452
131. The Flick Amendment_____455

132. Virginia Sues to Recover Berkeley and Jefferson Counties_____457
133. The Constitution of 1872_____462
134. J. H. Diss Debar's Promotional Campaign_____464

XII. The Bourbon Years, 1871-1897

135. Tax Exemptions and Fiscal Policy, 1863-1883_____471
136. The Great Railway Strike of 1877_____474
137. The Floating Capital_____476
138. Archibald W. Campbell: Republican Profile_____478
139. Resources and Advantages of West Virginia, 1880-1900_____479
140. Johnson N. Camden Defends Standard Oil_____482
141. A Protest Against Absentee Ownership, 1884_____483
142. Railroad Discrimination Against the Short Haul_____485
143. A Liberal Democrat in the Statehouse_____487
144. Conditions in an Early Mining Town_____490
145. The Beginning of Rural Free Delivery_____492

XIII. The Progressive Era

146. Establishment of the West Virginia Geological and Economic
     Survey _____497
147. Reforming the Tax Laws_____500
148. Establishment of a Department of Archives and History, 1905___505
149. Establishment of a State Department of Mines_____508
150. The Failure of the Conservation Movement_____510
151. The Maryland Boundary Dispute_____513
152. The Virginia Debt Controversy_____516
153. The Temperance and Prohibition Movement_____518
154. The Paint Creek-Cabin Creek Strike, 1912-1913_____522
155. Mother Jones—"Angel of the Miners"_____529
156. West Virginia in World War I_____533

XIV. Between World Wars

157. The Hitchman Case, 1917_____539
158. The March on Logan and the Treason Trials_____544
159. West Virginia Tries to Pre-empt Natural Gas_____551
160. State 4-H Camp at Jackson's Mill_____553
161. West Virginia Enacts a Gross Sales Tax_____555
162. The Tax Limitation Amendment, 1932_____558
163. West Virginia Establishes a Conservation Commission, 1933_____560
164. The Roosevelts Come to Arthurdale_____566
165. West Virginia's Contribution to World War II_____573

XV. Education in West Virginia

166. Test Oath Required of Teachers_____583
167. Superintendent White's Report_____584
168. The Normal Schools_____587

169. West Virginia University_____592
170. Alexander L. Wade, *A Graduating System for Country Schools*__598
171. *Up From Slavery*—Negro Education in West Virginia_____600
172. Progress in Education—Acts of 1939 and 1941_____605
173. West Virginia State Board of Education *et al* v. Barnette *et al.*___608
174. The Strayer Survey_____612
175. Location of the West Virginia Medical School_____617
176. Integration in West Virginia_____618
177. The Claude Worthington Benedum Foundation—Will of
         Michael L. Benedum_____620

XVI. Recent Years

178. The Little Report_____627
179. Public Welfare in West Virginia_____630
180. In Appreciation of Art_____631
181. Coal Production and Coal Reserves_____633
182. The Population Decline_____635
183. The Primary That Made a President: West Virginia 1960_____637
184. West Virginia Establishes a Department of Commerce, 1961____641
185. Railroad Mergers_____643
186. West Virginia: A "Paradoxical State"_____646
187. The Forum of the Future_____650

      INDEX _____657

ILLUSTRATIONS

1. View of Mountain—Frontispiece
2. George Washington as a Virginia Colonel of Militia__Opposite page 3
3. President Abraham Lincoln, c. 1862_____Opposite page 285
4. Senator John F. Kennedy and West Virginia Secretary of State
      Joe F. Burdett, February 6, 1960_____Opposite page 654

Part One: West Virginia In The Old Dominion

I. Claims and Exploration

George Washington as a Virginia Colonel of Militia.
Courtesy Library of Congress.

1. The Second Charter of Virginia, 1609

The first charter of Virginia, which was issued in April, 1606, authorized the London Company and the Plymouth Company to plant colonies between the thirty-fourth and the forty-first parallels and the thirty-eighth and forty-fifth parallels, respectively, but neither colony was to settle within a hundred miles of the other. Each company was granted control over an area which was to extend fifty miles north and fifty miles south along the seacoast from the first "Seat of their Plantation" and one hundred miles into the interior. The document included provisions for governing and exploiting the colonies and declared that every English subject in them should have and enjoy "all Liberties, Franchises, and Immunities" as "if they had been abiding and born" within the realm of England. The difficulties encountered in the settlement of Jamestown revealed the defects in the first charter and led the London Company to apply for a second one which increased the privileges of the Company and the territory under its jurisdiction and severed connection with the Plymouth Company. The vague "Sea to Sea" provision became a basis for Virginia's extensive western land claims. The original draft of the second charter was probably the work of Sir Edwin Sandys.

JAMES, BY THE GRACE OF GOD, King of *England, Scotland, France,* and *Ireland,* Defender of the Faith, &c. To all, to whom these Presents shall come, Greeting. WHEREAS, at the humble Suit and Request of sundry our loving and well-disposed Subjects, intending to deduce a Colony, and to make Habitation and Plantation of sundry our People in that Part of *America,* commonly called VIRGINIA, and other Parts and Territories in *America,* either appertaining unto Us, or which are not actually possessed of any *Christian* Prince or People, within certain Bounds and Regions, We have formerly, by our Letters-patents, bearing Date the tenth Day of *April,* *i*n the fourth Year of our Reign of *England, France,* and *Ireland,* and of *Scotland* the nine and thirtieth, GRANTED to Sir *Thomas Gates,* Sir *George Somers,* and others, for the more speedy Accomplishment of the said Plantation and Habitation, that they should divide themselves into two Colonies (the one consisting of divers Knights, Gentlemen, Merchants, and others, of our City of *London,* called the FIRST COLONY; And the other consisting of divers Knights, Gentlemen, and others, of our Cities of *Bristol, Exeter,* and Town of *Plimouth,* and other Places, called the SECOND COLONY). And have yielded and granted many and sundry Privileges and Liberties to each Colony, for their quiet settling and good Government therein, as by the said Letters-patents more at large appeareth: . . .

And we do also of our special Grace, certain Knowledge, and mere Motion, give, grant and confirm, unto the said Treasurer and Company, and their Successors, under the Reservations, Limitations, and Declarations hereafter expressed, all those Lands, Countries, and Territories, situate, lying, and being in that Part of *America,* called *Virginia,* from the Point of Land, called Cape of *Point Comfort,* all along the Sea Coast to the Northward, two hundred miles, and from the said Point of *Cape Comfort,* all along the Sea Coast to the Southward, two hundred Miles, and all that Space and Circuit of Land, lying from the Sea Coast of the Precinct aforesaid, up into the Land throughout from Sea to Sea, West and Northwest; And also all the Islands lying within one hundred Miles along the Coast of both Seas of the Precinct aforesaid; Together with all the Soils, Grounds, Havens, and Ports, Mines, as well Royal Mines of Gold and Silver, as other Minerals, Pearls, and precious Stones, Quarries, Woods, Rivers, Waters, Fishings, Commodities, Jurisdictions, Royalties, Privileges, Franchises, and Preheminences within the said Territories, and the Precincts thereof, whatsoever, and thereto, and thereabouts both by Sea and Land, being, or in any sort belonging or appertaining, and which We, by our Letters Patents, may or can grant, in as ample Manner and Sort, as We, or any our noble Progenitors, have heretofore granted to any Company, Body Politic or Corporate, or to any Adventurer or Adventurers, Undertaker or Undertakers of any Discoveries, Plantations, or Traffic, of, in, or into any Foreign Parts whatsoever, and in as large and ample Manner, as if the same were herein particularly mentioned and expressed; TO HAVE AND TO HOLD, possess and enjoy, all and singular the said Lands, Countries, and Territories, with all and singular other the Premises heretofore by these Presents granted, or mentioned to be granted to them, the said Treasurer and Company, their Successors and Assigns forever; To the sole and proper Use of them, the said Treasurer and Company, their Successors and Assigns forever; TO BE HOLDEN of Us, our Heirs and Successors, as of our Manor of *East-Greenwich*, in free and common Soccage, and not in Capite; YIELDING and PAYING therefore, to Us, our Heirs and Successors, the fifth Part only of all Ore of Gold and Silver, that from Time to Time, and at all Times hereafter, shall be there gotten, had, or obtained, for all Manner of Services.— *The Federal and State Constitutions, Colonial Charters, and Other Organic Laws . . .,* edited by Francis Newton Thorpe, VII, 3790-96.

2. The Expedition of Batts and Fallam

Western exploration in Virginia began with the establishment of the colony and steadily advanced during the seventeenth century in spite of Indian hostility and political troubles. Only through exploration could the colonists find the sources of the broad rivers of Virginia, open trade with the Indians, discover mineral resources, patent virgin lands, and establish British claims to the westernmost limits of the continent, as far, indeed, as the Pacific which some people supposed to be only ten days' march beyond the Alleghenies. The outstanding figure in early Virginia exploration was Abraham Wood, who rose from obscurity to a place on the Governor's Council. In 1646 Wood became commander of Fort Henry, which stood on the site of present day Petersburg, Virginia. In compensation for maintaining the post in a state of defense, Wood received six hundred acres of land with the buildings and other appurtenances of the fort, and exemption from all public taxes. In the summer of 1650, Wood and Edward Bland, a merchant of Charles City County, led a small expedition from Fort Henry into the Roanoke valley. This adventure provided the inspiration for Bland's narrative, The Discovery of New Brittaine, *published in London the following year, and induced Wood to send into this western area pack trains laden with the staples of the Indian trade. After his restoration as governor in 1660, William Berkeley not only gave his powerful support to western exploration, but, so he wrote to Lord Arlington in 1669, would have led a company of two hundred gentlemen "to find out the East India sea," and prospect for silver mines, if "unusual and continued Raynes" had not thwarted his plans. Although Berkeley never made the projected expedition, he encouraged John Lederer, a German physician of questionable veracity, to undertake three western journeys (1669-1670) which took the adventurer to the summit of the Blue Ridge.*

The first known expedition to reach a westward flowing stream, the New River, on September 13, 1671, was made under the auspices of Abraham Wood. If the explorers, Thomas Batts and Robert Fallam, did not actually enter what is now West Virginia, they probably came to its boundary in Giles County, Virginia. The account of their journey was written by Fallam.

THOMAS BATTS, THOMAS WOODS and Robert Fallows [Fallam] having received a commission from the honbl Major General Wood for the finding out the ebbing and flowing of the Waters on the other side of the Mountains in order to the discovery of the South Sea accompanied with *Penecute* a great man of the *Apomatack* Indians and Jack Weason, formerly a servant to Major General Wood with five horses set forward from the Apomatacks town . . . being Friday Sept. 1, 1671. That day we traveled above 40 miles, took up our quarters and found that we had travel'd from the *Okenechee* path due West.

Sept. 2. we traveled about 45 miles. . . .

Sept. 3. we traveled west and by south and about three o'clock came to a great swamp a mile and a half or two miles over and very difficult to pass. we led our horses thro' and waded twice over a River emptying itself in Roanoake River. . . . This day we traveled 40 miles good.

Sept. 4. We set forward and about two of the clock arriv'd at the *Sapiny* Indian town. . . . Here we were very joyfully and kindly received with firing of guns and plenty of provisions. We here hired a Sepiny Indian to be our guide toward the *Teteras,* . . .

Sept. 5. Just as we were ready to take horse and march from the *Sapiny's* about seven of the clock in the morning we heard some guns go off from the other side of the River. They were siven Apomatack Indians sent by Major General Wood to accompany us in our Voyage. . . . About eleven of the clock we set forward and that night came to the town of the *Hanathaskies* which we judge to be 25 miles from the *Sapenys,* . . . in an Island on the *Sapony* River, rich Land.

Sept. 6. About 11 of the clock we set forward from the *Hanathaskies;* but left Mr. Thomas Wood at the town dangerously sick of the Flux, and the horse he rode on belonging to Major General Wood was likewise taken with the staggers and a failing in his hinder parts. . . .

Sept. 7. We set forward about three of the clock we had sight of the mountains, we travelled 25 miles over very hilly and stony Ground our course westerly.

Sept. 8. We set out by sunrise and Travelled all day a west and by north course. About one of the clock we came to a Tree mark'd in the past with a coal M. A N I. About four of the clock we came to the foot of the first mountain went to the top and then came to a small descent, and so did rise again and then till we came almost to the bottom was a very steep descent. We travelled all day over very stony, rocky ground and after 30 miles travill this day we came to our quarters at the foot of the mountains due west. We past the *Sapony* River twice this day.

Sept. 9. We . . . travelled west and after a little riding came again to the Supany River where it was very narrow, and ascended the second mountain . . . After we were over that, we came to a very steep descent, at the foot whereof stood the

Tetera Town in a very rich swamp between a branch and the main River of Roanoke circled about with mountains. . . .

[Sept. 9-11.] Saturday night, Sunday and monday we staid at *Toteras. Perceute* being taken very sick of a fever and ague every afternoon, not withstanding on tuesday morning about nine of the clock we resolved to leave our horses with the *Toteras* and set forward.

Sept. 12. We left the town West and by North we travell'd that day sometimes southerly, sometimes westerly as the path went over several high mountains and steep Vallies crossing several branches and the River Roanoke several times all exceedingly stony ground until about four of the clock *Perceute* being taken with his fit and verry weary we took up our quarters by the side of Roanoke River almost at the head of it at the foot of the great mountain. Our course was west and by north, having travell'd 25 miles. At the *Teteras* we hired one of their Indians for our Guide and left one of the *Apomatock* Indians there sick.

Sept. 13. In the morning we set forward early. After we had travelled about three miles we came to the foot of the great mountain and found a very steep ascent so that we could scarse keep ourselves from sliding down again. It continued for three miles with small intermissions of better way. . . . When we were got up to the Top of the mountain and set down very weary we saw very high mountains lying to the north and south as far as we could discern. . . . A very small descent on the other side and as soon as over we found the vallies tending westerly. It was a pleasing tho' dreadful sight to see the mountains and Hills as if piled one upon another. After we had travelled about three miles from the mountains, easily descending ground about 12 of the clock we came to two trees mark'd with a coal MA. NI. the other cut in with MA and several other scratchments.

Hard by a Run just like the swift creek at Mr. Randolph's in Virginia, emptying itself sometimes westerly sometimes northerly with curious meadows on each [side]. Going forward we found rich ground but having curious rising hills and brave meadows with grass about man's hight. many rivers running west-north-west and several Runs from the southerly mountains which we saw as we march'd, which run northerly into the great

River. After we had travelled about 7 miles we came to a very deep descent where are found a great Run which emptied itself so we supposed into the great River northerly. . . . We went over the great run emptying itself northerly into the great River. After we had marched about 6 miles northwest and by north we came to the River again where it was much broader than at the two other places. . . . Here we took up our quarters, after we had waded over, for the night. Due west, the soil, the farther we went [is] the richer and full of bare meadows and old fields. . . .

Sept. 14. We set forward before sunrise our provisions being all spent we travel'd as the path went sometimes westerly sometimes southerly, over good ground but stony, sometimes rising hills and then steep Descents as we march'd in a clear place at the top of a hill we saw lying south west a curious prospect of hills like waves raised by a gentle breese of wind rising one upon another. Mr. Batts supposed he saw sayles: but I rather think them to be white cliffs. We marched about 20 miles this day and about three of the clock we took up our quarters to see if the Indians could kill us some Deer. being west and by north, very weary and hungry and Perceute continued very ill yet desired to go forward. We came this day over several brave runs and hope tomorrow to see the main River again.

Sept. 15. Yesterday in the afternoon and this day we lived a Dog's life—hunger and ease. Our Indians having done their best could kill us no meat. The Deer they said were in such herds and the ground so dry that one or other of them could spy them. About one of the clock we set forward and went about fifteen miles over some exceedingly good, some indifferent ground, . . . As we march'd we met with some wild gooseberries and exceeding large haws with which we were forced to feed ourselves.

Sept. 16. Our guides went from us yesterday and we saw him no more till we returned to the *Toras*. Our Indians went aranging betimes to see and kill us some Deer or meat. One came and told us they heard a Drum and a Gun go off to the northwards. They brought us some exceedingly good Grapes and killed two turkies which were very welcome and with which we feasted ourselves and about ten of the clock set forward and after we had travelled about 10 miles one of our Indians killed us a Deer and presently afterwards we had sight of a curious River like Apamatack River. Its course here was north and so as we suppose runs west about certain curious mountains we saw westward. . . . We understand the *Mohecan* Indians did here formerly live. It cannot be long since for we found corn stalks in the ground.

Sept. 17. Early in the morning we went to seek some trees to mark our Indians being impatient of longer stay by reason it was like to be bad weather, and that it was so difficult to get provisions. We found four trees exceeding fit for our purpose that had been half bared by our Indians, standing after one the other. We first proclaimed the King in these words: "Long live Charles the Second, by the grace of God King of England, Scotland, France, Ireland and Virginia and of all the Territories thereunto belonging, Defender of the faith etc." firing some guns and went to the first tree which we marked . . . CR with a pair of marking irons for his sacred majesty.

Then the next WB for the right honble Governor Sir William Berkley, the third thus: AW for the honourable Major General Wood. The last thus: TB: RF. P. for Perceute who said he would learn Englishman. And on another tree hard by stand these letters one under another TT. N.P. VE. R after we had done we went ourselves down to the river side; but not without great difficulty it being a piece of very rich ground where on the Moketans had formerly lived, and grown up with weeds and small prickly Locusts and Thistles to a very great height that it was almost impossible to pass. . . . When we came to the River side we found it better and broader than expected, much like James River at Col. Stagg's, the falls much like these falls. We imagined by the Water marks it flows here about three feat. It was ebbing Water when we were here. We set up a stick by the Water side but found it ebb very slowly. Our Indians kept such a hollowing that we durst not stay any longer to make further tryal. Immediately upon coming to our quarters we returned homewards and when we were on the top of a Hill we turned about and saw over against us, westerly, over a certain delightful hill a fog arise and a glimmering light as from water. We supposed there to be a great Bay. We came to the *Toteras* Tuesday night where we found our horses, and ourselves wel entertain'd. We immediately had the news of Mr. Byrd and his great company's Discoveries three miles from the *Tetera's* Town. We have found *Mohetan* Indians who having intelligence of our coming were afraid it had been to fight them and had sent him to the *Totera's* to inquire. We gave him satisfaction to the contrary and that we came as friends, presented him with three or four shots of powder. He told us by our Interpreter, that we had [been] from the mountains half way to the place they now live at. That the next town beyond them lived upon plain level, from whence came abundance of salt. That he could inform us no further by reason that there were a great company of Indians that lived upon the great Water.

Sept. 21. After very civil entertainment we came from the *Toteras* and on Sunday morning the 24th we came to the *Hanahaskies.* We found Mr. Wood dead and burried and his horse likewise dead. . . .

Sept. 25. on monday morning we came from thence and reached to the *Sapony's* that night where we stayed till wednesday.

Sept. 27. We came from thence they having been very courteous to us. At night we came to the *Apamatack* Town, hungry, wet and weary.

Oct. 1 being Sunday morning we arrived at Fort Henry. God's holy name be praised for our preservation.—John Clayton's Transcript of the Journal of Robert Fallam, in David I. Bushnell, Jr., "Discoveries Beyond the Appalachian Mountains in September, 1671," *American Anthropologist,* IX, (January-March, 1907), 46-53.

3. John Fontaine's Journal of The Spotswood Expedition

Colonel Alexander Spotswood (1676-1740) soldier, iron producer, deputy postmaster general of the British North American colonies, and lieutenant governor of Virginia (1710-1722), is most commonly remembered in West Virginia for the expedition to the Shenandoah Valley which he led in the summer of 1716. Spotswood was interested in locating good lands and mineral resources and in seeking an overland route to the Great Lakes for the purpose of promoting western trade. The Governor left Williamsburg on August 20 and arrived at Germanna, in the Rapidan valley, four days later. On the 29th, the exploring party of sixty-three men, including four Indians, which had assembled at this place, started westward with seventy-four horses, some dogs, a stock of provisions, and a variety of liquid refreshments. In the course of his journey from the Virginia capital to the Shenandoah (Euphrates) valley, Spotswood covered approximately 438 miles, some of which imposed "abundant fatigue" and required frequent shoeing of horses. In commemoration of the expedition the Governor presented to each of the gentlemen who accompanied him a golden horseshoe inscribed with the motto, Sic Juvat Transcendere Montes, *"Thus it was decided to cross the mountains." By instituting the Order of the Golden Horseshoe, Spotswood undoubtedly hoped to encourage westward exploration and settlement. It was to stimulate interest in the study of West Virginia among the school children of this state that the West Virginia Board of Education initiated the Knights and Ladies of the Golden Horseshoe contest in 1931. The only detailed account of the Spotswood expedition is the one written by John Fontaine, a young Huguenot who shared the Governor's interest in promising real estate. The first and last parts of Fontaine's journal covering the journey from Williamsburg to Germanna and return have been omitted in the following selection.*

29th. [*August 1716*]. In the morning we got all things in readiness, and about one we left the German-town to set out on our intended journey. At five in the afternoon, the Governor gave orders to encamp near a small river, three miles from Germanna, . . .

30th. In the morning about seven of the clock, the trumpet sounded to awake all the company, and we got up. . . . We had lain upon the ground under cover of our tents, and we found by the pains in our bones that we had not had good beds to lie upon. At nine in the morning, we sent our servants and baggage forward, and we remained because two of the Governor's horses had strayed. At half past two we got the horses, at three we mounted, and at half an hour after four we came up with our baggage at a small river, three miles on the way, which we called Mine River, because there was an appearance of a silver mine by it. We made about three miles more, and came to another small river, which is at the foot of a small mountain, so we encamped here and called it Mountain Run, ... We had good pasturage for our horses, and venison in abundance for ourselves, which we roasted before the fire upon wooden forks, and so we went to bed in our tents. Made six miles this day.

31st. At eight in the morning, we set out from Mountain Run, and after going five miles came upon the upper part of Rappahannoc River.... About five miles further we crossed the same river again, and two miles further we met with a large bear, which one of our company shot, and I got the skin. We killed several deer, and about two miles from the place where we killed the bear, we encamped upon Rappahannoc River. From our encampment we could see the Appalachian Hills very plain. We made large fires, pitched our tents, and cut boughs to lie upon, had good liquor, and at ten we went to sleep. . . . Made this day 14 miles.

1st, September. At eight we mounted our horses, and made the first five miles of our way through a very pleasant plain, which lies where Rappahannoc River forks. I saw there the largest timber, the finest and deepest mould, and the best grass that I ever did see. We had some of our baggage put out of order, and our company dismounted, by hornets stinging the horses. This was some hindrance, and did a little damage, but afforded a great deal of diversion. We killed three bears this day, which exercised the horses as well as the men. We saw two foxes but did not pursue them; we killed several deer. About five of the clock, we came to a run of water at the foot of a hill, where we pitched our tents.... On this day we made 13 miles.

2d. At nine we were all on horseback, and after riding about five miles we crossed the Rappahannoc River, almost at the head, where it is very small. We had a rugged way; we passed over a great many small runs of water, some of which were very deep and others very miry. Several of our company were dismounted, some were down with their horses, and some thrown off. We saw a bear running down a tree, but it being Sunday, we did not endeavour to kill anything. . . .

3d. About eight we were on horseback, and about ten we came to a thicket so tightly laced together, that we had a great deal of trouble to get through; our baggage was injured, our clothes torn all to rags, and the saddles and holsters also torn. About five of the clock we encamped almost at the head of James River, just below the great mountains. . . . We made all this day but eight miles.

4th. We had two of our men sick with the measles, and one of our horses poisoned with a rattlesnake. We took the heaviest of our baggage, our tired horses, and the sick men, and made as convenient a lodge for them as we could, and left people to guard them, and hunt for them. We had finished this work by twelve, and so we set out. The sides of the mountains were so full of vines and briers, that we were forced to clear most of the way before us. We crossed one of the small mountains this side the Appalachian, and from the top of it we had a fine view of the plains below. We were obliged to walk up the most of the way, there being abundance of loose stones on the side of the hill. I killed a large rattlesnake here, and the other people killed three more. We made about four miles, and so came to the side of James River, where a man may jump over it, and there we pitched our tents. As the people were lighting the fire, there came out of a large log of wood a prodigious snake, which they killed; . . .

5th. A fair day. At nine we were mounted; we were obliged to have axemen to clear the way in some places. We followed the windings of James River, observing that it came from the very top of the mountains. We killed two rattlesnakes during our ascent. In some places it was very steep, in others it was so that we could ride up. About one of the clock we got to the top of the mountain; about four miles and a half and we came to the very head spring of James River, where it runs no bigger than an man's arm, from under a large stone. We drank King George's health, and all the Royal Family's, at the very top of the Appalachian Mountains. About a musket shot from the spring, there is another which rises and runs down on the other side; it goes westward, and we thought we could go down that way, but we met with such prodigious precipices, that we were obliged to return to the top again. We found some trees which had been formerly marked, I suppose, by the northern Indians, and following these trees, we found a good, safe descent. Several of the company were for returning; but the Governor persuaded them to continue on. About five, we were down on the other side, and continued our way for about seven miles further, until we came to a large river, by the side of which we encamped. We made this day 14 miles. . . .

6th. We crossed the river which we called Euphrates. It is very deep; the main course of the water is north; it is four score yards wide in the narrowest part. We drank some healths on the other side, and returned; after which I went a swimming in it. We could not find any fordable place, except the one by which we crossed, and it was deep in several places. . . . The Governor had graving irons but could not grave anything, the stones were so hard. I graved my name on a tree by the river side; and the Governor buried a bottle with a paper inclosed, on which he writ that he took possession of this place in the name and for King George the First of England.*

*. . . For this expedition they [members of the party] were obliged to provide a great quantity of horse shoes, (things seldom used in the lower parts of the country, where there are few stones;) upon which account the Governor, upon their return, presented each of his companions with a golden horse shoe, (some of which I have seen studded with valuable stones, resembling the heads of nails,) with this inscription on the one side: *Sic juvat transcendere montes*; and on the other is written the tramontane order. This he instituted to encourage gentlemen to venture backwards, and make discoveries and new settlements; any gentleman being entitled to wear this Golden Shoe that can prove his having drunk his Majesty's health upon Mount George.   HUGH JONES, 1724

We had a good dinner, and after it we got the men together, and loaded all their arms, and we drank the King's health in champagne, and fired a volley, the Princess's health in Burgundy, and fired a volley, and all the rest of the Royal Family in claret, and a volley. We drank the Governor's health and fired another volley. We had several sorts of liquors, viz.; Virginia red wine and white wine, Irish usquebaugh, brandy shrub, two sorts of rum, champagne, canary, cherry punch, water, cider, etc.

. . . We called the highest mountain Mount George, and the one we crossed over Mount Spotswood.

7th. At seven in the morning we mounted our horses, and parted with the rangers, who were to go farther on, and we returned homewards; . . . —W. W. Scott, *A History of Orange County Virginia*, pp. 106-11.

4. The Fairfax Line–Thomas Lewis's Journal of 1746

Thomas, sixth Lord Fairfax, inherited through his mother, Lady Catherine, daughter of Thomas Lord Culpeper, a princely domain of more than five million acres which included seven counties of present West Virginia—Grant, Hardy, Hampshire, Mineral, Morgan, Berkeley, and Jefferson—and eighteen counties of Virginia. In order to protect and administer his rich inheritance, the bachelor proprietor of the Northern Neck first came to Virginia in 1735 for a stay of two years. He returned in 1747, and making his seat at Greenway Court, he remained in Virginia until his death late in 1781 at the age of ninety-one. During the Revolution Fairfax was a Loyalist, although an inoffensive one, and since his heirs were British subjects, Virginia confiscated his estate following his death. What with conflicting grants, overlapping boundaries, Virginia's confiscatory measures, and the treaties of 1783 and 1794 with Great Britain, the Northern Neck properties were the center of much litigation. Two cases are especially notable. The first one, Hite et al vs. Fairfax et al., was initiated in 1749 by Joist Hite, a land speculator who sought to obtain confirmation of his own and other claims within the boundaries of the Northern Neck; the case was not settled until 1786, some years after Hite's death. The second one made constitutional history as Martin vs. Hunter's Lessee, when Justice Joseph Story asserted the supremacy of the United States Supreme Court over the highest court in any state in cases in-

volving the supreme law of the land which included treaties. In reversing the decision of Virginia's Court of Appeals and thus invalidating the grant of nearly eight hundred acres of the Fairfax holdings obtained by David Hunter, the Supreme Court confirmed the title of the Fairfax devisee. But by that time, the Martin heirs of Lord Fairfax had conveyed their Virginia properties to John Marshall and his brother and brother-in-law, James M. Marshall and Rawleigh Colston.

The Northern Neck comprised the land between the Potomac and the Rappahannock from the Chesapeake Bay as far westward as the sources of these rivers. But where, exactly, were the fountains of these streams? On this question rested the validity of land claims and the respective rights of Virginia and Fairfax to dispose of ungranted and waste lands and to collect quitrents in this area. In response to a petition of Lord Fairfax, in 1733 the Privy Council issued an order for the appointment of commissioners to determine the western termini of the Northern Neck. Both the commissioners for the crown and those for the proprietor appointed surveyors to locate the headwaters of the Rappahannock and Potomac, an assignment which was accomplished in a little over two months late in 1736. On the basis of the ensuing reports, the King in Council decided in 1745 that the western boundary of the Fairfax domain began at the first spring of the Rapidan or the South Branch of the Rappahannock and extended in a straight line northwest "to the place in the Alagany Mountains where that part of the River . . . Potomack which is now called Cohongoroota alias Cohongoronton first arises." The task of establishing the "Fairfax line" was entrusted to a second joint commission who appointed Peter Jefferson, the father of Thomas Jefferson, and Robert Brook as surveyors for the Crown and Benjamin Winslow and Thomas Lewis for Lord Fairfax.

The twice-replaced Fairfax stone at the first fountain of the Potomac River has special significance in West Virginia history because it became an important witness for the defense—Virginia and later West Virginia—in their boundary disputes with Maryland whose western limit was fixed at the meridian of the fountain of the Potomac by the grant of Charles I to Lord Baltimore. Maryland went so far as to contend that the Potomac began at

*the head of the South Branch, not of the North Branch where the
Fairfax Stone had been placed. The brief prepared by Charles J.
Faulkner of Martinsburg in 1832 stated the case for Virginia with
convincing clarity. Had Maryland succeeded in establishing her
most extensive claim, Virginia would have lost large portions of
Pendleton, Hardy, Hampshire, Randolph, and Preston Counties.*

*Thomas Lewis, the author of the following journal, was the
first surveyor of Augusta County. His journal provides the only
detailed account of the survey of the Fairfax Line in 1746, and
despite its careless composition, presents a rare view of the Appalachian divide in all its primeval ruggedness.*

Sunday 5th, [October, 1746] . . . Seting off at all Adventures
we fell into a valley Between two Spurs of the mont we had all-
most precipices on eithe hand the valley very narrow full of
Loges & Brush & Exceding Rockey & a very great Decent We
had like Been Killd with Repeated falls in this Case you may Be
Sure or horses were in a miserable Condition the lose Rocks were
often So very Complesant as to Convey us a Considrable way
Down & had like very offten proved fatal to us—we at length
got to the Bottom. . . . hardly any of us Escaping without Broken
Shins or Some other missfortune

Monday 6th . . . hearing the Comisrs were about 5 or six miles
Blow us on ye aforsaid Branch mr Brook Road Down to them
& after piching our tent Colo. Jefferson & I Went Down the River to Discover Some Inhabitants that we might get Some provision Saw but one familey of poor Duch people from whom we
Could have no Supply Then Returned to our Camp Mr. Brook
not Returning till in the night Did not Bring us Such a Supply of
provision as we thought proper to pursue our Journey with. The
land on this Branch is Exceding good for about ¼ of a mile in
Breadth. . . .

Tusday 7th . . . Sent a messenger by whom we wrote to the
Comisioners for Some more provisions . . .

Wensday 8th Began where we left off. . . . hearing the
Comisioners were then Encamped about 3 miles Down the River We Road Down to them where we Spent the Evening

Thursday 9th . . . moved with the Bagage up to the line where we Encam'pd oposite to Coburns Went to see Coburn who with his Wife & miller a Bucksom lass Repay'd the Visite in the Evining we Spent very meriley

Friday 10th This Being the farthest Setlement we were obliged to Lye By in Order to be Supplyd with a fresh Cargo of provision that the Farrer might have time to fasten our horses Shoes & the men have time to wash their Shirts &c.

Saturday 11th . . . Encampd on Looneys Creek which Runs into the South Br. about ¼ of a mile Below where we Crost the River & is about the Same Distance at this place. . . .

Munday 13th . . . we had very Difficult access to the top of the Alleganey mountain where was a precipice about 16 feet high & were very hard Set to get a place where there was any probeability of our asending when we had gaind the Sumit there was a Level as far as we Could see to Right & left Clear of timber about a Quarter of a mile wide Covered with Large flat Rocks & marshey tho on the tope of the highest mountain I ever Saw. . . .

Tusday 14th . . . This River was Calld Styx [one of the head streams of the Blackwater River?] from the Dismal apperance of the place Being Sufficen to Strick terror in any human Creature ye Lorals Ivey & Spruce pine so Extremly thick in ye Swamp through which this River Runs that one Cannot have the Least prospect Except they look upwards the Water of the River of Dark Brownish Cooler & its motion So Slow that it can hardly be Said to move its Depth about 4 feet the Bottom muddy & Banks high, which made it Extremly Difficult for us to pass the most of the horses when they attempt'd to asend the farthest Bank tumbling with their loads Back in the River. most of our Bagage that would have been Damaged by the water were Brought over on mens Shoulder. . . . We got all our Bagage over as it Began to grow Dark So we were Obliged to Encamp on the Bank & in Such a place where we Could not find a plain Big enough for one man to Lye on no fire wood Except green or Roten Spruce pine no place for our horses to feed And to prevent their Eating of Loral tyd them all up least they Should be poisoned.

Wensday 15th. As Soon as light Lodging our hungary horses Set forward In hopes of getting through Swamp and Lorals Begining at the Bank where we left off Last night. . . .

The Swamp, . . . is prodigiously full of Rocks & Cavitys those Covered over with a very Luxuriant Kind of moss of a Considerable Depth. the fallen trees of which there was great numbers & Naturly Large were vastly Improven in Bulk with their Coats of moss The Spruce pines of which . . . there are great Plenty their Roots Grow out from the trunk a Considrable hight above the Surface, Covered over & Joyned togither in Such a manner as makes their Roots appear like Semie Globs the Loral & Ivey as thick as they can well grow whose Branches growing of an Extraordinary length are So well Woven together that without Cutting away it would be Imposibable to force through them provided they grew on agood Even Surface their Roots together with the pines are Spread over the Rocks & under the moss like archs In what Danger must we be, in Such a place all Dangerous places Being Obscured under a Clock of moss Such thickets of Loral to Strugle with whose Branches are all most as Obstinate as if Composed of Iron. Our horses and often our Selves fell into Clefts & Cavitys without Seeing the danger Before we felt the Effects of it. . . . frequently we had the Roots to Cut & the Rocks to Break to free our horses of whom four or five might have been Seen Engaged at a time. . . .

Friday 17th . . . We went So Slow our provision Begining to fail it was Juged Necesary to Eate very Sparingly Went to Sleep on the Strength of our Breakfast after atoilsom Day Work . . .

Saturday 18th mr. Brook and I, aSoon as it was light Set off with our men With out Breakfast & Began where we left off . . . It was a very Discouraging Circumstance, to find all the Waters Runing to the left hand or West ward Directly Contrary to our Expectation So that Instead of Crossing the Branches of Potowmack we Crost those of Missisipia which made us Con-Clude we were Considerably to the West Ward of the head Spring of Potowmack. . . .

Monday 20th Capt Winslo who was one of them that Surveyd up the River in 1736 Set off very Earley in the morning with three other hands up the Creek in order to Discover whither this was the head of the River or not after we we Decampd And

Removed about a mile to the Westward to get Better food for our horses. & there Piched our tents Sent Some hands to the NW. ward to See what they could Discover. . . .

Tusday 21 those Sent to ye N.W. ward came Back about 9 Otheclock & Informd us that the Branches of Allegsney were not above four or five miles ahead of us & that there was but few & very Small Branches Between us & them. About 3 in the afternoon Capt Winslo Returned who had the good fortune to find the marked trees at the head Spring mentioned in their Journal of 1736 This piece of good News was So very agreeable yt it Seemd Inspire every one with New life & vigour & was then Resolved to Run a traverse to the Spring head from where we left off on Sunday night Accordingly mr Brook & I with the Chain Cariers Went to the place & from near Thence West 400 poles to our present Camp where we left off Being late. . . .

The land or Soil on the N.W. Side the River is Black & very moist a great maney Small Springs and Ouzey places & prety Stoney & hilley Exceding well timbred with Such as very Large Spruce pines great multituds of Beach and Shugartrees Chery Trees the most and finest I ever Saw Some three or four foot Diameter thirty or forty foot without a Branch. Some few oaks Chesnuts and Locusts tho' not maney &c

Wensday 22 . . . S 80 E 6 poles to the Spring head where we found the Following old marks to (viz.) aSpruce pine md RB. BW. IF. BL. FF. 1736 [R. Brooke, B. Winslow, Joshua Fry] a Beach P. G 1736 ABeech JS. &a Black aBeach W.MAYO. two Beaches & two Spruce pines markd with three notches three way Each & one Large Spruce pine Blazed three Ways We Dined on a Loyn Roasted Vension about three O'Clock at the Spring head Drank his Majestys health. . . .

Thursday 23d. Returned to the Spring Where we made the following marks (viz) a Beach mark, d G.R. on one Side (G.R. —King George) and FX on the other Side on a nother Beach (FX—Fairfax) G. FX. W. BEVERLEY 1746 on one of the old notched Beches Ld. FX on another Beech FRY. Lun. LOMAX. P. HEDGMAN 1746. a Small Spruce pine for the Corner PJ. on the Beech markd W. MAYO. is new markd T. LEWIS 1746 on another Beech R. BROOKE Sur. 1746. JAMES LOYDE on a nother Beach J GENN 1746. on the pine old mark'd RB. is new

mark,d TB aSmall pine mark,d JA. 1746. another pine markd
JOHN RAIN. GG. aSmall Beech W.O. JJ. JL. 1746 I. H. on the
Beach markd P. G. 1736 is markd WR 1746 P. J. 1746 & PH.
on another Beach WB WR. 1746. y3 aStone by the Corner pine
mark'd FX on a Beech markd A. C. This Done we Bid adue to
the head Spring about ½ hour after nine OClock. . . . —*The Fairfax Line, Thomas Lewis's Journal of 1746,* edited by John W.
Wayland, pp. 22-42.

5. Western Counties

*West Virginia once formed a part of Orange County which
was established in 1734. Morgan ap Morgan of "Opeckon," reputed to be the first permanent settler in this state, served as
justice of the peace of Orange County and as vestryman of Frederick Parish. Both of these offices carried considerable distinction in the eighteenth century. The justices, who as a group
composed the county court, were appointed by the governor of
the colony; the vestrymen, who were members of a self-
perpetuating body of twelve men, were chosen in the first instance by the freeholders and householders. In 1738 Frederick
and Augusta Counties were created from the western part of
Orange County; when the new counties were organized Winchester and Staunton became their respective county seats. The
oldest county in West Virginia, Hampshire, was formed in 1754
from a portion of Frederick and Augusta.*

*The provision in the following act regarding the killing of
wolves was repealed six years later, when the assembly in response to the "humble suit" of the westerners, authorized the
payment of six shillings as the reward for killing an old wolf and
two and a half shillings for killing a young one.*

I. WHEREAS great numbers of people have settled themselves
of late, upon the rivers of Sherrando, Cohongoruton, and Opeckon, and the branches thereof, on the north-west side of the Blue
ridge of mountains, whereby the strength of this colony, and it's
security upon the frontiers, and his majesty's revenue of quit-

rents, are like to be much increased and augmented: For giving encouragement to such as shall think fit to settle there,

II. *Be it enacted, by the Lieutenant-Governor, Council, and Burgesses, of this present General Assembly, and it is hereby enacted, by the authority of the same,* That all that territory and tract of land, at present deemed to be part of the county of Orange, lying on the north west side of the top of the said mountains, extending from thence northerly, westerly, and southerly, beyond the said mountains, to the utmost limits of Virginia, be separated from the rest of the said county, and erected into two distinct counties and parishes; to be divided by a line to be run from the head spring of Hedgman river, to the head spring of the river Potowmack: And that all that part of the said territory, lying to the northeast of the said line, beyond the top of the said Blue ridge, shall be one distinct county, and parish; to be called by the name of the county of Frederick, and parish of Frederick: And that the rest of the said territory, lying on the other side of the said line, beyond the top of the said Blue ridge, shall be one other distinct county, and parish; to be called by the name of the county of Augusta, and parish of Augusta.

III. *Provided always,* That the said new counties and parishes shall remain part of the county of Orange, and parish of Saint Mark, until it shall be made appear to the governor and council, for the time being, that there is a sufficient number of inhabitants for appointing justices of the peace, and other officers, and erecting courts therein, for the due administration of justice; . . .

IV. *And be it further enacted,* That after a court shall be constituted in the said new counties respectively, the court for the said county of Frederick be held monthly, upon the second Friday; and the court for the said county of Augusta, be held upon the second Monday, in every month. . . . And for the better encouragement of aliens; and the more easy naturalization of such who shall come to inhabit there,

V. *Be it further enacted,* That it shall and may be lawful, for the governor, or commander in chief, of this colony, for the time being, to grant letters of naturalization to any such alien, upon a certificate from the clerk of any county court, of his or their having taken the oaths appointed by act of parliament to be taken instead of the oaths of allegiance and supremacy; and taken and subscribed the oath of abjuration, and subscribed the test, in like manner as he may do, upon taking and subscribing the same before himself.

VI. And for the more easy paiment of all levies, secretary's, clerks, sherifs, and other officers fees, by the inhabitants of the said new counties, *Be it further enacted*, That the said levies and fees shall and may be paid in money, for tobacco, at three farthings per pound, without any deduction. And that the said counties be and are hereby exempted from public levies, for ten years.

VII. *Provided nevertheless*, That from and after the passing of this act, no allowance whatsoever shall be made to any person, for killing wolves, within the limits of the said new counties. Any law, custom, or usage, to the contrary hereof, notwithstanding.

VIII. And, for the better ordering of all parochial affairs in the said new parishes, *Be it enacted, by the authority aforesaid*, That the freeholders and housekeepers of the same, respectively, shall meet, at such time and place, as the governor, or commander in chief, of this dominion, for the time being, with the advice of the council, shall appoint, by precept under his hand, and the seal of the colony; to be directed to the sherifs of the said new counties, respectively, and by the said sherifs publickly advertised; and then and there elect twelve of the most able and discreet persons of their said parishes, respectively; Which persons so elected, having taken the oaths appointed by law, and subscribed to be conformable to the doctrine and discipline of the church of England, shall, to all intents and purposes, be deemed and taken to be the vestries of the said new parishes, respectively.—Hening, *Statutes at Large*, V, 78-80.

6. Expedition of Celoron

Prior to the French and Indian War, the Ohio Valley was one of the several areas involved in the battle of the maps. In 1749 the Marquis de la Galissonniere, Governor of Canada, ordered Captain Celoron de Blainville with a detachment of 270 men, including Iroquois and Abenaki Indians, to descend the Ohio and take possession of the region drained by that river in the name of Louis XV, King of France. The expedition carried leaden plates engraved by Paul de Brosse, which were buried at strategic points on alternate banks of the Ohio to assert French sovereignty over this valley. Journals of the mission were kept by Celoron and Father Bonnecamps, a Jesuit mathematician who was the chaplain, sailing master, and cartographer of the expedition. The three plates which have been found thus far are similar except for the places and dates of deposit which appear to have been coarsely engraved, probably with a knife. The following passage is from the Bonnecamps Journal, and the inscription is from the plate buried at the mouth of the Kanawha. The Illinois cattle mentioned by Father Bonnecamps was the buffalo.

... "I WILL ONLY TELL YOU THAT WE BURIED THREE PLATES OF LEAD at the mouths of three different rivers, the 1st of which was called Kanonouaora [Wheeling Creek], the second, Jenanguekona [Muskingum], and the 3rd, Chinodaichta. It was in the neighborhood of this river that we began to see the illinois cattle; but, here and elsewhere, they were in such small numbers that our men could hardly kill a score of them. It was, besides, necessary to seek them far in the woods. We had been assured, however, at our departure, that at each point we should find them by hundreds, and that the tongues alone of those which we should kill would suffice to support the troops. This is not the first time when I have experienced that hyperbole and exaggeration were figures familiar to the Canadians."—*The Jesuit Relations and Allied Documents,* edited by Reuben G. Thwaites, LXIX, 177-79.

(Translation from the French)

In the year 1749, reign of Louis XV., King of France, We, Celoron, commandant of a detachment sent by Monsieur the Marquis de la Galissoniere, Commandant General of New France, to re-establish tranquillity in some Indian villages of these cantons, have buried this plate at the mouth of the river *Chinodashichetha,* the 18th August, near the river Ohio, otherwise Beautiful River, as a monument of renewal of possessions, which we have taken of the said river Ohio, and of all those

which fall into it, and of all the lands on both sides, as far as to
the sources of said rivers; the same as were enjoyed or ought
to have been enjoyed, by the preceding Kings of France, and
that they have maintained it by their arms and by treaties, especially by those of Ryswick, Utrecht, and Aix-la-Chapelle.—
Wills De Hass, *History of the Early Settlement and Indian Wars
of Western Virginia*, pp. 50n-51n.

7. Instructions to Christopher Gist and Second Journey of Gist

*By the middle of the eighteenth century settlers had penetrat-
ed into Augusta County, which included most of Virginia west
of the Blue Ridge at the time of its organization in 1745. Staunton, the county seat, was surveyed by John Lewis, who had come
to the Valley of Virginia in 1732 with his three sons, Andrew,
Thomas, and William, all of whom, together with a younger
brother, Charles, became leaders on the Virginia frontier. Another pioneer of Augusta was John Peter Salley, a German emigrant
from Pennsylvania. On March 16, 1742, Salley accompanied John
Howard on an expedition authorized by the Governor of Virginia "to travel . . . westward" to the Mississippi River "in order
to make Discovery of the Country." In compensation for his
services Howard was promised "ten hundred thousand Acres of
Land" to be shared with other members of the expedition. The
brief journal kept by Salley told how the six explorers who had
covenanted to go on the journey went down the Kanawha Valley
by land and by water in a boat covered with buffalo hide, between mountains that contained "great plenty of coals." On the
lower Mississippi the party was arrested by the French and imprisoned in New Orleans, but Salley managed to escape and return to Virginia in May, 1745. After the indecisive peace of 1748
between Great Britain and France, the initiative for western expansion in Virginia was taken by land companies, notably the
Ohio and the Loyal, which received grants of five hundred
thousand and eight hundred thousand acres, respectively. Rival-
ry between the companies was keen, as each sought out the best*

areas for settlement. For this purpose the Loyal Company employed Dr. Thomas Walker who, with five companions, left his home in Louisa County, March 6, 1750. Going by way of southwest Virginia, the Walker expedition went through Cumberland Gap, then swung northward to the Kentucky River and eastward to the Tug and to the New River, the last of which they crossed with some difficulty just below the mouth of the Greenbrier. As they ascended the Greenbrier at a maximum pace of ten miles a day, they noted that the land was "very good in many places" and that there were some inhabitants on the branches of this stream.

The agent of the Ohio Company was the famous Christopher Gist. In 1750-51 and again in 1751-52 he explored a large area within the boundaries of western Maryland, southwestern Pennsylvania, Ohio, Kentucky, and West Virginia. The Ohio Company's instructions to Gist and sections of his journal covering his second journey are given below.

AFTER YOU HAVE RETURNED FROM WILLIAMSBURG and have executed the Commission of the President & Council, . . . otherwise as soon as You can conveniently You are to apply to Col. Cresap for such of the Company's Horses, as You shall want for the Use of yourself and such other Person or Persons You shall think necessary to carry with You; and You are to look out & observe the nearest & most convenient Road . . . from the Company's Store at Wills's Creek to a Landing at Mohongeyela; from thence You are to proceed down the Ohio on the South Side . . . as low as the Big Conhaway, and up the same as far as You judge proper, and find good Land—You are all the Way to keep an exact Diary & Journal & therein note every Parcel of good Land, . . . with the Breadth, Depth, Course and Length of the several Branches falling into the Ohio, & the different Branches any of Them are forked into, . . . observing also the Produce, the several Kinds of Timber and Trees, observing where there is Plenty and where the Timber is scarce; and You are not to omit proper Observations on the mountainous, barren, or broken Land, that We may . . . judge what Quantity of good Land is contained within the Compass of your Journey, for We woud not have You omit taking Notice of any Quantity of good Land, tho not exceeding 4 or

500 Acres provided the same lies upon the River Ohio & may be convenient for our building Store Houses & other Houses for the better carrying on a Trade and Correspondence down that River.

1751.—Pursuant to my Instructions hereunto annexed from the Committee of the Ohio Company bearing Date 16th July 1751

Monday Nov 4.—Set out from the Company's Store House in Frederick County Virginia opposite the Mouth of Wills's Creek and crossing Potomack River went W 4 M to a Gap in the Allegany Mountains upon the S W Fork of said Creek—This Gap is the nearest to Potomack River of any in the Allegany Mountains, and is accounted one of the best, tho the Mountain is very high, The Ascent is no where very steep but rises gradually near 6 M, it is now very full of old Trees & Stones, but with some Pains might be made a good Waggon Road; this Gap is directly in the Way to Mohongaly, & several Miles nearer than that the Traders commonly pass thro, and a much better Way. . . .

Sunday 24.—Set out . . . over the S Fork and encamp'd on the SW Side about 1 M from a small Hunting Town of the Delawares from whom I bought some Corn—I invited these Indians to the Treaty at the Loggs Town, the full Moon in May, as Col. Patton had desired Me; they treated Me very civilly, but after I went from that Place my Man informed Me that they threatened to take away our Guns and not let Us travel. . . .

From Saturday 30 to Friday Dec. 6.—We searched the Land several Miles round and found it about 15 M from the Foot of the Mountains to the River Mohongaly the first 5 M of which E & W is good level farming Land, with fine Meadows, the Timber white Oak and Hiccory— . . . The Land nearer the River is about 8 or 9 M wide, and the same Length is much richer & better timbered, with Walnut, Locust, Poplars and Sugar-Trees, but is in some Places very hilly, the Bottoms upon the River 1 M, and in some places near 2 M wide.

Saturday 7.—Set out W 6 M and went to an Indian Camp and invited them to the Treaty at the Loggs Town at the full Moon in May next; at this Camp there was a Trader named

Charles Poke who spoke the Indian Tongue well, the Indian to whom this Camp belonged after much Discourse with Me, complained & said "my Friend You was sent to Us last Year from the Great Men in Virginia to inform Us of a Present from the Great King over the Water, and if You can bring News from the King to Us, why cant You tell Him something from Me? The Proprietor of Pensylvania granted my Father a Tract of Land begining eight Miles below the Forks of Brandy Wine Creek and binding on the said Creek to the Fork and including the West Fork & all its Waters on both Sides to the Head Fountain— The White People now live on these lands, and will neither let Me have Them, nor pay Me any Thing for Them—My Father's Name was Chickoconnecon, I am his eldest Son, and my Name is Nemicotton [Nemacolin]—I desire that You will let the Governor and Great Men in Virginia know this—It may be they will tell the great King of it, and he will make Mr Pen or his People give Me the Land or pay Me for it—This Trader here Charles Poke knows the Truth of what I say, . . . —This I was obliged to insert in my Journal to please the Indian.

Sunday Dec. 8.—Stayed at the Indian Camp.

Tuesday 17.—Set out W 5 M . . . to Licking Creek . . . ; upon this Creek We lodged at a hunting Camp of an Indian Captain named Oppaymolleah, here I saw an Indian named Joshua who spoke very good English; he had been acquainted with Me several Years, and seemed very glad to see Me, and wondered much where I was going so far in those Woods; I said I was going to invite all the great Men of the Indians to a Treaty to be held at Loggs Town, the full Moon in May next, where a Parcel of Goods, a Present from the King of Great Britain, would be delivered Them by proper Commissioners, and that these were the Goods which I informed them of last Year, by Order of the President of Virginia, Col. Lee, . . . Joshua informed Them what I said, and they told Me, I ought to let the Beaver know this, so I wrote a Line to him by Joshua, who promised to deliver it . . . —This Beaver is the Sachemore or Chief of the Delawares. It is customary among the Indian Chiefs to take upon Them the Name of any Beast or Bird they (f)ancy, the Picture of which they always sign instead of their Name or Arms. . . .

From Saturday 21 to Tuesday, Janry 7.—We stayed at this Place [a branch of Licking Creek], We had a good Deal of Snow & bad Weather—My Son had . . . his Feet frost-bitten, which kept Us much longer here than We intended however We kill'd Plenty of Deer Turkeys &c and fared very well—The Land hereabouts very good but to the W and SW it is hilly.

1752

Wednesday Janry 8—My Son's Feet being somewhat better, We set out S 30 W 5 M, S 45 W 3 M, the Land middling good but hilly—I found my Son's Feet too tender to travel, and we were obliged to stop again. . . .

Thursday [February] 13.— . . . In this Day's Journey We found a Place where a Piece of Land about 100 Yards square & about 10 Feet deep from the Surface had slipped down a steep Hill, somewhat more than it's own Breadth, with most of the Trees standing on it upright . . . In the Place from whence it removed was a large Quarry of Rocks, in the Sides of which were Veins of several Colours, particularly one of a deep yellow, about 3 Feet from the Bottom, in which were other small Veins some white, some a Greenish Kind of Copperas: A Sample of which I brought in to the Ohio Company in a small Leather Bag No 1— . . . Not far from here We encamped in the Fork of a Creek.

Friday 14.—We stayed at this Place—On the NW Side of the Creek on a rising ground by a small Spring We found a large Stone about 3 Feet Square on the Top, and about 6 or 7 Feet high; it was all covered with green Moss except on the SE Side which was smooth and white as if plaistered with Lime. On this Side I cut with a cold Chizzel in large Letters,

THE OHIO COMPANY

FEBY 1751   [old style]

BY CHRISTOPHER GIST

. . . Thursday [March] 5.—Set out N 30 E 9 M to a Creek called Neemokeesy [Fishing Creek] where We killed a black Fox & two Bears—Upon this Creek We found a Cave under a Rock about 150 Feet long & 55 feet wide; one Side of it open facing the Creek, the Floor dry—We found it had been much used by Buffaloes & Elks who came there to lick a kind of salt-ish Clay . . . in the Cave, and of which I took a sample in a Leather Bag N. 2.

Friday March 6.—We stayed at the Cave—Not very far from it We saw a Herd of Elks near 30 one of which my Son killed.

Saturday 7.—Set out N 30 E 7 M to the Ohio River—The Bottoms here were very rich and near 2 M wide; but a little higher up, the Hill seemed very steep, so that We were obliged to leave the River & went E 6 M on very high Land; then N 9 M thro' very good high Land tolerable level to a Creek called Wealin or Scalp Creek where We encamped. . . .

Tuesday 10.—We hunted up and down these Creeks . . . ; in our Way to the Conhaway—They run near parallel at about 3 or 4 M Distance, for upwards to 30 M—The Land between Them all the Way is rich & level, chiefly Low Grounds & finely timbered with Walnuts, Locusts, Cherry Trees, & Sugar Trees. . . .

Thursday 12.—I set out for Mohongaly crossed it upon a Raft of Logs from whence I made the best of my Way to Potomack—I did not keep exactly my old Tract but went more to the Eastward & found a much nearer Way Home: and am of Opinion the Company may have a tolerable good Road from Wills Creek to the upper Fork of Monhongaly, from whence the River is navigable all the Way to the Ohio for large flat bottomed Boats —The Road will be a little to the Southward of West, and the Distance to the Fork of Mohongaly about 70 M—While I was at Mohongaly in my Return Home an Indian, who spoke good English, came to Me & said—That their great Men the Beaver and Captain Oppamylucah (these are two Chiefs of the Delawares) desired to know where the Indian's Land lay, for that the French claimed all the Land on one side the River Ohio & the English on the other Side; . . . after some Consideration "my Friend" said I, "We are all one King's People and the different Colour of our Skins makes no Difference in the King's Subjects; You are his People as well as We, if you will take Land & pay the King's Rights You will have the same Privileges as the White People have, and to hunt You have Liberty every where so that You dont kill the White Peoples Cattle & Hogs"—To this the Indian said, that I must stay at that

Place two Days and then he woud come & see Me again, He then went away, and ... returned as he promised, and ... said that the great Men bid Him tell Me I was very safe that I might come and live upon that River where I pleased—that I had answered Them very true ... & for his Part he would come to see Me at Wills's Creek in a Month.

March—From Thursday 12 to Saturday 28. We were traveling from Mohongaly to Potomack for as We had a good many Skins to carry & the Weather was bad We traveled but slow

Sunday 29.—We arrived at the Company's Factory at Wills's Creek.—William M. Darlington, *Christopher Gist's Journals with Historical, Geographical and Ethnological Notes and Biographies of his Contemporaries,* pp. 67-79.

II. Two Wars: The French and Indian and Dunmore's

8. Report on the Present State of Virginia

*Robert Dinwiddie, a Scottish merchant with considerable ex-
perience in colonial affairs, was appointed lieutenant-governor
of Virginia in July, 1751, and arrived in the colony the following November. During his more than six years as chief executive of the colony, Dinwiddie's main concern was to check the
aggressive policy of France in North America, particularly in
the Ohio valley. It was he who sent Major George Washington
in October, 1753, to Fort Le Boeuf with a message to the French
commander that "the lands upon the River Ohio, in the western parts of the Colony of Virginia, are so notoriously known
to be the property of the Crown of Great Britain that it is a matter of equal concern and surprise to me, to hear that a body
of French forces are erecting fortresses and making settlements upon that river. . . ." In January 1754, Dinwiddie ordered Captain William Trent to erect a fort on the Ohio, and
shortly afterward dispatched Washington with a small force of
raw recruits to support Trent. Both expeditions met with ad-
versity. The first one, during the absence of Trent, was compelled by a superior French force to abandon the unfinished
fort. The second one, under Washington, surprised a French
party encamped a few miles from Great Meadows and in the
ensuing encounter defeated the enemy and killed their commander, Joseph Coulon de Jumonville. The French had their
revenge early in July when they forced Washington to surrender Fort Necessity which had been hurriedly constructed at
Great Meadows. Dinwiddie foresaw the intensity of the coming
struggle for empire and urged the Virginia legislature, other
colonial executives, and the British government to prepare
for it. His report to the Lords Commissioners, part of which is
given below, attributes the outbreak of hostilities to French ag-*

gression, and gives a succinct account of the government, economy, state of defense, resources, and population of colonial Virginia.

. . . . THE AIR [OF VIRGINIA] IS TEMPERATE; . . . The Western Boundary as yet is not well known, nor can it be expected to be fully known for some Ages. The British Subjects have for some years settled within a few Miles of the River Ohio, on the other side of the Allagany Mount's, w'ch settlem't was approved of by the Ind's, and a Grant of the Land was made by H. M'y, the K. of G. B., by the Six Nat's at the Treaty of Lancaster. These settlem'ts I was willing to fix as our pres't Boundary to the Westw'd, as it is part of the Lands belonging to the five Nat's, w'ch, by the Treaty of Utritch, is expressly allowed to be under the Dom'n of the Crown of G. B., and as further, the Lake Champlain, formerly called Lake Iroq[u]ois, and the Co'try So'w'd of it, as also the Lakes Ontorio and Erie have, by all ancient authors, both Fr. and English, been allowed to belong to the five Nat's of Ind's, and in Course, by the above Treaty, to be under the Protect'n of the B. Crown. Notwithstand'g the above Treaty, the Fr. have, subsequent thereto, built several Forts on the Lands belong'g to the Five Nat's, and a remarkable strong one at Crown Point to the So'w'd of Lake Champlain. The Treaty of Aix la Chapelle, confirmi'g the Treaty of Utritch, has no weight with the Fr., but it appears y't the Conquest of ye whole Cont't seems to be the object of their Attent'n. The Fr., since the above Treaties, have erected many Fortresses on the Lands belong'g to the Five Nat's, . . . and contrary to Law and Justice, erect these Forts as the Marks of Possess'n, and they have been constantly increasing their Forces by importing Numbers of People from France in a Private Manner, not to be notic'd, or observed by the Powers in Europe. They have, for the last seven years, robb'd our Subjects, trading with the Ind's in our back Co'try, and sent their Persons Prisoners to Quebeck, all w'ch is a most notorious Infract'n of the above Treaties. Not satisfied with these clandestine and Private Robberies, they have now taken off the Mask, and y's last Sumer declared, in this part of the World, y'r Intent's. I was ordered by H. M'y to build

some Forts on His Lands on the River Ohio. In Obedience thereto I ordered out some Soldiers and Tradesmen to begin a Fort
on the Forks of Monongahela, till I was qualified by our Assembly to send stronger Forces to y't Fort, and to build some
others. The Fr., with an armed Force from Canada, came down
the River Ohio, surpriz'd our People, took Possess'n of His
M'y's Forts, and robbed and plundered all our poor settlers y't
were near to y't River, some of whom had lived peacibly
there upwards of 10 Years. I raised w't Men the small Pittance
our Assembly granted in Feb'y last, enabled me to do, who,
with an Independ't Co'y H. M'y was pleased to order from So.
Car., on their march to the Ohio, were attacked by the Fr. and
Ind's, with a much superior Force, many of our Men were
killed and the rest obliged to such a Capitulat'n as their inferiority of numbers and the situat'n of their Affairs compelled
them to comply with. These Transact's in the Time of .tranquil
Peace between the two Crowns, I conceive is with't Preced't,
and I am convinc'd there is no conduct'g an Expedit'n with't
Aid from Home, and an Act of the B. Parliam't to oblige the
Colonies to raise Money for their own Protect'n. But to ret'n
to the present State of Virg'a. The establish'd Constitut'n of
the Gov't of Virg'a is as follows: A chief Gov'r, appointed by
His M'y, who always resides in G. B.; A L't Gov'r, appointed
also by H. M'y, who presides over the Affairs of Gov't; A
Council, consist'g of 12 Gent'n, appointed by Mandamus from
H. M'y. The Dom'n has now 50 Counties, who elect two Members for each co'ty; one for the College of W. and M'y, one for
the City of W'msb'g, one for Jas. Town, and one for the Borough
of Norfolk, in all 104 Memb'rs, who are called at Meet'g, the
Ho. of Burgesses. The Lieut. Gov'r, Council, and Ho. of Burgesses, are the Gen'l Assembly of this Colony, and are impowered to
enact Acts for the good Gov't of the Co'try. These Acts are duly transmitted to G. B., soon after each Session, for His M'y's
Assent and Approbation; w'n they receive H. M'y's Sanc'n they
become Laws. The administrat'n of Justice. First There are in
each Co'ty, Courts held monthly by Persons commissioned by
the Gov'r, . . . And for the City of W'msburg, there is a Court
of Hustings held Monthly, before the Mayor, Recorder and Al-
dermen, . . . There is the like Court in the Bor'o of Norfolk;

these are the inferior Courts in this Gov't, and from their Judgem't, an Appeal lies to the Gen'l Court. . . . The Gen'l Court consists of the Gov'r and Members of the Council, any five whereof make a Quorum; this Court is held in Apr. and Oct'r, and has Jurisdict'n of all Causes, real, Personal and mixt, at comon Law, bro't hither, originally exceeding the Value of £10 Sterling, or by Appeal or Supercedeas . . . from the Inferior Courts, all Criminal Offences are here tryable, and it is also a Court of Chancery for matters of great Value. But, by a late Act of Assembly, no Appeal . . . lies from the Judgem't or Decree of any inferior Court, unless the Debt or Damage, or Thing in dem'd (exclusive of the Costs) exceeds the Value of 5£; Except'g only where the Title or Bounds of Lands are in Question, and from the Gen'l Court an Appeal lies to the King and Council in any Causes of 300£ St'g and upwards; Secondly, There are two Courts of oyer and terminer held Yearly, the one the second Friday in June, the other the second Tuesday in Dec'r, wherein all Criminals y't happen to be comitted after the respective Gen'l Courts, are tried. The Judges here, are only such as are Members of the Council, . . . Thirdly, For the punishm't of Slaves committ'g Cappital Crimes, a Com'o. of Oyer and Terminer is issued by the Gov'r, directed to the Justices of the Peace in the Co'ty where the offence is comitted, to try the Offenders, on Proof of the Fact by Witnesses, with't any Jury, and on Convict'n, the Comiss'rs award Execution, and set a Value on the Slave, w'ch Valuat'n is afterwards p'd the Owner by the Gen'l Assembly as an Encouragement to the People to discover the Villain[ie]s of their Slaves; . . . There is a Court of the Comissary of the Bishop of London, w'ch only relates to the Punishm't of the Imoralities of the Clergy, and proceeds by Monition, Suspension, or Deprivation, as the Nature of the Offence deserves, and from thence there lies an Appeal to the Delegates appointed by His M'y's Comiss'n in England. . . . the Gov'r is invested with a Power to pardon all Crimes and Offences, Treason and willful Murder only excepted, . . .

The Gov'r has also a Power to remit all Fines and Forfeitures occurring to the Crown, under the Value of 10£ St'g, and if above, he may suspend the levying such Fines and Forteitures untill H[is] M'y's Pleasure is known, but this Indulgence does not reach to the Inhabitants of the No'ern Neck, the Fines, &c., being granted to L'd Fairfax, the Proprietor thereof....

The Number of Inhabitants, from the most exact Acc'ts I can have, of White and Black, are 230,000, and the[y] Annually increase in Numbers. There are 50 Counties, each has a Co'ty Lt., Colo., Lieut. Colo. and Major, and according to the largeness of the Co'ty, their Militia is divided into compa's, each Company hav'g a Capt., Lieut. and Ensign, and our Militia may now amo. to 27,000 Men from 21 to 60 Years of Age. In order to bring the Militia into good Discipline, and a proper Use of their Arms, I divided this Dom'n into four Districts, and appointed experienc'd Persons to be Adjutants, to teach the officers, and y'n the private Men their Exercise, w'ch I hope, will in Time bring the Militia into good Order and Discipline; for our whole Dependence (under God) must be on them, for we have no Forts in y's Dom'n.... [Of the] Indians: The tributary Ind's, subject to the Rules of this Gov't, are much reduced and very inconsiderable; there are at pres't only the Pamunkey and Nottaways, their Numbers together, are not above 60 fight'g Men, they are seated among the Inhabit'ts and live in Peace and Amity with them. The other Nat's of Ind's y't are near us, and profess Fr'dship and League with the English, are the Six Nat's to the No'wards, the Catawbas, Cherokees, Chickasaws, and Creeks to the So'w'd. The different Nat's on the River Ohio, the Picts, Twightwees, and Shawnesse to the Westw'd, if they be not seduced by the Fr., who are between Us and them. This Colony has always been happy, and in firm Peace with the Ind's till lately, the Fr. have, by Threats and fair Promises, seduced some of the Ind's from the B. Interest, and with great injustice invaded H. M'y's Lands, plundered and Robbed many of his Subjects, and carried many of them to Quebeck. The Fr. do not make regular Settlements, but build Fortresses as marks of Possession, with't Justice or any Shadow of Right to the Lands where they build their Forts, and make Incursions among our Frontier Settlem'ts (who lie scattered for the Benefit of the best Lands) and rob them of their Cattle, Corn, &c., and often murder them.

This is the miserable Situat'n of this Colony at Pres't and with't Aid from G. B., by the Infatuation and Neglect of the Assemblies on this Cont't, must rem'n a Prey to the Enemy's Depredations.—R. A. Brock, *The Official Records of Robert Dinwiddie*, I, 380-90.

9. Advertisements

"Its true, we have been beaten, most shamefully beaten, by a handful of Men!" Washington lamented shortly after the terrible defeat of General Edward Braddock in July, 1755. Governor Dinwiddie saw in the military disaster a judgement of the Almighty and proclaimed September 24 as a day of general fast to expiate the "national Guilt." At the same time the indomitable Governor recommended the payment of bounties for Indian scalps. In order to bolster the courage and calm the panic of the frontiersmen of Hampshire, Frederick, and Augusta counties, many of whom were abandoning their homes for safer areas, Dinwiddie and Washington, who were in charge of frontier defense, issued the following advertisements.

WHEREAS IT HAS BEEN REPRESENTED TO ME, That many of the Inhabitants of the County of *Augusta,* have most shamefully deserted their Plantations, for Fear of the Enemy, which a small Number of them, with a proper Spirit, might easily have destroyed, and that they are still so afraid, as to think of leaving every Thing that they have, and seek for Settlements in some other Country; I thought it might not be amiss to inform them, in this public Manner, That they may return to their Estates with the utmost Security: That the Five Companies of Rangers, and an independent Company, consisting of such as have voluntarily offered to assist in defending the Frontiers, are stationed in the best Manner to provide for their Security; and the Men under Col. *Washington,* will all be disposed of, so as to answer the same Purpose.

ROBERT DINWIDDIE

—*The Virginia Gazette,* (Hunter), September 26, 1755.

[October 13, 1755.]

An inconceivable Panick which prevailed amongst the people of this County, induced me to write the following Advertisement:

Whereas divers timorous persons run through the Country and alarm its Inhabitants by False Reports, of the Indians having attacked and destroyed the Country, even Winchester itself, and that they are still proceeding: This is to give Notice to all people, that I have great reason to believe that the Indians who committed the late Cruelties (though no lower that the South Branch) are returned Home, as I have certain Accounts that they have not been seen nor heard of these ten days past: And I do advise all my Countrymen, not to be alarmed on every false Report they may hear, as they must now be satisfied, from the many false ones that have been made; but to keep to their Homes and take care of their Crops; as I can venture to assure them, that in a short time the Frontiers will be so well Guarded, that no mischief can be done, either to them or their Plantations, which must of course be destroyed, if they desert them in so shameful a manner.—*The Writings of George Washington,* edited by John C. Fitzpatrick, I, 208-209.

10. Preston's Journal of the Sandy Creek Expedition

Several plans were advanced for the construction of a chain of forts to guard the Virginia frontier. An act of the Virginia legislature passed in March, 1756, provided for a line of fortifications beginning "at Henry Enochs, on Great-Cape-Capon" and extending to "the South-Fork of Mayo-River" in Halifax County. A council of war held at Augusta Court House, July 27, 1756, proposed the building of a cordon of fourteen forts covering 250 miles and garrisoned by 680 men. In November, 1756, Washington recommended the construction of additional forts, from ten to thirty miles apart, covering 360 miles, to be garrisoned by two thousand men. Since he considered the Potomac valley especially vulnerable to invasion, five of the forts were to be located on the South Branch, two on Patterson's Creek, one on the Cacapon, and one, Fort Maidstone, on the Potomac at the mouth of the Great Cacapon in Morgan County. Early in 1757, Washington reported to Earl Loudoun, the Commander in Chief of the British forces in America, that although the military appropriations of Virginia were "very considerable," the frontier would never be safe until the French were dislodged from Fort Duquesne. Washington had many complaints to lay before Loudoun, in particular, the lack of a plan of operations and the faulty system of recruiting, paying, disciplining, feeding, and clothing the militia, whose members were generally "indolent and careless, and always unguarded."

That Washington was not exaggerating regarding these military problems is well attested by William Preston's account of the Sandy Creek expedition led by Major Andrew Lewis in 1756. Of Irish birth (1720-1781), Andrew Lewis, son of John Lewis, settled after his marriage near the site of present-day Salem, Virginia. Although his public career included service as county lieutenant and justice of the peace and as member of the Virginia House of Burgesses, of the Convention of 1775, and of the executive council of Virginia, Lewis is best known for his military achievements of which the Big Sandy expedition, however, is not one. This ill-planned, badly-provisioned, and poorly-led campaign against the Shawnee towns was a military failure except insofar as it contributed to cementing the friendship of the Cherokees, some of whose braves participated in the abortive adventure. A force of approximately 340 men set off from Fort Frederick near Ingles Ferry on February 18. Going by way of Bear Garden, Burke's Garden, and the head of the Clinch, the expedition reached the head of the Big Sandy on February 28. The House of Burgesses cleared Lewis of any responsibility for the failure of the campaign.

SATURDAY 28TH. [1756]. We marched at 10 o'clock & passed several Branches of Clinch and at length got to the head of Sandy Creek. . . .

Tuesday ye 2nd. A number of the Indians went out Early to make what Discoveries they could of ye Enemy—About 10 oClock some of them Returned & Reported that they had seen a Large Camping Place of ye Enemy where they had been about 3 Days ago with Sundry signs of Horses which had been stolen by them. The Cherokees Desired to stay that day at their Camp to Range the woods which they did, . . . This Day we were put to half alowance of Beef which was almost Exhausted. . . .

Wednesday 3d. . . . We March'd until Sunset or nigh that time & advanced only 9 or ten miles being much Retarded by the River & mountains which Closed in on Both sides . . . each man had but half a pound of flour & no meat but what we could kill, & that was very scarce. we Encampd on ye Creek at a place where no food was for the Horses. Wch. occasioned many to stray away. . . .

Fryday 5th. We marched about nine oClock this morning & with great difficulty Proceeded 15 miles on our Journey the River being very deep & often to cross almost killed the men, and more so as they were in utmost extremity for want of Provisions. this Day my 4th horse Expired & I was left on foot with a Hungry Belly which increased my woe—& indeed it was the Case with almost Every man in the Company. . . .

Saturday 6th. . . . The Cherrokees proposed to make Bark Canoes to carry themselves down the River which was Imediatly put in Practice. Major Lewis set men to work to make a Large canoe to carry down the amunition & the small Remains of our Flour which was then almost Exhausted. The men murmured very much for want of Provisions & numbers threatned to Return home so that I was much affraid a mutiny would Ensue. I spoke to the major & let him know the General murmur of the soldiers which very much concern'd him & had no way to please them but to order a Cask of Butter to be Divided among them which was no more than a taste to Each man. it Rained very hard all that night which still added [?] to our misfortune as we had no tents, nor indeed hardly any other necessaries for such a journey.

Sunday 7th. . . . It was agreed upon by the Officers that Capt. Smith Capt. Breckinridge Lt. Morton Capt. Dunlap & myself, with our Comp. & part of Mountgomiries Vollonteers 130 in number should proceed Down the Creek 15 miles & no furthur in search of Hunting Ground. . . . Our hunger & want still increased, as we Could not get any flesh meat & had but one pound of flour alowed to Each man until the major with the Remainder of the men could overtake us. . . . It was agreed upon by a Great number of the Soldiers to break off homeward next morning & my two Seargants told me their Intention & that they with severals perhaps all of my men would return with the [yer?] Companies that they were fainty & weak with hunger . . . & that there was no game in the mountains nor no appearance of a Level Country, that their half Pound of flour per day could not support them & that small Quantity would soon be done, I Proposed to kill horses & Eat which they Refused to Comply with. They said that might do if they were Returning to Support them home but it was not Diet Proper to Sustain men on a long march against an Enemy, however I Persuaded them to make a further Tryal down the River the next Day . . .

Monday 8th. We . . . proceeded down the River about 3 miles where the mountains Closed so nigh the water that we Could not Pass. We took up a Branch & passed a very high Mountain & going down another Branch we met part of the men who had been at the River & could not git down any further. . . . We Encamped at the River to which Place one Elk was brought & Divided to the no small Joy of Every man in Company, for by that Time hunger appeared in all our Faces & most of us were got Weak & Feeble & had we not got that Relief I Doubt not but several of the men would have died with hunger, their Cries and Complaints were Pitiful & shocking & more so as the officers could not give them any help, for they were in equal want with the men, our march was 7 miles.

Tuesday 9th. This morning the Vollunteers killed two Buffaloes & an Elk which gives us a further Relief, (however, the Men still Continued to murmur). . . . A Great number of our young men went out to hunt and view the Country, . . . & Reported that they had Climbed a very great mount in order to take a view of the Country & that there seemed to be Several prodigious great mountains before them . . . that the River seemed to Bear westward & no possabillity of taking Horses down the River & that they saw no Game. This account very much disturbed the men. In short they agreed to a man to Return next morning. I called the officers together & it was Concluded that Each Captain should try to advise his men to stay untill Majr. Lewis would arrive with the Remainder of the men. . . .

Wednesday 10th. The men were prepar'd to Return. I told the men that if they should go before Major Lewis Came, that I would be blamed for it & my Character would suffer they agreed to stay, as did also all the other Companies untill a Letter could be sent to Majr. Lewis, Lt. Morton was imediatly Dispatched with two men & a letter wherein I set forth the Disorder & Confusion that was among us . . . & Requested him to come that Evening or next morning if Possable, for our meat was then done & the men had nothing to support them. . . .

Thursday 11th. Notwithstanding the Promises the men made the Day before of staying untill the major would Come they were all in Readiness for a march homewards but after many Arguments & Perswasion I Prevailed on them to Tarry that Day for the Majors arrival as also for And'w Lynam who had been out 3 days making what Discoveries he could. I procured a little Venison for their support that Day about 12 oClock two Indians came down in a Canoe who gave us to understand that the Companies would be down that night; In the afternoon Andrew Lynam & Wm. Hall Returned & Reported that they had been fifteen miles down the River that they see a Great Buffalo Road & fresh signs of Buffalos & Elks & see great numbers of Turkies & they were of opp'ion that game was Plenty. They see an old Fort which they believed to be a hunting Fort built by the Indians, and they think the main mountain was not above two miles below them but did not choose to venture themselves to make any further Discoveries as they Judged this to be sufficient to Encourage the men to Pursue their Journey. This account Pleased the Officers very much; But it Rather increased the mutiny among the Men for they Looked upon the Report to be formed only to Draw them so much farther from home, & said were the game ever so plenty it was Impossible to support 340 men by it as there was nothing Else to Depend upon & if they Proceeded any Further they must Inevitably Perish with hunger which they Looked upon to be more Inglorious than to Return & be yet serviceable to their Country when properly Provided for. These & many other weighty Arguments they made use of but thro the whole they laid great part of our misfortunes on the co-m-es for not Providing properly for such a Number of Men as we had not above 15 Days Provisions when we Left Fort Frederick to support us on a Journey of near 300 miles as we suppose Mr. Morton arrived & Informed me that he had had Delivered my Letter to ye major who could hardly believe the Contents & said he had often seen the like mutiny among soldiers & it might Easily be settled &&& 8 of Capt. Smiths men went off & Bledsher & Gredi[?] wth ym.

Fryday 12th. . . . The Soldiers being all Ready to march up ye Creek 8 or 10 of my Company had their Bundles on their Backs & was about to march, after spending some time Reasoning with them about going I was obliged to Disarm them & take their Blankets by force. They had not been Disarmed above half an Hour untill 5 of them went off Privately & left their guns. I soon missed them & sent Wm. Robinson & one other man after them who met them at some Distance & Brought them back to Camp. Capt. Wodson arived & with some of his Company & Informed us that his Canoe overset & lost his Tents with every thing valluable in her. That Major Lewis's Canoe was sunk in the River & that ye Major Capt. Overton Lt. Gun & one other man had to swim for their Lives & that several things of Vallue was Lost particularly five or six fine Guns. Major Lewis, Lt. McNeal, & Mr. Chew arrived who Informed us of their being shipwrecked. . . .

Saturday morning ye. 13th. Major Lewis give Orders to Each Capt. to Call his Compy together imediatly . . . & the Major Told the Soldiers that he was Informd of their Design to go home . . . that he hoped they would alter their Intentions of Desertion & Mutiny & would pursue the journy, he Likewise set forth the Ill Consequence that would Certainly attend such Conduct & that they would be well Supported when they Got into the hunting ground which . . . must be very nigh & horses would support them for some time notwithstanding all that Could be said they appear'd obstinatly bent to go home for if they went forward they must Perish or Eat horses neither of which They were willing to do. Then the major Stepped off some yards Distance & Desired all that was willing to Serve their Country & share his Fate to go with him all the Officers & some private men not above 20 or 30 join'd him upon which Mountgomeries Vollunters marched off & was Imediatly followed by my Company & Smiths. 4 Private men and my Lts. staid with me.... A small quantity of wet meal was brought in, I see about one pound given to 12 men & one of them bought a share which he gave 2/ for, one Jesse Mays offered 13 Day hire as a Packhorsman for 2 lb. of Bears meat so that it is Impossable to Express the abject Condition we were in both before & after the men Deserted us, . . . —From William Preston's Journal, Draper Mss. IQQ 96-123, State Historical Society of Wisconsin.

11. Washington's Proposals for Frontier Defense

No one felt the plight of the frontiersmen more keenly than Washington. "I SEE their situation," he wrote from Winchester on April 22, 1756, "know their danger, and participate their sufferings, without having it in my power to give them further relief, than uncertain promises." Fort Ashby, on Patterson's Creek, in present Mineral County, had just been attacked. A skirmish with the Indians at Fort Edwards on the Capon River had resulted in the death of Captain John Mercer. Enoch's Fort in Hampshire County was evacuated and scarcely a family remained in the county. In every communication Washington reported some new setback and stressed the urgency of the situation on the Virginia frontier. His proposals for the defense of the area were outlined in a letter of April 24, 1756, to John Robinson, Speaker of the House of Burgesses.

Winchester, April 24, 1756

Dear Sir: . . .

The deplorable situation of this people is no more to be described, than my anxiety and uneasiness for their relief....

You may expect, by the time this comes to hand, that, without a considerable reinforcement, Frederick county will not be mistress of fifteen families. They are now retreating to the securest parts in droves of fifties. In short, every thing has too melancholy an appearance for pen to communicate. I have therefore sent an officer, whose good sense and judicious observations will be a more effectual way of transmitting an account of the people's distresses.

I wish the Assembly had given two thousand men, instead of fifteen hundred, and that I had been acquainted with the dispositions they intended to make. Since I am ignorant of *this*, I hope it will not be thought presuming when I offer my sentiments upon the subject.

We are, Sir, first to consider, that if a chain of forts is to be erected upon our frontiers, it is done with a design to protect the people. Therefore, if these forts are more than fifteen and eighteen miles, or a day's march, asunder, and garrisoned with less than eighty or an hundred men each, the intention is lost, and for these reasons. 1st, if they are at greater distances, it is inconvenient for the soldiers to scout, and allows the enemy to pass between without being easily discovered, and when discovered so soon pursued. And secondly, if they are garrisoned with less than eighty or an hundred men, the number is too few to afford detachments. Then, again, our frontiers are so extensive, that, were the enemy to attack us on the one side, before the troops on the other could get to their assistance, they might overrun and destroy half the country. And it is more than probable, if they had a design upon the first, they would make a feint upon the other. Then we are to consider what sums the building of twenty forts would cost, and the removing stores and provisions to each, and in the last place, we are to consider where and when this expense is to end. For, if we do not endeavour to remove the cause, we are liable to the same incursions seven years hence as now, if the war continues, and they are allowed to remain on Ohio.

I shall next give the reasons, which I think make for a defensive plan. If the neighbouring colonies refuse us their assistance, we have neither strength or abilities or ourselves to conduct an expedition; or, if we had, and were the whole to join us,

I do not see to what purpose, since we have neither a train of artillery, artillery-men, engineers, &c, to execute any scheme beyond the mountains against a regular fortress. Again, we have not, that I can see, either stores or provisions, arms or ammunition, wagons or horses, in any degree proportioned to the service; and to undertake an affair, where we are sure to fall through, would be productive of the worst consequences, and another defeat would entirely lose us the interest of every Indian. . . .

I would beg leave, . . .to propose that there should be a strong fort erected at this place, for a general receptacle of all the stores, &c, and a place of residence for the commanding officers, to be garrisoned with one company for the security of the stores, and to serve as escorts for all wagons, that are going higher up, because it is the most public and most convenient for intelligence of any in the country, and the most convenient to the part that will ever be attacked by *numbers*, it lying directly on the road to Fort Duquisne, from whence, and their Indian allies, who are still up higher, we have the greatest reason to apprehend danger. It also lies convenient to the inhabitants for raising the militia when occasion requires.

I have found by experience, that being just within the inhabitants is absolutely necessary to give orders for the defence of the people; . . . For the people so soon as they are alarmed, immediately fly inwards, and at this time there is not an inhabitant living between here and Fort Cumberland, except a few settlements upon the Manor about a fort we built there, and a few families at Edward's, on Cacapehon, with a guard of ours, which makes this very town at present the outmost frontiers, and though a place trifling in itself, is yet of the utmost importance, as it commands the communication from east to west, as well as from north to south, for at this place do almost all the roads center, and secures the great roads of one half of our frontiers to the markets of the neighboring colonies, as well as to those on Rappahannock and Potomack &c. At Fort Cumberland I would have one company garrisoned to secure the place, to procure the earliest intelligence, and to cover all detachments that may be sent towards the Ohio, which is all the use it can ever be of. In the next place, I would propose, that a good fort should be erected between this and Fort Cumberland, which shall be in a line with the chain of forts across the country, and be garrisoned with two companies. . . .

These three forts that I have already spoken of will employ four companies, which will be a tolerable body, if the companies are large, which they would be, according to the scheme I sent you. And it would be a trifling expense to augment each company to one hundred privates, which will make two thousand, exclusive of officers, which were included in the scheme last sent.

After this is done, I would post the remaining companies equidistant, or at proper passes, along our frontiers, agreeable to the enclosed sketch, and order communications to be opened between fort and fort, and large detachments scouting between to discover the tracts of the enemy.

And now, sir, one thing to add, which requires the Assembly's attention, and that is, what vale, or upon what part of our frontiers these forts are to be built? For I am to tell you that the Great Ridge or North Mountain, so called in Evans's map, to which I refer, is now become our exterior bound, there not being one inhabitant beyond that on all the Potomack waters, except a few families on the South Branch, and at Joseph Edwards's, on Cacapehon, (which I have already mentioned,) guarded by a party of ours. So that it requires some consideration to determine whether we are to build near this to protect the present inhabitants; or on the South Branch, or Patterson's Creek, in the hopes of drawing back those, who have forsaken their dwellings,

If we do not build there, that country will ever want settlers; and if we *do,* there is so great a blank, with such a series of mountains between, that it will be next to impossible to guard the people effectually. . . . —*The Writings of George Washington,* edited by John C. Fitzpatrick, I, 331-36.

12. Preston's Register

Colonel William Preston (1729-1783) of Augusta County has been credited with the authorship of a unique record of the captives and casualties of the French and Indian War in Virginia. This document attests with statistical conciseness what the commanders of the western outposts were reporting to their superiors. "As the Inhabitants on Green Briar, New Rivr. and Holstens are all scattered from their plantations and have Left the best Crops of corn in the Colony," wrote Captain Peter Hogg in 1755, "it will become a Settlement for the Indians during the Winter if more Companies are not Sent up to protect the farmers while they gather their Corn." Equally dire was the news from the upper Potomac where nothing was to be seen but "Desolation and murder heightened with all Barbarous Circumstances, and unheard of Instances of Cruelty." If the Indians spared the lives of young women, continued Colonel Adam Stephen, it was only to "Carry them away to gratify the Brutal passions of Lawless Savages." Besides serving as a general epitaph, the register provides a roster of western Virginia pioneers. One of the victims listed was Preston's own uncle, Colonel James Patton, a leading figure in the early annals of Augusta County, which once included a large part of present West Virginia.

A Register of the Persons who have been either Killed, Wounded or taken Prisoners by the Enemy in Augusta County, as also of such as have made their Escape.

DATES	PERSONS NAMES	PLACES	
[1754]	Robt. Foyles, his wife & 5 children	Monongalia	[Killed]
[October]	Steven Lyon	Holstons River	"
	John Goldman	"	"
	Benjamin Harrison	"	"
[1755]	———— Burk	"	[Prisoner—Escaped]
[May 3]	Mary Baker	"	[Wounded]
[June 18]	Sam. Stalnacker	"	[Prisoner—Escaped]
	Sam Hydon	"	[Prisoner]

	Adam Stalnacker	"	[Killed]
	Mrs. Stalnacker	"	"
	A Servant man	"	"
	Mathias Counce	"	"
	Micheal Houck	"	"
[July 3]	James Mcfarland	N. River	"
	John Bingeman	"	"
	Mrs. Bingeman	"	"
	Adam Bingeman	"	"
	John Cook	"	"
	Henry Zin	"	"
	A young child	"	"
	Nathaniel Welshire	"	[Wounded]
	Dutch Jacob &	"	[Wounded—Prisoner]
	His Wife	"	[Prisoner—Escaped]
	Frederick Stern	"	[Wounded]
	Mrs. Bingeman Jun	"	"
	Mrs. Davies	"	"
	Isaac Freeland his wife & 5 children	"	[Prisoners]
	Bingeman's Son & Daughter & a stranger	"	"
[July 12]	Lieut. Wright & Two soldiers	Reed Creek	[Killed]
[July 30]	Colo. James Patton	N. River	"
	Caspr. Barrier	"	"
	Mrs. Draper & 1 child	"	"
	James Cull	"	[Wounded]
	Mrs. English &	"	[Prisoner—Escaped]
	her 2 children	"	[Prisoners]
	Mrs. Draper Junr.	"	[Prisoner]
	Henry Leonard	"	"
[August 12]	Morrice Griffith	Vauses	[Prisoner—Escaped]
[September]	Henry Boughman	Green Brier	[Killed]
	John Cause & his father-in-law	"	"
	Walter Fishpough	"	"
	George White	"	"
	Old Christopher	"	"
[1755]	Mrs. Cousler	"	"
	An old man his wife & a school master	"	"
[September]	John Thomas	"	"
	Mrs. Fishpough & 5		

	children, Couslers Daughter & Mrs.		
	Freny	"	[Prisoners]
	Corporal Bennet	"	[Killed]
	2 girls called Landsisco	So. Branch	[Prisoners]
[1756]	Robt. Looney & a		
[February]	Dutchman	Reed Creek	[Killed]
[March]	John See		"
	Michael Motes		"
	Patrick Smith		"
	Moses Man		[Prisoner]
	Vallentine Harman	N. River	[Killed]
	Jacob Harman & Son	"	"
	Andr. Moses	"	"
[June]	Thos. Davies	Roanoke	[Prisoner—Escaped]
[25]	Capt. John Smith	Ft. Vause	[Prisoner—Returned]
	Peter Looney	"	[Prisoner—Escaped]
	Wm. Bratton	"	[Prisoner—Returned]
	Joseph Smith	"	"
	Wm. Pepper	"	[Prisoner]
	Mrs. Vause her 2 Daughters, a Negro, 2 young Indians & a servant man	"	[Prisoners]
	Ican Medley & 2 Daughters	"	"
	James Bell	"	"
	Christopher Hicks	"	"
	———— Cole	"	" & Burned in ye town [?]
	———— Graham	"	[Prisoner]
	Benjamin Davies	"	"
[June 25]	Lieut. John Smith	"	[Killed]
	John Tracey	"	"
	John English	"	"
	Mrs. Mary English	"	[Prisoner]
	Wm. Robinson	"	[Wounded]
	Thos. Robinson	"	"
	Saml. Robinson	"	"
	Robt. Pepper	"	"
[September] [11, 12, 13, 14]	Ensign Madison	Jacksons Riv.	[Killed]
	Nicholas Carpenter	"	"
	———— Fry	"	"
	Steven Lowel	"	"
	James Mais	"	"

Date	Name	Location	Status
	James Montgomery	"	"
	Nicholas Nut	"	"
	John Bird	"	"
	George Kinkead	"	"
[September]	Mrs. Boyl	"	"
	3 children names Parsinger	"	"
	Joseph Swobe	"	[Wounded]
	———— Willson	"	"
	5 children belonging to Charles Boyl	"	[Prisoners]
	David Gallaway	"	[Prisoner—Escaped]
	Mrs. McConell	"	"
	Joseph Carpenter	"	"
	Mrs. Bird & 6 children	"	[Prisoners]
	Mrs. Kinkead & 3 children	"	"
	Mrs. Parsinger & 2 children	"	"
	5 children called Carpenter	"	"
	Saml. Brown a Boy	"	"
	———— Swobe a Boy	"	"
[October 12]	John Robinson	Vauses	[Killed]
	John Walker	"	[Prisoner]
[1757]	Jacob Peters lost		
[February]	6 children	S. Branch	[Prisoners—Escaped]
[March]	Wm. Bradshaw & Son	Craigs Creek	[Prisoners]
[May 14]	Andw. Arnold	Jacksons River	[Killed]
	Henry Lawless	"	"
[May 16]	John Moor	Cowpasture	"
	Mrs. Moor & 5 children	"	[Prisoners]
	George Meese &	South Branch	[Killed]
	his 2 Sons	"	[Prisoners]
	———— Shudec	"	[Killed]
	Henry Lawrence	"	"
	Michael Freeze & Wife	"	"
[July]	Mark Tollet	Jacksons River	"
	A servant man	"	[Prisoner]
	James Allen	"	[Wounded]
	———— Swobe	"	"
[25]	Robt. Renicks	Forks of Jam. River	[Killed]
	Thos. Moor	"	"
	Mrs. Renick & 7 children	"	[Prisoners]

	Mrs. Denis	"	"
	John Crawford Jur.	Craigs Creek	[Killed]
	Jno. & Alex.		
	Crawford	"	[Wounded]
[September]	Serg't Henry	Fort Dinwiddle	[Killed]
	James Stewart	Cowpasture	"
	James Stewart Jun.	"	[Prisoner]
	James McClung	"	"
	2 childn. named		
	Cartmill	"	"
[October]	James McFerrin	Catawba	[Killed]
	Wm. McFerrin	"	[Prisoner]
[November]	3 Dutch People, I don't		
	know their names	Brocks Gap	[1 Killed—2 Prisoners]
	John States	"	[Killed]
[1758]			
[January]	Abm. Merchant	"	"
	Wm. Ward a Boy	Ft. Dinwiddie	[Prisoner]
	a soldier of Capt.		
	Woodwarde	Roanoke	
	a serv. man of Bryan's	"	
[March 19]	Wm. Clepole	Brocks	[Killed]
	Peter Moser	Sth. Branch	"
	Nicholas Frank	"	"
	John Coonrad	"	"
	John Cuningham & 2		
	others, there names		
	forgot	"	[Prisoners]
	George Moser	"	[Wounded]
	Adam Harper	"	"
[March]	A Servt. man kill'd &		
	maid & one child	Cow Pasture	[2 prisoners]
[20]	James Gatlive	Roanoke	[Killed]
	Joseph Love	"	"
	Wm. Love	"	"
	A Servt. Maid & Child	"	[Prisoners]
	Snodgrass a girl	Catawbo	[Prisoner]
[April 24]	John McCreery Jr.	Cow-pastr.	"
	Wm. McCreety	"	"
[27]	Capt. Jam. Dunlap	S. Branch	[Killed]
	Josiah Willson	"	"
	John Hutchinson	"	"
	Thomas Caddon	"	"
	Henry MCullam	"	"
	John Wright	"	"
	Thos. Smith	"	"

	Robt. McNully	,,	,,
	Wm. Elliott	,,	,,
[April 27]	Mrs. Elliott	,,	,,
	Ludwick Falck & wife	,,	,,
	Adam Little	,,	,,
	————— Brock	,,	,,
	John Ramsay	,,	,,
	Wm. Burk	,,	,,
	————— Reeney	,,	,,
	Wm. Woods	,,	,,
	John McCulley	,,	,,
	Thos. Searl	,,	,,
	James Gill	,,	,,
	John Guy & a Stranger	,,	,,
[28]	Capt. Sybert w.th 16 Persons, names not known	So. Fork	,,
	24 prisoners at that same place missing	,,	[Prisoners]
[May]	Moses Moore	Jacksons Riv.	[Prisoner]

—Draper Mss. 1QQ83, State Historical Society of Wisconsin.

13. William Fleming to Governor Fauquier

Conditions improved on the western Virginia frontier in 1758 when General Jeffrey Amherst ordered General John Forbes to undertake the long contemplated offensive against Fort Duquesne. Instead of taking Braddock's road, Forbes moved westward by way of Loyalhanna and Fort Ligonier. The cautious advance of the English and their judicious distribution of presents and concessions among the Indians who deserted the French at this critical hour ensured success to the expedition. Before retreating down the Ohio, the French burned Fort Duquesne. When the English rebuilt it, to the great uneasiness of the Indians, it was renamed Fort Pitt and once more resumed its role as the Gibraltar of the Mountains. Although the Treaty of Paris of 1763 eliminated France as a colonial power in North America, the Indians continued to menace the frontier. In the spring of 1763 under the leadership of the great Ottawa chief, Pontiac, they attacked from Detroit to the Virginia frontier taking several forts, investing others, including Fort Pitt, and capturing or killing two thousand persons. The decisive defeat of the Indians at Bushy Run by Colonel Henry Bouquet in August, 1763, relieved Fort Pitt as well as the Virginia frontier which had been weakened by the disbandment of a regiment of militia. The Virginia troops subsequently called out by the governor of that colony were placed under the command of Adam Stephen and Andrew Lewis, the latter in accordance with the suggestion contained in the following letter.

Sir:

Since the last Reduction of the Regiment I have had in this County which enables me to inform your Honor of some particulars I think it a duty incumbent on me to do. I can assert that in Eight years service I never knew such a general Consternation as the late Irruption of Indians has occasioned Should they make a second attempt I am affraid the County will be laid desolate which I attribute to the following reasons. The sudden unexpected and great Slaughter of the People, their being destitute of Arms & Ammunition. The County Lieutn. being at a distance and not exerting himself, his orders are neglected the most of the Militia officers being unfitt persons or unwilling not to say affraid to meet an Enemy too busy with their harvest to run a risk in the Field. The Inhabitants left without protection without a person to Head them have nothing to do but fly. As the Indians are saving & Caressing all the Negroes they take should it be productive of an Insurrection it may be attended with the most serious Consequences—Sir I hope you will excuse my freedome in mentioning the above or assuring you that the Militia will always be unequal to the task on an Invasion. No doubt the Legislature will find some defects in the Militia law which on a revisal may be remedied. if the Militia Commissions in this & other Frontier Countys were only given to Persons and who would be active in the defense of their Country some good might be expected. this depends on an Active County Lieutn. such a person your Honor need not be at a loss for in this County while *Colo. Lewis* is alive. I am sensible of the disadvantages the Colony labours under at present with reguard to its Currcy.

which may be a great hinderence to the raising of men for its defence yet if three or foure hundred men active & good woodsmen which might easily be done were to be draughted out of the Militia of this County, Companied & Officerd by Persons who had seen Service and Continued for two or three months as exigence requires not in Forts but constantly to raing beyond the Inhabitants. I think they might prevent anymore mischief being done or at least preserve the County from being ruined. these troops might be paid in Tobacco ... Arms & Powder for any number of men is not to be got in this County. The Bearer Lieutn. Cunningham waits on you to offer his service. He has servd with & under me some years I can assure your Honor he is a good & deserving officer.

I am & c.

[Wm. Fleming to
Govr. Fauquier.]

Stanton
July 26, 1763
—Draper Mss. 3ZZ50-51, State Historical Society of Wisconsin.

14. The Royal Proclamation of 1763

Pontiac's Conspiracy emphasized the need for a revised Indian policy designed to maintain peace on the frontier. The Royal Proclamation of October 7, 1763, in addition to providing for the government of the newly acquired provinces of Quebec, East Florida, West Florida, and Grenada, granted lands to veterans, regulated the Indian trade, and forbade "for the present" the purchase or settlement of lands west of the sources of the streams flowing into the Atlantic.

By the KING. A PROCLAMATION. GEORGE, R.

WHereas we have taken into our royal consideration the extensive and valuable acquisitions in America, secured to our crown by the late definitive treaty of peace concluded at Paris the 10th day of February last; and being desirous that all our loving subjects, as well of our kingdoms as of our colonies in America, may avail themselves, with all convenient speed, of the great benefits and advantages which must accrue therefrom to their commerce, manufactures, and navigation; we have thought fit, with the advice of our privy council, to issue this our royal proclamation, hereby to publish and declare to all our loving subjects, that we have, with the advice of our said privy council, granted our letters patent under our great seal of Great Britain, to erect within the countries and islands, ceded and confirmed to us by the said treaty, four distinct and separate governments, stiled and called by the names of Quebec, East Florida, West Florida, and Grenada, and limited and bounded as follows, viz.: . . .

And whereas we are desirous, upon all occasions, to testify our royal sense and approbation of the conduct and bravery of the officers and soldiers of our armies, and to reward the same, we do hereby command and impower our governors of our said three new colonies, and other our governors of our several provinces on the continent of North America, to grant, without fee or reward, to such reduced officers as have served in North America during the late war, and are actually residing there, and shall personally apply for the same, the following quantities of land, subject, at the expiration of ten years, to the same quit-rents as other lands are subject to in the province within which they are granted, as also subject to the same conditions of cultivation and improvement, viz.

To every person having the rank of a field officer, 5000 acres.

To every captain, 3000 acres.

To every subaltern or staff officer, 2000 acres.

To every non-commission officer, 200 acres.

To every private man 50 acres.

We do likewise authorise and require the governors and commanders in chief of all our said colonies upon the continent of North America to grant the like quantities of land, and upon the same conditions, to such reduced officers of our navy of like rank, . . .

And whereas it is just and reasonable, and essential to our interest, and the security of our colonies, that the several nations or tribes of Indians, with whom we are connected, and who live under our protection, should not be molested or disturbed in the possession of such parts of our dominions and territories as, not having been ceded to, or purchased by us, are reserved to them, or any of them, as their hunting-grounds; we do therefore, with the advice of our privy council, declare it to be our royal will and pleasure, that no governor, or commander in chief, in any of our colonies of Quebec, East Florida, or West Florida, do presume, upon any pretence whatever, to grant warrants of survey, or pass any patents for lands beyond the bounds of their respective governments, as described in their commissions; as also that no governor or commander in chief of our other colonies or plantations in America, do presume for the present, and until our further pleasure be known, to grant warrant of survey, or pass patents for any lands beyond the heads or sources of any of the rivers which fall into the Atlantic Ocean from the west or north-west; or upon any lands whatever, which not having been ceded to, or purchased by us, aforesaid, are reserved to the said Indians, or any of them.

And we do further declare it to be our royal will and pleasure, for the present, as aforesaid, to reserve under our sovereignty, protection, and dominion, for the use of the said Indians, all the land and territories not included within the limits of our said three new governments, or within the limits of the territory granted to the Hudson's Bay Company; as also all the land and territories lying to the westward of the sources of the rivers which fall into the sea from the west and north-west as aforesaid; and we do hereby strictly forbid, on pain of our displeasure, all our loving subjects from making any purchases or settlements whatever, or taking possession of any of the lands above reserved, without our special leave and license for that purpose first obtained.

And we do further strictly enjoin and require all persons whatever, who have either wilfully or inadvertently seated themselves upon any lands within the countries above described, or upon any other lands, which not having been ceded to, or purchased by us, are still reserved to the said Indians as aforesaid, forthwith to remove themselves from such settlements.

And whereas great frauds and abuses have been committed in the purchasing lands of the Indians, ... in order, therefore, to prevent such irregularities for the future, and to the end that the Indians may be convinced of our justice and determined resolution to remove all reasonable cause of discontent, we do, with the advice of our privy council, strictly enjoin and require, that no private person do presume to make any purchase from the said Indians of any lands reserved to the said Indians within those parts of our colonies where we have thought proper to allow settlement; but that if at any time any of the said Indians should be inclined to dispose of the said lands, the same shall be purchased only for us, in our name, at some public meeting or assembly of the said Indians, to be held for that purpose by the governor or commander in chief of our colony respectively within which they shall lie: and in case they shall lie within the limits of any proprietaries, conformable to such directions and instructions as we or they shall think proper to give for that purpose: and we do, by the advice of our privy council, declare and enjoin, that the trade with the said Indians shall be free and open to all our subjects whatever, provided that every person who may incline to trade with the said Indians, do take out a license for carrying on such trade, from the governor or commander in chief of any of our colonies respectively, where such person shall reside, and also give security to observe such regulations as we shall at any time think fit, by ourselves or commissaries, to be appointed for this purpose, to direct and appoint for the benefit of the said trade: and we do hereby authorize, enjoin, and require the governors and commanders in chief of all our colonies respectively, as well those under our immediate government, as those under the government and direction of proprietaries, to grant such licenses without fee or reward, taking especial care to insert therein a condition that such license shall be void, and the security forfeited, in case the person, to whom the same is granted, shall refuse or neglect to observe such regulations as we shall think proper to prescribe as aforesaid . . .

Given at our Court at St. James's, the 7th day of October 1763, in the third year of our reign.—*The Annual Register* . . . *For the Year 1763*, Seventh Edition, 208-13.

15. Proclamation of Governor Fauquier

Violations of the injunction in the Proclamation of 1763 against settlement west of the Appalachian watershed evoked the following warning from Francis Fauquier, Lieutenant Governor of Virginia. Fauquier was appointed to this position in January, 1758. He served as Virginia's chief executive until his death at Williamsburg on March 3, 1768.

WHEREAS I Have lately received letters from his Excellency Major General Gage, and Major William Murraye, commanding officer at fort Pitt, informing me that several people of Virginia have seated themselves on lands belonging to the Indians, to the westward of the Allegheny mountains, and contiguous to the river Cheek, in disobedience of his Majesty's commands (notified by two proclamations of the 7th of October 1763, and the 10th of April 1766) in violation of the friendship subsisting between us and the said Indians, and in contempt of the dreadful consequences . . . apprehended from such unjust and licentious proceedings: I have therefore, to put a stop to these and all other the like encroachments for the future, thought fit, by and with the advice of his Majesty's Council, to issue this proclamation, in his Majesty's name, hereby strictly enjoining and requiring all persons who have made such settlements immediately to evacuate the same, and to pay the strictest obedience hereafter to his Majesty's commands herein signified; which if they shall fail to do they must expect no protection or mercy from Government, and be exposed to the revenge of the exasperated Indians.

GIVEN under my hand, and the seal of the colony, at WILLIAMSBURG, this 31st day of July, 1766, and in the 6th year of his Majesty's reign.

FRANCIS FAUQUIER
GOD SAVE THE KING
—*The Virginia Gazette*, Purdie and Dixon, August 1, 1766.

16. Dunmore's War – Letter of Devereux Smith

The relentless advance of the Virginia and Pennsylvania fron-
tiersmen into the Ohio valley, checked only momentarily by the
Proclamation of 1763, was the basic cause of Dunmore's War in
1774. Indian title to land south of the Ohio had been relinquished
by the Six Nations in the Treaty of Fort Stanwix (1768) and by
the Cherokees in the Treaties of Hard Labour and Lochaber
(1768, 1770). A vast and fertile area was thus opened to land
speculators, bounty claimants, and restless pioneers, to whom
"the Lands further off," as Lord Dunmore, royal governor of Vir-
ginia put it, always seemed better than those nearby. Before the
Revolution, isolated settlements appeared in the Kanawha, Buck-
hannon, Cheat, and Greenbrier valleys and on the southern bank
of the upper Ohio. North of the Ohio were the Delawares, some
of whom had accepted Christianity and now wished to live in
peace with the whites. Their neighbors, the Shawnees, however,
led by their Chief Cornstalk, together with the Mingoes, were
fiercely determined to resist the aggressive Virginians. In coping
with the Indian menace, the Virginians could expect little co-
operation from the Pennsylvanians because of the boundary dis-
pute that resulted in the establishment of two rival jurisdictions
in the area of the Forks of the Ohio—Westmoreland County by
Pennsylvania and the District of West Augusta by Virginia. Dr.
John Connolly, a justice of the District, emphasized Virginia's
authority by renaming Fort Pitt Fort Dunmore.

By the opening of 1774, an Indian uprising seemed imminent.
The panic-stricken pioneers of the valleys of southwest Virginia
began to abandon their homes for the more secure settlements
to the east; along the Ohio the number of outrages committed by
both whites and Indians increased alarmingly. On April 21, Dr.
Connolly issued a circular which could only result in an Indian
war, or so thought Devereux Smith, the author of the following
letter, who was a justice of Westmoreland County and a bitter
foe of Connolly.

Pittsburgh, June 10, 1774

. . . On the 15th of *April,* Mr. *William Butler* sent off a canoe loaded with goods for the *Shawanese* Towns, and on the 16th it was attacked about forty miles from here by three *Cherokee Indians,* who had waylaid them on the river bank. They killed one white man, and wounded another, and a third made his escape. They plundered the canoe of the most valuable part of the cargo and made off; but as they were *Cherokees,* we were sure they did this for sake of plunder alone, therefore thought no more of it than the loss. As Mr. *Butler* was under the necessity of sending people to assist in bringing his peltry from the *Shawanese* Towns, he sent off another canoe on the 24th of *April,* in care of two *Indians,* who were well known to be good men, and two white men. On the 27th, about ninety miles from here, they were fired upon from shore, and both the Indians were killed, by *Michael Cresap,* and a party he had with him; they also scalped the *Indians.* Mr. *Cresap* then immediately followed the above mentioned *Shawanese* Chiefs some small distance lower down, where they were encamped, and fired upon them, killed one and wounded two more. The *Indians* fled to the *Delaware* Towns, which were the nearest, and are greatly exasperated at this treatment, as they did not expect any such thing from the *English.* About that same time, a party, headed by one *Greathouse,* barbarously murdered and scalped nine *Indians* at the house of one *Baker,* near *Yellow Creek,* about fifty-five miles down the river. Owing to these cruelties committed by *Cresap* and *Greathouse,* the inhabitants of *Rackoon* and *Wheeling* fled from that settlement, and are chiefly gone to *Virginia.* After *Cresap* had been guilty of these cruelties, he returned to *Maryland,* but has since came back with a party of men. . . . On the 21st of *April, Conolly* wrote a letter to the inhabitants of *Wheeling,* telling them that he had been informed, by good authority, that the *Shawanese* were ill disposed towards white men, and that he, therefore, required and commanded them to hold themselves in readiness to repel any insults that might be offered by them. This letter fell into the hands of *Cresap,* and he says that it was in consequence of this letter, and the murder committed by the *Cherokees* on Mr. *Butler's* people, that he committed the hostilities above mentioned.

I am informed, that on the 6th day of *May,* Mr. *Croghan* sent Captain *White Eyes,* (one of the *Indian* Chiefs,) in company with some of our traders, to acquaint the *Shawanese* and *Delawares* that the outrages which had been committed by some of our ill disposed white people, were without the least countenance from Government. This *Indian* promised to use his best endeavours to accommodate matters, and returned the 24th of *May,* and brought with him ten white men, who had been protected by the *Delawares* eight days, in their towns, and guarded safe to this place. He also brought a speech from the *Delawares,* from which we have great reason to believe they are not inclined for war. We also believe that they will endeavour to preserve the lives of the traders that are now amongst the *Shawnese.* He also brought from the *Shawanese* Chief (called the *Hardman*) an answer to a speech sent to them by Mr. *Croghan* upon this occasion, in which he signifies that the *Shawanese* are all warriors, and will not listen to us until they have satisfaction of us for what injuries they have received from the *Virginians,* &c.

White Eyes informs us that a Mingo man called *Logan,* (whose family had been murdered in the number,) had raised a party to cut down the *Shawanese* Town traders at the *Canoe* Bottom, on *Hockhocking Creek,* where they were pressing their peltry; but we have heard since that the *Shawanese* have taken them under their care until matters are further settled, but *God* knows what fate they have met with; we hope they are still alive, and if it be so they have a chance to come in, if the outrageous behaviour of the *Virginians* do not prevent them. The sixth of this month we had an account from *Muddy Creek,* (empties into the river *Monongahela,* near *Cheat* river,) that the Indians had killed and scalped one white man, his wife, and three children, and that three more of the same man's children were missing, and has since been confirmed. We suppose this to be *Logan's* party, and that they will do more mischief before they return. About the 20th of *May,* one *Campbell,* lately from *Lancaster,* was killed and scalped near *Newcomer's* Town, and one *Proctor,* at *Wheeling,* by a party of *Shawanese* and *Mingoes.*

The *Virginians* in this part of the country seem determined to make war with the Indians at any rate. The one half of this country is ruined to all intents and purposes, which, a few months ago, was in a flourishing way. *Conolly* has embodied upwards of one hundred men, and will have this fort in good order in a short time. He is gathering in all the provisions he can possibly get from the country, which, he says, will be paid for by the Government of *Virginia*. The militia here, by *Conolly's* orders, shoot down the cattle, sheep and hogs, belonging to the inhabitants, as they please; they also press horses, and take by force any part of our property they think proper, and tell us that they have the authority so to do; therefore you may judge of our situation at present. . . .

June 12. Mr. *Conolly* purposes to march from this place to-morrow with two hundred men to build a stockade fort at *Wheeling Creek*, and another near *Hockhocking Creek;* and says he will send parties, at the same time, against the *Shawanese* Towns; and I am of opinion that they will make no distinction betwixt *Shawanese* and *Delawares* as they are determined to have a general war. Mr. *Croghan* has set off this morning to *Williamsburg*, as he says, to represent the state of this country to Lord *Dunmore* and Council, as also to acquaint them of Mr. *Conolly's* rash conduct at this place, which he seems to disapprove of. We are this day informed, that the three children before mentioned, that were missing near *Muddy Creek*, were found dead, and scalpled, and two other men in sight of a fort that is lately built on *Dunkard Creek*, up the river *Monongahela*, all supposed to be done by *Logan's* party. The inhabitants of the town are busily employed in stockading it round about, yet have no reason to expect anything better than ruin and destruction. . . .

I am, sir, your most obliged humble, servant,

Devereux Smith

—*American Archives*, Fourth Series, I, 467-70.

17. Lord Dunmore's Proclamation, April 25, 1774

The Governor of Virginia attributed the alarming situation on the frontier to the obstructionist policy of the Pennsylvania authorities and to Indian disturbances.

WHEREAS, I have reason to apprehend that the Government of *Pennsylvania*, in prosecution of their claim to *Pittsburg* and its dependencies, will endeavour to obstruct his Majesty's Government thereof, under my administration, by illegal and unwarrantable commitments of the officers I have appointed for that purpose, and that that settlement is in danger of annoyance from the *Indians* also; and it being necessary to support the dignity of his Majesty's Government, and protect his subjects in the quiet and peaceable enjoyment of their rights, I have therefore, thought proper, by and with the advice and consent of his Majesty's Council, by this Proclamation in his Majesty's name, to order and require the officers of the militia in that district, to embody a sufficient number of men to repel any insult whatever; and all his Majesty's liege subjects within this Colony, are hereby strictly required to be aiding and assisting therein, as they shall answer the contrary, at their peril. And I do further enjoin and require the several inhabitants of the territory aforesaid, to pay his Majesty's quit rents, and all public dues, to such officers as are, or shall be appointed to collect the same, within this Dominion, until his Majesty's pleasure therein shall be known.

Given under my hand, and the seal of the Colony, at *Williamsburg*, this 25th day of *April*, 1774, in the fourteenth year of his Majesty's reign. DUNMORE

GOD SAVE THE KING

—*American Archives,* Fourth Series, I, 283

18. Answer of the Shawnees to the Virginians

In May, 1774, Dr. Connolly held a conference at Fort Pitt with the Six Nations and with the Delawares, Shawnees, and other Indians involved in the recent frontier incidents. To the message of "condolence" sent by Connolly and the Indian agents, George Croghan and Alexander McKee, and delivered by the Delaware chief, White Eyes, the Shawnees made the following reply.

"BROTHERS: (Captain *Conolly,* Mr. *McKee,* and Mr. *Croghan,*) We have received your Speeches by *White Eyes,* and as to what Mr. *Croghan* and Mr. *McKee* says, we look upon it all to be lies, and perhaps what you say may be lies also; but as it is the first time you have spoke to us, we listen to you and expect that what we may hear from you will be more confined to truth than what we usually hear from the white people. It is you who are frequently passing down and up the *Ohio,* and making settlements upon it, and as you have informed us that your wise people were met together to consult upon this matter, we desire you to be strong and consider it well.

"BRETHREN: We see you speak to us at the head of your warriors, who you have collected together at sundry places upon this river, where we understand they are building forts, and as you have requested us to listen to you, we will do it, but in the same manner that you appear to speak to us. Our people at the Lower Towns have no Chiefs amongst them, but are all warriors, and are also preparing themselves to be in readiness, that they may be better able to hear what you have to say.

"You tell us not to take any notice of what your people have done to us; we desire you likewise not to take any notice of what our young men may now be doing, and as no doubt you can command your warriors when you desire them to listen to you, we have reason to expect that ours will take the same advice when we require it, that is, when we have heard from the Governour of *Virginia.* . . .—*American Archives,* Fourth Series, I, 479-80.

19. Dunmore Takes the Offensive – Letter to Andrew Lewis

As violent incidents and military preparations increased along the Virginia frontier, Lord Dunmore took the offensive against the Shawnees. He instructed Colonel Andrew Lewis to lead a force to the mouth of the Great Kanawha and there await the arrival of the Governor who planned to bring his troops from Pittsburgh down the Ohio to Point Pleasant. The following letter is a poor copy of one which Dunmore sent to Lewis from Winchester on July 24, 1774.

Sir—I receivd your's and Colo. Charles Lewis Letters, the general Confederacy of Different Indian Nations their repeated Hostilities there were six Men Murderd on Dunkard Creek on the 18th instant the Discovery of Indians & universal Alarm throughtouth all the frontiers of the Colony & the unhappy situation of the Divided Peopel settled over the Alagany Mountain's makes it necessary for going [in] Person to Fort Dunmore to put Matters under the best Regulation to Support that Country for a Barrier give the Enemies a Blow that will Breake the Confederacy, & render their plans abortive I intend to take as [many] men from this quarter as I Can get in order in some short time & Desire you to raise a respectable Boddy of Men and join me either at the mouth of the Greate Kanaway or Wailen as is most Convenient for you the Indians having Spies on the Frontiers the[y] may Bring all the Force of the Shawnees against you in your march to the Mouth of the Kenawey so I would have you Consider in What Time You Could get them and other things ready so as to meet me at eny Place at Ohio in as Short time as you Can let me know the same by the return of the express and forward the Letter to Colo. Wm. Preston with the greatest Dispatch as I want his Assistance as well as that of your Brother, *Charles Lewis.* The Expences the Expence [sic] of the numerous scouting Parties in the Different Counties forming an Expensive Frontere Will soon exceed the Expencis of an Expedition Against their Towns which will be more effectiaul & we may as well depend on the House of burgess providing for the Expedition as for a greater Expence of Acting on the Defensive at eny rate we know the Old Law Still in force as far as it goes we are sure of being reimbersed I wish you would Acquaint Colo. Preston of Contents of this Letter that those he Sends Out may joine you and Pray be explicit as you Can as to the time & place of Meeting I need not inform You how necessary Dispatch is.

I am Sir Your most Obt. & very H.ble Ser

DUNMORE

Winchester July 24th 1774
Colo. Lewis
—Draper Mss. 3QQ141, State Historical Society of Wisconsin.

20. Colonel William Fleming's Journal of the Expedition Led by Colonel Andrew Lewis Against the Ohio Indians

Of the several accounts of Colonel Andrew Lewis's expedition from Camp Union (Lewisburg) to Point Pleasant and into Ohio, the one found in the Orderly Book of Colonel William Fleming (1729-1795) of Botetourt County is the best. Fleming was severely wounded at the Battle of Point Pleasant on October 10, and the entries in his journal from October 9-17 were written by John Todd, who, on the 17th, crossed the Ohio with the main body of Lewis's troops and marched for the Indian towns. Fleming was left in charge of the camp at Point Pleasant, which was partially fortified with breastwork after the battle. Meanwhile, the forces under Dunmore moved down the Ohio to the mouth of the Hockhocking River, where they erected a stockade called Fort Gower. Before news of the Battle of Point Pleasant reached Dunmore, he decided to advance to the Indian villages in Ohio and ordered Lewis to join him there. The Indians, humbled by their defeat at Point Pleasant, were ready to sue for peace when the Governor opened negotiations with them at Camp Charlotte. The advance of Lewis and his victorious band in Ohio, however, alarmed both the Indians, who feared an attack against their towns, and Dunmore, who felt that the threat of renewed hostilities would prevent a speedy conclusion of peace. The Governor, therefore, instructed Lewis to halt, but the Colonel evaded the command. Dunmore then came in person to Lewis's camp and ordered the forces to return to Point Pleasant, which they reached on October 27 and 28. The following is a condensed version of Lewis's operations written by Fleming in his Orderly Book.

Viz.—In consequence of a Plan laid down by my Lord Dunmore, in which the Forces under Colo. Andw. Lewis were to Join His Lordship at the Mouth of New River, Camp Union at the big levels of Green Brier was appointed the place of Rendevouse for the Augusta Botetourt & Fincastle County troops, at which place they were Assembling from August ye. 27th. Septr. ye. 2d. we were Alarmed by a report that Stewarts Fort, four miles from Camp was Attack'd by Indians. A party being sent out found that only one man had been fired at and escaped with a verry slight wound but next day Septr. ye. 3d. McGuire a Countryman was brought in from another Quarter into Camp much wounded & had a bullet cut out of his Cheek. Septr. ye 4th. Parties as the day before were sent out in quest of the Enimy, and discovered three or four who had horses, but had no Opportunity of firing on them, tho they recovered the horses, and several Buffalo hide halters a tomhawk &c. were found. These Indians being a Party who had, as was customary come in to do what mischeif was in their power, and then push home with as many horses as they could pick up. The 5th. Parties on horseback had orders to scour the woods for two or three miles round camp. And a Capt. &c: & fifty private went in pursuit of the Enemy discovered yesterday.

Col: Andw. Lewis Joind the troops Septr. 1st. as Commander in Chief.

6th. Colo. Charles Lewis with the greatest part of the Augusta troops and Arbuckles Compy. from Botetourt march'd from Camp union with all the Cattle collected there at that time and [four?] hundred pack horses loaded with Flower, Salt, & Tools, for [the] mouth of Elk River, and had orders to build a small store house, for the provisions. And get Canoes made, sufficient to transport the Flower &c: from that Place down the New River to the Ohio. The 10th. One of Our Spies came in from Gauly and reported that on the 6th. Inst he discovered a party of Indians with horses on their return from the Inhabitants, And on the morning of the ninth another party coming in, from this time we have reason to believe that Our motions were narrowly watched by the Enemy.

Septr. the 12th Colo. Andw. Lewis with the Botetourt troops & Capts. Shelby Russels & Bufords Compies left Camp Union & took with them all the Beeves & Pack horses that we were then Collected. In the Evening a man from Colo. C. Lewis party came into Camp & reported that Colo. Fields from Culpepper County who Joind us with about 30 men & had marchd after Colo. C. Lewis on the 10 Inst. his men being out hunting had one of them shot down by an Indian, but that the Indian was kild before he scalpd him. This Indian proved to be a Tawa.

19th Crossed Gauly Mountain, which I take to be a Continuation of that Chain of mountains caled the Alegany Mountain, to the Northward and we Met with sudden & frequent Showers of Rain as is usual near these Mountains. It is pritty difficult to Cross being about a mile & half in Ascent & as much in descent

The 21st we fell in with New River or the Big Kanhaway a little below Kellys Place. and marching down the River Eight or Nine miles passed two curious Springs, the Vapour of which kindles quick as Gunpowder & burns with a surprizing force.

The 23. we Joind Col: C. Lewis who was encamped on the Banks of Elk river about a mile above its influx into New River by Computation 108 Miles from Camp Union.

Imployed to the 30th. in building a storehouse & making Canoes for transporting the stores. The 24th Scouts were sent different ways for the discovery of the Enimy. The 25th One of the Scouts that had Crosed the Kanhaway returnd & reported that about four miles from Camp, a Small party of Indians had passed them in the Night with horses on their way down the Kanhaway. Colo. Lewis sent some Scouts this

Evening to the Ohio to wait on his Lordship, As we expected about this time His Excellency with the Troops from the Northward would be arrived. And the 29th One of them returnd when about 15 miles from the Ohio, on their discovering Indian fires on the banks of the Kanhaway, and this Scout likewise on his way up discovered another party of Indians.

The 30th. Cros'd the Elk & marchd down to its mouth where we encamped. Octr. 1st.

The Troops were ordered to form two Colums in their march from this, each Colum made two grand divisions The Botetourt Troops formd the Right, the Augusta the left Colum. Capt. Jno Lewis of Botetourt with his Company Marchd advanced a little way in the front of the Colums—the Bullocks & Pack horses fell in betwixt the Front & Rear divisions, and had each Flank covered with One hundred Men. 6th. reach'd the Junction of the Great Kanhaway with the Ohio. we here met with a lettar from My Lord Dunmore The Spies sent from Elk came in this Evening, and told us they had quitted their Canoe, after sending back the Messenger formerly mentiond, and came by land to the point, where not finding His Lordship, they had continued amongst the hills, without being discovered by several parties of Indians that were hunting Buffaloes. Colo Lewis sent up by some of our Spies a lettar in return to His Lordships to Hockhocking. The 8th. Some messengers from My Lord with lettars came down by water & returnd in a few hours—

The 10th. some men who had left Camp at about three miles distance, fell in with a large Party of Indians a little after day break. One of Capt Russels men was shot down one escaped, & brought us the first intelligence which in a few minutes was confirmed by several Others being chased into Camp—Imagining this to be some scouting party, Colo. Lewis ordered a detachment from every Company. so as to make up One hundred & fifty men from each line, to go in quest of them Colo. Charles Lewis led the Augusta Detachment And had with him Capts Dickinson, Harrison & Skidmore, & Colo. Fleming the Botetourt. and had with him Capts Shelby, Russel, Buford & Love. & the Augusta line marchd on the Right near the foot of the hills. The Botetourt along the Banks of the Ohio, at about

200 Yards distance: We Marched Briskly ¾ of a mile or better from Camp, the Sun then, near an hour high, when a few guns were fired on the Right, & succeeded by a heavy fire, which in an Instant extended to the left and the two lines were hotly engaged. Early in the ingagement Colo. Charles Lewis on the Right received a mortal wound, and was led out of the Field. He died in a few houres, much beloved, universally esteemed, & greatly lamented by the whole troops. Soon afterward Colo. Fleming on the left, was daingerously wounded in the breast & Arm & Obleedged to quit the Field. The Fire continuing very warm & the Indians pushing our men, forced them to re-treat 150 or 200 Yards, but being timely supported by rein-forcements sent from Camp, they recovered the ground they had lost, & in turn drove the Enimy: Colo. Fields who came out with reinforcement was unhappily kild. the Action continued verry warm till near twelve o'Clock, when the Fire tho pritty constant was not so heavy. As the Enimy whenever they met with an advantagious piece of ground in their retreat, made a resolute stand, during which some of them were employed to remove their dead, dying & wounded, in the Afternoon they had gained such an advantagious post that it was thought im-prudent to Attempt to dislodge them, & firing ceased on both sides about half an hour before Sunset, from this place the Enemy made a final retreat and crossed the Ohio with their wounded. Some of their dead were slightly covered in the Field of Battle, some were drag'd down, & thrown into the Ohio And others they had scalped themselves to prevent our people—whilst this passed in the Field, Colo. Lewis was fully imployed in Camp, in sending necessary reinforcements where wanted on the different quarters. The Troops were encamped on the Banks of the N[ew] River & Ohio, extending up both Rivers near half a Mile the Point betwixt the Rivers was full of large trees & very brushy, from the furthest extent of the tents on both Rivers he cleared a line across & with the brush & trees made a breastwork and lined it with the men that were left in Camp. The following is a list of the kild and Wounded Those markd with Asterisks died after the engagement Kild of the Augusta line, Colo. Charles Lewis° Colo. Jno. Field, Capt. Saml. Wilson, Lieutt. Hugh Allen. Eighteen private[s].

Wounded of the Augusta line Capts. Dickinson. Skidmore Lieutts. Leard & Vance with 51 private[s]. Kild of the Botetourt line Capts. Murray, Robt. McClennachan* Jas. Ward* Thos. Buford*. Lieutts. Bracken & Goldman, with Ensign Cundiff & 17 Private[s]. Wounded Colo. Fleming Lieut. Robison & 35 private[s]. We had the morning of the engagement upwards of Eleven hundred effective men.

About 12 o'Clock at Night Colo Christian with part of the Fincastle troops came into Camp—The 11th. Large parties were sent out in search of the Enimy when they found all the Indians had crosd the Ohio.

The 12th Imployed in gathering in the dispers'd Bullocks & horses & in clearing the Camp of Underwood. this day the Guns Blankets &c taken from the Indians, sold by Vendue amounted to near £100. The 13th. the Express that first went to his Lordship returnd with Instructions for Colo Lewis to march towards the Shawnese Towns and Join His Lordship at a certain place by the way

The 14th. 15th. & 16th. imployed in finishing a store house & running up a breastwork, which was Raised two logs high, with part of a Bastion. we cros'd the Ohio the 17. After leaving all our Indisposed, lame, & those Judged unfit for Duty at the point, and the 18th. begun our march for the Shawnese Towns, when about 15 miles from them we had an Express from His Lordship Accquainting us a Peace with the Indians was Almost concluded, inviting Colo. Lewis & such of [his] Officers as he choose to come over to his Camp. We continued to march forward & in some houres afterwards another express arrived with the News that Peace was concluded & brought orders for the Army to halt, as the place was inconvenient for the Troops to encamp, we marched on to west [?] which the Indians observing struck them with a dread that we were going to Attack their towns, as we by a mistake of the Guide had got rather betwixt his Lordships Camp & the Towns & much nearer than we imagined. All the Indians with his Lordship, immediately quitted His Camp, except White Fish, who with Gibson a trader, Attended His Lordship to Our Army. My Lord informd us the Shawnise had agreed to all his Terms, and that as Our Presence could be of no service, but rather a hindrance to the peace being concluded he ordered the whole to return, which we did the next day. We reached the Point the 28th where we found the Breast work very near compleated from which Place we filed off homeward by [MS. torn].—Draper Mss. 2ZZ 71 (48-56), State Historical Society of Wisconsin.

21. Logan's Speech

The celebrated and controversial reply of Chief Logan to Lord Dunmore's invitation to attend the peace conference in Ohio was delivered by John Gibson, fur-trader, Indian interpreter, Logan's brother-in-law, and eventually secretary of Indiana Territory. Thomas Jefferson reproduced Logan's message in the NOTES ON THE STATE OF VIRGINIA *as an example of Indian eloquence equal to the orations of Demosthenes and Cicero. Because Logan, in his speech, had accused Michael Cresap of wiping out Logan's family, the kinsmen of Cresap, together with Jefferson's political enemies, later charged that Jefferson had fabricated Logan's speech. Documentary evidence disproves these charges. And Jefferson was entirely correct in contending that the Indian's reply was well-known before it appeared in his* NOTES. *That Cresap had taken no part in the Yellow Creek atrocities in which Logan's relatives were murdered was indeed true; but it was likewise true that on another occasion a party under Cresap had killed Indians. The first of the two following documents, a portion of John Gibson's deposition relative to the murder of Logan's family, gives the setting for Logan's speech which follows.*

This Deponent further saith that in the year 1774, he accompanied Lord Dunmore on the Expedition against the Shawnese and other Indians on the Siota, that on their arrival within 15 Miles of the towns, they were met by a flag, and a white man of the name of Elliot, who informed Lord Dunmore that the Chiefs of the Shawnese had sent to request his Lordship to halt his army and send in some person, who understood their language; that this Deponent, at the request of Lord Dunmore and the whole of the officers with him, went in; that on his arrival at the towns, Logan, the Indian, came to where this deponent was sitting with the Corn-Stalk, and the other chiefs of the Shawnese, and asked him to walk out with him; that they went into a copse of wood, where they sat down, when Logan, after shedding abundance of tears, delivered to him the speech, nearly as related by Mr. Jefferson in his notes on the State of Virginia; that he the Deponent told him then that it was not Col. Cressap who had murdered his relations, and that although his son captain Michael Cressap was with the party who killed a Shawnese chief and other Indians, yet he was not present when his relations were killed at Baker's, near the mouth of Yellow Creek on the Ohio; that this Deponent on his return to camp delivered the speech to Lord Dunmore; and that the murders perpetrated as above were considered as ultimately the cause of the War of 1774, commonly called Cressap's war.

Sworn and subscribed the 4th April,
  1800, at Pittsburgh, before me,

                                        JOHN GIBSON.

JER. BARKER.

—Thomas Jefferson, *Notes on the State of Virginia*, edited by William Peden, p. 234. Copyright, 1954, by the University of North Carolina Press. By permission.

"I appeal to any white man to say, if ever he entered Logan's cabin hungry, and he gave him not meat; if ever he came cold and naked, and he clothed him not. During the course of the last long and bloody war, Logan remained idle in his cabin, an advocate for peace. Such was my love for the whites, that my countrymen pointed as they passed, and said, 'Logan is the friend of white men.' I had even thought to have lived with you, but for the injuries of one man. Col. Cresap, the last spring, in cold blood, and unprovoked, murdered all the relations of Logan, not sparing even my women and children. There runs not a drop of my blood in the veins of any living creature. This called on me for revenge. I have sought it: I have killed many: I have fully glutted my vengeance. For my country, I rejoice at the beams of peace. But do not harbour a thought

that mine is the joy of fear. Logan never felt fear. He will not
turn on his heel to save his life. Who is there to mourn for
Logan?—Not one."—Thomas Jefferson, *Notes on the State of Virginia*, edited by William Peden, p. 63. By permission.

22. Fort Gower Address and Resolutions, November 5, 1774

Rumblings of revolution were heard in Virginia prior to Dunmore's offensive against the Indians. On May 26, 1774, the Governor peremptorily dissolved the House of Burgesses because it had adopted a resolution designating June 1 as a day of fasting, humiliation, and prayer to protest the commercial stangulation of Boston under the terms of the Boston Port Act. The following day, a number of the burgesses met in the Apollo Room of the Raleigh Tavern at Williamsburg and signed an agreement recommending that the local Committee of Correspondence communicate with committees in other colonies on the expedience of calling a general congress. The First Continental Congress met in Philadelphia on September 5. Before its adjournment on October 26, 1774, it adopted the Declaration and Resolves and the Association—a non-importation, non-consumption, and non-exportation agreement, which the local revolutionary committees zealously enforced. The campaign in Ohio temporarily removed Dunmore's forces from the revolutionary currents, but the officers, on their return march, held a meeting at Fort Gower and adopted a patriotic resolution, tempered, like most of the resolutions of this period, by professions of loyalty to the King.

AT A MEETING OF THE OFFICERS under the command of his
Excellency the Right Honourable the Earl of *Dunmore* convened at *Fort Gower, November* 5, 1774, for the purpose of
considering the grievances of *British America,* an Officer present addressed the Meeting in the following words:

"GENTLEMEN: Having now concluded the campaign, by the assistance of Providence, with honour and advantage to the Colony and ourselves, it only remains that we should give our country the strongest assurance that we are ready, at all times, to the utmost of our power to maintain and defend her just rights and privileges. We have lived about three months in the woods without any intelligence from *Boston,* or from the Delegates at *Philadelphia.* It is possible, from the groundless reports of designing men, that our countrymen may be jealous of the use such a body would make of arms in their hands at this critical juncture. That we are a respectable body is certain, when it is considered that we can live weeks without bread or salt; that we can sleep in the open air without any covering but that of the canopy of Heaven; and that our men can march and shoot with any in the known world. Blessed with these talents, let us solemnly engage to one another, and our country in particular, that we will use them to no purpose but for the honour and advantage of *America* in general, and of *Virginia* in particular. It behooves us then, for the satisfaction of our country, that we should give them our real sentiments, by way of resolves, at this very alarming crisis."

Whereupon the meeting made choice of a Committee to draw up and prepare Resolves for their consideration, who immediately withdrew; and after some time spent therein, reported that they had agreed to and prepared the following Resolves, which were read, maturely considered, and agreed to, *nemine contradicente,* by the Meeting, and ordered to be published in the *Virginia Gazette*:

Resolved, That we will bear the most faithful allegiance to his Majesty King George the Third, whilst his Majesty delights to reign over a brave and free people; that we will, at the expense of life and every thing dear and valuable, exert ourselves in support of the honour of his Crown and the dignity of the *British* Empire. But as the love of Liberty, and attachment to the real interests and just rights of *America* outweigh every other consideration, we resolve that we will exert every power within us for the defense of *American* liberty, and for the support of her just rights and privileges; not in any precipitate, riotous, or tumultuous manner, but when regularly called forth by the unanimous voice of our countrymen.

Resolved, That we entertain the greatest respect for his Excellency the Right Honourable Lord *Dunmore,* who commanded the expedition against the *Shawanese;* and who, we are confident, underwent the great fatigue of this singular campaign from no other motive than the true interest of this country.

Signed by order and in behalf of the whole Corps,

BENJAMIN ASHBY *Clerk.*

—*American Archives,* Fourth Series, I, 962-63.

23. Dunmore's Report to Lord Dartmouth, Secretary of State For The Colonies, December 24, 1774

Governor Dunmore's official account of the "war" that bears his name is long, explanatory, and exculpatory. In reviewing its background and course, the Governor referred to the lawless temper of the pioneers and the many acts of violence committed by both Indians and whites, including the inhuman affair at Baker's Bottom near the mouth of Yellow Creek which annihilated the family of Chief Logan. Of particular interest are Dunmore's report of the peace settlement at Camp Charlotte in Ohio and his denunciation of the Pennsylvania authorities.

. . . I have had, My Lord, frequent opportunities to reflect upon the emigrating Spirit of the Americans, Since my Arrival to this Government. There are considerable bodies of Inhabitants Settled at greater and less distances from the regular frontiers of, I believe, all the Colonies. In this Colony Proclamations have been published from time to time to restrain them: But impressed from their earliest infancy with Sentiments and habits, very different from those acquired by persons of a Similar condition in England, they do not conceive that Government has any right to forbid their taking possession of a Vast tract of Country, either uninhabited, or which Serves only as a Shelter to a few Scattered Tribes of Indians. Nor can they be easily brought to entertain any belief of the permanent obligation of Treaties made with those People, whom they consider, as but little removed from the brute Creation. . . . I only think it my duty to State matters as they really are: and this being a true Account of them, three Considerations offer themselves for His Majesty's Approbation. The first is, to Suffer these Emigrants to hold their Lands of, and incorporate with the Indians; the dreadfull Consequence of which may be easely foreseen, and which I leave to your Lordships Judgment. The Second, is to permit them to form a Set of Democratical Governments of their own, upon the backs of the old Colonies; a Scheme which, for obvious reasons, I apprehend cannot be allowed to be carried into execution. The last is, that which I proposed to your Lordship, to receive persons in their Circumstances, under the protection of Some of His Majesty's Governments already established, and, in giving this advice, I had no thought of bringing a Dishonour upon the Crown. On the contrary, the measure appeared to me as the wisest, and Safest that could be entered into under the Circumstances above mentioned. . . .

The last quarrel with the Indians, as far as the Virginians were concerned in it, took its rise from, or rather never Subsided after, the expedition of Mr. Bouquet. . . .

In hopes of preventing the effects, which were Naturally to be dreaded from these repeated violences of the Indians; . . . I wrote to Mr. Stuart the Indian agent . . . to desire, that he would use his endeavors to perswade the Indians to give up the offenders: But the Indians Shifted the accusation from one tribe to an other; that, in Short, the application had no effect. . . .

It happned that, soon after the murder of young Russel and his party, a man who had been of that party, and the only one who had escaped, was at a horse race at a Place upon the Frontiers, and that two Indian Men and one Woman should come there also. The man immediately fell upon the Indians and murdered one of them, notwithstanding the interposition of all the other People: all they could do was to save the other Indian and the woman. . . .

This however was the first Indian blood drawn by our People Since the treaty of Mr. Bouquet. Nor was this followed by any other act of hostelity till about the 27th. of last March, that five Indian Cannoes, containing fourteen Indians, going down the Ohio, were followed by one Michael Cressop, a Maryland Trader, with a party of fifteen Men, and a Skirmish ensued in which one Indian and one of Cressops people were killed; but Sixteen keggs of rum, Some Saddles and bridles were taken from the Indians. About the 26th. of April following, two Indians, who were with a white man in a Cannoe on the river, were fired upon from the Shore and killed. This likewise is attributed to Cressop.

Soon after this, an affair of more importance happned, and which indeed is marked with an extraordinary degree of Cruelty and Inhumanity. A party of Indians, with their women, happening to encamp on the side of the Ohio opposite to the house of one Baker, who, together with a Man of the name of Gratehouse, called to, and invited the Indians to come over and drink with them; two men and as many women came accordingly, and were, at first, well received, but Baker and Gratehouse, who by this time had collected other People, contrived to entoxicate the Indians, and they then Murdered them. Soon after two more came over from the Indian Party in Search of their Companions and these met with the same fate. The remainder of the Indian Party growing uneasy at not Seeing their friends return, five of them got into a Cannoe to go over to the house, but they were soon fired upon by Baker and Gratehouse, and two of the Indians killed and the other three wounded. . . .

The Indians, however, had recently repeated their blows, and given too much cause to these People, not much less Savage than themselves, to Justify their Sanguinary deeds. They had in the beginning of February killed Six men and two Negroes, and, towards the end of the same month, a Trading Cannoe was attacked, the men murdered and the Goods carried to the Shawnese towns. . . .

The event of this Action [Battle of Point Pleasant], proving very different from what the Indians had promised themselves, they at once resolved to make no further efforts against a Power they saw so far Superior to theirs; but determined to throw themselves upon our Mercy: And, with the greatest expedition, they came in Search of the body with which they knew I marched, and found me near their own Towns the Day after I got there.

They presently made known their intentions, and I admitted them immedeately to a Conference, wherein all our differences were Settled. The terms of our reconciliation were, briefly, that the Indians should deliver up all prisoners without reserve; that they should restore all horses and other valuable effects which they had carried off; that they Should not hunt on our Side the Ohio, nor molest any Boats passing thereupon; That they Should promise to agree to such regulations, for their trade with our People, as Should be hereafter dictated by the Kings Instructions, and that they Should deliver into our hands certain Hostages, to be kept by us untill we were convinced of their Sincere intention to adhere to all these Articles. The Indians, finding, contrary to their expectation, no punishment likely to follow, agreed to everything with the greatest alacrety, and gave the most Solemn assurances of their quiet and peacable deportment for the future: and in return I have given them every promise of protection and good treatment on our Side . . .

The Assertion of the Proprietary Governor, [of Pennsylvania] and the intelligence, which your Lordship informs me, you have received thro' a variety of other Channals; all Spring from the same Source: from the Malevolence which that Gentleman thinks he has cause to manifest towards me. . . .

Instead of manefesting any disposition to reconcile the different opinions, respecting the disputed boundary between this Colony, and his Province, his mode of proceeding was, with no little confidence, to exact a full complyance with his demands of this Government, or we were to Suffer the Consequences, . . .

It is an easy matter to make people believe that Duty to His Majesty, and Zeal for his Service and interest, could not have been my real motive for interfering in this affair; but that it proceeded from views of emolument to myself. The Philadelphia Papers, and I dare Say other means, have been used to make it believed, that I acted only in conjunction with a parcel of Land Jobbers, and not by the advice of His Majestys Council or by any good Authority; the Natural inference to be drawn being, that by such means I am procuring Grants of land: The Indian disturbances have been also wonderfully aiding to Mr. Penn's purpose, and he has not neglected them.

The trade carried on with the Ohio Indians has been almost engrossed by the Province of Pennsylvania, which they have draw[n] to themselves, artfully enough, but with what degree of propriety or right I must leave to your Lordships Judgment, by repeated treaties held of their own Authority, and at such times and for such purposes as they think fit. The Traders in General are composed of the most worthless Subjects, such as fail in all other occupations, and become in a manner outcasts of Society. These Men, we have full proof, have made it their constant business to discredit the Virginians (who lye much more convenient for carrying on a Trade with these Indians than the Pennsylvanians) and make the Indians consider them in the most odious light. We know that these Men have bought the Plunder, which the Indians carried off in their incursions.—If the Indians took Skins, they could Sell them cheaper than those they got themselves by hunting, and at the expence of Gun Powder;—if horses, they knew nothing of their value, and anything would purchase them.—It was a lucrative trade to these People, and the means of it, which were the disturbances between the Indians and the Virginians, were encouraged by them. . . .

I am My Lord . . .
Dunmore

—Draper Mss. 15J4-48, State Historical Society of Wisconsin.

III. The Revolution

24. Letter From Fort Blair (Point Pleasant), June 12, 1775

Despite the defeat of the Indians at Point Pleasant and the favorable terms of the provisional treaty negotiated by Lord Dunmore at Camp Charlotte, the western Virginia frontier was uneasy at the outbreak of hostilities in Massachusetts in April, 1775. Committees of safety were organized for both Westmoreland County and the District of West Augusta. The latter committee wrote Congress that it feared Dunmore's designs with regard to the Indians and asked Virginia and Pennsylvania to send commissioners to negotiate with the Indians. The Shawnees, who had given hostages to Dunmore during the previous autumn, were clamoring for the return of their braves and for the peace treaty which the royal governor had promised. But in 1775 revolutionary fires in eastern Virginia prevented Dunmore from fulfilling his western commitments; consequently, his agent, Dr. Connolly, whom the western patriots rightly suspected of being a Tory, assembled the Mingoes and Delawares, but not the Shawnees, at Pittsburgh in early summer and completed a treaty which the Virginia convention approved in July, 1775. One of the last executive acts of Dunmore was to order the abandonment of Fort Dunmore and Fort Blair. The provincials immediately seized Fort Dunmore and renamed it Fort Pitt. The Indians, during the summer of 1775, burned Fort Blair which had been situated at the confluence of the Kanawha and the Ohio. The following letter written by Captain William Russell (1748-1794), a justice of Fincastle County, a commander of a company at the Battle of Point Pleasant, and a colonel and brigadier general by brevet in the Revolution, shows the burgeoning revolutionary spirit in the West.

Fort Blair June 12th 1775

Dear Mjr.

I Recd. your welcome Letter by Thomas Tays; which, be assure'd, in this remote Department, contributed more than a little to my Satisfaction.

I had some Days before the Receipt of yours, been favour'd with the shocking Acct. of three Battles being fought near the City of Boston, between the Brittish Troops, and Americans; tho', must acknowledge my great joy, in our victories obtained over the Enemies Tyranic Pride.

The unheard of Acts of Barbarity, committed by the Brittish Troops, will doubtless stir up every lover of his Country, to be Zealous, and forward in it's defence, to support our Liberty; tho', I doubt not, but many sychophants to Brittains Interest, will now appear Patriots;—as long as our Arms prove Victorious; . . . I have, as long as in my power, procrastinated our departure from this Garison, expecting that ere now, we should Receive some Orders from the Convention, that might countermand the Governors Letter to me; but as none such have yet come to hand, I am this Morning preparing to start off our Cattle up Sandy, and expect, that Commd. will leave this Wensday, or thursday at farthest, and shall Decamp myselfe, with a Convoy to the other stores next Monday, and expect to overtake the Stock, at the big painted Lick about sixty Miles up Sandy.

I expect you have hear'd of Colo. Preston's Orders, to Majr. Engles to take possession of the Cattle, and Horses in my care at this Garison; but, as I found not a word, in his Lordships Orders to me, Similar to the Colonels pretended authority, I took the oppinion of my officers, who judged it most to the Interest of the Country, that I should keep together the Stock and Stores, and Convoy them into the Settlement, and dispose of them my selfe, unless contra Orders come to me from the Convention. . . . The Garison we intend to let remain, as I think the [des]truction of it at this time might prove Injurious to the Country.

[The] Corn Stalk left me, last Thursday; and in the space of four Days [conve]rsation, I discovered, that it is the Intention of the Pick Tribe of Indians [to be tr]oublesome to our new Settlements, whenever they can; and he further assured me, that the Mingoes behave in a very unbecoming manner [fr]equently upbraiding the Shawanees, in cowardly making the Peace; [?] call them big knife People; that the Corn Stalk can't well account for their Intentions. if this be true, and a rupture between England and America has really commenced, we shall certainly Receive Trouble at the hands of those People in a short Time, as they got the news of the Battles in the Shawanee Towns, eight, or ten Days before the Corn Stalk came here; Tho' I am confident, the Shawanees will always be our Friends. The Corn Stalk brought me two of the Horses taken by that party of Cherrokees; who, murdered the People on Kentucke in March. The Shawanees took the Rascal, who had them; but, he made his escape from them, it is supposed he is return'd to the Cherokee Nation. It appears to have been the Pics, that fired on Boons Camp when the two Men were kill'd, out of his Party. I had Resolved when I left home to go from this Place to Kentucke; and especially since I Recd. my other Warrant; but hearing of the Troublesome Times, in the Country, I am greatly purplex'd in mind, to hear more certain acct. how affairs are likely to go in Virginia; nor can I fall upon any method, to save the Stores so effectual, from the danger of the Indians, as to bring them into the Settlements; . . .

I have wrote several Letters to Colo. Henderson, since I returnd to this Post, and have had it in my power, to calm the Minds of several Compys. who, have gone down this River, so that I hope, the new Country about Kentucke will Settle quickly: I have also Wrote Majr. Connelly, so that I wood fain hope, our wishes, and endeavours may prove effectual, to the speedy Settling that Country.

I have heard the Convention is to meet some Time this Month; and have wrote to Inform Colo. Christian, respecting the present Temper, of the neighbouring Tribes of Indians, to the Shawanees: which, I think is really necessary, the Convention should be made acquainted with, that they may judge accordingly; and as your Letter to me got brook open on new River, his may also, and probably miscarry; therefore, think it best to send off Henry Boyer, and Geo: Oxen as an express, one with this Letter to you, and the other to let my Family know of my coming, and withall to have some Horses taken out to Sandy, to carry in the Stores upon. . . .

[William Russell]

[To Col. William Fleming]

—Draper Mss. 4QQ19, State Historical Society of Wisconsin.

25. Addresses at The Conference Held In Pittsburgh September, October, 1775

Since both the colonial authorities and the British wished to enlist the sympathy and support of the Indians in the coming struggle, both sent agents into the Indian country with presents and propaganda messages. In the fall, 1775, a delegation of Ottawa, Wyandot, Mingo, Shawnee, Delaware, and Seneca Indians met at Pittsburgh with the commissioners of Indian Affairs appointed by the Continental Congress and the Virginia Convention. The resulting pledges of peace, amity, and neutrality given by the Indians enabled many frontier riflemen to leave their homes and enlist in the Continental Army. Dr. Thomas Walker (1715-1794), explorer, soldier, scientist, politician, and land speculator was a commissioner for Congress and Virginia at the Pittsburgh conference and presided over the joint meetings.

AT A MEETING of the Commissioners for Indian Affairs as well those from Congress as those from Virginia October 10th 1775 Present Lewis Morris Thomas Walker James Wilson James Wood Andrew Lewis John Walker Adam Stephen Comrs. . . .

The Gentlemen from the Congress then withdrew and the Commissioners from Virginia Opened their Business with the following Speech delivered by John Walker *To the Mingoes Wiandots Delawares Shawnese and Tawaas Friends and Bretheren* we are sent here by the Grand Council of our Country, the big knife, to take you by the hand and Welcome you to this Council fire, to which we have Invited all the Ohio Indians and other Neighbouring Nations: you have Accepted the Invitation and we are heartily Glad to see you, this Council we hope, will be called the Blessed Council of Peace, and the Fame of it handed Down thro' all Generations *A String to Each Nation* . . .

Brothers you have no doubt heard of the dispute between us and some of our Fathers evil Counsellors beyond the Great Water, in this dispute your Interest is Involved with ours so far as this, that in Case those People with whom we are Contending shou'd Subdue us, your *Lands* your *Trade* your *Liberty* and all that is dear to you must fall with us, for if they wou'd Distroy our flesh and Spill our Blood which is the same with theirs; what can you who are no way related to or Connected with them Expect? and further, Suppose you were Inclined to Join our Enemies, how Cou'd you Act in Conjunction with them? they Cannot Pass through us to your Country Neither cou'd you get to them. Notwithstanding all this, we only ask of you to Stay at home, to take Care of your Women and Children, and follow other Usual Occupations: we are not Affraid these People will Conquer us, they Can't fight in our Country, and you Know we Can; we fear not them, nor any Power on Earth

Brothers the thirteen great Colonies of this Extensive Continent, Comprehending in the whole, at least One Million of Fighting Men, are now so firmly United and Inseparably bound together by one lasting Chain of Freindship, that we are no more to be Considered as Distinct Nations, but as one great and Strong Man, who if Molested in any one of his Members, will not fail to Exert the Combined force of his whole Body to Punish the Offender. . . .

Brothers If any other Nation or Nations shou'd take up the Tomhawk and Endeavour to Strike us it wou'd be Kind in you to give us Notice and Use your best Endeavours to Prevent the Stroke, for it must be your Interest to live in Peace and Amity with such near and Powerfull Neighbours and this is all we Ask *A String to Each Nation.* . . .

Brothers the Wiandots . . . we desire you will give Ear to no Idle reports you may hear from the Commanding Officer at

Fort Detroit who will Endeavour to deceive you we have already discovered Many of their Falshoods we desire to live in Peace with you, and hope you will Acquaint your Neighboring Nations with what we have said *A String*

Brothers the Delawares we Esteem you a Wise people for not engaging in the War last Summer and you may depend upon our Friendship agreeable to Lord Dunmores Promise *A String*

Brothers the Shawanese we have returned you your Hostages safe and Trust they can say nothing but good of us It is our Earnest desire to live in Peace with you, shou'd any of our People Molest you, we will Endeavour to bring them to Justice and shou'd any of yours Molest us we Expect you will Punish them *A String* ...

To the whole Nations Present we have reason to Believe great Uneasinesses and Jealousies have Prevailed Amongst you respecting our Intention of making Encroachments on your Lands we take this Opportunity to Assuring you that we have not the most Distant thought of Possessing any part of your Lands you must all be sensible that the Lands on this side Ohio as far down as the C[h]erokee River was Purchased at the Treaty of Fort Stanwix by Sir William Johnston for the King of England who has since sold it to his Childeren on this Continent and which they now Expect to Enjoy in Peace *A Belt*

Brothers we Expect you have brought with you and are ready to Deliver up all our Flesh and Blood our Negroes and all that belongs to us and that you are prepared to make restitution for all Damages agreeable to the Terms Stipulated between you and Lord Dunmore last Fall *A String* ...

Corn Stalk then Spoke as follows *Brothers the Bigknife* as you have desired we shou'd deliver you your flesh and Blood and your Negroes we will give you an Answer to morrow respecting that Matter

————————

At a Conference Continued and held with the Shawanese on the 11th October 1775 Present Thomas Walker, Andrew Lewis, James Wood John Walker Adam Stephen Commrs

The Cornstalk addressed the Commissioners *My Old Brothers the Bigknife* In our Councils last fall when we were settling every thing we made ourselves one Body and Promised to Each Other at the same time that if any Mischeif shou'd happen through the inadvertency of foolish Young People that we wou'd not keep it a Secreet from one another but Seriously Consider and have it rectified when I left home I Assembled my Young Men and told them I was going to Treat with my Bretheren the English and if any foolish People shou'd spread any bad reports not to listen to it as I had nothing in my heart but what was good we had not forgot where the Mischeif a rose from the foolish People who are endeavouring to Overset our Friendship . . .

Brothers listen to me when we held a Council last Fall you desired us to deliver up your Flesh and Blood your Negroes your Horses and every thing that belonged to you . . . we Immediately Complied and Delivered you up all your flesh and Blood your Negroes and Horses and all that belonged to you not only at that time but when they were Demanded twice before . . . last spring when some of the Cherokees robbed your People on the Kentucke we Immediately set off took two of the Horses from them and delivered them at the Mouth of Kanhawa and when the Negro Woman made her Escape from that Place and Came to our Towns on her being Demanded we delivered her . . . but told him as the [two] Children were Bagat by our People we thought it very hard they shou'd be made Slaves of as the Negro Woman is delivered up she will soon have more Children at the same time they Demanded Horses from us we Informed them we had delivered up all the Horses we had belonging to the White People and that Many of our People had delivered up their own Horses in leiu of yours which cou'd not be found we likewise told them that ours was not the only Nation who had stolen their Horses . . .

Brothers I now Inform you we have delivered up all we possibly can and as we are one People I hope you will not Ask more of us. . . . —*The Revolution on the Upper Ohio, 1775-1777*, edited by R. G. Thwaites and L. P. Kellogg, pp. 90-105.

26. New State Movements – Proposed State of Westsylvania

The chronic discontent of the frontiersmen resulting from uncertain land titles, inefficient and corrupt local government, inadequate military protection, remoteness from the seat of government, eastern political domination, and the machinations of land speculators was aggravated during the Revolution and Confederation period by conflicting jurisdictional claims over some western areas. These factors were responsible for the several attempts to create new western states during this formative period in American history. The proposed states of Vandalia and Westsylvania would have included all of Trans-Allegheny Virginia and large segments of present Kentucky and, in the case of Westsylvania, of western Pennsylvania, as well. The two projects had their origin in the negotiations at Fort Stanwix in 1768, when the Six Nations conveyed to the Indiana Company a large tract of land bounded by the Little Kanawha in the south, by the "Laurel Hill" and the Monongahela on the east, by the southern Pennsylvania line on the north, and by the Ohio River on the west—in short, territory almost wholly in present West Virginia. On the basis of this grant, the Vandalia, or Grand Ohio Company, was organized in 1769 for the purpose of obtaining a still larger grant from which a new colony would be created with its seat at the confluence of the Kanawha and Ohio. With stubborn persistency the Indiana-Vandalia group which included such outstanding figures as Benjamin Franklin, Sir William Johnson, George Morgan, and Samuel Wharton, sought confirmation of their ambitious project, first from the British government, then, after the break with Great Britain, from Virginia and the Continental Congress. But Virginia statesmanship was more than a match for the claimants' adroit maneuvers both in and out of Congress. The eleventh amendment of the Federal Constitution rendering a state immune against private suit gave the coup de grace to their final efforts.

The Vandalia interests were probably the instigators of a movement in 1776 to create a fourteenth state to be named Westsylvania. Shortly after the adoption of the Declaration of Independence, "The Inhabitants of the Country West of the Allegheny Mountains," as the anonymous petitioners called themselves, sent a memorial to Congress in which they called attention to their many grievances and asked as a corrective the formation of "The Province & Government of Westsylvania." In forming the Alleghenies, they said, "Nature itself" had fixed the eastern boundary of the proposed state. That this abortive scheme did not have the unanimous approval of the westerners may be seen from the following memorial to the Virginia legislature.

IN THE SENATE, Wednesday, October 30th. 1776—

A Memorial of the Committee of West Augusta to the House of Delegates was read, representing that David Rogers Esqr. a member of this House and others did in the month of June last Set on foot a Scheme for erecting a Government within Certain limits therein described, and offered a Memorial for that purpose to a Number of people at Pittsburgh for their perusal, that after opposition was made to the Scheme, their advertisements were dispersed without any Signature, directing the people to choose men to meet & Consult whether application should be made to Congress for laying off the Country within the said Limits into a new Government or whether they would not immediately proceed to Colonize themselves by their own authority, and Send Delegates to Congress to represent them as the fourteenth link in the American Chain, that in July when the Ordinance of Convention made it necessary that Committee men should take an oath, Mr. Rogers and others refused to take the oath, and persisted in using all their influence to make proselytes to their favorite Scheme of a new Government.... —Draper Mss. 4NN32, State Historical Society of Wisconsin.

27. The Murder of Chief Cornstalk

Fort Randolph, named for Peyton Randolph, Virginia patriot and President of the First Continental Congress, was built as a replacement for Fort Blair by Captain Matthew Arbuckle in the early summer of 1776. This post was an important link in the chain of defense along the Ohio, a chain which included Beech Bottom Fort, Fort Henry at Wheeling, and Grave Creek Fort. During the Revolution, the western front, with headquarters at Pittsburgh, suffered from lack of supplies and manpower, local dissensions, and a series of mediocre and generally unpopular commanders—Generals Edward Hand, Lachlan McIntosh, Daniel Brodhead, and William Irvine. In spite of their difficulties, however, the isolated garrisons vigilantly guarded the frontier. "I intend keeping out Spies both up, Down, & over the Ohio Constantly & shall always endeavour to Protect the Inhabitants on the Frontiers to the utmost of my power," reported Captain Arbuckle on November 2, 1776. But so anxious were the frontiersmen to defend themselves that they often failed to distinguish between friend and foe among the Indians. This failure not only nullified all efforts to maintain peace with the Indians but also occasioned inhuman acts. Such was the murder of Chief Cornstalk at Fort Randolph late in 1777. Captain John Stuart (1749-1823), a pioneer and magistrate of Greenbrier County, gives an eye-witness account of Cornstalk's murder in the following document.

. . . THE PRECEEDING YEAR 1777 the Indians again began under the influence of british agents to manifest signs of commencing hostilities, and the Corn Stak warrior with the young Redhawk paid a visit to Capt. Arbuckle's garison he made no secret of the disposition of the Indians declaring that he was opposed to joining the war on the side of the British, but that all the rest of the nation but himself and his wife were determined to engage in it, and of course he should have to run with the stream (as he expressed it) on which Capt. Arbuckle thout proper to detain him, the young Redhawk and another fellow as hostages to prevent the nation from joining the British. In the course of that summer our new Government [ordered] an army to be raised of volenteers and General Hand was appointed to the command, who as soon [as] sufficient force could be collected at fort Pit was to begin his march down the River to point pleasant and there to meet a reinforcement expected to be raised in Augusta and Botetourt counties. . . . we collected in all 30 or 40 men and joined the rest of the men on their march under Colo. Skelleran, to point pleasant when we arrived there, there was no account of General Hand or his army . . . we concluded to remain at the garison until General Hand would arrive, or some accounts from him; during our stay two young men of the name of Hamilton, and Gilmore, crossed the kanawha one day to hunt deer; on their return to camp some Indians had approached to view our encampment and had concealed themselves in the weeds of the top of the bank at the mouth of the kanawha; and as Gilmore came along they killed him on [the] bank Capt. Arbuckle and myself were standing on the point of the opposite bank when the gun fired and wondered what any one was doing there firing contrary to orders; when we Saw Hamilton run down the bank and call out that Gilmore was killed; Gilmore was one of the company of Capt. John Hall . . . Halls men instantly jumped in to a canoe and went to the relief of Hamilton brought the corpse of Gilmore down the bank scalped and covered with blood, he was put into canoe and as the[y] passed the River I observed to Capt. Arbuckle the[y] would be for killing the hostages as soon as the canoe would land but he supposed they[y] would not commit so great an out rage on the innocent who were not accessary to Gilmore's murder.

but the canoe was scarcely landed in the creek when the cry was raised let us kill the Indians in the fort and every man with his gun in his hand came up the bank pale as death with rage; Capt. Hall was at their head. Captain Arbuckle and myself met them endeavering to disuade them from so unjustifyable an action but they cocked their guns threatened us with instant death if we did not desist and rushed into the fort. On the preceeding day Corn Stalk's son had come from the nation to see his father and to know if he was alive: when he came to the River his father was that instant delineating a map of the country and waters between the Shawanee town and the Mississippi at our request with Chalk upon the floor: he instantly knew the voice of his son, went out and answered him, when the young fellow crossed over and they embraced each other in the most tender and affectionate manner. The next day the Interpreter's wife who had been a prisoner with the Indians and had recently left them, hearing the uproar and seeing the men coming to kill the Indians for whom she seemed to have an affection, run to their cabin informed them the people were coming to kill them and that the[y] said the Indians that killed Gilmore came with Elinipsies the day before: he utterly denied it declared he knew nothing of them, and trembled exceedingly; his father incouraged him told him not to be afraid, for the great Spirit above had sent him there to be killed: the men advanced to the door, the Corn Stalk arose and met them, seven or eight bullets were fired into him, and his son was shot dead as he sat upon a stool. Redhawk made an attempt to go up the chimney but was shot down, the other Indian was shamefully mangled. I grieved to see him so long a dying. Thus died the great Cornstalk warrior who from personal appearance and many brave acts was undoubtedly a Hero. I have no doubt if he had been spared but he would have been friendly to the Americans for nothing could have induced him to make the visit to the garison at that critical time, but to communicate the temper and disposition of the Indians, and their design of taking part with the British: on the day he was killed we held a council in which he was present; his countenance was dejected and he made a Speech all of which seemed to indicate an honest and manly disposition. he acknowledged that he expected himself and his party would have to run with the stream, for all the Indians or the Indians on the lakes and to the north were joinin the British. . . . When he made his speech in council with us he seemed impressed with an awful presentment of his approaching fate for he repeatedly said, when I was a young man and went to war I thought that might be the last time, and I would return no more but now I am here among you and you may kill me if you please, I can die but once and its all one to me now or at another time. this sentiment concluded every period of his Speech he was killed one hour after. A few days afterwards General Hand arrived but had no troops and we were dismissed and returned home Shortly before Christmass. Not long after we left the garison a small party apeared in sight of the fort; Lieutenant More was ordered with a party to pursue them, they had come to retaliate the murder of Cornstalk: Moore had not advanced ¼ of a mile when he fell into an ambuscade and was killed with 1 or 2 more of him men. —Draper Mss. 6NN105-12, State Historical Society of Wisconsin.

28. Defense of Virginia – Letter of Patrick Henry to William Fleming

Anticipating renewed hostilities with the Shawnees, Governor Patrick Henry of Virginia ordered Colonel William Fleming to make preparations for the defense of western Virginia. At the same time, the Governor deplored the lawless conduct of the frontiersmen which necessitated these measures.

Williamsburg, Feby 19th 1778.

SIR The Murder of the Shawanese Indians will no doubt bring on Hostilities with that People. In order to ward off the Stroke which may be expected it is necessary to have every Gun in your County put into good order & got ready for Action. Lead may be had from the Mines. An order for one pound for each Man of your Militia accompany's this. Powder it is said is plenty among you. If it cant be had otherwise send to Richmond for it. Let trusty Scouts be kept in constant Action towards the Enemys Country to discover their Movements & give Information of approaching Danger. Proper Stockades or Defences to receive the more helpless part of the People should be provided in time and fixed at Places judiciously chosen, that the able Men may be at liberty to assail the Enemy & range the Frontiers as occasion may require. These Stockades should be provided at the Expence of your People & are not meant to be garrisoned only as particular Exigencies may make necessary. I think no Neighbourhood ought to be without one where the Enemy can possibly penetrate. In case of Attack you are to draw out such Force from the Militia as you judge sufficient to chastise the Invaders. Let the pursuit of Scalping Parties, be close, hot and determined, for if Vengeance is taken on the foremost Partys, others will be intimidated. I wish to reinforce Capt. Arbuckles Garrison with a Company of fifty Men officered in the usual manner from your County and that they should march thither without delay. Volunteers enlisted for this Business to serve six Months in it, I would prefer, but if they are not to be got without loss of Time let the Militia be drafted. For I expect the Indians very shortly on the Frontiers. I beg the favour of you to confer with *Col. Preston* on the propriety of establishing a Post to preserve the Communication with Fort Randolph, perhaps some Place near the mouth of Elk River might answer this purpose and also check the Inroads of the Savages if the Garrison was alert and diligent to intercept their Parties.

I am at a loss for Officers in Green Bryar and wish for a recommendation from your County Court of such as are proper; That Place will be attacked tis likely and if no other Expedient can be found I must fill up the Commissions in Council, where the Individuals cannot be known. . . . I wish the Lead to be carefully preserved for the purpose of Defence & not given to the Men but as Occasions call for it, except in exposed Places, where the People must be trusted with it. I think the Garrison proposed near Elk need not consist of more than sixty Men, but I submit it to you and Col. Preston to do for the best being on the Spot.

You will perceive my Views go no further than defensive Operations. I know how impossible it is to render them completely effectual against the Enemies you have to oppose. But offensive Measures set on foot against these Indians at this time after their late Treatment, would be too full of Injustice to escape general Execration. Policy & even Self preservation may ere long call for such Measures. But even then it may be doubted if Provisions purchased in your parts would answer the Design.

Having now done every thing which I can foresee to be necessary for protecting the Frontiers, I must tell you Sir that I really blush for the occasion of this War with the Shawanese. I doubt not but you detest the vile Assassins who have brought it on us at this critical Time when our whole Force was wanted in another Quarter. But why are they not brought to Justice? Shall this Precedent establish the Right of involving Virginia in War whenever any one in the back Country shall please? I need not argue to shew you Sir the fatal tendency of such Conduct. You see it & I fear your County will feel indiscriminately that Misery which ought to visit only the guilty Authors of the Mischief. Some say the People of your Country will not suffer the Apprehension of the Murderers. I desire it may be remembered, that if the frontier people will not submit to the Laws, but thus set them at Defiance, they will not be considered as entitled to the protection of Government, and were it not for the miserable Condition of many with you, I should demand the Offenders previous to every other Step. For where is this wretched Business to end? The Cherokees, the Delawares and every other Tribe may be set on us in this manner this Spring for what I know. Is not this the work of Tories? No Man but an Enemy to American Independance will do it, and thus oblige our People to be hunting after Indians in the Woods, instead of facing Genl. Howe in the field—search into the Matter and depend upon it the Murderers are Tories—the Honor of your Country is at Stake and it is time to decide whether these Villains are to meet with punishment or whether the greater Number will espouse their Interests. I desire you to the utmost, at all hazards & to the last Extremity to support and assist the civil Magistrate in apprehending and bringing these offenders to Justice.

If the Shawenese deserved Death, because their Countrymen committed Hostilities, a Jury from the Vicinage will say so and acquit the accused who must be judged by his Neighbours feeling the same Resentments and Passions with themselves. But they are Traytors I suspect and Agents for the Enemy, who have taken this method to find employment for the brave back Woodsmen at home, and prevent their joining Genl. Washington to strike [a de]cisive Stroke for Independency at this critical time.

Urge these things Sir with that Spirit and Warmth the Subject demands—prepare your People for their own Defence against the Indians to vindicate their Honor from the rude Attack now made on it, and let them be shewn to the World as possessing the other Virtues which usually accompany Courage.

In the Confidence that what I now press, I mean the bringing the Murderers of the Indians to Justice, will be done, Government will loose no Time in lending its best Aids to protect your Country. I fear something essential for the frontier Defence, may have escaped me, But your part must be in concert with your Neighbours to point out what yet remains to be done for your Safety. If a Reinforcement of fifty Men more is necessary at Fort Randolph they will be sent on your and Col. Preston's writing to me.

I have it much at Heart to bring the Indians to treat on the Subject of our Difference with them. Perhaps the Grenadier Sqaw may be useful in this Business, please to confer on this matter with *Col. Preston* and let every possible Effort be made to bring on a Treaty. The Expences necessary for the Attempt I will pay on Demand. I forbear to mention particulars for beginning this Work as they must be better judged of on the spot, but at all Events try it vigorously. . . . —Draper Mss. 15ZZ17-20, State Historical Society of Wisconsin.

29. Attack on Fort Donnally, May 29, 1778

On April 3, 1778, in compliance with the orders of Governor Henry, Colonels Fleming and Preston sent a conciliatory message to the Shawnees assuring them that everything would be done to bring the murderers of Cornstalk to justice. The bearer of this olive branch was the tall Grenadier Squaw, Nonhelema, a sister of the murdered chief, who was also called Katy by the garrison at Fort Randolph for whom she frequently acted as interpreter. Nonhelema's mission was fruitless and

the expected retaliatory raid against Fort Randolph came in
May, 1778. When the Indians were frustrated in both their
hopes of taking the fort and starting negotiations, they moved up
the Kanawha Valley. Again the Grenadier Squaw came to the aid
of her white friends, this time by assisting John Pryor and Philip
Hammond to disguise as Indian warriors prior to their depar-
ture from the fort to warn the exposed settlers. The two scouts
succeeded in slipping past the Indians at Lewisburg and reach-
ing the house of Colonel Andrew Donnally. On receiving the
alarm, Donnally's neighbors gathered into his stockaded house
to prepare for the anticipated attack which began at dawn, May
29. The narrator of this episode was Captain John Stuart.

THE NEXT YEAR 1778 in the month of May a small party appeared in sight of the fort [Randolph], but decamped aparently
in great terror, the garison was aware of their sediction and
none pursued them; finding their scheme did not succeed,
their whole army rose up at once in sight of the fort, extending
across the point from the banks of Ohio to the banks of Kanawha
and commenced a fire on the garison for several hours, but
without effect; at length one of them had the presumption to
advance so near the fort as to request the favour of being per-
mited to come in to which Capt. McKee assented, and the
stranger verry composedly walked in. Capt arbuckle was then
in Greenbrier on a visit to his family. Not long after the introduction of the stranger a gun went off by accident, the Indians without raised a hedeous yell: but the fellow Instantly
jumped up in one of the bastions and, giving the sign to his
friends that all was well. Finding they could make no impression on the garison they concluded to come on to greenbrier and
collecting all the cattle about the Garuson for provisions on their
march set off up the kenawha in ample order to finish their
campaign and take vengeance on us for the death of Corn
Stalk. Capt. McKee discovering their rout, and concludin what
was their design; dispatched general Hammon and John Prior
in pursuit of them [with] orders if possable to pass them undiscovered and give the people notice of their aproach. This
hazerdous enterprize was executed by them with great fidelity
the Indians had marched two days before them; but they pur-

sued them with such speed that they overtook and passed them at Mecllungs medows within 20 miles of Lewisbergh; (well known by the name of Camp union) it was in the evening; and Mclungs family had removed farther in among the inhabitants being the frontier house on the way to point pleasant. Here the Indians were regaling themselves and walking about on rising ground near the house viewing the situation of the place and great extencive medows which afford a verry agreeable prospect. From these medows Hammon and Prior had a ful view of the whole of their army undiscovered and pursued on with all speed to Colonel andrew Donnallies, where the[y] gave the alarm [of the] aproach of the Indians consisting according to their last estimate of about 200 warriors. Colo. Donnally lost no time in collecting in all his neighbours that night and dispatched a man to my house to inform me before day 20 odd men including Hammon and prior was collected and the[y] had the advantage of a stockade fort round the house. There was women and children to the amount of 60 in the fort. On the next day the[y] kept a good lookout in momentary expectation of the Indians. Colonel Sam Lewis was present at my house when we received by Donnallies message and we lost no time to alarm the neighbours and collect as many men as we could at Camp union all the next day. All were busy; some flying with their families to the inco[?]d Settlement and others securing their property so that in the course of the next day we had not collected near 100 men. On the following day we dispatched two Scouts to Donnely's verry early in the morning who soon returned with inteligence that the Indians had attacked the fort, as the[y] had aproached within about a mile and heard a brisk firing we determined to give all the relief we could to the beseiged and collected all the men in the fort that was willing to go which amounted to 68 including Colo. Lewis Capt. Arbuckle and myself. we drew near Donnally's house about 2 oclock P M. but heard no firing; for Sake of expedition we had left the road for a nearer way that led to the back of the house and escaped falling into an embuscade place on the road not far from the house, which might have been fatal to us as we were greatly inferior to the Indians in point of number.

We soon discovered one Indian in a rye field looking earnestly at the house; Charles Gatliff and myself fired at him and we saw others run in the rye near where he stood. We all run directly to the fort, and the people who at first hearing the guns on the back side of the house supposed it was another party of Indians and were all at the port holes ready to fire on us, but some discovering who we were opened the gates for us and we all got in safe, one man only was shot through a fold of his hunting shirt. When we got to the fort we found 4 men only were killed, 2 who were coming to the fort fell into the midst of the Indians and were killed. A servant of Dunmores [Donnally?] was killed before the door on their first attack, and one was shot in a bastion in the fort. the Indians had commenced their attack about day light when all in the fort were fast asleep except the centry, Phil Hammon and an old negro. The house composed one part of the front of the fort and was double Hammon and the negro was in the kitchen and where a hogshead of water against the door The Indians had laid down 3 guns at a stable about 50 yards from the house and made their attack at the kitchen door with their tomhawks and war clubs when Hammon let the door open and killed the Indian on the threshold who was in the act of spliting the door. the negro had a musket loaded with swanshot and was jumping about on the floor asking Hammon where he would shoot, who told him to fire away among them for the yard was covered as thick as the[y] could stand, which he did and I believe with good effect, for a war club lay in the yard with a swan shot in it. he is now upwards 80 years old has long been abandoned by his Master as well as his wife who is as aged as himself and has made out to preserve a miserable existance for themselves these many years past with their own endeavours; this is the negro whom our Assembly at the last session refused to grant a small pention to support his wretched condition which must soon terminate, on his humble petition suppor[t]ed by certificates from the most respectable men in our country of his meritorious services on that occasion, which was a means of preserving the lives of many citizens then in the house. The firing of Hammond awakened the people in the other end of the house and up stairs where the chief of the men were lying

wh[o] fired out of the windows so briskly upon the enemy
that when we got into the fort 17 lay dead in the yard. After dark
a fellow drew near the fort and called out in the English language that he wanted to make peace and we invited [him] to
come and consult on the terms, but he declined our civility.
The[y] departed that night but not before the[y] draged off
their Slain out of the yard and we never after found where
the[y] burried them, nor the[y] never afterwards viseted
greenbrier more than once or twice in Small parties, and the
last persons murdered by them was an old man and his wife
of the name of Monday in the year 1780. thus ends our war
in Greenbrier with the Indians.—Draper Mss. 6NN112-18, State
Historical Society of Wisconsin.

30. Military Grants

*Virginia rewarded her military veterans with handsome
grants from her vast public domain. Much of the land in
present West Virginia was acquired in this manner by men who
had served in the French and Indian War and in the Revolution. The following act was passed in 1779 to provide land
bounties for the officers and soldiers of the Virginia line in the
Continental and state forces and for the officers and sailors in
the Virginia navy.*

II. And whereas no law of this commonwealth hath yet ascertained the proportions or quantity of land to be granted, at
the end of the present war, to the officers of the Virginia line
on continental or state establishment, or to the officers of the
Virginia navy, and doubts may arise respecting the particular
quantity of land due to the soldiers and sailors, from the different terms of their enlistments; *Be it enacted,* That the officers who shall have served in the Virginia line on continental
establishment, or in the army or navy upon state establishment to the end of the present war; and the noncommissioned
officers, soldiers, and sailors upon either of the said establishments, their heirs or legal representatives, shall respectively
be entitled to and receive the proportion and quantities of land

following; that is to say, every colonel, five thousand acres; every lieutenant colonel, four thousand five hundred acres; every major, four thousand acres; every captain, three thousand acres; every subaltern, two thousand acres; every non-commissioned officer who having enlisted for the war, shall have served to the end thereof, four hundred acres; and every soldier and sailor under the like circumstances, two hundred acres; every non-commissioned officer, who having enlisted for the term of three years, shall have served out the same, or to the end of the present war, two hundred acres; and every soldier and sailor under the like circumstances, one hundred acres; every officer of the navy the same quantity of land as an officer of equal rank in the army. And where any officer, soldier, or sailor shall have fallen or died in the service, his heirs or legal representatives shall be entitled to and receive the same quantity of land as would have been due to such officer, soldier, or sailor respectively, had he been living. . . . —Hening, *Statutes at Large*, X, 159-62.

31. Loyalism in Western Virginia – Garret Van Meter to Jefferson, April 14, 1781

Loyalism persisted in western Virginia throughout the Revolution in spite of the vigilance of patriots and the imposition of oaths of loyalty to the State of Virginia and the United States. Late in 1775, John Connolly, confident that his skillful diplomacy would secure the Indians' support to the royal cause, tried to launch from Detroit a counter-revolutionary offensive in Virginia. The detection of this plot and the arrest of Connolly did not stamp out loyalism in this area. In March, 1778, Alexander McKee, Matthew Elliott, Simon Girty, Robert Surphlitt, and John Higgins escaped from Fort Pitt to aid the British in the West. Shortly afterward, General Edward Hand warned that if a few men were not stationed at Fort Pitt immediately "to encourage the timerous, tho' well affected, and over-awe the Tory faction, this whole country [would] be abandoned or over-

*run by the enemy in a short time." Similar concern was later
expressed by General Daniel Brodhead. "I learn more and
more of the disaffection of many of the inhabitants on this side
the mountain," he wrote in December, 1780. "The King of
Britain's health is often drunk in companies; & I believe those
wish to see the Regular Troops removed from this department,
& a favorable opportunity to submit to British Government."
In southwest Virginia loyalism became increasingly evident as
the British advanced through the Carolinas, shaking the isolated frontiersmen's confidence in the success of the Revolution
and seeking their support or neutrality with promises of amnesty and financial rewards. In 1779 Colonels William Preston
and William Campbell and Major Walter Crockett suppressed a
design to seize control of the lead mines in Montgomery County. The following year a more formidable conspiracy in this
area was crushed by the local military authorities assisted by
Colonel Charles Lynch, whose name became synonymous with
ruthlessness and disregard of due process of law. Disaffection, if not overt loyalism was also evident in Hampshire,
Berkeley, and Greenbrier counties during the governorship of
Thomas Jefferson. Not only did some of the residents of these
counties withhold the provisions, clothing, and wagons which
they were required by law to furnish to the state, but they also
protested against calls for military service. The lenity employed in dealing with these disaffected elements may be explained by fear in official quarters that summary proceedings
might occasion "Rebellion or Bloodshed" at a time when northwestern Virginia was menaced by the Indians, the southern
part of the state by Cornwallis, and the eastern, by a formidable enemy invasion.*

Sir   Hampshire April 14th. 1781

Inclosed you have the Return of our Two Battalions and as
I Received instructions from General Clarke not to march the
Malitia untill Further Orders, So I have Gave orders for the
full of your Excellencies Demand but am afraid the orders will
not Be Comply'd with by Reason of the Disaffected people
amongst us (a Collecter of one of the Divisons for making up
the Cloathes and Beef was Interrupted in the Execution of his

office. A certain John Claypole Said if all the men were of his mind they would not make up any Cloathes, Beef or men and all that would Join him Should turn out. Upon which he Got all the men present to five or Six and Got Liquor and Drank king George the thirds health, and Damnation to Congress). Upon which Complaint was made to three majistrates upon which there was a warrant Issued for Several of them and Guard of Fifty men with the Sherriff. When they Came to the Place they found Sixty or Seventy men Embodied with arms. After Some time they Capitulated. The Sherriff Serv'd the precept on the Said John Claypole but he refused to Come with him or Give up His arms but agreed to Come Such a time which time is Passt. Inclosed you have a Copy of a Letter they Sent me and the answer I sent them. I was Informed there was One Hundred and fifty of them to Gether the next Day. I am informed there are Several Deserters Amongst those People, Some from the English Prisoners, Some Eighteen months men and Some Eight month men which they Support and Conceal. As for farther Particulars I Refer you to Mr. Woodrow the Bearer Hereof. So leave it to your Excellencies wisdom to order Such Measures as you think proper.—Executive Papers, Box EP-8, Virginia State Library.

32. The Second Siege of Fort Henry – Report of Colonel Ebenezer Zane and Exploit of Elizabeth Zane

The annals of early West Virginia are replete with stories of heroism, some of which persist in spite of contradictory or even lack of documentary evidence. This frontier lore, so vividly described by Alexander Scott Withers in his CHRONICLES OF BORDER WARFARE *(Clarksburg, 1831), has overshadowed West Virginia's substantial contributions of manpower and supplies to the revolutionary cause. Settlers of this area served in the state and Continental forces throughout the Revolution; a num-*

ber of the men in the gallant band which George Rogers Clark
led to victory in the Illinois country in 1778-1779 were from
western Virginia; some inhabitants, like those of Holliday's
Cove in the summer of 1777, "declared the[y] would stay &
Difend themselves as long as the[y] could" against the Indians. Women also assisted in the defense of their families and
homes and of the rude stockades where they took refuge in time
of attack. One of the most important forts in the Ohio valley
was at Wheeling. It was built in June, 1774, and named Fort
Fincastle, for one of Lord Dunmore's titles. During the Revolution the name was changed to Fort Henry, in honor of Governor
Patrick Henry of Virginia. Joseph Doddridge, the frontier historian of West Virginia, spent part of his boyhood in the neighborhood of the fort which he described as substantially built
of squared timbers pointed at the top and furnished with bastions and sentry boxes at the angles. The fort covered an area of
a little more than half an acre and contained a house for officers
and barracks for the men. Fort Henry was attacked several
times during the Revolution, and the sieges of 1777 and 1782 are
among the most thrilling episodes of the early West.

The second siege of Fort Henry in September, 1782, brought
frontier acclaim to the pioneering Zane family of Wheeling.
Colonel Ebenezer Zane had been placed in charge of the garrison at Wheeling, but while the fort was under attack he remained in his fortified dwelling house which served as a magazine and as a second outpost. His brother, Captain Silas Zane,
was the commander of the fort during the three days' siege.
Their young sister, Elizabeth or Betty, saved the fort by re-
plenishing its supply of powder. The father of this intrepid trio
and of two other brothers, Jonathan and Andrew, was probably
William Zane who had moved from the Philadelphia area to the
South Branch valley after breaking with the Society of Friends
to which his family belonged. Aside from the details of her exploit, very little is known about Betty Zane. According to family tradition she was attending school in Philadelphia at the
time Fort Henry was attacked in 1777. Also according to tradition she stood in the sentry box of the fort when it was be-
sieged in 1782 and assisted the defenders in reloading their
guns. Elizabeth was twice married, first to John MGloughlin

*by whom she had five daughters, then to Jacob Clark by whom
she had a daughter and a son, Ebenezer. She died in 1823 and
was buried in the Walnut Grove Cemetery, Martins Ferry,
Ohio.*

*Ebenezer Zane's report of the attack to General William Ir-
vine and an early newspaper account of the gunpowder exploit follow.*

Wheeling, *September* 17, 1782.

Sir:— On the evening of the 11th instant, a body of the enemy
appeared in sight of our garrison. They immediately formed
their lines round the garrison, paraded British colors, and demanded the fort to be surrendered, which was refused. About
twelve o'clock at night, they rushed hard on the pickets in order to storm, but were repulsed. They made two other attempts
to storm before day, but to no purpose.

About 8 o'clock next morning, there came a negro from them
to us and informed us that their force consisted of a British
captain and forty regular soldiers and two hundred and sixty
Indians. The enemy kept a continual fire the whole day. About
ten o'clock at night, they made a fourth attempt to storm to no
better purpose than the former. The enemy continued around
the garrison until the morning of the 13th instant, when they
disappeared. Our loss is none. Daniel Sullivan, who arrived
here in the first of the action, is wounded in the foot.

I believe they have driven the greatest part of our stock
away, and might, I think, be soon overtaken.

--Washington-Irvine Correspondence, edited by C. W. Butter-
field, pp. 397-98.

A Philadelphia paper has recently published a full account
of the attack on the fort at Wheeling in the fall of 1782 from
which we extract an incident, *which we have repeatedly heard
related,* one of *our informants being an eye witness.* When the
alarm was given by a ranger that the Indians were coming,
the fort having for some time been unocupied by a garrison,
and *Colonel Zane's house,* which stood near it, having been
used for a *magazine,* those who retired into the fort had to take
with them a supply for its defense. The *powder* became Exhausted by reason of the long siege. In this Emergency it be-

came necessary to renew the stock from the abundant store in *Col. Zane's house.* Accordingly it was proposed that one of the fleetest men should Endeavor to reach the house, obtain the powder and return to the fort. *Col. Zane's sister* was in the fort and at once volunteered to bring the powder. She was young, active, and athletic with courage to dare anything. On being told that one of the men would run less risk by reason of his fleetness, she replied—"*Should he fall his loss would be more severely felt: You have no men to spare,* and *a woman will not be missed in defending the fort.*" She was then told to go, and divesting herself of some heavy clothing, started out through the gate like a deer. The sight so amazed the savages that they cried "*squaw, squaw*" and not a shot was fired at her. Arriving at the house, *Col. Zane* fastened a cloth about her waist, and poured into it a *a quantity of powder,* when she again ventured out. The Indians now discovered the object of the "*squaw*" and bullet after bullet whizzed past her head. She reached the fort in safety, although a bullet hole was found in her dress. The powder Enabled the brave little band to hold out against the besiegers who were at last compelled to retire without having accomplished their object.

—Draper MSS. 4ZZ22, State Historical Society of Wisconsin.

IV. From Frontier to Towns and an Occasional Mansion

33. Notes On The Settlements and Indian Wars

Frontier society was coarse, but hospitable; individualistic, yet permeated with the spirit of mutual helpfulness; dangerous, and yet primevally peaceful. A vivid portrayal of this society is found in Notes on the Settlement and Indian Wars ... *by Joseph Doddridge (1769-1826), whose family moved to the western part of Washington County, Pennsylvania, near the Virginia border, early in 1773. Endowed with remarkable versatility, Doddridge attended Jefferson Academy in Pennsylvania, was ordained a minister in the Protestant Episcopal Church, studied medicine with the eminent Dr. Benjamin Rush, and was elected corresponding member of the Philadelphia Academy of Natural Science. From his home in Wellsburg, Brooke County, Doddridge practiced his professions in both Virginia and Ohio. His writings, in addition to the* Notes, *include a* Treatise on the Culture of Bees, *a short play,* Logan, the Last of the Race of Shikellemus, *an unfinished series of letters entitled "The Russian Spy," and some poetry.*

The Furniture for the Table, for several years after the settlement of this country, consisted of a few pewter dishes, plates and spoons; but mostly of wooden bowls, trenchers and noggins. If these last were scarce, gourds and hard shelled squashes made up the deficiency.

The iron pots, knives and forks, were brought from the east side of the mountains along with the salt and iron on pack horses.

. . . "Hog and hominy" were proverbial for the dish of which they were the component parts. Johnny cake and pone were at the outset of the settlements of the country, the only forms of bread in use for breakfast and dinner. At supper, milk and mush was the standard dish. When milk was not plenty, which was often the case, owing to the scarcity of cattle, or the want of proper pasture for them, the substantial dish of hominy had to supply the place of them; mush was frequently eaten with sweetened water, molasses, bears oil, or the gravey of fried meat.

Every family, besides a little garden, for the few vegetables which they cultivated, had another small enclosure containing from half an acre to an acre, which they called a "Truck patch," in which they raised corn for roasting ears, pumpkins, squashes, beans and potatoes. These, in the latter part of the summer and fall, were cooked with their pork, venison and bear meat for dinner, and made very wholesome and well tasted dishes. The standard dinner dish for every log rolling, house raising, and harvest day was a pot pye, or what in other countries is called "Sea pye." . . .

The fort consisted of cabins, blockhouses, and stockades. A range of cabins commonly formed one side at least of the fort. Divisions, or partitions of logs separated the cabins from each other. The walls on the outside were ten or twelve feet high, the slope of the roof being turned wholly inward. A very few of these cabins had puncheon floors, the greater part were earthen.

The blockhouses were built at the angles of the fort. They projected about two feet beyond the outer walls of the cabins and stockades. Their upper stories were about eighteen inches every way larger in dimension than the under one, leaving an opening at the commencement of the second story to prevent the enemy from making a lodgment under their walls. In some forts instead of blockhouses, the angles of the fort were furnished with bastions. A large folding gate made of thick slabs, nearest the spring closed the fort. The stockades, bastions, cabins, and blockhouse walls were furnished with port holes at proper heights and distances. The whole of the outside was made completely bullet proof.

It may be truly said that necessity is the mother of invention; for the whole of this work was made without the aid of a single nail or spike of iron, and for this reason, such things were not to be had.

In some places, less exposed, a single blockhouse, with a cabin or two constituted the whole fort.

Such places of refuge may appear very trifling to those who have been in the habit of seeing the formidable military garrisons of Europe and America; but they answered the purpose, as the indians had no artillery. They seldom attacked, and scarcely ever took one of them.

The families belonging to these forts were so attached to their own cabins on their farms, that they seldom moved into their fort in the spring until compelled by some alarm, as they called it; that is, when it was announced by some murder that the indians were in the settlement.

. . . I well remember that, when a little boy, the family were sometimes waked up in the dead of night, by an express with a report that the indians were at hand. The express came softly to the door, or back window, and by a gentle tapping waked the family. This was easily done as an habitual fear made us ever watchful and sensible to the slightest alarm. The whole family were instantly in motion. My father seized his gun and other implements of war. My step mother waked up, and dressed the children as well as she could, and being myself the oldest of the children, I had to take my share of the burthens to be carried to the fort. There was no possibility of getting a horse in the night to aid us in removing to the fort. Besides the little children we caught up what articles of clothing and provision we could get hold of in the dark, for we durst not light a candle or even stir the fire. All this was done with the untmost dispatch and the silence of death. The greatest care was taken not to awaken the youngest child.

To the rest it was enough to say *indian* and not a whimper was heard afterwards. Thus it often happened that the whole number of families belonging to a fort who were in the evening at their homes, were all in their little fortress before the dawn of the next morning. In the course of the succeeding day, their household furniture was brought in by parties of the men under arms.

...For a long time after the first settlement of this country, the inhabitants in general married young. There was no distinction of rank, and very little of fortune. On these accounts the first impression of love resulted in marriage; and a family establishment cost but a little labour and nothing else....

In the first years of the settlement of this country, a wedding engaged the attention of a whole neighborhood; and the frolic was anticipated by old and young with eager expectation....

In the morning of the wedding day, the groom and his attendants assembled at the house of his father for the purpose of reaching the mansion of his bride by noon, which was the usual time for celebrating the nuptials; which for certain must take place before dinner....

The march, in double file, was often interrupted by the narrowness and obstructions of our horse paths, as they were called, for we had no roads; and these difficulties were often increased, sometimes by the good, and sometimes by the ill will of neighbors, by felling trees and tying grape vines across the way. Sometimes an ambuscade was formed by the way side, and an unexpected discharge of several guns took place, so as to cover the wedding company with smoke....

Another ceremony commonly took place before the party reached the house of the bride, after the practice of making whiskey began, which was at an early period. When the party were about a mile from the place of their destination, two young men would single out to run for the bottle.... The start was announced by an indian yell; logs, brush, muddy hollows, hill and glen, were speedily passed by the rival ponies. The bottle was always filled for the occasion, so that there was no use for judges; for the first who reached the door was presented with the prize, with which he returned in triumph to the company. On approaching them he announced his victory over his rival by a shrill whoop. At the head of the troop, he gave the bottle first to the groom and his attendants, and then to each pair in succession to the rear of the line, giving each a drams; and then, puting the bottle in the bosom of his hunting shirt, took his station in the company.

The ceremony of the marriage preceeded the dinner, which was a substantial backwoods feast of beef, pork, fowls, and sometimes venison and bear meat roasted and boiled, with plenty of potatoes, cabbage, and other vegetables. During the dinner the greatest hilarity always prevailed; although the table might be a large slab of timber, hewed out with a broad axe, supported by four sticks set in auger holes; and the furniture, some old pewter-dishes, and plates; the rest, wooden bowls and trenchers; a few pewter spoons, much battered about the edges, were to be seen at some tables. The rest were made of horns. If knives were scarce, the deficiency was made up by the scalping knives which were carried in sheaths suspended to the belt of the hunting shirt.

After dinner the dancing commenced; and generally lasted 'till the next morning. The figures of the dances were three and four handed reels, or square sets and jigs. . . . The jigs were often accompanied with what was called cutting out; that is, when either of the parties became tired of the dance, on intimation the place was supplied by some one of the company without any interruption of the dance. In this way a dance was often continued till the musician was heartily tired of his situation. Toward the latter part of the night, if any of the company, through weariness, attempted to conceal themselves, for the purpose of sleeping they were hunted up, paraded on the floor, and the fiddler ordered to play "Hang on till tomorrow morning."

About nine or ten o'clock a deputation of the young ladies stole off the bride, and put her to bed. In doing this, it frequently happened that they had to ascend a ladder instead of a pair of stairs, leading from the dining and ball room to the loft, the floor of which was made of clapboards, lying loose and without nails. This ascent one might think, would put the bride and her attendants to the blush; but as the foot of the ladder was commonly behind the door, which was purposely opened for the occasion, and its rounds at the inner ends were well hung with hunting shirts, petticoats, and other articles of clothing, the candles being on the opposite side of the house, the exit of the bride was noticed but by few. This done, a deputation of young men in like manner stole off the groom, and placed him snugly by the side of his bride. The dance still continued; and if seats happened to be scarce, which was often the case, every

young man, when not engaged in the dance, was obliged to offer his lap as a seat for one of the girls; and the offer was sure
to be accepted. In the midst of this hilarity the bride and groom
were not forgotten. Pretty late in the night, some one would
remind the company that the new couple must stand in need
of some refreshment: black Betty, which was the name of the
bottle, was called for, and sent up the ladder; but sometimes
black Betty did not go alone; I have many times seen as much
bread, beef, pork, and cabbage sent along with her, as would
afford a good meal for a half dozen hungry men. The young
couple were compelled to eat and drink, more or less, of whatever was offered them. . . .

. . . A day was appointed shortly after their marriage for
commencing the work of building their cabin. The fatigue party
consisted of choppers, whose business it was to fell the trees
and cut them off at proper lengths. A man with a team for
hauling them to the place, and arranging them, properly as-
sorted, at the sides and ends of the building, a carpenter, if
such he might be called, whose business it was to search the
woods for a proper tree for making clapboards for the roof.
The tree for this purpose must be straight grained and from
three to four feet in diameter. The boards were split four feet
long, with a large frow, and as wide as the timber would allow. They were used without planing or shaving. Another division were employed in getting puncheons for the floor of the
cabin; this was done by splitting trees, about eighteen inches
in diameter, and hewing the faces of them with a broad
axe. . . .

In the morning of the next day the neighbours collected for
the raising. The first thing to be done was the election of four
corner men, whose business it was to notch and place the logs.
The rest of the company furnished them with the timbers. In
the meantime the boards and puncheons were collecting for
the floor and roof, so that by the time the cabin was a few
rounds high the sleepers and floor began to be laid. The door
was made by sawing or cutting the logs in one side so as to
make an opening about three feet wide. This opening was secured by upright pieces of timber about three inches thick
through which holes were bored into the ends of the logs for the

purpose of pinning them fast. A similar opening, but wider, was made at the end for the chimney. This was built of logs and made large to admit of a back and jams of stone. At the square, two end logs projected a foot or eighteen inches beyond the wall to receive the butting poles, as they were called, against which the ends of the first row of clapboards was supported. The roof was formed by making the end logs shorter until a single log formed the comb of the roof. On these logs the clapboards were placed, the ranges of them lapping some distance over those next below them and kept in their places by logs, placed at proper distances upon them.

The roof, and sometimes the floor, were finished on the same day of the raising. A third day was commonly spent by a few carpenters in leveling off the floor, making a clap board door and a table. This last was made of a split slab and supported by four round legs set in auger holes. Some three leged stools were made in the same manner. Some pins stuck in the logs at the back of the house supported some clap boards which served for shelves for the table furniture. A single fork, placed with its lower end in a hole in the floor and the upper end fastened to a joist served for a bed stead, by placing a pole in the fork with one end through a crack between the logs of the wall. This front pole was crossed by a shorter one within the fork, with its outer end through another crack. From the front pole, through a crack between the logs of the end of the house, the boards were put on which formed the bottom of the bed. Sometimes other poles were pinned to the fork a little distance above these, for the purpose of supporting the front and foot of the bed, while the walls were the supports of its back and head. A few pegs around the walls for a display of the coats of the women, and hunting shirts of the men, and two small forks or bucks horns to a joist for the rifle and shot pouch, completed the carpenter work.

In the mean time masons were at work. With the heart pieces of the timber of which the clapboards were made, they made billets for chunking up the cracks between the logs of the cabin and chimney, a large bed of mortar was made for daubing up those cracks; a few stones formed the back and jambs of the chimney.

The cabin being finished, the ceremony of house warming took place, before the young couple were permitted to move into it.

The house warming was a dance of a whole night's continuance, made up of the relations of the bride and groom, and their neighbors. On the day following the young couple took possession of their new mansion. . . .

For the bite of a rattle, or copper snake, a great variety of specifices were used. I remember when a small boy to have seen a man bitten by a rattlesnake brought into the fort on a man's back. One of the company dragged the snake after him by a forked stick fastened in its head. The body of the snake was cut into pieces of about two inches in length, split open in succession, and laid on the wound to draw out the poison, as they expressed it. When this was over, a fire was kindled up in the fort yard and the whole of the serpent burned to ashes, by way of revenge for the injury he had done.

After this process was over, a large quantity of chestnut leaves was collected and boiled in a pot. The whole of the wounded man's leg and part of his thigh were placed in a piece of chestnut bark, fresh from the tree, and the decoction poured on the leg so as to run down into the pot again; after continuing this process for some time, a quantity of the boiled leaves were bound to the leg. This was repeated several times a day. The man got well; but whether owing to the treatment bestowed on his wound, is not so certain.

A number of native plants were used for the cure of snake bites. Among them the white plantain held a high rank. This was boiled in milk and the decoction given the patient in large quantities. A kind of fern, which from its resemblance to the leaves of walnut, was called walnut fern, was another remedy. A plant with fibrous roots, resembling the seneka-snake root, of a black color and a strong, but not disagreeable smell, was considered and relied on as the indian specific for the cure of the sting of a snake. A decoction of this root was also used for the cure of colds. Another plant which very much resembles the one above mentioned, but violently poisonous, was sometimes mistaken for it and was used in its place. . . .

Cupping, sucking the wound, and making deep incisions which were filled with salt and gun powder, were amongst the remedies for snake bites. . . . —Joseph Doddridge, *Notes on the Settlement and Indian Wars Of the Western Parts of Virginia & Pennsylvania* (1824), pp. 108-50.

34. "Laws," from Notes On The State of Virginia

One of the best sources of information on Virginia is Thomas Jefferson's NOTES ON THE STATE OF VIRGINIA, *written during the Revolution in reply to a set of queries circulated by Francois Marbois, the secretary of the French legation at Philadelphia, among various members of the Continental Congress. The preparation of the* NOTES *was a congenial task for Jefferson, whose store of knowledge about his native state was both varied and profound. Despite Jefferson's modest appraisal of this work, it has been hailed as a thoughtful commentary on early Virginia and a noteworthy exposition of eighteenth century American liberalism.*

Although Jefferson was much more familiar with eastern Virginia than with the western part of the state, he was well qualified to write on the latter. He described the Great Kanawha as "a river of considerable note for the fertility of its lands, and still more, as leading towards the headwaters of James (and Roanoke) river(s)." He mentioned the limitless deposits of coal and the many salt springs in the "western country." "The area at Bullet's lick [Kanawha County] is of many acres," he wrote. "Digging the earth to the depth of three feet, the water begins to boil up, and the deeper you go, and the drier the weather, the stronger the brine." He noted the numerous caves and mineral springs of western Virginia, and its important gas deposits. At Burning Springs, seven miles above the mouth of the Elk River, he stated that there was "a hole in the earth of the capacity of 30 or 40 gallons" from which issued a gaseous stream so strong as to move the sand about its mouth. But what was still more wonderful, Jefferson contin-

*ued, "on presenting a lighted candle or torch within 18 inches
of the hole, it flames up in a column of 18 inches diameter,
and four or five feet height, which sometimes burns out within
20 minutes, and at other times has been known to continue
three days, and then has been left still burning." Though the
two sections of Virginia divided by the lofty Alleghenies differ-
ed in resources and topography, they were one politically and
were subject to the laws which Jefferson briefly described in
Query XIV, "Laws."*

The state is divided into counties. In every county are appointed magistrates, called justices of the peace, usually from
eight to thirty or forty in number, in proportion to the size of
the county, of the most discreet and honest inhabitants. They
are nominated by their fellows, but commissioned by the governor, and act without reward. These magistrates have jurisdiction both criminal and civil. If the question before them be
a question of law only, they decide on it themselves; but if it
be of fact, or of fact and law combined, it must be referred to
a jury. In the latter case, of a combination of law and fact, it
is usual for the jurors to decide the fact, and to refer the law
arising on it to the decision of the judges.... These judges execute their process by the sheriff or coroner of the county, or
by constables of their own appointment. If any free person
commit an offence against the commonwealth, if it be below
the degree of felony, he is bound by a justice to appear before
their court, to answer it on indictment or information. If it
amount to felony, he is committed to jail, a court of these justices is called; if they on examination think him guilty, they
send him to the jail of the general court, before which court
he is to be tried first by a grand jury of 24, of whom 13 must
concur in opinion: if they find him guilty, he is then tried by a
jury of 12 men of the county where the offence was committed,
and by their verdict, which must be unanimous, he is acquitted
or condemned without appeal. If the criminal be a slave the
trial by the county court is final. In every case however, except
that of high treason, there resides in the governor a power of
pardon. In high treason, the pardon can only flow from the
general assembly. In civil matters these justices have juris-

diction in all cases of whatever value, not appertaining to the department of the admiralty. This jurisdiction is twofold. If the matter in dispute be of less value than 4 1/6 dollars, a single member may try it at any time and place within his county, and may award execution on the goods of the party cast. If it be of that or greater value, it is determinable before the county court, which consists of four at the least of those justices, and assemblies at the court-house of the county on a certain day in every month. From their determination, if the matter be of the value of ten pounds sterling, or concern the title or bounds of lands, an appeal lies to one of the superior courts.

There are three superior courts, to wit, the high-court of chancery, the general court, and court of admiralty. The first and second of these receive appeals from the county courts, and also have original jurisdiction where the subject of controversy is of the value of ten pounds sterling, or where it concerns the title or bounds of land. The jurisdiction of the admiralty is original altogether. . . .

There is one supreme court, called the court of appeals, composed of the judges of the three superior courts, assembling twice a year at stated times at Richmond. This court receives appeals in all civil cases from each of the superior courts, and determines them finally. But it has no original jurisdiction. . . .

Debtors unable to pay their debts, and making faithful delivery of their whole effects, are released from confinement, and their persons for ever discharged from restraint for such previous debts: but any property they may afterwards acquire will be subject to their creditors.

The poor, unable to support themselves, are maintained by an assessment on the titheable persons in their parish. This assessment is levied and administered by twelve persons in each parish, called vestrymen, originally chosen by the housekeepers of the parish, but afterwards filling vacancies in their own body by their own choice. . . . The poor who have neither property, friends, nor strength to labour, are boarded in the houses of good farmers, to whom a stipulated sum is annually paid. To those who are able to help themselves a little, or have friends

from whom they derive some succours, inadequate however to
their full maintenance, supplementory aids are given, which enable them to live comfortably in their own houses, or in the
houses of their friends. Vagabonds, without visible property
or vocation, are placed in workhouses, where they are well
cloathed, fed, lodged, and made to labour. . . . Their [the
poor's] situation too, when sick, in the family of a good farmer,
where every member is emulous to do them kind offices,
where they are visited by all the neighbours, who bring them
the little rarities which their sickly appetites may crave, and
who take by rotation the nightly watch over them, when their
condition requires it, is without comparison better than in a
general hospital, where the sick, the dying, and the dead are
crammed together, in the same rooms, and often in the same
beds. The disadvantages, inseparable from general hospitals,
are such as can never be counterpoised by all the regularities
of medicine and regimen. Nature and kind nursing save a much
greater proportion in our plain way, at a smaller expence, and
with less abuse. One branch only of hospital institution is wanting with us; that is, a general establishment for those labour-
ing under difficult cases of chirurgery. The aids of this art are
not equivocal. But an able chirurgeon cannot be had in every
parish. Such a receptacle should therefore be provided for
those patients: but no others should be admitted.

Marriages must be solemnized either on special licence,
granted by the first magistrate of the county, on proof of the
consent of the parent or guardian of either party under age,
or after solemn publication, on three several Sundays, at some
place of religious worship, in the parishes where the parties
reside. The act of solemnization may be by the minister of any
society of Christians, who shall have been previously licensed
for this purpose by the court of the county. Quakers and Men-
onists however are exempted from all these conditions, and marriage among them is to be solemnized by the society itself.

A foreigner of any nation, not in open war with us, becomes
naturalized by removing to the state to reside, and taking an
oath of fidelity: and thereupon acquires every right of a native
citizen: and citizens may divest themselves of that character,
by declaring, by solemn deed, or in open court, that they

mean to expatriate themselves, and no longer to be citizens of this state.

Conveyances of land must be registered in the court of the county wherein they lie, or in the general court, or they are void, as to creditors, and subsequent purchasers.

Slaves pass by descent and dower as lands do. Where the descent is from a parent, the heir is bound to pay an equal share of their value in money to each of his brothers and sisters.

Slaves, as well as lands, were entailable during the monarchy: but, by an act of the first republican assembly, all donees in tail, present and future, were vested with the absolute dominion of the entailed subject.

Bills of exchange, being protested, carry 10 per cent. interest from their date.

No person is allowed, in any other case, to take more than five per cent. per annum simple interest, for the loan of monies.

Gaming debts are made void, and monies actually paid to discharge such debts (if they exceed 40 shillings) may be recovered by the payer within three months, or by any other person afterwards.

Tobacco, flour, beef, pork, tar, pitch, and turpentine, must be inspected by persons publicly appointed, before they can be exported.

The erecting iron-works and mills is encouraged by many privileges; with necessary cautions however to prevent their dams from obstructing the navigation of the watercourses. . . .

The laws have also descended to the preservation and improvement of the races of useful animals, such as horses, cattle, deer; to the extirpation of those which are noxious, as wolves, squirrels, crows, blackbirds; and to the guarding our citizens against infectious disorders, by obliging suspected vessels coming into the state to perform quarantine, and by regulating the conduct of persons having such disorders within the state.

The mode of acquiring lands, in the earliest times of our settlement, was by petition to the general assembly. If the lands prayed for were already cleared of the Indian title, and the as-

sembly thought the prayer reasonable, they passed the property by their vote to the petitioner. But if they had not yet been
ceded by the Indians, it was necessary that the petitioner
should previously purchase their right. This purchase the assembly verified, by enquiries of the Indian proprietors; and being
satisfied of its reality and fairness, proceeded further to examine
the reasonableness of the petition, and its consistence with
policy; and, according to the result, either granted or rejected
the petition. The company also sometimes, though very rarely,
granted lands, independantly of the general assembly. As the
colony increased, and individual applications for land multi-
plied, it was found to give too much occupation to the general
assembly to enquire into and execute the grant in every special case. They therefore thought it better to establish general
rules, according to which all grants should be made, and to
leave to the governor the execution of them, under these rules.
This they did by what have been usually called the land laws,
amending them from time to time, as their defects were developed. According to these laws, when an individual wished a portion of unappropriated land, he was to locate and survey it by
a public officer, appointed for that purpose: its breadth was to
bear a certain proportion to its length: the grant was to be executed by the governor: and the lands were to be improved in
a certain manner, within a given time. From these regulations
there resulted to the state a sole and exclusive power of taking
conveyances of the Indian right of soil: since, according to
them, an Indian conveyance alone could give no right to an
individual, which the laws would acknowledge. The state, or
the crown, thereafter, made general purchases of the Indians
from time to time, and the governor parcelled them out by special grants, conformed to the rules before described, which it
was not in his power, or in that of the crown, to dispense with.
Grants, unaccompanied by their proper legal circumstances,
were set aside regularly by *scire facias,* or by bill in Chancery.
Since the establishment of our new government, this order of
things is but little changed. An individual, wishing to appropriate to himself lands still unappropriated by any other, pays
to the public treasurer a sum of money proportioned to the
quantity he wants. He carries the treasurer's receipt to the

auditors of public accompts, who thereupon debit the treasurer with the sum, and order the register of the land-office to give the party a warrant for his land. With this warrant from the register, he goes to the surveyor of the county where the land lies on which he has cast his eye. The surveyor lays it off for him, gives him its exact description, in the form of a certificate, which certificate he returns to the land-office, where a grant is made out, and is signed by the governor. This vests in him a perfect dominion in his lands, transmissible to whom he pleases by deed or will, or by descent to his heirs if he die intestate. . . .

I. Crimes whose punishment extends to *Life*.

1. High treason.		Death by hanging. Forfeiture of lands and goods to the commonwealth.
2. Petty treason.		Death by hanging. Dissection. Forfeiture of half the lands and goods to the representatives of the party slain.
3. Murder.	1. by poison	Death by poison. Forfeiture of one-half as before.
	2. in Duel.	Death by hanging. Gibbeting, if the challenger. Forfeiture of one-half as before, unless it be the party challenged, then the forfeiture is to the commonwealth.
	3. in any other way.	Death by hanging. Forfeiture of one-half as before.
4. Manslaughter.		The second offence is murder.

II. Crimes whose punishment goes to *Limb*.

1. Rape,
2. Sodomy, ⎫ Dismemberment.
Retaliation, and the forfeiture of half the lands and goods to the sufferer.
3. Maiming,
4. Disfiguring, ⎫

III. Crimes punishable by *Labour*.

1. Manslaughter, 1st offence.   Labour VII. years for the public.   Forfeiture of half as in murder.

2. Counterfeiting money.	Labour VI. years.	Forfeiture of lands and goods to the commonwealth.
3. Arson 4. Asportation of vessels.	Labour V. years.	Reparation threefold.
5. Robbery. 6. Burglary	Labour IV. years.	Reparation double.
7. Housebreaking. 8. Horse stealing.	Labour III. years.	Reparation.
9. Grand Larceny.	Labour II. years.	Reparation. Pillory.
10. Petty Larceny.	Labour I. year.	Reparation. Pillory.
11. Pretensions to witchcraft, &c.	Ducking.	Stripes.
12. Excusable homicide. 13. Suicide. 14. Apostacy. Heresy.	to be pitied, not punished.	

—Thomas Jefferson, *Notes on the State of Virginia* edited by William Peden, pp. 130-32, 133-36, 144-45. By permission.

35. An Act For Establishing A Town At Warm Springs

In 1776 the Virginia legislature passed the following act for establishing a town at Warm Springs, also called Bath, now Berkeley Springs, Morgan County, West Virginia. The humane provision for assisting "poor infirm persons" was prompted by the number of such people taking the waters who, as Washington reported, lacked "the means of obtaining any other relief."

WHEREAS it hath been represented to this general assembly, that the laying off fifty acres of land in lots and streets for a town at the Warm Springs, in the county of Berkeley, will be of great utility, by encouraging the purchasers thereof to build convenient houses for accommodating numbers of infirm persons, who frequent those springs yearly, for the recovery of their health:

Be it therefore enacted by the General Assembly of the commonwealth of Virginia, That fifty acres of land adjoining the said springs, being part of a larger tract of land, the property of the right honourable Thomas lord Fairfax, or other person or persons holding the same by a grant or conveyance from him, be, and the same is hereby vested in Bryan Fairfax, Thomas Bryan Martin, Warner Washington, the reverend Charles Mynn Thruston, Robert Rutherford, Thomas Rutherford, Alexander White, Philip Pendleton, Samuel Washington, William Ellzey, Van Swearingen, Thomas Hite, James Edmundson, and James Nourse, gentlemen, trustees, to be by them, or any seven of them, laid out into lots of one quarter of an acre each, with convenient streets, which shall be, and the same is hereby established a town, by the name of Bath.

And be it farther enacted, by the authority aforesaid, That so soon as the said fifty acres of land shall be so laid off into lots and streets, the said trustees, or any seven of them, shall proceed to sell the said lots at publick auction for the best price that can be had, the time and place of which sale shall be previously advertised for three months in the Virginia Gazette, the purchasers to hold the said lots respectively subject to the condition of building on each of the said lots a dwelling-house twelve feet square at least, to be finished fit for habitation within twelve months from the day of sale; and the said trustees, or any seven of them, shall, and they are hereby empowered to convey the said lots to the purchasers thereof in fee simple, subject to the condition aforesaid, and pay the money arising from the sale thereof to the said Thomas lord Fairfax, or the person or persons holding the same under him, his or their executors, administrators, or assigns.

And be it farther enacted, That all the said Warm Springs, except one large and convenient spring suitable for a bath, shall be, and the same are hereby vested in the said trustees, in trust, to and for the publick use and benefit, and for no other purpose whatsoever.

Provided always, and be it farther enacted, That after the said lots and streets shall be laid out as aforesaid, such and so many of the lots, whereon any house or houses already built by the said Thomas lord Fairfax may happen to be, shall not be sold by the said trustees, but shall be and remain to the said lord Fairfax, or his grantees, his or their heirs or assigns, for ever; and that it shall and may be lawful for all and every person or persons who may have built any houses upon the lands hereby directed to be laid off into a town, within six months after the same shall be so laid off, to remove or otherwise dispose of the said houses to their own use. . . .

And be it farther enacted, That if the purchaser of any lot shall fail to build thereon within the time before limited, the said trustees, or the major part of them, may thereupon enter into such lot, and may either sell the same again, and apply the money, or appropriate the lot, or part of it, towards accomodating such infirm persons as may resort to the said springs, and should be so poor as to be unable to accommodate themselves, and so in like manner, as often as any forfeiture shall occur, to the end that a fund may be established on the best foundation which such forfeitures will afford, together with any donations which may be made to the said trusees for aiding the same, to extend the benefit of the said waters to such poor infirm persons.

And be it farther enacted, by the authority aforesaid, That it shall not be lawful for any person or persons, inhabitants of the said town of Bath, owners of any swine, to suffer the same to go at large in the limits of the said town; and if any swine belonging to any inhabitant of the said town shall be found running or going at large within the said limits, it shall and may be lawful for any person whatever to kill and destroy every such swine so running at large.

Provided always, That such person shall not convert any such swine to his or her own use, but shall leave the same where it shall be so killed, and give immediate notice to the owner thereof, if known, and if not, then such person shall immediately inform the next justice of the peace thereof, who may order the same to the use of any poor person or persons he shall think fit.

Provided also, That nothing herein contained shall be deemed or taken to hinder any person or persons from driving any swine to or through the said town, or limits thereof, in order to sell the same, or in their removal from one plantation to another.—Hening, *Statutes at Large*, IX, 247-49.

36. An Act To Regulate The Inoculation of Smallpox

The primitive state of public health and the awful dread of smallpox which prevailed well into the nineteenth century are reflected in the following act of 1777.

I. WHEREAS the smallpox, at this time in many parts of the commonwealth, is likely to spread and become general, and it hath been proved, by incontestible experience, that the late discoveries and improvements therein have produced great benefits to mankind, by rendering a distemper which taken in the common way is always dangerous and often fatal comparatively mild and safe by inoculation, and the act for regulating the inoculation of the smallpox having been found in many instances inconvenient and injurious, makes it necessary that the same should be amended:

II. *Be it therefore enacted by the General Assembly,* That any person, having first obtained, in writing, to be attested by two witnesses, the consent of a majority of the housekeepers residing within two miles, and not separated by a river, creek or marsh, a quarter of a mile wide, and conforming to the following rules and regulations, may inoculate, or be inoculated for the smallpox, either in his or her own house, or at any other place. No patient in the smallpox shall remove from the house where he or she shall have the distemper, or shall go abroad into the company of any person who hath not before had the smallpox or been inoculated, or go into any publick road where travellers usually pass, without retiring out of the same, or giving notice upon the approach of any passenger, until such patient hath recovered from the distemper, and hath been so well cleansed, in his or her person and clothes, as to be perfectly free from infection, under the penalty of forty shillings for every offence, to be recovered, if committed by a married woman, from her husband, if an infant, from the parent or guardian, and if by a servant or slave, from the master or mistress.

III. Every physician, doctor, or other person undertaking inoculation at any house, shall cause a written advertisement to be put up at the nearest publick road, or other most notorious adjacent place, giving information that the smallpox is at such house, and shall continue to keep the same set up so long as the distemper or any danger of infection remains there, under the penalty of forty shillings for every day that the same shall be omitted or neglected, to be paid by the physician or doctor if the offence shall be committed when he is present, or by the master, mistress, manager, or principal person of the family respectively, if the offence is committed in the absence of the physician or doctor. Every physician, doctor, or other person, undertaking inoculation at any publick place or hospital for the reception of patients, shall before he discharges the patients, or suffers them to be removed from thence, take due care that their persons and clothes are sufficiently cleansed, and shall give such patients respectively a certificate under his hand that in his opinion they are free from all danger of spreading the infection, under the penalty of three pounds for every offence; and every person wilfully giving a false certificate shall be subject to the penalty of ten pounds.

IV. If any person who hath not had the smallpox, other than those who have been or intend to be inoculated, shall go into any house where the smallpox then is, or intermix with the patients, and return from thence, any justice of the peace of the county, on due proof thereof, may, by warrant, cause such person to be conveyed to the next hospital where the smallpox is, there to remain until he or she shall have gone through the distemper, or until the physician or manager of the hospital shall certify that in his opinion such person cannot take the same; and if such person shall not be able to pay the necessary expenses, the same shall be paid by the county.

V. Every person wilfully endeavouring to spread or propagate the smallpox without inoculation, or by inoculation, in any other manner than is allowed by this act, or by the said recited act, in special cases, shall be subject to the penalty of five hundred pounds, or suffer six months imprisonment, without bail or mainprise. . . . —Hening, *Statutes at Large,* IX, 371-73.

37. Washington's Journey, 1784

George Washington's insatiable hunger for land led him to Trans-Allegheny Virginia, where he obtained patents for tracts of rich bottom land aggregating somewhat more than 33,000 acres. "Any person . . . who neglects the present oppertunity of hunting out good Lands and in some measure marking and distinguishing them for their own (in order to keep others from settling them) will never regain it," he wrote in 1767. Three years later, accompanied by Dr. James Craik and some servants, he started westward to locate the property he desired. On October 20, 1770, he and Craik embarked at Fort Pitt in a large canoe which carried seven additional passengers, including Captain William Crawford, the courageous frontiersman, surveyor, and trusted agent of Washington. On the 31st they arrived at the confluence of the Ohio and Kanawha; the following morning they set off in their canoe "to discover what kind of Lands lay upon the Kanhawa." Washington advertised in glowing terms the western Virginia lands he acquired and tried "to seat" prior to the Revolution. In 1784 the General returned to the Trans-Allegheny for the purpose of protecting his land titles and of obtaining information on the best connections between the eastern and western rivers, a project which, together with the improvement of the Potomac navigation, received his enthusiastic attention for the remainder of his life.

HAVING FOUND IT INDISPENSABLY NECESSARY to visit my Landed property West of the Apalachean Mountains, and more especially that part of it which I held in Co-partnership with Mr. Gilbert Simpson.—Having determined upon a tour into that Country, and having made the necessary preparations for it, I did, on the first day of this Month (September) set out on my journey.

Having dispatched my equipage about 9 O'clock A. M:, consisting of 3 Servants and 6 horses, three of which carried my Baggage, I set out myself in company with Doctor James Craik; . . .

. . . *3d.* Having business to transact with my Tenants in Berkeley; and others who were directed to meet me at by Brother's (Colo. Charles Washington's), I left Doctr. Craik and the Baggage to follow slowly, and set out myself about Sun Rise for that place—where after Breakfasting at Keys's ferry I arrived about 11 O'clock.—distant abt. 17 Miles.

Colo. Warner Washington, Mr. Wormeley, Genl. Morgan, Mr. Trickett and many other Gentlemen came here to see me—and one object of my journey being to obtain information of the nearest and best communication between the Eastern and Western Waters; and to facilitate as much as in me lay the Inland Navigation of the Potomack; I conversed a good deal with Genl. Morgan on this subject, who said, a plan was in contemplation to extend a Road from Winchester to the Western Waters, to avoid if possible an interference with any other State. but I could not discover that Either himself, or others, were able to point it out with precision. He seemed to have no doubt but that the Counties of Frederk., Berkeley and Hampshire would contribute freely towards the extension of the Navigation of Potomack; as well as towards opening a Road from East to West.

4th. Having finished my business with my Tenants (so far at least as partial payments could put a close to it) and provided a Waggon for the transportation of my Baggage to the Warm springs (or Town of Bath) to give relief to my Horses, which from the extreme heat of the Weather began to Rub and gaul, I set out after dinner, and reached Catpn. Stroads a Substantial farmers betwn. Opecken Creek and Martinsburgh—distant by estimation 14 Miles from my Brothers.

Finding the Captn. an intelligent Man, and one who had been several times in the Western Country—tho' not much on the communication between the North Branch of Potomack, and the Waters of Monongahela—I held much conversation with him—

the result of which so far as it respected the object I had in view, was, that there are two Glades which go under the denomination of the Great glades—one, on the Waters of the Yohiogany, the other on those of Cheat River; and distinguished by the name of the Sandy Creek Glades.—that the Road to the first goes by the head of Pattersons Creek—that from the accts. he has had of it, it is rough;—the distance he knows not. That there is a way to the Sandy Creek Glades from the great crossing of Yohiogany (or Braddocks Road) and a very good one; but how far the Waters of Potomack above Fort Cumberland, and the Cheat River from its Mouth are navigable, he professes not to know—and equally ignorant is he of the distance between them.

He says that old Captn. Thos. Swearengen has informed him, that the Navigable Water of the little Kanhawa comes within a small distance of the Navigable Waters of the Monongahela, and that a good Road, along the Ridge, may be had between the two and a young Man who we found at his House just (the Evening before) from Kentucke told us, that he left the Ohio River at Weeling (Colo. David Shepperds) and in about 40 Miles came to Red Stone old Fort on the Monongahela, 50 Miles from its Mouth. . . .

5th. Dispatched my Waggon (with the Baggage) at day light; and at 7 O'clock followed it.—bated at one Snodgrasses, on Back Creek and dined there; about 3 Oclock P. M. we arrived at the Springs, or Town of Bath after travelling the whole day through a drizling Rain, 30 Miles.

6th. Remained at Bath all day and was showed the Model of a Boat constructed by the ingenious Mr. Rumsey, for ascending rapid currents by mechanism; the principles of this were not only shown, and fully explained to me, but to my very great satisfaction, exhibited in practice in private under the injunction of Secresy, untill he saw the effect of an application he was about to Make to the Assembly of this State, for a reward.

The Model, and its operation upon the water, which had been made to run pretty swift, not only convinced me of what I before thought next to, if not quite impracticable, but that it might be turned to the greatest possible utility in inland Navigation; and in rapid currents; that are shallow—and what adds vastly to the value of the discovery, is the simplicity of its works; as they may be made by a common boat builder or carpenter, and kept in order as easy as a plow, or any common impliment of husbandry on a farm.

Having obtained a Plan of this Town (Bath) and ascertained the situation of my lots therein, which I examined; it appears that the disposition of a dwelling House, Kitchen and Stable cannot be more advantageously placed than they are marked in the copy I have taken from the plan of the Town; to which I refer for recollection, of my design; and Mr. Rumsey being willing to undertake those Buildings, I have agreed with him to have them finished by the 10th of next July....

Having hired three Pack horses—to give my own greater relief—I sent my Baggage of this day about one Oclock, and ordered those who had charge of it, to proceed to one Headricks at 15 Miles Creek, distant abt. ten Miles, to night, and to the old Town next day.

8th. Set out about 7 Oclock with the Doctr. (Craik) his Son William, and my Nephew Bushrod Washington, who were to make the tour with us.—about ten I parted with them at 15 Miles Creek, and recrossed the Potomack (having passed it abt. 3 Miles from the Springs before) to a tract of mine on the Virginia Side which I find exceedingly Rich, and must be very valuable—the lower end of the Land is rich white oak in places springey; and in the winter wet.—the upper part is exceedingly rich and covered with Walnut of considerable size many of them....

24th. The Cheat at the Mouth is about 125 yds. wide—the Monongahela near dble. that—the colour of the two Waters is very differt., that of Cheat is dark (occasioned as is conjectured by the Laurel, among which it rises, and through which it runs) the other is clear; and there appears a repugnancy in both to mix, as there is a plain line of division betwn. the two for some distance below the fork; which holds, I am told near a Mile.—the Cheat keeps to the right shore as it descends, and the other the left.

The Line which divides the Commonwealths of Virginia and Pennsylvania crosses both these Rivers about two Miles up each from the point of fork and the Land between them is high as the line runs being a ridge which seperates the two Waters —but higher up the fork a good road (it is said) may be had from one River to the other.

From the Fork to the Surveyors Office, which is at the house of one Pierpoint, is about 8 Miles along the dividing Ridge—at this Office I could obtain no information of any Surveys or Entrie made for me by Captn. Wm. Crawford; but from an examination of his books it appeared pretty evident that the 2500 acres which he (Crawford) had surveyed for and offered to me on the little Kanhawa (adjoining the large survey under the proclamation of 1754) he had entered for Mr. Robert Rutherford—and that the other tract in the fork between the Ohio and little Kanhawa had been entered by Doctr. Briscoe and Sons.

Pursuing my enquiries respecting the Navigation of the Western Waters, Captn. Hanway proposed, I would stay all Night, to send to Monongahela Ct. House at Morgan town, for Colo. Zachl. Morgan and others; who would have it in their power to give the best accts. that were to be obtained, which, assenting to, they were sent for and came, and from them I received the following intelligence viz—

That from the fork of Monongahela and Cheat, to the Court House at Morgan Town, is, by Water, about 11 Miles, and from thence to the West fork of the former is 18 More—from thence to the carrying place between it and a branch of the little Kanhawa, at a place called Bulls town, is about 40 Miles by Land—more by Water—and the Navigation good. The carrying place is nine Miles and an half between the navigable parts of the two Waters; and a good Road between; there being only one hill in the way, and that not bad—hence to ye Mo. of the Kanhawa is 50 Miles.

That from Monongahela Court House 13 Miles along the New Road which leads into Braddock's Road, East of the winding ridge, and McCulloch's path, to one Joseph Logston's on the North branch of Potomack is about 40 Miles—that this way passes through Sandy Creek glades, and the glades of Yohiogany, and may be good—but, if the Road should go from Clark's Town on the Western fork of Monongahela, 15 Miles below the carrying place to the aforesaid Logston's it would cross the Tyger Valley River (the largest branch of Monongahela) above the falls therein, go through the glades of Monongahela; cross Cheat River at the Dunkers bottom (25 Miles from its Mouth) and thence through the Glades of Yohiogany—in all fm. ye Kaha. 85 Miles.

That the Cheat River where it runs through the Laurel hill is, in their opinion, so incomoded with large Rock stones, rapid and dashing water from one Rock to another, as to become impassable; especially as they do not think a passage sufficient to admit a Canal can be found between the Hills and the common bed of the River—but of these matters none of them pretended to speak from actual knowledge, or observation; but from Report, and partial views.

That from these rapids to the Dunkers bottom, and four Miles above, the Navigation is very good;—after which for 8 Miles, the River is very foul, and worse to pass than it is through the Laurel hill; but from thence upwards thro' the horse Shoe bottom, and many Miles higher, it is again good, and fit for transportation; but (tho' useful to the Inhabitants thereof) will conduce nothing to the general plan, as it is thought no part of the Cheat River runs nearer to the navigable part of the No. branch of Potomack than the Dunkers bottom does, which they add is about 25 Miles of good road. From the Dunkers bottom to Clarkes Town they estimate 35 Miles, and say the Tyger Valley fork of the Monongahela affords good navigation above the falls which is 7 Miles only from the Mouth, and is a Cateract of 25 feet.

25th. Having obtained the foregoing information, and being indeed somewhat discouraged from the acct. given of the passage of the Cheat River through Laurel hill and also from attempting to return by the way of the Dunkers bottom, as the path it is said is very blind and exceedingly grown up with briers, I resolved to try the other Rout, along the New Road to

Sandy Creek; and thence by McCullochs path to Logstons; and accordingly set out before Sunrise.

Within 3 Miles I came to the River Cheat abt. 7 Miles from its Mouth—at a ferry kept by one Ice; of whom making enquiry, I learnt that he himself, had passed from the Dunkers bottom both in Canoes and with Rafts. That a new Canoe which I saw at his Landing had come down the day before only, . . . That the difficulty of passing these rapids lies more in the number of large Rocks which choak the River, and occasion the water not only (there being also a greater dissent here than elsewhere) to run swift, by the meandering thro' them renders steerage dangerous by the sudden turnings. That from his ferry to the Dunkers bottom, along the River, is about 15 Miles; and in his opinion, there is room on one side or the other of it at each of the Rapids for a Canal.

This acct. being given from the Man's own observation, . . . left no doubt on my Mind of the practicability of opening an easy passage by Water to the Dunker bottom. . . .

The Road from Morgan Town, or Monongahela Ct. House, is said to be good to this ferry—distance abt. 6 Miles. . . . —*The Diaries of George Washington 1748-1799*, edited by John C. Fitzpatrick, II, 279-305. Copyright 1925, by The Mount Vernon Ladies' Association of the Union. By permission.

38. An Act in Behalf of James Rumsey

James Rumsey (1743-1792), inventor, jack-of-all-trades, and author of A Short Treatise on the Application of Steam *and* A Plan Wherein the Power of Steam is Fully Shewn, *came to Bath, now Berkeley Springs, from Maryland, in 1783. While working in secret on a mechanically propelled boat, he tried to earn a livelihood by keeping a store and a boarding house, engaging in the building trade, and acting as superintendent of construction for the Potomac Company. General Washington's interest in Rumsey's experiments influenced the Virginia legislature to grant the inventor a ten-year*

*monopoly to construct and navigate his boats on Virginia wa-
ters. Similar rights were granted to him by the Maryland legislature. In December, 1787, Rumsey demonstrated his steamboat on the Potomac, near Shepherdstown, before a number of
spectators including General Horatio Gates. The boat, according to one report, "made a progress of four miles in one hour
against the current of Potowmac river, by the force of steam,
without any external application whatsoever, impeled by a
machine that will not cost more than twenty guineas for a ten-
ton boat, and that will not consume more than four bushels of
coal, or the equivalent of wood, in twelve hours." Impressed
with his achievements, some members of the American Philosophical Society formed the Rumseian Society to promote
Rumsey's projects which included, in addition to the steamboat,
an improved steam boiler, improved saw and grist mills, and
a plan for raising water by means of a steam pump. In 1788
Rumsey went to England to patent his improvements and to
obtain the capital which he so desperately needed and continuously sought. On the eve of success with a "beautiful Vessel
Burthen 101 & 45/94 tons," which he named the* COLUMBIAN
MAID, *he died in London and was buried in St. Margaret's
Church. The following act was passed in 1784.*

I. WHEREAS it is represented to this present general assembly,
that James Rumsey hath invented boats which are constructed
upon a model that will greatly facilitate navigation against the
current of rapid rivers, whereby great advantages may be derived to the citizens of this state; and whereas the said James
Rumsey hath made application for the sole and exclusive right
and privilege of constructing and navigating such boats for the
term of ten years as a recompence for this invention:

II. *Be it therefore enacted,* That the said James Rumsey, his
heirs, executors, and assigns, shall have the sole and exclusive
right and privilege of constructing and navigating boats upon
his model, in each and every river, creek, bay, inlet, or harbour
within this commonwealth, for and during the said term of ten
years, to be computed from the first day of January, one thousand seven hundred and eighty-five. If any person, other than
the said James Rumsey, his heirs, executors, or assigns, shall

during the term aforesaid, either directly or indirectly, construct, navigate, employ, or use, any boat or boats upon the model of that invented by the said James Rumsey, or upon the model of any future improvement which the said Rumsey may make thereon, he or they, for every boat so constructed, navigated, employed or used, shall forfeit and pay for every such offence the sum of five hundred pounds, to be recovered with costs, by action of debt, to be founded on this act, in any court of record; one half to the use of the party who will sue for the same, and the other half to the use of the said James Rumsey. *Provided always,* That the exclusive right and privilege hereby granted, may at any time during the said term of ten years, be abolished by the legislature, upon paying to the said James Rumsey, his heirs, executors, or assigns, the sum of ten thousand pounds current money of Virginia.—Hening, *Statutes at Large,* XI, 502.

39. The Virginia-Pennsylvania Boundary Dispute – Report of the Commissioners

The protracted boundary dispute between Pennsylvania and Virginia stemmed from the provision in the Pennsylvania charter fixing the western boundary of that colony at five degrees west of the Delaware River. The Pennsylvanians contended that the line should run due north from five degrees west of the Delaware in the latitude of the Mason-Dixon line; the Virginians held that the line should run five degrees west following the meanders of the Delaware River. At the request of the Continental Congress the controversy was held in abeyance during the first years of the Revolution. In 1779 commissioners appointed by the two states decided in favor of Pennsylvania, thereby reducing the Northern Panhandle of present West Virginia to its present narrow boundaries and depriving Virginia of the control of the entrance to the Ohio Valley.

AGREEABLY TO THE COMMISSION given by the state of Pennsylvania to John Ewing, David Rittenhouse, John Lukens, and Thomas Hutchins, and by the state of Virginia to James Madison, Robert Andrews, John Page, and Andrew Ellicott, to determine by astronomical observations the extent of five degrees of longitude west from the river Delaware in the latitude of Mason's and Dixon's line, and to run and mark the boundaries which are common to both states, according to an agreement entered into by commissioners from the said two states at Baltimore in 1779, and afterwards ratified by their respective assemblies; we, the underwritten commissioners, together with the gentlemen with whom we are joined in commission, have by corresponding astronomical observations, made near the Delaware and in the western country, ascertained the extent of the said five degrees of longitude: And the underwritten commissioners have continued Mason's and Dixon's line to the termination of the said five degrees of longitude, by which work the southern boundary of Pennsylvania is completed. The continuation we have marked by opening vistas over the most remarkable heights which lie in its course, and by planting on many of these heights in the parallel of latitude, the true boundary, posts marked with the letters P & V, each letter facing the state of which it is the initial. At the extremity of this line, which is the south west corner of the state of Pennsylvania, we have planted a squared unlettered white oak post, around whose base we raised a pile of stones. The corner is in the last vista we cut, on the east side of the hill, one hundred and thirty four chains and nine links east of the meridian of the western observatory, and two chains and fifty four links west of a deep narrow valley thro' which the said last vista is cut. At the distance of fifty one links and bearing from it north twenty three degrees east stands a white oak marked on the south side with three notches, and bearing south twelve degrees west, and at the distance of twenty nine links stands a black oak marked on the north side with four notches.

The advanced season of the year and the inclemency of the weather have obliged us to suspend our operations: but we have agreed to meet again at the south west corner of Pennsyl-

vania on the sixteenth day of next May, to complete the object
of our commission. Given under our hands and seals, in the
county of Washington in Pennsylvania, this 18th day of November, 1784.

JOHN EWING, (L. S.)
DAVID RITTENHOUSE, (L. S.)
THOMAS HUTCHINS, (L. S.)
ROBERT ANDREWS, (L. S.)
ANDREW ELLICOTT, (L. S.)

—Hening, *Statutes at Large,* XI, 555-56.

40. Adam Stephen on the Ratification of the Federal Constitution

*Trans-Allegheny Virginia was predominantly in favor of the
ratification of the Constitution, despite the dire warning of
Patrick Henry that the northwest would "sip sorrow" under
the proposed Federal government. Among the westerners who
approved the ratification of the Constitution was Adam Stephen (?-1791), a delegate from Berkeley County to the Virginia
Convention of 1788. Of Scottish origin, Stephen had practiced
medicine in Fredericksburg and had taken part in the French
and Indian War and in the suppression of Pontiac's conspiracy
before settling in Berkeley County. During the Revolution he
rose to the rank of major general, but his conduct at the Battle
of Germantown in October, 1777, led to his dismissal from the
army. His Berkeley home to which he retired was probably
"The Bower," near Leetown in present Jefferson County.*

MR. STEPHEN addressed the chairman, but in so low a voice that
he could not be distinctly heard.—He described in a feeling
manner the unhappy situation of the country, and the absolute
necessity of preventing a dismemberment of the confederacy.
I was, says he, sent hither to adopt the constitution as it is, but
such is my regard for my fellow-citizens, that I would concur
in amendments. The gentlemen on the other side have adduced
no reasons or proofs to convince us, that the amendments should

become a part of the system, before ratification. What reason have we to suspect, that persons who are chosen from among ourselves, will not agree to the introduction of such amendments as will be desired by the people at large?—In all safe and free governments, there ought to be a judicious mixture of three different kinds of government. This government is a compound of those different kinds. But the democratic kind preponderates as it ought to do. The members of one branch are immediately chosen by the people; and the people also elect in a secondary degree the members of the other two.—At present we have no confederate government. It exists but in name.—The honorable gentlemen asked where is the genius of America? What else but that genius has stimulated the people to reform that government, which woeful experience has proved to be totally inefficient. What has produced the unison of sentiments in the states on this subject? I expected that filial duty and affection would have impelled him to enquire for the genius of Virginia—that genius which formerly resisted British tyranny, and in the language of manly intrepidity and fortitude said to that nation— *thus far and no farther shall you proceed*. What has become of that genius which spoke that magnanimous language—that genius which produced the federal convention? Yonder she is in mournful attire, her hair dishevelled—distressed with grief and sorrow—supplicating our assistance, against gorgons, fiends and hydras, which are ready to devour her, and carry desolation throughout her country. She bewails the decay of trade and neglect of agriculture—her farmers discouraged—her ship-carpenters, blacksmiths and all other tradesman unemployed. She casts her eyes on these, and deplores her inability to relieve them. She sees and laments that the profits of her commerce goes to foreign states. She further bewails that all she can raise by taxation is inadequate to her necessities.—She sees religion die by her side—public faith prostituted, and private confidence lost between man and man. Are the hearts of her citizens so deaf to compassion that they will not go to her relief? If they are so infatuated, the dire consequences may be easily forseen.—Expostulations must be made for the defection of Virginia, when congress meets. They will enquire where she has lately discovered so much wisdom—she that gave an immense tract of country [Northwest Territory] to relieve the general distresses?—Wherein consists her superiority to her friends of South-Carolina and the respectable state of Massachusetts, who to prevent a dissolution of the union, adopted the constitution, and proposed such amendments as they thought necessary, placing confidence in the other states, that they would accede to them?—After making several other remarks, he concluded that in his opinion, they were about to determine whether we should be one of the United States or not.—*Debates and Other Proceedings of the Convention of Virginia . . . 1788*, Taken in Shorthand, by David Robertson, Second Edition, pp. 459-60.

41. Journal of Col. John May of Boston, 1789

The tremendous risks and difficulties involved in early western commerce were offset by rewards sufficiently handsome to attract merchants from as far away as New England. Such a one was Colonel John May of Boston who twice adventured into the Ohio area in 1788 and 1789. His second journey, which took him to Wheeling, began on April 23, 1789, and ended in the middle of the following December. May sent five tons of goods by water to Baltimore; here he loaded them into five wagons bound for "the wilderness." Riding ahead of the cargo, he traveled to Pittsburgh by way of Shippensburg, Bedford, and Redstone. When the wagons failed to arrive as expected, May, sick with worry and fatigue, left Pittsburgh to look for them and finally encountered them at Greensburg. His relief was short-lived, however, for near Redstone he learned that a violent hurricane had blown down "half the trees on the Alleghany mountains," and rendered the road utterly impassable. Since the only remaining route to the Ohio was by water, the merchandise was transferred to a boat. But the departure was delayed until some of the stock was sold in order that the wagoners could be paid and until the river rose to a navigable level. "O Lord," May despairingly exclaimed, "how long are we to stay prisoners on this

Monongahela river?" At Philadelphia May sold the skins and furs which he had obtained in Wheeling. The ginseng he sent to Baltimore where it was transferred to a Boston-bound vessel. Only the account of May's stay in Wheeling is given below.

WE STOPT THREE DAYS AT PITT, one night at Big Beaver, & one day & two nights at Buffalo, & at 12, noon, on the 11th August, arrived safely at Wheeling. [Where May had rented a store from Ebenezer Zane]. Next day unloaded the big boat, & put up the goods in the store. The situation is a pleasant & agreeable one; the store a new one, high on the bank of the Ohio, with a beautiful island, three miles long, stretching directly in front. From the new store, there is a delightful prospect, not only of this island, but a view also of two miles down the river. ... Here the boats going either to or from the settlements, either above or below, always stop; here I am handy to the farmers; & here I can watch the markets at Marietta, & send them such supplies as are needed. . . .

Saturday, 12th. Warm & lowery. Have pickled 5 gallons of the best & largest peaches my eyes ever beheld. It takes only three of them to weigh a pound. Picked them all with my own hand, & took none but those which seemed to be the very best. The pickles I mean to send to Mrs. Harmar, Mrs. Battelle, Mrs. Zieglar. They will furnish something of a variety to them. Have also cut & dried a bushel of elegant peaches to put into the spirit to give it a flavor. . . .

Thursday, 17th. . . . Did considerable business, chiefly loading two floats down the river, Benjamin Hulen's & Jacob Fowler's, both bound for the Big Kenawha.

Friday, 18th. Awoke as usual just at the break of day. . . . Found people waiting for me. Purchased forty deer skins, & had them in my store before sunrise, a transaction which restored me a great deal to a better feeling. . . . Today Mr. John White came down the river. With him I traded to the amount of $25, and sent friend William (Breck) at Muskingum about £40 worth of goods. . . .

Monday, 21st. Foggy morning, but fine clear day, the sun very hot. We have had no rain for fourteen days. The Ohio lower than ever known; can be forded in many places. This gives great opportunity for the savages to cross over & do mischief, which has been frequent this summer. According to the best computation I can make, the Indians have killed in various places about fifty men & women, taken a number of prisoners, & carried off many horses. . . .

Thursday, 24th. Fine dry weather, but not much business. In the evening arrived Dr. Downer, with others from the South East. These Yankees certainly are not a quiet people, like the folks 'round here. . . .

Monday, 28th. . . . This afternoon some road makers were driven in by a party of Indians, how large I know not. These inroads are not infrequent, so common in fact that we think but little of them, perhaps not nearly so much as we should. I am generally prepared for them, with two pistols and two guns, properly loaded, besides a tomahawk at the head of my bed.

Tuesday, 29th. Nights as restless as ever, & I drag through my days heavily. Make out to do some business. Have taken in today several little parcels of sang (ginseng), bought 32 fox & wild-cat skins, received a canoe load of flour, whiskey, &c, &c.

Wednesday, 30th. Remarkably fine weather. The bottom of the river almost bare. The Indians, in several places, murdering, scalping, plundering.

Thursday, October 1st. . . . My landlord & several others gone a hunting. The Indians killed eight men, three days ago, at a little distance from this place. The next day, they killed or carried off into captivity four families. As I always sleep by myself in a lone log-store, I keep my arms constantly in good order. Tonight I shall load these arms, two with buck shot, and a ball in the other, besides my pistols which I lay at the head of the bed. If the yellow devils come, I intend to give them a proper blazing. . . .

Saturday, 3rd. This morning, my landlord came home, bringing with him the carcases of seven fine deer, some of them as fat as mutton. We shall live now on venison instead of bacon. A very cold, raw & lowery day; but one of the best days for business have had yet. Have taken in near 200 lbs of ginseng, 70 odd deer skins & bear skins, to the amount of upwards of

£25, and delivered out the pay in goods, without help from any body; & this just what I like.

Sunday, 4th. A cold uncomfortable day.... A Mr. Jones, a baptist preacher from near Philadelphia, came here last night, & preached today. I heard him all day. He is more than a middling preacher, & an agreeable companion to boot. This is the second time I have heard preaching since I left Boston. Although there is a holding forth every Tuesday by preachers of a certain stamp; whose yelling as if they would split their throats & damnation doctrine disgust me entirely....

Monday, 5th. The weather warmer. The river shrunk almost to nothing. Business dull, so am I.

Tuesday, 6th. Rose at 5, determined to mope no longer. Took my gun, & was over the hill just as the sun rose. Spied two fine turkeys at roost on a very high tree, fired at them with 13 buck shot, & killed them both. Was back home again when the sun was an hour high, & felt quite elated. Took in considerable sang (ginseng) & that about all.

Wednesday, 7th. ... Have been hard at work all day handling sang. Have striven not a little to buy 2000 lbs of sang from a Kentucky Dutchman, but he was solicitation proof; but I am determined to go at him again....

Thursday, 8th. ... Have been playing out my best cards to the Dutchman, but have not trumped him yet. Have kept his skin full, which is the way to deal with men of his kidney, & tried to prevent correspondence on his part with the many packers who come here for cargoes, lest he should send off his sang elsewhere.

Friday, 9th. Have had a good share of custom today, taken near a hundred weight of sang, by driblets, also some peltry. My Dutchman still holds out. During the night considerable rain with thunder.

Saturday, 10th. After some manoeuvring, marching & counter-marching, attacks & feints, the bargan completed, my Dutchman capitulated; & was allowed to march out with all the honors of war. Closed the bargain with him for 1700 lbs. sang. Had to employ all my tactics, however; for two other men, as I have since found out, were working against me all the time....

Monday, 12th.... This morning a passenger down the river gave information of two lads, respectively 10 & 12 years of age, by name Johnstone, taken prisoners by two Indians in the Christian dress & wearing beaver hats. These Indians hung 'round till almost night, looking for horses, but finding none retired into the wilderness about 6 miles, taking the boys with them; & there, making a fire, laid down to sleep, each Indian having a boy on his arm. The boys, of course, did not rest quiet, but when they thought the Indians sound asleep, slipped down towards the fire. There they concerted a plan of killing the Indians, & escaping. The eldest took the lead. He seized one of the rifles, aimed it at the head of one of the Indians, & then passed it into the hands of his younger brother, enjoining him to fire when he saw him, the elder, strike the tomahawk into the head of the other savage. This was completed, according to plan, the boys got safe away, &, coming back, informed the inhabitants that they heard their captors say, there were fifty warriors lurking 'round, about 25 miles off. This roused the people in alarm.

Tuesday, 13th.... A number of the stoutest & bravest men mustering to go on a hunt after the Indians made a considerable parade.

Our braves returned having found one of the Indians dead, but the other, with a ghastly wound, only half dead. He looked so horribly, they dared not go near him, but let him escape....

Wednesday, 21st. Am using the day packing sang & putting casks in order. Wagon load of salt of John McCall, at 21/ per bushel, & shall load him back tomorrow. This the third wagon which has been here since it was settled. As to the Indians, they keep lurking 'round us. Some days two, & others three, are seen lurking about,—spies no doubt. As I sleep in a lone building, I keep my arms all loaded, near at hand, & ready to use at any moment.

Thursday, 22nd. Rose very early, & by 10 o'clock had loaded & sent away John McCall with seven large casks of ginseng & ten bundles of deer skins & furs. The whole weight 2000 lbs. ... What sang I have taken is very good, but the people were loath to dig it at 1/6, and I would not take it if dug before the first of September. In 15 days from that time, there came a frost

& rain, which knocked it all down, so that the diggers had only 15 days to work in. Some years it is good to gather till the middle of November. If it had been so this year it would have made some thousand weight difference in our favor.

Friday, 23d. . . . In the space of one month I have taken in upward 2800 lbs sang, some of it quite green (this I have 3 for 1) & most of it wants sunning two, three, or four days, and, on account of showers sometimes, must be taken in three or four times a day. I have also taken about 1400 lbs of deer skins & furs. These also must be aired & packed in the nicest order. . . .

Sunday, 25th. Late in the last evening, arrived two boats from Marietta. I saw them two miles off, & knew them at once. . . . In one of the boats came as passenger a Mrs. Bilderback, who with her husband was taken by the savages at Short Creek, 8 miles from here, early in last July. The day after she was taken she was separated from her husband, & committed to the care of one Indian, who travelled with her alone fifteen days. When the rest of the band joined them, they had killed her husband, & brought his clothes to her, & showed them as a trophy. She was carried back into the wilderness to many of the Indian towns, & thence to the Miamis, where she was released. She is a young woman of about twenty-three years of age; & left behind her two children, one of which was a nursing child. When she went away from this place, I gave her calico enough to make slips for her children. These Kentuck fellows give me some annoyance. I went to my store on some little piece of business, when a number of them crowded in, drunk & noisy, and I could not get rid of them for two hours. I was obliged to pick a quarrel with one of them, & push him out. . . .

Friday, 30th. Employed in settling accounts, & arranging matters with Mr. Breck, packing sang, deer skins, &c. . . .

Sunday, November 1st. Feeling somewhat at leisure, I put on my ruffled shirt and best clothes, which I have not done before since I came here, & went up the river, two miles, in a canoe, to visit a Mr. Martin & lady, who live on the Indian shore. We dined on venison, corn pork, & plenty of roots & vegetables. This Mr. Martin married a daughter of my landlord, some time ago, & went on to the place where he is now living, this

Spring. He has a fine family already, has built a house, raised ten acres of corn, put in ten acres of wheat, & withal added another baby to the family. If people out here—such is the fertility of the soil, & such the abundance of good things—can manage to build them a log-hut near some good spring of water, & plant them a little land with corn, they are rich enough. The woods will furnish them with plenty of superfluities. Turkey are much more numerous here than in our country, & as yet much fewer people to eat them. . . .

Thursday, 5th. Another cold day. But I had business enough to keep me warm, dispatching my skins & sang, (14 horse loads) weight about 2900 lbs. This carried on horses 250 miles. Each horse has a bell, & there is a driver to every five horses. Tomorrow I set my face towards HOME.—"Journal of Col. John May of Boston, Relative to a Journey to the Ohio Country, 1789," *Pennsylvania Magazine of History and Biography,* XLV, 155-69. By permission of The Historical Society of Pennsylvania.

42. Daniel Boone's List

Daniel Boone came to the Kanawha Valley in 1789, and settled first at Point Pleasant, then at Charleston which became the seat of Kanawha County on its establishment in 1788. Although Boone's stay in the county was brief—by 1795 he was back in Kentucky—he left some characteristic marks in what is now West Virginia. He located and surveyed many acres in the Guyandotte, Twelve Pole, and Big Sandy valleys. His brushes with the Indians and his hunting and trapping exploits enhanced his already colorful reputation. Once it was officially though erroneously reported that "old Colo. Boon" had been taken prisoner and his son, Daniel, had been killed by savage marauders. In October, 1789, Boone was named lieutenant colonel of the Kanawha County militia, but his commission for this office did not arrive until April, 1791. In the latter year Boone became a delegate from Kanawha County to the Virginia legislature and in December he successfully applied for a contract to provision the militia of the county. As a legislator Boone was totally inconspicuous and as a quartermaster he was down-right inefficient, at least according to the complaints lodged against him. That Boone was no scribe is very evident from the following letter.

[December 12, 1791]

For Kanaway County, 68 Privets; Lenard Cuper, Capt. at Pint plesent, 17 men; Joell Dane, Insine at Bellville, 17 men; John Young, Scout at Elke, 17 men; John Morris, Juner, Insine at the Bote yards, 17 men.

Two Spyes or Scutes Will be Nesesry at the pint to sarch the Banks of the River at the Crosing plases. More would be Wanting if the could be aloude. Those Spyes Must be Compoused of the inhabitence who Well Know the Woods and waters from the pint to belville, 60 mildes—No inhabitence; also, from the pint to Alke, 60 miles, No inhabitence; from Alke to the Bote yards, 20 Milds, all inhabited.

This from Your Most Obedient

[Daniel Boone]

—*Calendar of Virginia State Papers,* edited by Wm. P. Palmer and Sherwin McRae, V, 410.

43. The Whiskey Rebellion

The Federal Excise Act of 1791 which levied a tax on distilled spirits was bitterly opposed by the specie-starved westerners of the Monongahela Valley who not only consumed large quantities of whiskey but also used it as an article of trade. The climax came in the summer and fall of 1794 when an insurrection led by angry Scotch-Irish elements in Pennsylvania was suppressed by a strong militia force called out by President Washington and placed under the command of Governor Henry Lee of Virginia. Although the center of the insurrection was in Pennsylvania, dissatisfaction with Federalist policies was also evident in neighboring Maryland and Virginia. In August, 1794, "Banditti" from western Pennsylvania, as Governor Lee put it, used threats and "other evil doings" to compel a collector stationed at Morgantown to abandon his post. In September militia was used to disperse a crowd that had gathered in Martinsburg to erect a liberty pole. The whiskey tax was the major, but not the only cause of these disturbances, as the following resolves from Ohio County indicate.

RESOLUTIONS ADOPTED BY A MEETING of delegates consisting of two members duly elected from each militia company in Ohio county, in the State of Virginia, held in West Liberty, on the 8th and 9th days of September, 1794:

1. *Resolved,* As the opinion of this committee, That we conceive the excise system to be oppressive in its nature, and hostile to the liberties of the people, in particular to those of the Western country, and a nursery of vice; and the funding system a nursery to the excise; the revenue arising from thence is a nursery and support to sycophants.

2. *Resolved,* That a direct tax on real property would discourage the men of wealth from engrossing lands profusely, and would afford the industrious men of middle and low class an equal privilege with those of the rich—which ought to be the true object of a republican government.

3. *Resolved,* That we draft a remonstrance, praying the Congress of the United States of America to repeal the Act for raising a revenue from spirits distilled from the growth of the United States and stills; a land office west of the Ohio river be opened, and the free navigation of the Mississippi river be immediately procured: That William McKinley, Archibald Woods, John Connell, Robert McClure, and Robert Stephenson, do prepare and draft the same.

4. *Resolved,* That we hold a correspondence with our brethren in the neighbouring counties of Virginia and Pennsylvania.

5. *Resolved,* That the inhabitants of the United States, west of the Allegheny mountains, are entitled, not only by nature, but by treaty, to the free navigation of the Mississippi river; The Tardy and ineffectual negociations pursued by government, are observed with concern and regret, as they are uniformly veiled with the most mysterious secrecy, which is a violation of the political rights of the citizens in general, as it declares that the people are unfit to be trusted with important facts.

6. *Resolved,* That the taking citizens of the United States from their respective counties, to be tried for real or supposed of-

fences, is a violation of the rights of free citizens, and ought not to be exercised by the judicial authority.

7. *Resolved,* That the withholding the country west of the Ohio river from being settled, is repugnant to the true interest of the people. A generous land office ought to be opened, in order that the citizens in the Western country may have an equal privilege of procuring lands with Europeans, and those of our fellow citizens whose situation is not so remote from the seat of government.

8. *Resolved,* That the exorbitant wages allowed to the officers of the general government ought to be reduced and the wages of the soldiers in the army of the United States be immediately advanced.

9. *Resolved,* That we are ready and willing at the risk of our lives and property to support just and equitable laws, to deny our confidence to those members of government and others whose interest is different from that of the people at large, and at the same time revere those members who act from true republican principles, such as a Madison, a Findley, &c., &c.

10. *Resolved,* That the above be printed in the Pittsburgh *Gazette.*

Adjourned until the 18th inst.

Signed by order of the Committee.

DAVID CHAMBERS, *Chairman*

Attest:

Archibald Woods, *Clerk.*

—*Pennsylvania Archives,* Second Series, IV, 228-29.

44. Blennerhassett Island

The tragedy of the "Deserted Isle" began in 1798, when Harman Blennerhassett, a wealthy member of the Irish gentry, brought his talented young wife, Margaret, to the island in the Ohio which bears his name. Here Blennerhassett created an Eden "whose romantic loveliness" was the wonder of the Ohio Valley. His library, scientific apparatus, and musical instruments enabled him to pursue his cultural interests, while his capital investment, which he estimated at $50,000, permitted him to lead *the life of a country gentleman. In 1805, Aaron Burr, politically discredited and without resources, but full of confidence in the success of his devious scheme to enlist recruits for an expedition to the Southwest, arrived on the island. Two years later, at the treason trials of Burr and Blennerhassett, William Wirt, floridly but not untruthfully described what transpired: Burr, "winding himself into the open and unpracticed heart of Blennerhassett, found but little difficulty in changing the native character of that heart, and the objects of its affections. By degrees, he in-fuse[d] into it the poison of his own ambition; he breathe[d] into it the fire of his own courage; a daring and desperate thirst for glory. . . ." The collaboration of Blennerhassett in Burr's con-spiracy brought to the Irishman separation from his family, im-prisonment, loss of property, and the bitter discovery that he had been the dupe of Burr. After his acquittal, Blennerhassett vain-ly sought to mend his fortune in the South, in Canada, and back in his native country. He died in 1831 on the Island of Guernsey. In 1842 the indomitable Mrs. Blennerhassett returned to the United States to seek indemnification from Congress for damages done to the island property by the Wood County mi-litia in December, 1806. Her memorial stated that "the resi-dence of her family . . . noted for its elegance and high state of improvement" had been left by the militia "in a compara-tive state of ruin and waste." Before her claim could be de-cided, Mrs. Blennerhassett died in New York. Her nostalgic lament, "The Deserted Isle," written while she was in Canada, tells of the desolation of Blennerhassett Island not only by "ruffians" immune "to refinement's polishing," but also by the "black'ning fire" which destroyed the mansion in 1811. The fol-lowing description of the island in its happier days was writ-ten by the English actor, John Bernard, (1756-1828), who visit-ed it in the summer of 1800.*

AFTER A SLOW BUT DELIGHTFUL PASSAGE of twelve days we at length reached the goal of our journey—the fairy creation of Blennerhasset. To describe the effect of its appearance I do not hope; I can only endeavor, by means of a few details, to place the scene before my reader and leave the filling-up to his imagination.

Blennerhasset is an island about a mile in circumference, lying in the bed of the Ohio, which had been made the retreat of a man of equal taste and affluence. The ground rose gradually on all sides to its centre, and on this favorable spot was the house, erected in the style and splendor of a Persian pavilion. It was but sixty feet square, consisting of two stories, connected with wings by a semi-circular veranda, luxuriantly covered with myrtle, and commanded an extensive range of one of the loveliest regions in the world. The grounds were laid out with that better modern taste which superseded the monotonous straight lines and close-cropped Puritanic borders of old English gardening. Everywhere were contrasts and surprises, evidencing an eye that had surveyed the best effects of Europe; and, to crown the whole, walks, lawns, and shrubberies were blooming with all the flowers and fruits, and vocal with all the melody a generous clime so liberally dispenses to this Italy of the West. The effect of this contrast between the perfection of wild and cultivated loveliness, of this discovery of a triumph of Art in the very stronghold of Nature, was perfectly entrancing. What changes may have since occurred in it by storm, caprice, or a conformity to the tastes of a surrounding population I know not, but until I go to my grave I must bear with me, as of a dream, the remembrance of the beautiful Blennerhasset. All that I could learn of the owner and creator of this Paradise was that he was a European recluse who had arrived in these regions about the period of the French Revolution, and, after purchasing the island, lived on it in seclusion, devoting himself to its adornment. Mr. Clay computed that the estate could not have cost less than the building of a town, and that the mere purchase and transport of materials must have involved an expenditure sufficient to have procured a handsome property in any part of the Union.—John Bernard, *Retrospections of America 1797-1811*, pp. 188-89.

V. Education and Religion

45. Education in Western Virginia – Kanawha County

The common schools of old Virginia formed the basis for the public school system of West Virginia. Many of these schools were held in rude structures located in abandoned "old" fields, and in barns, lofts, and private homes; in some communities the same building served as schoolhouse and church. The teachers, most of whom were men, generally had little education and still less professional identity. Some common schools were organized by itinerant schoolmasters who contracted with groups of parents to teach their children for a stipulated sum. In 1810 the Virginia legislature established, from the proceeds of all escheats, fines, and forfeitures, the Literary Fund for the encouragement of learning. This Fund was increased in 1816 by the appropriation of the debt due from the United States to Virginia. As differences of opinion arose on how the Fund should be used—whether for higher education, for academies and colleges, or for elementary schools—the Act of February 21, 1818, compromised by allocating $15,000 annually to the proposed University of Virginia, and $45,000 annually to the counties of Virginia, to be distributed according to their white population, for the purpose of instructing poor children in the three R's. The county appropriations were placed under the control of school commissioners appointed by the county courts. In 1832 twenty-two of the twenty-five counties comprising present West Virginia reported that during school periods varying in extent from 40 to 81 days, 5,872 poor children out of a total population of 9,255 were in attendance. The rate of tuition was from two to four cents per day. In 1850, over thirteen hundred common schools were being used for the education of poor children in the western counties excepting Logan, which made no report, and Kanawha, Jefferson, and Ohio which had adopted the district free school system. Far less *numerous, but offering broader and more advanced courses of study than the common schools, were the academies and colleges, which were largely financed by tuition fees supplemented by grants from the Literary Fund for payment of teachers' salaries.*

The development of education in western Virginia from privately financed to limited public education may be seen in the following records from Kanawha County. This was the first county in the Trans-Allegheny to establish district free schools under the Act of March 5, 1846, as amended March 10, 1847, which provided instruction on the elementary level for all white children above the age of six. The first selection is a contract for private teaching. The second one is an agreement between the superintendent, Herbert P. Gaines, and the subscribers of Mercer Academy in Charleston. The third selection contains excerpts from the reports of the School Commissioners of Kanawha County. The fourth is an abstract of accounts for the tuition of pauper children.

ARTICLES OF AGREEMENT Made and Agreed upon between Ruel Daggs of the county of Kanawha of the one part and Nicks Smith of the county and State afore Said of the other part and State of Virginia this thirteenth day of April 1812 the condition of the above Obligation is such that the Sd Nicks Smith Obligates him Self to teach Six months each year and to Endeavour to Learn the Sd R D Girls to Spell read and Write if they will Learn and the boys as far as his Abbillities will Allow on the Sd Daggs Pr [?] Land But in case that the Said Smith should Die or the Sd Daggs should Sell or move of the the Widow is not to be Accountable for the Scooling And for the Sd Services the sd Daggs Agrees to Give the sd Smith and mary his wife During both their Lifetimes as their just right and property unmolested a certain track or parcel of Land where he now resides and bound as follows. . . . But in case the Sd Daggs Should Sell or rent his place the Sd Smith and mary his wife, place that they now Live on to be Eximped. During both their Lifetimes as their Just right and property Unmolested T Sd Daggs allows Sd Smith and his Wife the use of peaches for their own use untill they can raise an orchard. for the true performances of the Same we bind each and either of us in the penal Sum of five hundred Dollars Lawfull Money of the State of Virginia the failers and in So doing we Interchangeably Set our hands and Seals this thirteenth of April 1812.... —Manuscript in Kanawha County Records, West Virginia University Library.

ARTICLES OF AGREEMENT made and entered into the 20th day of October in the year of our Lord one thousand eight hundred and twenty three, by and between Herbert P. Gaines of the county of Kanawha and Commonwealth of Virginia, of the one part; and the subscribers to said agreement of the other part, witnesseth;—

That the said Gaines, on his part, for the consideration hereafter mentioned, hereby agrees to superintend the education of all pupils who may be admitted into the Academy in the town of Charleston, during the present session, which commenced this day and will terminate on the fifth day of April 1824.—

He farther agrees to use his utmost exertions to facilitate the progress of learning and the dissemination of correct, moral and honorable principles amongst his pupils; in which arduous and important duties, as well as in the course of general education, he will be aided by one or more competent assistants, during the period aforesaid.—

And the subscribers to this agreement on their part, do hereby severally and individually agree to pay to said Gaines, his executors, administrators and assigns, the prices for tuition, as set forth in, and graduated by, the classes following, viz;—

Class No 1.—comprehending scholars in the highest department of said seminary,—$15 per session. Those admitted into this class will be taught Surveying, both theoretically and practically, Navigation, Plane and Spherical Trigonometry, Euclid's Elements of Geometry, Algebra, Moral and Natural Philosophy, Astronomy, the use of the Celestial Globe, Chemistry, Political Economy and Natural, National [?] and Municipal Law.—

Class No 2—Will be taught the Latin, Greek and French Languages, Book keeping, by single and double entry, Logic, Rhetorick, Mensuration [?] of superfices and solids, Gauging,

Dialing, the use of the Terrestrial Globe and Conveyancing, [blotted] so far as it can be acquired without a knowledge of the laws and the peculiar effect and application of judicial decisions, upon the subject.—Terms $12 per session.—

Class No 3,—Will be taught English Grammar, Composition, Elocution, History, Geography and the construction of Maps, and Arithmetic. Terms $10 per session.—

Class No 4—Will be taught Spelling, Reading and Writing. —Terms $8 per session.—

The said subscribers hereby farther bind themselves to contribute their proportional part, indispensably necessary to defray the expense in furnishing fuel for said Academy, during such part of the term aforesaid that it may be required, as also towards the rent of a stove, in the event of the trustees of sd Academy not purchasing one.—

And finally, the said subscribers also respectively agree to furnish the scholar or scholars [?] sent by each, with suitable books &c &c during said period, or the period they may continue them at school; nor will they, or either of them, encourage his or her scholar or scholars in wilfully and unnecessarily absenting himself or herself from said seminary; they the said subscribers being well aware that "a constant attendance to studies, is the main wheel on which education turns."—Manuscript in Kanawha County Records, West Virginia University Library.

[1834]

... The Commissioners consider the term "indigent" as applying to those children only, who have no means of obtaining Schooling, but through the aid of the literary fund—and the Commissioners in extending that aid, have endeavored to confine strictly the benefit of the fund to such—The ages of the children schooled vary from 6 to 15 years—The Commissioners are of opinion that the quotas allowed this County are insufficient for the education of all the poor children of the county, entitled to the benefit of aid from the school fund, and hope that the quotas in succeeding years to be allowed, will be so far increased as to enable the Commissioners to extend aid to many who are now entirely without the means of education. The Commissioners are grateful in being able to certify that the children enjoying the benefit of the fund during the past year have generally made good progress and that their Teachers or the most of them are known to this Board to be men of good moral character and capable of instructing in the Common rudiments of education.

[1837]

... The children they [Commissioners] consider as coming within the meaning of the term "indigent" are 1st Poor orphans who have lost both parents—2nd The children of poor women who are widows—And 3rd The children of such poor persons as the commissioners deem unable to pay for their education—said children being between the ages of seven & fifteen years—either girls or boys; they have heretofore given no preference to either sex—It will be seen that a large unexpended balance remains in the hands of our Treasurer; this has been occasioned by the law of 30th March last authorizing the payment of old outstanding claims; the commissioners being desirous not to expend such an amount, as to leave any of those just claims unpaid—It is believed that the unexpended balance before mentioned together with their quota for 1838 (particularly should there be a new surplus quota of the magnitude of the last) will give so large an amount of funds, that every poor child in our County living in the neighborhoods where common schools are established may participate largely in its benefits. These schools are sometimes visited by the Commissioners, though not with that frequency that the importance of their charge requires; ... [the] teachers are sometimes examined by commissioners as to their qualifications; in all cases the teachers employed are the best to be procured for the pay.

[1838]

... Again a large unexpended balance remains in the hands of their Treasurer; the board attributes this to the hardness & scarcity of the Times, many heads of families who in former years joyfully sent their children to our schools, being forced during the past season to keep them at home, in order that their labor might contribute towards the support of their respective families.—Manuscript in Kanawha County Records, West Virginia University Library.

ABSTRACT OF SCHOOL MASTERS ACCOUNTS for the tuition of poor
Children paid by the Treasurer of the School Commissioners of
Kanawha County for the year ending 1840.

Names of School Commissioners who entered the poor Children and directed payment of the account—	Names of School Masters	No. poor children taught	Whole No. of days attendance of all the Childn. at ea. School	Price of tuition pr. day
Alexander W. Quarrier	Rob. Mitchell 2 accts.	11	490	4 Cts.
	H. McNaughton	4	261	,,
	John Williams 2 accts.	20	1027	,,
	Saml. V. Fleck 2 "	28	1558	,,
	S. Roberson	13	105	,,
	Wm. Hensley 2 accts	12	406	,,
	Jo B. Chilton	13	566	,,
	Ann Howe	1	90	,,
	W. Brisco	5	70	,,
	Jos. Asbury	4	353	,,
	H. Shoemaker	3	140	,,
	M. Arnold	21	1324	,,
Francis Thompson	James J. Straughan	17	488	,,
	Cornelius Turley	11	500	,,
	W. B. Southerland	12	406	,,
	J. M. Walden	8	392	,,
David Ruffner Esq.	Jas. J. Straughan 3	82	2460	,,
	T. H. Le Forge 2 acct	31	2230	,,
	Geo. W. Taylor 2 "	30	2145	,,
	W. Sneed	16	664	,,
	A. G. Walker 2 accts.	20	817	,,
	C. Payne	12	229	,,
John Slack	Chr. D. Arnold	14	539	,,
	Martha Slack	5	158	,,
Joel Shrewsbury	Ro Milburn	3	350	,,
Samuel Handley	J. B. McGinnis	4	80	,,
	N. Holcomb 2 accts	24	543	,,
	Allen Love 2 "	12	474	,,
	D. S. Montague 2 "	24	810	,,
	Jane E. Paul	5	274	,,
	Otho Brisco	13	352	,,
John Hansford	J. M. Walden	6	231	,,
	H. H. Wood 2 accts	12	261	,,
John C. Thomas	Wm. Dudding	6	344	,,
	Jo. Asbury	3	170	,,
A. Coon	J. L. Eustace	6	178	,,
	Wm. Harless	2	110	3¾
	Geo. S. Loyd	2	60	4 ct.

James B. Rust	V. R. Rust	7	112½	,,
William Millan	A. Woolfe	12	496	,,
	Fanny Thayer	11	284	,,
		545	22547½	

No. of Teachers—   38

   ,, Children in Treasurers Acct   545   ——   Boys—260

      Do actually sent   452   ——   Girls—192

Same from children in successive Bills   93   452

Elementary Books principally used viz—

                        Websters Spelling Book

Pupils 1st Book   Angels 2nd Reader   Angels 4th Reader Testament

History U. States   Moral Instructor — English reader — Websters

History Smileys arithmatic Pikes do — Smiths Grammar,

Geography and Arithmatic — Peter Parleys works — Life of Wash-

ington — Life of Franklin   New York reader   &c &c —

                        David Ruffner   President

teste A.W. Quarrier   Clk of Board

—Manuscript in Kanawha County Records, West Virginia University Library.

46. Abstract of School Commissioners' Reports

The Second Auditor of Virginia administered the Literary Fund, whose permanent capital, in September, 1833, amounted to $1,551,857.47, from which a revenue of $78,340.61 was derived. The following selection shows the disbursements of the Fund for the counties in present West Virginia.

ABSTRACT OF SCHOOL COMMISSIONERS' REPORTS for the year 1832, received between 30th September, 1832, and 1st October, 1833.

COUNTIES (of present West Virginia)	No. of common schools attended by poor children	No. of poor children in each county.	No. of poor children sent to school.	Average number of days attendance of each poor child at school.	Rate of tuition per diem in each county.	Average amount paid for each poor child, including all expenses.	Expenditures in 1832, for tuition, and all other expenses.
Berkeley	34	530	349	70	3¼ cts.	$2.45	$854.14
Brooke	29	410	268	72	2½	1.98	530.13
Cabell	17	200	117	55	4	2.40	280.76

Fayette	—	—	—	—	—		—	—
Greenbrier	20	500	239	50	4		2.25	537.90
Hampshire	48	800	545	40	4		1.67	912.14
Hardy	21	250	100	76	4		3.32	332.23
Harrison	86	900	754	48	2½		1.29	976.13
Jackson	—	—	—	—	—		—	—
Jefferson	31	350	217	78	4		3.25	705.26
Kanawha	24	450	298	64	4		2.73	814.72
Lewis	34	500	235	50	2½		1.30	304.99
Logan	—	—	—	—	—		—	—
Mason	19	175	127	53	3¾		2.23	283.41
Monongalia	80	1000	637	51	2½		1.39	889.15
Monroe	25	450	192	54	3½		2.05	395.40
Morgan	9	150	66	57	3 2/3		2.46	162.75
Nicholas	18	150	99	52	3		1.82	179.80
Ohio	40	500	282	81	21-12 [2½]		1.84	520.06
Pendleton	36	400	356	40	3¼		1.45	515.43
Preston	23	220	190	49	3		1.61	306.14
Pocahontas	17	120	100	60	3		2.11	211.29
Randolph	22	350	197	40	3 1/3		1.37	280.64
Tyler	20	450	216	51	2		1.20	259.46
Wood	34	400	288	40	3		1.27	366.34

—Joseph Martin, *A New and Comprehensive Gazetteer of Virginia . . .*, pp. 78-80.

47. An Act Incorporating the Trustees of Bethany College

Bethany College at Bethany, Brooke County, is the oldest permanent institution of higher learning in present West Virginia. A denominational school under the Disciples of Christ, the college owes its founding in 1840 to the vision and energy of Alexander Campbell who became its first president by action of the trustees. The following act of incorporation passed March 2, 1840, has never been amended.

(1) BE IT ENACTED BY THE GENERAL ASSEMBLY, That there be and is hereby created and established at or near Bethany, in the county of Brooke, in this Commonwealth, a seminary of learn-

ing for the instruction of youth in the various branches of science and literature, the useful arts, agriculture, and the learned and foreign languages.

(2) And be it further enacted, that the said seminary shall be called and known by the name of "BETHANY COLLEGE."

(3) And be it further enacted, that Alexander Campbell, Albert G. Ewing, Samual Church, Henry Langley, James T. McVay, Ro. Y. Henley, Samual Grafton, William Stewart, Josiah Crumbacker, Adamson Bentley, Robert Nichols, Campbell Tarr, Matthew McKever, John Andrews, Ro. H. Forrester, Thomas Campbell, Robert Richardson and John C. Campbell, be and are hereby constituted and appointed trustees of said college, who, and their successors shall be a body politic and corporate by the name of "THE TRUSTEES OF BETHANY COLLEGE," and shall have perpetual succession and a common seal, which seal they may alter at pleasure; and by the name aforesaid they and their successors shall be capable in law and shall have full power and authority to acquire, hold, possess, purchase, receive and retain, to them and their successors forever, any lands, tenements, rents, goods, chattels, or interest of any kind whatsoever, which may be given to them, or be by them purchased, for the use of said college; to transfer, convey and dispose of the same in any manner whatsoever they shall adjudge most useful to the interests and legal purposes of the institution; and by the same name to sue and implead, and be sued and impleaded, answer and be answered in all courts of law and equity; to select and employ a treasurer, and such other officers, agents and servants as they may see proper; to elect and employ such president, professors, instructors, and tutors for the benefit of said college, as they may deem necessary; to make, ordain, establish and execute, or cause to be executed, all such by-laws, rules and ordinances, not inconsistent with the constitution and laws of the United States, or of this commonwealth, as they may think necessary for the welfare of said college, the good government of the professors, instructors, tutors, agents and students of the same; and generally to do all acts necessary and proper to promote the welfare and prosperity of said institution.

(4) And be it further enacted, That the President of the college, by and with the advice and consent of the trustees, shall have power from time to time to ordain, regulate and establish the mode and course of instruction and education to be pursued in said college; and together with such professors, instructors and tutors as the corporation may designate, shall be styled "The Faculty of the College," and shall have power to adopt and enforce such rules as may be deemed expedient for the good government of the institution; ...

(5) And be it further enacted, That the first meeting of the trustees designated in the third section of this act, shall be held at Bethany aforesaid, on the second Monday in May next, or at any time afterwards, on a day agreed on by any three or more of said trustees, ... After a president shall have been elected, he shall preside in all meetings of the board of trustees unless unavoidably absent; ...

(6) And be it further enacted, that the said president and trustees or any seven of them, shall have full power and authority to meet at such times as they shall think necessary for the examination of any candidates for literary degrees; and they are hereby authorized and empowered to confer such degrees on such persons as in their opinion shall merit the same, in as ample a manner as any other college of this commonwealth can do, and under their common seal to grant testimonials thereof, signed by the president and seven of the trustees at least. ....

(7) And be it further enacted, That the said trustees or a quorum of them, shall annually elect a treasurer for said college, ...

(8) And be it further enacted, that the said trustees, or a quorum of them, shall have power to remove or suspend the president or any of the professors, instructors or tutors, at any time, two-thirds of such quorum concurring and also, two-thirds concurring, to remove any of the trustees for good cause. And when there shall be a vacancy in said board of trustees, occasioned by death, removal, resignation or refusal to act, the remaining trustees or a quorum of them, shall supply the vacancy. It shall also be lawful for any three of the trustees, or the president, or the professors for the time being, or a ma-

jority of them, to call a meeting of the trustees whenever, they or he, as the case may be, shall deem it expedient, by giving at least ten days notice of such meeting, in the mode prescribed in the fifth section of this act.

(9) And be it further enacted, That whenever any trustee shall absent himself from three successive annual meetings of the board of trustees, without assigning a sufficient reason at the fourth, the trustees of said college . . . shall have power . . . to declare his seat vacant, and proceed to the election of a new trustee to supply such vacancy.

(10) And be it further enacted, That the said trustees and their successors are hereby authorized, so far as their funds may warrant, to admit gratuitously, in whole or in part, as their respective cases may require, such person or persons as they may think proper.

(11) And be it further enacted, That the trustees of said college shall have power to establish a department of agriculture in said college; provided nevertheless, that no pupil or student in the college aforesaid shall be required to study or labor in said department, in any manner contrary to the wishes of the person or persons at whose charge, and by whom such pupil or student has been placed in the institution aforesaid.

(12) . . . It shall be the duty of the said board of trustees, when thereto required, to make a report of the general condition of the college to the president and directors of the literary fund, to be by them communicated to the general assembly.

(13) And be it further enacted, That the said board of trustees shall never be less than twelve nor more than thirty in number. . . .

(14) And be it further enacted, That nothing herein contained shall be construed as at any time to authorize the establishment of a theological professorship in the said college.

(15) This act shall be in force from the passing thereof.

—*Charter and By-Laws of Bethany College* (1956), pp. 7-13.

48. Religion in Western Virginia
Philip Vickers Fithian:
Journal

The three most numerous denominations of the Protestant faith in West Virginia—the Presbyterian, Baptist, and Methodist—have roots extending far back into the eighteenth century. In the 1730's Presbyterians built meetinghouses on Opequon Creek, Cedar Creek, Bullskin Creek, and probably Tuscarora Creek, all of which were visited by ministers of the Donegal Presbytery. By the 1740's this presbytery was sending ministers into the South Branch Valley. After the Revolution the Presbyterians of Greenbrier County, under the leadership of Reverend John McCue organized congregations at Lewisburg, Spring Creek, and Good Hope. The fine "Old Stone Church" at Lewisburg was erected in 1796 during the ministry of Reverend Benjamin Grigsby. In the next century Presbyterianism spread to all parts of the Trans-Allegheny under the vigorous leadership of such men as Reverend John McElhenney.

The Baptists also made considerable progress, despite what they regarded as "persecutions," especially after the adoption of the famous Virginia Statute for Religious Freedom in 1786. The subsequent revival, which lasted until about 1792, resulted in the conversion and baptism of thousands, and produced great changes among the Baptists, "some for the better, and others for the worse." Their preachers, explained the Baptist historian, Robert Semple, became "much more correct in their manner of preaching: A great many odd tones, disgusting whoops and awkward gestures, were disused: In their matter also, they had more of sound sense and strong reasoning." But as "their piety became more rational" and their membership more prominent, he added, the Baptists lost "a great deal of that simplicity and plainness, that rigid scrupulosity about little matters," which had given them moral strength. The Baptists, too, had great leaders in John Alderson, John Corbley, James Sutton, Josiah Osburne, John Garrard, and others.

The first Methodist societies in present West Virginia were organized in the Eastern Panhandle. In 1778 the Berkeley circuit, composed of Berkeley and Jefferson counties, was established under the ministry of Reverend Edward Bailey, whose untimely death in 1780 was mourned by that most fervent missionary and first Bishop of the Methodist Episcopal Church of America, Francis Asbury. Before the end of the Revolution Methodist preachers were laboring in the South Branch Valley "to seek" the whiskey-drinking, "prayerless" outcasts of that area whose conduct shocked respectable settlers. The Greenbrier circuit was organized in 1787, one year after the completion of a little log meetinghouse, the now venerable Old Rehoboth Church. The Red Stone Circuit, which included the Monongahela Valley, was formed in 1784. The following year one of its most zealous ministers, Wilson Lee, organized a Methodist society in Wheeling. Reverend Henry B. Bascom, who from an itinerant in the Guyandot circuit rose to become President of Transylvania University, editor of the SOUTHERN QUARTERLY RE-VIEW, *and finally Bishop of the Methodist Episcopal Church South, organized a Methodist church in Charleston about 1815.*

Philip Vickers Fithian (1747-1776), the author of the following selection, is best known for his delightful DIARY *written while he was tutor of the children of Robert Carter of Nomini Hall. A graduate of the College of New Jersey (Princeton), he was licensed to preach by the Philadelphia Presbytery in December, 1774. After serving a year as an itinerant minister, he became a chaplain in the Revolutionary army. His untimely death in 1776 reflects the deplorable state of the medical corps at this time.*

MARTIN'SBURG

THE COUNTY-TOWN—Berkely has lately been taken off from Frederick—This Village derives its Name from Col: Martin, a Nephew of Lord Fairfax—It is yet in Infancy—Two Years ago the Spot was high Woods—There are now perhaps thirty Houses, they have already built a Prison of Stone & strong—And are now making a Courthouse of no inconsiderable Size & Eligance —Probably, if American Liberty be established, for which we are now contending even in Blood, this, with many other infant

Villages, in a Series of Years, will be populous & wealthy Towns, grand in Appearance, & busy with Commerce—Especially if the Navigation up this long River can be effected— But the Glory of America, her Wealth, & Inhabitants, and inchanting Habitations, are remote yet, & to be obtained by Time, & Industry—

Expence to Day o/o. Distance 15 miles.

MAY 20 [1775]

We visited Mr. Vance, Minister of Tuscarora Congregation— He gave us Liberty to visit & preach in the neighbouring Vacancies til the meeting of Presbytery—He lives at the Foot of the North-Mountain, in a pleasant Situation—Partakes, I observe, of the Virginian Spirit, & hands round the "Sociable Bowl"—

—We dined at Capt: Mitchel's—On our Return, Andrew & I, for the Sake of Meditation, took a Ramble into the long Bosom of a tall, dark Wood—We chose, at some Distance from each other, a green shady Spot; threw ourselves carelessly on the cool Grass; far from human Observation, & only in the View of that Being we were preparing to serve—This, surely, is the exactest Copy I have ever seen of what Horace calls "Nemus." "Secret Grove."

> "Scriptorum Chorus omnis amat
> "Nemus" — — —

It brought fresh to my Mind what I used to read in Virgil at the Grammar-School—

> — — "Hic secura Quies
> "Et nescia fallere Vita—
> — — "Hic frigida Tempe
> "Mugitusque Boum, mollesque
>   Sub Arbore Somni."

Here's Easy Quiet, a secure Retreat, &c. Expence 4/.

SUNDAY, MAY 21

—A rainy Morning: the Country here is very dry, and needs Refreshment—Mr. Hunter & I preached at Falling-Water Meeting-House—It stands on the Potowmack, is well situated, &, I am told, is a numerous Society—To Day, however, we had but few Hearers, the Day was bad & the Notice short—The People gave good Attention—Sing the Scotch, or as they call them David's Psalms—The Congregation is chiefly made up of Country-Irish, & half-Scotch—Most of them Presbyterians— We dined at one Bowlands.—He could tell me many things of home—Once he was through Cohansie—Saw, he tells me, & conversed, with Mr. Green, the Leeks, & others, of Deerfield— Mr. Greenman, Craig, & others of Pittsgrove—It is pleasant, it is desireable, to hear of Home—Two waggons, fully loaded, went past, going, with Families to the back Settlements—They tell us many are going back almost daily!—*Philip Vickers Fithian: Journal, 1775-1776,* edited by Robert G. Albion, pp. 11-13. Copyright 1934, by Princeton University Press. By permission.

49. The Journal of the Reverend Francis Asbury

The "imperfect Journal" of Bishop Francis Asbury (1745-1816), a portion of which was published in his lifetime, gives an inspiring and detailed account of the founding of Methodism in America. The following gleanings from his JOURNAL *cover some of his activities in present West Virginia.*

[1776]

Thursday, [July] 18. After riding forty miles to-day, we reached the springs: [Berkeley] and at first we found it difficult to obtain lodgings. But after a while I procured a good lodging with Mr. Merryman. Here was work enough for a preacher, if he desired to be faithful. My soul was happy; and I felt myself totally delivered from the fear of man—determined, by the grace of good to discharge my duty. . . .

Wednesday, [July] 24. The congregation was rather increased; many were affected, and one man fell down. It clearly appears that I am in the line of my duty, in attending the springs: there is a manifest check to the over-flowing tide of immorality, and the prejudices of many people are in a great degree removed. So that I hope my visit to this place will be for the benefit of the souls of some, as well as for the benefit of my own body; though preaching in the open air, to a people who are almost strangers to a praying spirit, is more disagreeable to my feelings, and a much greater cross than travelling and preaching in a circuit.

[1781]

Saturday, June 2. Preached at Martinsburg: afterward returned to Brother Bruce's; he is a lily among the thorns. . . .

Thursday, 7. I set out for the south branch of Potomac—a country of mountains and natural curiosities. . . . We found some difficulty in crossing Great Capon River; three men very kindly carried us over in a canoe, and afterward rode our horses over the stream, without fee or reward: about five o'clock we reached William Rannell's [?]; . . .

Friday, 8. Not being able to cross the South Branch, we had to bear away through the mountains, and to go up one of about two hundred yards' elevation; in some places the breaks in the slate served for steps, in other parts of the ascent there were none: we at length reached the place appointed, and preached to about twenty, as I think, prayerless people, on Isaiah 1v, 6, 7 . . .

Sunday, 10. I preached at eleven o'clock to about two hundred people with a degree of freedom. I then rode to Richard William's. On my way I had a view of a hanging rock that appears like a castle wall, about three hundred feet high, and looks as if it had been built with square slate stones; at first glance a traveller would be ready to fear it would fall on him. I had about three hundred people; but there were so many wicked whisky drinkers, who brought with them so much of the power of the devil, that I had but little satisfaction in preaching.

Monday, 11. . . . From Williams's I crossed the South Branch and went to Patterson Creek. I came to a Dutch settlement [Fort Ashby in Mineral Co.]: the people love preaching, but do not understand class meeting, because they are not enough conversant with the English tongue; and we cannot all do as John Hagerty and H. Weidner, who speak both languages; could we get a Dutch preacher or two to travel with us, I am persuaded we should have a good work among the Dutch. I love these people; they are kind in their way. . . .

I am now in a land of valleys and mountains, about ten or fifteen miles from the foot of the Alleghany—a mountain that, at this part of it, is two days' journey across; thither some of our preachers are going to seek the outcasts of the people. . . .

Wednesday, 20. We had hard work crossing the Fork Mountain, being sometimes obliged to walk where it was too steep to ride. I was much blessed in speaking to about ninety Dutch folks, who appeared to feel the word. Here is a spring [Spring Run] remarkable for its depth, and the quantity of water it discharges sufficient for a mill within two hundred yards from the source, which sometimes in freshets throws its mass of waters considerably above the ordinary level of the surface. . . .

Thursday, 21. Last evening I rode a mile and a half to see some of the greatest natural curiosities my eyes ever beheld: they were two caves, [probably Seldon Cave] about two hundred yards from each other; their entrances were, as in similar cases, narrow and descending, gradually widening towards the interior, and opening into lofty chambers, supported, to appearance, by basaltic pillars. In one of these I sung,

"Still out of the deepest abyss."

The sound was wonderful. There were stalactites resembling the pipes of an organ, which, when our old guide, father Ellsworth, struck with a stick, emitted a melodious sound, with variations according to their size; walls, like our old churches; resemblances to the towers adjoining their belfries; and the natural gallery, which we ascended with difficulty: all to me was new, solemn, and awfully grand. There were parts which we did not explore; so deep, so damp, and near night. I came away filled with wonder, with humble praise, and adoration. . . .

[1784]

Friday, [June] 25. We had hard work in crossing a mountain six miles over, and it was still worse the next day in crossing the greater mountain. I found it very warm work, though stripped. We struggled along nevertheless, and met with about four hundred people at Strader's, to whom I spoke on 2 Cor. xiii, 5,—I hope not in vain. While I was at prayer, a large limb fell from a sycamore tree in the midst of the people, yet not one received the least injury; some thought it was a trick of the devil; and so indeed it might have been. Perhaps he wanted to kill another, who spoke after me with great power.

Sunday, 27.... I was assisted to speak feeling words to some souls at Isaac Van Meter's, though in pain and weariness. Thence I hasted to preach at six o'clock at Conrad Hoffman's, a third time this day.... About ten o'clock at night I came to brother Samuel Dew's, very weary, and lodged there....

Sunday, [July] 4. At Cheat River we had a mixed congregation of sinners, Presbyterians, Baptists, and it may be, of saints: I had liberty, and gave it to them as the lord gave it to me—plain enough. . . .

Three thick—on the floor—such is our lodging—but no matter: God is with us. . . .

[1785]

Tuesday, [June] 28. Rode to the Springs called Bath; now under great improvement. I preached in the play-house, and lodged under the same roof with the actors. Some folks, who would not hear me in their own neighborhood, made now a part of my audience, both night and morning. Leaving Bath I came to Brother Dew's (on the South branch of the Potomac) very unwell....

Sunday, [July] 10. . . . A long, dreary ride, brought us to Morgantown. I preached and baptized, and was much spent.

[1788]

Monday, [June] 30. Crossed the high mountains, and came to Hogg's in Green Brier.

Tuesday, July 1. I enlarged on Gal. iii, 22. We then rode to Alexander M'Pherson's, a serious family on Sinking Creek, where I preached with some freedom. After crossing some considerable mountains, and preaching occasionally, on *Friday* we arrived at the Sweet Springs: here I preached and the people were very attentive.

Saturday and Sunday, 5, 6. I had large congregations at Rehoboth. I preached with some satisfaction.

Monday, 7. Our troubles began; it being the day we set out for Clarksburg. Thirty miles brought us to Watt's, on the Great Levels.

Tuesday, 8. Reached M'Neal's, on the Little Levels, where almost the whole settlement came together, with whom I found freedom on Matt. xi, 28-30. Our brother Phoebus had to answer questions propounded to him until evening.

Wednesday, 9. We rode to the Clover Lick, to a very remote and exposed house. Here we found good lodgings for the place. The former tenant had made a small estate by keeping cattle, horses, &c., on the *range,* which is fertile and extensive.

Thursday, 10. We had to cross the Alleghany mountain again, at a bad passage. Our course lay over mountains and through valleys, and the mud and mire was such as might scarcely be expected in December. We came to an old, forsaken habitation in Tyger's Valley. Here our horses grazed about, while we boiled our meat. Midnight brought us up at Benjamin Jones's, after riding forty, or perhaps fifty miles. The old man, our host, was kind enough to wake us up at four o'clock in the morning. We journeyed on through devious lonely wilds, where no food might be found, except what grew in the woods, or was carried with us. We met with two women who were going to see their friends, and to attend the quarterly meeting at Clarksburg. Near midnight we stopped at William Anglin's, who hissed his dogs at us; but the women were determined to get to quarterly meeting, so we went in. Our supper was tea. Brothers (William) Phoebus and (Valentine) Cook took to the woods; old ───────── gave up his bed to the women. I lay on the floor on a few deer skins with the fleas. That night our poor horses got no corn; and next morning they had to swim across Monongahela. After a twenty miles' ride we came to Clarksburg, and man and beast so outdone that it took us ten hours to accomplish it. I lodged with Col. Jackson. Our meeting was held in a long, close room belonging to the Baptists. Our use of the house it seems gave offense. There attended about seven hundred people, to whom I preached with freedom; and I believe the Lord's power reached the hearts of some. After administering the sacrament, I was well satisfied to take my leave. We rode thirty miles to Father Haymond's, [near present Fairmont] after three o'clock, Sunday afternoon, and made it nearly eleven before we came in. About midnight we went to rest, and rose at five o'clock next morning. My mind has been severely tried under the great fatigue endured both by myself and my horse. O, how glad should I be of a plain, clean plank to lie on, as preferable to most of the beds; and where the beds are in a bad state, the floors are worse. The gnats are almost as troublesome here, as the mosquitoes in the lowlands of the sea-board. This country will require much work to make it tolerable. The people are, many of them, of the boldest cast of adventurers, and with some the decencies of civilized society are scarcely regarded, two instances of which I myself witnessed. The great landholders who are industrious will soon show the effects of the aristocracy of wealth, by lording it over their poorer neighbours, and by securing to themselves all the offices of profit or honour. On the one hand savage warfare teaches them to be cruel; and on the other, the preaching of Antinomians poisons them with error in doctrine: good moralists they are not, and good Christians they cannot be, unless they are better taught.

Tuesday, 15. I had a lifeless, disorderly people to hear me at Morgantown, to whom I preached on "I will hear what God the Lord will speak." It is a matter of grief to behold the excesses, particularly in drinking, which abound here. I preached at a new chapel near Colonel Martin's, and felt much life, love, and power. Rode to the widow Robinson's, and refreshed with a morsel to eat; thence to M. Harden's, where, though we had an earth floor, we had good beds and table entertainment.

[1790]

Friday, [July] 16. We had twenty miles to Green Brier courthouse: —here some sat as critics and judges. We had to ride thirty-one miles without food for man or horse, and to call at three houses before we could get water fit to drink—all this may serve to try our faith or patience.

Saturday, 17. Some very pointed things were delivered relative to parents and children, from Gen. xviii, 19. After being in public exercises from ten till two o'clock, we rode in the afternoon twenty miles to the little levels of Green Brier. On my way I premeditated the sending of a preacher to a newly-settled place in the Kenhaway county.

Sunday, 18. We had a warm sermon at M'Neal's, at which many were highly offended; but I trust their false peace is broken. There are many bears in this part of the country; not long since, a child in this neighbourhood was killed by one.

Monday, 19. Rode to Thomas Drinnon's, whose wife was killed, and his son taken prisoner by the Indians.

[1792]

Friday, [July] 6. We had a long ride to Morgantown: we came in at eleven o'clock, being much fatigued. I discoursed on the likeness between Moses and Christ, in the academical church. This building is well designed for a school and a church. I directed Esquire Morgan to one of our local preachers as a teacher. . . .

[1793]

Friday, [June] 7. We rode to Bath, that seat of sin: here we continued to rest ourselves: my public work was a sermon on the Sabbath. A number of our society from various parts being here, I have an opportunity of receiving and answering many letters. I am afraid I shall spend nine or ten days here to little purpose; I employ myself in reading Thomas a Kempis and the Bible: I also have an opportunity of going alone into the silent grove, and of viewing the continent, and examining my own heart. I hope for some relief from my rheumatic complaint which has so oppressed me for six months past. The people here are so gay and idle, that I doubt there being much good done among them. The troubles of the east and west meet me as I pass.

[1796]

Monday, [May] 23. I rode to Rehobeth chapel, in the sinks of Green Brier, where we held conference with a few preachers. Here I delivered two discourses. *Thursday,* crossed Green Brier River, and had to pass along a crooked and dangerous path to Benton's. My mind is in peace.

Friday, 27. I felt my self very heavy, my mind unprepared for the congregation at Gilboa meeting house, and could not preach with any satisfaction. After meeting the society, I came away much clouded. We came off from brother Crawford's about four o'clock, aiming at the Little Levels; but darkness came on, and we had to climb and blunder over the point of a mountain, in descending which my feet were so squeezed that the blood was ready to gush out of the pores: I could hardly help weeping out my sorrow: at length we came to brother Hamilton's, where the kindness of the family was a cordial, and we went to rest about ten o'clock, and all was well.

Sunday, 29. I was very warm in body and mind at M'Neal's. In the afternoon (contrary to my sentiment and practice on the Lord's day) we took our departure, purposing to reach Morgantown on *Wednesday* evening, in order to attend an appointment made for me on *Thursday,* the second of June. We reached my old friend Drinnon's, who received us gladly, and entertained us kindly. Next day (*Monday*) we opened our campaign through the mountains, following a path I had thought never to travel again. Frequently we were in danger of being plucked off our horses by the boughs of the trees under which we had to ride. About seven o'clock, after crossing six mountains and many rocky creeks and fords of Elk and Monongahela Rivers, we made the *Valley of Distress,* called by the natives Tyger's Valley. We had a comfortable lodging at Mr. White's; and here I must acknowledge the kindness and decency of the family, and their readiness to duty, sacred and civil. Thence we hastened on at the rate of forty-two miles a day. We had to ride four miles in the night, and went supperless to *the Punchins* [floor?], where we slept a little on hard lines.

After encountering many difficulties, known only to God and ourselves, we came to Morgantown. I doubt whether I shall ever request any person to come and meet me at the levels of Green Brier, or to accompany me across these mountains again, as brother Daniel Hitt has now done. O! how chequered is life! . . . —*The Journal and Letters of Francis Asbury,* edited by Elmer T. Clark, I, 192-93, 404-408, 461-63, 490-91, 575-79, 645-46, 718, 759-60; II, 88-89.

50. Camp Meetings

Camp meetings not only provided an avenue to salvation, but also a release from the monotony of daily existence. Hundreds and even thousands flocked to these open-air revivals to hear the passionate exhortations of preachers and to participate in the singing, praying, shouting, and confessing which often lasted far into the night. Since women as well as men attended the meetings and among the latter there were usually a few "sons of Belial," drunk and looking for trouble, it became necessary to adopt rules to prevent the gatherings from degenerating into what some observers thought, indeed, they often were—western saturnalia. John Waller (1741-1802), the author of the following camp-meeting regulations, was a well-known Baptist preacher. Daniel Hitt, whose letter follows, was one of the faithful companions of Bishop Asbury.

I. No female, on any account whatever, shall be permitted to stay in the camp, later than an hour by sun at night; nor appear in the camp, earlier than an hour by sun in the morning.

II. The persons in the camp, shall depend for sustenance, during the camp meeting, on the friendly hospitality of the neighbourhood.

III. Any person in camp, waking at any period of the night, may pray or sing, without disturbing the slumbers of others.— Robert B. Semple, *A History of the Rise and Progress of the Baptists in Virginia*, pp. 407-408.

Alexandria district, Fredericksburg, December 3, 1804

Soon after the general Conference, I commenced my first rout of quarterly meetings at Front Royal, in Winchester circuit, on the 2nd and 3rd of June; ... From thence the week following we were at a place called Hedges chapel, in Berkeley circuit; ...

I commenced my second rout of quarterly meetings with a regular camp-meeting on Bullskin, near the white house in Jefferson: this began on 11th of August, and continued till the morning of the 20th, and was conducted under the following regulations: at sunrise, each day, at the blowing of the trumpet, the people assembled at the stand for morning prayer: after morning prayers, I detained all the official characters in council: the design of this council was to correct any improprieties that might appear, and suggest any thing that might be adopted to the advantage and prosperity of the meeting. From morning prayer till 10 o'clock, we got breakfast: at 10 o'clock there was preaching; at 3 o'clock we took a cold cut; then sang, prayed, and preached again.

As soon as evening preaching began, certain men, before appointed for the purpose, took their station, some round and through the congregation, and some others about the tents and wagons; the former of those continued their station during public exercise. The latter, with substitutions, continued (generally) through the whole night. The business of these men, was to detect any and all misconduct in their power; by this means we continued (with but little variation) from the 11th to the morning of the 20th day, when we struck tents, blew the trumpets and journeyed; in which time we calculated on about sixty-four or sixty-five converted. Hallelujah, praise the Lord. It seemed as if I could live and die at such a place and in such exercise.

On the 13th of October we had another camp-meeting at Pipe-creek in Maryland; ... I think a well regulated camp-meeting, is one of the best institutions in the world, to quicken and stir up believers, and to get souls converted to God. I would give it as my opinion, not to continue nor have a sabbath day in the time of a camp-meeting. Whenever I have attended, there has been more mischief on that day, than in a whole week besides, and generally less good is done. At all events, the conductors of these meetings should be very strict, and keep the greatest decency and order possible.

DANIEL HITT

—*Magazine of the Jefferson County Historical Society,* XIV (December, 1948), 15.

51. Constitution and Covenant of Simpson Creek Baptist Church

The Simpson Creek Baptist Church of Bridgeport, reputed to be the oldest Baptist church west of the Alleghenies, was organized before the Revolution. Not until November 12, 1831, however, did it adopt the following covenant, which is still in effect.

WE, THE UNDERSIGNED, being all members of the regular Baptist Church of Jesus Christ, called Simpson Creek, in Harrison County, Virginia, do agree to be governed by the following Constitution and Covenant:

We believe in one God the Creator of all things, known to us as Father, Son, and Holy Ghost. We believe the Holy Scriptures to be the revealed will of God, and the rule of our faith and practice, learning from them through the influence of the Holy Spirit, the fall of our federal head and representative (and ours in Him) by disobedience to the commands of God, thereby being made liable to all the miseries of this life, to death and the pains of hell forever.

We believe further that our Almighty Sovereign not willing that we should be eternally punished, entered into a covenant with His eternal Son, ordered in all things and sure, that He, God and Son, who knew no sin, should become sin for us that we might become the righteousness of God in Him, that He should magnify the law of God and make it honorable so that God can be just and the justifier of all that believe in Jesus.

Trusting therefore in the faithfulness of God, through this strong consolation in the Gospel of His dear Son, ... we do with humility and fear, ... enter into the following covenant with each other: We take God the Father, Son and Holy Spirit of our God and the only proper object of all religious worship. ...

Having devoted ourselves to the Lord Jesus, we give ourselves to one another by the will of God, and agree to be kindly affectionate toward each other with brotherly love, realizing that we have one Master and that we are all brethren.

We believe that it will be for the declarative glory of God, the prosperity of Zion and the advancement of the Redeemer's Kingdom on earth, that we follow the primeval example of the Lord, to join in Church fellowship. . . .

Therefore, we think it our indispensable duty as well as our privilege to meet together as often as God in His providence shall permit in the house appointed for His worship that we may thereby renew our strength by waiting on the Lord in the way of his appointment; . . .

We believe it a duty incumbent on us to keep the ordinances of God's house in their primitive purity as they are held out to us in the gospel.

1st. The preaching of the word as becomes sound doctrine of Godly edifying, and not to doubtful disputation which genders strife.

2nd. That the ordinance of baptism be only administered to those who make a profession in Christ and that the mode be by immersion.

3rd. That the celebration of the Lord's Supper be as represented to us by our Lord Jesus by bread and wine.

4th. We agree that we ought to have bowels of compassion toward our indigent brethren, and that we will minister to their necessities of such things as the Lord shall give us.

5th. That all things may be done in decency and good order, we agree that there be officers appointed by this Church to have the care and oversight thereof, to-wit:

First. A pastor to go in and out before us and to minister to us in Holy things.

Second, Deacons to serve in the administration of the Lord's Supper and to watch over the flock with and without a pastor.

Third. Clerk to keep a record of all matters and things that appertain to the Church.

Fourth. We further agree to hold our business meetings on the Saturday before the first Lord's Day in each month, and that our communion be on the first Lord's Day of every third month.

Fifth. That the Church alone judge of the propriety of receiving candidates for membership in her own body, or of excluding or otherwise dealing with those who walk disorderly.

And now we do with our whole hearts and hands agree to and with each other, as in the presence of God, to carry this covenant into effect as far as God by His grace may enable us.

Entered into at our November meeting, 1831.—J. William Bonner, *History of the Simpson Creek Baptist Church,* pp. 25-29. Copyright by J. William Bonner. By permission.

VI. Economic Developments and Tourist Attractions

52. John Marshall in West Virginia

An astute observer of ante-bellum Virginia once remarked that this state was considerably behind New York and Pennsylvania in internal improvements for the following reasons: "First, her habitual caution and prudence in legislation, requiring demonstration of its utility before she will embark her capital in any new enterprize; second, the sectional jealousies of different portions of the state ...; third, the mismanagement of her first enterprizes in this field." Yet despite the formidable Allegheny barrier which divided Virginia into two distinct sections farsighted Virginians began soon after the Revolution to advance plans for welding the state by means of east-west lines of communication. The proposals to connect the Chesapeake Bay with the Ohio River by way of the Potomac, and the Tidewater with the Ohio by way of the James and Kanawha rivers were among the most persistent and ambitious. In 1812 the General Assembly of Virginia ordered a survey of the headwaters of these last two rivers to determine the "practicability of extending their navigation to the base of the chain of mountains that divide them." A portion of the optimistic report of the commissioners of this expedition, one of whom was John Marshall, is given below.

Your Commissioners proceeded down the Greenbrier river in the boat in which they ascended the James. The season had been remarkably dry, and the water was declared by the inhabitants to be as low as at any period within their recollection. It frequently spreads over a wide bed covered with large stone, and is, in its present unimproved state, and at the season when it was viewed, so very shallow, for the greater part of its course, as not to swim an empty boat. . . . In part of the river the shoals are frequent and long, and the falls, . . . considerable. At the great falls, which is the most important of them, the descent is twelve feet in forty-eight poles. There is no perpendicular fall at this place, but one continued rapid, with large rocks, irregularly interspersed through the bed of the river. Near the mouth of the river there is a flat rock, which continues for about two hundred and forty poles, with many irregular apertures or fissures through which the water passes. Although, in the usual state of the river, this rock is covered with water of sufficient depth for navigation; yet, such was the drought of last autumn, it was necessary to drag the boat over its whole extent. . . .

But, from the best information your Commissioners can obtain, and they believe it to be correct, the Greenbrier is seldom so low at any season as it was during the last autumn; and it seldom if ever fails, for eight or nine months in the year, to be at least two feet higher than when viewed by your Commissioners; a depth of water unquestionably sufficient for the purposes of navigation. . . .

On an attentive consideration of the obstacles which were found by your Commissioners to be great, while the river remains in the state in which they viewed it, they are unanimously and decidedly of opinion, that its navigation may be rendered as safe, as certain, and as easy as that of the James, at all times, except when the water is unusually low. The rocks are in general loose, and may be removed without extraordinary difficulty, so as to afford a tolerably smooth passage to boats; and by collecting the water into narrow channels, a sufficient depth may be obtained, with the exception of a short period in a very dry year, to swim any boat which can be brought at the same time down James river. But so scanty is the supply of water in a time of uncommon drought, that doubts are entertained whether there may not be a short season of the year during which, unless a considerable expense be incurred, the navigation must be suspended. Though aided by men and horses, ten days of unremitting labour were consumed in passing from the mouth of Howard's creek to the mouth of Greenbrier river, a distance not much exceeding forty-eight miles. In the month of June, the same voyage, if not retarded by measuring the river, might have been performed in a single day. Some of your Commissioners, however, are of the opinion, that the Greenbrier may, without great additional expense, be rendered at all times passable for boats carrying half a load.

In addition to the shallowness of the water, ... and to the rocks which have been mentioned, the obstructions to the navigation of the Greenbrier consist in its falls, and in the general rapidity of its current.

The great falls alone are of sufficient magnitude to merit particular attention. These unquestionably admit of being rendered navigable, either by opening a sluice judiciously through them, or by locks. The latter would be most expensive, but would leave the navigation less laborious.

The rapidity of the current may be estimated by observing that the descent in forty-eight miles and eighty-four poles, is three hundred and sixty-two feet ten inches; between seven and eight feet to the mile.

This current will present no difficulty to a boat descending the river. To one ascending it, the labour will be considerable, but not so considerable as in some parts of James river..

The New River, or that part of the Great Kanawha which is above the mouth of Gauley, having to search its intricate way, and force a passage through a long chain of lofty and rugged mountains, whose feet it washes, exhibits an almost continued succession of shoals and falls, from which the navigator is sometimes, though rarely, relieved by a fine sheet of deep placid water.

The difficulties encountered in descending this river were of a character essentially different from those which were experienced in the Greenbrier. Uncommon as had been the drought, the supply of water was abundant. The boat sometimes, though rarely, rubbed upon a shoal; but in every such case it was apparent that a sufficient passage might be opened without much labour or expense. . . .

The distance from the mouth of Greenbrier to Bowyer's Ferry, is forty miles one quarter and forty-six poles, and the descent is four hundred and sixty-six feet seven inches; ... In general, there is much sameness in the appearance of this part of the river. . . .

Brook's Falls are about four miles and one fourth below the mouth of Greenbrier. The water descends thirteen feet seven inches in fifty poles. . . . The boat was navigated through this place.

A much more formidable obstruction is the falls at Richmond's Mill. These are designated in the neighbourhood by the name of the "Great Falls of New river," but are generally called at a distance, "Lick Creek Falls."

At this place the water may with propriety be said to fall perpendicularly twenty-three feet. . . . A small distance lower down is another fall of three or four feet.

Here, for the first time, the boat was taken out of the water and let down by skids.

The ground along which a canal may be carried around these falls, pursuing the course of Richmond's mill race, was measured, and the elevation taken. The descent was found to be twenty-two feet nine inches, in one hundred and eighty-one poles. . . .

From Bowyer's Ferry to the Falls of the Great Kanawha, was estimated at nineteen miles and fifty-eight poles, in which distance the river falls three hundred and thirty-one feet; that is, seventeen feet to a mile. . . . For a part of this space, the scene is awful and discouraging. The vast volume of water which rolls down New river, and which, far above the ferry, often spreads, without becoming shallow, over a bed three or four hundred yards wide, is seldom more than one hundred or one hundred and fifty yards wide. In some places, for a mile or more in continuation, it is compressed by the mountains on each side, into a channel of from twenty to sixty yards wide; and even these narrow limits are still more narrowed by enormous rocks which lie promiscuously in the bed of the river, through which it is often difficult to find a passage wide enough for the admission of a boat. In some places the bank is formed of rugged and perpendicular cliffs of entire rock, which appear to be twenty, thirty, and forty feet high; in others, enormous, but unconnected, rocks dip into the water. . . .

Immediately above the mouth of Gauley, the river opens and presents a beautiful sheet of deep smooth water, which is succeeded by the rocks over which it dashes, and forms the Great Falls of Kanawha. The height of these falls is twenty feet four inches. With its name the river loses its wild and savage aspect. It is no longer confined by rugged cliffs, by mountains barely separated from each other, nor interrupted by enormous masses of rocks which are scarcely to be avoided. . . .

The boat which conveyed your Commissioners, passed from the mouth of Greenbrier, to the place where their expedition terminated, without being taken out of the water, except at the Great Falls of New river, and at the Great Falls of the Kanawha. It was navigated in the usual way through all the other difficult places which abound in New river, except two—both below Bowyer's Ferry. Through these it was conducted by ropes.

The boat was not laden, nor was it empty. In addition to the number of hands usually employed in navigation, it carried between two and three thousand weight. The greater part of this burthen was taken out in the most difficult places; but in many of considerable magnitude, it remained in the boat. Where the vessel was guided by ropes, the necessity of resorting to this expedient was occasioned solely by the intervention of rocks, which can be removed.

It is also worthy of notice, that this voyage was performed by boatmen, who, having never before seen the river, were reduced to the necessity of selecting their way at the moment, without the aid of previous information. . . .

Should New river be rendered a safe and easy channel of communication, between the Ohio and the commercial towns on James river, the subject will assume a more important aspect, and the advantages may be estimated on a larger scale. Not only will that part of our own State which lies on the Kanawha and on the Ohio, receive their supplies and send much of their produce to market through James river, but an immense tract of fertile country, a great part of the States of Kentucky and Ohio, will most probably give their commerce the same direction. All that part of the State of Kentucky which lies above Louisville, and all that part of the State of Ohio whose trade would pass through the river of that name, might reasonably be expected to maintain a large portion of their commercial intercourse with the Atlantic States, through the James or the Potomac.... It is far from being impossible, that even the south western parts of Pennsylvania may look down one of these rivers for their supplies of goods manufactured in Europe....

In times of profound peace, then, the States on the Ohio would make sacrifices of no inconsiderable magnitude, by restricting their importations to a single river. But, in time of war, their whole trade might be annihilated. When it is recollected that the Mississippi empties itself into the Gulph of Florida, which is surrounded by foreign territory; that the island of Cuba and the coast of East Florida completely guard the passage from its mouth to the ocean; that the immense commerce flowing down its stream, hold forth irresistible allurements to cruizers, the opinion seems well founded, that scarcely a vessel making for that place could reach its port of destination....

The price of transportation from Richmond, up James river to the mouth of Dunlop's creek, thence across the Alleghany to Greenbrier, and down to the mouth of the Great Kanawha, will certainly depend on the goodness of the road and the degree of perfection to which the navigation may be carried. Your Commissioners believe that a sound national economy would dictate such improvements as would reduce the price of freight, although the labor employed in making them might be procured by an augmentation of toll, and some expenditure of public money....

The advantages to accrue to the United States, from opening this new channel of intercourse between the eastern and the western States, are those which necessarily result to the whole body from whatever benefits its members, and those which must result to the United States, particularly from every measure which tends to cement more closely the union of the eastern with the western States. . . .

All which is respectfully submitted to the General Assembly, by

> John Marshall,
> James Breckenridge,
> William Lewis,
> James M'Dowell,
> William Caruthers,
> Andrew Alexander.

—From "Report of the Commissioners Appointed to View Certain Rivers within the Commonwealth of Virginia in the Year 1812", in *Messages and Documents of Virginia* (Richmond, 1829), pp. 3-5, 7-8.

53. The Kanawha Salt Industry

The salt licks of the Kanawha Valley provided salt for the Indians long before the coming of the white man into this area. In 1797 Elisha Brooks erected the first salt furnace on the property of Joseph Ruffner who had recently purchased from the Clendenins a tract of rich bottom land extending from the mouth of Campbell's Creek to Malden. After considerable experimentation in boring and tubing a well, Ruffner's two sons, Joseph and David, launched salt manufacturing as one of the leading industries in the valley. By 1827 the Kanawha salt works were producing 787,000 bushels of salt which, with the products of the Bulltown salines in Lewis, now Braxton, County and those of the Big Sandy in Cabell County, accounted for about one-fifth of the entire domestic production. The success of the Kanawha operations reduced the price of salt in the Trans-Allegheny from two, three, and even five dollars to one dollar per bushel. Such was the pace of production that during the War of 1812 the price of Kanawha salt was usually from seventy-five to eighty-seven and a half cents, despite the heavy demands of contractors supplying the Army of the Northwest at handsome profits. Following the war, decreased demand, increased competition from

*new works farther west and foreign importations not only de-
pressed the price—in 1826 it reached a new low of twelve cents
a bushel—but also forced some furnaces to remain idle.*

*Meanwhile in order to bring some stability to the industry the
Kanawha producers organized a salt trust in 1817. To combat
competition from abroad which increased as salt became an important part of the cargo of steamboats returning upstream
from New Orleans, they persistently advocated protection. Appealing to patriotism as well as to economic interests, the manufacturers pointed out that three-fourths of all the salt imports
came from the British Empire which closed its markets to American breadstuffs and other agricultural products and imposed a
heavy tax on American tobacco. The trust agreement of the Kanawha producers and a description of the salt works are given
below.*

ARTICLES OF AGREEMENT, Association and Copartnership made
and entered into this tenth day of November, in the year of our
Lord one thousand eight hundred and seventeen, By and Between the undersigned Subscribers, towit, Danl. Ruffner, Tobias
Ruffner, David Ruffner, Wm. Steele of Ky., Stephen Radcliff,
Aron Stockton, John Reynolds, John Shrewsbury, Saml. Shrewsbury, John D. Shrewsbury, Joel Shrewsbury, Leonard Morris,
Charles Morris, Wm. Steele & Co., Charles Brown, Andr. Donnally, Isaac Noyes, Bradford Noyes, John J. Cabell, Joseph Lovell, who are owners of salt works, salt interests and appurtenances thereunto, in the County of Kanawha and State of Virginia, do for the purpose of manufacturing and disposing of salt
on a general and uniform plan and method, form themselves into a company under the name and title of the Kanawha Salt
Company, who for the government and management of their
affairs, do adopt the following articles.

Article 1st. This Company shall commence and go into operation on the first day of January, one thousand eight hundred and
eighteen, and shall cease & expire on the thirty first day of
December, one thousand eight hundred and twenty two.

2nd. On the first Mondays in January and July in each year
(or so soon thereafter as convenient) the Subscribers or a majority of them shall by Ballot elect five Directors out of the Sub-

scribers, who shall continue in office and manage the affairs of the Company the following six months, or until there shall be a new election. It shall also be the duty of the directors to appoint a President out of their own body, who with the Directors or a majority of them shall superintend and manage the affairs of the Company, during the term of their service, and shall have power at any time to call a general meeting of the Subscribers whenever they may think the interest of the Company require such meeting. . . .

4th. It shall be the duty of the President and Directors to receive all the salt manufactured by the Subscribers, or under or through them or any of them, to regulate and fix the price from time to time and the terms on which the same shall be sold, make sale thereof, and if necessary, to transport the same to distant markets, to make and close all and any contracts relative thereto, receive the money, notes, or other proceeds of said salt, keep regular books and accounts of all transactions of the company, and make a fair dividend of the net proceeds of all sales of salt (after deducting all proper and necessary expenses & losses if any shall have occurred) among the Subscribers agreeable to their respective interests and proportions hereafter allotted and assigned to each of them, provided, however, that no subscriber shall at any time receive a greater dividend than he may be entitled to for the quantity of salt which he shall actually [have delivered].

It shall be the duty of the President and Directors to declare dividends monthly, on such day or days as they may think proper, if necessary and required by any of the Subscribers, and to enable the President and Directors to discharge their duties, they are hereby authorized to employ from time to time the proper clerks, agents, &c, and form all necessary correspondence.

5. It shall be the duty of the President and directors and they are hereby authorized from time to time, to borrow as much money from Banks or other persons as may be necessary for the discharge of any debts, contracts, or purchases, heretofore made or which may be hereafter made for the use and benefit of said company, or for any other purpose deemed advisable and necessary by the President & Directors, and also to detain from

the dividend of each Subscriber his necessary proportion which may be required for the discharge of all and any debts, contracts or purchases made, or to be made for the benefit of said Company.

6. All salt made by the Subscribers or through or under them and each of them shall be of good quality, and by them well packed and sealed in good and sufficient Barrels, and deposited in some convenient situation under cover on the bank of the Kanawha River, which salt shall have been packed at least ten days before delivered to the proper agent of the Company, whose duty it shall be to weigh the same, and mark on the head of each Barrel the name of the manufacturer, and the gross weight of each Barrel and give a Receipt therefor to the owner, who upon returning said Receipt to the proper clerk of the Company, shall be entitled to a credit for the amount thereof, on the books of the Company, and it shall be the duty of each manufacturer of salt to deliver over to the proper agent of the Company, once a month at least, all salt he may have on hand, and it shall also be the duty of the President and Directors to receive the same or cause it to be received if required, and no Subscriber shall be at liberty to lease or transfer his furnace or furnaces to any person or persons, during the existence of this Company, without giving the President & Directors, for the time being, a sufficient quaranty [sic] that all salt manufactured or to be manufactured at said furnaces shall be punctually delivered as specified in this Article.

7th. It shall be the duty of the President and Directors, and they are hereby required to ascertain by actual inspection or other means the quality of all salt manufactured, before, or at the time it shall be delivered, and also to attend to the quality and situation of the Barrels, and make the necessary deduction if necessary, from the price, as may be just and necessary, in consequence of its bad quality or deficiency in Barrels, and whereas many salt manufacturers make use of Tallow in the manufacture of salt, which is found by experience to injure its quality. It is therefore recommended that no tallow be used in the manufacture of salt by any of the Subscribers during the continuance of this company, and if it should be discovered to have been used, it shall be the duty of the President and Directors to cause a sufficient and just deduction to be made in the price of such salt.

8. The quantity of salt to be manufactured by all the Subscribers in the year one *one* thousand eight hundred & eighteen shall not exceed four hundred & fifty Thousand Bushels, and the proportional quantity of salt to be manufactured by each Subscriber, or any person or persons, manufacturing, for or under them or any of them shall not exceed the following quantities, (to-wit), Danl. Ruffner nine thousand Bushels, Joseph Lovell Twenty five thousand Bushels, Tobias Ruffner Twenty Thousand Bushels, David Ruffner forty thousand Bushels, Wm. Steele of Kentucky Twenty thousand Bushels, Aron Stockton Twenty thousand Bushels, John Reynolds twelve thousand Bushels, Stephen Radcliff Ten thousand Bushels, John Shrewsbury, Saml. Shrewsbury and Jno. D. Shrewsbury Thirty two thousand Bushels, Joel Shrewsbury Thirty thousand Bushels, Leonard & Charles Morris thirty three thousand Bushels, Wm. Steele & Co. fifty three thousand Bushels, Charles Brown Sixteen thousand Bushels, Andr. Donnally forty thousand Bushels, Isaac & Bradford Noyes thirty thousand Bushels, John J. Cabell Twenty thousand Bushels. And if any of the subscribers should at any time think that the quantity of salt assigned and allotted him to manufacture is too small, it shall be determined by the Ballance of the Subscribers or a majority of them who are disinterested in the property for which the quantity is limited, and should the Subscribers or a majority of them at any time think during the continuance of this Company that the quantity of salt described for any one Subscriber to manufacture too great or more than he is entitled to make, taking into consideration his situation and quantity of wood and water, the ballance of the Subscribers or a majority of them shall ascertain and fix the quantity which he shall manufacture, which decision shall be binding.

9th. The following Property and salt interests already purchased are—Saml. Slack's L. Joseph Alderson's Land & Salt interest, Wm. Grant's & John Alderson's Land & Salt interest, Robt. Lewis' Andr. Worth & Martin Worth's Land & Salt interest, Levi Patrick Lots & Salt interest, and John Fields Lots and Salt interest, shall be paid for by the Company, and be and

remain their joint Property, according to their respective proportional quantities of salt described for each to manufacture,
and if the following property can at any time be purchased or
leased by the President & Directors or any Subscriber thereto,
at fair and reasonable price, the same shall be done, in like
manner to be paid for by the Company and for their benefit as
before described, (to-wit Eli Jarretts Land and Salt interest,
James Jarrets Land and Salt interest, Jno. Wilson's Salt interest, Reuben Slaughter & Partners Land & Salt interest and
Jno. Andersons and the heirs of Silas Reynolds Dec. Land &
Salt interest, and any other Lands and Salt interests in the
County of Kanawha aforesaid, that the President and Directors
(with the advice of the Subscribers hereto) shall purchase or
direct to be purchased or leased or otherwise procured, and
shall, if procured be under the control of the President and Directors for the time being.

10th. It is understood that there are several of the Subscribers
to this Agreement, who have their furnaces leased for some
time to some. It is therefore agreed and understood that any subscriber so situated shall not be responsible for the delivery of
more salt than actually belongs to him or comes under his control until the expiration of such lease. . . .

12th. As it is suggested that there is too great a quantity of
salt manufactured for the demand of the present year, the
Subscribers hereto enguages [sic] to take all legal and proper
means in their power to lessen the quantity to be manufactured
by themselves and others from this time until the first day of
January next, and as Messrs, Steele, Donnally & Steele were
the purchasers of the salt made in the County of Kanawha of
the present year, the members of that Company, Subscribers
hereto, on their part Pledge themselves that should any of the
salt of the present year remain on hand unsold after the first
day of January next, that they will not sell or dispose of the
sum at any lower price than shall be established by the President & Directors of the Present Company.

13. And for the True and faithful performance of all and each
of the articles & provisions herein contained the Subscriber or
Subscribers delinquent or not observing on his or their part,
bind themselves, their heirs & assigns to the Subscriber or Sub-

scribers observing & performing on his or their part in the penal Sum of Fifty Thousand Dollars.

In Testimony whereof they have hereinto Respectively Subscribed their names And set their Seals the day and year before mentioned. . . .

Memorandum. It is agreed by the subscribers to the above agreement that the land & salt interest of John Worth heretofore purchased of him by Messrs. Steele, Donnally accidentally omitted in the 9th article of the above agreement, shall be taken & paid for by the Subscribers on the terms agreed on by said Steele, Donnally & Steele with said Worth, in the same manner as the other properties mentioned in the said 9th article.

In Testimony Whereof we have hereunto set our hands and affixed our seals on the 26th day of January, in the year 1818. . . . —Typewritten copy, in West Virginia Department of Archives and History.

KANAWHA SALT WORKS. These valuable works are situated on the Kanawha river, commencing near Charleston, and embracing a distance of 15 miles above, on each side of the river. The salt water is obtained anywhere within that distance, by boring or sinking a shaft, from three to five hundred feet below the bed of the river, through a solid rock, from which it is brought to the surface through the surrounding fresh water, in copper tubes, and is raised to the bank of the river by steam engines, and is thrown into cisterns, whence it is conveyed to the furnaces. There are at present about 60 furnaces, manufacturing about one million two hundred thousand bushels annually, and the quantity is only limited by the demand. The adjacent hills abound with stone coal of a superior quality, which lies in horizontal strata, varying in thickness from 4 to 7 feet. The coal is conveyed from the mines to the furnace on rail roads. There has been for the last year a furnace manufacturing allum salt by steam, which is said to be equal to the imported article. At this furnace 100 bushels of this salt are made per day. Several others are erecting on the same plan, and will soon be in operation. The exports of the salt from these works in 1832, is estimated as being worth to the proprietors $250,000. Seldom has it fallen to the lot of any region of country to possess such inexhaustible sources of mineral wealth on the borders of a fine navigable river, leading to a region of country which will one day be filled with almost boundless multitudes of people.—Joseph Martin, *A New and Comprehensive Gazetteer of Virginia* . . . , pp. 380-81.

54. Report of Claudius Crozet

Claudius Crozet (1789-1864), noted engineer and teacher, was born in France, fought with Napoleon at Wagram, followed the Emperor to Russia, and supported him during the fateful days before Waterloo. After his migration to the United States in 1816, Crozet taught engineering and mathematics at West Point until he became Principal Engineer and Surveyor of Public Works for the state of Virginia in 1823. In Virginia Crozet made numerous turnpike and canal surveys, especially in the western part of the state. Largely through his efforts the Northwestern Turnpike was completed by 1840, and in the next two years the Staunton and Parkersburg and the Giles, Fayette and Kanawha turnpikes were located. His recommendations for lock and dam improvements on the James and for railway connections between the upper courses of the James and Kanawha were rejected in 1831 in favor of a proposal for a continuous canal over this route. Crozet was extremely sanguine concerning the future of railroads. He maintained that a state should not try "to preserve that which has ceased to be best, and reject that which new inventions have rendered most desirable, because what has been done before, might lose part of its usefulness." In the periods when Crozet was not serving Virginia as an engineer, he contributed to the state's educational progress as professor at Virginia Military Institute and as Principal of Richmond Academy. The following report of Crozet was made in 1828.

No where has the kind hand of Providence been more profusely bountiful than in Virginia; blessed with a mild climate and a fertile soil; producing cotton and the best tobacco, besides the common staples of the northern States, to which she even exports her flour; abounding with rich mines; her coal nearer to tide water than that of any other State. Virginia is no less favored in her geographical position: she occupies in the Union an important central situation, and the mouth of the Chesapeake, her fine harbour, always open, strongly protected against aggression, is equal to even that of New-York.

She possesses, besides, perhaps more than any other State, the elements of manufacture; she has, in abundance, water power, coal, iron and raw materials. . . .

The importance of a more immediate connection on the east and west appears to be so generally appreciated, that it is needless to say much on this subject: public opinion, of late years, has manifested itself very conclusively by the operations and enquiries which have been instituted, with a view to the Union of the Ohio to the Chesapeake by a canal; and likewise, by the active efforts of Baltimore to effect the same object by a rail-way.

These exertions must awaken the attention of Virginia. The most direct line from the Ohio to the mouth of the Chesapeake, is evidently through her territory, and it was only, I think, the widely circulated report, that a water communication through the State was impracticable, which could have induced public opinion to foster exclusively the connexion emphatically called the Ohio and Chesapeake canal.

In my report of 1826, . . . I suggested the importance and probable success of a more careful examination of the mountains, which divide the eastern and western waters: the search has since been made, and a connexion found to be practicable between James River and the Kanawha, and also between New River and the Roanoke. This latter, expecially, offers facilities that have not been found anywhere else: the Roanoke can also be connected with James River, through Botetourt county.

Whether, by canal or rail-way, therefore, a connexion through Virginia is proved to be more practicable than by any other routes. . . .

In regard to the rail-road, by looking at the map of Virginia, it will appear obvious that a line from Baltimore to the Ohio, will cross at right angles the cluster of formidable ridges which divides the Potomac from the Ohio, and encounter so many steep mountains and deep vallies, that the road must, either be immensely expensive, or very circuitous.

Whereas, from the head of the valley of James river, or of Roanoke, there is only one ridge to be passed over; after which, the valley of New River may be pursued down to the Ohio. The superiority of this route is so obvious, that it has even been proposed to carry the rail-road from Baltimore by way of Covington to the Ohio. . . .

Here would be no portage, no transshipment of produce, and all their consequent expenses. The same boats and men might continue from the Ohio over the Alleghany to tide water. With such advantages before him, who would think of taking a circuitous route from the State of Ohio, with the additional inconvenience and expenses of shifting the produce twice at a portage, and twice more at the lakes, besides the dangers attending their navigation, and all that, perhaps, to be stopped at least four months by ice? By the connexion through Virginia, things must undoubtedly be reversed, and the trade descend, instead of ascending the rivers through the State of Ohio.

To these considerations must be added the fact which has been communicated to me by the Hon. Judge Summers, that, during the last dry season, the water in the Ohio, below the Great Kanawha, was about 18 inches over the bars; and above that point, and up to Wheeling, only from 13 to 15; whereas, the Kanawha, as stated in the memorial of the citizens of Kanawha county to the General Assembly, affords 20 inches in the shallowest places. . . .

The time has arrived, I think, when a system must be adopted to prosecute, with a steady step, all the improvements tending to these great benefits. Their progress must be gradual: but, after the completion of the improvement of James river, it is confidently expected that the means for the prosecution of the great scheme of connexion, will develop themselves rapidly.—From C. Crozet, "Report of the Principal Engineer, Made in 1828, on His Survey of James River in 1827," in *Messages and Documents* (Richmond, Virginia, 1829), pp. 43-44.

55. The National Arsenal at Harpers Ferry

In 1830 only six towns in present West Virginia had a population which reached or exceeded one thousand. Four of them —Charlestown, Harpers Ferry, Martinsburg, and Shepherdstown —were in the Eastern Panhandle and the remaining two —Wheeling and Wellsburg—in the Northern Panhandle. The cultural facilities in these and smaller towns consisted of "houses of public worship," common schools, academies, religious and aid societies, and weekly newspapers. Physical needs were supplied by a variety of stores, including apothecary shops, and small artisan establishments. To these common features Martinsburg added a woolen manufactory and a foundry "with a cupola furnace, and water power." Wellsburg had glass and pottery works, a large cotton factory running 1200 spindles, a steam sawmill which cut 3,000 feet of plank in twelve hours, two printing offices, breweries, and a carpet factory. Charlestown had a branch of the Bank of the Valley. A landmark of Harpers Ferry was its Catholic church, "one of the handsomest and neatest buildings in the state," ornamented "by a beautiful steeple" and containing a "fine toned organ." On the economic side the town pointed with pride to its projected canal and rail facilities and, above all, to the national arsenal and armory which could manufacture fourteen hundred muskets a month. The operations of this arsenal and of the Hall's Rifle Works, also located in Harpers Ferry, are described in the following selection.

THE NATIONAL ARSENAL at Harper's Ferry is an object worthy of attention. Eighty or ninety thousand stand of arms are usually kept there, and as these are sent off to other depositaries [sic] their place is supplied from the extensive manufactory adjacent. It is interesting to observe the facility with which a weapon, so complicated as the musket, is produced. A bar of iron is forged into a rough tube, the interior of which is formed into a smooth surface by drills turned by the power of water.

At first, the barrel, strongly fastened, is moved slowly forward, whilst the drill, a cylindrical rod of iron, terminating in a rectangular bar, ten or twelve inches long, revolves with rapidity, but without progressive motion; the barrel is surrounded by water, which, though constantly renewed, becomes warm to the touch. The barrel is not made cylindrical by a single drill, a succession is employed, until, in the application of the finer drills, the barrel, only fastened in the middle, is left free to adapt itself to the motion of the drill.

The outside of the barrel is polished by enormous grindstones, turning with great rapidity. These stones are guarded by thick cheeks of wood.... The barrel passing through these cheeks, bears against the stone, and is drawn across it with a motion resembling that of a screw.

The stocks are shaped by a machine, the idea of which seems to have been borrowed from an admirable contrivance in the celebrated Block Machinery of Brunel. The writer was struck immediately with the resemblance, and, on inquiry, found that the inventor, Blanchard, had previously introduced the use of Brunel's machinery in this country.

... This machine will shape a musket stock in about eight seconds.

The limits of this article will not permit us to describe the operations by which the minute parts of the muskets are completed. The whole gives employment when in full work to about two hundred and fifty men, and at such times fourteen hundred muskets have been finished in a month. The average cost is about eleven dollars for each musket, and a good workman will earn two dollars a day. About a dozen of the workmen are from England, chiefly from the Armory Mills which were worked during the war near Deptfort in Kent. The muskets are lighter, and in this respect preferable to the English; the workmen did not hold the iron, which is chiefly from Massachusetts, in the same esteem. The establishment is governed by a superintendant who receives fourteen hundred dollars a year, and conducted by a master armorer at sixty dollars per month, and four assistants at forty dollars.

We must not quit this part of the subject without mentioning Hall's rifle, which is loaded at the breech, and of which there is a separate manufactory here. The barrel is formed of two portions by being cut asunder a few inches from the breech. And on touching a trigger, placed before the ordinary one, the lower portion is raised out of the stock by a spring, and may be loaded as a pistol. When pressed down again the parts perfectly coincide, and the movable part of the barrel is retained in its place by a catch.—Joseph Martin, *A New and Comprehensive Gazetteer of Virginia* ... , pp. 370-72.

56. Wheeling City c. 1830

The largest and most promising town in western Virginia was Wheeling which boasted in 1830 of having the largest white population of any town in the state and a growth that was "altogether unexampled" in Virginia.

WHEELING CITY ... The origin of this place was Wheeling fort, built early in the Revolutionary war, which stood on the breast of a high bank, at the point of which the U. S road reaches the Ohio river. Wheeling advanced at first but slowly. It was laid out as a village early in 1783, and in 1820 contained 1,567 inhabitants. Within the last thirteen years the advance has been rapid,—in 1830 the population was 5,222 and now, 1834, is estimated at 8,000—among whom are 14 resident attorneys, 12 regular physicians, and 11 clergymen. It contains about 500 houses, 9 houses of public worship, (2 Presbyterian, 1 Episcopalian, 2 Methodist, 1 Catholic, 1 Friends or Quakers, 1 regular Baptist, and 1 Campbellite, &c.

There are a number of very excellent institutions here. 1st. The Wheeling Institute, contains 4 departments, viz:—infant—primary—classical, and female—under the superintendence of six teachers, and contains from 150 to 160 pupils.

2nd. The Wheeling Lancasterian Academy. 3d. The Wheeling Classical Academy. 4th. The Wheeling Female Seminary. 5th. The Wheeling University, (not yet organized,) and nine common English preparatory schools.

The rear of this town is skirted by a range of hills which approaches within a short distance of the river. These hills, which abound with inexhaustible quantities of stone coal, from their proximity to the town are of the greatest convenience to the numerous manufactories;—a number of them having coal within a few yards of their fires. This place is one of the first manufacturing towns in the western country, and ranks, in point of population, the fourth in the state. There are at all times not less than 26 steam engines in operation. The Wheeling Iron Works, owned by Messrs, Shanberger & Agnew, roll 1000 tons of iron annually—about 300 tons of which are cut into nails of various sizes—the balance being bar, boiler, sheet, hoop iron, &c.—giving employment to a great number of hands, and consuming 150,000 bushels of stone coal annually. These works are calculated to produce double or treble the quantity pr. annum, if there were a demand for it. There are also 4 iron foundries, employing 70 hands, & consuming about 130,000 bushels of coal annually, 4 steam engine builders, giving employment to 70 hands and consuming 60,000 bushels of stone coal annually—5 glass houses and 2 glass cutting establishments —giving employment to 193 hands, and consuming 260,000 bushels of stone coal, 3 steam flour mills, consuming 75,000 bushels per annum, 1 brewery, 2 steam distilleries, consuming 50,000 bushels, 2 cotton factories, 2 woollen factories and carding machines, consuming 70,000 bushels, 2 paper mills, 70,000 bushels, 2 steam saw mills, 50,000 bushels, 1 copperas, 1 white and 1 sheet lead factory, consuming 8,000 bushels of stone coal annually.

There are 2 tobacco factories and 1 glue factory, 1 coach and wagon maker, 1 edge tool maker, 3 chair makers, 1 comb maker, 2 merchant tailors, giving employment to a great number of hands, 4 silversmiths, 18 blacksmiths, and 3 white smiths, 2 steam planing machines, 3 tanners and curriers, 5 saddlers, 17 boot and shoe factories, 6 painters and glaziers, 3 cabinet makers, 3 coppersmiths and tin plate workers, 5 hatters, 2 wire workers, 2 coopers, 1 rope maker, 2 water pump manufactories, 2 soap and tallow chandleries, 10 bake houses, 6 livery stables, 1 stone and earthen pottery, 7 brick yards, 12 master stone and brick masons, 5 stone cutters, 6 plasterers, 7 carpenters and undertakers, 1 book bindery, 1 brass foundry, 3 window glass and hollow ware manufactories, consuming 175,000 bushels of coal annually, 3 printing offices, (2 issuing a weekly, and 1 a tri-weekly paper,) 1 book and job office, 2 book stores, 1 reading room, and a very extensive circulating library, 12 apothecaries' shops, 1 Lyceum, a Masonic Hall and Theatre.

The aggregate number of manufactories in the town of Wheeling for domestic goods are 113, using annually upwards of 1,000,000 bushels of coal, and giving employment to more than 1,300 hands. There are 65 wholesale and retail stores, vending annually goods to the amount of $1,500,000, 7 commission and forwarding houses, for the sale of goods consigned, and for receiving and forwarding merchandize and produce. These houses, from Nov'r 1832, to Nov'r 1833, forwarded to Baltimore and the District of Columbia, by wagons 2,671 hogsheads of tobacco, and by steam, keel and flat boats, to the west and south, and by wagons to Baltimore and Philadelphia, merchandize and produce equal to at least 11,000 tons.... There is owned in Wheeling, in whole and in part, from 17 to 20 steam boats, worth from 200 to $230,000. The arrivals and departures of steam boats at and from this port during the past year were, 738. Wheeling is by a law of Congress a port of entry, so that goods from any port of Europe may be imported direct without payment of duties at New Orleans.

There is now running to and from Wheeling eight lines of daily stages, east, west and north—1 tri-weekly line, 1 semiweekly and 1 weekly. The number of passengers arriving and departing weekly by steam boats and stages are variously estimated at from 350 to 400.—The Baltimore and Ohio wagon transportation company with a capital of $200,000 (one-fourth of which is paid in) transports goods and produce between Wheeling and Baltimore. One wagon arrives and departs daily at and from each of those places, with a load weighing from 2¼ to 2½ tons and occupies 8 days upon the road. Arrangements are in progress to increase the number of daily arrivals and departures from one to three wagons, and eventually to five.

. . . The public water works are now nearly completed, worked by a steam engine of 120 horse power; . . . These, together with the erection of public stone wharves, sewers,

&c. &c. of the most permanent kind, cost the corporation within the last 2 years an expenditure of upwards of $40,000. A stone bridge has lately been erected over Wheeling creek at this place, at a cost of $17,000.—Boat building for the last few years has been carried on here extensively. At low water, steam boats ascend no higher than this place. From the fact of its having a more permanent navigation the whole year round than any other point, it is made the general route of travellers. It also possesses one of the finest markets in the western country. The Baltimore and Ohio rail-road it is supposed will strike the Ohio river at this place. Considering all these advantages, there remains no doubt that in the course of a few years Wheeling will become one of the most important places in the west. The northwestern bank of Virginia is located here. It may not be considered irrelative to state that the present population of Wheeling is estimated at about 8,000 souls; shewing an increase in the last four years, (since the census of 1830) of about *fifty per cent.*; and, in the last 15 years, of about *eight hundred* per cent! The colored part of the population, both slaves and free blacks—amounting to less than two hundred—it is highly probable that Wheeling contains already, the largest *white population* of any town or city, in the state; and, in reference to its manufactories and commerce, if not the first, is doubtless, the second town in the commonwealth. A growth so rapid, is believed to be altogether unexampled in Virginia; and but seldom surpassed even in the rapidly filling districts of the "great west."

This town, the capital of Ohio county, . . . at the termination of the eastern, and commencement of the western division of the great "Cumberland," or "National Road:" possessing unexampled facilities and advantages for manufacturing, in the abundance and low cost of all materials, and especially of *fuel;* (coal, costing, delivered at the factories, but on to three cents per bushel:) surrounded by a country of uncommon fertility, and remarkable for health—cannot but continue to advance in business, population and wealth.—Joseph Martin, *A New and Comprehensive Gazetteer of Virginia . . .*, pp. 406-408.

57. Formal Opening of the Wheeling Bridge, 1849

The controversial and ill-fated bridge over the Ohio at Wheeling, designed by Charles Ellet, Jr., was reputed to be the largest structure of its kind in the world at the time of its completion in October, 1849. Two years were required for its construction, and an expenditure of nearly a quarter of a million dollars. From its inception the bridge became the target of bitter attack from Pittsburgh shipping and boat-building interests who contended that since the span would be only thirty feet above high water mark, it would interfere with navigation on the Ohio. When these objections failed to halt the project, aptly designated as the "Bridge of Size," Pennsylvania appealed to the United States Supreme Court for an order to have the bridge removed as a nuisance. The Court ruled in favor of unobstructed navigation of the river and directed the Wheeling Bridge Company to alter the bridge in accordance with this decision by February 1, 1853. Wheeling then asked Congress to declare the bridge a post-road and to require steamboats to adjust their smoke-stacks to existing conditions. This request, which had the support of state rights advocates, champions of railroads, and friends of Wheeling, received the approval of Congress in August, 1852. But Wheeling's triumph was short-lived. On May 17, 1854, a violent gale left the bridge a "tangled ruin." A new bridge which utilized the towers and cables of the original structure, but had a narrower floor, was completed early in 1856.

THE CITIZENS OF WHEELING will long remember the 15th of November, the day appointed for the formal opening of the Wire Suspension Bridge erected by the citizens of Wheeling over the Ohio river.

The morning was ushered in by the sound of cannon, and at an early hour strangers began to gather in from all quarters, the bridge was lined with vehicles, and all around seemed life and animation.

The splendid band from Zanesville was brought in by the Ohio Stage Company and dispensed their music in a manner soul-inspiring.

The firing of cannon continued for a great portion of the day, and the crowds along the Bridge sensibly increased until 3 o'clock, when the ladies assembled, and with their escorts passed over to the Island and returned. With them the hour seemed given up to enjoyment, friend met friend, and gaiety and good feeling reigned supreme. We had there the pleasure of meeting more lovely and happy faces than we have ever seen before for months. A continuous train of human beings moved along the work from 3 o'clock until dark.

At 6 o'clock, the thousand lamps, hung upon the wires, were lighted almost simultaneously and presented an elegant and graceful curve of fire, high above the river, that was never excelled in beauty. It forcibly reminded one of Mr. Clay's remarks, a few days since, when looking at the work from a distance, while his face glowed with pride and exultation—"Take that down! you might as well try to take down the rainbow."

The illumination was under the superintendance of Mr. Williams, the clerk of the company, and reflected much honor on him for taste and industry. Soon after the lamps were lighted, we strove to effect an entrance to the bridge, but the crowd was so dense we gave it up in despair. . . .

Judge Wilson, of Steubenville, Ohio, being called upon . . . observed that, in reference to the National Road, of which the new Bridge now forms a part, it was constructed, or rather intended to be constructed, as far as the Ohio river, by the appropriation of two per centum of the avails of the public lands in Ohio. This two per cent was soon expended, and, if the completion of the road had depended upon that fund alone, it would not, in all probability, have reached Wheeling to this day—and the magnificent and beneficial structure, the erection of which we are now assembled to witness and celebrate, would not have been thought of. . . .

Now that this splendid and useful structure is completed, what do we hear? Why some few smoke pipes of steamboats, have been constructed so high that they cannot get along without doing as is done at all other places where bridges are constructed over navigable streams—to wit, letting down a portion of said smoke pipes! And because these few smoke pipes have no hinges attached by which this can be effected, why, forsooth, the Bridge must be pulled down!—the Ohio river must remain without a Bridge, unless it be elevated in the air to such height as a rifle bullet would hardly reach it! But I need not take up the time of this assemblage in adverting to such absurdities—absurdities which, however far they may be countenanced by the technicalities of law, are revolting to public opinion and the common sense of all. The time is near at hand at which many such structures will grace the beautiful Ohio; and I venture to predict, that it will not be long before this smoke pipe farce, like all other absurdities, will end in smoke. . . . —*The Daily Wheeling Gazette,* November 17, 1849.

58. Public Improvements in the Trans-Allegheny

The four grand divisions into which Virginia was officially divided—the first, or Tidewater; the second, or Piedmont; the third, or Valley; and the fourth, or Trans-Allegheny—emphasized the sectional character of its government. In the logrolling that followed, the western legislators came out fourth best, as may be seen from the following report on appropriations and expenditures for internal improvements. In spite of the westerners' persistent efforts to correct this unfavorable situation, transportation facilities in trans-montane Virginia continued to be inadequate, especially in the southern part which had no railway service until after the Civil War.

. . . It will appear by the corrected statements herewith presented, that the entire expenditures of the state, on works of internal improvement, exclusive of the James River and Kanawha work, up to 30th September, 1850, have been as follows: In the first, or Tide-water, division, $2,552,681.72. In the second, or Piedmont, division, $1,401,461.85. In the third, or Valley, division, $1,294,406.72, and in the fourth, or Trans-Alleghany, division, $1,021,968.61. And the entire expenditures, inclusive of the James River and Kanawha improvement, are as follows: In the first grand division $3,383,678.12. In the second grand division $4,903,830.65. In the third grand division $1,956,108.92; and in the fourth grand division $1,184,968.21....

FOURTH GRAND DIVISION OF THE STATE.— (FROM THE ALLEGHANY MOUNTAINS TO THE OHIO RIVER.)

Name of Corporation or State Improvement	Total amount subscribed, or appropriat'd by state to each improvement.	Total expenditures of state.
Cheat River Toll Bridge	6,000.00	1,153.12
Coal River Navigation Company	6,000.00	4,000.00
Monongalia Navigation Company	8,180.00	8,180.00
Guyandotte Navigation Company	45,000.00	4,500.00
Buchanan Turnpike Company	5,400.00	1,350.00
Clarksburg and Buchanan Turnpike Co.	9,000.00	8,066.22
Charleston and Pt. Pleasant T'pike Co.	28,800.00	28,800.00
Clarksburg and Philippi T'pike Co.	6,000.00	1,320.00
Giles, Fayette and Kanawha T'pike Co.	30,000.00	27,491.60
Harrisville Turnpike Company	6,000.00	3,000.00
Holliday's Cove Turnpike Company	12,000.00	4,733.33
Jacksonville and Bent Mt. T'pike Co.	6,000.00	472.50
Lewisburg and Blue Sulphur Springs T'pike Co.	5,000.00	4,950.00
Morgantown and Bridgeport T'pike Co.	13,200.00	3,600.00
Marshall and Ohio Turnpike Company	12,000.00	7,822.50
Red and Blue Sulphur Springs T'pike Co.	8,800.00	7,456.66
Russell and Washington Turnpike Co.	6,675.00	3,577.50
Weston and Fairmont Turnpike Co.	12,000.00	9,000.00
Williamsport Turnpike Company	3,000.00	1,889.32
Weston and Gauley Bridge T'pike Co.	27,000.00	6,065.33
Wheeling, West Liberty and Bethany T'pike Co.	21,000.00	14,541.18
Wellsburg and Washington T'pike Co.	7,133.33	7,071.01
White and Salt Sulphur Springs T'pike Co.	4,000.00	4,000.00
Wellsburg and Bethany T'pike Co.	16,200.00	7,144.00
Beverly and Fairmont Road	42,000.00	26,745.01
Fancy Gap Road From N. Carolina to Wytheville	2,000.00	1,976.20
Huttonsville and Huntersville Road	15,000.00	750.00
Ice's Ferry Road	4,200.00	1,358.00

Floyd Courthouse and Hillsville Road	9,000.00	1,410.00
Little Stone Gap Road	3,600.00	3,287.90
Penn., Morgantown and Beverly Road	3,000.00	1,214.26
Loan to Ohio River and Md. Road	84,534.00	23,611.08
North Western Road, (Macadamizing)	120,000.00	62,896.11
Richlands and Kentucky Line Road	19,000.00	9,865.81
Sistersville and Salem Road	11,000.00	10,512.89
Tazewell Courthouse and Richlands Road	8,000.00	162.50
Tazewell Courthouse and Fancy Gap Road	19,200.00	3,150.00
Staunton and Pkersbg. Road, Bridging	30,800.00	23,778.97
ADD THE FOLLOWING	$ 675,722.33	$ 340,903.00
Amount expended for improvements in the fourth grand division, as per First Auditor's statement H.	138,205.52	138,205.52
Add estimates of statement E., exclusive of James River and Kanawha Co.	1,812,578.47	542,860.09
Total exclusive of James River and Kanawha Company	2,626,506.32	1,021,968.61
Add James River and Kanawha Company	162,999.60	162,999.60
Total,	$2,789,505.92	$1,184,968.21

—"Report of the Committee on the Second Auditor's Report," Appendix, *Journal, Acts and Proceedings of a General Convention of the State of Virginia . . . Assembled at Richmond . . . Eighteen Hundred and Fifty.*

59. Opening of the Baltimore and Ohio Railroad at Wheeling

The arrival of the Baltimore and Ohio Railroad at Wheeling in January 1853 was the occasion for a splendid celebration which the WHEELING DAILY INTELLIGENCER *reported in proud detail down to the menu at the Lucullan banquet.*

YESTERDAY MORNING DAWNED UPON THOUSANDS who had come by steamboats, by coaches, on horses and on foot, from near and far, to participate in the commemoration of one of the greatest works of the age—the completion of an unbroken link connecting the Chesapeake with the waters of the Ohio.

At an early hour the streets were thronged with a multitude of all ages, sexes and conditions, which was increased by the successive arrivals of various steamers crowded with passengers. Among them we noticed the steamer Wm. Knox, with a large number of the citizens of Marietta, and the American Star, with a handsome uniformed company, the "Steubenville Grays," commanded by Capt. Webster. This company and the Bridgeport Artillery, commanded by Capt. Grubb, presented an imposing appearance in our streets.

By noon a dense crowd was assembled along the line of the track in Centre Wheeling, as far as the eye could see, awaiting the arrival of the cars.

At 2 o'clock the military, and the First Ward Hose and the Hope Fire Companies formed into line, and were conducted by the Marshals to the line of the track on the south side of the creek.—In the morning a dispatch was received, announcing that the cars had reached Cumberland in the night, and might be expected here at 3 or 4 o'clock which they would undoubtedly have done, had not a slight accident, news of which was received last night by the arrival of the mail train, caused a delay of several hours. It was the breaking of an axle-tree of the locomotive, which caused the detention, but no injury to any of the passengers.

Last night the Suspension Bridge was brilliantly illuminated along its entire length with 1010 lights, and its long curve of radiance stretching in mid air, against the "dark vaulted heavens," looked really like a triumphal Rainbow spanning the storms which have beat in vain against its majestic form.

8½ o'clock P. M.—The mail train has arrived with about 50 passengers, mostly from Baltimore.

5 Minutes of 2 o'clock, A. M. The first train of passenger cars has arrived, and several hundred of the citizens of Baltimore have been conducted to the McLure House, led by Capt. Holland's Band of Independent Blues, whose soul-stirring music

peals out upon the morning air, which wafts back a heart-felt welcome from all our citizens.

The formal reception of the President and Directors of the Road, and the City's guests, will take place at the Court House to-day at 11 o'clock.

THE RECEPTION

At about noon on Wednesday, the President and Directors of the Company, the Chief Engineer, Benj. H. Latrobe, Esq., Governor Johnson, of Virginia, Governor Lowe, of Maryland, the members of the Legislature, and the great concourse of the invited guests, were escorted to the Court House, where his Honor, Mayor Nelson and the City Council were in waiting, and where the ceremonies of a formal reception took place.

After a brilliant overture had been performed by Captain Holland's Band, of Baltimore, his Honor Mayor Nelson, addressed the distinguished President of the Company, Thos. Swann, Esq., as follows:

On behalf of the city of Wheeling, and in their name, permit me to bid your [sic] and your respected associates, welcome to our city—and to congratulate you on the auspicious consumation of the enterprise which you have carried forward with so much zeal and with such signal ability. . . .

THE BANQUET

In the evening the two spacious rooms of Washington Hall presented a scene of splendor but rarely witnessed. In each hall, 104 feet in length, there were five tables bearing a most sumptuous repast, and elegantly decorated. The supper was furnished by Mr. Wm. Guy of Baltimore and was worthy his unrivalled reputation in such matters. At each end of the halls, above the seats of the Presidents' and officers, very large and gorgeous National flags were displayed. In the first story, Capt. Holland's Band of Baltimore, and in the second story, the German Band of this city, enlivened the proceedings with the choisest music.

Governor Johnson, of Va., Mr. Swann, members of the Legislatures and Directors of the Company, and other distinguished persons occupied seats beside the Mayor in the first hall, and Governor Lowe, of Maryland, and others of like distinction occupied similar positions in the second hall, beside the President, S. Brady, Esq. . . .

At 7 o'clock about 1000 persons sat down to the table, to discuss the following bill of fare:

Stewed Oysters:
Val au Vent of Oysters.

Entrees—Hot

Lamb Chops with Green Peas;
Form of Rice, a la Financier;
Cutlets of Veal, Truffle Sauce;
Buffalo Tongues, Gardineer's Sauce.

Cold and Ornamental Dishes

Beef, a la mode,
Boned Turkey, with Truffles on a forne,
Ham decorated with Jelly,
Chicken Salad, French style,
Game Patta, modern style,
Lobster Salad, New York style,
Fillets of Chicken, En Belveue,
Beef Tongue, decorated with Jelly,
Pressed Corned Beef, Maryland style,
Rounds of spiced beef, decorated with Pickles,
Turkey Olio.

Roast Dishes

Turkey,	Saddle of Mutton,
Chicken,	Saddle of Mutton,
Beef,	Capons with Mushrooms.

Ornamental Pieces

The Horn of Plenty,
Emblem of Commerce,
The Alleghany Mountains over Pettybone's Tunnel,
Nuga, Baskets filled with Fruit,
Coupe Garnee de Freeau.
Napolitans,
        do. Mille Faielle,

Pyramid of Orange,
Pyramid of Lady's Finger,
Pyramid of Maccaroni.

Ices

Oranges, Apples, Raisins, Nuts, &. . . .

The company dispersed at a late hour, long to remember the celebration of the opening of the Baltimore and Ohio Railroad to Wheeling.—Wheeling *Intelligencer*, January 12, 14, 1853.

60. Extension of Railway Facilities

The second railroad to be constructed in western Virginia before the Civil War was the Northwestern Virginia which ran from Grafton, on the Baltimore and Ohio, to Parkersburg, and connected the Baltimore and Ohio with the lines to Cincinnati and St. Louis. The road was completed in 1857 at which time Peter G. Van Winkle succeeded Thomas Swann as its president. The time table for the special train which was run to celebrate the opening of the new road and a description of the two largest cities—Clarksburg and Parkersburg—served by it are given below.

AT SIX O'CLOCK A.M., having breakfasted, we resumed our seats in the cars, placed in two trains, the conductors shouted "all aboard," the whistle sounded, and away we sped on our journey towards the Ohio at Parkersburg, via the Northwestern Virginia Railroad. The following special Time Table had been prepared for our train, and was run with scrupulous exactitude.

TIME TABLE for Special Passenger Train from Grafton to Parkersburg, Tuesday, June 2d, 1857.

Stations	Miles	Time	Remarks
Grafton _____leave	___	6.00 A.M.	
Webster _____	4	6.10 "	
Simpson's _____	8	6.19 "	
Flemmington _____	10	6.24 "	
Bridgeport _____	17	6.40 "	
Clarksburg _____arrive	22	6.52 "	

"	leave	___	6.55	"	
Wilsonburg	_____	26	7.05	"	
Salem	_____	36	7.28	"	
Long Run	_____	41	7.40	"	
Smithson	_____	46	7.51	"	
West Union	_____	50	8.00	"	
Central	_____arrive	52	8.05	"	
"	leave	___	8.08	"	
Toll Gate	_____	58	8.22	"	
Pennsboro'	_____	62	8.32	"	
Ellenboro'	_____	67	8.46	"	
Cornwallis	_____	72	8.58	" T Meet Tonnage Trains East.
Cairo	_____	74	9.03	"	
Petroleum	_____arrive	82	9.23	"	
"	leave	___	9.26	"	
Walker's	_____	90	9.45	"	
Kanawha	_____	94	9.56	"	
Claysville	_____	97	10.03	"	
Parkersburg	_____arrive	104	10.20	"	

(To be used only on the 2d June.)

The regular Passenger and Freight Trains, East and West, will be run as usual upon this day. . . .

Clarksburg, Va., twenty-two miles from Grafton, prettily located in a more open country, is the centre of a grazing district, from which Baltimore obtains a considerable instalment of her finest beef. It is the county town of Harrison, one of the richest portions of the State. Here we were greeted by a large and good-looking collection of the natives, of both sexes. An immense business is done on the line of the road in staves, of which we saw enough apparently to barrel the Mississippi,—or, if that figure is not strong enough—coop up all the whiskey which floats down the "father of waters" and its tributaries. The country traversed by the road is exceedingly rich in minerals. Of coal its supplies are inexhaustible. . . .

[Parkersburg] presents on every side abundant evidence of vigorous growth and extraordinary prosperity. During the last year an excellent hotel—the "Swann House"—has been erected. The building is of brick, contains forty chambers, can accommodate about one hundred persons, and is doing a flourishing business. The town contains also six modern-built church edifices, occupied by as many different denominations. It also boasts a sound bank, two daily papers—the Gazette and News, —a number of steam flour and saw mills, and several manufactories. One of the latter, a wooden ware establishment, uses up every particle of wood brought within its walls, turning out every thing in the shape of wooden ware. from a whiskey barrel to a match box.—W. Prescott Smith, *The Book of the Great Railway Celebrations of 1857*, pp. 164-67.

61. Charles Ellet, Jr., Proposes Meadow River Reservoir

The great American engineer, Charles Ellet (1810-1862), was assistant engineer of the Chesapeake and Ohio Canal Company, chief engineer of the James River and Kanawha Canal Company (1836-1839), builder of the suspension bridge over the Ohio River at Wheeling, and one of the most enthusiastic promoters of Virginia's inland waterways. The feasibility of his proposal for controlling floods by impounding surplus water in upland dams has been amply demonstrated in West Virginia in recent years. The salient points of his scheme, presented in 1858, may be seen in the following excerpts from his recommendations for a Meadow River reservoir in the area of Big Sewell Mountain and Laurel Mountain.

To ENABLE WELL LOADED COAL BOATS to descend the river with regularity and certainty, we must secure a depth of not less than *six feet* at all seasons of the year—if not all the time, as would be preferable, at least at stated periods, occurring frequently enough to satisfy the actual necessities of the trade.

To accomplish this purpose, I propose to secure water enough in artificial reservoirs, on the tributaries of the Kanawha, to maintain a depth of 4 feet *permanently* in the channels; *and then, by greater discharges of this reserved water, to produce a flood of two feet, on top of the permanent depth of 4 feet, once in every seven or every ten days, so that fleets of colliers drawing 5½ feet of water, may be dispatched that often down the Kanawha*. . . .

These first results I propose to attain by the construction of a single reservoir, on one of the small tributaries of the river, at a site where a dam of moderate height will convert a large natural meadow or swamp into a considerable mountain lake. . . .

Within the space inclosed by several of these mountains, viz., the Big Sewell, Little Sewell, Laurel Mountain, Meadow Mountain, the Cold Knob, Keeney's Knob, &c., are found the "meadows" of Meadow River, one of the principal tributaries of the Gauley. . . .

I propose to convert this entire area into an artificial lake, by forming a mound of earth, or a stone dam, across its outlet. This dam will be 68 feet high from the low water surface of the river to the bottom of the waste for the discharge of the surplus water.

The length of the mound will be 140 feet at the bottom, where the banks of the river draw near together, and 875 feet at the surface of the lake—68 feet above the river.

The length of the lake thus formed will be 21 4/10 miles. It will cover an area of 10,800 acres or 16 9/10 square miles. . . .

This great basin will hold no less than 13,587,815,000 cubic feet of water. It will receive the drainage from 209 2/10 square miles of territory, the whole of which, exclusive of the meadows which will form the bottom of the lake, is composed of steep, and, to a considerable extent, very elevated mountains, from the slopes of which the rains and melted snows will descend rapidly into the reservoir. . . .

The [Meadows] dam will either be a stone wall or a mound of earth, depending on the character of the foundation, which is believed, though not positively ascertained, to be a sandstone rock. Large detached masses of sandstone cover the slopes of the mountain and the bed of the river, which cannot be satisfactorily examined without their removal. There can scarcely be a doubt, however, that the bottom of the channel, immediately under these loose masses, is solid rock, in place. . . .

If the dam is formed of earth, its width at the level of the surface of the water will be 100 feet; and at the foundation over 300 feet.

Fifty feet of the width of the mound, at top, will be reserved for mill seats, leaving space for a landing and road way, 34 feet wide, between the edge of the lake and the front of the mills. If formed of earth, the top of the bank will be raised about 5 feet above the bottom of the waste.

The mills of this dam will be supplied from the lake by pipes passing through the mound, below the lowest level to which the water will be reduced. The loss of water which will be caused by its application for milling purposes, will be too small to be worthy of any consideration here. When there is a small surplus, as there may sometimes be, unless the dam is raised somewhat higher, it will be just as well to allow the water to be used in driving machinery as to run to waste; and when there is a deficiency, and water must be furnished to the rivers below, for the benefit of their navigation, it is just as well to let it do service on its passage, as to flow away idly into the streams to be supplied. . . .

But, I am not yet quite prepared to decide whether it would be best, in this position, to construct a mound of earth, or a dam of solid masonry. That question should be reserved until the site is cleared of all superincumbent material, and the character of the foundation clearly ascertained. This question is not merely one of economy, but of safety. A mound of the most ample dimensions will be much cheaper than a wall; but it can only be safely adopted where a perfectly reliable connection can be formed with the natural bottom. . . .

ESTIMATE OF THE COST OF THE DAM, IF RAISED 68 FEET ABOVE LOW WATER IN MEADOW RIVER

Preparation of the foundations—assumed to be the removal of 2500 cubic yards of loose rock, at $0.40 ___ $	1,000
35,000 cubic yards of plain masonry, laid in hydraulic cement, at $5.00 _____	175,000
21 wickets, at $500 each _____	10,500
800 lineal feet of cut coping, 7 feet wide, at $5.00 _____	4,000
Probable cost of the dam _____	$190,500
Add for contingencies _____	25,000
Total estimated cost _____	$215,500

The damages which will be occasioned by this work are difficult to estimate.... The *average* value of the uncultivated and untamed meadows, may be set down at $5 an acre, and that of the cultivated portions, with one or two exceptions, where the soil is capable of easy drainage, and the improvements are better, at about $17 an acre. I shall estimate both these items, however, somewhat higher; adding something for the increased value which this property will acquire, in consideration of its adaptation to the purpose in view....

ESTIMATE OF DAMAGES

8500 acres, uncultivated, at $7.00	$ 59,500
1800 ” cultivated, at $20,000	36,000
500 ” ” at $50.00	25,000
Cost of new turnpike, &c.,	5,000
Cost of altering three small mills on Meadow River below the dam	3,000
	$128,500
Add for contingencies, 20 per cent	25,700
	$154,200
Total estimated damages	$154,200
Estimated cost of the dam	215,500
Estimated cost of Meadow Lake	$369,700

HEALTH, AS AFFECTED BY THE RESERVOIRS ...

It must be understood that the lakes which I propose are not shallow collections of stagnant water; but masses of pure, fresh water, to be annually supplied and annually changed. Many of them, like Meadow Lake, will be placed high up in the mountains, where they will occupy glades now subject to frequent overflows, which, after barely covering a dense vegetation, subside and leave the moistened grass and weeds exposed to the sun. The lakes which I propose will substitute a permanent mass of deep water for these occasional inundations....

The dense growth of timber and underbrush which now covers a great portion of the meadows, will be much in the way of the steamboats which will be used on the lake, and care must therefore be taken gradually to remove it....

The water of the Ohio, in the dry summers, is now for many weeks stagnant in the pools. Along its course of a thousand miles, many cities and large manufacturing towns have grown up, and are rapidly increasing in population, and, consequently, pouring an increased volume of filth into the stagnant river. ... The river itself is the common receptacle of all the contents of the sewers and gutters, and other disgusting products of all the cities on its banks.

It is from the river, thus polluted, that the people of the Ohio Valley now derive their supply of water for domestic uses. It is scarcely to be doubted that the day is not distant, when these great and increasing cities will be driven to the necessity of purifying this tainted water, for the preservation of the health of their citizens. ... —Charles Ellet, Jr., *Report on the Improvement of the Kanawha ... by Means of Artificial Lakes*, pp. 17-76.

62. The Springs of Virginia

The mineral springs of western Virginia attracted men and women in search of diversion, as well as hypochondriacs and invalids. Warm Springs, or Bath, as Berkeley Springs was once called, enjoyed considerable popularity even before the Revolution. In August, 1761, George Washington wrote that there were about two hundred people at Warm Springs "full of all manner of diseases and complaints," and two or three doctors who probably came to take the waters rather than to practice their profession. Food was plentiful, but lodgings were so inadequate that Washington was thankful that he had brought a tent and a marquee from Winchester. Although the road to the Springs was bad and it was predicted that the waters would "soon begin to lose their virtues," the number of visitors to the spa increased year by year, accommodations improved, a playhouse was built, and social life became so "gay and idle," that Bishop Asbury referred to Bath as "that seat of sin."

By the middle of the nineteenth century the spas of Virginia offered comfortable, even genteel, accommodations for an increasingly large, and cosmopolitan clientele. White Sulphur

Springs in Greenbrier County, the most fashionable of them all, survived the impact of social change to become one of the most beautiful and famous resorts in the United States. The following accounts of Berkeley Springs, Red Sulphur Springs, and White Sulphur Springs explain the popularity of the Virginia spas.

AUGUST 31 [1775]

WARM SPRINGS [Berkeley Springs] by 4 Evening. Met with Col Calendir on the Way. Back-Creek Swimming high. Cloudy sloppy Day.

Huge Stone tumbled from the Mountain directly to the Drinking-Spring.

Fray between Mr. Fleming & Mr. Hall concerning an Account. Mr. Hall wrung Mr. Fleming's Nose. I took Lodging at Mrs. Baker's. Mr. Miller, an aged, Rheumatic Invalid taken ill in the Bath.

SEPTEMBER 1775
FRYDAY SEPT: 1

Drank early & freely of the Waters. About four Hundred now present. Near one Half of these visibly indisposed. Many in sore Distress. I made several new Acquaintances. Col: Lewis of Fredericksburgh; Dr. Holmes, Mr. Finley, & Mr. Williamson of Alexandria—Mr. Blain of Maryland; Mr. Washington, Major Willis, Morrow. I met also with some old ones: Capt Blackwell; George Lewis an old fellow Student; Mr. Parks; Mr. Stephens, & Mrs. Mitchell of this Colony. Parson Allen of Frederick in Maryland left Bath this Morning. It is said he has been mobbed by the Ladies. Tickets going about for a Ball this Evening. Parson Wilmore said to be the verriest *Buck* in Town. With Col: Callendir, Dr. Holmes, Mr. Blain, Finley, Morry & Hunter, walked over the Mountain to the Cold Spring. Spoke here with Miss Slemons, white, feeble, weak Maid. Mr. Diggs of York in this Government the Picture of Decrepitude.

EVENING

In one Part of the little bush Village a splendid Ball—At some Distance, & within hearing, a Methodist Preacher was haranguing the People. Frequent Writings on the Plates, &c—In

our dining Room Companies at Cards. Five & forty, Whist, Alfours, Callico-Betty &c. I walked out among the Bushes here also was—Amusements in all Shapes, & in high Degrees, are constantly taking Place among so promiscuous Company. The Observation, when on the Spot, to see it in real Life. I can picture it out but sadly, is curious & improving.

Mr. Biddle one of the Delegates for the Province of Penn. in the Con. Congress is here & much disordered with the Rheumatism.

SATURDAY SEPT. 2

From twelve to four this Morning soft & continual Serenades at different Houses where the Ladies lodge. Several of the Company, among many the Parson, were hearty. Miss ———— said to be possess'd of an Estate in Maryland of ten thousand Pounds is accused by the Bloods as imperious & haughty. An Accusation against one—for breaking, in the Warmth of his Heart, through the Loge & entering the Lodging Room of buxom Kate—Unfortunate Scot, he was led to this immediately stimulated by a plentiful Use of these Vigor-giving Waters— He came to recruit his exhausted System. He was urged—he was compell'd, by the irresistable Call of renewed Nature.

But breaking Houses is breaking the Peace,—And, salacious Caledonian, if it be made appear that you broke last Night into buxom Kate's House, & then & there was *unable* to make her *full* Satisfaction, for such Conduct—It were as well you had been in the Bushes too—!—*Philip Vickers Fithian: Journal, 1775-1776,* edited by Robert G. Albion, pp. 123-27. By permission.

RED SULPHUR SPRINGS, . . . These celebrated waters are situated in lat. 37° 30' 25" N., long. 3° 14' 50" W. from Washington. . . . They receive their name from a deposite of a rich crimson color. This deposite rests on another of white, and is itself of a gelatinous consistence. The water issues from various fissures, in a stratum of soft slate stone, within a space of about 24 by 8 ft. Heretofore, they were but partially collected, three-fourths having been permitted to waste; but the present proprietor having, in the autumn of 1833, opened the native stone, and obtained a vast increase in the quantity, has collected them in two fountains of white marble. The temperature of the water is preceisely 54 deg. of Fahr.; it is peculiarly pleasant, though so strongly impregnated with sulphuretted hydrogen. Hundreds of persons now living can bear testimony to its extraordinary effects in the cure of pulmonary disease: it is therefore superfluous to offer farther evidence of its value in checking that frightful enemy of mankind. . . . It remains that we should notice its effects in other diseases, and here we must express our astonishment, that physicians have turned to so little account the knowledge of its powers in pulmonary complaints, and in the reduction of arterial action. . . .

The writer hazards the opinion that it will be found no less efficacious, in calming nervous irritability, than in reducing arterial action. He has experienced this effect in his own person, and has witnessed it in others. . . .

That these waters are most singularly efficacious in *uterine* diseases, and restoring the health of delicate females is a fact too well established, to admit of controversy, and one which we deem it peculiarly important, should be known, as these are probably the only mineral waters in Virginia that are suited to such cases.

The writer is of opinion, that the *tonic* property of these waters is *consequent* on their sedative property.—They do not belong to the ordinary class of tonics; they do indeed, invigorate the stomach in a remarkable manner—a fact which is clearly proved by the rapid increase of weight, many persons gaining from one to two pounds a day for several successive days; but whilst they effect this, they are most usually producing one or two evacuations a day, and acting freely on the kidneys and skin. From what has been said, it may be perceived that we believe the water to be *directly sedative, indirectly tonic, alterative, diuretic* and *diaphoretic.*

It has been found efficacious in all forms of consumption, scrofula, jaundice and other bilious affections, chronic dysentery and diarrhea, dyspepsia, diseases of the uterus, chronic rheumatism and gout, dropsy, gravel, neuralgia, tremor, syphilis, scurvy, crysipetas, tetter, ring-worm and itch; and it has long been celebrated as a vermifuge. That there are many other diseases, to which its medicinal properties are applicable, there can be little doubt, and we can state one fact highly important, which is, that we have never known it to do a positive injury. If the patient has gone away in a worse condition, it is because the disease had progressed so far as to be incurable, or the failure may be clearly traced to some imprudence on his own part. . . . The writer has had some experience in the use of the Red Sulphur water, and does not hesitate to say, that in his opinion, its efficacy is impeded by *all stimulants*. Ardent spirits, strong coffee, strong tea, meat diet, especially at night, should be avoided. The patient should live on a strictly vegetable diet. Milk, maple molasses, cold bread, buckwheat cakes, rice, rye mush, bread-pudding, stewed peaches and various other articles of a similar character are best suited to the action of the water. These combined with its judicious use, moderate exercise, and a calm mind, afford the best prospect of a cure. . . . It is highly important to invalids to lay aside the use of all medicines if possible, but more particularly the use of opium. The latter interferes very much with the action of the water. . . . —Joseph Martin, *A New and Comprehensive Gazetteer of Virginia . . .* , pp. 393-95.

THE WHITE SULPHUR SPRING is in the county of Greenbriar, western Virginia, embosomed in a beautiful valley, where the mountains recede on a sudden, forming at first an irregular opening, which at a little distance widens into an extensive plain. The main road runs directly through the valley, passing on one side the enclosure containing the spring and the principal improvements; then crossing the longs meadows and finally losing itself in the shade of the mountain at the further end.

When we arrived at the springs, the company were going to dinner, and all the walks and avenues leading from the different cabins were streaming with lively forms. A band of music was playing gaily in the portico of the dining hall; and the whole face of things had the look of enchantment. . . .

The grounds are laid out very prettily with gravel walks intersecting the green lawns, and the area is bordered on all sides by rows of neat cabins, some of them of a very attractive appearance. The whole looks like a well laid out little town. . . .

On the front square stands a large frame building containing the dining room, the public room, and the offices. A portico runs the whole length of this edifice, forming a fine promenade in wet weather. Near to this in a similar building is the ball room, with lodging apartments above.

Immediately in front of these, on the acclivity of the hill, which overlooks the plain, and sweeping round before you, is Alabama Row, which extends as far as the large centre building, where it is joined by Paradise Row, which has a similar range. The cabins which form these ranges are all built of brick, with little piazzas in front. Carolina Row, fronts the walk, from the spring, beyond which are, Baltimore—Virginia—and Georgia Rows. There are besides many beautiful cabins on various parts of the premises, which are reserved for private families, who spend their summers here.

A new row of six ornamental veranda cottages has lately been erected on a line with Paradise Row, and four large brick buildings on the hill beyond, the latter being occupied by Carolineans. The accommodations are at present sufficient for six hundred persons. A large hotel is about being erected in the course of another year, which will accommodate several hundred more. At present each family or party reside in a separate cabin, being lords of their own castles for the time being, which is perhaps the most preferable mode of living.

The noble fountain is immediately in front of Spring Row, and can be seen from any part of the square. It is ornamented by a handsome dome, supported by twelve pillars, which is surmounted by a statue representing Hygeia. There are circular seats beneath, and the area is roomy enough for near one hundred persons seated and standing.

The water flows in an octagonical basin about three feet and a half in depth, and gushes from an aperture in the white rocks, which line the sides of the reservoir. It sparkles in the glass like liquid crystal, and it gives the frame of the invalid new vigor at every draught. . . .

Such a place as the White Sulphur so well fashioned and provided for by nature, cannot fail to become, in a very few years, the resort of thousands of persons, in search of health, and the head quarters of fashion, when the first people of the land will gather from all quarters, and meet to reciprocate mutual good feelings. In less than forty months from the present time, it may be predicted, a railroad will sweep by, within a short distance of the Warm Spring Mountain, and the inhabitants of Union, will find it but three days travel to New York, which less than twenty years since, was the journey of a month.

The receipts at these springs are now very large, but the expenses are great. A considerable amount is annually appropriated for improvements, and by the summer of 1840, when the projected ones shall be completed, there will be accommodations for more than twelve hundred persons.

There is one great comfort here, in the good bedding and clean white sheets, not always to be had at watering places. The cabins are neat, small, but comfortable, generally having two rooms, many of them four. . . .

It is now the middle of August, [1838] and the White Sulphur and the whole neighbourhood is thronging with company. . . .

The opening of the mail—a scramble for letters and papers—expectation on tiptoe for the news—arrival of the Great Western—fourteen days from Liverpool—coronation of Queen Victoria—Washington deserted—President at the springs, and the citizens at Piney Point. . . .

The president of the United States is here, [Martin Van Buren] and many other distinguished persons. Ladies of fashion and belles from the principal cities—foreign ministers—members of the cabinet, senators—and representatives, prominent judges—officers of the army and navy, and polished private gentlemen, all combining to make the present company, as elegant and select as any party ever assembled at a watering place.

There is great attraction at the ball-room at present, and it is brilliantly attended every evening by the light and gay hearted. . . . —Mark Pencil, *The White Sulphur Papers* . . . , pp. 23-40.

VII. Sectionalism and Slavery–From Argument to Violence

63. The Constitutional Convention of 1829-1830

Sectionalism, the basic cause of the dismemberment of Virginia during the Civil War, became alarmingly evident in the forensic outburst at the Virginia Constitutional Convention of 1829-1830, held in Richmond. The convention included in its membership two venerable Ex-Presidents of the United States, James Madison and James Monroe, Chief Justice John Marshall, and a distinguished representation of younger men, among them John Tyler. The outstanding figures from western Virginia were Philip Doddridge and Alexander Campbell of Brooke County, both of whom were leaders of the reform bloc. Charles S. Morgan of Monongalia County and Lewis Summers of Kanawha also ably supported the cause of reform. The main issues before the convention concerned suffrage and representation: the reformers favored white manhood suffrage and apportionment of representation based upon white population; the conservatives defended freehold qualification for voting and advocated apportionment upon white population and taxation combined. On these, as well as on less controversial points the conservatives, led by Benjamin W. Leigh, were victorious. Instead of adopting a basis for representation, the convention approved a plan which gave to the counties west of the Blue Ridge fifty-six delegates in the House and thirteen in the Senate and to the eastern counties seventy-eight in the House and nineteen in the Senate. It also provided that after 1841 and at intervals thereafter of not less than ten years, the General Assembly, with the concurrence of two-thirds of each house, should have authority to make reapportionments of delegates and senators, with the number of the former not to exceed one hundred and fifty, and of the latter, thirty-six. Although voting privilege was extended to include lease holders and house-keepers, more than thirty thousand men were still excluded from the polls. In the referendum on the constitution 26,055 votes were cast in favor of ratification and 15,563 against. Brooke County proudly registered unanimous rejection. Dismayed by the outcome of the Convention, the west threatened dismemberment as the only recourse left to the Trans-Allegheny for obtaining political and economic relief.

The following selections are from the convention addresses delivered by Philip Doddridge, Alexander Campbell, and Charles S. Morgan.

[MR. DODDRIDGE:] The greatest grievance proposed to be remedied, is the inequality in the representation, and this especially in the House of Delegates; the next, in point of magnitude and general concern, is the freehold restriction on the electoral franchise. The latter of these will claim more particular attention, when the third resolution of the Legislative Committee shall come under consideration. As to the first, the distribution of representation, as conferred by the Royal charter of Government, may have been tolerably fair and equal at the date of that charter. There were then but few counties or settlements, perhaps not more than six or seven, in the Colony. They were all contiguous; they had but one interest, and but one pursuit, which was agricultural. Each county had its frontier. When war existed on the border, it affected all; when peace reigned, all enjoyed it alike. In the process of time, this state of things became materially changed. When the settlements extended far from the Capital, owing to the unprotected state of the country, and the sparseness of population, frontier counties were exposed to almost continual wars, while the interior enjoyed the blessings of profound peace. With few, and but short intervals, this state of things continued until Wayne's victory. Whatever may have been the justness, or equality of representation, at the beginning of the Royal Government, great changes were made before the Revolution. Around Williamsburg, the seat of Government, counties and settlements were sub-divided into small precincts, to each of which a representation of two members in the House of Burgesses was allowed, while no more was allowed to the large counties farther removed from the influence of Executive favor, and to those on the frontier. No more, indeed, was allowed to all West Augusta. Hence, if we look at the map, we will perceive representation distributed in double, treble, or even quadruple proportions round Williamsburg; and this representation grew up to be so unequal, and the consequent evils so intolerable, as no longer to be borne with. In consequence, public opinion, in 1816, was brought to bear on the Senate, and in the session which commenced in that year, representation in that body, was distributed and apportioned on the basis of white population. I mention this fact now, in order to meet and refute a positive assertion, here and elsewhere, that the proposition to equalize representation on the basis of white population, is a new, cruel, and unheard of innovation!

Since the year 1790, scarcely one session passed, in which petitions were not received in the General Assembly, praying for a reform of abuses in this particular, and in the law of suffrage. From the counties of Patrick and Henry, these petitions were as regularly looked for as the commencement of the session. In 1815, a bill was brought into the House of Delegates, for making a new arrangement of the counties in districts, for the choice of Senators, on this very abused white basis. At that time two-fifths of the free white population, were represented by *four* Senators, while the other three-fifths had *twenty*. This inequality was sensibly felt by those of our citizens who lived west of the Blue Ridge; and it is impossible for any gentleman to resist the conviction, that from that inequality, there must have resulted much misrule and practical evil. Every exertion was made, by western members, to pass that bill. Every effort, however, failed. The bill was nailed to the table after the second reading, and although motions were repeatedly made to take it up for consideration, they were scornfully rejected, by a silent vote.

At this time, 1815, there was not, in the House, one eastern constitutional lawyer, who did not maintain that no Legislative act could change the districts. They argued, that the same power that made the Constitution, had ordained the districts, and that they were as sacred as the Constitution itself, and could only be altered by a general Convention of the people.

One of the natural consequences of this doctrine was, that large assemblage of distinguished men, commonly called the Staunton Convention of 1816. That body addressed to the General Assembly, of 1816, an able memorial, praying for the passage of a law, to take the sense of the people on calling a Convention. Numerous petitions were, at the same time, received from various quarters of the State, on the same subject, and uniting in the same prayer. All who felt deeply aggrieved by the unjust rule of apportionment, looked forward to such a law, and to a Convention, as the only means of redress. All demanded that basis which we now demand. . . .

In 1790, the whole white population east of the Blue Ridge, was 314,523, and the whole population west, 127,594; 1800, east of the Ridge, 336,389, and west, 177,476; 1810, east of the Ridge 338,837, and west 212,726; 1820, east of the Ridge 348,873, and west 254,308; 1829, by estimate, east 362,745, and west 319,516.

The balance of white population in 1790, in favor of the east was 185,932; in 1800, 159,903; in 1810, 126,114; in 1820, 94,965; and by estimate in 1829, 43,229. . . .

. . . The doubt is as to that majority which the Bill of Rights declares have the power to alter or amend the Constitution: whether the majority there spoken of, is composed of men, or of men and wealth. Surely the Declaration of Rights means numbers alone: that is the plain English of the text, which might be safely left to the decision of any man or woman, having a common knowledge of our mother tongue. Local interests, and slave property, existed in 1776, as well as now. These interests and localities bore the same relations and ratios to each other as now, yet they are neither alluded to nor provided for by the Bill of Rights or Constitution. Had it been intended to take property into the scale of representation, this silence could not have been observed. This brings me to the conclusion, that slaves were not regarded in 1776 as an element of society, but merely as property. The Convention of that day, left representation where they found it; based on the freehold qualification, just as it had been based in the Colony, when there was scarcely a slave in it. . . .

I will now call the attention of the Committee to the state of our representation in this body. We have been elected here by a ratio marked by injustice. The Senatorial apportionment of 1816 was founded on the Census of 1810, which was unequal, to be sure; but that was then the last enumeration to which we could refer. In this body, we are apportioned by the same Census of 1816, although that of 1820 was in being, and could have been resorted to. For this injustice, no reason was, or ever will be assigned, except that those who practiced it, had the power to do so. This measure was a poor expedient for appeasing a discontented people. By it, the west were deprived of more than four members on this floor. By the Census of 1820, we were entitled to 40 293-603 members, instead of 36, and by the present population to 42 229-682. Yet, notwithstanding this injustice, I hope the cause of the people will triumph. The majority here may be small indeed, but I hope they will represent at least two-thirds of the inhabitants of the whole State. . . . —*Proceedings and Debates of the Virginia State Convention of 1829-30*, pp. 80-89.

Mr. CAMPBELL (of Brooke,) then addressed the Chair, in nearly the following terms:

. . . When I rise to address an assemblage composed of such illustrious patriarchs, sages and politicians; . . . I cannot but feel embarrassed and intimidated. But, Sir, this embarrassment arises most of all, from the fears which I entertain, that I may not be able to do justice to the cause which reason and conscience have compelled me to espouse. . . . But I am compelled to contribute my mite; and well, I am assured, that it will be a very small contribution indeed.

I am a *man*, Sir, and as such I cannot but feel interested in every thing which concerns the prosperity and happiness of man.

. . . I am not, Sir, believe me, under the influence of district or local feelings. In all matters to be discussed here, I am a Virginian. I feel myself inspired with that spirit, which regards the interest of every man, slave-holder or non-slave-holder in the State. If I lived in Northampton, I would advocate the same principles which I now do in coming from Brooke. It was *principles,* Mr. Chairman, which brought me here. *Principles, Sir,* which reason, observation and experience convinced me, are inseparably connected with the temporal prosperity of men; and of our State of Virginia: And principles, Sir, which are not to be sacrificed. I know, Sir, that local interests, and district feelings, can only yield to principles. Animosities and contention must arise between rival interests, unless fellow-citizens are determined to be governed by principles. . . .

But, Sir, it is not the increase of population in the west which this gentleman [from Culpeper] ought to fear. It is the energy which the mountain breeze and western habits impart to these emigrants. They are regenerated; politically, I mean, Sir. They soon become *working politicians;* and the difference, Sir, between a *talking* and a *working* politician, is immense. The Old Dominion has long been celebrated for producing great orators; the ablest metaphysicians in policy; men that can split hairs in all abstruse questions of political economy. But at home, or when they return from Congress, they have negroes to fan them asleep. But a Pennsylvania, a New-York, a Ohio, or a western Virginia Statesman, though far inferior in logic, metaphysics, and rhetoric, to an old Virginia Statesman, has this advantage, that when he returns home, he takes off his coat, and takes hold of the plough. This gives him bone and muscle, Sir, and preserves his Republican principles pure and uncontaminated. . . .

This gentleman [from Northampton] starts with the postulate, that there are two sorts of majorities; on numbers and interests; in plain English, of men and money. I do not well understand, why he ought not to have added, also, majorities of talent, physical strength, scientific skill, and general literature. These are all more valuable than money, and as useful to the State. A Robert Fulton, a General Jackson, a Joseph Lancaster, a Benjamin Franklin, are as useful to the State, as a whole district of mere slave-holders. Now, all the logic, metaphysics and rhetoric of this Assembly, must be put in requisition to shew, why a citizen, having a hundred negroes, should have ten times more political power than a Joseph Lancaster, or a Robert Fulton, with only a house and garden. And if scientific skill, physical strength, military prowess, or general literature, in some individuals, is entitled to so much respect, why ought not those majorities in a community to have as much weight as mere wealth? . . .

I have been sorry, very sorry, Sir, to observe in sundry gentlemen on this floor, a disposition to treat us as aliens, or as persons, who have no *common interest* with the people of the east. We have given them no reason to suspect our want of fellow-feeling, or of common interest. Let gentlemen but reflect upon the circumstances of this State in the year 1814. When all the militia east of the Blue Ridge were employed, or chiefly employed in patrolling the counties on the seaboard, and generally east of the Ridge, in order to preserve that property for which a guarantee is now demanded: I say, when your militia, Mr. Chairman, were all needed to prevent insurrections amongst your own discontented population, who was it that fled to your succour and protection from an invading enemy, who were disposed to harrass your seaboard, and to augment the discontents of your slaves? The Valley and the west volunteered their aid. Yes, Sir, the single county of Shenandoah gave you twelve hundred men to fight your battles, or rather, the battles of their own State. They made a common cause with you. And, Sir, the bones of many a gallant and brave citizen of the west, lie in the sands of Norfolk. Men, too, who had no suffrage, no representation in your government, sacrificed not their property only, but **their** lives also, in your defence. . . . Yes, Sir, from the very shores of the Ohio, from my own county of Brooke, they marched to your succour, and hazarded their all, their earthly all, in defence of that very country, and that very Government, which treated many of them as aliens of the land of their nativity.

We have been told that nearly 3-4ths of the tax has been paid by the counties east of the Blue Ridge. But these gentlemen tell us nothing about who fight the battles of the country. But, Sir, the disproportion between the east and the west, in the taxpaying department, will every day diminish. As the west increases in population and improvement, its ability to pay will increase, and its property will increase in value.

It were endless, Sir, to notice the many objections made against the surrender of power, or rather, the arguments offered, to retain a power already assumed and possessed. I will only remark, that it is said, that if the *white basis* should obtain, there will be endless discontentment among many of the citizens of this Commonwealth. But, Sir, if the *black basis*, or the *money basis*, as it should be called, should obtain, would it diminish, or terminate discontentment or complaint? No, Sir; in that case, a majority, a large majority of the freeholders, would be irreconcileably discontended. And, Sir, if discontents, murmurs and complaints must, on any hypothesis, exist, the question is, whether in policy and in justice, they had not better be confined to the minority, than spread through a majority of the citizens of this Commonwealth; . . . —*Proceedings and Debates of the Virginia State Convention of 1829-30*, pp. 116-24.

MR. MORGAN OF MONONGALIA, then rose and addressed the Committee as follows: . . .

The number of freehold-voters in the State, may be estimated at 45,000, and not more. I shall consider them as of that number. From the free white population of 1820, and the hypothetical increase since that time, there are now in the State more than 140,000 free white male citizens over 21 years of age. Deduct from this number the voters, and you find 95,000 free white men excluded from the polls. But, Sir, deduct from this last number, 5, 10, or if you please, 15,000 for paupers and others who ought to be excluded, and you still have 80,000; leaving the Government in the hands of little more than one third of the people. I am then justified in saying that the Government is in the hands of the few; that it is held and exercised by that few, who hold it by virtue of their freehold estates. I ask you, now Sir, if our Government be not to some extent aristocratical in its form? It is so considered by some men of great wisdom, and I believe generally by the people of the other States of this Union. . . .

When I use this argument to prove the aristocratical principles of our Government, I do it with due respect to the opinions of all the members of this body, and also, with due respect to the freeholders who sent me here; whose opinions and interests I wish to represent. But, Sir, from these facts, I must contend that the Right of Suffrage ought greatly to be extended. The freehold

Suffrage is contrary to the genius of our people; and I may well say, contrary to the genius of the people of all these United States. Is it not unwise to contend for a principle so much opposed to the will of the great body of the people? . . .

A few days ago we were told that wealth and political power could not be divorced; that capital and labour could not be separated; and that labour must be represented. Yes, Sir, on the present occasion, we find that labour is only to be represented by the votes of *freehold-labourers;* and the whole power of the Government is to be placed at the control of the capital of the country, if possible. It is not for me, however, to reconcile these inconsistencies in gentlemen's arguments. I hesitate not to say, that those sixty or eighty thousand persons, to whom it is proposed to extend the Right of Suffrage, constitute the great mass of actual productive labourers of the State. Mr. Chairman, I believe it cannot be otherwise.

We have been told that we shall have a war of the poor against the rich, and that the right of property will be destroyed, if the amendment be adopted. It is not so, and no man can or ought to believe it. If the people of the East, West or South, have given us examples worthy of our imitation, we can fear no such thing. There has been no instance of war upon property in any of our sister States. It is just as secure in them as in Virginia. . . .

It has been argued, that General Suffrage has a tendency to bring together the rich and the poor, and that the one will have means, and be able to buy up the other, to the prejudice of the liberty of the people. This argument always comes from those who advocate the power of the few over the many. Yes, Sir, from the real aristocracy of the country. It is an argument to be found in nearly all the treatises of theoretical writers, who support aristocracies. The object is to alarm the people with fear that the poor will be bought, and made engines of their own ruin. It is only for purposes of alarm, and is not true. If the Constitution shall require of electors, the payment of a small tax just before elections, there will be a possibility of an improper influence, if there can be candidates corrupt enough to buy, having the means to buy, and voters base enough to sell their votes. But I know of no case of corruption, in any of the States, having such a qualification. Cases of mere suspicion, perhaps, have occurred. If the payment of taxes be made a qualification, they ought not to be required immediately before the election, but some one or two years preceding, at a time when they cannot be paid with a view of any particular election. But, Sir, I would not tax a man merely to qualify him to vote, although it may be proper, in this way, to require a man justly and honestly to pay the public demands. All free men ought to vote, because they are free men. Then they will act independently. Such men can never be purchased by the cash of candidates, or the power of demagogues. No, the poor will be as independent in their opinions, as the greatest land-holders of the State.—*Proceedings and Debates of the Virginia State Convention of 1829-30*, pp. 377-82.

64. The Ruffner Pamphlet (1847)

Henry Ruffner, minister, educator, missionary, and author, was born in Page County, Virginia, January 16, 1790. In the fall of 1796 he moved to the Kanawha Valley, where his father, David Ruffner, engaged in the production of salt. Ruffner's formal education began at the classical academy in Lewisburg established by the eminent Dr. John McElhenney and continued at Washington College (now Washington and Lee University) which granted him the A. B. degree in 1813. After a year of theological study followed by travel in the United States, Ruffner was licensed to preach, and in 1818 was ordained a minister by the Lexington Presbytery. During Ruffner's first brief, but fruitful ministry in the Kanawha region, he organized two churches—one in Charleston and one in Teay's Valley, did extensive missionary work, and directed the newly-established Mercer Academy in Charleston. From 1819 to 1848 Ruffner was at Washington College, first as professor of ancient languages, then as president of the institution. In 1838 Princeton conferred on him the degree of D. D. and in 1849 Washington College awarded him the LL. D. On his return to the Kanawha Valley, Ruffner took charge of the church established by his father at

Malden, farmed, made political addresses, and continued his varied literary pursuits. He died at Malden, December 17, 1861.

The famous address which Henry Ruffner made before the Franklin Society in Lexington, Virginia, in 1847, exemplified the moderate, though generally disapproving attitude of western Virginians toward slavery. Ruffner had as little use for the abolitionists with their "fanatical violence" as for the "nullifiers" who were threatening the dissolution of the Union. The originality of Ruffner's proposal for gradual emancipation of slavery in "West Virginia" lay in his contention that a state, in this case Virginia, like the United States, could live peaceably part slave and part free. "An amendment of the constitution," he argued, "could easily provide for the security of slaveholders in East Virginia against all unjust legislation, arising from the power of the anti-slavery principles of the West." In pleading for the end of slavery in western Virginia, Ruffner also called attention to grievances which intensified sectionalism in this area.

... Now it is admitted on all hands, that slave labor is better adapted to agriculture, than to any other branch of industry; and that, if not good for agriculture, it is really good for nothing.

Therefore, since in agriculture, slave labor is proved to be far less productive than free labor,—*slavery is demonstrated to be not only unprofitable, but deeply injurious to the public prosperity.*

We do not mean that slave labor can never earn any thing for him that employs it. The question is between free labor and slave labor. He that chooses to employ a sort of labor, that yields only half as much to the hand as another sort would yield, makes a choice that is not only unprofitable, but deeply injurious to his interest.

Agriculture in the slave States may be characterized in general by two epithets—*extensive—exhaustive*—which in all agricultural countries forebode two things—*impoverishment—depopulation.* The general system of slaveholding farmers and planters, in all times and places, has been, and now is, and ever will be, to cultivate much land, badly, for present gain—in short, to kill the goose that lays the golden egg. They cannot do otherwise with laborers who work by compulsion, for the benefit only of their masters; and whose sole interest in the matter is, to do as little and to consume as much as possible....

Of all the States in this Union, not one has on the whole such various and abundant resources for manufacturing, as our own Virginia, both East and West. Only think of her vast forests of timber, her mountains of iron, her regions of stone coal, her valleys of limestone and marble, her fountains of salt, her immense sheepwalks for wool, her vicinity to the cotton fields, her innumerable waterfalls, her bays, harbors and rivers for circulating products on every side;—in short every material and every convenience necessary for manufacturing industry....

...What must you think has caused Virginians in general to neglect their superlative advantages for manufacturing industry?—to disregard the evident suggestions of nature, pointing out to them this fruitful source of population, wealth and comfort?

Say not that this State of things is chargeable to the *apathy* of Virginians. That is nothing to the purpose, for it does not go to the bottom of the subject. What causes the apathy? That is the question. Some imagine that they give a good reason when (leaving out the apathy) they say, that Virginians are devoted exclusively to agriculture. But why should they be, when their agriculture is failing them, and they are flying by tens of thousands from their worn out fields to distant countries? Necessity, we are told by these reasoners, drove the New Englanders from agriculture in their barren country, to trade and manufactures. So it did: Necessity drives all mankind to labors and shifts for a living. Has necessity, the mother of invention, ever driven Virginians to trade and manufactures? No; but it drives them in multitudes from their native country. They cannot be driven to commerce and manufactures. What is the reason of that? If a genial climate and a once-fertile soil wedded them to agriculture, they should have wedded them also to their native land. Yet when agriculture fails them at home, rather than let mines, and coal beds, and waterfalls, and timber-forests, and the finest tide rivers and harbors in America, allure them to manufacturers and commerce, they will take their negroes and emigrate a thousand miles. This remarkable fact, that they will quit their country rather than their ruinous system of agriculture, proves that their institution of slavery disqualifies them to pursue any occupation, except this same ruinous system of agriculture. . . .

The AGRICULTURE of West Pennsylvania is much better conducted, and much more prosperous, than that of West Virginia. We have calculated its productiveness from the census tables, in the manner before described; and we find that the farming industry of West Pennsylvania yields the annual value of two hundred and twelve dollars to the hand; that of West Virginia, one hundred and fifty-eight dollars to the hand. This result is substantially correct; for the lands of West Pennsylvania are much more highly valued, than those of similar natural qualities in West Virginia. This is true, both in the Great Valley, and West of the Alleghany. Mark that fact, fellow-citizens; it is worthy of deep consideration; it is full of meaning. Lands in West Virginia are much cheaper than similar lands in the free country North of Virginia. Yet rather than buy and cultivate these good cheap Virginia lands, Northern farmers go farther, pay more, and fare worse;—so they do, and so they will. They look upon all Virginia as an *infected country;*—and so it is.

Next, the *Iron-making Business.*

West Virginia had, in 1840, as good natural resources, in every respect, for making iron, as West Pennsylvania. Yet, according to the census of 1840, (when no stone-coal was used in iron furnaces,) West Virginia made only 14,660 tons of cast and of bar iron, a year; when West Pennsylvania, made 116,530 tons. The value of the West Virginia iron was 515,000 dollars, that of West Pennsylvania iron was 4,763,000 dollars. The West Virginia iron masters made seventy per cent on their capital, and 390 dollars worth to the hand—chiefly slaves. The West Pennsylvania iron masters made 109 per cent on their capital, and 720 dollars worth to the hand:—all free laborers. . . .

The iron business has since increased in West Virginia; it has increased vastly more in West Pennsylvania.

Next, *Manufactures.*

If to the value of the cast and the bar iron of each country, we add the value of the manufactures of iron and steel, of wool, cotton and leather, we get a total of 770,000 dollars in West Virginia, and about six millions of dollars in West Pennsylvania.

The cost of constructing new buildings, amounted, in West Virginia, to about one-fourth of what it did in West Pennsylvania; indicating an increase in wealth and population at the same comparative rate.

Manufactures make towns, and towns make good markets for farmers; the larger the towns, the better the markets, and the more valuable the lands near them. The Pennsylvania towns are larger and more numerous than the Virginia towns, both in the Valley and West of it. The boast of our West Virginia is the good city of Wheeling. Would that she were six times as large, that she might equal Pittsburg, and that she grew five times as fast, that she might keep up with her.

We glory in Wheeling, because she only, in Virginia, deserves to be called a manufacturing town. For this her citizens deserve to be crowned—not with laurel—but with the solid gold of prosperity. But how came it, that Wheeling, and next to her, Wellsburg—of all the towns in Virginia—should become manufacturing towns?—Answer: They breathe the atmosphere of free States, almost touching them on both sides.—But again; seeing that Wheeling, as a seat for manufactures, is equal to Pittsburg, and inferior to no town in America, except Richmond; and that moreover, she has almost no slaves:—why is Wheeling so far behind Pittsburg, and comparatively so slow in her growth?—Answer: She is in a country in which slavery is established by law.

Thus it appears, fellow-citizens, by infallible proofs, that West Virginia, in all her parts and in all her interests, has suffered immensely from the institution of slavery.

The bad policy of the Legislature in former times, in respect to roads and land surveys west of the Alleghany, did great injury to the country. But after allowance is made for this, a vast balance of injury is chargeable to slavery, and to nothing else. In the Great Valley, where the other causes had little or no operation, the effects of slavery are most manifest and most pernicious. In those parts West of the Alleghany, upon the Ohio and its navigable waters, where want of roads and disputed land titles did least injury—there too the corrosive touch of slavery has also shown its cankerous effects. . . .

OUTLINES OF A SCHEME
FOR THE REMOVAL OF SLAVERY

1. Let the farther importation of slaves into West Virginia be prohibited by law. . . .

2. Let the exportation of slaves be fully permitted, as heretofore; but with this restriction, that children of slaves, born after a certain day, shall not be exported at all after they are five years old, nor those under that age, unless the slaves of the same negro family be exported with them. . . .

3. Let the existing generation of slaves remain in their present condition, but let their offspring, born after a certain day, be emancipated at an age not exceeding 25 years. . . .

4. Let masters be required to have the heirs of emancipation taught reading, writing and arithmetic: and let churches and benevolent people attend to their religious instruction. . . .

5. Let the emancipated be colonized. . . .

Now, fellow-citizens, it is for you to determine whether the slavery question shall be considered, discussed and decided, at this critical, this turning point of your country's history; or whether it shall lie dormant until the doom of West Virginia is sealed. May heaven direct your minds to the course dictated by patriotism, by humanity and by your own true interest.

A SLAVEHOLDER OF WEST VIRGINIA.

—Henry Ruffner, *An Address to the People of West Virginia,* Bridgewater, Va., 1933, pp. 20-40.

65. Speech of George W. Summers at the Convention of 1850-51

Western discontent mounted in the two decades following the Convention of 1829-30, when the eastern-dominated legislature of Virginia obstinately refused to consider reapportionment of representation in spite of the fact that census reports showed that the white population west of the Blue Ridge had outstripped that of the eastern section of the state. Western leaders rightly contended that as long as their section continued to be unfairly represented they could expect no redress of other injus-

tices, particularly on the score of internal improvements. Protest conventions were held in Charleston, Clarksburg, and Lewisburg urging constitutional revision and western political solidarity. The "exposition" of grievances submitted to the General Assembly by citizens of Kanawha County in August, 1841, warned that if the Assembly withheld remedial action, the petitioners would hold "solemn council" with their fellow-citizens who shared the "present political degradation." The memorialists of Kanawha pointed out that each delegate of the western district represented 7,578 white people, in contrast to 5,472 for the Valley representatives, 4,738 for the Piedmont, and 4,737 for the Tidewater. A similar situation prevailed in the Senate. The Kanawha citizens denied that the slave holders had anything to fear from western influence in legislation; far more dangerous, they held, was the "partial disfranchisement of the West," a section which was "but in the infancy of its future strength," as western increase in property values, slaves included, amply demonstrated. "The white population compose the people," the memorialists declared, "in whom all power is vested, and from whom all delegated power is derived, and towards whom all our public functionaries stand in the relation of trustees and servants"; yet the eastern people, with a minority of the white population, ran the government of Virginia as it was now organized. Although the reform movement preceding the Convention of 1850-51 was largely sectional, there was general support, even in the east, of the proposal for manhood suffrage.

The achievements of the Convention of 1850-51 represented a well-earned victory for the west. While no principle of representation was adopted, the white population as reported in the census of 1850 was the determining factor in apportioning membership in the House of Delegates, and the door was left open for the adoption in 1865 of the white or suffrage basis for the Senate, in which, for the time being, thirty seats were allotted to the east and twenty to the west. Before, the west had controlled only 41 per cent of the total representation in the Legislature; now it had 51 per cent. The other desired reforms were also obtained—manhood suffrage, direct election of judges and local officials, as well as of the chief executive. Every western county voted in favor of the reformed constitution. And the first governor chosen by direct vote of the people was Joseph Johnson of Harrison County, a Democrat who had served in Congress and at the recent convention.

In this finest hour of western Virginia as a member of the Old Dominion, the section had rare leadership in such men as Charles J. Faulkner of Berkeley, Joseph Johnson and Gideon D. Camden of Harrison, John S. Carlile of Barbour, Waitman T. Willey of Monongalia, Benjamin Smith and George W. Summers of Kanawha, and others. Their unbroken front as much as the justice of their cause accounted for their success. The most outstanding delegate of this able group was George W. Summers (1804-1868), who was made chairman of the committee on representation. Summers was born in Fairfax County, Virginia, and moved to Kanawha County as a child. After his graduation from Ohio University, he studied law under his brother, Judge Lewis Summers of the General Court of Virginia. A staunch Whig, Summers served in the Virginia house of delegates and the Federal Congress, and was a member of the Virginia conventions of 1850-51 and 1861, in the last of which he voted against the Ordinance of Secession. Although he was defeated in his bid for the governorship of Virginia in 1851, the following year he was elected judge of the Eighteenth Judicial Circuit of Virginia, where he served for six years. At the outbreak of the Civil War, Summers retired from public life, but continued to practice law until his death in Charleston. Summers' forensic tour de force at the reform convention, a "noble effort" which received tremendous applause, was delivered on March 18, 1851, in support of the suffrage or white basis for representation.

... Mr. Chairman, the moment you depart from the majority principle, and determine to place the power of government in the hands of a minority of the people, you abandon the true principles of republicanism and create an aristocracy more or less concentrated, in proportion to the numbers of which such minority may be composed, but still not the less an aristrocracy. ...

Suppose this were an original question—imagine, for a moment, that instead of being here in this representative assembly, the whole people had assembled together at some central point in the Commonwealth, to agree upon the terms on which they were to live together as one people—to make a government for themselves and by themselves, instead of through us, their deputies. Suppose in this assembly one-fourth, or one-third of the whole number, being east of the Blue Ridge, should set up a claim to govern the residue by taking the legislative power into their own hands, and for the reason, that having the larger amount of property, they would be called upon to make the largest contribution in taxes to the support of government. How would this pretension be received and treated by the three-fourths, or the two-thirds who had come to the assembly from the west side of the mountains! They would say: "if we unite in forming a government with you, it must be on terms of perfect equality. We are willing to mingle our people with your people, and our destiny with your destiny, and to be governed by the will of a majority of the whole, properly expressed in such forms as we shall agree upon. We came, not to surrender any rights which we possess, but by union with you to have those rights better guarded and preserved, and in turn to preserve and guard yours. . . . If you have most property we have most men. If you will be called upon to make the largest contribution in peace, we will be called upon to make the largest contribution in war. If you have the money to furnish arms, and construct defences, we have the soldiers to wield them. If you have the means to purchase peace, we have the physical force to compel and to maintain it. . . ."

. . . What is representation, but the product of suffrage; and of what value is equal suffrage unless equal representation flows from it? What boots it, that fifteen hundred voters in Kanawha are, without regard to their respective fortunes, equal each to the other, and rejoice in this equality, if five hundred other voters, in some eastern county, because of their greater amount of property, can send to the legislature the same representation, to silence and neutralize the voice of the fifteen hundred as effectually as if it had never been uttered. . . . What a mockery, to talk about the equality of men and the equality of suffrage, and at the same time take away all quality of result! . . . Away with your semblance of equality. Do not tell us of equality at the polls, and inequality in the halls of legislation. Do not tell me that one hundred and twenty thousand voters west of the Blue

Ridge, having precisely the same right of suffrage, shall send sixty-eight members to the house of delegates, only, while one hundred thousand voters east of the mountains shall send eighty-two members. . . .

It has been somewhat amusing to witness the array which has been made on this floor, of the vast amount of property held in eastern Virginia and the enormous taxes which are borne by the people. At the same time we are taunted with our poverty. Certain counties of the West are pointed to, as paying less than the cost of their representation. The east is so abounding in riches that she cannot come into an equal co-partnership with us at all. I venture to say that western Virginia not only bears an equal burthen with eastern Virginia, but that in proportion to the value of our property, we pay more. We pay at the same rate on lands and other taxable property. We have the same subjects of taxation which the east has. If our cattle, household furniture, &c., are untaxed, the same property is untaxed in the east. But then, there is other property on this side of the mountain not taxed. Slaves under twelve years of age are not subjects of taxation. This class, by the computation of the gentlemen from Richmond, (Mr. R. G. Scott,) amounts in value in eastern Virginia to more than sixty millions of dollars. Admit that they are unproductive, you take very good care not to exclude from taxation, the forest and mountain lands of the west, however unproductive they may be. . . .

. . . You will remember, Mr. Chairman, that some twenty-three years ago, when the Baltimore and Ohio railroad company was first incorporated by the State of Maryland, an application was made to the legislature of Virginia to permit that work to pass through her territory. The preference of that company was, if the consent of the state could have been obtained, to pass with their improvement from Harper's Ferry through the great valley of Virginia and to the Ohio river by way of the ravine of the Kanawha, terminating at Guyandotte or Point Pleasant. The legislature of Virginia refused permission to terminate that work at any point on the Ohio, south of the mouth of the little Kanawha. Several attempts were subsequently made to procure the removal of this restriction, all of which were unsuccessful. . . . Upon what ground was this rejection of the application to which I have referred, and the subsequent adherence to the same policy, predicated? It was upon the ground, that the trade of central Virginia and of Southwestern Virginia, belonged legitimately to her own citizens—that the route to the rich regions beyond her borders, through the Kanawha valley, was a pearl too precious to be thrown away. These sources of wealth must be sacredly preserved, to pour their fertilizing stream through our own soil—to swell the business and population of Virginia cities—to stimulate Virginia enterprize and capital, and to make Virginia herself, what she ought to be, the first in power and prosperity of all the States of this Union.

You refused to permit others, to put sickle into the jocund harvest which you saw ripening for yourselves. But what did you do, when you rejected this application? Why you solemly promised that Virginia should do herself, and with her own means, the work which others offered to construct, and which would have been constructed and finished long ago, but for that refusal. How has this promise been performed and fulfilled? Why, in 1832, when the application was distinctly made, and the legislature vehemently urged to make good this promise and to enter at once upon the construction of this central connection, with the means and credit of the commonwealth, it was declined. . . .

You speak of the comparative poverty of western Virginia. Why, sir, her very geographical position is capital. A straight line across the North American continent from the Pacific to the Atlantic passes through her borders. . . . Virginia in the munificence of her bounty, gave away the "Northwest Territory" to cement the union of these States, and to aid in the defraying the expenses of our war of independence. Shall she not seek to participate, at least, in the benefit of commercial relations with the great Commonwealths which have been carved out and are now flourishing upon the soil which was once her very own? . . .

. . . Can we disguise it from ourselves, that we have not done our duty, and our whole duty to this old Commonwealth. What was her rank and condition among the States of this confederacy in the beginning, and what is it now? . . .

What have we done for the common mind—how have we provided for the education of our people? In what way are we to answer, in an age like this, for the humiliating fact that eighty-three thousand of our adult white population cannot even read that book "which is the history of their race and the record of their redemption?"

... Gentlemen speak of western schemes and western improvements, and of the eastern people being plundered of their money to construct works in the west. Mr. Chairman, I am a western man, but I am also a Virginian. I trust I have a proper appreciation of the interests and the honor of the whole State. I have no hesitation in believing that the central connection [James River-Kanawha] to which I have alluded, whenever made, will bring benefits to eastern Virginia five-fold more important and valuable than the west can ever derive from it. The eastern end of the line will be the commercial end, while ours will be the producing end....

Gentlemen assure us that the growing west will soon have the legislative power, even upon the plan which they propose—they foretell that in ten or twelve years the sceptre will pass over the mountains. With the same breath they inform us, that while they might be willing to trust the present generation, they know not who is to come after us. I have already shown what may be the workings of the system, and that we may never obtain this power, whatever may be our increase. But suppose it be true that a few years will change the balance, even on your own principle. Is it better to do what is right now, and thereby cement the affections of your western brethren, or retain power for mere power's sake, through a few more years of strife and discontent, and then let it pass to them, angered with recollections of past injustice, and smarting with the sting of past inflictions?

But this minority rule is sought to be justified upon the ground that it can perpetrate no wrong upon the majority. It can impose no taxes which its own members will not equally feel. Are there no subjects of taxation to be found west of the mountains which do not exist on this side? My colleague (Mr. Smith) stated the other day that salt might be taxed. He omitted to state, however, that the legislature in 1815, actually did impose a tax of twelve and a half cents per bushel upon that article. A tax to that amount on the quantity made at this time in the county of Kanawha alone, would impose a larger sum than is levied upon all the slaves in the Tide-water district. What would forbid the taxing of the lime-kilns of the valley and the mineral springs? . . .

Again, we have between ninety and a hundred thousand more white inhabitants west of the mountains than there is on the east side. What forbids the raising of the needed revenue for the State by a *per capita* tax on the white inhabitants alone? . . .

The advocacy of the mixed basis has, so far, proceeded upon the ground, exclusively, that it is necessary to protect eastern Virginia from excessive taxation, and improper appropriation. We have answered to this, that the west is as much interested in the proper exercise of these powers, as is the east. In addition to this, we have offered to insert in the constitution, any and all reasonable guaranties for the safety and quiet of our eastern brethren.

. . . A good deal has been said in this discussion about slave property and the necessity for its protection. We have said to our eastern brethren that we cannot consent to put the reins of government in the hands of a minority of the people for the purpose of protecting slaves or any other species of property. We deny that slaves are entitled to be represented as persons or as property . . .

. . . I am a protection man, in reference to slave property, as I am in reference to all other property, but as a slave holder, all I ask of the government is "hands off." Make no discrimination between the slave holder and the non-slaveholder. . . . If you wish to preserve this institution, in security and quiet, amid all the dangers which threaten us without, I pray you, do not use it as the means of injustice towards your own people at home. Do not consign a majority of your white population, to political inferiority, because they have not as large an interest as owners in this property, as you have . . .

Mr. Chairman, the gentleman from Fauquier, (Mr. Scott,) said that there was "a proclivity to disunion sentiment in eastern Virginia." In speaking of the people of western Virginia, he said he looked upon our growth "with the pride of a Virginian and the sympathy of a brother," and that he looked to our people for important aid in the preservation of the Union of these

States. In this expression of sentiment he has but done justice to the western people. They do love this Union, not with a fitful, occasional, temporary attachment, but with a devotion as firm and unshaken as the mountains among which they dwell, and as constant as the flow of the streams which issue from their base. It was to the people of "West Augusta" that the thoughts of Washington's great soul were directed, when, in the darkest hour of the revolution, and when all was disaster and dismay around him, despair filled every heart but his own, he declared that though stripped of all means of attack or defence, if he was given the ability to erect a standard, however tattered and torn, upon the hills of "West Augusta," he could yet call around him the men, who would lift up and restore the bleeding fortunes of his country. Sir, our people are the children of that old "West Augusta." [Applause.] The descendants of those to whom Washington looked for succor and support, are as determined to preserve the independence and Union of these States, as their fathers were to achieve these blessings.

What portion of the United States is more interested in perpetuating this Union than western Virginia? Our geographical position renders it essential to our happiness and safety. While eastern Virginia is situated between the slave States of North Carolina and Maryland, western Virginia is bounded to a great extent by the free States of Pennsylvania and Ohio. If dissolution should come, civil discord and the strife of battle would come with it. In such an event, ours would be the Flanders of America, where embattled hosts would meet and contending armies decide the fate of nations. It would be the red pathway between the North and South....

Gentlemen, you are excitable upon this subject of slave property; you ought to be to a certain extent. It is all right that you should be vigilant. But you are sometimes a little too excitable, and you had better have some cool men, with mountain air fanning their temples, to help you when you go into these consultations down south. Sir, in the event of conflict and of war, we have been told here that the east would like very well to have our help. We will give you our help, but we must come in as equals and brethren—equals in the cabinet as well as in the field—equals in the power to declare the war as well as to wage it. . . .

Gentlemen express surprise that the people of the west should consider themselves degraded by this inequality which is sought to be forced upon them, . . . When our people see that some five thousand eastern inhabitants can send a member to this body, and that it requires some nine thousand of themselves to do the same thing, is it not easy for them to perceive that you claim superiority, and that by consequence, theirs is a position of inferiority. . . .

What is a government worth unless the people love it? What is a government worth unless the people feel that they are free under it? What is freedom but equality of political rights? I would ask gentlemen to remember the advice of old Burleigh to Queen Elizabeth, "win hearts and you have their swords and purses." . . . You cannot induce our people to take this constitution by bespangling it all over with constables and sheriffs, and other elective officers. They will not surrender the great principles of civil liberty for baubles. They are no longer children, to have a sugar stick thrown to them to quiet them. They know and understand that 500,000 people in one section of the State, ought not to be subjected to the rule and dominion of 400,000 people in another section. Humble as I am, if I had a voice that could reach every cabin and hamlet that stand scattered among the green valleys and swelling hills of the west, it should be heard imploring the people to dash this drugged beverage from their lips, spice it as you may. . . .

We are here to try this great issue of popular rights and of popular equality. Send us not away with sorrow in our hearts, and with reproaches upon our tongues. Put not this yoke upon us. We appeal to you in the name of a half million of free citizens. We entreat you, by every recollection of the past and by every hope of the future—as American citizens—as Virginians—as brethren rocked in the same cradle, and nurtured upon the bosom of a common mother—by the tombs of our ancestors yet remaining amongst you—by all the ties that bind families together, and by all the warning lessons of national injustice which history has recorded for our instruction and our admonition, we entreat, we beseech, that you do not perpetrate this great wrong upon us and upon our posterity. [Great applause.]—*Supplement to the Enquirer, Whig, Examiner, Times, Republican, and Republican Advocate,* April, 1851.

66. Taxation and Finance–Constitution of 1851

The slave-holding conservatives in Virginia did not capitulate to the reformers without obtaining concessions, as may be seen from the following provisions on taxation.

22. TAXATION SHALL BE EQUAL and uniform throughout the commonwealth, and all property other than slaves shall be taxed in proportion to its value, which shall be ascertained in such manner as may be prescribed by law.

23. Every slave who has attained the age of twelve years shall be assessed with a tax equal to and not exceeding that assessed on land of the value of three hundred dollars. Slaves under that age shall not be subject to taxation; and other taxable property may be exempted from taxation by the vote of a majority of the whole number of members elected to each house of the General Assembly.

24. A capitation tax, equal to the tax assessed on land of the value of two hundred dollars, shall be levied on every white male inhabitant who has attained the age of twenty-one years; and one equal moiety of the capitation tax upon white persons shall be applied to the purposes of education in primary and free schools; but nothing herein contained shall prevent exemptions of taxable polls in cases of bodily infirmity. . . . —*New Constitution of . . . Virginia, Adopted by the State Convention . . . on the 31st Day of July,* 1851, p. 20.

67. Alexander Campbell on the Fugitive Slave Law

Western Virginia, located as it was at the crossroads between East and West and North and South, held a generally moderate position on the question of slavery. In 1860 only one county in this area, McDowell—in recent years the West Virginia county with the largest Negro population—reported no Negroes, either free or slave; Calhoun, Hancock, and Webster each had fewer than ten slaves. On the other hand, Berkeley, Greenbrier, Hampshire, Hardy, and Monroe counties each had well over one thousand slaves, and Kanawha had over two thousand. Jefferson led with 3,960 slaves and 511 free Negroes; the white population of the county numbered 10,064. The Federal Fugitive Slave law provided by the Compromise of 1850 aroused violent protests from the abolitionists. The position of many western Virginians, including members of the clergy, on the controversial slave law is candidly stated in the following essay from the MILLENNIAL HARBINGER, *whose publisher, editor, and chief contributor was the Reverend Alexander Campbell of Bethany College. Campbell was not, and never had been, an apologist for slavery. Indeed, in the "Prospectus" announcing the publication of the* HARBINGER *in 1830, he stated that he intended to discuss in the periodical the* "Injustice *which yet remains in many of the political regulations under the best of political governments, when contrasted with the* justice *which Christianity proposes . . ." and "disquisitions upon the treatment of African slaves, as preparatory to their emancipation, and exaltation from their present degraded condition."*

STILL, WE ARE NOT AT ALL INSENSIBLE to the fact, that slavery in the United States has been so conducted, on the part of very many professors of Christianity, owners of large and small estates, as to outrage both humanity and the Bible, Old Testament and New. But who so destitute of reason and observation, as not to perceive and admit that the abuse of any thing, human or divine, is no valid objection against the thing itself. . . .

We desire to be impartial on this subject, being neither in love with slavery nor abolitionism, as they both stand before us. . . .

But we are entreated and urged, on both sides, to express our ideas and views of the "Fugitive Slave Law," now the standing topic—the burthen of the year 1851. Both citizens and brethren, at the North and at the South, have requested it, and urged it upon our attention. We shall yield to their importunities.

The first question that I propound to myself on this subject, in sustaining my position, and to those who oppose it, is—*What does the Constitution of the United States itself require of me and of them, as citizens of the United States, in reference to American slavery?* To which I answer, in the words of the Constitution—*"No Person held to service or labor in one State, under the laws thereof, escaping into another, shall, in consequence of any law or regulation therein, be discharged from such service or labor, BUT SHALL BE DELIVERED UP, on the claim of the party to whom such service or labor shall be due."* This is not the statute of *ninety-three* nor of *fifty-one*, but the *Constitution of the United States.* Every officer in this government is sworn to support it. . . . *I am sworn to support it;* and it is presumable that every . . . *citizen* of the United States is religiously and morally bound to support it.

How, then, can any enlightened American citizen, native or naturalized, be held guiltless by the Judge of all, of perjury or of rebellion, while endeavoring to prevent a fellow-citizen of another State, from recovering one "held to his service by the laws" of his own State, under the sanction of the Constitution of the United States, which he is most solemnly bound to sustain?

The second question is, What is *the law* of the United States on the subject? . . .

The law of Congress passed in 1793, and that passed in 1851, obviously agree in the following items: 1. It is declared to be a *criminal offence* to resist the due execution of the law; to "knowingly and wilfully obstruct or hinder the claimant in the arrest of the fugitive; to rescue such fugitive from the claimant when arrested; to harbor or conceal such person after notice that he or she is a fugitive from labor. . . ."

It is taught and believed in most of the free States, by many opposed to this law, that it inhibits, on civil pains and penalties, any citizen of a free State from showing any act of sympathy or kindness to a runaway slave; such as feeding, clothing, lodging him, or giving him any directions, suspecting or knowing him to be a runaway; and thus virtually forbids the charities due to suffering humanity. I do not so interpret or understand the law, and neither so understands it any one whose calm and deliberate judgment I respect. The law, as I read it, only says, "Thou shalt not harbor or conceal such fugitive, *so as to prevent the discovery and arrest of such person, after notice or knowledge of the fact that such person is a fugitive from service or labor aforesaid.*" The "notice and knowledge of the fact" is neither rumor nor suspicion, but *legal* notice and knowledge. And as stated by some of those who enacted this law, "This deprives no one of the privilege of extending charities to the fugitive. You may feed, clothe, and lodge him, provided you do not 'harbor or conceal him, so as to prevent discovery and arrest, after notice or knowledge that he is a fugitive.'" And this I learn to be "the construction put upon a simular provision in the old law, by the highest judicial tribunal in the land." ...

... I am sorry to see ministers of the gospel of the Protestant denomination—especially those of the Baptists at the North—in the late movements at Boston, so outraging their own profession as ministers of peace, and every Christian principle, by condescending to come down from their sacred desks into the streets, to inflame a tumultuous mob, and to inspire an unlawful assembly to resist the government of our own, as well as that of our Lord's, creation and ordination. This union with political demagogues, most of whom have their own aggrandizement and elevation incomparably more at heart and in their eye, than the emancipation or elevation of their alleged down-trodden brethren at the South, is most revolting. ...

No one regrets, more than I, the existence of slavery in the United States, nor the means which are employed to break it down. It is not enough to remonstrate against it, by showing a better way, but we must chide and denounce our less fortunate brethren, who happened to be born and brought up in the midst of it, and under laws which, were they ever so unanimous, they could not annul. They should not be held up to public scorn, and treated as man-stealers and robbers, because they are not able, nor, under the present circumstances, willing, to encounter all the responsibilities consequent upon an indiscriminate and universal emancipation of those providentially placed under their care and protection, and in which no free State seems willing to co-operate, so far as to permit them to locate and settle amongst them, or to send back to Africa the descendents of those whom their fathers imported, we know not on what condition, nor by what authority, and for whom, in most cases, they received a full remuneration. . . .

To conclude for the present, as a philosopher and a Christian I would say to the North, let the South have their slaves, and throw no impediment in the way. Let them, on the present compromise fill up their own territory, or emancipate them, as they please; and rather sympathize with them than upbraid them on account of misfortunes which they have inherited, rather than superinduced upon themselves and their children.

A. C.

—Alexander Campbell, "Slavery and the Fugitive Slave Law," *The Millennial Harbinger*, Series 4, I (July, 1851), 386-92.

68. An Affair of Honor—the Clemens-Wise Duello

The tense, sometimes violent, political climate of the decade preceding the Civil War provided the background for the duel fought between Congressman Sherrard Clemens (1820-1881) of Wheeling and O. Jennings Wise, editor of the Richmond En-quirer and son of Governor Henry A. Wise of Virginia, in which Clemens was seriously wounded. This cause celebre had its start in a note submitted by Clemens to the Enquirer, in which he announced that Judge John W. Brockenbrough had authorized him to state that the Judge declined "the use of his name" in the coming canvass for the governorship. In a subsequent communication to the Enquirer, Brockenbrough admitted that

266 THE THIRTY-FIFTH STATE

*he had told Clemens that "he did not seek or desire" the gov-
ernorship, but added with characteristic political coyness, that
he would not "shrink" from serving the state in that capacity if
he were "tendered" the nomination for the office. The ENQUIRER
saw in Clemens's allegedly authorized statement an attempt to
undermine the candidacy of Brockenbrough and advance that
of John Letcher, the Democratic favorite of the Valley, who had
become suspect among the ardently pro-southern Democrats because of his endorsement of the* Ruffner Pamphlet. *When the*
ENQUIRER *ended a long tirade against Clemens by charging him
with "an act of gross treachery towards Judge Brockenbrough,
perpetrated under the guise of personal and political friendship" and "an act of political trickery, intended to enure to the
benefit of some political aspirant, for the accomplishment of
which he has not failed to resort to public and wilful misrepre-
sentation," the Wheeling congressman challenged Wise to a
duel. The affair of honor, although widely condemned in the
press, had no adverse effect on the political aspirations of either
Clemens or Letcher. Clemens was returned to Congress in 1859
and two years later, as a member of the Secession Convention,
he voted against the Ordinance of Secession. John Letcher, after
publicly purging himself of abolitionist sentiments, was elected
governor of Virginia in 1859, largely with western support. The
following account of the duel was written by Charles Irving,
who delivered the challenge.*

A CARD

Richmond, 18th September, 1858.

Having heard various rumors with reference to the difficulty
between the Hon. Sherrard Clemens and O. Jennings Wise,
Esq., and conceding the justice of criticism upon the seconds
in allowing the exchange of four shots, *in the absence of a knowledge of facts,* I deem it but proper to give the public those
facts, and to allow them to decide upon whom rests the responsibility of the result.

On the 16th of September, at the request of Mr. Clemens, I
delivered to Mr. O. J. Wise a challenge, which was accepted,
and for arrangements I was referred to Mr. T. P. Chisman. The
challenge was based upon an editorial in the *Enquirer,* which

Mr. Clemens regarded as deliberate insult. By arrangement, the parties were to meet at or near sunrise, at the Fairfield Race Course, on Friday, the 17th, and both parties had the liberty of selecting one outside friend in addition to a surgeon. Before the hour fixed the parties were on the field. Mr. Pryor was requested by Mr. Clemens to go with him, and consented to do so, with the understanding that he would have no connection with the matter whatever, and that he might be useful in the event of Mr. Clemens being wounded, or to effect an accommodation. Mr. Geo. Ritchie was upon the field as the outside friend of Mr. Wise, accompanied by Dr. —————— as surgeon. Dr. —————— was the surgeon for Mr. Clemens. As soon as convenient, and without any propositions of amicable adjustment by the friends of either party, the distance (ten paces) was measured by the seconds, and the pistols loaded. Before rehearsing the word as to be given, the principals were brought together, each exchanging the ordinary salutations. They were then put in position and weapons handed them. Mr. Irving, who had won the word, then gave it in the unusual manner, whereupon both principals fired deliberately, but without effect. Mr. Pryor then came forward, and, remarking that both gentlemen had vindicated their honor, asked if the affair could not be settled without proceeding farther. Mr. Irving replied that he desired an adjustment if consistent with the honor of Mr. Clemens, and, as evidence of that feeling, he withdrew the challenge for the time. Mr. Chisman asked to see Mr. Wise, and returned with the reply from Mr. Wise that if the challenge was withdrawn, and Mr. Clemens satisfied, it was all right, and that they would leave the field; but, if withdrawn for explanation, Mr. Wise declined all explanations of his article, as he honestly believed every word of it. Mr. Irving then said that as explanations were refused, Mr. Clemens had no honorable option but to demand another fire, and the seconds proceeded to load. After the second fire without effect, Mr. Irving again withdrew the challenge, and proposed to refer the whole matter to the friends of the parties upon the field, and announced his entire readiness to abide their decision. This proposition, was understood to meet the approval of both Mr. Ritchie, the outside friend of Mr. Wise, as also of his surgeon. It was, however, rejected by Mr.

Wise. Still desirous of adjusting the matter, and, from that feeling, disregarding *punctilio*, Mr. Irving requested Mr. Ritchie to ask Mr. Wise if no accommodation was possible. Mr. Ritchie returned, after conversing with Mr. Wise, and stated that there was none.

Mr. Irving then demanded the third fire which was also without effect. Mr. Pryor then proposed the following terms of accommodation, which were read to Mr. Wise, who remarked in reply, that it was a matter for the seconds to decide. Mr. Chisman, the second of Mr. Wise, then declined to sign the paper. Here is the statement as drawn up by Mr. Pryor:

"Messrs. Wise and Clemens having met and exchanged shots three times, in our opinion their honor is entirely vindicated, and we insist that they be withdrawn from the field by their seconds."

Accordingly they were withdrawn by their respective seconds.

This proposition was understood to have received the concurrence of both Mr. Wise's surgeon and Mr. Ritchie. After its rejection Mr. Irving stated to Mr. Chisman that he withdrew Mr. Clemens from the field, and would appeal to the public; and that in so doing he intended no reflection upon him, but, as a matter of course, would be willing to assume such responsibilities to others as might attach to such publication.—The parties were preparing to leave the field when Mr. Clemens, hearing the facts from his surgeon, and with the belief that the result of such publication would involve Mr. Irving in collision with Mr. Wise, came forward and protested against his withdrawal under such circumstances, and appealed to Mr. Irving to continue his services.—After some conversation with Mr. Clemens, Mr. Irving agreed to continue as his friend, and the challenge was renewed.

The fourth fire being inevitable at this stage, Mr. Pryor stated in the presence of the other party, that the affair had gone far enough, and that he would not farther countenance the matter by his presence, and retired from the field.

On the fourth fire Mr. Clemens was shot through the thigh, and fell.

Such are the facts, which I am confident no friend of either party will contradict. The public can decide upon whom rests the responsibility of this continued prosecution of the affair to so serious a result. Whatever the consequences, I feel the consciousness of having done everything that a gentleman could do to accommodate the matters.

Respectfully,
C. Irving.

—Wheeling *Intelligencer*, October 1, 1858.

69. John Brown's Raid

The tragically quixotic raid of John Brown at Harpers Ferry in October, 1859, foreshadowed with alarming emphasis the impending conflict between the free North and the slave-holding South. The gaunt, intrepid abolitionist had already shed blood in Kansas for the cause of emancipation and had led a group of Negro fugitives to Canada shortly before his arrival in Virginia early in July, 1859. After renting a farm about five miles from Harpers Ferry on the Maryland side of the Potomac, Brown spent the remainder of the summer and the early fall gathering arms and recruits for his projected attack on Harpers Ferry and the Federal armory and arsenal located at the point where the Baltimore and Ohio bridge entered Virginia. The foray began on the evening of October 16. With incredible boldness the little band commanded by Captain Brown cut the telegraph lines, posted guards at the bridges over the Potomac and Shenandoah, seized the armory and arsenal, occupied the Hall's Rifle works, took prominent citizens, including Colonel Lewis W. Washington, as hostages, and detained the east-bound Baltimore and Ohio train which arrived around 1:25 A. M. The only casualty up to this point was, ironically, a local Negro employee of the railroad, who was shot dead by one of Brown's guards on the bridge. At 3 A. M. the raiders notified the conductor that the train could proceed, but he delayed giving the necessary orders until Brown reassured him that the bridge was safe by accompanying him across it in advance of the train. "You doubtless wonder that a man of my age should be here with a band of armed men," Brown said to him, "But if you knew my past history you would not wonder at it so much." The following morn-

ing the stunned town began to recover from the effect of the nocturnal stroke. The Lutheran church bell was rung and arms were distributed to the outraged citizens. Before noon of the 17th the militia began to arrive. By mid-afternoon Brown's situation was desperate. Some of the raiders lay dead or wounded. With retreat virtually cut off, Brown assembled the remnant of his band, the hostages, and the slaves he had armed in a small brick building called the engine-house. During the night Colonel Robert E. Lee arrived with Federal troops. To his demand for surrender, Brown replied that he would do so only upon condition that he and his men should be allowed to escape. When the little fortress was taken by assault on the morning of October 18, Brown was injured by sword strokes inflicted by a marine lieutenant. The bloodstained liberator was carried to the office of the paymaster of the armory where he was interviewed by Governor Henry A. Wise of Virginia. "In the midst of enemies, whose home he had invaded; wounded and a prisoner, surrounded by a small army of officials, and a more desperate army of angry men; with the gallows staring him full in the face, he lay on the floor, and, in reply to every question, gave answers that betokened the spirit that animated him," wrote an eye-witness of the dramatic scene. Eight of the raiders, besides Brown's two sons, Watson and Oliver, were killed in the attack; six others followed John Brown to the gallows, and five managed to escape. Technically Brown had a fair trial, as the Governor of Virginia boasted and the defendant admitted. Against the advice of his counsel, the unchastened abolitionist scorned to seek refuge in a plea of insanity. On the contrary, he saw in his death a means of furthering his cause. "I feel astonished that one so vile and unworthy as I am would even be suffered to have a place anyhow or anywhere amongst the very least of all who when they come to die . . . were permitted to pay the debt of nature in defense of the right and of God's eternal and immutable truth," he wrote his sisters. The indictment of Brown and his co-defendants in the Judicial Circuit of Virginia at Charles Town, and his profoundly moving statement following his conviction are given below.

JUDICIAL CIRCUIT OF VIRGINIA, Jefferson County, to-wit: The Jurors of the Commonwealth of Virginia, in and for the body of the County of Jefferson, duly impanelled, and attending upon the Circuit Court of said county, upon their oaths present that John Brown, Aaron C. Stephens, alias Aaron D. Stephens, and Edwin Coppoc, white men, and Shields Green and John Copeland, free negroes, together with divers other evil minded, and traitorous persons to the Jurors unknown, not having the fear of God before their eyes, but being moved and seduced by the false and malignant counsel of other evil and traitorous persons, and the instigations of the Devil, did, severally, on the sixteenth seventeenth and eighteenth days of the month of October, in the year of our Lord eighteen hundred and fifty nine, and on divers other days before and after that time, within the Commonwealth of Virginia and the County of Jefferson aforesaid, and within the jurisdiction of this Court with other confederates to the Jurors unknown feloniously and traitorously make rebellion and levy war against the said Commonwealth of Virginia; and to effect, carry out and fulfill their said wicked and treasonable ends and purposes, did then and there, as a band of organized soldiers, attack, seize, and hold, a certain post and place within the county and state aforesaid, and within the jurisdiction aforesaid, known and called by the name of Harpers ferry, and then and there did forcibly capture, make prisoners of, and detain divers good and loyal citizens of said Commonwealth, to-wit: Lewis W. Washington, John H. Allstadt, Archibald M. Kitzmiller, Benjamin J. Mills, John E. P. Dangerfield, Armstead Ball, John Donoho, and did then and there slay and murder, by shooting with fire arms, called Sharps Rifles, divers good and loyal citizens of said Commonwealth, to-wit: Thomas Boerly, George W. Turner, Fontaine Beckham; together with Luke Quinn—a soldier of the United States; and Hayward Shephard a free negro, and did then and there, in manner aforesaid, wound divers other good & loyal citizens of said Commonwealth—and did then and there feloniously and traitorously establish and set up, without authority of the Legislature of the Commonwealth of Virginia, a government, separate from and hostile to the existing government of said Commonwealth; and did then and there hold and exercise divers offices, under said usurped Government, to-wit the said John Brown as commander-in-chief of the military forces, the said Aaron C.

Stephens, alias Aaron D. Stephens as captain; the said Edwin Coppoc as Lieutenant and the said Shields Green, and John Copeland as soldiers; and did then and there require and compel obedience to said officers; and then and there did hold and profess allegiance and fidelity to said usurped Government; and under color of the usurped authority aforesaid, did then and there resist forcibly and with warlike arms, the execution of the laws of the Commonwealth of Virginia, and with fire arms, did wound and maim divers other good and loyal citizens of said Commonwealth, to the jurors unknown, when attempting, with lawful authority, to uphold and maintain said Constitution and laws of the Commonwealth of Virginia—and for the purpose, end, and aim of overthrowing and abolishing the Constitution and laws of said Commonwealth, and establishing in the place thereof another and different government, and a constitution and laws hostile thereto, did then and there feloniously and traitorously, and in military array, join in open battle and deadly warfare, with the civil officers and soldiers, in the lawful service of the said Commonwealth of Virginia; and did then and there shoot and discharge divers guns and pistols charged with gunpowder and leaden bullets against and upon divers parties of the militia and volunteers embodied and acting under the command of Colonel Robert W. Baylor and of Colonel John Thomas Gibson, and other officers of said Commonwealth, with lawful authority, to quell and subdue the said John Brown, [*et al*] . . . and other rebels and traitors assembled, organized, and acting with them as aforesaid—to the evil example of all others, in like case offending, and against the peace and dignity of the Commonwealth—

2nd Count And the Jurors aforesaid, upon their oaths aforesaid, do further present that the said John Brown, [*et al*] . . . did each severally maliciously and feloniously conspire with each other, and with a certain John E. Cook, John Kagi, Charles Tidd, and others to the jurors unknown, to induce certain slaves, towit Jim, Sam, Mason, and Catesby—the slaves and property of Lewis W. Washington, and Henry, Levi, Ben, Jerry, Phil, George and Bill—the slaves and property of John H. Allstadt, and other slaves to the Jurors unknown, to rebel and make insurrection against their masters and owners, and against the Government, and the Constitution and laws of the Commonwealth of Virginia: and then and there did maliciously and feloniously advise said slaves, and other slaves to the jurors unknown, to rebel and make insurrection against their masters and owners, and against the Government, the Constitution and laws of the Commonwealth of Virginia; to the evil example of all others in like cases offending, and against the peace and dignity of the Commonwealth.

3rd Count. And the Jurors aforesaid upon their oaths aforesaid further present that the said John Brown, [et al] ... did make an assault, and with firearms called Sharps rifles, and other deadly weapons to the Jurors unknown, then and there charged with gunpowder and leaden bullets, did then and there ... shoot and discharge the same against the bodies severally and respectively, of the said Thomas Boerley George W. Turner, Fontaine Beckham, Luke Quinn, and Hayward Shephard and that the said John Brown, [et al] ... did strike penetrate and wound the said Thomas Boerley, [et al] ... each severally, to-wit the said Thomas Boerley in and upon the left side—the said George W. Turner in and upon the left shoulder—the said Fontaine Beckham in and upon the right breast, the said Luke Quinn in and upon the abdomen—and the said Hayward Shephard in and upon the back and side, giving to the said Thomas Boerley, George W. Turner, Fontaine Beckham, Luke Quinn and Hayward Shephard, ... each one mortal wound; of which said mortal wounds they ... each died; ...

4th Count And the Jurors aforesaid upon their oaths aforesaid further present, that the said John Brown, [et al] ... did strike, penetrate and wound the said Thomas Boerly, [et al] ... giving to the said Thomas Boerly, [et al] each one mortal wound; of which said mortal wounds, they ... then and there died; and that the said John Copeland, then and there feloniously, willfully and of his malice aforethought, was present, aiding, helping, abetting, comforting and assisting the said John Brown, [et al] ... in the felony and murder aforesaid, in manner and form aforesaid to commit. And so the Jurors aforesaid upon their oaths aforesaid, do say that the said John Brown, Aaron C. Stephens alias Aaron D. Stephens, Edwin Coppoc, Shields Green, and John Copeland, then and there, ... in the manner aforesaid and by the means aforesaid, feloniously, willfully and of their and each of their, malice aforethought did kill and murder against the peace and dignity of the Commonwealth of Virginia. —Photostat Copies of Papers on the Trial of John Brown, West Virginia University Library.

The Clerk asked John Brown whether he had anything to say why sentence should not be pronounced upon him.

John Brown. I have, may it please the Court, a few words to say. In the first place, I deny everything but what I have all along admitted, of a design on my part to free slaves. I intended certainly to have made a clean thing of that matter, as I did last winter when I went into Missouri, and there took slaves without the snapping of a gun on either side, moving them through the country, and finally leaving them in Canada. I designed to have done the same thing again on a larger scale. That was all I intended to do. I never did intend murder or treason, or the destruction of property, or to excite or incite the slaves to rebellion, or to make insurrection. I have another objection, and that is that it is unjust that I should suffer such a penalty. Had I interfered in the manner, which I admit, and which I admit has been fairly proved—for I admire the truthfulness and candor of the greater portion of the witnesses who have testified in this case— had I so interfered in behalf of any of the rich, the powerful, the intelligent, the so-called great, or in behalf of any of their friends, either father, mother, brother, sister, wife, or children, or any of that class, and suffered and sacrificed what I have in this interference, it would have been all right, and every man in this Court would have deemed it an act worthy of reward rather than punishment. This Court acknowledges, too, as I suppose, the validity of the law of God. I see a book kissed, which I suppose to be the Bible, or at least the New Testament, which teaches me that all things whatsoever I would that men should do to me, I should do even so to them. It teaches me further to remember them that are in bonds as bound with them. I endeavored to act up to that instruction. I say I am yet too young to understand that God is any respecter of persons. I believe that to have interfered as I have done, as I have always freely admitted I have done in behalf of His despised poor, is no wrong, but right. Now, if it is deemed necessary that I should forfeit my life for the furtherance of the ends of justice, and mingle my blood further with the blood of my children and with the blood of millions in this slave country whose rights are disregarded by wicked, cruel, and unjust enactments, I say let it be done.

Let me say one word further. I feel entirely satisfied with the treatment I have received on my trial. Considering all the circumstances, it has been more generous than I expected. But I feel no consciousness of guilt. I have stated from the first what was my intention, and what was not. I never had any design against the liberty of any person, nor any disposition to commit treason or excite slaves to rebel or make any general insurrection. I never encouraged any man to do so, but always discouraged any idea of that kind. Let me say also in regard to the statements made by some of those who were connected with me, I fear it has been stated by some of them that I have induced them to join me; but the contrary is true. I do not say this to injure them, but as regretting their weakness. Not one but joined of his own accord, and the greater part at their own expense. A number of them I never saw, and never had a word of conversation with till the day they came to me, and that was for the purpose I have stated. Now, I am done.—*The Life, Trial and Execution of Captain John Brown,* compiled by Robert M. Dewitt, pp. 94-95.

70. John Brown's Death and Last Words as Reported by Porte Crayon

David Hunter Strother (1816-1888), the author of the following account of the execution of John Brown, was a leading genre illustrator and author of ante-bellum Virginia. His sketches of southern Negroes and Appalachian mountaineers accompanying his lively tales of adventure delighted thousands of readers of HARPER'S NEW MONTHLY MAGAZINE, *who knew him as "Porte Crayon." Born into a substantial, well-connected family of Martinsburg, Berkeley County, he attended Jefferson College and*

*studied painting with Pietro Ancora, Samuel F. B. Morse, and
various teachers in France and Italy, where he remained for
three years. His profitable connection with* Harper's Monthly
*began in 1853 and continued until after the Civil War. At the
outbreak of the conflict, to the dismay and surprise of many of
his southern friends, Strother joined the Federal army. After his
resignation from the army in 1864 with the rank of colonel, Strother served for one year as adjutant general of Virginia under
Governor Francis Pierpont with the rank of brigadier general by
brevet. Strother's post-war literary efforts were not successful,
and it was only through an appointment as consul general to
Mexico (1879-1885) that he was able to stave off financial difficulties. On his retirement, Strother lived at Berkeley Springs and
Charles Town until his death at the latter place.*

On Friday, December 2nd the notorious John Brown was executed at Charlestown, Virginia, according to the sentence of the
law. It may be a matter of curiosity to the public, to know how
a man, whose late acts have created so much disturbance, de-
ported himself in his last hours. Although very guarded in his
conversation on the subject, it was quite evident that up to a certain date, he indulged in the hope of a rescue or possibly a pardon. When, however, he ascertained that the Court of appeals
had confirmed the sentence, and saw the formidable military
preparations made to insure its execution, there was a marked
change in his manner. The great gulf between the simple probability and the gorgon head of certainty was not passed without a
visible struggle. He became more thoughtful & serious, less dog-
matic in the expression of his opinions, and somewhat softened
toward those who had treated him with civility & consideration
(and this included all whose official duties had brought them in
contact with him during his confinement).

He expressed a disinclination to receive visitors and sent for
his wife whom he had heretofore refused to see. Their meeting,
which took place in the afternoon of the 1st of December is represented to have been a most businesslike affair without visible
emotion on either side.

On the morning of the 2nd, Brown sent for an eminent legal
gentleman of Charlestown to write his will, or rather a codicil to
a former will disposing of some property which had been over-

looked. His manner then was cold & stony, his discourse altogether of business. After the completion of the writing, he enquired sharply and particularly about a dollar which had been mentioned in one of his letters but which had not come to hand. He was assured that all the money enclosed in letters had been delivered to him. This he insisted was an error, he had the letter mentioning the enclosure but the money was not there.

Unwilling to dispute, the gentleman said that the note might have been dropped accidentally and if found, the amount would be transmitted to his wife.

But Brown was by no means satisfied, and at length informed his visitor that in consideration of the service just rendered in writing his will, he might keep the dollar.

This the Lawyer politely but peremptorily declined, as he intended to accept no remuneration for what he had done, and again expressed a doubt as to whether the money had been sent.

The letter was produced. In the body of the writing the enclosure of the dollar was named, but on the margin, it was noted in pencil that it had been withdrawn & sent to his wife.

Thus was the mystery cleared up, to the very great apparent satisfaction of the old man and thus was concluded the last business transaction of his life. An hour after he was called on by the officers who were to convey him to the place of execution. His farewell scene with his late followers and fellow prisoners was peculiar and characteristic. To Coppock and the two negroes he gave a scolding and a quarter each, remarking that he had now no further use for money. To Stephens who had occupied the same room with him he also gave a quarter, and charged them all to die like men and not to betray their friends. To Cook he gave nothing but sharp & scathing words charging him with falsehood & cowardice. Cook denied the charges and attempted to dispute the points with his former commander but was authoritatively silenced. As to the question of veracity between them, circumstances seem decidedly to favour the truth of Cook's statement, and he may be readily excused for not caring to prolong a dispute with a man on his road to the gallows. Governor Wise and others, who were imposed upon by Brown's apparent frankness during his first examination at Harpers Ferry, have long since had occasion to change their opinions in regard to his honesty & veracity.

However, of all these matters I was not an eye nor ear witness, but had them from those who were.

As early as nine o clock on Friday morning, the field (adjoining the town of Charlestown), which had been selected for the place of execution, was occupied by a considerable body of soldiers, horse, foot, & artillery. A line of sentinels encircled the enclosure preventing access by the fences and a guard of infantry and artillery was posted at the gate by which spectators were required to enter.

I repaired to the field some time before the appointed hour that I might choose a convenient position to witness the final ceremony. The gibbet was erected on a gentle swell that commanded a view of the country for many miles around. From the scaffold which I ascended the view was of surpassing beauty. On every side stretching away into the blue distance were broad & fertile fields dotted with corn shocks and white farm houses glimmering through the leafless trees—emblems of prosperity and peace. Hard by was the pleasant village with its elegant suburban residences and bordering the picture east & west were the blue mountains thirty miles apart. In the Blue Ridge which lay to the eastward appeared the deep gap through which the Potomac and Shenandoah pour their united streams at Harpers ferry, eight miles distant.

Near at Hand stood long lines of soldiers resting on their arms while all the neighboring hills in sight were crowded with squadrons of cavalry. The balmy south wind was blowing which covered the landscape with a warm & dreamy haze reminding one rather of May than December. From hence thought I, the old man may see the spot where his enormous crime first took the form of action—he may see the beautiful land his dark plots had devoted to bloody ruin, he may see in the gleaming of a thousand swords and these serried lines of bayonets—what might be well calculated to make wiser men than he, thoughtful.

At eleven o clock escorted by a strong column of soldiers the Prisoner entered the field. He was seated in a furniture waggon on his coffin with his arms tied down above the elbows, leaving

the forearms free. The driver with two others occupied the front seat while the jailer sat in the after part of the waggon. I stood with a group of half a dozen gentlemen near the steps of the scaffold when the Prisoner was driven up. He wore the same seedy and dilapidated dress that he had at Harpers ferry and during his trial, but his rough boots had given place to a pair of particoloured slippers and he wore a low crowned broad brimmed hat (the first time I had ever seen him with a hat). He had entirely recovered from his wounds and looked decidedly better & stronger than when I last saw him. As he neared the gibbet his face wore a grim & greisly smirk which, but for the solemnity of the occasion might have suggested ideas of the ludicrous. He stepped from the waggon with surprising agility and walked hastily toward the scaffold pausing a moment as he passed our group to wave his pinioned arm & bid us good morning. I thought I could observe in this a trace of bravado—but perhaps I was mistaken, as his natural manner was short, ungainly and hurried. He mounted the steps of the scaffold with the same alacrity and there as if by previous arrangement, he immediately took off his hat and offered his neck for the halter which was as promptly adjusted by Mr. Avis the jailor. A white muslin cap or hood was then drawn over his face and the Sheriff not remembering that his eyes were covered requested him to advance to the platform. The Prisoner replied in his usual tone, "you will have to guide me there."

The breeze disturbing the arrangement of the hood the Sheriff asked his assistant for a pin. Brown raised his hand and directed him to the collar of his coat where several old pins were quilted in. The Sheriff took the pin & completed his work.

He was accordingly led forward to the drop the halter hooked to the beam and the officers supposing that the execution was to follow immediately took leave of him. In doing so, the Sheriff enquired if he did not want a handker-chief to throw as a signal to cut the drop. Brown replied, "no I dont care; I dont want you to keep me waiting unnecessarily."

These were his last words, spoken with that sharp nasal twang peculiar to him, but spoken quietly & civilly, without impatience or the slightest apparent emotion. In this position he stood for five minutes or more, while the troops that composed the escort were wheeling into the positions assigned them. I stood within a few paces of him and watched narrowly during these trying moments to see if there was any indication of his giving way. I detected nothing of the sort. He had stiffened himself for the drop and waited motionless 'till it came.

During all these movements no sound was heard but the quick stern words of military command, & when these ceased a dead silence reigned. Colonel Smith said to the Sheriff in a low voice— "we are ready". The civil officers descended from the scaffold. One who stood near me whispered earnestly—"He trembles, his knees are shaking." "You are mistaken," I replied, "It is the scaffold that shakes under the footsteps of the officers." The Sheriff struck the rope a sharp blow with a hatchet, the platform fell with a crash—a few convulsive struggles & a human soul had gone to judgement.

Thus died John Brown, the strange, stern old man; hard and uncouth in character as he was in personal appearance, undemonstrative and emotionless as an indian. In the manner of his death there was nothing dramatic or sympathetic. There was displayed neither the martial dignity of a chieftain nor the reckless bravado of a highwayman—neither the exalted enthusiasm of a martyr nor the sublime resignation of a christian. His voice and manner were precisely the same as if he had been bargaining for a sixpence worth of powder slightly anxious to get through the job but not uncivilly impatient. A stony stoicism, an easy indifference, so perfectly simulated that one could hardly perceive it was acting.

As with John Brown, so it seemed with the spectators around him. Of Sympathy there was none—of triumph no word nor sign. The fifteen hundred soldiers stood mute and motionless at their posts—The thousand civic spectators looked on in silence. At the end of half an hour the body was taken down & placed in the coffin —the people went home, the troops wheeled into columns & marched to their quarters, and the day concluded with the calm & quiet of a New England sabbath.

No man capable of reflection could have witnessed that scene without being deeply impressed with the truth that then & there was exhibited, not the vengeance of an outraged people, but the awful majesty of the law.—Boyd B. Stutler, "An Eyewitness Describes the Hanging of John Brown," *American Heritage*, VI, (February, 1955), 6-9. Courtesy of American Heritage Publishing Co., Inc.

Part Two: West Virginia

VIII. A House Divided—Secession and Reorganization

President Abraham Lincoln, c. 1862. Photograph by
Mathew B. Brady. Courtesy Library of Congress.

71. The Presidential Election of 1860 in West Virginia

In the presidential election of 1860 John Bell, the nominee of the Constitutional Union Party, carried Virginia by a plurality of 358 over his nearest opponent John C. Breckinridge, nominee of the Southern faction of the Democratic Party, who received 74,323 votes. Stephen A. Douglas, nominee of the Northern Democrats, and Abraham Lincoln, the Republican nominee, polled 16,290 and 1,929 respectively.

The voters from counties in present West Virginia cast 5,742 ballots for Douglas, a dedicated Unionist, and 1,402 for Lincoln. They gave Breckinridge who appealed to West Virginia Democrats as a Kentuckian, a Union man, a states rights' advocate, and a party regular, a plurality of 911 over Bell. The distribution of votes among the candidates for President in the West Virginia counties is given below.

	Republican Lincoln	Constitutional Union Bell	Democrat Breckinridge	Democrat Douglas
Barbour	0	422	910	39
Berkeley	0	913	830	106
Boone	0	121	204	24
Braxton	0	274	227	46
Brooke	173	173	450	76
Cabell	0	316	161	407
Calhoun	0	19	285	1
Clay	0	119	35	0
Doddridge	0	143	356	91
Fayette	0	381	241	65
Gilmer	0	117	268	119
Greenbrier	0	993	505	16
Hampshire	0	878	1,054	75
Hancock	254	33	262	85
Hardy	0	894	355	74
Harrison	0	931	1,191	107
Jackson	0	388	500	61
Jefferson	0	959	458	440
Kanawha	0	1,176	513	52

Lewis	0	332	604	247
Logan	0	100	271	6
Marion	1	569	1,337	137
Marshall	0	928	809	108
Mason	0	716	439	297
McDowell	0	35	37	0
Mercer	0	443	432	13
Monongalia	0	622	601	757
Monroe	0	693	520	83
Morgan	0	308	254	20
Nicholas	0	345	152	48
Ohio	771	1,202	915	716
Pendleton	0	400	217	133
Pleasants	0	140	166	119
Pocahontas	0	163	333	30
Preston	110	562	942	239
Putnam	0	400	327	38
Raleigh	0	230	69	14
Randolph	0	259	243	143
Ritchie	12	224	544	73
Roane	0	237	264	16
Taylor	0	647	575	26
Tucker	0	22	99	23
Tyler	0	315	423	197
Upshur	0	331	589	54
Wayne	0	326	166	82
Webster	0	66	52	5
Wetzel	0	90	607	153
Wirt	0	150	255	16
Wood	81	832	832	56
Wyoming	0	60	29	9
Totals	1,402	20,997	21,908	5,742

—*The Tribune Almanac for 1861,* New York, pp. 50-51.

72. The Virginia Ordinance of Secession

The election of Abraham Lincoln as President and the re-sulting secession movement in the lower South precipitated a crisis in Virginia. In response to a widespread demand Governor John Letcher, a Douglas Democrat and a Unionist, re-luctantly called an extra session of the General Assembly to meet on January 7, 1861. Ostensibly called to consider sale of the James River and Kanawha Company to a French concern, the assembly actually met to determine what the policy of Virginia would be in the secession crisis. After adopting a res-olution denying the right of the Federal government to coerce a state, the assembly approved the reorganization of the state militia and authorized an election on February 4 to choose delegates to a convention. In this election voters were asked to decide whether or not important decisions of the convention would be referred to the electorate for ratification or rejection. The voters approved the reference proposal and elected approximately 50 steadfast Unionists, 30 uncompromising secessionists, and 72 moderates who deplored secession but denied the right of the Federal government to coerce a state. The moderates organized the convention and with the help of the Unionists defeated every secessionist move until after the firing on Fort Sumter. Then came President Lincoln's call for troops and Governor Letcher's curt refusal to supply Virginia's quota. Virginia promptly took steps to sever its ties with the Union: On April 17 the convention adopted by a vote of 88 to 55 an ordinance of secession, effective when ratified by a vote of the people at the spring election on May 23.

No. 1.—An ORDINANCE to repeal the ratification of the Constitution of the United States of America, by the State of Virginia, and to resume all the rights and powers granted under said Constitution.

The people of Virginia, in their ratification of the constitution of the United States of America, adopted by them in convention on the twenty-fifty day of June in the year of our Lord one thousand seven hundred and eighty-eight, having declared that the powers granted under the said constitution were derived from the people of the United States, and might be resumed whensoever the same should be perverted to their injury and oppression; and the federal government having perverted said powers, not only to the injury of the people of Virginia, but to the oppression of the southern slaveholding states:

Now, therefore, we the people of Virginia do declare and ordain, that the ordinance adopted by the people of this state in convention on the twenty-fifty day of June in the year of our Lord one thousand seven hundred and eighty-eight, whereby the constitution of the United States of America was ratified, and all acts of the general assembly of this state ratifying or adopting amendments to said constitution, are hereby repealed and abrogated; that the union between the state of Virginia and the other states under the constitution aforesaid is hereby dissolved, and that the state of Virginia is in the full possession and exercise of all the rights of sovereignty which belong and appertain to a free and independent state.

And they do further declare, that said constitution of the United States of America is no longer binding on any of the citizens of this state.

This ordinance shall take effect and be an act of this day, when ratified by a majority of the votes of the people of this state, cast at a poll to be taken thereon on the fourth Thursday in May next, in pursuance of a schedule hereafter to be enacted.

Done in convention, in the city of Richmond, on the seventeenth day of April in the year of our Lord one thousand eight hundred and sixty-one, and in the eighty-fifth year of the commonwealth of Virginia.—*Ordinances Adopted by the Convention of Virginia in Secret Session in April and May 1861, Acts of the General Assembly of the State of Virginia, Passed in 1861, Richmond, 1861, Appendix.*

73. How the West Virginia Delegates Voted on the Ordinance of Secession

Of the fifty counties which were soon to comprise West Virginia, all except McDowell sent delegates to the Virginia convention which convened at Richmond, February 13, 1861. Since delegates to the Convention were chosen on the basis of population, some western Virginia counties sent one delegate, several two, while other counties with widely dispersed populations jointly sent one delegate. Of the 47 delegates who represented West Virginia counties in the Virginia convention, commonly called the Secession Convention, 15 voted for adoption of the Ordinance of Secession, 28 voted against adoption, and 4 did not vote. Allen C. Hammond of Berkeley who did not vote on roll call later cast his ballot in favor of secession, while George W. Berlin of Upshur County and Alpheus F. Haymond of Marion, who had voted against the secession ordinance, were permitted to change their votes to the affirmative.

Below is a list of West Virginia counties and delegate districts with their delegates arranged in columns showing how each finally voted on the Ordinance of Secession.

	For Secession	Against Secession	Not Voting
Barbour	Samuel Woods		
Berkeley	Allen C. Hammond	Edmund Pendleton	
Braxton, Clay Nicholas, Webster		Benjamin W. Byrne	
Brooke		Campbell Tarr	
Cabell		William McComas	
Doddridge, Tyler		Chapman J. Stuart	
Fayette, Raleigh	Henry L. Gillespie		
Gilmer, Calhoun, Wirt		C. B. Conrad	
Greenbrier		Samuel Price	
Hampshire		Edward Armstrong David Pugh	
Hancock		George McC. Porter	
Hardy			Thomas Maslin
Harrison		John S. Carlile	Benjamin Wilson
Jackson, Roane	Francis P. Turner		
Jefferson	Alfred H. Barbour	Logan Osburn	
Kanawha		George W. Summers Spicer Patrick	
Lewis		Caleb Boggess	
Logan, Boone, Wyoming	James Lawson		
Marion	Alpheus F. Haymond	Ephriam B. Hall	
Marshall		James Burley	
Mason		James M. Couch	
McDowell (not represented)			
Mercer	Napoleon B. French		
Monongalia		Waitman T. Willey Marshall M. Dent	
Monroe	Allen T. Caperton John Echols		
Morgan	Johnson Orrick		
Ohio		Sherrard Clemens Chester D. Hubbard	
Pendleton		Henry H. Masters	
Pocahontas			Paul McNeil

Pleasants,		
Ritchie	Cyrus Hall	
Preston		William G. Brown
		James C. McGrew
Putnam		James W. Hoge
Randolph,		
Tucker	John N. Hughes	
Taylor		John S. Burdette
Upshur	George W. Berlin	
Wayne		Burwell Spurlock
Wetzel	Leonard S. Hall	
Wood		John J. Jackson

—J. H. Brenaman A *History of Virginia Conventions*, pp. 53-56.

74. Last Train From Richmond

William H. Edwards (1822-1909), lawyer, businessman and internationally famous naturalist, came to the Kanawha Valley in the 1850's. Born in the Catskills, he was the great-great-grandson of the eminent New England evangelist Jonathan Edwards. After graduating from Williams College, Edwards studied law in New York City and in 1846 made a trip to South America. In 1847 he published VOYAGE UP THE AMAZON *which described the wildlife of the Amazon forests.*

Edwards settled at Coalburg on the Kanawha near Charleston, acquired extensive holdings of wild lands, opened coal mines, operated coal barges, built railroads, and busied himself in related enterprises. In the meantime he published many articles and papers while writing THE BUTTERFLIES OF NORTH AMERICA, *published 1872-1897.*

Edwards sustained a keen interest in public affairs. He went as an observer to Richmond during the secession crisis and was there on April 17, when the Virginia convention adopted the Ordinance of Secession. The excerpt below describes events and relates some of his experiences.

I WENT FROM NEW YORK TO RICHMOND on Monday, April 8th, 1861, at the request of the Hon. Allen T. Caperton, who was there as a member of the Legislature. . . . In the convention, the Hon. George W. Summers and Dr. Spicer Patrick were members from Kanawha. It was a gathering of the ablest men of the State. Ex-President Tyler was one of them, and so was ex-Governor Wise. From one of the lower counties came Jeremiah Morton, whom I had known as a stockholder in one of the cannel coal-oil companies of Paint Creek, in Kanawha county, and also as one of the recently organized White Sulphur Springs Company. . . .

On the day I left there was no symptom of present disturbance, at any rate. So when I reached Washington, I saw nothing to indicate a coming storm. Passing through Alexandria, I noticed a pole from which flew a new style of flag, and someone remarked that this was the emblem of the Confederacy, but there was no talk about it. People were keeping their opinions to themselves. That was all to Richmond. I put up at Ballard's Exchange Hotel, where I found Mr. Caperton and several friends from the Western counties. Judge Summers was one of these. He, in connection with John Tyler, William C. Rives and others, had represented Virginia in a peace deputation that met in Washington late in February or early in March, but which had been unable to obtain assurances or promises from the incoming administration. The Judge was a Union man then and always, and he expressed to me his disquiet at the situation. Indeed he was very much dispirited. He spoke of desperate efforts that were being made to take Virginia over to the Confederacy, and what the result would be he could not conjecture. Dr. Patrick felt in the same way, as did others whom I knew. All agreed that the sooner this convention separated the better for Virginia. I was surprised at this feeling, as from what I had heard at home I had not believed that Virginia could be made the cat's paw of the cotton States.

On successive days I attended the meetings of the convention, and listened to no end of speeches, some few sensible, deprecating excitement and hasty action, but the most were fiery and breathed of war and blood. The Union men had already had their say, and had no wish now to protract the session, and the talking was mostly left to the other side. The extremists, on the other hand, were desirous of nothing so much as delay. If they could prolong the session a few weeks only, something might turn up to "fire the Southern heart," and force the State out. John Tyler was ardent for secession, and talked interminably. So did Wise and Morton, and all three made long speeches on nothing. It seemed to me that these men were acting on a preconcerted plan. . . .

One of the most outspoken of the Union men was John S. Carlile, from Harrison county. I had made his acquaintance some years previous in the Western Part of the State—a bright, able man. He fought Wise and Morton strenuously. Being a Democrat, he was very obnoxious to the secessionists.

. . . On Sunday I took a walk to the suburbs with Mr. Caperton, and he expressed himself as being greatly disturbed at the situation. He said that messengers were coming in from his county and from Greenbrier and the adjoining counties, and the country was reported as wild for secession. He did not believe that the contagion could be resisted. He thought that if Virginia cast her lot with the Southern States it would make for peace. The government would not dare to attack the Confederacy, with the addition of Virginia, and in time, through the good offices of his State, the two sections would be brought together again. I suggested that he use his great influence in his district, and that Mr. Price should do the same, and resist this ruinous action of the convention before the people, as Judge Summers and Col. Ben Smith and Lewis Ruffner would do in Kanawha; and I assured him that it was a great mistake to assume that the North would not fight for the Union.

. . . That day, 15th April, President Lincoln issued the call for 75,000 troops, of which Virginia was expected to furnish her quota. This added fresh fuel to the sufficiently hot fire. I went with a gentleman that evening to the Powhatan House, the headquarters of the extremists, to see what was going on. We found Mr. Morton enthroned in the lobby, haranguing, and evidently feeling extra good. Presently he addressed me personally: "Sir, if all my coal in Kanawha were diamonds, and the White Sulphur ran pearls, I would give the whole to have Virginia go out. Why, sir, in twenty years grass would be growing in the streets of New York, and Norfolk would be the bigger city." . . .

I had gone to bed that night when Mr. Caperton came to my room and advised me to leave town in the morning, else there was no telling when I might be able to get away. He said that some fellows had just been through the house carrying a rope in search of Carlile. That gentleman probably had notice, for he had already left. He walked a few miles up the Fredericksburg road and boarded the train in the morning.

On Monday, April 17th, the convention passed the ordinance of secession, big with disaster to Virginia. It was to be submitted to the voters a month later, but the managers proceeded as if the State were already out, as in fact it was.

I left Richmond early, and heard afterwards that I had taken the last train that left for the North for many a day. . . .—William H. Edwards, "A Bit of History," *The West Virginia Historical Magazine Quarterly,* II, (July, 1902), 59-64.

75. Mayor Sweeney's Proclamations

The secession of Virginia placed the western Virginian in the agonizingly difficult position of having to decide immediately whether he would support his state or his country. Nevertheless some withheld judgment while others optimistically subscribed to the belief expressed by the Kingwood CHRONICLE *that "The North will not invade us if we stand firm where we are, and the east has not the means of compelling us to abandon our defenseless homes." Indeed, as the war clouds darkened security became the concern of the borderland and many sought it in neutrality. The impact of the secession crisis in northwestern Virginia was reflected in proclamations of Andrew James Sweeney (1827-1893), Democratic mayor of Wheeling. The first proclamation, issued on April 19, 1861, anticipated the official announcement of the adoption of the Virginia secession ordinance, the second set apart Thursday, May 9, 1861, as a day of fasting and prayer.*

MAYOR'S OFFICE,
Wheeling, April 19, 1861.

WHEREAS APPREHENSIONS EXIST IN THE MINDS of many citizens, that violations of the peace of the city may occur in the present excited state of the public mind, upon questions of political import, I deem it advisable to issue this my proclamation, calling upon all good citizens to preserve the public peace and order, at all times, and under all circumstances, and invoking them to refrain from harshness of speech, and from any act which might lead to violence of any kind to any person or property whatsoever, and to render aid to the authorities in maintaining the public peace, protecting property, and in suppressing lawless violence by whomsoever attempted.

A. J. SWEENEY, Mayor.

I do heartily concur in the above proclamation and will use all my official powers to maintain its observance.

A. P. Woods, Chief J. P.

—West Virginia Collection, West Virginia University Library.

MAYOR'S OFFICE.
Wheeling, May 4, 1861.

Whereas, at a meeting of the City Council, held on Friday evening, 3d inst., a resolution was unanimously adopted recommending the observance of a day of fasting, humiliation and prayer, therefore I, A. J. Sweeney, Mayor of the city of Wheeling, fully impressed with the imminence of the danger which threatens our beloved country, and trusting in the mercy of Almighty God to avert it, do earnestly recommend to the people and the several Pastors and congregations of this city to set apart Thursday, the 9th day of May, for the purpose named, and that they observe it, by engaging in public services and devotional duties according to their usages on such solemn occasions.

And further, I recommend that all persons engaged in business of any kind whatever in this city, do close their several establishments and abstain from their ordinary pursuits on that day.

A. J. SWEENEY, Mayor.

—Wheeling *Intelligencer,* May 7, 1861.

76. The Clarksburg Convention, April 22, 1861

Soon after the adoption of the Ordinance of Secession by the Virginia convention on April 17, 1861, most of the delegates from the western counties who had voted against secession returned to their homes. There they found not only the resistance movement against secession already under way but also a strong sentiment for the creation of a new state. Of the several mass meetings then gathering at county seats throughout northwestern Virginia, the one held at Clarksburg on Monday, April 22, 1861, set the stage for action on a broader scale. Led by John S. Carlile, a delegate from Harrison County just returned from the Richmond convention, more than a thousand citizens listened to speeches and adopted resolutions denouncing secession and recommending appointment of delegates by the northwestern counties to a convention to meet on May 13.

Printed on April 22, 1861, in an extra edition of the Clarksburg WESTERN VIRGINIA GUARD *as an "Address of the Convention to the People of Northwestern Virginia," this call for action was distributed Revere-like by railroad and horseback throughout northwestern Virginia as well as in the upper Potomac counties.*

WHEREAS, THE CONVENTION now in session in this State, called by the Legislature, . . . has, contrary to the expectation of a large majority of the people of this State, adopted an ordinance withdrawing Virginia from the Federal Union.

And Whereas, By the law calling said Convention, it is expressly declared that no such ordinance shall have force or effect, or be of binding obligation upon the people of this State, until the same shall be ratified by the voters at the polls.

And Whereas, We have seen with regret that demonstrations of hostility, unauthorized by law, and inconsistent with the duty of law-abiding citizens, still owing allegiance to the Federal Government, have been made by a portion of the people of this State against the said Government.

And Whereas, The Governor of this Commonwealth has, by proclamation, undertaken to decide for the People of Virginia, that which they have reserved to themselves, the right to decide by their votes at the polls, and has called upon the volunteer soldiery of this State to report to him and hold themselves in readiness to make war upon the Federal Government, which Government is Virginia's Government, and must in law and of right continue so to be, until the people of Virginia shall, by their votes, and through the ballot-box, that great conservator of a free people's liberties, decide otherwise.

And Whereas, The peculiar situation of Northwestern Virginia, separated as it is by natural barriers from the rest of the State, precludes all hope of timely succor in the hour of danger from other portions of the State, and demands that we should look to and provide for our own safety in the fearful emergency in which we now find ourselves placed by the action of our State authorities, who have disregarded the great fundamental principle upon which our beautiful system of Government is based, to-wit: "That all governmental power is derived from the consent of the governed," and have without consulting the people, placed this State in hostility to the Federal Government by seizing upon its ships and obstructing the channel at the mouth of Elizabeth river; by wresting from the Federal officers at Norfolk and Richmond the custom houses; by tearing from the Nation's property the Nation's flag, and putting in its place a bunting, the emblem of rebellion, and by marching upon the National Armory at Harper's Ferry; thus inaugurating a war without consulting those in whose name they profess to act.

And Whereas, The exposed condition of Northwestern Virginia requires that her people should be united in action, and harmonious in purpose—there being a perfect identity of interests in times of war as well as in peace—Therefore,

Be it Resolved, That it be and is hereby recommended to the people in each and all of the counties composing Northwestern Virginia to appoint delegates, not less than five in number, of their wisest, best, and discreetest men, to meet in Convention on the 13th day of May next, to consult and determine upon such action as the people of Northwestern Virginia should take in the present fearful emergency. . . .—*How West Virginia Was Made*, edited by Virgil A. Lewis, pp. 33-34.

77. The Southern Rights Convention, April 26, 1861

In spite of the predominance of Unionist strength in north-western Virginia, there was strong secessionist sentiment in many counties. To counteract the influence of the "Clarksburg Resolutions," adopted April 22, 1861, the secessionists sponsored a states' rights meeting which met in Clarksburg on April 26. Presided over by former Governor Joseph Johnson, this body endorsed the secession ordinance, condemned the proposal to dismember the state, and urged citizens to arm for the defense of Virginia. Former Governor Johnson and sixty other citizens of Harrison County signed the call to this convention.

TO THE
SOUTHERN RIGHTS
MEN
OF HARRISON COUNTY.

War is upon us! A most fearful, terrible and devastating war has been inaugurated by the present administration; it has been forced upon the people of the South, and the proclamation of Lincoln calling for 75,000 men, to carry out the infamous behests of the North, to murder the citizens of our sister Southern States, is published in our midst, and Virginia is called upon to furnish her quota of men, and means for the slaughter of those who know their rights, and dare maintain them. Georgia, Alabama, Mississippi, South Carolina, Texas, Florida, and Louisiana, and after them Virginia, and the other Southern States, are to be trampled under the iron heel of Black Republican despotism. The battle cry and shout of an insolent and vindictive Northern fanatic, who claims by the votes of your enemies to be your master, is now heard; he is now arming a civil war, and inciting blood and rapine at the hands of the slave; is now calling upon you to aid him in coercion, to carry fire and sword into the homes of those to whom you are endeared by every tie of consanguinity, of interest and affection.

FREEMEN OF HARRISON! will you stand by and permit this war to be waged without any interference or remonstrance? you are bound to assume a position: the fanatical North calls upon you; the outraged, injured and gallant people of the South call upon you; the honor, the independent State-rights men of Virginia call upon you, and you this day have to decide which voice you will obey.—The Union is dissolved, it cannot be cemented again and made a Union by the spilling of blood. The independence of the Southern seceded States should be at once acknowledged; civil war and destruction should not wrap this land in flames, and internecine strife should not be forced upon us. FREEMEN OF HARRISON! this dark and bloody drama which Abraham Lincoln is desiring to open up before the country the people of Virginia by

PROMPT ACTION,

may avert; we invite you to meet with us in solemn assembly; let every man come to Clarksburg on

FRIDAY, THE 26th DAY OF APRIL,

to take counsel together and take such action as the circumstances then surrounding us may require.

We do not propose to you to go to war, but we want the great heart of the people to beat audibly, as we know it does silently, responsive to our Southern sisters in this perilous hour of their sad calamity. We are opposed to coercion;—we deplore the necessity of revolution. We therefore invite you to meet with us and say that no hostile forces whose aim shall be the degradation of the South, shall pollute the soil of Virginia with impunity.

Come one! Come all! We may under the providence of the God of armies, make such a start that others may be induced to follow, or at least wipe out the stain and stigma of being looked upon as coercionists and the minions of the bloody crew who are preparing to destroy our homes, and worse than all, the liberties of the Commonwealth.—West Virginia Collection, West Virginia University Library.

78. The Baltimore and Ohio in a Dilemma

Opened to the Ohio in 1853, the main line of the Baltimore and Ohio Railroad, 379 miles long, extended across Maryland and Virginia, from Baltimore to Wheeling. With branch lines and supporting connections on the Potomac and the Ohio, the road was situated to compete for the trade and travel of the industrial North, the planting South, and the agricultural West. But with roots deep in slave soil and tendrils reaching into free states, the line occupied an unenviable position at the beginning of the Civil War. The unique position of the road at the outbreak of hostilities in April, 1861, was the subject of a trenchant editorial by Archibald W. Campbell, militant editor of the Wheeling INTELLIGENCER.

THIS ROAD, IN ITS GEOGRAPHICAL POSITION, is to be deeply sympathized with. It is most unfortunate. Its case resembles that of the amphibious animal that could not live on land, and died in water. It is in a position in which it can be neither flesh nor fowl—neither for the Government, nor completely with the traitors. The main stem runs through 379 miles of country, and through every kind of country, at that. And the public sentiment which it traverses, is not less varied than the soil it passes over. The terminus at one hand is among the mobocracy; at the other end, here in Wheeling, among good, order-loving Union men. At Harper's Ferry it is completely under military despotism, and every train has to run the gauntlet of cannon and armed espionage. At Cumberland it passes through loyalty and Union, and from that point on west, it might be said to be all right.

The Government seems to be deliberating as to what they shall do about this road. We see it noticed that the Secretary of War has notified John W. Garrett, that in case he carries troops, arms, or ammunitions of war for the conspirators, that the road will be condemned under the treason act of the Government. And this will be just what the Government will have to do. No road should be permitted to run an hour, after it is found that they are giving aid and comfort to the Government enemies.

We should be very sorry to see the Baltimore road stopped, because, despite all Wheeling's old prejudices against it, it is really her efficient ally. But if, as is reported, Letcher is to send troops and arms over its rails for the traitors, the Secretary of War should close it from the go. It is the duty of the Union men of Wheeling to at once make themselves acquainted with this fact; to know whether troops or arms will be brought here by this route. It should be known at once.

And we have this much to say in connection, that if ever troops or arms *are* brought over it into our midst, it will be the sorriest day that ever the Baltimore road or any other road saw. Ohio and Pennsylvania will wipe out the last vestige of its existence. Those great States never intend that their borders shall be laid waste by any willing or unwilling instrument of the conspirators. And if it shall prove to be the misfortunes of that road that the control of it has passed from its own hands, then the sooner the Government knows it and acts upon it the better. As a measure of safety the road should surrender its whole working establishment into the hands of the Government. This loyal act would be warmly remembered by the people East and West after these troublesome times shall have passed away. It is the only hope which the road has for a future.—Wheeling *Intelligencer*, April 27, 1861.

79. Judge George W. Thompson's Instructions to the Ohio County Grand Jury, May 10, 1861

Among those who counselled moderation when civil war threatened in 1861 was George Western Thompson (1806-1888) of Wheeling. Born in Ohio County, Virginia, and graduated from Jefferson College, Pennsylvania, he had read law in Richmond, practiced in St. Clairsville, Ohio, and moved to Wheeling in 1837. He held several state and Federal offices as a Democrat and in the legislative contest for governor in 1848 ran second to John B. Floyd, the successful candidate. While serving in the United States House of Representatives from 1851 to 1852, he secured passage of a bill which declared that the bridge over the Ohio River at Wheeling was part of a postal route, thereby nullifying a decision of the United States Supreme Court which had ordered its removal. In 1852 Thompson was elected judge of the Twelfth Judicial Circuit of Virginia, a post which he held until mid-year 1861, when the reorganized General Assembly removed him because he refused to take the prescribed oath of allegiance to the United States and to the restored government. Meanwhile, Thompson gained prominence as a Confederate sympathizer when two of his sons joined the Confederate army. Indeed his alleged pro-Southern sympathies twice caused his arrest by Federal authorities. Both times he was released—in 1861 by order of his friend, Secretary of War Edwin M. Stanton; two years later by order of Federal Judge John J. Jackson.

Although Judge Thompson stoutly defended the Union in the secession crisis, he vigorously opposed the reorganization of the Virginia government. On May 10, 1861, three days before the First Wheeling Convention opened, his instructions to an Ohio County Circuit Court grand jury pinpointed the constitutional dilemmas then facing Virginians. The charge so impressed the jurymen that twenty asked for copies. The Wheeling INTELLIGENCER *obliged and printed the address in full.*

WE ARE CONVENED AGAIN UNDER THE MOST SOLEMN and affecting circumstances to the discharge of our respective duties. Surrounded as we are by excited passions, under the influence, as we must be, of conflicting emotions arising out of our relations to the double sovereignties which constitute our form of government, and both of which now claim our allegiance, we are in a conflict in which we must determine the fatal choice. Fatal it must be, let the choice be as it may, for upon that choice depends our line of conduct, whether our aid and our sympathies shall be with the government of the Union, or with the action of a majority of the people of the State in opposition to that government....

... You, each of you have this day sworn to discharge your duties to the Commonwealth of Virginia....

The oath is of a double aspect; it enforces your duties to the Commonwealth, and it purges your hearts from all ill will and fear and favor as it regards individuals or classes in the community. Upon this solemn adjuration you are called upon to discharge these twofold duties.

But upon him who presides over your deliberations, and whose duty it is to give you in charge the law in regard to all matters touching your present service, a more comprehensive, if not a more solemn duty is imposed....

Before I was permitted to take my seat upon this bench and administer the law between man and man; between man and the Commonwealth in the enforcement of its criminal laws, I was obliged to take an oath to support the Constitution of the United States....

. . . This brings us to the extremely delicate questions which are dividing us among ourselves and disturbing the consciences of just and upright men. This oath to support the Constitution of the United States is obligatory on all, whether it has been taken in fact or not. The taking of the oath is but the formal declaration of the natural allegiance.... The obligation on all is the same: the moral obligation of that allegiance bears on all alike. It is the obligation on you and me in the discharge of these our duties....

But the State is a part of the Constitution of the United States, and the General Government is bound by obligations to the State, as high and solemn as those which bind the State to the General Government. By sub-section fifteen of Section VIII of the first article of the Constitution of the United States, the General Government is bound to provide for calling forth the militia to execute the laws of the Union, suppress insurrections and repel invasions. The first power here "to execute the laws of the United States" may be to enforce a judgment between two or more States, and to enforce the rights of the weak. Under the third article of the Constitution of the United States, it may be and is its duty to suppress any insurrection against the Constitution and laws of the State, committed by its own citizens, or its slaves, and it is its duty to repel any invasion of one State whether by a foreign nation or citizens of another State, and this whether they come in to aid an insurrection or otherwise....

But the obligation of the general Government does not stop here. By the third section of the fourth article, it is provided that "New States may be admitted by the Congress, into this Union; *but no new State shall be formed or erected within the jurisdiction of any other State;* nor any State be formed by the junction of two or more States, or parts of States, *without the consent of the Legislatures of the States concerned,* as well as of the Congress." Here is the obligation of the general Government to suppress insurrection; to prevent by force or any other manner than that provided for by the Constitution, the division of a State. . . .

But in the present unhappy condition of affairs, the general Government claims to be in the most solemn discharge of its constitutional functions, and this from the necessity of its own self preservation. It would then be fallacious, unseasonable and the most guilty ambition on the part of our rulers to permit, much less to aid in the division of the State by lawless and insurrectionary movements—to break the Constitution to save the Constitution.

An armed force on the soil of Virginia, of its own citizens moving towards such purpose would be traitors to Virginia. An armed force from another State aiding in such a movement, would be traitors against the General Government; it would be procuring in a change in the form and internal regulation of the Government by violence, which the Constitution says shall be done by peace, and by consent of the States and of Congress. . . .

No man can strike at the sovereignty of the State without striking at the welfare and sovereignty of the Union. Destroy the States and the Union is gone forever, and central despotism is established on their ruins. . . . Those who are in haste to show their loyalty to the Constitution of the Union by setting up a broken and divided sovereignty against the State, do not see, or will not maintain their true loyalty to the Constitution which they so ardently support and so earnestly maintain, but which they violate in their very zeal for its maintainance. . . .

Be assured, gentlemen of the jury and my fellow citizens, that our greatest security is in our mutual confidence and in a manly determination to support the law. Let those whose passions, or whose other necessities or impulses, drive them to arms, go to the scenes of conflict and carnage, and there offer themselves to that side which best represents their views and feelings, and leave their own community, their wives, their children and their parents in peace.—Wheeling *Intelligencer,* May 17, 1861.

80. Resolutions Adopted by the First Wheeling Convention, May 15, 1861

Twenty-seven counties of western Virginia responded to the call of the Clarksburg meeting of April 22, and together sent 436 representatives to a convention which met in Washington Hall at Wheeling on May 13, 1861. After a spirited but futile debate on the extent of their powers, the delegates elected John Moss of Wood County as president. Since most of the delegates had been irregularly chosen, this meeting was like the parent one at Clarksburg, a revolutionary rather than a constituent body.

Whatever their differences on other matters, the delegates were unanimous in their opposition to secession. However the convention divided sharply on the course it should follow. One faction led by John S. Carlile of Harrison County and Campbell Tarr of Brooke County advocated the immediate formation of a new state, while another led by General John J. Jackson of Wood County, Waitman T. Willey of Monongalia, and Francis H. Pierpont of Marion, urged postponement of action until Virginians had balloted on the Ordinance of Secession. Although a minority at the beginning of the discussions, the latter faction prevailed, as can be seen in the resolutions adopted by an almost unanimous vote on Wednesday, May 15. The Convention then adjourned—but not until it had taken steps to prepare an address to the people of Virginia and provide for the election of delegates to another convention to be convened at a time and place designated by a central committee. The Convention authorized this committee to issue the call in the event the voters of Virginia ratified the Ordinance of Secession.

1. *Resolved,* That in our deliberate judgment the ordinance passed by the Convention of Virginia, on the 17th day of April, 1861, known as the ordinance of secession, by which said Convention undertook in the name of the State of Virginia, to repeal the ratification of the Constitution of the United States by this State, and to resume all the rights and powers granted under said Constitution, is unconstitutional, null and void.

2. *Resolved,* That the schedule attached to the ordinance of secession, suspending and prohibiting the election of members of Congress for this State, is a manifest usurpation of power, to which we ought not to submit.

3. *Resolved,* That the agreement of the 24th of April, 1861, between the Commissioners of the Confederate States and this State, and the ordinance of the 25th of April, 1861, approving and ratifying said agreement, by which the whole military force and military operations, offensive and defensive, of this Commonwealth, are placed under the chief control and direction of the President of the Confederate States, upon the same principles, basis and footing as if the Commonwealth were now a member of said Confederacy; and all the acts of the executive officers of our State in pursuance of said agreement and ordinance, are plain and palpable violations of the Constitution of the United States, and are utterly subversive of the rights and liberties of the people of Virginia.

4. *Resolved,* That we earnestly urge and entreat the citizens of the State every where, but more especially in the Western section, to be prompt at the polls on the 23rd instant; and to impress upon every voter the duty of voting in condemnation of the Ordinance of Secession, in the hope that we may not be involved in the ruin to be occasioned by its adoption, and with the view to demonstrate the position of the West on the question of secession.

5. *Resolved,* That we earnestly recommend to the citizens of Western Virginia to vote for members of the Congress of the United States, in their several districts, in the exercise of the right secured to us by the Constitution of the United States and the State of Virginia.

6. *Resolved,* That we also recommend to the citizens of the several counties to vote at said election for such persons as entertain the opinions expressed in the foregoing resolutions for members of the Senate and House of Delegates of our State.

7. *Resolved,* That in view of the geographical, social, commercial and industrial interests of Northwestern Virginia, this Convention is constrained in giving expression to the opinion of their constituents to declare that the Virginia Convention in assuming to change the relation of the State of Virginia to the Federal Government, have not only acted unwisely and unconstitutionally, but have adopted a policy utterly ruinous to all the material interests of our section, severing all our social ties, and drying up all the channels of our trade and prosperity.

8. *Resolved,* That in the event of the Ordinance of Secession being ratified by a vote, we recommend to the people of the Counties here represented, and all others disposed to co-operate with us, to appoint on the 4th day of June, 1861, delegates to a General Convention, to meet on the 11th of that month, at such place as may be designated by the Committee hereinafter provided, to devise such measures and take such action as the safety and welfare of the people they represent may demand,—each County to appoint a number of Representatives to said Convention equal to double the number to which it will be entitled in the next House of Delegates; and the Senators and Delegates to be elected on the 23d inst., by the counties referred to, to the next General Assembly of Virginia, and who concur in the views of this Convention, to be entitled to seats in the said Convention as members thereof.

9. *Resolved,* That inasmuch as it is a conceded political axiom, that government is founded on the consent of the governed and is instituted for their good, and it cannot be denied that the course pursued by the ruling power in the State, is utterly subversive and destructive of our interests, we believe we may rightfully and successfully appeal to the proper authorities of Virginia, to permit us peacefully and lawfully to separate

from the residue of the State, and form ourselves into a government to give effect to the wishes, views and interests of our constituents.

10. *Resolved*, That the public authorities to be assured that the people of the North West will exert their utmost power to preserve the peace, which they feel satisfied they can do, until an opportunity is afforded to see if our present difficulties cannot receive a peaceful solution; and we express the earnest hope that no troops of the Confederate States be introduced among us, as we believe it would be eminently calculated to produce civil war.

11. *Resolved*, That in the language of Washington in his letter of the 17th of September, 1787, to the President of Congress, "in all our deliberations on this subject we have kept steadily in view that which appears to us the greatest interest of every true American, the consolidation of our Union, in which is involved our prosperity, felicity, safety and perhaps our national existence." And therefore we will maintain and defend the Constitution of the United States and the laws made in the pursuance thereof, and all officers acting there-under in the lawful discharge of their respective duties.

12. *Resolved*, That John S. Carlile, James S. Wheat, C. D. Hubbard, F. H. Pierpont, Campbell Tarr, G. R. Latham, Andrew Wilson, S. H. Woodward, and James W. Paxton, be a Central Committee to attend to all the matters connected with the objects of this Convention; and that they have power to assemble this Convention at any time they may think necessary.

13. *Resolved*, That each county represented in this Convention, and any others that may be disposed to co-operate with us, be requested to appoint a Committee of five, whose duty it shall be to correspond with the Central Committee, and to see that all things necessary, be done to carry out the objects of this Convention.

14. *Resolved*, That the Central Committee be instructed to prepare an address to the people of Virginia, in conformity with the foregoing resolutions, and cause the same to be published and circulated as extensively as possible.—West Virginia Collection, West Virginia University Library.

81. John S. Carlile and Waitman T. Willey Find Common Ground

Following the adoption of resolutions in the evening of May 15, 1861, postponing action on the formation of a new state, the First Wheeling Convention adjourned SINE DIE *to await the results of the election of May 23, when the voters of Virginia balloted on the Ordinance of Secession. Before adjournment, however, that body heard spirited addresses by John S. Carlile and Waitman T. Willey who were leaders of opposing factions at the opening of the convention but now stood together on a platform of "unity of action and singleness of purpose." Both spoke for the Union and for a new state.*

[MR. CARLILE:]

I feel that upon us of Northwestern Virginia, and upon our efforts, depend to a very great extent, the restoration of harmony to the whole of our beloved land, and the preservation and perpetuity of those free institutions under which we have been born and reared. This is a government to love: and I cannot for a moment contemplate its destruction without feeling as I never deemed myself capable of feeling in contemplating any subject short of utter annihilation. When I left the Virginia Convention, on the evening on which the Ordinance of Secession passed, and walked solitary and alone to my lodgings, and felt that a home and country remained not to me, I felt as sad at heart as I could have felt had I just returned from the burial ground, having deposited in their last resting place my wife and children. Entertaining these sentiments, placing this estimate upon this government, I have resolved to do all that I can, in any and every position, to preserve it, and aid and co-operate with my fellow-citizens in its preservation. And I believe that preservation is to be secured by and through the agency of this portion of Virginia; by and through the erection of a new State; by and through, it may be, scenes of blood, accomplished by deeds of daring, but deeds that will result to effect its accomplishment. Let each and all determine for himself, and get his neighbors to determine with him. Be the means to be used what they may, come life or come death, it shall be accomplished. . . .

[MR. WILLEY:]

I do not despair of the Republic . . . If we could have two weeks longer until the election, I verily believe, the disheartening anticipation of my friend from Harrison to the contrary notwithstanding, to use a vulgar, but expressive phrase, which may be well applied to this ordinance of secession, we would "knock it into a cocked hat." (Laughter.) Why, sir, I am credibly informed that these soldiers, of whom we have heard so much, and from whom we anticipate so much danger, and who are said to be quartered and posted all over the State for the purpose of public intimidation, have pledged their lives that their own blood shall crimson the streets, but they will cast their votes on the 23rd of this month, against the ordinance of secession . . .

Fellow-citizens, the first thing we have got to fight is the Ordinance of Secession. Let us kill it on the 23d of this month. (Applause.) Let us bury it deep beneath the hills of Northwestern Virginia. Let us pile up our glorious hills on it; bury it deep so that it will never make its appearance among us again. (Applause.) Let us go back home and vote, even if we are beaten upon the final result, for the benefit of the moral influence of that vote. If we give something like a decided preponderating vote of a majority in the Northwest, that alone secures our rights. (Applause.) That alone, at least, secures an independent State if we desire it. . . .

We have to go to work now. We must appeal to the people; appeal to their patriotism; and let us defeat the ordinance of secession in Northwestern Virginia at least. My advices from the valley are, that where, some weeks since, a Union man dare not hold up his head, he has come out now, and is shaking his fist at his adversary. They are getting bold and numerous; and I should not be surprised if the upper and lower valley, even Jefferson county, right under the shadow of—or rather casting its shadow upon—Harper's Ferry, and under the in-

fluence and intimidation of the soldiery there, . . . should all give
majorities against the ordinance. . . .—Virgil A. Lewis, *How
West Virginia Was Made*, pp. 66, 68-70.

82. Keynote Address at the Second Wheeling Convention, June 11, 1861

*Events moved rapidly following the adjournment of the First
Wheeling Convention. On May 23 the voters of Virginia ratified
the Ordinance of Secession, thanks to decisive majorities in
the Tidewater, the Piedmont, and the Valley. But west of the
Alleghenies, except in southern and central counties, Virginians
cast equally decisive majorities against ratification. The occupation of northwestern Virginia by Union forces under General
George B. McClellan a week later assured the election of delegates to the proposed convention at Wheeling. There on
June 11 about one hundred delegates from thirty-four counties
organized the Second Wheeling Convention with Arthur I. Boreman of Wood County as president. More than a third were
members of the Virginia general assembly, several were sent
by military authorities, some were self-appointed. Of the forty-
four Virginia counties west of the Allegheny divide, fifteen sent
no delegates, while such far-off eastern counties as Alexandria,
Fairfax, Hardy, Hampshire, and Jefferson had representation.*

*The first formal action of the Convention was the adoption
of resolutions thanking General McClellan for military protection, justifying the presence of Union troops on Virginia soil,
and expressing hope for the recovery of Colonel Benjamin F.
Kelley who had suffered a painful wound at the battle of Philippi. Arthur I. Boreman delivered the following address as
he became permanent chairman.*

. . . THE CONVENTION OF VIRGINIA AT RICHMOND, so far as
they have the power, have by the passage of an Ordinance of
Secession withdrawn us from the Union of our fathers. They
submitted their action to a vote of the people as they pro-

claimed it, but in a way that made that vote a mockery. The vote in form has ratified the Ordinance of Secession—thus in the estimation of that Convention withdrawing us from the United States of America. Under these circumstances Western Virginia is placed in a peculiar position.—The States north of us and some of the Slave States have made no effort by an official body to withdraw from the Union. States south of us have gone according to their opinions out of the Union. Elsewhere there are no efforts being made in any of them by any regularly constituted bodies to retain their places in the Union, while here in Western Virginia we have determined that by the help of Him who rules on high we will resist the action of that Richmond Convention, which has practiced upon us a monstrous usurpation of power, violated the Constitution of the country and violated every rule of right. We have determined I say, to resist it, and under this determination we are found here to-day to take definite action. If you gentlemen, will go with me, we will take definite, determined and unqualified action as to the course we will pursue. We will take such action as will result in Western Virginia, if not the whole of Virginia, remaining in the Union of our fathers. I am satisfied that the members of this Convention concur with me almost unanimously.

Then in this Convention we have no ordinary political gathering. We have no ordinary task before us. We come here to carry out and execute, and, it may be, to institute a government for ourselves. We are determined to live under a State Government in the United States of America and under the Constitution of the United States. It requires stout hearts to execute this purpose; it requires men of courage—of unfaltering determination; and I believe, in the gentlemen who compose this Convention, we have the stout heart and the men who are determined in this purpose. The definite line of action to be pursued, it is not for me to indicate. . . .—Virgil A. Lewis, *How West Virginia Was Made*, pp. 82-83.

83. Dennis B. Dorsey, Jr., Urges Immediate Statehood

Whether the Second Wheeling Convention should proceed immediately to the formation of a new state or reorganize the government of Virginia became the overriding issue in that body upon meeting, June 11, 1861. The leading exponent in the Convention of the plan to create a new state without delay was Dr. Dennis B. Dorsey, Jr., of Monongalia County, who introduced a resolution on the second day of the Convention which declared that "this mode of meeting the present exigencies of Western Virginia, is preferable to that of reconstructing the Government of Virginia; inasmuch as it is equally legal and yet does not impose upon us the calamity of an over-burdening State debt—no part of which we owe in equity—or the scarcely less disastrous calamity of repudiating that debt, and thus ruining the financial credit of the State."

The issue was clearly drawn two days later when John S. Carlile, now a convert to the restoration policy of the national administration, introduced a substitute resolution providing for the reorganization of the Virginia state government. Delegate Dorsey spoke in opposition to the Carlile resolution.

. . . IT IS A REVOLUTIONARY MOVEMENT ALTOGETHER. Both plans are revolutionary; and if the General Government can recognize one, it can the other. I may say that I know from private conversations with those who know something about the views of the Administration, that they expect us not to quibble about technicalities, not to be squeamish about little points of law, in our action in this convention; and if we are afraid of little points of law, if we are squeamish, really, about these little technicalities, it is time for us to begin to tremble already. We have already done acts which viewed in the light of formal law, are treasonable....

. . . We propose to do something in due form of law, and yet we have already trembled about the forms of law, and not only that, but we propose to override all forms of law in carrying out the plan that is now proposed by this committee. It is the understanding, though not formally proposed in the report of that committee, that we shall overhaul the Constitution of Virginia, change its provisions, make such arrangments in the change of those provisions, as will enable us to carry out this project of reconstructing the State Government. In fact, the project itself is a change of the Constitution of Virginia as to some of its specific laws.

Well then, shall the simple consideration of the expectation of the United States, and the desire of the Administration indicated in a variety of ways, decide us as between these two plans that are proposed to the members of this Convention? I admit, Mr. President, that there is some force in the proposition that is made. I admit there is some propriety in the accomplishment of the object which the administration propose to accomplish by the action of this Convention, in accepting the plan proposed and suggested by the committee. I can see that the design is to introduce this same plan in all the border States. The design is, as rapidly as the troops advance to establish a similar government to this proposed in the report of the committee—establish a simple government and call on the Union men of the Commonwealths in the various States, to rally around the government. I see it will have a mighty moral influence in the border States in which such government shall be established, and also on the States still further South. But then here I ask that the Administration shall not solicit us to do that, while we have local interests embarrassing us of such a character. If we had no complication of interests in this matter, it might be kind, prudent and appropriate, for the Administration to request us indirectly, as it has, to take such action. But, Sir, if this action anticipated is the desired thing—if the effort of this new project upon the border States and the States South of them, is the desirable thing, I suggest that Western Virginia shall be separated from Eastern Virginia, and then that Eastern Virginia, as pressure is removed, shall enter into this enterprise, and establish a provisional government, and set the precedent the Administration desires this Convention to set.

. . . The interests of Eastern and Western Virginia are entirely antagonistic. There is an "unnatural connection" between them and us. They will of course keep us down, as they have already done, if it be possible to for the purpose of meeting their little bills. It is very convenient to have somebody for this purpose. They will burden us as they always have done. That they have the majority is evident when we remember that all the Southern portion of Western Virginia, considering the Blue Ridge as the line, sympathizes with Eastern Virginia. Their interests are the same as hers. They lie along the line of Tennessee and Kentucky, connected with Eastern Virginia by railroads. That section of the country is filled up with persons who emigrated from the Eastern part of the State, and their sympathies are all there. Unless we in Western Virginia are a united people, it is impossible for us to carry out this project. I insist that we shall not enter into a plan to put ourselves at the mercy of Eastern Virginia and our neighbors who sympathize with her, any more, and I propose therefore that this plan shall proceed just so far, with the understanding that immediately as soon as Congress has taken action on the case, or as soon as the Administration has recognized this government that is proposed to be set up, a separation shall be made. And I make these remarks, Mr. President, more for the purpose of committing this convention to the design, than for the purpose of objecting to this plan of itself considered. I do not object to the legality of it, or the principle upon which it proceeds, or any formal arrangement, except the verbal one I mentioned. They are all legal as we can get. But I object that no provision has been made, specific and definite, for the separation of Virginia, Western from Eastern, just as soon as it is possible to do it, and come as near meeting the technicalities as the nature of the case will allow.

In a word, Sir, I deem that the separation of Western Virginia from Eastern is the paramount object in the minds of Western Virginians; and I hope, Sir, indeed I believe, that that is a paramount object in the minds of a majority of the members of this convention. What I want is, that they shall explicitly say so, inform, if they choose; or, if not then, in the formal documents that are being successively presented by this committee; or they should do it in a specific resolution; or, if not in that way, they should say so in debate. . . .—Virgil A. Lewis, *How West Virginia Was Made*, pp. 102-106.

84. Chester D. Hubbard Supports Restoration of Virginia Government

Of the many speeches made in the Second Wheeling Convention in support of the proposition to restore the Virginia State government, the remarks by Chester D. Hubbard (1814-1891) of Ohio County set the high-water mark of effective speaking in the Convention. Brief, eloquent, and punctuated with forceful argument, the speech contained the elements of a masterpiece. That the first duty of the people of northwestern Virginia was to the Union and the wishes of the national administration was the theme of his Lincoln-like remarks delivered June 18, 1861.

WE ARE NOT HERE TO CREATE A STATE, but to save one; not here to create a government, but to help save a government. Let us go forward in the great work, and not haggle about what our taxes will be hereafter, or questions of that character. Let us save this government, let us save Virginia, and then save the Union; for the banner we are lifting up here, will be the banner for the salvation of the country. As the arms of the government go forward and rescue our State from revolution, we must save what they gain. I hope we shall say nothing more now about the division of the State; our first and highest object is to perpetuate the Union and the government, and the next to rescue and save Virginia. If we find in the future that we cannot remain in the State, and that we can do better to separate, I shall be as willing as any other man. I believe this movement will not stop with Virginia, but will spread all over the seceded States, as they are delivered from the military despotism that now rules them. Let us not fall short of our duty in this hour or hesitate in the course which is before us, as true men. Let us go forward as Virginia in the Union.—Virgil A. Lewis, *How West Virginia Was Made,* pp. 123-124.

85. Governor John Letcher's Proclamation to the People of Northwestern Virginia, June 14, 1861

John Letcher (1813-1884) served as governor of Virginia from 1859 to 1863. Born in Lexington, a graduate of Washington College, and a lawyer by profession, Letcher launched his political career in the 1840's as editor of a Democratic newspaper at Lexington. In the 1850's he represented the eleventh Virginia district in Congress, where as a self-appointed watchdog on government spending he earned the sobriquet of "Honest John." In 1847 he endeared himself to many in western Virginia when he signed the anti-slavery address commonly called the "Ruffner Pamphlet," and in the constitutional convention of 1850-51 he championed the cause of the west in its fight for the white basis of representation in the General Assembly. Although he virtually repudiated the "Ruffner Pamphlet" during the gubernatorial campaign of 1859, Letcher retained the support of the west, especially of the northwest, which contributed 4,500 votes to his 5,569 majority for the governorship. After the presidential election of 1860, in which he supported Douglas, Letcher refused to call the General Assembly into special session but finally convened that body on January 7, 1861. Unable to prevent the authorization of a convention, Letcher championed the peace movement wholeheartedly. He opposed secession until President Lincoln called for troops to restore Federal authority in the seceded states. With the adoption of the Virginia Ordinance of Secession, Letcher became an enthusiastic Confederate. His concern for the territorial integrity of Virginia and determination to establish the Confederate boundary at the Ohio River and the Mason and Dixon Line became an obsession.

On June 14, 1861, Governor Letcher issued two proclamations directed to the people of northwestern Virginia. In the first he announced the adoption of the Ordinance of Secession by the Virginia voters at the election held on May 23, and gave the vote as 125,950 for and 20,373 against ratification. He estimated the vote in certain counties controlled by hostile forces at 11,961 for rejection and 3,234 for ratification. Letcher also proclaimed the constitution of the Provisional Government of the Confederate States of America in force throughout Virginia.

In the second proclamation, which follows, Letcher appealed directly to the people of the northwest where the restoration of the Virginia government was under way at Wheeling. This proclamation was published at Huttonsville and circulated in counties occupied by Confederate troops.

THE SOVEREIGN PEOPLE OF VIRGINIA unbiassed and by their own free choice have by a majority of nearly one hundred thousand qualified voters, severed the ties that heretofore bound them to the government of the United States, and united this Commonwealth with the Confederate States. . . .

The State of Virginia has now the second time in her history asserted this right, and it is the duty of every Virginian to acknowledge her act when ratified by such majority, and to his willing co-operation to make good the declaration. All her people have voted, each has taken his chance to have his personal views represented.

You as well as the rest of the State have cast your vote fairly and the majority is against you. It is the duty of good citizens to yield to the will of the State. The bill of rights has proclaimed "that the people have a right to uniform government, and that, therefore, no government separate from or independent of the government of Virginia ought to be erected or established within the limits thereof." The majority thus declared therefore have a right to govern.

But notwithstanding this right that exercise has been regarded by the people of all sections of the United States, as undoubted, and sacred, yet the government at Washington now utterly denies it, and by the exercise of despotic power is endeavoring to coerce our people to abject submission to their authority. Virginia has asserted her independence. She will maintain it at every hazard. She is sustained by the power of her sister Southern States, ready and willing to uphold her cause. Can any true Virginian refuse to render assistance?

Men of northwest, I appeal to you by all the considerations which have drawn us together, as one people heretofore, to rally to the standard of the Old Dominion.

By all the sacred ties of consanguinity, by the intermixture of blood of East and West, by common paternity, by friendships hallowed by the thousand cherished recollections, by memories of the past, by the relics of the great men of other days, come to Virginia's banner and drive the invaders from your soil. There may be traitors in the midst of you who for selfish ends have turned against their mother, and would permit her to be ignominiously oppressed and degraded, but I cannot —will not believe that a majority of you are not true sons who will give your blood and your treasure for Virginia's defence. I have sent for your protection such troops as the emergency enabled me to collect in charge of a competent commander. I have ordered a large force to go to your aid, but I rely with the utmost confidence upon your own strong arms to rescue your friends and altars from the pollution of a reckless and ruthless enemy. The State is invaded at several points, but ample forces have been collected to defend her.

There has been a complaint among you that the Eastern portion of the State has enjoyed an exemption from taxation to your prejudice. The State by a majority of 95,000 has put the two sections on an equality in this respect. By a display of magnanimity in the vote just given, the east has, by a large majority, consented to relinquish this exemption and is ready to share with you all the burdens of government, and to meet all Virginia's liabilities. They come now to aid you as you came in former days to aid them. The men of the Southern Confederate States glory in coming to your rescue. Let one heart, one mind, one energy, one power, nerve every patriot arm in a common cause. The heart that will not beat in unison with Virginia now is a traitor's heart; the arm that will not strike home in her cause now is palsied by a coward fear.

The troops are posted at Huttonsville—come with your own good weapons and meet them as brothers.

Given under my hand and under the seal of the Commonwealth, this 14th day of June, 1861, and in the 85th year of the Commonwealth.—*Calendar of Virginia State Papers*, XI, 152-53.

86. West Virginia's Declaration of Independence, June 17, 1861

A committee of the Second Wheeling Convention, headed by John S. Carlile, reported on June 13, "A Declaration of the People of Virginia." The report was discussed at length on the floor of the convention, amended, and unanimously adopted on June 17. Carlile, who had drafted the report with his own hand, said it was a happy coincidence and an auspicious omen that "we have 56 votes recorded in favor of our declaration, and we may remember that there were just 56 signers of the Declaration of Independence." Another member of the convention remarked that the date of passage was the anniversary of the Battle of Bunker Hill, while still another observed that it was on June 17, 1789, that the States General declared itself the National Assembly and began the French Revolution. The declaration was engrossed on parchment and signed by all members of the Convention on June 20, 1861.

"A Declaration of the People of Virginia" is one of the most important state papers in West Virginia history. It contains a statement of principles, a strong indictment of the Virginia secession convention, an urgent recommendation for the reorganization of the Virginia government, and a list of grievances which impelled the Convention to action. An inspired paraphrase of the famous Declaration adopted at Philadelphia, July 4, 1776, the pronouncement was in a very real sense West Virginia's declaration of independence.

THE TRUE PURPOSE OF ALL GOVERNMENT is to promote the welfare and provide for the protection and security of the governed, and when any form or organization of government proves inadequate for, or subversive of this purpose, it is the right, it is the duty of the latter to abolish it. The Bill of Rights of Virginia, framed in 1776, re-affirmed in 1830, and again in 1851, expressly reserves this right to a majority of her people. The act of the General Assembly, calling the Convention which assembled at Richmond in February last, without the previously expressed consent of such majority, was therefore a usurpation; and the Convention thus called has not only abused the powers nominally entrusted to it, but, with the connivance and active aid of the executive, has usurped and exercised other powers, to the manifest injury of the people, which, if permitted, will inevitably subject them to a military despotism.

The Convention, by its pretended ordinances, has required the people of Virginia to separate from and wage war against the government of the United States, and against citizens of neighboring States, with whom they have heretofore maintained friendly, social and business relations:

It has attempted to subvert the Union founded by Washington and his co-patriots, in the purer days of the republic, which has conferred unexampled prosperity upon every class of citizens, and upon every section of the country:

It has attempted to transfer the allegiance of the people to an illegal confederacy of rebellious States, and required their submission to its pretended edicts and decrees:

It has attempted to place the whole military force and military operations of the Commonwealth under the control and direction of such confederacy, for offensive as well as defensive purposes:

It has, in conjunction with the State executive, instituted wherever their usurped power extends, a reign of terror intended to suppress the free expression of the will of the people, making elections a mockery and a fraud:

The same combination, even before the passage of the pretended ordinance of secession, instituted war by the seizure and appropriation of the property of the Federal Government, and by organizing and mobilizing armies, with the avowed purpose of capturing or destroying the Capital of the Union:

They have attempted to bring the allegiance of the people of the United States into direct conflict with their subordinate allegiance to the State, thereby making obedience to their pretended Ordinances, treason against the former.

We, therefore, the delegates here assembled in Convention to devise such measures and take such action as the safety and welfare of the loyal citizens of Virginia may demand, having maturely considered the premises, and viewing with great concern the deplorable condition to which this once happy Commonwealth must be reduced unless some regular adequate remedy is speedily adopted, and appealing to the Supreme Ruler of the Universe for the rectitude of our intentions, do hereby, in the name and on the behalf of the good people of Virginia, solemnly declare, that the preservation of their dearest rights and liberties and their security in person and property, imperatively demand the reorganization of the government of the Commonwealth, and that all acts of said Convention and Executive, tending to separate this Commonwealth from the United States, or to levy and carry on war against them, are without authority and void; and that the offices of all who adhere to the said Convention and Executive, whether legislative, executive or judicial, are vacated.—*Ordinances of The Convention, Assembled at Wheeling, on the 11th of June, 1861*, pp. 39-40.

87. John S. Carlile Supports Reorganization of the Virginia Government

Defeated at the First Wheeling Convention in his effort to form a new state without the consent of Virginia, John S. Carlile (1817-1878) led the movement in the second convention to reorganize the state government. Born at Winchester and tutored by his mother, Carlile had clerked in a store, managed a store of his own, studied law, and practiced his profession at Beverly and Philippi before moving to Clarksburg. He served as a Democrat in the Virginia senate from 1847 to 1851 and as a delegate to the Constitutional Convention of 1850-51. He became a Know-Nothing and was elected to Congress on the American Party ticket in 1855. When he failed of re-election in 1857, he rejoined the Democrats and in 1861 won a seat in the Thirty-Seventh Congress by an overwhelming majority. Carlile represented Harrison County in the Virginia convention and opposed secession with such vigor that he remained in Richmond at the hazard of his life. When he returned to

Clarksburg he rallied the Unionists to the convention of April 22, which set in motion the chain of events that eventually led to the formation of West Virginia.

Carlile made his last notable contributions to the partition of Virginia as chairman of the Committee on Business in the Second Wheeling Convention. He wrote the stirring address, "A Declaration of the People of Virginia", and led the forces that carried the day for the plan to restore the Virginia government. Little wonder that the restored General Assembly in July, 1861, elected him to fill the United States Senate seat made vacant by the resignation of Virginia Senator R. M. T. Hunter.

Carlile's speeches in the Second Wheeling Convention reveal a complete reversal of the position he first held at the May convention. On June 18, 1861, he delivered an address in opposition to a resolution introduced by D. D. T. Farnsworth of Upshur County, who wished to commit the convention and restored government to the creation of a new state without delay.

IN RELATION TO THIS THING OF DIVIDING, I find that even I, who first started the little stone down the mountain, have now to apply the rubbers to the gentlemen who have outrun me in the race, to check their impetuosity. Those who know what I have done in behalf of this movement, and would do now, if practicable, know that it is from no lack of sympathy with their desire, that I am now drawing the brakes. I believe I know the people of Harrison county, and of all the counties of Northwestern Virginia, for in some capacity I have served them nearly all, except these Panhandle counties—and they know just as well as we do, and have probably found it out a little in advance of us, that at this time a division of the State cannot be effected, for the reason which they see in the Constitution of the United States, that it is only through it, and by virtue of its provisions, that a division can be had. They know another thing, too, that a separation is worth nothing without the perpetuity of the Government to which we desire to attach ourselves, and that they must first address themselves to maintaining the Government. . . .

In an hour like this when the question is: shall we save the State; when we are particularly helpless to save it ourselves; when the very Government itself has by this rebellion been bankrupted; when it is engaged in this death struggle to maintain its own existence, and when we have come here to aid, if we can, this effort of the Government in this struggle,— why should we now be discussing that which is utterly impossible and which more belongs to days of peace than to the hours of war? That is the question to put to ourselves. If we could divide the State today, who would desire to do so under existing circumstances. In a short time the power of this Government may be established. Then we may be acknowledged as the Government of Virginia; then we can provide for that which is essential to our interest. . . .

There is no man within the limits of this State that is more thoroughly convinced than I am and have been for long years of the necessity of this separation. There is no power on earth that can prevent it. But it cannot take place now, and we are but embarrassing our movements, which must first be addressed to the perpetuity of the government and the maintenance of our free institutions before we can act on what is and must be a secondary consideration. . . .—Wheeling *Intelligencer*, June 19, 1861.

88. The Reorganization Ordinance Adopted June 19, 1861

The Second Wheeling Convention adopted without a dissenting vote on June 19, 1861, an ordinance for the reorganization of the Virginia state government on a loyal Union basis. This ordinance provided for the appointment by the Convention of a governor, lieutenant governor, attorney general, and an advisory council; reconstituted the General Assembly on a loyal basis; and prescribed the tenure of all others in the service of the State, counties, and municipalities. Among its provisions was a requirement that officials, old and new, should take an oath of allegiance to the United States and to the reorganized gov-

*ernment of Virginia. Provision was also made for the appoint-
ment or election of the successors to officeholders who refused
to take the loyalty oath.*

The People of the State of Virginia, by their Delegates assembled in Convention at Wheeling, do ordain as follows:

1. A Governor, Lieutenant-Governor and Attorney General
for the State of Virginia, shall be appointed by this Convention,
to discharge the duties and exercise the powers which pertain to
their respective offices by the existing laws of the State, and to
continue in office for six months, or until their successors be
elected and qualified; . . .

2. A Council, to consist of five members, shall be appointed
by this Convention, to consult with and advise the Governor respecting such matters pertaining to his official duties as he shall
submit for consideration, and to aid in the execution of his official orders. Their term of office shall expire at the same time
as that of the Governor.

3. The Delegates elected to the General Assembly on the
twenty-third day of May last, and the Senators entitled under
existing laws to seats in the next General Assembly, together
with such Delegates and Senators as may be duly elected under
the Ordinances of this Convention, or existing laws, to fill vacancies, who shall qualify themselves by taking the oath or affirmation hereinafter set forth, shall constitute the Legislature
of the State, to discharge the duties and exercise the powers
pertaining to the General Assembly. They shall hold their offices from the passage of this Ordinance until the end of the
terms for which they were respectively elected. They shall assemble in the City of Wheeling, on the first day of July next,
and proceed to organize themselves as prescribed by existing
laws, in their respective branches. A majority in each branch
of the members qualified as aforesaid, shall constitute a quorum
to do business. A majority of the members of each branch thus
qualified, voting affirmatively, shall be competent to pass any
act specified in the twenty-seventh Section of the fourth Article
of the Constitution of the State.

4. The Governor, Lieutenant-Governor, Attorney General,
members of the Legislature, and all officers now in the service

of the State, or of any county, city or town thereof, or hereafter
to be elected or appointed for such service, including the Judges
and Clerks of the several Courts, Sheriffs, Commissioners of the
Revenue, Justices of the Peace, officers of the city and municipal corporations, and officers of militia, and officers and privates of volunteer companies of the State, not mustered into the
service of the United States, shall each take the following oath
or affirmation before proceeding in the discharge of their several duties:

"I solemnly swear (or affirm,) that I will support the Constitution of the United States, and the laws made in pursuunce
thereof, as the supreme law of the land, anything in the Constitution and laws of the State of Virginia, or in the Ordinances of
the Convention which assembled at Richmond on the 13th of
February, 1861, to the contrary notwithstanding; and that I will
uphold and defend the Government of Virginia as vindicated
and restored by the Convention which assembled at Wheeling,
on the 11th day of June, 1861." . . . —*Ordinances of the Convention, Assembled at Wheeling, on the 11th of June, 1861*, pp. 40-
42.

89. Francis H. Pierpont's Inaugural Address, June 20, 1861

*In the evening of June 19, 1861, members of the Second
Wheeling Convention who had only that day adopted an ordinance providing for the restoration of the Virginia government,
held a caucus in the Custom House and unanimously nominated
Francis H. Pierpont as candidate for governor. Born in Monongalia County, Virginia, January 25, 1814, Pierpont had moved as
a youth with his parents to Fairmont, Marion County. After
graduating from Allegheny College at Meadville, Pennsylvania,
he had taught school and read law. Admitted to the bar in Harrison County, Virginia, in 1841, he returned a year later to Fairmont. Here he built up a lucrative practice, served as counsel
for the Baltimore and Ohio Railroad, and prospered in the coal-
mining business.*

Pierpont had taken an active part in state and local elections as a Whig but had not been a candidate for office. Although a critic of the pro-slavery influence in Virginia politics, he held no brief for abolitionism. Too conservative to embrace Republicanism in the presidential election of 1860, he had supported the candidates of the Constitutional Union Party. After the adoption of the Ordinance of Secession by the Virginia Convention on April 17, 1861, Pierpont joined with other moderates in the fight to reorganize the Virginia state government. He was elected governor of the restored Commonwealth by the unanimous vote of the Convention on June 20, and immediately inaugurated. Without peer as a leader in both the reorganization and new-state movements, Pierpont was in a real sense the "father of West Virginia." Before taking the oath of office he spoke briefly to the Convention on the issues which divided Virginia.

THIS DAY AND THIS EVENT mark a period in the history of constitutional liberty. They mark a period in American history. For more than three-quarters of a century our government has proceeded, in all the States and in all the territories, upon which our fathers erected it—namely: upon the intelligence of the people; and that in the people resides all power, and that from them all power must emanate.

A new doctrine has been introduced by those who are at the head of the revolution in our Southern States—that the people are *not* the source of all power. Those promulgating this doctrine have tried to divide the people into two classes; one they call the laboring class, the other the capital class. They have for several years been industriously propagating the idea that the capital of the country ought to represent the legislation of the country, and guide it and direct it; maintaining that it is dangerous for the labor of the country to enter into the legislation of the country. This, gentlemen, is the principle that had characterized the revolution that has been inaugurated in the South; they maintain that those who are to have the privilege of voting ought to be of the educated class, and that the legislation ought not to be represented by the laboring classes.

We in Western Virginia, and, as I suppose in the whole of Virginia, adopted the great doctrine of the fathers of the Republic that in the people resides all power; and that embraced *all* people. This revolution has been inaugurated with a view of making a distinction upon the principles that I have indicated. We of Western Virginia have not been consulted upon that subject. The large body of your citizens in the eastern part of the State have not been consulted upon that subject.

American institutions lie near to the heart of the masses of the people, all over this country, from one end of it to the other, though not as nearly perhaps in Louisiana, Georgia and Texas, as in some of the Western and Northern States.

This idea has been covertly advanced only in portions of Virginia. She has stood firm by the doctrines of the fathers of the Revolution up to within a very short period. Its propagators have attempted to force it upon us by terror and at the point of the bayonet. We have been driven into the position we occupy today, by the usurpers at the South, who have inaugurated this war upon the soil of Virginia, and have made it the great Crimea of this contest. We, representing the loyal citizens of Virginia, have been bound to assume the position we have assumed today, for the protection of ourselves, our wives, our children, and our property. We, I repeat, have been *driven* to assume this position; and now we are but recurring to the great fundamental principle of our fathers, that to the loyal people of a State, belongs the law-making power of that State. The loyal people are entitled to the government and governmental authority of the State. And, fellow-citizens, it is the assumption of that authority upon which we are now about to enter. . . . —Virgil A. Lewis, *How West Virginia Was Made*, pp. 144-45.

IX. West Virginia: The Thirty-Fifth State

90. The Edward Bates Letter

The Second Wheeling Convention which reconvened in the United States custom house in that city on August 6, 1861, authorized appointment of a committee, consisting of one member from each county represented, to study "the whole subject of a division of this State"; on the following day, the Convention tabled a motion by D. D. T. Farnsworth of Upshur County, declaring it to be "unwise at this time" for the Convention to take action for a division of the State. That the new-state men held a majority in the Convention was further attested on August 13, when James G. West of Wetzel County, Chairman of the Committee on Division of the State, submitted the report of the committee in the form of a skeleton ordinance proposing the creation of a new state and outlining the means and methods to be employed. The Convention debated the issue until August 20, when it adopted the ordinance providing for the creation of a new state to be called "Kanawha." It was in this debate that Delegate A. F. Ritchie of Marion County, an opponent of immediate division, sent to the desk a letter, dated August 12, 1861, he had received from Edward Bates, Attorney General of the United States.

I HAVE THOUGHT A GREAT DEAL UPON THE QUESTION of dividing the State of Virginia into two States; and since I came here, as a member of the government, I have conversed with a good many, and corresponded with some of the good men of Western Virginia in regard to that matter. In all this intercourse, my constant and earnest effort has been to impress upon the minds of those gentlemen the vast importance—not to say necessity—in this terrible crisis of our national affairs, to abstain from the introduction of any new elements of revolution, to avoid, as far as possible, all new and original theories of government; but, on the contrary, in all the insurgent Commonwealths to adhere, as closely as circumstances will allow, to the old constitutional standard of principle, and to the traditional habits and thoughts of the people. And I still think that course is dictated by the plainest teachings of prudence.

The formation of a new State out of Western Virginia is an orginal, independent act of Revolution. I do not deny the power of Revolution (I do not call it right—for it is never prescribed, it exists in force only, and has and can have no law but the will of the revolutionists.) Any attempt to carry it out involves a plain breach of both the constitution—of Virginia and the Nation. And hence it is plain that you cannot take that course without weakening, if not destroying, your claims upon the sympathy and support of the General Government; and without disconcerting the plan already adopted both by Virginia and the General Government, for the reorganization of the revolted States, and the restoration of the integrity of the Union. That plan, I understand to be this: When a State, by its perverted functionaries, has declared itself out of the Union, we avail ourselves of all the sound and loyal elements of the State —all who owe allegiance to, and claim protection of the Constitution, to form a State Government, as nearly as may be, upon the former model, and claiming to be the very State which has been, in part, overthrown by the successful rebellion. In this way we establish a constitutional nucleus around which all the scattered elements of the Commonwealth may meet and combine and thus restore the old State in its original integrity.

This, I verily thought, was the plan adopted at Wheeling, and recognized and acted upon by the General Government here. Your Convention annulled the revolutionary proceedings at Richmond, both in the Convention and the General Assembly, and your new Governor formally demanded of the President the fulfillment of the constitutional guarantee in favor of Virginia—Virginia, as known to our fathers and to us. The President admitted the obligation and promised his best efforts to fulfill it; and the Senate admitted your Senators not as representing a new and nameless State, now for the first time heard of in our history, but as representing "the good old Commonwealth."

Must all this be undone, and a new and hazardous experiment be ventured upon, at the moment when danger and difficulties are thickening around us? I hope not—for the sake of the nation and the State, I hope not. I had rejoiced in the movement in Western Virginia, as a legal, constitutional and safe refuge from revolution and anarchy—as at once an example and fit instrument for the restoration of all the revolted States.

I have not time now to discuss the subject in its various bearings: What I have written, is written with a running pen, and will need your charitable criticism.

If I had time I think I could give persuasive reasons for declining the attempt to create a new State at this perilous time. At another time, I might be willing to go fully into the question, but now I can say no more.—Virgil A. Lewis, *How West Virginia Was Made*, pp. 219-20.

91. An Ordinance Establishing the State of Kanawha

After completing the work of reorganizing the Virginia State government, the Second Wheeling Convention adjourned on June 25, 1861, to meet again on the first Tuesday in August, unless otherwise ordered by the governor. Meanwhile Governor Pierpont convened the General Assembly on July 1, and that body took the last important steps toward obtaining recognition of the restored government by the United States as it enacted legislation to meet the war emergency, filled the remaining vacancies in state offices, and elected two United States Senators. The assembly was importuned to take initial action toward the formation of a new state but refused to consider the matter on grounds of expediency and a conviction that such a step should be taken in the Convention.

The important act of the Second Wheeling Convention which met again on August 6 was the adoption on August 20 of an ordinance providing for the formation of a new state, named

"Kanawha." *The ordinance, which follows, was ratified by the voters at an election held October 24, 1861, when delegates were also elected to a constitutional convention.*

WHEREAS, it is represented to be the desire of the people inhabiting the Counties hereinafter mentioned, to be separated from this Commonwealth, and to be erected into a separate State, and admitted into the Union of States, and become a member of the Government of the United States:

The People of Virginia, by their Delegates assembled in Convention at Wheeling, do ordain that a new State, to be called the State of Kanawha, be formed and erected out of the territory included within the following described boundary; beginning on the Tug Fork of Sandy River, on the Kentucky line where the Counties of Buchanan and Logan join the same; and running thence with the dividing lines of said Counties and the dividing line of the Counties of Wyoming and McDowell, to the Mercer County line, and with the dividing line of the Counties of Mercer and Wyoming to the Raleigh County line; thence with the dividing line of the Counties of Raleigh and Mercer, Monroe and Raleigh, Greenbrier and Raleigh, Fayette and Greenbrier, Nicholas and Greenbrier, Webster, Greenbrier and Pocahontas, Randolph and Pocahontas, Randolph and Pendleton, to the south-west corner of Hardy County; thence with the dividing line of the Counties of Hardy and Tucker, to the Fairfax Stone; thence with the line dividing the States of Maryland and Virginia, to the Pennsylvania line; thence with the line dividing the States of Pennsylvania and Virginia, to the Ohio river; thence down said river, and including the same, to the dividing line between Virginia and Kentucky, and with the said line to the beginning; including within the boundaries of the proposed new State the Counties of Logan, Wyoming, Raleigh, Fayette, Nicholas, Webster, Randolph, Tucker, Preston, Monongalia, Marion, Taylor, Barbour, Upshur, Harrison, Lewis, Braxton, Clay, Kanawha, Boone, Wayne, Cabell, Putnam, Mason, Jackson, Roane, Calhoun, Wirt, Gilmer, Ritchie, Wood, Pleasants, Tyler, Doddridge, Wetzel, Marshall, Ohio, Brooke and Hancock.

2. All persons qualified to vote within the boundaries aforesaid, and who shall present themselves at the several places of

voting within their respective Counties, on the fourth Thursday in October next, shall be allowed to vote on the question of the formation of a new State, as hereinbefore proposed; and it shall be the duty of the Commissioners conducting the election at the said several places of voting, at the same time, to cause polls to be taken for the election of Delegates to a Convention to form a Constitution for the government of the proposed State.

3. The Convention hereinbefore provided for may change the boundaries described in the first section of this Ordinance, so as to include within the proposed State the Counties of Greenbrier and Pocahontas, or either of them, and also the counties of Hampshire, Hardy, Morgan, Berkeley and Jefferson, or either of them, and also other Counties as lie contiguous to the said boundaries, or to the Counties named in this section; if the said Counties to be added, or either of them, by a majority of the votes given, shall declare their wish to form part of the proposed State, and shall elect Delegates to the said Convention, at elections to be held at the time and in the manner herein provided for. . . .

If on the day herein provided for holding said election, there shall be in any of the said Counties any military force, or any hostile assemblage of persons, so as to interfere with a full and free expression of the will of the voters, they may assemble at any other place within their County, and hold an election as herein provided for. It shall be the duty of the Commissioners superintending, and officers conducting said election, and the Clerks employed to record the votes, each before entering upon the duties of his office, to take, in addition to the oath now required by the general election law, the oath of office prescribed by this Convention. . . .

6. It shall be the duty of the Governor, on or before the fifteenth day of November next, to ascertain and by proclamation make known the result of the said vote; and if a majority of the votes given within the boundaries mentioned in the first section of this Ordinance, shall be in favor of the formation of a new State, he shall so state in his said proclamation, and shall call upon said Delegates to meet in the City of Wheeling, on the 26th day of November next, and organize themselves into a

Convention; and the said Convention shall submit, for ratification or rejection, the Constitution that may be agreed upon by it, to the qualified voters within the proposed State, . . .

8. It shall be the duty of the Governor to lay before the General Assembly, at its next meeting, for their consent according to the Constitution of the United States, the result of the said vote, if it shall be found that a majority of the votes cast be in favor of a new State, and also in favor of the Constitution proposed to said voters for their adoption.

9. The new State shall take upon itself a just proportion of the public debt of the Commonwealth of Virginia prior to the first day of January, 1861, to be ascertained by charging to it all State expenditures within the limits thereof, and a just proportion of the ordinary expenses of the State Government, since any part of said debt was contracted; and deducting therefrom the monies paid into the Treasury of the Commonwealth from the Counties included within the said new State during the same period. All private rights and interests in lands within the proposed State, derived from the laws of Virginia prior to such separation, shall remain valid and secure under the laws of the proposed State, and shall be determined by the laws now existing in the State of Virginia. . . .

10. When the General Assembly shall give its consent to the formation of such new State, it shall forward to the Congress of the United States such consent, together with an official copy of such Constitution, with the request that the said new State may be admitted into the Union of States.

11. The Government of the State of Virginia as reorganized by this Convention at its session in June last, shall retain, within the territory of the proposed State, undiminished and unimpaired, all the powers and authority with which it has been vested, until the proposed State shall be admitted into the Union by the Congress of the United States; and nothing in this Ordinance contained, or which shall be done in pursuance thereof, shall impair or affect the authority of the said reorganized State Government in any County which shall not be included within the proposed State.—*Ordinances of the Convention, Assembled at Wheeling, on the 11th of June, 1861,* pp. 54-59.

92. Naming West Virginia

At the election held on October 24, 1861, voters in thirty-five Virginia counties ratified the ordinance authorizing the formation of a state to be called "Kanawha" and also sent 53 delegates to the Constitutional Convention which met in the Custom House at Wheeling on November 26. After the Committee on Boundary suggested in its report of December 3 the inclusion of thirty-one additional counties, Delegate Harmon Sinsel of Taylor County offered a motion to amend the proposed draft of Article I of the constitution by striking out the word "Kanawha." When the Sinsel motion was adopted and the convention left to choose a new name, "Allegheny" received 2 votes, "Augusta" 1, "Kanawha" 9, and "West Virginia" 30. Other proposed names were Columbia, New Virginia, and Potomac.

Some of the considerations which led the Constitutional Convention to revoke the action of the Second Wheeling Convention and favor the name "West Virginia" appear in the debate on the Sinsel motion.

[MR. SINSEL OF TAYLOR.] Mr. President, one reason I have for striking it out is that I am a Virginian; I was born and raised in Virginia, and I have ever been proud of the name. I admit that Virginians have done wrong—that many of them in this rebellion have disgraced themselves; but that has not weaned me from the name. When we look back to history and see the origin of the name—Virginia, from the Virgin Queen—the queen who swayed the scepter of England with so much glory and renown—we might almost go back a little further to Virginia, the Virgin. It always makes me think of the Virgin Mary, the mother of our blessed Redeemer. It is a name that I almost revere; and I am utterly opposed to leaving it out and substituting the name "Kanawha" in its stead.

[MR. PARKER OF CABELL.] . . . There is within the boundary of the new State a large county of the same name as the one proposed for the State—the county of Kanawha, which has been one of the most prominent points within the boundaries of the new State. In looking over the United States, I believe we can find no instance where any subdivision of a state bears the name of the state itself. . . . Well, I suppose the reason is that it shall not create confusion, in postal and other connections with other parts of the country, and the outside world. And it seems to me that so prominent a county, known so well as Kanawha—the county of Kanawha is the prominent point in our new State. Now, we get up the name of the State—we attach to it the name of Kanawha—well, it strikes me we can find some other, more proper name at this time. . . . Now we give the name of the State of Kanawha, to the county of Kanawha, to the post office at Kanawha court house, and it seems to me we shall get into confusion. Therefore I can see no peculiar claim that Kanawha has. There is a very pretty river there of this name—nice river —but there is no particular euphony in the name; or perhaps no claim from historical considerations.

[MR. BROWN OF KANAWHA.] . . . That ordinance prescribes definitely the name of the State proposed to be erected; and it becomes a question not whether this or that or any other name shall be the name of the new State but submits the question definitely to the people within the proposed boundaries whether they will form the new State as proposed with the name prescribed. . . .

That there is a very obvious propriety in that name seems to me very clear; . . . We see that in the name of the state right across the way here; in our sister State of Kentucky, which was the daughter of Virginia; in the State of Tennessee named after the river of that name,—even changed in the case of Tennessee, for the original name of the territory was Franklin, and they began in the early stages of that territory to form a state of that name, but they afterwards changed it and adopted the name of Tennessee, after one of the principal rivers in the territory. You go into Nebraska—you find a territory there named after the chief river of that territory. We have the same thing in the State of Kansas. Pursue the cases around you, within these Western States, and you find that the chief rivers have been the chosen example for the naming of the states. . . .

It has been said by gentlemen that they cherish the name of Virginia, from the source, from the Virgin Queen after whom it was named, but, sir, when this was mentioned, I confess my mind reverted to the fact that that virgin was not above suspicion (laughter) that the history that tells the truth tells of dalliances not to the credit of the virgin, and we need seek no honor or pleasure in the recollection. I only regret that our old mother state has been caught in dalliance from which we are trying to rid ourselves by a division of our territory. . . .

[MR. LAMB OF OHIO.] . . . I want to have the new State, not merely in substance, but even in name. A resident of the state as I have been more than thirty years, I have no hesitation in proclaiming to this Convention and my constituents that there is nothing in the conduct of the State of Virginia to the people of western Virginia that entitles her or the name of our attachment. . . .

[MR. WILLEY OF MONONGALIA.] . . . So far as I have had any communications with my constituency, I have understood from them that there was some reason why they were very much opposed to the name of Kanawha. Amongst some that they assigned is one that it is a very hard name to spell (Laughter). For myself, Mr. President, I will say that I have no objections personally. I have no objection to any name that is convenient, though I will say that in this case I think the rose would smell sweeter by some other name (Laughter). . . .

[MR. VAN WINKLE OF WOOD.] . . . I think it [Kanawha] is one of the most euphonious words with which I am acquainted. Almost every letter in it has a soft and musical sound. . . .

Well, sir, one gentleman tells us that he is a Virginian. Now, what I very much fear from the indications thrown out all around us on this subject is that several gentlemen intend *to be* Virginians after we have separated from Virginia. . . . If we are so servile to old Virginia, now that we are about casting off the fetters, if we cannot forget our servile habits but must cringe and bow the knee to Old Virginia—I think, sir, this movement had better stop precisely where it is now.

. . . If we could have Virginia by itself I would take it and be thankful for it; but if we must have West Virginia or New Virginia, or, as the world will think, Little Virginia, I shall most certainly feel if it is persisted in after the discussion that has taken place, and under the circumstances—that it comes before us as a compromise—I certainly shall think that at least there is a strong affection somewheres for the fleshpots of Egypt (Laughter).

[Mr. STUART OF DODDRIDGE.] I am not actuated alone by a wish to conform to the wishes of my constituents, but, from my heart I love the name of Virginia; I love the people and the territory of Virginia; and I am unwilling to array all the wrongs and evils she has done, and look at the dark side of Virginia alone; but I would sometimes look at the brighter side, and that is the side my people look upon. And they are attached to the name; . . . It is a familiar name. It is a name I have listened to ever since I have been able to speak—that of West Virginia. It is familiar all over this broad land of our country—West Virginia. Something attaches to the name that ennobles us in the eyes of the country. . . .

[Mr. BATTELLE OF OHIO.] I desire to make a single remark, . . . It is this: not only did the ordinance passed by the former convention fix the name, but it has been ratified by solemn vote of the people. And I find, so far as I understand my powers and duties here, no longer to go behind that vote of the people. . . .

I will further say that should it be the pleasure of the Convention, in the exercise of a very questionable power, as it seems to me, to strike out Kanawha, I shall be opposed to substituting either New Virginia or West Virginia. We are now forming a new State. I for one would want a new name—a fresh name— a name which if it were not symbolical of especially new ideas would at least be somewhat indicative of our deliverance from very old ones. But the consideration I have first named is the one which will control my vote in opposing the striking out of the name of Kanawha.—*Debates and Proceedings of the First Constitutional Convention of West Virginia, 1861-1863,* edited by Charles H. Ambler, Frances Haney Atwood and William B. Mathews, I, 81-103.

93. Gordon Battelle's Plea for a Free State

The most sensitive of the issues which confronted the First Constitutional Convention was the slavery question. Leading a small but resolute group of delegates determined to incorporate an emancipation provision in the constitution was Gordon Battelle (1814-1862) of Ohio County. Twice he introduced resolutions designed to prohibit the importation of slaves into the new state for residence and to provide for the gradual emancipation of slaves. The Battelle resolutions met the opposition of the pro-slavery delegates and of a controlling bloc of moderates who believed that action on emancipation was inexpedient and untimely. Undaunted, Battelle brought his resolutions once again before the Convention on February 12, 1862, and with them another resolution providing that the article on slavery containing his resolutions be submitted separately for ratification or rejection at the time of the constitutional referendum. Although the Battelle resolutions were tabled without debate, the first section providing that "No slave shall be brought, or free person of color come into this state for permanent residence" was incorporated into the constitution next day.

Denied the opportunity to debate the question of emancipation on the floor of the Convention and restrained by a cloture rule limiting debate to ten minutes, Battelle took the issue to the people in a notable address which was widely read throughout northwestern Virginia. Although without effect in the decisions of the Convention, the address rallied supporters outside, where at unofficial polls opened in twenty or more counties the voters approved gradual emancipation by decided majorities.

Gordon Battelle died August 7, 1862, but it was his position on gradual emancipation which Congress accepted in the "Willey Amendment" and imposed as a condition for admission of West Virginia into the Union. The following passages have been taken from Battelle's "An Address to the Constitutional Convention and the People of West Virginia."

... THE INJURIES WHICH IT [SLAVERY] INFLICTS upon our own people are manifold and obvious. It practically aims to enslave not merely another race, but our own race. It inserts in its bill of rights some very high sounding phrases securing the freedom of speech; and then practically and in detail puts a lock on every man's mouth and a seal on every man's lips who will not shout for and swear by the divinity of the system. It amuses the popular fancy with a few glittering generalities in the fundamental law about the liberty of the press, and forthwith usurps authority, even in times of peace, to send out its edict to every postmaster, whether in the village or at the cross roads, clothing him with a despotic and absolute censorship over one of the dearest rights of the citizen. It degrades labor by giving it the badge of servility; and it impedes enterprise by withholding its proper rewards. It alone has claimed exemption from the rule of uniform taxation; and then demanded and received the largest share of the proceeds of that taxation. Is it any wonder in such a state of facts, that there are this day, of those who have been driven from Virginia, mainly by this system, men enough with their descendants, and means and energy, scattered through the West, of themselves, to make no mean State? ...

... God help us all! for I fear that none of us is wholly innocent in this business. Our own slave code—organic and statute, written and unwritten—has furnished the fruitful soil whence has sprung full armed—perjury and rebellion, and treason and war....

... I take it for granted that we all desire, in behalf of the new State which we are seeking to inaugurate, that it shall at once, and with no tardy pace, enter upon that high and honorable career of prosperity that has been so long and so iniquitously denied us as a people; that our virgin lands shall be tilled; that our immense mineral wealth shall be disembowelled, that school houses and churches shall crown our hill tops, and that the whole land shall smile with fruitful fields and happy homes. To the attainment of ends so desirable, we will all agree that it is indispensable that population, capital and enterprise, shall flow into our borders, and through our valleys; and above all that we must have as that which lies at the base of all material prosperity, *labor;* and that labor must be *free.*...

... We have seen it [slavery] year by year driving out from our genial climate, and fruitful soil, and exhaustless natural resources, some of the men of the very best energy, talent, and skill among our population. We have seen also in times of peace, the liberty of speech taken away—the freedom of the press abolished—and the willing minions of this system in hunting down their victims, spare from degradation and insult, neither the young, nor the gray haired veteran of seventy winters, whose every thought was as free from offense against society, as is that of the infant of days. And last but not least, we have seen its own chosen and favored interpreters, standing in the very sanctuaries of our political zion, throughout the land, blaspheming the holy principles of popular liberty to which the very places where they stood had been consecrated, by dooming my child and every man's child that must live by labor to a virtual and helpless slavery. And as the natural outgrowth of all this, we have seen this huge barbaric raid against popular rights, and against the world's last hope. It has been the merit of other attempted revolutions that their motive at least was a reaching upward and forward after liberty; it is the infamy of this that it is a reaching backward and downward after despotism. . . . —G. Battelle, *An Address to the Constitutional Convention of the People of West Virginia*, pp. 3-5, 8.

94. The Baltimore and Ohio Makes a Panhandle

Once committed to the task of drafting a constitution, the Convention proceeded to establish the boundaries of the new state. On November 28, 1861, the president of the Convention appointed a special committee to study the boundary question. In its report, submitted five days later, the committee not only recommended the inclusion of certain northwestern counties that had not participated in the election of October 24, but also of eighteen counties in the Valley of Virginia. For days the Convention debated the question of extending the boundary of West Virginia to the Blue Ridge only to strike out county after coun-

ty. Finally, after refusing to incorporate upper and middle Shenandoah Valley counties mainly because of slavery, the Convention adopted a resolution providing for the inclusion in the new state of the counties of Pendleton, Hardy, Hampshire, Frederick, Jefferson, Berkeley, and Morgan—all east of the Alleghenies.

The determining factor in the proposal of the constitutional convention to include these counties was the Baltimore and Ohio Railroad. In a speech delivered in the Convention, December 11, 1861, Waitman T. Willey of Monongalia County presented the main argument for the establishment of the eastern boundary of West Virginia on the Potomac River.

[MR. WILLEY.] And now, sir, I make this proposition: that we want all the territory to be included in this new State embraced within the counties of Pendleton, Hardy, Hampshire, Morgan, Frederick, Berkeley and Jefferson. I believe the inclusion of this territory is essential to the welfare of this new State. I believe that if we cannot include this territory, our new State enterprise will be crippled in all its future efforts to increase in population, in wealth and in power, as a State. Sir, the Baltimore and Ohio Railroad is the great artery that feeds our country. It conveys into our center, or by its ramifications of necessity infuses through the entire body politic of this new State the life-blood of its existence. We cannot do without it. It has been intimated by gentlemen that that Road is made and will exist and still extend its benefits to the new State although we shall not include these counties within the limits of the new State. Sir, it may be true; but I beg gentlemen to remember another fact: that unless this whole line of railroad is included in this new State its operations and its benefits will be embarrassed to the full extent of the power of eastern Virginia legislation; its utility will be crippled; it will be taxed as far as reason and decency—and further than there—will allow; and every influence of eastern Virginia will be arrayed against the successful working of this road. That has been the case hitherto, Mr. President. We have but to advert to the history of the legislation of Virginia to see the fact in time past. Every available artifice has been resorted to to cripple the energies or utility of that railroad.... —*Debates and Proceedings of the First Constitutional Convention*, I, 438.

95. Restored Virginia Gives Consent

After the voters had ratified the constitution at elections held on the following April 3, 1862,* Governor Pierpont took the next important step in state-making. The Constitution of the United States provides that no state shall be formed or created within the jurisdiction of any other state without the consent of its legislature. Consequently on April 18, 1862, Pierpont issued a call to the General Assembly of the restored Virginia government to convene at Wheeling on May 6. He defended the legality of the restored government in an open letter addressed "To the People of Virginia," saying that it was not the object of the Wheeling convention to set up a new government in the State or any other than the one under which they had always lived; nor had it effected any changes in the constitution of Virginia other than the one which prescribed the number in the General Assembly necessary to a quorum.

After the two houses, consisting of ten senators and thirty-one delegates present, had organized, Governor Pierpont laid before them copies of the ratified West Virginia constitution with a strong recommendation that the Assembly grant its consent for statehood. Those who urged that the movement was revolutionary, he said, did not understand the history, geography and social relations of the State.

*The convention fixed the date of the referendum on the first Thursday in April but authorized county election officers to open polls later for cause, "if so done as not to delay the submission of the result to the Legislature for its action." The election was held April 3, 1862, in a majority of the twenty-six counties which reported returns up to April 18, when Governor Pierpont issued the call for a special session of the General Assembly. Of the 14,567 votes cast in these counties, 14,199 were for ratification of the constitution, 368 against ratification. Counties reporting later brought these totals up to 18,862 for ratification and 514 against. No elections were held in many of the central, southern and eastern counties.

The General Assembly responded with the appointment of a joint committee of seven which on May 8 reported a bill authorizing the proposed division of the State. This the General Assembly enacted on May 13, 1862.

Passed May 13, 1862.

1. Be it enacted by the General Assembly, That the consent of the Legislature of Virginia be, and the same is hereby given to the formation and erection of the State of West Virginia, within the jurisdiction of this State, to include the counties of Hancock, Brooke, Ohio, Marshall, Wetzel, Marion, Monongalia, Preston, Taylor, Tyler, Pleasants, Ritchie, Doddridge, Harrison, Wood, Jackson, Wirt, Roane, Calhoun, Gilmer, Barbour, Tucker, Lewis, Braxton, Upshur, Randolph, Mason, Putnam, Kanawha, Clay, Nicholas, Cabell, Wayne, Boone, Logan, Wyoming, Mercer, McDowell, Webster, Pocahontas, Fayette, Raleigh, Greenbrier, Monroe, Pendleton, Hardy, Hampshire, and Morgan, according to the boundaries and under the provisions set forth in the consitution for the said State of West Virginia and the schedule thereto annexed, proposed by the convention which assembled at Wheeling, on the twenty-sixth day of November, eighteen hundred and sixty-one.

2. Be it further enacted, That the consent of the Legislature of Virginia be, and the same is hereby given, that the counties of Berkeley, Jefferson and Frederick, shall be included in and form part of the State of West Virginia whenever the voters of said counties shall ratify and assent to the said constitution, at an election held for the purpose, at such time and under such regulations as the commissioners named in the said schedule may prescribe.

3. Be it further enacted, That this act shall be transmitted by the executive to the senators and representatives of this commonwealth in congress, together with a certified original of the said constitution and schedule, and the said senators and representatives are hereby requested to use their endeavors to obtain the consent of congress to the admission of the State of West Virginia into the Union.

4. This act shall be in force from and after its passage. —*Acts of the General Assembly, Extra Session, 1862, p. 3.*

96. Senator Willey Presents West Virginia's Application for Statehood

Waitman T. Willey shares with Francis H. Pierpont a preeminent place as a leader of the West Virginia statehood movement. Born in Monongalia County, Virginia, October 11, 1811, Willey moved with his parents to Marion County where he attended subscription schools. After graduating from Madison College at Uniontown, Pennsylvania, he took up law and entered politics at Morgantown. Meanwhile, he gained prominence as a Methodist lay leader and temperance crusader throughout northwestern Virginia. He served as a delegate to the Constitutional Convention of 1850-51, but was defeated in 1852 as candidate for Congress on the Whig ticket and again in 1859 as candidate for lieutenant governor. He was elected delegate from Monongalia County to the Virginia convention of 1861, where he made a notable address and voted against the secession ordinance.

Following his return from Richmond, Willey supported the reorganization movement but opposed the plan of Carlile for immediate statehood on the ground that it contemplated treason against the United States, against Virginia, and against the Confederacy. Willey expounded his "triple treason" views in public addresses and as a member of the First Wheeling Convention joined the moderates in securing postponement of action on the statehood issue until the voters had balloted on the secession ordinance. Despite his conservative leanings and reputation as an obstructionist, the reorganized General Assembly elected him to the United States Senate to fill the vacancy created by the withdrawal of James M. Mason.

On May 29, 1862, Senator Willey presented West Virginia's application for statehood, together with supporting documents, to the United States Senate. In a characteristically long speech, he then recited the events which had led up to the application for statehood—from the adoption of the Ordinance of Secession on April 17, 1861, to the action of the General Assembly at Wheeling on May 13, 1862, which had given its formal consent as required by the Constitution of the United States. Willey surveyed the grounds of law and equity on which the new-state movement was founded, and summarized fundamental social and economic causes which had estranged eastern and western Virginia.

First. Let us consider the population. I have prepared the following table, showing the white and slave population in each of the forty-four counties of the proposed new State, and also the per cent. of slave population in each county, according to the census of 1860. . . . Thus, in 1860, the aggregate white population was three hundred and thirty-four thousand nine hundred and twenty-one; and the aggregate slave population was twelve thousand two hundred and seventy-one. It is but fair to say that, in consequence of the ravages of the war, the number of white inhabitants has, perhaps, not increased since the taking of the census; and the number of the slaves has, doubtless, diminished two or three thousand. Thus also it will be seen that the per cent. of slaves in 1860 was only about four per cent., and certainly does not now amount to three per cent. We have, therefore, the requisite number of inhabitants.

Secondly. I respectfully solicit the attention of Senators to the geographical position of the proposed new State. Look at the map. Observe how this territory lies, like a wedge driven in between the State of Ohio on one side, and the States of Pennsylvania and Maryland on the other, and is completely cut off from all convenient intercourse with East Virginia by the Alleghany mountains, the sky-kissing summits of which are proposed as the eastern boundary of the new State. . . .

Third. This application for admission as a new State is predicated on considerations of industrial and commercial necessity. The people living within the limits of the projected new State never had, and never can have, any trade or commerce with Eastern Virginia. There is no means of getting back and forth between the two sections by any direct and convenient way. There never has been; there never can be. The impediments are insuperable. . . .

Fourth. The difference of social institutions and habits of the people indicate the propriety of this division of the State. The existence of negro slavery is said, and I think correctly, by its friends, and by those who own slaves and yet are not its friends, to require a system of laws and municipal regulations adapted to the peculiar necessities and relations necessarily growing out of that institution. But slavery never can exist to any considerable extent in the territory proposed to be embraced in the new State. It never has flourished there. It never can. . . .

Mr. President, in view of these considerations, I think I am authorized to say that the division of the State of Virginia asked for is a physical, a political, a social, an industrial and commercial necessity. It is necessary for the preservation of harmonious and fraternal relations between the eastern and western sections of the State. It is indispensable to the development of the great natural resources of West Virginia, and to the prosperity and happiness of its inhabitants. . . .

Fifth and lastly. A few words in relation to the resources of the new State. Its area will be at least respectable—greater than very many of the other States of the Union. It will contain about twenty-four thousand square miles. It will embrace immense mineral wealth. It will include water power more than sufficient to drive all the machinery of New England. It contains the finest forests of timber on the continent. It includes the Great Kanawha salines and the Little Kanawha oil wells. It abounds in iron ore; and its coal fields are sufficient to supply the consumption of the entire Union for a thousand years. Much of it is well adapted to the production of all the valuable cereals; and all of it is unrivaled for the growth of grass and for grazing. . . . —*Congressional Globe*, May 29, 1862, p. 2418.

97. Senator John S. Carlile and the Willey Amendment

Senator Benjamin Wade of Ohio, chairman of the Committee on Territories, brought the West Virginia Bill (Senate Bill No. 365) to the floor of the Senate on June 23, 1862. To the surprise of its supporters the measure provided for the gradual emancipation of slaves and the inclusion of fifteen additional counties. Even more surprising was a proposed enabling act au-

thorizing the call of a new convention to write a new constitution. These provisions had been added to the bill by Senator John S. Carlile, a member of the committee, who had stood at the forefront of the West Virginia movement since the Clarksburg convention of April 22, 1861. His apparent change of heart as reflected in the West Virginia Bill, his subsequent opposition to the Willey Amendment, and finally his untiring efforts to delay statehood disappointed constituents and colleagues alike.

But Carlile was the Talleyrand rather than the Judas of West Virginia statehood. A Democratic prodigal and a Know-Nothing orphan in the 1850's; a Democrat during the War and a Republican after; author of the plan to form a new state immediately at the May convention, then architect of the restored government in the June convention; a small-state advocate at home and a large-state advocate in Congress; a proslavery man, an antislavery man, a states' righter and a nationalist, —Carlile had a long record of expediency. His reversal of position on the dismemberment of Virginia at that late day bore a close relation to the growing opposition by the Democratic Party to the rising power of the Radical Republicans in Congress, who were not only uniting behind the West Virginia Bill but also striving to turn the struggle for the Union into a war to abolish slavery. Whatever the motives of Carlile, his plan contemplated a delay which might well prove fatal to the new-state movement.

The West Virginia Bill became further tangled in the slave controversy when Senator Charles Sumner of Massachusetts offered an amendment providing for the admission of West Virginia as a free state. Therefore when the Senate rejected both the Sumner amendment and the Carlile proposal to remand the constitution to a new convention, Senator Waitman T. Willey offered the amendment providing for gradual emancipation which has since borne his name. The "Willey Amendment" eliminated the provision of the original constitution which excluded free persons of color from the state, while retaining the provision prohibiting the entry of slaves for permanent residence. It also contained a provision for emancipation of children of slave-mothers at birth and a schedule for the emancipation of others under twenty-one years of age.

*The Willey Amendment appears below along with excerpts
from the Carlile-Willey debate on the question of a referendum
on the amendment.*

THE CHILDREN OF SLAVES born within the limits of this State
after the fourth day of July, eighteen hundred and sixty-three,
shall be free; and all slaves within the said State who shall, at
the time aforesaid, be under the age of ten years, shall be
free when they arrive at the age of twenty-one years; and all
slaves over ten and under twenty-one years, shall be free when
they arrive at the age of twenty-five years; and no slave shall
be permitted to come into the State for permanent residence
therein.—Section 7, Article XI, *Constitution of 1863.*

[WAITMAN T. WILLEY:]
    In a matter like this, and especially after the voluntary ex-
pression of the people at the polls in regard to the subject
involved in this amendment at the election when they adopted
this constitution, it does seem to me there is no necessity for
sending this question back to them; but let the people of West
Virginia, in convention assembled, to be reconvened under the
authority and power reserved in the schedule annexed to the
constitution, say whether they will assent to this proposition or
not, as I think they have a perfect right to do, without going
through all these formalities again, without imposing upon our
people the trouble and expense that it necessarily would impose
upon them, and accomplish as satisfactorily, I am sure, the object designed by us all, as if there is another election held. The
people do not want to be troubled with it in my humble estimation, and there is no necessity for doing it. The proposition,
as I have presented it, is almost a literal copy of the celebrated Missouri resolution. The question of the adoption by the
people of the State of Missouri of the condition prescribed by
Congress was not submitted to the people even in convention
assembled, but to the Legislature; and if the Legislature consented they were thereupon to be admitted into the Union without any further proceedings whatever. I follow this precedent,
and I go a little further, as we have it in our power to do, by
submitting it not to the Legislature of the new State, but to

the people themselves in convention to be assembled under the authority which I have mentioned. I hope my colleague will withdraw his proposition.—*Congressional Globe*, July 14, 1862, p. 3309.

[JOHN S. CARLILE:]

In this case, the members of the convention to whom my colleague proposes to submit these conditions precedent to our admission, changing the Constitution proposed by them as essentially as if you were to turn day into night, were elected last fall. They submitted a constitution—the one now before the Senate—to the people, recognizing all existing rights of property and social institutions as they now exist. This constitution the people adopted. These conditions change the fundamental law, interfere with the existing rights of the people, propose that their own domestic institutions shall be changed at the bidding of Congress, if some thirty or forty gentlemen who last year composed a convention shall assent thereto. Three hundred and forty thousand people, in everything pertaining to their government, represented by fifty thousand voters, are to be bound by these gentlemen who met last year to frame for, and propose to this people a constitution which, if adopted, was to be the organic law. . . .

It will be remarked, too, by the Senate that there are three fundamental conditions now in the amendment of my colleague, which must be accepted before the assent of Congress, if his bill shall pass, can be given to the admission of the State of West Virginia: first, upon the fundamental condition that all slaves born after the 4th of July, 1863, shall be free; second, that all slaves under the age of twenty-one years shall be free upon arriving at that age; third, that the clause in the constitution excluding free negroes from the limits of that State shall never be so construed as to authorize the passage of any law on the part of the Legislature excluding from it citizens of the several States of this Union. . . .

. . . Mr. President, the people of West Virginia not only desire an admission into the Union; but they wish to preserve their liberties under the Constitution of the United States, and I shall be mistaken if they surrender the high privilege of freemen, that of forming for themselves, free and untrammeled, their own organic law. They will never consent that this Congress shall prescribe for them a form of government. Such exercise of power has never been submitted to by the people of this country since the day our fathers declared the independence of the colonies; prior to that, forms of government were prescribed for them by the British Crown. The exercise of such a power by Congress, if submitted to by the people of West Virginia, would not only affect them, but it would be an assertion of power over a free people that would alarm the fears of the patriot and encourage the traitor in arms. The people of West Virginia value constitutional liberty; they do not look alone to their interests, isolated and disconnected from the interests of their fellow-citizens throughout the entire country. . . . —*Congressional Globe,* July 14, 1862, pp. 3310, 3311-12.

98. The House Debate on West Virginia Statehood

John Armor Bingham, who represented the Ohio congressional district which bordered the West Virginia northern panhandle counties, piloted the West Virginia statehood bill through the House of Representatives. Bingham was a Radical Republican and prominent after the war in the impeachment and trial of President Andrew Johnson.

Bingham succeeded in bringing the West Virginia statehood bill to its third reading in the House on July 16, 1862, but when Representative Joseph E. Segar of Virginia objected to placing the measure on its final passage the House postponed further consideration until the second Tuesday in December. Bingham's motion on December 9, 1862, to place the bill on its passage precipitated a debate which lasted the better part of two days. The House of Representatives then passed the bill on December 10, 1862, by a vote of 96 for to 55 against.

Opponents contended that Virginia had not legally consented to the formation of West Virginia, while supporters of the bill declared the right of a loyal minority to govern a state in the presence of disloyalty and rebellion. The passages which follow have been taken from speeches in the House by Republican Representatives Martin F. Conway, of Kansas, and John A. Bingham, who presented the overriding constitutional arguments on the West Virginia statehood issue.

[MR. CONWAY:]

... This bill is not so much for the admission of a new State as it is for the division of an old one. Nevertheless, I would have no objection to that, were it presented under proper conditions. But the Constitution of the United States requires that no State shall be divided unless the assent of its Legislature be first obtained....

I do not regard this proposed division of Virginia as having received that assent from the Legislature of the State which the Constitution requires. Here, of course, however, is a question; and the question turns on whether the State of Virginia of which a Mr. Pierpont is Governor, is the lawful State or not. I do not believe that it is....

It is true, the President of the United States has recognized this as the actual State of Virginia; and acting upon his sanction the Senate has admitted its Senators into that body. But this is of no binding force upon us. On the contrary, if the President and Senate are wrong in so grave a matter, it is the more important that the House of Representatives should be right.

The argument in favor of the validity of the Wheeling government is that the original State of Virginia fell into treason and became null and void, and caused a vacuum which could only be filled in this way. Now this is entirely unsatisfactory to me; for, in the first place, I do not see how a State can fall into treason; and secondly, if it should, what right Mr. Pierpont would have to assume the office of Governor over any other individual who might wish it. Where did the law come from which gave him his warrant? From a mob or a mass meeting? Neither mobs nor mass meetings make laws under our system.

... The utter and flagrant unconstitutionality of this scheme —I may say, its radically revolutionary character—ought to expose it to the reprobation of every loyal citizen and every member of this House. It aims at an utter subversion of our constitutional system. Its effect would be to consolidate all the powers of the Government in the hands of the Executive. With the admission of this new State, the President will have substantially *created* four Senators—two for Virginia and two for West Virginia. He will also have substantially *created* fifteen electoral votes for President, as belonging to the State of Virginia, and six or eight as belonging to the new State, besides the number of members of this House to which West Virginia will be entitled, and also the number which may come in hereafter from the so-called Virginia itself, under Mr. Pierpont's certificate. . . .

. . . A State is either in the Union or it is out of it. If it is in the Union it is of course to be respected as such. If it is out, then it is a foreign State, and its territory is liable to be conquered and held as other territory, subject to the sovereignty which has conquered it. . . .

In my judgment, a State can only be out of the Union (unless through a constitutional amendment) when its people have accomplished a revolution, or, in other words, have by force of arms become either a belligerent Power or absolutely independent. In my opinion, the situation with regard to our seceded States is that they are out of the Union by having acquired at least a belligerent character, thus securing an international status incompatible with their Federal relations. This places them to us in the position of a foreign Power with whom we are at war, and makes their territory subject to our sovereign will whenever we take it from them.

The true policy of this Government, therefore, with regard to the seceded States, is to hold them as common territory wherever and whenever our arms are extended over them. This obviates the terrible dangers which I have alluded to, and is in harmony with the highest considerations of public utility, as well as with sound legal principles. At any rate, I hope that Congress will not fail to set itself firmly against that scheme which looks to a reorganization of southern power on the ruins of our constitutional system. . . . —*Congressional Globe,* December 9, 1862, pp. 37-38.

[MR. BINGHAM:]

...I say, that if the majority of the people of Virginia have turned rebels, as I believe they have, the State is in the loyal minority, and I am not alone in that opinion. I repeat, where the majority become rebels in arms, the minority are the State; that the minority, in that event, have a right to administer the laws, and maintain the authority of the State government, and to that end to elect a State Legislature and executive, by which they may call upon the Federal Government for protection 'against domestic violence,' according to the express guarantee of the Constitution. To deny this proposition is to say that when the majority in any State revolt against the laws, both State and Federal, and deny and violate all rights of the minority, that however numerous the minority may be, the State government can never be re-organized, nor the rights of the minority protected thereby so long as the majority are in the revolt....

...The majority have become traitors. When the Representatives whom they had elected, who were required by the existing constitution of Virginia, as well as by the Federal Constitution, to take an oath to support the Constitution of the United States, went to Richmond, joined in this conspiracy, lifted up the hand of treason and rebellion against the Government, foreswore themselves, and, in short, entered into a deliberate article of bargain and sale with Alexander H. Stephens, vice president of the southern confederacy, transferring the State of Virginia to that confederacy, they surrendered all right to represent any part of the people of Virginia; as a Legislature they utterly disqualified themselves to execute that trust.

...I am not going to quarrel with good friends if they differ with me as to final conclusions, but I am not going to stand here and allow the Representatives of the people, on a question of this magnitude, to shirk their responsibility. I say it without the fear of contradiction, because it has been affirmed by every branch of this Government, legislative, executive and judicial, more than once, that when the storm of revolution shakes the civil fabric of a State of the Union, the ultimate and final arbiter to determine who constitute the legislative and executive government of that State, and hold its great trust of sovereignty, is the Congress of the United States, or the President acting by authority of an act of Congress. . . .

I think I have said enough to satisfy the gentlemen who have done me the kindness to attend to what I have said, that the Legislature which assembled at Wheeling, Virginia, was the Legislature of the State of Virginia; and that it remains with you alone to determine whether it shall be or not. If you affirm that it is, there is no appeal from your decision. I am ready, for one, to affirm it, and upon the distinct ground that I do recognize, in the language of Mr. Madison, even the rights of a minority in a revolted State to be protected, under the Federal Constitution, both by Federal law and by State law. I hold, sir, that the Legislature assembled at Wheeling, then, is the legal Legislature of the State; that it had power to assent to this division of the State of Virginia; and that it is wholly immaterial to me whether a majority of the counties of that State refused, by reason of their treason, to co-operate in the election of Delegates and Senators to that Legislature. On the subject of granting the admission of the proposed State, to which that body has assented, it is enough for me to know there is a sufficient number of loyal men within the limits of the proposed State to maintain the machinery of a State government, and entitle them to Federal representation. That is the only rule heretofore recognized by Congress in the matter of admitting new States duly organized. . . .

It is because I have confidence in the people that I am willing to send this bill to them. I want to see them vote on it, from the base of the Alleghenies to the beautiful waters of the Ohio. I have been among that people. I know something of their character. I have seen eight or ten thousand of them in convention assembled, for the laudable purpose of holding up the arm of the Government against this unmatched treason and rebellion. I believe that they are loyal. I believe that they are the friends of free institutions. We have some evidence of it in the constitution now before us; and we will have additional evidence in that instrument as they will amend it, if you pass this bill. . . . —*Congressional Globe*, Dec. 10, 1862, pp. 57-58.

99. The Cabinet Divides: The Case For and Against

West Virginia achieved statehood on the tide of nationalism which swept the Union during the Civil War. However, having passed the Senate by a vote of 23 to 17 in July, 1862, and the House of Representatives by 96 to 55 in the following December, the West Virginia Bill had still another gauntlet to run. That the Lincoln administration gave its support to the restoration of the Virginia government at Wheeling was not surprising in view of military considerations and Federal responsibility under the Constitution to protect the state against invasion as well as guarantee it a republican form of government. But the use of the reorganized government as an agency for the creation of a new state was another matter. President Lincoln was for good reason deeply troubled by the West Virginia movement. Senator Orville H. Browning of Illinois, a member of the Senate Committee on Territories, went to the Executive Mansion in the evening of December 15 and there handed him the enrolled bill creating the State of West Virginia. "He was distressed at its passage," said Browning, "and asked me how long he could retain it before approving or vetoing. I told him ten days. He wished he had more." Browning stated that he told the President he "would not now lay it before him, but would retain it and furnish him a copy . . .".

Lincoln had remained cool toward the formation of West Virginia because it embarrassed his plan to use the Restored Government of Virginia as a pilot state in his reconstruction program; he had doubts as to the constitutionality of the scheme; and he had also to consider that conservative Republicans and practically all of the Democrats opposed the creation of West Virginia.

Soon after receiving the enrolled bill Lincoln acted upon a suggestion of Attorney General Edward Bates and addressed a memorandum to each member of his cabinet asking for answers to these questions: "1st Is the said Act constitutional? 2nd., Is the said Act expedient?" Blair, Seward, and Stanton returned statements under date of December 26; Bates, De-

cember 27; Chase and Welles, the 29th. Chase, Stanton and Seward urged approval on grounds of legality and expediency, while Blair, Bates and Welles urged a veto on grounds of unconstitutionality and inexpediency. The statements submitted to the President by Secretary of State William H. Seward and by Postmaster General Montgomery Blair contain the main arguments for and against the admission of West Virginia to statehood.

[SECRETARY OF STATE WILLIAM H. SEWARD:]

Western Virginia is organized unquestionably with all the constitutional elements and faculties of a State, and with a republican form of government. It, therefore, has a title to be a candidate for admission into the Federal Union. Congress has power to admit new States, but is a power restricted within certain limitations. One of these limitations is that no new State shall be formed or erected within the jurisdiction of any other State without the consent of that State as well as the consent of the new State and the consent of Congress. It is an undisputed fact that the new State of Western Virginia has been both formed and erected within the jurisdiction of the State of Virginia. Has the consent of the State of Virginia to the formation and erection of the State of West Virginia been given, or has it not been given? Upon this point the constitutionality of the Act of Congress now before me turns. The constituted and regular authorities of a State called the State of Virginia sitting at Wheeling, within the jurisdiction of that State, claiming to be the State of Virginia, and acting as such, have in a due and regular manner declared and given the consent of the State of Virginia to the formation and erection of the State of West Virginia within the jurisdiction of the State of Virginia. Thus far the case seems simple and clear. But is is just at this point that a complication begins. If we would unfold it successfully we must first state the existing facts in regard to the constitutional position of the State of Virginia, as well as those which belong to the formation and creation of the new State of West Virginia.

About the month of April, 1861, an insurrection against the Federal Union broke out within the State of Virginia. The constituted authorities, with the seeming consent of a majority of the People of the State, inaugurated a revolutionary war which they have carried to the extreme points of pronounced independence and of the setting up of a pretended revolutionary and belligerent government. The organized political body which has committed this treason, having broken and trampled under its feet the Constitution, and even the Union, of the United States, is still standing in that treasonable attitude within the jurisdiction of the State of Virginia, but it has been dislodged from that portion of that jurisdiction which is contained within the new State of West Virginia. This organization has not given its consent to the formation and erection of the State of Western Virginia, and in its present attitude it is clear that it neither can nor will give that consent. The State of Virginia having thus fallen into revolution, the people living within that part of its jurisdiction which is embraced within the new State of West Virginia, adhering in their loyalty to the State of Virginia and also to the United States, availed themselves of the fortune of the civil war to discard the treasonable authorities of Virginia, reorganized the State, and with all needful forms and solemnities chose and constituted the public functionaries for the state as nearly in conformity with the constitution of Virginia as in the revolutionary condition of that State was practicable. . . .

. . . It seems to me that the political body which has given consent in this case is really and incontestably the State of Virginia. So long as the United States do not recognize the secession, departure, or separation of one of the States, that State must be deemed as existing and having a Constitutional place within the Union, whatever may be at any moment exactly its revolutionary condition. A State thus situated cannot be deemed to be divided into two or more states merely by any revolutionary proceeding which may have occurred, because there cannot be constitutionally two or more States of Virginia. There must and can be, in the view of the Constitution, at all times only one State of Virginia. Here are two distinct political bodies, each asserting itself to be that one State of Virginia. Some constituted power must decide this dispute. The point in dispute necessarily affects the Federal Union. No matter whether the one or the other of these two bodies is the real State of Virginia, the Federal Union has authority to maintain within the

State, which cannot and must not be left in abeyance, and the body which is truly the State of Virginia has rights and holds obligations upon the Federal Union which must be conceded and fulfilled. The United States must therefore decide for themselves, so far as their rights and responsibilities extend, which of the two political bodies asserting themselves respectively to be the State of Virginia is truly the State, and which is not. ... It is a practical question, to be decided by the United States upon the grounds of public necessity or expediency, with a view to the best and permanent interests of the State of Virginia and of the United States. As I have already intimated, the question has been heretofore decided by the United States in favor of the new and against the old organization. The newly organized State of Virginia is therefore, at this moment, by the express consent of the United States, invested with all the rights of the State of Virginia, and charged with all the powers, privileges and dignity of that State. If the United States allow to that organization any of these rights, powers and privileges, it must be allowed to possess and enjoy them all. If it be a state competent to be represented in Congress and bound to pay taxes, it is a state competent to give the required consent of the State to the formation and erection of the new State of West Virginia within the jurisdiction of Virginia. . . .

Upon the question of expediency I am determined by two considerations. First. The people of Western Virginia will be safer from molestation for their loyalty, because better able to protect and defend themselves as a new and separate State, than they would be if left to demoralizing uncertainty upon the question whether, in the progress of the war, they may not be again re-absorbed in the State of Virginia, and subjected to severities as a punishment for their present devotion to the Union. The first duty of the United States is protection to loyalty wherever it is found. Second. I am of the opinion that the harmony and peace of the Union will be promoted by allowing the new State to be formed and erected, which will assume jurisdiction over that part of the valley of the Ohio which lies on the South side of the Ohio river, displacing, in a constitutional and lawful manner, the jurisdiction heretofore exercised there by a political power concentrated at the head of the James river.

[POSTMASTER GENERAL MONTGOMERY BLAIR:]

... The argument for the fulfillment of the constitutional provisions applicable to this case rests altogether on the fact that the Government organized at Wheeling (in which a portion of the District in which it is proposed to create the new State is represented with a few of the Eastern Counties) has been recognized as the Government of the State of Virginia for certain purposes by the Executive and Legislative branches of the Federal Government, and it is contended that by these acts the Federal Government is estopped from denying that the consent given by this Government of Virginia to be creation of the new State, is a sufficient consent within the meaning of the Constitution. It seems to me to be a sufficient answer to this argument to say: *First,* that it is confessedly merely technical, and assumes unwarrantably, that the qualified recognition which has been given to the Government at Wheeling for certain temporary purposes, precludes the Federal Government from taking notice of the fact that the Wheeling Government represents much less than half the people of Virginia when it attempts to dismember the State permanently. Or, *Second,* that the present demand, of itself, proves the previous recognitions relied on to enforce it, to be erroneous. For, unquestionably, the 4th article of the Constitution prohibits the formation of a new State within the jurisdiction of an old one without the actual consent of the old State, and if it be true that we have so dealt with a third part of the people of Virginia as that to be consistent we should now permit that minority to divide the State, it does not follow that we should persist, but on the contrary it demonstrates that we have heretofore been wrong, and if consistency is insisted on, and is deemed necessary, we should secede from the positions heretofore taken.

... It has been said with truth that Western Virginia has been a stepchild to the Eastern portion of the State where hitherto all political power has resided—And it is the injustice and oppression—the disfranchisement—and unequal taxation which has been exercised by the ruling class in the commonwealth for many long years which has alienated the people of the West. These wrongs have been familiar to me from childhood for among the people of Kentucky they found warm sympathy.

It is not therefore from want of sympathy with them that I oppose their wishes at this moment—But it is because in my view of the situation at present the days of their tyrants have passed away never to return and the hour is near when they have but to reach forth their hands and redress not only their own grievances but to restore the old commonwealth to honor & power in the Sisterhood of States—Each county as we remove the armed rebel hordes now overrunning the State will affiliate with the free government of the west & of the Union and the men of the west who have lead the vanguard of freedom in the State will naturally control the policy of the Regenerated State—what a glorious prospect thus opens to a state with one front on the Ocean with such a port as Hampton Roads, and another front on a great tributary of the Mississippi River. Give the people of the west time to consider this subject in the light of events which cannot be distant and which will open to their view the power they will possess to make the State of Virginia one of the greatest of the new world and they will thank the Statesman who refused his sanction to their wishes formed amidst the exasperations of civil war and a sense of wrongs which they will soon see can never be perpetrated again.

If ever there was case of hasty legislation calling for the interposition of the Executive this bill is one of that kind. No measure of such importance to the interests of a great people was ever passed through Congress with so little discussion. The condition of the country when the bill was before the Senate & House of Repesentatives seems to have so occupied the attention of the able men in those bodies, that they seem with rare exceptions not to have appreciated the importance of the measure, and it lead to but little discussion in either house. The only consideration which seems to have invoked favor or opposition was the fact that a free state was to be made of the part to be erected into a new State. This consideration would weigh with me if I believed the Union was to be divided and that the Eastern portion of the State was to be left the Rebels & to Slavery. But I look for neither result. I do not believe disunion possible & I shrink from a measure which looks like preparing for it. . . .

The idea that the mountains which divide the sections require the proposed political division has become obsolete by the use of Railroads and Canals. What sane man would propose to divide the State of Pennsylvania which is divided physically by the same ranges of Mountains? What irreparable mischief would have been done to that magnificent State if such a sacrifice had been made of her real & permanent interests on account of some temporary wrongs, as is now proposed with respect to the interests of Virginia for reasons not worth a thought to a Statesman. It may at this moment please the Western Virginians to favor a measure so cruel to the great interests of the State—But in my judgment the time is not far removed when no man among them would regard the measure otherwise than a Western Pennsylvanian would now regard a proposition to dismember that State—and I believe if the President refuses his sanction to the measure because it is pernicious to their best interests, the people of West Virginia will soon see in such refusal a thoughtfulness for their welfare which will endear his name to them forever.

I think the measure will be distasteful to the people generally. The legality of the act will be questioned and the reply we have to give is as I have said technical only. . . . In dismembering the State which has still a hold on the hearts of our people as the land of Washington, Jefferson, Madison, Monroe and other immortal names, there should therefore be no room for debate on the legality of the act.—William H. Seward to Abraham Lincoln, and Montgomery Blair to Abraham Lincoln, December 26, 1862, Lincoln Papers, Library of Congress.

100. Final Pleas for the Statehood Bill

While President Lincoln studied the West Virginia statehood bill in December, 1862, anxious friends of the new state, notably Governor Francis H. Pierpont and Archibald W. Campbell, showered him with letters and telegrams intended to show that a denial of statehood would destroy the Union cause in western Virginia.

Born in Jefferson County, Ohio, Archibald W. Campbell (1833-1899) was the son of Dr. A. W. Campbell and nephew of the eminent Alexander Campbell. After graduating from Bethany College in 1852 he studied law at Hamilton College where he formed a friendship with William H. Seward. A disciple of Seward and a pioneer Virginia Republican leader, Campbell had headed the anti-slavery forces in that state since 1856, when he became editor of the Wheeling DAILY INTELLIGENCER and directed the campaign of John C. Fremont for President. Unsuccessful in his fight for Wheeling as the Republican National Convention site in 1860, he attended the Chicago convention as a Seward delegate from Virginia; following the defeat of his idol for the presidential nomination he cast his vote for Cassius M. Clay of Kentucky before joining the victorious Lincoln ranks. As editor of the DAILY INTELLIGENCER, postmaster at Wheeling and confidant of Lincoln, Campbell exerted a determining influence on the troubled course of events in western Virginia throughout the Civil War.

On December 20, 1862, Campbell joined Pierpont and fifteen others in a dispatch which reached the President on the day after he received the enrolled bill. Finally on December 30, 1862, after drafting a letter to President Lincoln, Campbell persuaded Governor Pierpont to send a supporting letter. This document has been preserved in the Robert Todd Lincoln Papers and is, to all appearance, the communication which as the President told Pierpont in April, 1865, finally decided him to sign the West Virginia statehood bill.

The joint telegram of December 20, the Campbell letter, which apparently reached the President's desk after he had signed the bill, and the deciding Pierpont letter are given in full below.

Time Received 1:00 P. M.   United States Military Telegraph
                                                              War Department
                                              Wheeling, Va. Dec. 20th 1862
A. Lincoln
Prest U. S.

Great feeling exists throughout the bounds of the new state in reference to your delay in signing the bill for the new state. We represent almost every section of the proposed new state

& regard your delay as a calamity to the Union cause. It puts arguments into the mouths of the disloyal. We entreat you for the cause of the country not to hesitate to sign the bill. Do not think of allowing it to become a law simply by default. Give us the morale of positive action. Its failure will ruin the Union cause in Western Va. We speak what we know.

F. H. Pierpont Gov.

L. A. Hagans Secy of the Commonwealth

Saml. Crane Auditor

Campbell Tarr Treas'r

Daniel Pollsley Lieut Gov.

Edward M. Norton U. S. Marshal

A. W. Campbell Postmaster

Thos. Hornbrook Collector

Geo. C. McPorter Speaker house Delegates

Members of house of delegates:

H. W. Crothers

Geo. C. Bowie

Leroy Kramer

Jas. Burley State Senator

J. R. Dickey Cash. People's bank

J. W. Paxton Pres't N. W. bank Va.

N. P. Hildrath Cashr. Savings bank

C. D. Hubbard Prest bank of Wheeling

Daily Intelligencer Office
Wheeling, Va. Dec 31st 1862

To His Excellency
    President Lincoln
Dear Sir

I would be thankful if in the multiplicity of your calls you could spare time enough to read a few words, in addition to those already brought to your attention, in reference to our new State of West Virginia.

I write to you, Mr. President, as your ardent political and personal friend—as one who labored as hard in the cause of your election, and, since then, in the cause of the Union as any man in the country. Before the people, on the stump & in my newspaper I have never ceased for a day to do my uttermost to make friends for your administration and the great cause of the Union.

With these claims of sincerity and anxiety upon your attention, I ask you to consider the true situation of our people in reference to the effort, long continued, made & making by them for a new State. I do not propose to go over the historical part of the effort. I wish simply to call your attention to the present feeling and the future danger connected with a veto of the bill that has passed Congress. No people were ever more united in a wish than are our people for a new State. South Carolina, in my opinion, was never as much united for secession. Not a citizen of prominence in all our forty eight counties, with the single exception of Senator Carlile, opposes it. He, for his opposition in the Senate, together with his defection from the Union cause, has been more thoroughly and universally repudiated by our people than any public man ever has before by his constituency, so far as I can recall. Some twenty five large county meetings have requested his resignation, and at the same time have endorsed the bill for the new state as it had passed the Senate & has since passed the House. Numberless smaller meetings have done the same thing. Not a meeting, however insignificant, held anywhere for months past in any of the counties of the proposed state have neglected to endorse the bill. In addition, the legislature have endorsed it, & have formally requested the House to pass it while it was pending there in the early part of this month. Many members of that legislature, as many as were thought necessary, together with the Governor, Lieut Gov. and others, a few days ago, united in a dispatch to you praying you to sign the bill and make it a law.

Do not these mutliplied evidences convince you, Mr. President, that there is a general & earnest & persistent public sentiment demanding the New State? I doubt not they do. A people could not be more deeply excited on the issue of any question, of a political kind, than our people for the result, in your hands, of their long effort & their long deferred hope of a new state. The feeling against the ordinance of Secession, in the canvass, strong as it was, was mild in comparison with the present feeling. Indeed there is no comparison. A veto of the bill would be a disaster, the consequences of which I dread to contemplate. I verily believe that it would be a death blow to our Union sentiment. I can not see that there would be any coherency in it in the future. It would have lost the central magnet. It would be utterly disintegrated and demoralized. With our people the Union and the New State are convertible terms. Crush the one and you, as certain as death, in my opinion, crush the other. In the present prospects of our national affairs the expectation of a new state keeps thousands from falling away, and I see in a veto the sure melting away of our Union strength. Destroy the hope of a new state and our people see themselves remanded again to Eastern Va & again identified and committed to her fortunes. A crushed minority sentiment, thoroughly disloyal, would soon warm into life and prestige. Mr. Carlile with all his better and worse affiliations, now under ban, would rise and ride the wave.

Mr President, as your friend, as an original, unconditional and unchangable Union man, I say to you that, for the sake of the cause, now so far imperilled & so precious in its issue, you can never afford to veto the new State bill. If it was given me above all things to decide what could be most harmful to the cause of the Union among 300,000 people I would say a veto of this bill. And so would say every loyal man here. So say nine loyal newspapers against one disloyal. So say all our people in authority from the governor down to every sheriff.

To sum up all, Mr President, I will say that a veto of the bill, in my earnest and most deliberate opinion, will be the death warrant of Unionism in Western Va.

Very sincerely & respectfully

A. W. Campbell

Wheeling Va Decr 30 62

To His Excellency—

The President of the U. S.—

Sir.

Mr. A. W. Campbell has read me a letter addressed to you on the subject of the new state. I hope you will read the letter. It contains the truth in my opinion. The Union men of West Va. were not originally for the Union because of the new state. But the sentiment for the two have become identified. If one is stricken down I dont know what is [to] become of the other.

I am & c

F. H. Pierpont

—Lincoln Papers, Library of Congress.

101. President Lincoln on the Admission of West Virginia

The West Virginia Bill came to Lincoln's desk on a very dark night of the war. The ever-present danger of foreign recognition of the Confederacy, the failure of the compensated emancipation program, the uncertainties surrounding the success of the emancipation policy proclaimed in September, the triumph of the Democrats in the election of 1862, the meddling of Congress in the President's conduct of the war, the military stalemate in the West, the incompetence and carnage at the battle of Fredericksburg, and the threatened defection of the Radical Republicans cast long shadows across the path of Lincoln. In his memorable message to Congress early in December he had stated the plight of the country in those timeless lines which began: "The dogmas of the quiet past are inadequate to the stormy present. The occasion is piled high with difficulty and we must rise high with the occasion." Attorney General Bates declared that a determining factor in Lincoln's decision to sign the West Virginia statehood bill was the need to placate the Radical Republicans who supported the West Virginia movement and who after the battle of Fredericksburg were clamoring for the removal from the Cabinet of Secretaries Seward and Stanton.

Whatever the exigencies of the hour, President Lincoln signed the West Virginia Bill before retiring in the evening of December 31, 1862, and stated his reasons.

THE CONSENT of the Legislature of Virginia is constitutionally necessary to the bill for the admission of West Virginia becoming a law. A body claiming to be such Legislature has given its consent. We can not well deny that it is such, unless we do so upon the outside knowledge that the body was chosen at elections, in which a majority of the qualified voters of Virginia did not participate. But it is a universal practice in the popular elections in all these States to give no legal consideration whatever to those who do not choose to vote, as against the effect of the votes of those who do choose to vote. Hence it is not the qualified voters, but the qualified voters, *who choose to vote,* that constitute the political power of the State. Much less than to non-voters, should any consideration be given to those who did not vote, *in this case:* because it is also a matter of outside knowledge, that they were not merely neglectful of their rights under, and duty to, this government, but were also engaged in open rebellion against it. Doubtless among these non-voters were some Union men whose voices were smothered by the more numerous secessionists; but we know too little of their number to assign them any appreciable value. Can the government stand, if it indulges Constitutional constructions by which men in open rebellion against it, are to be accounted, man for man, the equals of those who maintain their loyalty to it? Are they to be accounted even better citizens, and more worthy of consideration, than those who merely neglect to vote? If so, their treason against the Constitution, enhances their constitutional value! Without braving these absurb conclusions, we cannot deny that the body which consents to the admission of West Virginia, is the Legislature of Virginia. I do not think the plural form of the words "Legislatures" and "States" in the phrase of the Constitution "without the consent of the Legislatures of the States concerned" has any reference to the *new* State concerned. That plural form sprang from the contemplation of two or more old States, contributing to form a new one. The idea that the new state was in danger of being admitted without its own consent, was not provided against, because it was not thought of, as I conceive. It is said, the devil takes care of his own. Much more should a good spirit—the spirit of the Constitution and the Union—take care of its own. I think it can not do less, and live.

But is the admission into the Union, of West Virginia, expedient. This, in my general view, is more a question for Congress, than for the Executive. Still I do not evade it. More than on any thing else, it depends on whether the admission or rejection of the new State would, under all the circumstances tend the more strongly to the restoration of the National authority throughout the Union. That which helps most in this direction is most expedient at this time. Doubtless those in remaining Virginia would return to the Union, so to speak, less reluctantly without the division of the old state than with it; but I think we could not save as much in this quarter by rejecting the new state, as we should lose by it in West Virginia. We can scarcely dispense with the aid of West Virginia in this struggle; much less can we afford to have her against us, in Congress and in the field. Her brave and good men regard her admission into the Union as a matter of life and death. They have been true to the Union under very severe trials. We have so acted as to justify their hopes; and we can not fully retain their confidence, and co-operation, if we seem to break faith with them. In fact, they could not do so much for us, if they would.

Again, the admission of the new State turns that much slave soil to free; and thus, is a certain, and irrevocable encroachment upon the cause of the rebellion.

The division of a State is dreaded as a precedent. But a measure made expedient by a war, is no precedent for times of peace. It is said the admission of West Virginia is secession, and tolerated only because it is our secession. Well, if we can call it by that name, there is still difference enough between secession against the Constitution, and secession in favor of the Constitution.

I believe the admission of West Virginia into the Union is expedient.—Abraham Lincoln, December 31, 1862, Lincoln Papers, Library of Congress.

102. The West Virginia Statehood Law

The controversial statehood bill which President Lincoln signed on December 31, 1862, named the forty-eight counties contained in the application for statehood and declared West Virginia to be one of the United States of America with three seats in the House of Representatives. The bill required the people of the State to incorporate in their constitution provisions for the gradual emancipation of slaves as embodied in the Willey Amendment. When these qualifications were fulfilled and certified, the President of the United States was authorized to issue his proclamation of statehood, effective sixty days from the date of the proclamation. The act is given in full below.

WHEREAS THE PEOPLE inhabiting that portion of Virginia known as West Virginia did, by a Convention assembled in the city of Wheeling on the twenty-sixth of November, eighteen hundred and sixty-one, frame for themselves a Constitution with a view of becoming a separate and independent State; and whereas at a general election held in the counties composing the territory aforesaid on the third day of May° last, the said Constitution was approved and adopted by the qualified voters of the proposed State; and, whereas the Legislature of Virginia, by an act passed on the thirteenth day of May, eighteen hundred and sixty-two, did give its consent to the formation of a new State within the jurisdiction of the said State of Virginia, to be known by the name of West Virginia, and to embrace the following named counties, to wit: Hancock, Brooke, Ohio, Marshall, Wetzel, Marion, Monongalia, Preston, Taylor, Tyler, Pleasants, Ritchie, Doddridge, Harrison, Wood, Jackson, Wirt, Roane, Calhoun, Gilmer, Barbour, Tucker, Lewis, Braxton, Upshur, Randolph, Mason, Putnam, Kanawha, Clay, Nicholas, Cabell, Wayne, Boone, Logan, Wyoming, Mercer, McDowell, Webster, Pocahontas, Fayette, Raleigh, Greenbrier, Monroe, Pendleton, Hardy, Hampshire, and Morgan; and whereas both the Convention and the Legislature aforesaid have requested that the new State should be admitted into the Union, and the Constitution aforesaid being republican in form, Congress doth hereby consent that the said forty-eight counties may be formed into a separate and independent State. Therefore—*Be it enacted by the Senate and House of Representatives of the United States of America in Congress assembled.* That the State of West Virginia be, and is hereby, declared to be one of the United States of America, and admitted into the Union on an equal footing with the original States in all respects whatever, and until the next general census shall be entitled to three members in the House of Representatives of the United States; *Provided, always,* That this act shall not take effect until after the proclamation of the President of the United States hereinafter provided for.

It being represented to Congress that since the Convention of the twenty-sixth of November, eighteen hundred and sixty-one,

°But see No. 95 above.

that framed and proposed the Constitution for the said State of West Virginia, the people thereof have expressed a wish to change the seventh section of the eleventh article of said Constitution by striking out the same and inserting the following in its place, viz: "The children of slaves born within the limits of this State after the fourth day of July, eighteen hundred and sixty-three, shall be free; and that all slaves within the said State who shall, at the time aforesaid, be under the age of ten years, shall be free when they arrive at the age of twenty-one years; and all slaves over ten and under twenty-one years shall be free when they arrive at the age of twenty-five years; and no slave shall be permitted to come into the State for permanent residence therein:" Therefore—

Sec. 2. *Be it further enacted,* That whenever the people of West Virginia shall, through their said Convention, and by a vote to be taken at an election to be held within limits of the said State, at such time as the Convention may provide, make, and ratify the change aforesaid, and properly certify the same under the hand of the president of the Convention, it shall be lawful for the President of the United States to issue his proclamation stating the fact, and thereupon this act shall take effect and be in force from and after sixty days from the date of said proclamation.

APPROVED, December 31, 1862.—*The Statutes at Large, Treaties, and Proclamations of the United States,* XII, 633-34.

103. The Issue of Compensated Emancipation

On the second day of the recalled session of the Constitutional Convention which convened in Wheeling, February 12, 1863, to consider the terms of admission imposed by Congress, a committee of five was appointed with instructions to study the propriety of incorporating into the constitution a section providing for compensation by the State of West Virginia to the owners of slaves freed by the Willey Amendment. In its report on February 14, 1863, the committee submitted to the Convention a res-

olution expressing the opinion that loyal owners of slaves would be "entitled to recover from the State the actual value of such slaves at the time of emancipation" under existing constitutional and legal guarantees. Nevertheless, the compensation proposal was debated at length until tabled on February 18 by a vote of 28 for and 26 against. The leading proponent in the convention of an explicit guarantee of compensation to loyal slaveholders was James H. Brown of Kanawha County and among those who opposed him were Elbert H. Caldwell of Marshall and Moses Tichenell of Marion County.

MR. BROWN. . . . We are proposing to take from a portion of our people property which belongs to them under the laws of the land; which is guaranteed to them by the Constitution of the country and the laws of our State. . . . In the very act that carries emancipation it provides indemnity for the owner. They would not put upon the record a stain. And that too by the most ultra men, who deny the right of property in human beings. Could it be supposed then that in the assembly of the sovereign people of West Virginia a member should express the sentiment of a readiness to take his neighbor's property without a compensation? I hardly think it would. It will not do any member of this Convention the injustice to believe that there is a man here that would; that there is an individual here that would be willing to put his hand into his neighbor's pocket and take from him his property without compensation at the hands of the public that does the act. Well, this question stands upon a principle of high and acknowledged right of a recognized law and constitution as applicable to the old world and its monarchies as to the new world and its republics. We have adopted a Constitution which in express terms asserts that proposition, that no private property shall be taken for public use without just compensation. There it is, written as plain as possible for the hand of man to write it, but we are not the authors of it. We have not the honor of its origin, because our fathers penned and placed it there. We only copy it out of one instrument into another. That Constitution has been adopted and ratified by the people of West Virginia, and they have therefore ratified and approved that doctrine as their doctrine, whether re-asserted by this Convention or not and re-adopted by them in their vote at the polls. . . .

MR. CALDWELL. . . . I regret that this proposition has been introduced. The gentleman from Kanawha thinks it can do no harm. Sir, I am satisfied it will do a great deal of harm. If I thought it would do no harm at all I would most cheerfully go with him. I do not oppose it because I expect my property to be taxed to pay the compensation for his slaves. I do not object to it; willingly, cheerfully, would I incur the tax; but, sir, it will do the harm in this way. Only a few days ago, a German who had lived in western Virginia twenty years in my presence paid to the sheriff of my county a tax on land amounting to over ninety dollars. I had a conversation with him as to this new State and he told me he was a new State man. Yes, and he went further; he was for a free State. "I desire to have a new State, and I want a free State; and they tell me" this simple German said, "you will have to build a capitol, a penitentiary and asylums of one description and another, and the result would be it would increase our taxes." Well, sir, when our enemies have taken the stand, they will go to this poor Dutchman, and they will tell him: "Don't you see by the expression of the opinion of this Convention that there is a provision in this Constitution that our property—we have no interest in slaves—must be taxed to pay these slave-holders for their slaves; and the Convention has gone out of its way to pass a resolution and declare that in their opinion that is what this provision means." Now, sir, there is the harm; and for these reasons I cannot give my consent to the resolution.

MR. TICHENELL. . . . Let this Convention come out and formally recommend that the people pay for all the slaves. They will seize that, and we will lose hundreds and thousands of votes; and before God today I am afraid we will lose it if we pass this resolution. The gentleman from Kanawha argues there is probably more in his region of country than we are aware of. Well, now I will admit some few individuals might vote for it that would not if we do not adopt this resolution; but while I am free to admit that thing, if you will compare hands with the whole country and then look at the small proportion of the persons who have this species of property, the argument can be brought to bear upon the masses and used with much greater effect the other way. While a small number of slaves holders might be led to vote against the Constitution because the Convention refused to declare their slaves should be paid for, a much greater number of non-slave-holders might be brought to vote against it if the Convention made this kind of formal declaration or pledge. It is a knife that will cut both ways. The question is in which way will it do most harm. I appreciate that gentleman's views and believe him entirely sincere in his wish to promote the success of the new State; but I tell you every one I fear the consequences of this vote. You have the right to hold property and they cannot take it away from you. . . . —*Debates and Proceedings of the First Constitutional Convention*, III, 565-66, 575, 577-78.

104. President Lincoln's Statehood Proclamation, April 20, 1863

Following a long debate in the recalled session of the Constitutional Convention on the issue of compensated emancipation, the Willey Amendment was adopted on February 17, 1863, and next day incorporated in the constitution without a dissenting vote. In compliance with the schedule agreed upon by the Convention, the constitution was submitted to the voters for ratification or rejection on March 26, 1863. Undaunted by their failure to prevent the incorporation of the Willey Amendment into the constitution, state-rights Democrats led by John J. Davis, General John J. Jackson, and Sherrard Clemens joined with John S. Carlile in a campaign to defeat the constitution at the polls. Defenders of the Willey Amendment, including Peter G. Van Winkle, Governor Pierpont, and Senator Willey himself, took to the hustings along with Representative John A. Bingham of Ohio and other imported speakers. The results of the election announced on April 17, 1863, were 27,749 for ratification and 572 against—a decisive victory for the Willey Amendment.

The ratification of the constitution with the Willey Amendment by the West Virginia electorate was certified to the President on April 16, and four days later, April 20, 1863, President Lincoln issued the proclamation which admitted West Virginia to the Union as the thirty-fifth state.

PRESIDENT LINCOLN'S PROCLAMATION, APRIL 20, 1863
By the President of the United States of America.

A PROCLAMATION

Whereas by the Act of Congress approved the 31st day of December last the State of West Virginia was declared to be one of the United States of America, and was admitted into the Union on an equal footing with the original States in all respects whatever, upon the condition that certain changes should be duly made in the proposed Constitution for that State; and

Whereas proof of a compliance with that condition, as required by the second section of the act aforesaid has been submitted to me:

Now, therefore, be it known that I, Abraham Lincoln, President of the United States, do hereby, in pursuance of the act of Congress aforesaid, declare and proclaim that the said act shall take effect and be in force from and after sixty days from the date hereof.

In witness whereof I have hereunto set my hand and caused the seal of the United States to be affixed.

Done at the city of Washington, this 20th day of April, A.D. 1863, [SEAL] and of the Independence of the United States the eighty-seventh.

By the President: ABRAHAM LINCOLN.

WILLIAM H. SEWARD, *Secretary of State.*—James D. Richardson, ed., *A Compilation of the Messages and Papers of the Presidents 1789-1897*, VI, 167.

105. Governor Arthur I. Boreman's Inaugural Address, June 20, 1863

West Virginia's first governor, Arthur Ingram Boreman (1823-1896), was born and reared at Waynesburg, Pennsylvania. In the 1840's he went to Middlebourne, Tyler County, Virginia, now West Virginia, to read law in his brother's office and in 1845 was admitted to the bar. A year later he began practice in Parkersburg, Wood County, where he entered politics. A Whig, he represented Wood County in the Virginia house of delegates from 1855 to 1861. In the special session of the General Assembly, convened by Governor Letcher on January 7, 1861, he opposed authorization of a convention and after adoption of the secession ordinance became a leader of the partition movement. Boreman served as president of the Second Wheeling Convention which restored the government of Virginia and launched the West Virginia movement. He also held a circuit judgeship under the restored Virginia government until he became governor of West Virginia. He won that office without opposition in an election held May 28, 1863. In 1864 he was elected on the Union ticket for a full term, again without opposition; two years later, as a Republican, he defeated Conservative candidate Benjamin H. Smith of Kanawha County. Although Boreman assumed the governorship as a symbol of unity, he soon embraced Radical Republicanism, and as the war drew to a close obtained the enactment of legislation which effectively disfranchised and decitizenized former Confederates until 1871. Indeed, when Peter G. Van Winkle alienated the support of the Radical Republicans by his vote to sustain President Andrew Johnson in the impeachment trial in 1868, the West Virginia legislature refused to return him and sent Boreman to the Senate instead. After Boreman retired from that body in 1875, he practiced law at Parkersburg until 1888, when he won election as judge of the 5th judicial circuit court, a post he held until his death in 1896.

Boreman was inaugurated before a large crowd of soldiers and civilians on the grounds of the temporary capitol at Linsly

*Institute in Wheeling, following a colorful procession from the
McLure House. Senator Chester D. Hubbard of the reorganized
Virginia general assembly presided and the Reverend J. T.
McClure gave the invocation. Governor Francis H. Pierpont re-
viewed the events that had led to West Virginia statehood before
he introduced Governor Boreman. Boreman recapitulated the
unredressed grievances which had made the new state necessary
and pledged his administration to all-out war against the Confederacy.*

FELLOW CITIZENS:—To be permitted to participate in the most
humble capacity in the organization of the State of West Virginia would be an honor; but, to be called by the unanimous
voice of her people to accept the highest office in their gift, and
to the performance of its duties, at a time of so much difficulty
and danger as the present, excites in my heart the profound-
est gratitude toward them for the confidence thus reposed in
me. . . .

West Virginia should long since have had a separate State
existence. The East has always looked upon that portion of the
State west of the mountains, as a sort of outside appendage—
a territory in a state of pupilage. The unfairness and inequality of legislation is manifest on every page of the statute book;
they had an unjust majority in the Legislature by the original
Constitution of the State, and have clung to it with the utmost
tenacity ever since; they have collected heavy taxes from us,
and have spent large sums in the construction of railroads and
canals in the East, but have withheld appropriations from the
West; they have refused to make any of the modern improvements by which trade and travel could be carried on from the
one section to the other, thus treating us as strangers; our people could not get to the Capital of their State by any of the usual
modes of traveling, without going through the State of Maryland and the District of Columbia. The East and the West have
always been two peoples. There has been little intercourse between them, either social or commercial. Our people seldom
visit the East for pleasure. The farmers do not take their stock,
grain, wool and other agricultural products there to sell; the
merchants do not go there to sell or buy; the manufacturers

have no market there; indeed, we have had nothing to do with the Eastern people, except that our Senators and Delegates have gone to Richmond to sit in the Legislature, and our Sheriffs have gone there to pay in the revenue as an annual tribute from this section of the State for the inequality and unfairness with which we have always been treated by them. Our markets, our trade and our travel are North and West of Virginia, through natural channels, or those constructed through the enterprise of our own people, or such means as they could procure. The mountains intervene between us, the rivers rise in the mountains and run towards the Northwest; and, as if to make the separation more complete, Eastern Virginia adopted the fatal doctrine of secession, while the west spurned and rejected it as false and dangerous in the extreme. Thus nature, our commerce, travel, habits, associations, and interests, all—all say that West Virginia should be severed from the East.—And now, to-day after many long and weary years of insult and injustice, culminating on the part of the East, in an attempt to destroy the Government, we have the proud satisfaction of proclaiming to those around us that we are a separate State in the Union.

Our State is the child of the rebellion; yet our peace, prosperity and happiness, and, not only ours, but that of the whole country, depends on the speedy suppression of this attempt to overthrow the Government of our fathers; and it is my duty, as soon as these ceremonies are closed, to proceed at once to aid the Federal authorities in their efforts to stay its destructive hand. . . . The politicians of many of the Southern States, having an inordinate desire for place and power, and it becoming apparent that the great North-West was improving and increasing in population so rapidly that the controlling influence of the Government was soon surely to be with the free States, and that the South must surrender power which they had so long exerted to a majority of the people according to the principles of our Government, they became desperate, and determined if they could no longer control, they would destroy the Government. By fraud and falsehood, and by incendiary speeches, they influenced the public mind in the South, and induced them to believe that they were suffering great injury from the General Government; that the rights of the South were not only disregarded, but trampled under foot; that Mr. Lincoln was a sectional President, and that his election was the crowning act of insult and injustice; that if they submitted to it they were reduced to a state of degradation worse than slavery itself; and, fearing that the people still had some reverence and respect for the constitution, they insidiously taught the faithless doctrine that peaceable secession was in consonance with the Constitution, and absolved them from all their obligations to support the Government. . . . thus they inaugurated a war of rebellion, and have prosecuted it for over two years with a zeal and energy worthy of a better cause. It has assumed fearful proportions, and it demands all the energies of the Government authorities and of the loyal people to defeat its ruinous purposes.

. . . In the commencement of these difficulties we were part of a Southern State, whose convention passed an ordinance of secession, and this fact inclined many to sympathize with the South without reflecting whether it was right or wrong. We were situated between the South and the North, and in case of a collision it must necessarily result that ours would be contested territory; that if we adhered to the Union the South would deal with us much more severely than if we were a part of a Northern State, or of one that had not attempted to secede; and that we would be, what we have since been so truthfully called by many, the great "breakwater" between the North and those in rebellion in the South. All these matters were weighed and considered by us, but we determined, with a full belief of what would occur, and what has since occurred, that the Government was too good to be lost, and that the rights and immunities which we knew we were enjoying were too precious to be surrendered on the uncertainty of the results of experiments in the future. . . . Shall we object that slavery is destroyed as the result of the acts of those in rebellion, if the Union is thereby saved? But there are those who say that we should stop the war and make peace. . . . We want no compromise: we want no peace, except upon the terms that those in rebellion will lay down their arms and submit to the regularly constituted authorities of the Government of the United States. Then, and not till then, will the people of West Virginia agree to peace. . . .

I shall co-operate with the Federal authorities in all those measures deemed necessary for the suppression of the rebellion. While the war continues I must necessarily be engaged in attending to military matters, and to the defence of the State, and it may not, therefore, be expected that I shall give much time at present to the internal civil policy of the State; but even amidst surrounding difficulties and dangers they shall not be entirely forgotten.

I shall do whatever may be in my power during my term of office to advance the agricultural, mining, manufacturing and commercial interests of the State. And it shall be my especial pride and pleasure to assist in the establishment of a system of education throughout the State that may give to every child among us, whether rich or poor, an education that may fit them for respectable positions in society. . . .

Fellow-Citizens, we are about to part with him, who has for two years exercised the office of Governor of Virginia in our midst. And I here express how highly are appreciated, not only by myself, but by the whole loyal population of the State, his purity and fidelity, and the ability with which he has discharged the arduous and responsible duties of his office. We regret that he is to leave us, but we have the satisfaction of knowing that he is going to a new and important field where his ability and patriotism are still to be devoted to the good of his country.

If I shall only be able to discharge the duties of my office with as much satisfaction to the people and honor to myself as my predecessor, I shall expect the approbation of a generous public. I shall, no doubt, often do wrong, this is the lot of man; and while I shall always do that which honesty of purpose and my opinion of the good of the country dictates, I shall expect you to exercize that indulgence which is due to a public officer under the surrounding circumstances.—Wheeling *Intelligencer,* June 22, 1863.

106. The West Virginia State Seal, Coat of Arms and Motto

On June 22, 1863, the Legislature adopted a joint resolution providing for the appointment of a committee to "devise and report suitable devices and inscriptions for the seals of the State." The committee went to work immediately with Joseph H. Diss Debar (1820-1905) as a consultant and designer.

Diss Debar was eminently qualified to devise the state seal. Born in Alsace, France, and educated at Strasbourg, Colmar, and Mülhausen, he had studied art in Paris, emigrated to the United States in 1842, and come to West Union, Doddridge County in 1846 as an agent for French creditors of the estate of James Swan of Boston, who owned vast tracts of western Virginia wildlands. Entrusted with the sale of 10,000 acres, Diss Debar opened an office at West Union but soon moved to Parkersburg where he lived until the early 1850's. He then returned to Doddridge County and founded a colony of immigrants, which he named Saint Clara after his deceased wife. On the basis of the returns Diss Debar won election to the House of Delegates from Doddridge County in 1863 but the House seated his opponent. He decisively defeated the same opponent at the next election and served in the lower branch one year. In 1864 Governor Boreman appointed him Commissioner of Immigration, a post he held until 1871. Both as legislator and commissioner, he performed notable service in attracting immigrants and advertising the resources of the State. He moved to Philadelphia in 1872 and died there on January 13, 1905.

Diss Debar submitted the design of the seal to the committee early in September and the Legislature adopted it with minor changes on September 26, 1863.

THE JOINT COMMITTEE appointed to report suitable devices, &c., for the seals of the State, respectfully recommend the following:

The disc of the great seal to be two and one-half inches in diameter.

The *obverse* to bear the legend, "*State of West Virginia*," the constitutional designation of our republic, which, with the motto "*Montani semper liberi*," (in English, "Mountaineers always free,") is to be inserted in the circumference. In the centre, a rock with ivy, emblematic of stability and continuance, and on the face of the rock the inscription "June 20, 1863," the date of our foundation, as if "graved with a pen of iron in the rock forever." On the right of the rock a farmer clothed in the traditional hunting shirt peculiar to this region, his right arm resting on the plow-handles, and his left supporting a woodman's axe, indicating that while our territory is partially cultivated, is still in process of being cleared of the original forest. At his right, a sheaf of wheat and a cornstalk. On the left of the rock, a miner, indicated by a pickaxe on his shoulder, with barrels and lumps of mineral at his feet. On his left, an anvil, partly seen, on which rests a sledge hammer, typical of the mechanic arts, the whole indicating the principal pursuits and resources of the State. In front of the rock and figures, as if just laid down by the latter and ready to be resumed at a moment's notice, two hunter's rifles, crossed, and surmounted at the place of contact by the Phrygian cap, or cap of liberty, indicating that our freedom and independence were won and will be defended and maintained by arms.

The above to be also the legend, motto and device of the less seal, the disc of which should have a diameter of an inch and a half.

The reverse of the great seal to be encircled by a wreath composed of laurel and oak leaves, emblematic of valor and strength, with fruits and cereals, productions of our State. For device, a landscape. In the distance, on the left of the disc, wooded mountains, and on the right, a cultivated slope with the log frame house peculiar to this region. On the side of the mountain a representation of the viaduct on the line of the Baltimore and Ohio Railroad in Preston county, one of the great engineering triumphs of the age, with a train of cars about to pass over it. Near the centre, a factory, in front of which a river with boats on the bank, and to the right of it nearer the foreground a derrick and shed appertaining to the production of salt and petroleum. In the foreground a meadow with cattle and sheep feeding and reposing, the whole indicating the leading characteristics, production and pursuits of the State at this time. Above the mountains, &c., the sun emerging from the clouds, indicating that former obstacles to our prosperity are disappearing. In the rays of the sun, the motto *"Libertas e Fidelitate,"* (in English, liberty from loyalty,) indicating that our freedom and independence are the result of faithfulness to the principles of the Declaration of Independence and the National Constitution.

The committee further recommend that the above device and motto for the obverse of the great seal, be also adopted as the coat of arms of the State.—*Journal of the House of Delegates,* First Session, 1863, Appendix.

X. Four Years of Civil War

107. Charles J. Faulkner and the Bill of Rights, 1861

Perhaps the most famous of the arbitrary arrests made by the War and State departments during the Civil War was the detention and imprisonment of United States minister Charles J. Faulkner of Martinsburg, Virginia, following his return from France in the summer of 1861. Merely told that he was being held as a hostage for the safe return of a certain Henry S. Magraw of Pennsylvania, then in custody of Confederate authorities, Faulkner was sent first to Fort LaFayette in New York, then to Fort Warren at Boston. An entry in the RECORD BOOK *of the State Department entitled, "Arrests for Disloyalty" states that the Government had reliable information that Faulkner had conspired with the Confederates by urging the secession of Virginia, sending arms from France to the Confederacy, planning the military occupation of Washington, and by other disloyal acts including acceptance of the command of a Confederate regiment said to be waiting for him at Winchester. But there was no evidence of disloyalty beyond irresponsible rumor and no formal charges were ever filed against him.*

Born at Martinsburg, Virginia, now West Virginia, July 6, 1806, Faulkner, a staunch Democrat, had practiced law, served in both branches of the Virginia general assembly, sat as a delegate in the Constitutional Convention of 1850-51, and represented his district in Congress from 1851 to 1859. He won prominence as a member of the General Assembly in 1832-33, when he supported a policy of gradual emancipation of slaves in Virginia and delivered speeches condemning South Carolina's adoption of an ordinance of nullification. In 1859 President James Buchanan appointed him minister to France where he served until 1861.

Arrested on the day he submitted his final report to the State Department, Faulkner suffered indignities and was kept in close confinement until December, 1861, when he was sent across the Confederate lines in exchange for Congressman Alfred Ely, of New York, who had been captured by the Confederates at the battle of Bull Run. Banished to the Confederacy, he refused the offer of a Confederate commission but served unofficially on General Stonewall Jackson's staff, 1862-63. Following the war Faulkner resumed practice of law at Martinsburg, became a member of the West Virginia Constitutional Convention of 1872, and served in Congress from the Second West Virginia District from 1875 to 1877. He died November 1, 1884.

When promised his release in September 1861 on condition that he take an oath of allegiance to the United States, Faulkner, after declaring that the oath was without sanction or authority, replied to Secretary Seward in words that will live in the history of civil liberty. The passages below have been taken from Faulkner's letter to Seward.

FT. LaFAYETTE, *September 25, 1861.*

. . . To take the oath which you prescribe would under existing circumstances furnish no evidence of my loyalty. It might be proof of my subserviency and cowardice. It could afford no guarantee of heart-felt devotion to the Union. To say to a prisoner that the bars of his dungeon shall be forever closed upon him unless he swears to be true to the Government may make a hyprocrite and a knave. It cannot make a good citizen or a true patriot. Loyalty springs from the heart; it cannot be manufactured by thumbscrews, political tests or prisons.

. . . From the day of my arrest up to the present moment my tongue has been silenced and hands paralyzed in my defense. In the meantime calumny has been unceasing in its assaults upon me. In not one leading paper deserving patronage and support from the Government have I been represented otherwise than as a traitor. There is scarcely an act of official perfidy of which a minister could have been guilty that has not been falsely ascribed to me. Before I had even received a copy of your letter of the 11th of September writers having access to the bureaus of the Government were familiar with its contents and announced the test that was to be applied to me, and they accompanied it with the statement that although I was clearly and unquestionably guilty of treason and could upon the clearest evidence be convicted of it before a jury yet as an act of clemency I would be allowed to escape if I complied with this requirement of the Secretary of State. I cannot accept your clemency on such terms. I cannot rest under imputations which a submission to your requirement would only fortify and confirm. If I am guilty of any official infidelity or of treason let me be tried and punished. If I am innocent of all such charges I should be unconditionally released. It is not becoming a great Government thus to palter with the interests of human liberty. Neither would it be just to my own character to accept of any such equivocal order of release.

. . . During the period which led to the existing difficulties I was not only absent in Europe but I was there the accredited representative of the Government of the United States, and if a love and veneration for that system of government founded by the fathers of the Republic had been without their proper influence on my conduct my official position at least utterly forbade my having any participation directly or indirectly in any movement for the overthrow of the Federal Union. I have ever made it not less a matter of pride than of duty to punctiliously and scrupulously [be] faithful to every trust public or private with which I have been honored. Of this you have satisfactory proof in my correspondence and relations with your Department, and I have no doubt in the correspondence and testimony of my successor in office. As I have already informed you I returned to the United States under all the moral responsibilities of that trust although the legal tenure of my appointment had previously ceased. I came back to perform my duties as a citizen and a patriot. I came here as a free man to survey the field of action and to determine by the light of my own judgment the part which duty and patriotism required me to pursue in the present crisis. No one has ever heard from me in conversation or has ever learned from me by correspondence what that decision would be. Indeed ignorant of much that has transpired in the country during my absence I felt it due to my own character and position to reserve the decision of my course until after my return and until I had an opportunity of learning much that it was not possible for me to acquire satisfactorily abroad. I arrived here then without a single committal as to the future that

could swerve my judgment as to my course. I cherished the
hope, probably an idle and presumptuous one, that the position
of total noncomplicity with all the events that then embarrassed
the country might furnish, especially if I concluded to reside in
Virginia, an opportunity of some signal service to the country.
My purpose therefore was to retire upon my estate and there
await the progress of events to determine what extent this position which absence and accident gave me might be made useful
to the country. It is manifest that such a position which I allude
to required free and unconstrained action. It is a freeman alone
who can confer with freemen about their rights and interests.
They would not take counsel from a slave. But you prefer a
course that would rob me of all the merit of my position if my
conclusions led me to support the cause of the Union. It deprives me of all deliberation and free will. It proposes to rivet
patriotism upon me by fetters and to grind loyalty into me by
the horrors of the prison. It seeks to anticipate the regular conclusions of my own reason and judgment and to make me a patriot by the potent process of the dungeon. I cannot accept your
prescription. Arbitrary power and brute force have given you
control over my body but you can exercise none over the mind.
. . . —*War of the Rebellion: A Compilation of the Official Records of the Union and Confederate Armies*, ii, II, 472-76.

108. Pinkertons Spy on General Wise, 1861

*The most famous Civil War detective was the Scottish-born
Allan Pinkerton (1819-1884). After joining the Chicago police
force in 1850, he established a private detective agency which
soon solved several train robberies; in 1861 the Pinkerton agency
won national acclaim when it discovered a plot to assassinate
President-elect Abraham Lincoln. In May, 1861, Pinkerton accepted General George B. McClellan's invitation to organize a
secret service for the Department of the Ohio. As chief of Mc-*

Clellan's secret service under the name of "Major E. J. Allen,"
Pinkerton played his role so well that few knew his true identity
long after the war.

As McClellan prepared in the early summer of 1861 to move
against the Confederates in the Kanawha Valley, Pinkerton dis-
patched two of his operatives behind the Confederate lines to
probe public opinion and gather military information. His agents
landed at Guyandotte and made their way to Charleston in the
guise of sight-seeing Englishmen. The experiences of these men
provide an interesting chapter in Civil War espionage and bring
to the center of the stage two Confederate officers closely iden-
tified with West Virginia history—General Henry A. Wise, for-
mer governor of Virginia, and Captain George S. Patton, later
colonel of the Twenty-Second Virginia Infantry.

. . . In order to afford variety to the professions of my operatives, and because of his fitness for the character, I decided that
Price [Pryce] Lewis should represent himself as an Englishman
traveling for pleasure, believing that he would thus escape a
close scrutiny or a rigid examination, should he, by any accident, fall into the hands of the rebels. . . .

I concluded to send with him a member of my force who
would act in the capacity of coachman, groom and body servant,
as occasion should demand. The man whom I selected for this
role was a jolly, good-natured, and fearless Yankee named Samuel Bridgeman, . . .

At midnight, on the second evening, the boat landed at Guyandotte, and Samuel, with a great deal of importance, attended
to the transfer of his master and the equipage from the boat to
the wharf. Here they found a number of men in uniform, who
were ascertained to be representatives of the "Home Guard," . . .
Stopping at the hotel over night, they continued their journey
on the following morning. They drove leisurely along, and at
about ten o'clock they stopped at a farm-house to rest their
horses. They remained here until nearly three o'clock in the
afternoon, conversing with the old farmer, who seemed to be
much pained at the condition of affairs, but who had two sons
who had joined the rebel army. They renewed their journey in
the afternoon, and in about two hours reached the little village
of Colemouth, where there was a rebel encampment. On pass-

ing this they were halted by the guard, who inquired their business and destination. . . . The guard informed them that he could not let them pass, and asked Lewis to go with him to the Captain's headquarters, which was located in a large stone house, a few hundred yards distant. . . .

He greeted my operative pleasantly, and informed him that he regretted the necessity of detaining him, but orders had to be obeyed. Lewis related in substance what he had already stated to the guard, which statement the Captain unhesitatingly received, and after a pleasant conversation, he invited the detective to accept the hospitality of the camp. . . .

Supper was ordered, and in a short time the Captain and his guest were discussing a repast which was far more appetizing than soldiers' fare usually is. During the meal Sam stood behind the chair of Lewis, and awaited upon him in the most approved fashion, replying invariably with a deferential,

"Yes, my lord." . . .

Lewis, being an Englishman by birth, was very well posted about English affairs, and he entertained his host with several very well invented anecdotes of the Crimea, in which he was supposed to have taken an active part, and his intimacy with Lord Raglan, the commander of the British army, gained for him the unbounded admiration and respect of the doughty Captain.

From this officer Lewis learned that there were a number of troops in Charleston, but a few miles distant, and that General Wise, who was then in command, had arrived there that day.

After a refreshing sleep and a bounteous breakfast, Lewis informed the Captain that he would continue his journey toward Charleston, and endeavor to obtain an interview with General Wise. The Captain cordially recommended him to do so, and furnished him with passports which would carry him without question or delay upon the road. . . .

By this means he was enabled to acquire a wonderful amount of information, both of value and importance to the cause of the North, all of which was duly reported to me at headquarters, and by me communicated directly to General McClellan. . . .

Leaving no opportunity that offered, the detective took advantage of every available suggestion, and the result was he be-

came fully posted upon everything that was of importance, and was enabled to render such an account of his labors as was satisfactory in the extreme. Sam Bridgeman, too, had not been idle, but mingling freely with the soldiers, he had succeeded in learning much of the conditions of the country that was immense advantage in the after events of the campaign in Western Virginia.
—Allan Pinkerton, *The Spy of the Rebellion*, pp. 210-30.

109. The Union Advance and General George B. McClellan's Proclamations

Especially strategic at the beginning of the Civil War was Trans-Allegheny Virginia, which looked out upon 300 miles of the Ohio River. With the Virginia panhandle counties reaching up that stream to the latitude of Pittsburgh and within seventy miles of Lake Erie, this northernmost salient of the projected Confederacy was both a threat to the loyal states of Ohio and Pennsylvania and a peril to the corridor which united East and West. Rightly alarmed by Confederate occupation of the Kanawha Valley and of the key railroad junction at Grafton, Union men of northwestern Virginia sent urgent appeals to Major General George B. McClellan, who commanded the Department of the Ohio, requesting military protection for the loyal Union element and the region's railroads—the Baltimore and Ohio and the Northwestern Virginia. Apprehensive that the presence of Union troops would arouse state pride and produce adverse effects, McClellan hesitated until the last week of May 1861, when he sent troops across the Ohio to Parkersburg, Benwood and Wheeling with orders to occupy the railroad and proceed to Grafton.

As McClellan dispatched orders on May 26, 1861, to his commanders to cross into Virginia he issued two proclamations—one addressed to the western Virginians, the other to the troops under his command.

VIRGINIANS: The General Government has long enough endured the machinations of a few factious rebels in your midst.

Armed traitors have in vain endeavored to deter you from expressing your loyalty at the polls. Having failed in this infamous attempt to deprive you of the exercise of your dearest rights, they now seek to inaugurate a reign of terror, and thus force you to yield to their schemes, and submit to the yoke of the traitorous conspiracy dignified by the name of Southern Confederacy.

They are destroying the property of citizens of your State and ruining your magnificent railways. The General Government has heretofore carefully abstained from sending troops across the Ohio, or even from posting them along its banks, although frequently urged by many of your prominent citizens to do so. I determined to await the result of the late election, desirous that no one might be able to say that the slightest effort had been made from this side to influence the free expression of your opinion, although the many agencies brought to bear upon you by the rebels were well known.

You have now shown, under the most adverse circumstances, that the great mass of the people of Western Virginia are true and loyal to that beneficent Government under which we and our fathers have lived so long. As soon as the result of the election was known the traitors commenced their work of destruction. The General Government cannot close its ears to the demand you have made for assistance. I have ordered troops to cross the river. They come as your friends and brothers—as enemies only to the armed rebels who are preying upon you. Your homes, your families, and your property are safe under our protection. All your rights shall be religiously respected.

Notwithstanding all that has been said by the traitors to induce you to believe that our advent among you will be signalized by interference with your slaves, understand one thing clearly—not only will we abstain from all such interference, but we will, on the contrary, with an iron hand, crush any attempt at insurrection on their part. Now that we are in your midst, I call upon you to fly to arms and support the General Government.

Sever the connection that binds you to traitors. Proclaim to the world that the faith and loyalty so long boasted by the Old Dominion are still preserved in Western Virginia, and that you remain true to the Stars and Stripes.

THE THIRTY-FIFTH STATE   397

SOLDIERS: You are ordered to cross the frontier and enter upon the soil of Virginia. Your mission is to restore peace and confidence, to protect the majesty of the law, and to rescue our brethren from the grasp of armed traitors. You are to act in concert with the Virginia troops, and to support their advance. I place under the safeguard of your honor the persons and property of the Virginians. I know that you will respect their feelings and all their rights. Preserve the strictest discipline; remember that each one of you holds in his keeping the honor of Ohio and of the Union.

If you are called upon to overcome armed opposition, I know that your courage is equal to the task; but remember that your only foes are the armed traitors, and show mercy even to them when they are in your power, for many of them are misguided. When under your protection the loyal men of Western Virginia have been enabled to organize and arm, they can protect themselves, and you can then return to your homes with the proud satisfaction of having preserved a gallant people from destruction.—*Official Records*, i, II, 48-49.

110. General Robert E. Lee's Report on the Battle of Philippi

The advance of Union troops across the Ohio in late May and the defeat of the Confederates under Colonel George A. Porterfield at Philippi on June 3, 1861, was the first link in a chain of events which led to the expulsion of organized Confederate forces from northwestern Virginia. Following the occupation of the rail junction at Grafton by the Confederates in mid-May, 1861, Union General George B. McClellan who was stationed at Camp Dennison near Cincinnati moved brigades to Marietta and Bellaire, Ohio. Without the means to challenge a crossing of the Ohio, Colonel Porterfield, who commanded at Grafton, began on May 25 the destruction of bridges and tunnels of the Baltimore and Ohio and the Northwestern Virginia railroads. With the issue joined, McClellan dispatched troops across the Ohio to Wheeling, Benwood, and Parkersburg to co-operate with the 1st West Virginia Infantry, commanded by Colonel Benjamin F. Kelley, which had been ordered to proceed at once by rail from Wheeling toward Grafton. As McClellan's forces closed upon him, Porterfield withdrew on May 28 to Philippi, eighteen miles south of Grafton, where on the morning of June 3, 1861, after a sharp but almost bloodless engagement, Porterfield was routed and driven back to Beverly. There a military court was convened at his request to examine the circumstances of the retreat, commonly called the "Philippi Races." General Robert E. Lee approved the report of the court of inquiry in General Orders, No. 30, dated at Richmond, July 4, 1861.

1.—The court of inquiry, which convened at Beverly on the 20th ultimo, at the request of Col. G. A. Porterfield, of the Virginia Volunteers, to examine into the circumstances of the retreat of the Virginia forces from Philippi on the 3rd of June, under his command, has reported the following facts in the case:

. . . On the morning of the day just indicated, at between daybreak and sunrise, this command was attacked and taken by surprise; no alarm or intimation of the enemy's approach having been given by the guard or infantry pickets, until the enemy was within some four hundred yards of the place, and had commenced the fire from his artillery. By the examination it is shown that a main and picket guard, as strong as was consistent with the effective infantry force present, was regularly detailed and posted at distances sufficiently far out to accomplish the object in view, provided they knew and did their duty, which latter is strongly to be suspected, from the fact that, although in advance, they failed to give any intimation of the enemy's approach, a conclusion which is strengthened by the official report of the mounted officers, out with the scouting parties on the night of June 2, that they had neither seen an infantry picket nor been challenged by its sentinels, going from or returning to the town that night. It appears that, immediately upon the arrival of the command at Philippi, the officer in command, Colonel Porterfield, took measures to place his force, which was raw and new in service, under a course of instruction, and to select those, in his opinion, best fitted to instruct the sentinels and guards in their duties. The testimony shows that, while there was certain degree of confusion in some quarters, a portion of the command moved from the town in good order, and that the whole force, nearly, after passing some distance from the town, was reformed, and proceeded in order.

It is shown in the evidence that an expectation of attack or movement upon Philippi, shortly to be made, was entertained generally among the officers and others of the command, and that intelligence (how well founded is now known) was brought from time to time of the strength and supposed intent of the enemy.

The testimony sets forth that this had so far produced its effect as to induce the officer in command to call a meeting of his officers; that the result of their consultations and deliberations was an almost, if not unanimous decision in favor of immediate retreat; that when Colonel Porterfield returned to the room (from which he had been absent a short time) their opinion was conveyed to him to which he seemed loth to accede; yet, determined to make a further examination of the ammunition on hand, and to prepare the baggage and train for removal at a moment's notice.

No orders to march at any particular time were given, so far as can be gathered from the testimony, although it appears that an understanding or impression was had or entertained by some that the movement would not take place until morning, while some believed it contingent upon the weather. . . .

The court having been directed to express its opinion, as well as report the facts, presents the following:

1st. That the commanding officer, having received information, deemed by him sufficient to prepare for an early retreat, erred in permitting himself to be influenced by the weather, so far as to delay the execution of his plan.

2d. That the commanding officer did order dispositions to be made to prevent surprise; but a misunderstanding as to the time at which the scouts were to be called in, and a total want of proper vigilance on the part of the infantry pickets, caused a surprise, which distinct and definite instructions, properly executed, would have been avoided.

3d. That the commanding officer erred in not advancing and strengthening his picket beyond the usual limits under the circumstances.

4th. That the commanding officer exhibited upon the occasion decided coolness, self-possession, and personal courage, and exerted himself, as far as possible, to effect a retreat in good order.

II.—The commanding general having attentively considered the proceedings of the court of inquiry in the foregoing case, concurs in the opinion expressed by the court and in the statement of facts deduced from the testimony. These facts show that the position at Philippi was seriously threatened by a superior force of the enemy, distant only four hours' march; that Colonel Porterfield was aware of the danger of his position, and prudently prepared to evacuate it. His desire to prevent the occupation of the town by the enemy was worthy of all praise, and had he promptly sent back his baggage and ineffective men, arranged his plan of defense, and taken proper measures to secure information of the advance of the enemy, he might safely have retained his position, and either given battle or retired, as circumstances might dictate. It does not appear from the record of the court that any plan of defense was formed; but it does appear that the troops retired without his orders, and that the instructions to his advance guard were either misconceived or not executed. To these circumstances must be attributed the disaster that followed, and they call for heavy censure upon all concerned. The commanding general remarks with pleasure upon the coolness, self-possession, courage, and energy displayed by Colonel Porterfield at the moment of attack; but he cannot exonerate him from blame in not taking proper precautionary measures beforehand. Yet, in consideration of all the circumstances of the case, he does not think it necessary to do more than to express the opinion of the court, in the hope that the sad effects produced by the want of forethought and vigilance, as exhibited in this case, will be a lesson to be remembered by the army throughout the war.—*Official Records*, i, II, pp. 72-74.

111. General McClellan Faces a New Confederate Challenge

After the defeat of the Confederates at Philippi on June 3, 1861, General Robert E. Lee reformed and strengthened his forces at Beverly under a new commander, Brigadier General Robert S. Garnett. Garnett soon established strong positions on Rich Mountain and Laurel Hill astride turnpikes leading to the Baltimore and Ohio Railroad. From these positions he planned to move against Clarksburg, Grafton, and the Cheat River railroad bridge at Rowlesburg. With the railroad and the newly reorganized Virginia state government thus menaced, McClellan—still at headquarters near Cincinnati—now took the field in person with heavy reinforcements. At Grafton on June 23, 1861, he issued a proclamation designed to reassure civilians.

To the Inhabitants of Western Virginia:

The army of this department, headed by Virginia troops, is rapidly occupying all Western Virginia. This is done in co-operation with, and in support of, such civil authorities of the State as are faithful to the Constitution and laws of the United States. The proclamation issued by me under date of May 26, 1861, will be strictly maintained. Your houses, families, property, and all your rights will be religiously respected; we are enemies to none but armed rebels and those voluntarily giving them aid. All officers of this army will be held responsible for the most prompt and vigorous action in repressing disorder and punishing aggression by those under their command.

To my great regret I find that enemies of the United States continue to carry on a system of hostililties prohibited by the laws of war among belligerent nations, and of course far more wicked and intolerable when directed against loyal citizens engaged in the defense of the common Government of all. Individuals and marauding parties are pursuing a guerrilla warfare, firing upon sentinels and pickets, burning bridges, insulting, injuring, and even killing citizens because of their Union sentiments, and committing many kindred acts.

I do now, therefore, make proclamation, and warn all persons that individuals or parties engaged in this species of warfare—irregular in every view which can be taken of it—thus attacking sentries, pickets, or other soldiers, destroying public or private property, or committing injuries against any of the inhabitants because of Union sentiments or conduct, will be dealt with in their persons and property according to the severest rules of military law.

All persons giving information or aid to the public enemies will be arrested and kept in close custody, and all persons found bearing arms, unless of known loyalty, will be arrested and held for examination.—*Official Records*, i, II, 196.

112. Governor Francis H. Pierpont Requests Federal Military Assistance

The restored government of Virginia at Wheeling owed its existence in the main to the prompt movement of Union forces across the Ohio in May and the defeat of the Confederate Virginians at Philippi, June 3, 1861. That its future lay with the fortunes of Union arms west of the Alleghenies was equally evident. Not only did Confederate troops still occupy the Kanawha Valley with outposts on the Ohio at Guyandotte, Point Pleasant, and Ravenswood; but they had reorganized at Beverly with reinforcements under a new commander who had taken strong positions on Laurel Hill and Rich Mountain.

On June 21, 1861, Governor Francis H. Pierpont addressed a letter to President Abraham Lincoln describing conditions and urging Federal military assistance.

His Excellency the PRESIDENT OF THE UNITED STATES:

SIR: Reliable information has been received at this department, from various parts of this State, that large numbers of evil-minded persons have banded together in military organizations with intent to overthrow the government of the State, and for that purpose have called to their aid like-minded persons from other States, who, in pursuance of such call, have invaded this commonwealth. They are now making war on the loyal people of the State. They are pressing citizens against their consent into their military organizations, and seizing and appropriating their property to aid in the rebellion.

I have not at my command sufficient military force to suppress this rebellion and violence. The legislature cannot be convened in time to act in the premises. It therefore becomes my duty, as governor of this commonwealth, to call on the Government of the United States for aid to suppress such rebellion and violence. I therefore earnestly request that you will furnish a military force to aid in suppressing the rebellion and to protect the good people of this commonwealth from domestic violence. . . . FRANCIS H. PIERPONT, Governor.—*Official Records*, i, II, 713.

113. General George B. McClellan: "Napoleon of the West"

With Union defenses strengthened along the railroad in western Virginia from Parkersburg to Rowlesburg, the curtain lifted in the last week of June upon McClellan riding out of Clarksburg to play his final role of "Napoleon of the West." As his column took the road toward Rich Mountain, stringing up a telegraph line as it advanced, General Thomas A. Morris led a diversionary force south from Philippi to hold the Confederates under General Robert S. Garnett on Laurel Hill. McClellan's leading brigade, commanded by General William S. Rosecrans, occupied Buckhannon on the Staunton and Parkersburg Turnpike on June 30, and two days later McClellan joined with the main body. On July 11, his forces under Rosecrans turned the Confederate left on Rich Mountain after a sharp engagement and two days later compelled the surrender of the demoralized enemy force. Upon learning of this disaster, Garnett fell back from Laurel Hill toward the road junction at Beverly but, hearing that McClellan had already occupied the town, retraced his steps with the hope of making his escape over the

Leadsville and St. George road, which led northeastward to the Northwestern Turnpike at Red House, Maryland. Closely pursued, Garnett was overtaken and killed on July 13 in a rearguard action at Corrick's Ford, now in the town of Parsons, West Virginia. The remnant of his army, some 3,000 strong, however, extricated itself and retreated to safety behind the Confederate lines in the upper South Branch Valley.

McClellan's successful western Virginia campaign definitely fixed the Confederate line along the Alleghenies, rather than the Ohio River or, indeed, in the state of Ohio. At Rich Mountain he had fought the first important battle of the Civil War after Fort Sumter; for this engagement, small though it was, settled summarily the political destiny of northwestern Virginia, making possible the use of that area as the pilot state in President Lincoln's reconstruction policy, and subsequently the formation of West Virginia. This battle, too, was the last stroke in a campaign that removed an enemy salient through which ran the strategic Baltimore and Ohio Railroad.

Justly proud of his successes and of his victorious army, McClellan closed his western Virginia campaign with a Napoleonic flourish on July 16, 1861, at Beverly, where he issued a congratulatory address to his troops. This address had much to do in establishing McClellan's reputation and in his elevation to command at Washington.

Soldiers of the Army of the West!
I am more than satisfied with you.

You have annihilated two armies, commanded by educated and experienced soldiers, intrenched in mountain fastnesses fortified at their leisure. You have taken five guns, twelve colors, fifteen hundred stand of arms, one thousand prisoners, including more than forty officers—one of the two commanders of the rebels is a prisoner, the other lost his life on the field of battle. You have killed more than two hundred and fifty of the enemy, who has lost all his baggage and camp equipage. All this has been accomplished with the loss of twenty brave men killed and sixty wounded on your part.

You have proved that Union men, fighting for the preservation of our Government, are more than a match for our misguided and erring brethren; more than this, you have shown mercy to the vanquished. You have made long and arduous marches, often with insufficient food, frequently exposed to the inclemency of the weather. I have not hesitated to demand this of you, feeling that I could rely on your endurance, patriotism, and courage.

In the future I may have still greater demands to make upon you, still greater sacrifices for you to offer. It shall be my care to provide for you to the extent of my ability; but I know now that by your valor and endurance you will accomplish all that is asked.

Soldiers! I have confidence in you, and I trust you have learned to confide in me. Remember that discipline and subordination are qualities of equal value with courage.

I am proud to say that you have gained the highest reward that American troops can receive—the thanks of Congress and the applause of your fellow-citizens.—*Official Records*, i, II, 236.

114. War Upon the Rails

Since the Baltimore and Ohio Railroad provided the shortest route between the Potomac and the Ohio, its worth to the Union cause in the Civil War was obvious. Consequently the evacuation of Harpers Ferry by the Confederates in June, 1861, signaled the adoption by the Confederate government of a new policy toward the railroad. It was decided to appropriate the best of the rails, rolling stock, and machinery for use on Southern railways, then destroy the road in its entirety. In May Colonel Thomas J. Jackson, soon to earn the sobriquet of "Stonewall," had cleverly bagged 56 locomotives and hundreds of cars; and it now fell his lot to apply the "scorched earth" policy. The Confederate commander began the work of destruction on June 20, 1861. Of the impounded rolling stock which had crowded the tracks in the vicinity of Martinsburg since May 23, the Confederates destroyed 42 engines and approximately 300 cars. David Hunter Strother ("Porte Crayon") described the scene he witnessed at Martinsburg.

ON THE 20TH OF JUNE we started for Martinsburg. . . . As we approached Martinsburg late in the afternoon we heard a strange singing and screaming in the air which resembled the notes of a gigantic Aeolian. These sounds grew more distinct and definite as we advanced, and still nearer the town we perceived immense columns of black smoke rolling up between us and the setting sun, and tinging the whole landscape with a coppery hue. As these clouds rose from the direction of the railroad shops it was easy to imagine their origin; but the accompanying sounds were unaccountable, until, turning into one of the lower streets of the town, a scene was suddenly presented to us which more resembled a dream of Dante's Inferno than an exhibition of real life.

Jackson's brigade were performing a grand *"auto da fe"* upon the rolling-stock of the Baltimore and Ohio Railroad. The foreground of the picture was occupied by a ruin of classic form and beauty—that of the pillared viaduct which had been destroyed some weeks before. On the open space in front of the work-shops stood, ranged upon the tracks, between forty and fifty locomotives roasting amidst the flames of a thousand cords of wood, distributed, refreshed, and stirred up continually by a brigade of wild Confederates. The rocks, hills, and houses which surrounded the place of execution was crowded by many hundred spectators, the old men, wives, and children of those who had depended on the road for their subsistence.

Twilight was approaching, and as the lurid light of the fires prevailed the aspect of the scene grew still more unearthly. The rebel soldiers, with their bronzed faces, raggedly picturesque costumes, and fiendish activity, were not unworthy representatives of the familiars of Beelzebub. They worked in silence too, with the sullen and desperate look of men who were executing the work of Fate rather than their own will. Motionless and mute the groups of citizens looked on, terror-stricken, yet every pallid face lowering with dumb execration. The locomotives, as the flames licked their iron bodies, and the heated air rushed through the steamwhistles, . . . impressed the spectator with the idea that they were living victims, who moaned and shrieked with an agony surpassing human comprehension. . . .

June 21.—The dawn of morning dispelled these distempered fancies, but brought with it no reviving cheerfulness. Between dreams and realities there was not so much difference after all. On the railroad we could see the wilted and discolored bodies of the locomotives lying amidst the smoke and ashes of their funeral pyres. Their wailings had ceased, and the general feeling of relief thereat was expressed by one of the negroes, who thanked God they were "out of their misery."—"Personal Recollections of the War," *Harper's Magazine*, XXXIII, (July, 1866), 145-47.

115. Secessionist Sentiment in the Kanawha Valley, 1861

In response to urgent pleas from residents and threats to his communications in northwestern Virginia, victorious General McClellan invaded the Kanawha Valley in July, 1861. General Jacob D. Cox led the invading force into Virginia at Guyandotte, Point Pleasant, and Ravenswood, drove the Confederate defenders under General Henry A. Wise through Charleston to Gauley Bridge, and occupied Gauley Mountain. In contrast with the people of the Kanawha Valley, who were about evenly divided in their loyalties, a majority of the inhabitants along the New and the Greenbrier rivers supported the Confederacy. Almost to a man their officeholders were secessionists or neutralists. In June, 1861, the Fayette County Court, meeting hurriedly at Fayetteville, adopted the resolutions below.

WHEREAS our State has been invaded by a hostile army of Northern Fanatics, and we feel bound to resist said invasion to the last extremity, Resolved Therefore, First that we feel it to be our duty in accordance with an act of the Legislature passed January 19, 1861, to Levy on the people of the County from time to time as may be necessary to enable us to resist said invasion successfully, such amounts of money as we shall think practicable and expedient.

Resolved 2nd That we will then after money and property are exhausted, feel it to be our duty to Levy for said purpose on the credit of the County and when that also is gone we will eat roots and drink water and still fight for our liberty unto death. And Resolved 3rd That should any of the members of this Court feel friendly to the North, that we invite them or him peacefully and civilly to resign his or their commission.—Minute Book, 4, Fayette County Court, June 13, 1861, Fayetteville, Va.

116. The Battle of Carnifex Ferry, September 10, 1861

General William S. Rosecrans, who had served McClellan so well at the battle of Rich Mountain, succeeded him in the northwestern Virginia command. Though beaten by McClellan, Lee's Confederates still defended a line from the upper Tygart River basin to the lower valley of the New River. As part of his defense Rosecrans stationed the Seventh Ohio Infantry under Colonel Erastus B. Tyler at Keslers Cross Lanes near Summersville. There on the morning of August 26, 1861, while Confederate General Henry A. Wise held General Jacob D. Cox's Federals on Gauley Mountain, two thousand Confederates under General John B. Floyd scattered the Seventh Ohio at breakfast, and occupied the Gauley Bridge and Weston Turnpike at Summersville. Although satirized by General Wise as the "battle of the forks and spoons," the action at Keslers Cross Lanes severed the Union line of communications and supply, threatened Cox's army at Gauley Bridge, and provided Floyd with a base for operations against the Northwestern Virginia Railroad. Moreover, Floyd could now prevent the referendum on the new-state ordinance scheduled for October 24, 1861.

Rosecrans moved quickly to save his army at Gauley Bridge. He drove the Confederates out of Summersville on the morning of September 10, and in mid-afternoon attacked their camp at Carnifex Ferry with a force of six thousand. With an open field of fire in his front and his flanks protected by canyons and wilderness, Floyd beat back every assault without the loss of a man killed. Rosecrans finally withdrew to await dawn and renewal of the attack. During the night, however, Floyd abandoned his position and retreated across the Gauley. Carnifex

*Ferry marked still another failure of Confederate Virginia to re-
assert authority over the northwestern counties. The story of the
battle is here told in the reports of the opposing commanders.*

[GENERAL WILLIAM S. ROSECRANS:]

Having driven the enemy's pickets before us from Big Birch,
we bivouacked 8 miles above Summersville. The column began
to move at 4.15 on the morning of the 10th, and reached Summersville at 8 o'clock, having been delayed by a burned bridge.
Found the town evacuated by a regiment of infantry and a company of cavalry, which had retreated towards the intrenched
camp. Two cavalry prisoners, stragglers from their company,
were captured, from whom we found that Floyd was strongly
intrenched and confident of holding his position against great
odds in front of Carnifix Ferry.

From this point the column moved cautiously but rapidly forward over 4 miles of very bad roads, forming almost a defile,
and then over more open country, until the head of it reached
a point where the first road leading to the ferry diverges from
the lower road to Gauley Bridge, on which we were marching.
Reached there about 2 o'clock, and halted for half an hour for
the column and train to close up, and then began to move down
towards the rebels' position, said to be about 2½ miles distant.
Picket-firing commenced at the head of the column within three-
quarters of a mile. The First Brigade, under General Benham,
the Tenth Ohio ahead, led the column, and soon reached a
camp which had been abandoned, leaving some camp equipage
and private baggage, which gave rise to the impression in the
mind of the brigade commander that the enemy were in full retreat. Satisfied however, that we should find it was not so, I
directed Brigader-General Benham to move forward with his
brigade slowly and cautiously into the woods, for the purpose
of reconnoitering. He was directed to be very careful to feel
the enemy closely, but not to engage him unless he saw an evident opening. . . . Twenty-five minutes after the column left the
deserted camp terrific volleys of musketry and the roar of the
rebels' artillery told that we were upon them, and indicated the
right of their position, a point to which the Twelfth Ohio was
directed to proceed.

A message from General Benham reached me at the deserted camp, announced that an engagement had commenced, and that he wanted help. Having the Tenth and Thirteenth with him, McMullin's howitzer battery and two rifled cannon were sent forward to the head of the column, and he was informed that the Twelfth had been ordered to his left, on the right of the rebels' works. Orders were dispatched to hasten the coming up of the Second and Third Brigades, under Colonels McCook and Scammon, and I proceeded to the head of the column to ascertain the position of the First Brigade and reconnoiter and rebels' works more closely. Arrived there, I found the Tenth Ohio and the batteries in the position indicated on the accompanying plan, the Thirteenth and a portion of the Twelfth in the valley in the rear of the position marked twenty-eighth on this plan. I proceeded into the valley to examine the right of the rebels' position, and afterwards to the corn field, in the rear of which was the Tenth, to examine that portion of the rebels' works visible from that point. I then awaited report of a reconnoitering party which had gone through the woods still farther to the enemy's left, entirely invisible from our position. Heavy volleys of musketry and the discharge of artillery soon told that this party had made its appearance in front of an unknown part of the rebels' position. Meanwhile our skirmishers kept up a well-directed fire along the whole of the enemy's left, while Schneider's rifled battery, taking a more advantageous position, and McMullins' howitzer battery continued to play on the rebels' guns at the battery shown on the plan.

Meanwhile Col. W. S. Smith, of the Thirteenth, and Captain Margedant, acting engineer, reported the practicability of reaching the rebels' extreme right, if not turning it. . . . Lieutenant-Colonel Korff, with the Tenth and a portion of the Twelfth which had become detached from the remainder and passed over to our right, was directed to advance to the right of the corn field to attack the rebel center and left.

The storming column of eight companies of the Ninth and sixth companies of the Forty-seventh was formed in the position shown on the plan. By this time it became dusk, the men were exhausted, the brush thick and tangled, and the strength and condition of the rebels, as well as the extent of their works, very imperfectly known. . . .

Under these circumstances I deemed it prudent to withdraw our forces from the woods to the open fields in rear of the intrenched camp. . . . I arranged the troops in order of battle on ground still farther to the rear, looked after the train which remained at the point of our halt, and at 2 o'clock retired to an oat loft to sleep, leaving Colonel Ewing in command of the advanced guard posted in the woods. . . . Early the next morning one of our sentries brought a runaway negro, who reported that the enemy had abandoned their camp during the night, crossed the Gauley, and destroyed their boats. I ordered Colonel Ewing with his troops to verify the truth of the statement, which he soon did, returning with a stand of colors. Having taken possession of the camp and a few sick prisoners, I proceeded to the extremity of the camp, and saw that the ferry was gone, foot-bridge destroyed, and the enemy's column out of sight, with the exception of a few wagons. . . .

Finding we had no means whatever of crossing the ferry, which is here 370 feet wide, pursuit was impossible, though much desired. The rebels, aware of this, left a body of skirmishers to occupy the cliffs along Meadow River down to the ferry to prevent small parties from crossing.—*Official Records*, i, V, 129-31.

[GENERAL JOHN B. FLOYD:]

Information had reached me for some number of days that a heavy force was advancing towards my position from the direction of Clarksburg, in the northwestern part of the State. As these rumors became a certainty I made an effort to strengthen myself, first by re-enforcement, and secondly by intrenchments sufficient to withstand the very large force of the enemy. My orders to General Wise I send you copies of, and also copies of his replies.

I failed in procuring re-enforcement, but succeeded somewhat better in the construction of a temporary breastwork. At 3 o'clock in the evening of the 10th of September the enemy, under command of General Rosecrans, as we learned through prisoners, of whose advance I was fully aware, at the head of ten regiments, made his appearance before intrenchments, when the battle instantly commenced. Our lines were necessarily very extended for the purpose of protecting our position, and when manned left not one man for reserve. The assault was made with spirit and determination with small-arms, grape, and round shot from howitzers and rifled cannon. There was scarcely an intermission in the conflict until night put an end to the firing. The enemy's force is estimated certainly between 8,000 and 9,000 men, whilst our force engaged was less than 2,000. Upon the close of the contest for the night I discovered that it was only a question of time when we should be compelled to yield to the superiority of numbers. I therefore determined at once to recross the Gauley River and take position upon the left bank, which I accomplished without the loss of a gun or any accident whatever. Our loss, strange to say, after a continued firing upon us by cannon and small-arms for nearly four hours, was only 20 men wounded. The loss of the enemy we had no means of accurately estimating, but we are satisfied, from report of prisoners and other sources of information, it was very heavy. We repulsed them in five distinct and successive assaults, and at nightfall had crippled them to such an extent that they were in no condition whatever to molest us in our passage across the river. —*Official Records,* i, V, 146-47.

117. Harpers Ferry in Wartime, 1862

When General Frederick W. Lander's Union forces reoccupied Romney and Berkeley Springs and General Nathaniel P. Banks advanced into the lower Shenandoah Valley in February, 1862, the Confederates withdrew from the Baltimore and Ohio Railroad, which they had held along the upper Potomac almost continuously since April, 1861. With military protection, the railroad company then repaired and rebuilt the sections which the Confederates had destroyed. Work on the Harpers Ferry bridge began on March 4; bridgemen moved east from Hancock to span Sleepy Creek, Cherry Run, and Back Creek; and tracklayers opened the road to through traffic from the Ohio River to Chesapeake Bay on March 30, 1862.

Nathaniel Hawthorne, who visited Harpers Ferry with Baltimore and Ohio officials, described conditions there in early March, 1862.

ANOTHER OF OUR EXCURSIONS was to Harper's Ferry,—the Directors of the Baltimore and Ohio Railroad having kindly invited us to accompany them on the first trip over the newly laid track, after its breaking up by the Rebels. . . . The scenery grew even more picturesque as we proceeded, the bluffs becoming very bold in their descent upon the river, which, at Harper's Ferry, presents as striking a vista among the hills as a painter could desire to see. But a beautiful landscape is a luxury, and luxuries are thrown away amid discomfort; and when we alighted into the tenacious mud and almost fathomless puddle, on the hither side of the Ferry, (the ultimate point to which the cars proceeded, since the railroad bridge had been destroyed by the Rebels,) I cannot remember that any very rapturous emotions were awakened by the scenery.

We paddled and floundered over the ruins of the track, and, scrambling down an embankment, crossed the Potomac by a Pontoon-bridge, a thousand feet in length, over the narrow line of which—level with the river, and rising and subsiding with it— General Banks had recently led his whole army, with its ponderous artillery and heavily laden wagons. Yet our own tread made it vibrate. The broken bridge of the railroad was a little below us, and at the base of one of its massive piers, in the rocky bed of the river, lay a locomotive, which the Rebels had precipitated there.

As we passed over, we looked towards the Virginia shore, and beheld the little town of Harper's Ferry, gathered about the base of a round hill and climbing up its steep acclivity; so that it somewhat resembled the Etruscan cities which I have seen among the Apennines, rushing, as it were, down an apparently breakneck height. About midway of the ascent stood a shabby brick church, towards which a difficult path went scrambling up the precipice, indicating, one would say, a very fervent aspiration on the part of the worshippers, unless there was some easier mode of access in another direction. Immediately on the shore of the Potomac, and extending back towards the town, lay the dismal ruins of the United States arsenal and armory, consisting of piles of broken bricks and a waste of shapeless demolition, amid which we saw gun-barrels in heaps of hundreds together. They were the relics of the conflagration, bent with the heat of the fire, and rusted with the wintry rain to which they had since been exposed. The brightest sunshine could not have made the scene cheerful, nor have taken away the gloom from the dilapidated town; for, besides the natural shabbiness, and decayed, unthrifty look of a Virginian village, it has an inexpressible forlornness resulting from the devastations of war and its occupation by both armies alternately. Yet there would be a less striking contrast between Southern and New-England villages, if the former were as much in the habit of using white paint as we are. It is prodigiously efficacious in putting a bright face upon a bad matter.

There was one small shop, which appeared to have nothing for sale. A single man and one or two boys were all the inhabitants in view, except the Yankee sentinels and soldiers, belonging to Massachusetts regiments, who were scattered about pretty numerously. A guardhouse stood on the slope of the hill; and in the level street at its base were the offices of the Provost-Marshal and other military authorities, to whom we forthwith reported ourselves. The Provost-Marshal kindly sent a corporal to guide us to the little building which John Brown seized upon as his fortress, and which, after it was stormed by the United States marines, became his temporary prison. It is an old engine-house, rusty and shabby, like every other work of man's hands in this God-forsaken town, and stands fronting upon the river, only a short distance from the bank, nearly at the point where the pontoon-bridge touches the Virginia shore. In its front wall, on each side of the door, are two or three ragged loop-holes which John Brown perforated for his defence, knocking out merely a brick or two, so as to give himself and his garrison a sight over their rifles. Through these orifices the sturdy old man dealt a good deal of deadly mischief among his assailants, until they broke down the door by thrusting against it with a ladder, and tumbled headlong in upon him. I shall not pretend to be an admirer of old John Brown, any farther than sympathy with Whittier's excellent ballad about him may go; nor did I expect ever to shrink so unutterably from any apophthegm of a sage, whose happy lips have uttered a hundred golden sentences, as from that saying, (perhaps falsely attributed to so honored a source,) that the death of this blood-stained fanatic has "made the Gallows as venerable as the Cross!" Nobody was ever more justly hanged.

He won his martydom fairly, and took it firmly. He himself, I am persuaded, (such was his natural integrity,) would have acknowledged that Virginia had a right to take the life which he had staked and lost; although it would have been better for her, in the hour that is fast coming, if she could generously have forgotten the criminality of his attempt in its enormous folly. On the other hand, any common-sensible man, looking at the matter unsentimentally, must have felt a certain intellectual satisfaction in seeing him hanged, if it were only in requital of his preposterous miscalculation of possibilities.

But, coolly as I seem to say these things, my Yankee heart stirred triumphantly when I saw the use to which John Brown's fortress and prison-house has now been put. What right have I to complain of any other man's foolish impulses, when I cannot possibly control my own? The engine-house is now a place of confinement for Rebel prisoners.—Nathaniel Hawthorne, "Chiefly About War Matters by a Peaceful Man," *The Atlantic Monthly,* X, (July, 1862), 52-54.

118. Twisting the Rails, 1862

Reopened from the Ohio River to Chesapeake Bay on March 30, 1862, the Baltimore and Ohio Railroad became at once fair prize for the Confederates. There was momentary interruption to through traffic during the last weeks of General Stonewall Jackson's Valley campaign in May-June, 1862, but throughout the summer the Confederates were held at safe distance. During Lee's invasion of Maryland in September, 1862, however, the Confederate army destroyed bridges and rolling stock between Point of Rocks and Monocacy Junction in Maryland, while forces under Jackson cut the road both east and west of Martinsburg as they marched to seize Harpers Ferry. After the battle of Antietam the Confederate army occupied the railroad in force until late October and destroyed most of the road from Harpers Ferry to Back Creek, a distance of thirty-five miles. In his annual report President John W. Garrett informed the stockholders of the nature and extent of company losses.

GREAT DESTRUCTION OF COMPANY'S PROPERTY at Martinsburg. The polygonal engine house, the half round engine house, the large and costly machine shops, warehouse, ticket and telegraph offices, the Company's hotel and dining and wash house, master mechanic's house, coal bins, and houses, blacksmith shop and tool houses, pumping engine for water station and connecting pipes were all destroyed. The destruction of tracks also commenced and continued until the main track from near the 87th to the 108½ mile, and the second track from Martinsburg to 108½ mile, and all the sidings and switches at Duffield's, Kearneysville, Vanclievesville, Martinsburg and other points destroyed, making a total of 37½ miles of track, the crossties from which were burned to heat and bend the iron.—*Thirty Seventh Annual Report of the President and Directors to the Stockholders of the Baltimore and Ohio Railroad Company, p. 42.*

119. The Jenkins Raid, 1862

Born in Cabell County, Virginia, General Albert Gallatin Jenkins (1830-1864) was educated at Jefferson College in Pennsylvania and Harvard Law School. Before the Civil War Jenkins practiced law in Charleston and managed his 4,400-acre estate at "Green Bottom" on the Ohio. He sat as a delegate in the Democratic National Convention in 1856 and served as a representative from Virginia in the Thirty-fifth and Thirty-sixth Congresses. Although reluctant to take up arms against the United States, he raised a company of cavalry when Virginia seceded. Jenkins served under Floyd and Wise in the Kanawha Valley and soon was promoted from captain to colonel. He was elected representative to the Confederate Congress in 1862, but he preferred military duty and returned to the field with the rank of brigadier general. In June, 1863, his brigade led the Confederate advance guard into Pennsylvania, where he captured Chambersburg and marched to Harrisburg before rejoining the main army. Jenkins was severely wounded at Gettysburg and did not return to his command until the fall of 1863, when he was ordered to defend the Virginia and Tennessee Railroad. He was mortally wounded at the battle of Cloyd's Mountain, May 9, 1864, while rallying his troops against General George A. Crook's Union forces.

Jenkins led his 550 cavalrymen on a daring raid through West Virginia in the summer of 1862. Leaving Salt Sulphur Springs in Monroe County on August 24, he marched northeast to Beverly and from there to Buckhannon, Weston, Glenville, Spencer, Ripley, and finally to Ravenswood. There he crossed into Ohio. Returning to Virginia below the mouth of the Kanawha, he made his way up the Guyandotte to Raleigh Courthouse, where he reported to General William W. Loring. Besides reconnoitering Union defenses, Jenkins and his cavalry screened the advance of Loring's larger force into the Kanawha Valley. He also seized 5,000 stands of arms at Buckhannon, captured 300 prisoners at Spencer, and appropriated $5,525 from a Union paymaster at Ripley.

Jenkins' five-hundred-mile raid dramatized the inadequacy of Union defenses that had been weakened early in August by the transfer of 5,000 men from the Kanawha Valley to General John Pope's army in eastern Virginia. On September 4, 1862, Daniel D. T. Farnsworth of Buckhannon described the demoralizing effects of the raid in a revealing letter addressed to Governor Francis H. Pierpont.

DOUBTLESS YOU HAVE HEARD BEFORE THIS of this place being taken on Saturday, the 30th ultimo, by Jenkins' cavalry, some 1,000 strong, and destroyed all the Government stores, worth some two or three hundred thousand dollars, and then breaking open some of the private stores and made havoc with the goods. They rifled my store. I made my escape after standing with my gun until the fight was over. We had in a manner no force, only Capt. Marsh's company and our battery boys, but never did fight better, and had we a few more such we would have whipped them. Their loss was 9 killed and some 10 or 12 wounded. Ours 9 wounded, two have died, and more probably will. They acted more like demons than like men. They stole all the horses that they could get their hands on. We are in the most exposed condition that any people ever was. The whole rout from here to Pocahontas county is open. The same rout that

Jenkins came in at, and unless there is a great change in the management of affairs, and that soon, this country will be completely overrun.

I am in possession of information that I think can be relied on, that Jenkins was to make the rade, which he has for the purpose of weakening every point that he could, and to get all the volunteers and horses that he could get his hands on, and return amediately to Floyd, who is now in Pocahontas, and conduct him into this place for the purpose of holding it. Jenkins, with part of his force, has already made the circuit, and is doubtless now back to Floyd. The other part of his forces, I understand, were pushing on towards Harrisville, and thus you see it will take but a few days for the combined forces to be here. Unless a heavy force be sent us soon we will be completely overrun.

I am confident that there is a screw loose some place, and I fear it is in the head commander of this reagon. . . . —*Calendar of Virginia State Papers*, XI, 389-90.

120. Confederate Occupation of the Kanawha Valley, 1862

When General William Wing Loring learned that Cox's division had been transferred to Pope's army in 1862, he sent Jenkins on his famous raid and planned an invasion of the Kanawha Valley. Cox had left behind at Gauley Bridge Colonel Joseph A. J. Lightburn with approximately five thousand men to defend a front which extended from Summersville through Hawks Nest and Fayetteville to Beckley. Proceeding through Princeton and Beckley, Loring occupied Fayetteville, and driving Lightburn's forces before him, entered Charleston on September 13. Although Lightburn conducted a skillful retreat, he abandoned strategic positions and lost property valued at more than a million dollars, the most serious Union reversal in Trans-Allegheny Virginia. Loring held Charleston until October 8, when concentration of Union troops at Clarksburg and Point Pleasant caused him to fall back to Lewisburg.

At Charleston Loring promptly supervised the manufacture of salt and its removal to Confederate Virginia. He also issued a proclamation to the People of Western Virginia and an address to his army.

To the People of Western Virginia.

The Army of the Confederate States has come among you to expel the enemy, to rescue the people from the despotism of the counterfeit State Government imposed upon you by Northern bayonets, and to restore the country once more to its natural allegiance to the State. We fight for peace and the possession of our own territory. We do not intend to punish those who remain at home as quiet citizens in obedience to the laws of the land, and to all such clemency and amnesty are declared; but those who persist in adhering to the cause of the public enemy, and the pretended State Government he has erected at Wheeling, will be dealt with as their obstinate treachery deserves.

When the liberal policy of the Confederate Government shall be introduced and made known to the people, who have so long experienced the wanton misrule of the invader, the Commanding General expects the people heartily to sustain it not only as a duty, but as a deliverance from their taskmasters and usurpers. Indeed, he already recognizes in the cordial welcome which the people everywhere give to the Army, a happy indication of their attachment to their true and lawful Government.

Until the proper authorities shall order otherwise, and in the absence of municipal law and its customary ministers, Martial Law will be administered by the Army and the Provost Marshals. Private rights and property will be respected, violence will be repressed, and order promoted, and all the private property used by the Army will be paid for.

The Commanding General appeals to all good citizens to aid him in these objects, and to all able-bodied men to join his army to defend the sanctities of religion and virtue, home, territory, honor, and law, which are invaded and violated by an unscrupulous enemy, whom an indignant and united people are now about to chastise on his own soil.

The Government expects an immediate and enthusiastic response to this call. Your country has been reclaimed for you from the enemy by soldiers, many of whom are from distant parts of the State, and the Confederacy; and you will prove unworthy to possess so beautiful and fruitful a land, if you do not now rise to retain and defend it. The oaths which the invader imposed upon you are void. They are immoral attempts to restrain you from your duty to your State and Government. They do not exempt you from the obligation to support your Government and to serve in the Army; and if such persons are taken as prisoners of war, the Confederate Government guarantees to them the humane treatment of the usages of war.

By command of
MAJ. GEN. LORING
H. Fitzhugh,
Chief of Staff

HEAD QUARTERS
DEPARTMENT OF WESTERN VIRGINIA, CHARLESTON, VA.,
September 14, 1862.

General Order No.

The Commanding General congratulates the Army on the brilliant march from the Southwest to this place in one week, and on its successive victories at Fayette C.H., Cotton Hill, and Charleston. It will be memorable in history, that overcoming the mountains and the enemy in one week, you have established the laws, and carried the flag of the country to the outer borders of the Confederacy. Instances of gallantry and patriotic devotion are too numerous to be specially designated at this time; but to Brigade Commanders, and their officers and men, the Commanding General makes grateful acknowledgment for services to which our brilliant success is due. The country will remember and reward you.

By command of MAJ. GEN. LORING
H. Fitzhugh
Chief of Staff

—West Virginia Collection, West Virginia University Library.

121. Oil and Troubled Waters

The opening of the oil field along the Little Kanawha River on the eve of the Civil War marked the beginning of an important West Virginia industry. Although the first well was a "dry hole", others yielded oil in marketable quantities. William P. and John V. Rathbone drilled a well at Burning Springs in Wirt

County in December, 1860, which attracted nationwide attention, and a month later the firm of Camden, Byrne and Company struck a "gusher". There was a feverish rush of adventurers and speculators into the oil region, and Burning Springs soon became a thriving town crowded with hundreds of sheds and hovels, fit only for the stout-hearted. In their haste men paid scant attention to the secession movement, but the war ended the Burning Springs oil boom in the spring of 1861. The following extract has been taken from an article written by John Russell Young, future Librarian of Congress, who visited the western Virginia oil field in 1862.

Go to West Virginia, that you may climb the high hills and bow down before the sublimity of Almighty God. . . . Now that I write these lines far away from the Kanawha, and think of the Burning Spring, its mud, and rain, and greasy waters, and eager, avaricious, hungry men, in muddy boots—that glimpse of nature rises to the mind, and brightens all.

All along the river and on the banks of its tributary rivers, we find evidences of the great panic that suddenly strangled the enterprises of 1860. Every few rods we see the black and mouldering derrick and the unfinished well in the ground. The few brave men who remained have made princely fortunes—the Rathbones, Camdens, and McFarlands being among the oil-princes of this new domain. They made their money by buying these lands at low figures, sinking good wells, and disposing of their purchases to the companies recently formed in New York and Philadelphia. Around the Burning Springs there are but few wells throwing up oil, and these are not recently developed, but the remnants of wells that have produced as many as one thousand barrels per day in their time, the gas sending up the oil in a thick, rushing stream, as high as the tree-tops, so that no tank could hold it, and it rushed out into the river and covered the stream. The old "Eternal Centre" well is eccentric. It was discovered by one of the Rathbones in 1860, and when struck, the finder clapped his hands and shouted, for he had found, he said, "the eternal centre of the great oil basin." It does not flow in a stream, but every six hours sends forth a few barrels, making a yield of about twenty or twenty-five barrels a day. The other wells in this vicinity are pumping-wells, and some of them reach as high as fifty or a hundred barrels a day. And yet, in justice to those who have spent large sums here, it must be said, that when we speak of West Virginia we speak of a business that is in its absolute infancy. It is but a few weeks since men of capital visited it. They have invested largely in obedience to a scientific principle, and no doubt exists in the minds of men who have thrown their millions over these rude and rugged hills, that their investments all will come back to them again. . . . —[John Russell Young], "A Visit to the Oil Regions of West Virginia," *Derrick and Drill*, pp. 155-56.

122. The Jones-Imboden Raid, 1863

For boldness of conception and audacity of execution, the month-long invasion led by Brigadier General William E. Jones across the Alleghenies in the spring of 1863 had few parallels in Confederate cavalry history. Included in his objectives were the overthrow of the reorganized Virginia government at Wheeling and suppression of the West Virginia statehood movement. While screening a larger force under Brigadier General John D. Imboden, which moved from Staunton through Beverly to Weston, the column under Jones consisting of approximately twenty-five hundred horsemen—formerly the Ashby Cavalry—overran the northwestern Virginia area from the South Branch of the Potomac to the Monongahela, penetrated almost to the Ohio, and returned to eastern Virginia by way of the Great Kanawha Valley without the loss of a dozen sabers while inflicting galling losses wherever Union arms and Union installations beset its path. The Confederates demolished bridges, tunnels, rolling stock, and equipment of the Baltimore and Ohio Railroad; cut telegraph lines; destroyed industrial establishments and oil wells; captured and paroled prisoners; and drove off livestock.

Generals Jones and Imboden summarized their successes and failures in reports to General Robert E. Lee. The concluding paragraphs from their reports are given below.

[William E. Jones:]

At Weston we rested two days, during which time Colonel Harman returned with the re-enforcements from Beverly. Feeling confident much danger would attend the attack of Clarksburg, on consultation with General Imboden it was agreed he should move south, while my cavalry should assail the Northwestern Railroad toward Parkersburg.

This movement commenced on May 6. Colonel Harman, with the Twelfth and Eleventh Regiments and Thirty-fourth (Witcher's) Battalion Virginia Cavalry, moved on West Union, while, with the remainder of my command, I took the Parkersburg pike, to attack the railroad at Cairo. Both were entirely successful. Colonel Harman amused a strong infantry force with skirmishers while parties were burning the two bridges to the right and left of the town. . . . This work was done by hard marching, my command having traveled upward of 80 miles without unsaddling.

From here we moved on Oiltown, where we arrived on May 9. The wells are owned mainly by Southern men, now driven from their homes, and their property is appropriated either by the Federal Government or Northern men. This oil is used extensively as a lubricator of machinery and for illumination. All the oil, the tanks, barrels, engines for pumping, engine-houses, and wagons—in a word, everything used for raising, holding, or sending it off was burned. The smoke is very dense and jet black. The boats, filled with oil in bulk, burst with a report almost equaling artillery, and spread the burning fluid over the river. Before night huge columns of ebon smoke marked the meanderings of the stream as far as the eye could reach. By dark the oil from the tanks on the burning creek had reached the river, and the whole stream became a sheet of fire. A burning river, carrying destruction to our merciless enemy, was a scene of magnificence that might well carry joy to every patriotic heart. Men of experience estimated the oil destroyed at 150,000 barrels. It will be many months before a large supply can be had from this source, as it can only be boated down the Little Kanawha when the waters are high. My orders were in all cases to respect private property, irrespective of the politics and part taken in the war by the owners. Horses and supplies were to be gathered indiscriminately. Two saw-mills (private property) were burned by my order—one, at Fairmont, was engaged on a contract with the Federal Government in making gun-stocks, and had on hand many thousands; the other, at Cairo, would have been used to repair the damages done the railroad. I am aware my orders were in a few instances disobeyed. The library of Pierpont was burned, in retaliation for a like act on the part of the ambitious little man. One or two stores were plundered, but as far as practicable the goods were restored.

From Oiltown we marched by Glenville and Sutton to Summersville, where the command of General Imboden was again overtaken. Our exhausted condition and exhausted supplies rendered homeward movements necessary. . . .

In thirty days we marched nearly 700 miles through a rough and sterile country, gathering subsistence for man and horse by the way. At Greenland and Fairmont we encountered the enemy's forces. We killed from 25 to 30 of the enemy, wounded probably three times as many, captured nearly 700 prisoners, with their small-arms, and 1 piece of artillery, 2 trains of cars, burned 16 railroad bridges and 1 tunnel, 150,000 barrels of oil, many engines, and a large number of boats, tanks, and barrels, bringing home with us about 1,000 cattle, and probably 1,200 horses. Our entire loss was 10 killed and 42 wounded, the missing not exceeding 15.—*Official Records,* i, XXV, 119-20.

[JOHN D. IMBODEN:]

The results of the expedition were not as great, perhaps, as they would have been with favorable weather and good roads. . . . In the horrible conditions of the roads, I could not move with the celerity that was desirable, and deemed myself fortunate in being able, by pursuing an interior route, to keep the way of escape open at all times for General Jones, while he, being mounted, ventured to go much farther than I could do. I compelled the enemy to destroy large and valuable stores at Beverly, Buckhannon, Weston, Bulltown, Suttonville, and Big Birch; captured and brought away over $100,000 worth of horses, mules, wagons, and arms; burned their blockhouses and stockades; forced them to burn three important and valuable covered turnpike bridges; burned six or eight wooden railroad bridges west of Fairmont; enabled the Government agents to buy and bring out to places of safety over 3,100 head of fine cattle, at a cost—stated to me by Maj. [W. M.] Tate, who procured a large part of them—of $300,000 less than they would sell for anywhere within our lines. I was thirty-seven days gone, marched over 400 miles, subsisted my command on half-rations a great part of the time. I lost 1 lieutenant (Vincent), Nineteenth Cavalry, and 1 man in the Eighteenth Cavalry, killed, and left to fall into the hands of the enemy 3 men, wounded, at Beverly, and 8 sick, and 3 prisoners captured; a total loss of 16. I secured between 75 and 100 recruits for my own command, including the Twenty-fifth and Thirty-first Regiments, and Col. William L. Jackson got between 300 and 400. In this respect we were all disappointed. The people now remaining in the northwest are, to all intents and purposes, a conquered people. Their spirit is broken by tyranny where they are true to our cause, and those who are against us are the blackest-hearted, most despicable villains upon the continent. . . .

I have heard scarcely a complaint of any wrong done to private rights of persons or property by the men under my command. They were nearly all Northwestern Virginians, and had much to provoke them to vengeance upon a dastard foe, who had outraged their unprotected families, but, with the willing obedience of the true Confederate soldier, every man obeyed all orders to respect private rights, even of their traitor neighbors.—*Official Records,* i, XXV, 104-05.

123. The Great Skedaddle: Hunter's Retreat, 1864

One of the important military events in West Virginia history was the retreat of General David Hunter's Union army from Lynchburg, Virginia, to Charleston, West Virginia, in the summer of 1864. After the defeat of General Franz Sigel at New Market in May, 1864, General Hunter was assigned to command in the Shenandoah Valley with orders to march against Lynchburg. On June 5 he won the battle of Piedmont, and two days later occupied Staunton. There re-enforcements under Generals George Crook and William W. Averell, who had marched from West Virginia, raised his army to 18,000 with thirty guns. After destroying factories, military installations, and several miles of the Virginia Central Railroad east and west of Staunton, Hunter moved to Lexington, where he burned the Virginia Military Institute and the home of former Governor John Letcher.

When Hunter reached Lynchburg on June 17, he attacked its defenses without success and next day he met even stronger resistance. Convinced that the Second Corps of Lee's army under General Jubal A. Early had arrived, he retreated down the New and Kanawha Rivers and up the Ohio to Parkersburg, where his army boarded Baltimore and Ohio trains and moved to Martinsburg in a futile effort to oppose Early's advance into Maryland. Although Hunter described his campaign and withdrawal as a success for Union arms, his headlong flight from Virginia and the suffering of his men on the week-long march cast doubt on his military prowess and judgment.

For a week his troops traversed devastated country before supplies sent out from Gauley Bridge reached the head of his famished column. Hunter's army passed Sweet Springs in Monroe County on June 24 and reached Lewisburg on the James River and Kanawha Turnpike the following day. Private William B. Stark of the 34th Massachusetts Infantry, related in his diary the hardships of the march from Lewisburg to Meadow Bluff and across Big Sewell Mountain.

June 25th, 1864.—We wished to go into camp but were not permitted to do so. We marched through Lewisburg. Hundreds if not thousands of our troops strayed off and in and about here all night. I think they must have found some provisions. It was almost impossible to lift our feet from the ground. Our tobacco was gone. We passed some good farms but soon were in the wilderness again. Squad after squad now fell out.

On and on we went; at last we halted. Of course we did not pitch our tents. We had dispensed with almost everything of that kind long ago. All we wanted now was to lie down anywhere and be let alone. Our clothes were fast passing away. Many had worn out their shoes and were barefoot. I have stood it thus far and resolved to endure unto the end if possible.

I obtained permission of the surgeon to go in advance of the column. This may appear strange but it proved a benefit. We get an hour's start, push ahead, then stop and rest without fear of being left behind.

We expected to meet rations tonight and that gave us encouragement to travel on. I was fortunate enough to get about ½ lb. of meat. A calf came in sight and it was soon made meat of. This gave me a new start.

Everything that was eatable that came in our way was eaten, such as roots and herbs. We pealed the black birch trees and ate the bark. I picked some currants which I cooked and ate without sugar; they only added to my misery. The men and teams continued to give out. What Amunition we had left was thrown away to lighten our burthen. Most of the men threw away their ball cartriges. Trunk valises, Knapsacks and all kinds of baggage was thrown from the train and left or burned. Sugar belonging to the commissary department was thrown out. Some of the boys that was near at hand got a good supply. We did not suppose there was a pound of sugar on the train. If we had it would not have remained there long.

June 26th.—I crippled along, stopping when I could go no farther. I thought of leaving my equipments and breaking my Springfield but finally brought them through. Their weight was about 18 lb. and they were all that we had to protect ourselves. We came through Meadowbrook, a dismal swampy wilderness between mountains with corduroy roads and broken bridges. We did not get any rations here as we had expected. Rumor said that we would get them next day. Our Brigade halted and camped here for the night. Still in advance, I crossed over what is called Little Sue Mountain and encamped with the Second Brigade. . . .

Our Brigade was several miles in the rear and this was rough for the wounded. They suffered for want of food and care and were roughed about until they died. . . .

June 27th.—We marched at early dawn and were soon climbing the Big Sue Mountain, last of these monsters. Scouts had been sent through to Gauley bridge several days before to hurry up the supplies. Some of them had got safely through and the supplies were on their way to us. They had come as far as this mountain. . . . It was some 8 or 10 miles up this mountain, and about the same distance down. I happened to find some carrion where a beef had been killed a few days before. I managed to get some meat from the carcase. It was something like Sampsons riddle of old (Sweet out of the Strong). The carcase was not inhabited by bees, neither was there any honey found in it, yet it was virtually the same, for swarms of living creeping worms were there and yet the meat was sweet to the taste. Had a splendid meal. A few others shared with me.

I now felt strong and made better time. We now reached the mountain top and it was a grand sight. After traveling some 10 miles through the forest we came to the base and went into camp.

Rations came in just before dark. The mountains ring and echo back the shouts of joy. Cheer on Cheer now went up until we were hoarse and out of breath.

We were saved; bread and life was ours at last. Half rations were dealt out for one day. Many ate all that was given them at once but the wise kept oil in their lamps and had breakfast out of the fragments. And now cooling rain began to fall. We took off our caps and gave it welcome. The bread and the small rain gave new vigor to both mind and body and sweet peace to our souls. We slept sound and awoke cheered and refreshed. Thanks be to God!—William B. Stark, "The Great Skedaddle," *Atlantic Monthly*, CLXII, (July, 1938), 91-93. Copyright 1938, by the Atlantic Monthly Company, Boston 16, Massachusetts.

124. Rutherford B. Hayes in West Virginia, 1861-1864

Some of the most vivid descriptions of conditions in West Virginia during the Civil War were written by Rutherford B. Hayes, later President of the United States, who rose from major to colonel of the Twenty-third Ohio Infantry. First stationed at Weston, Beverly, and Huttonsville, he fought under Rosecrans at Carnifex Ferry, spent the winter of 1861-62 near Gauley Bridge and at Fayetteville, and commanded General Cox's ad-

vance guard which occupied Princeton in May, 1862. Although transferred with Cox's division to General Pope's army near Washington, Hayes later campaigned under Crook against the Virginia and Tennessee Railroad in May, 1864, and in Hunter's advance to Lynchburg and retreat down the Kanawha a month later. He ended his field service that autumn under Sheridan in the Shenandoah Valley, where he won promotion to brigadier general.

Hayes kept a diary and wrote many letters home. The following excerpts from his writings throw considerable light upon West Virginia and its people during the war years.

WESTON, VIRGINIA, Tuesday Morning, July 30, 1861.

Dear Uncle:—If you look on the map you can find this town about twenty-five miles south of Clarksburg, which is about one hundred miles east of Parkersburg on the Northwest Virginia Railroad. So much for the general location; and if you were here, you would see on a pretty sidehill facing towards and overlooking a fine large village, surrounded by lovely hills, almost mountains, covered with forest or rich greensward, a picturesque encampment, and on the summit of the hill overlooking all, the line of field officers' tents. Sitting in one of them, as [Henry] Ward Beecher sat in the barn at Lenox, I am writing you this letter. . . .

We enjoy this life very much. So healthy and so pretty a country is rarely seen. After a month's campaign here the Tenth has lost no man by sickness and has but seven sick. General Rosecrans takes immediate command of us and will have us with him in his operations against Wise. We shall have mountain marches enough no doubt. So far I stand it well as the best. . . .

This is the land of blackberries. We are a great grown-up armed blackberry party and we gather untold quantities.

Here there are nearly as many Secessionists as Union men; the women avow it openly because they are safe in doing so, but the men are merely sour and suspicious and silent. . . .

R. B. Hayes.

Send this to Lucy.
S. Birchard.

HEADQUARTERS 23d Reg't, O. V. INF., U. S. A.,
August 17, 1861.

Dear Uncle:—We are kept very busy, hunting up guerrillas, escorting trains, etc., etc. Attacking parties are constantly met on the roads in the mountains, and small stations are surrounded and penned up. We send daily parties of from ten to one hundred on these expeditions, distances of from ten to forty miles. Union men persecuted for opinion's sake are the informers. The Secessionists in this region are the wealthy and educated, who do nothing openly, and the vagabonds, criminals, and ignorant barbarians of the country; while the Union men are the middle classes—the law-and-order, well-behaved folks. Persecutions are common, killings not rare, robberies an every-day occurrence.

Some bands of Rebels are so strong that we are really in doubt whether they are guerrillas or parts of Wise's army coming in to drive us out. The Secessionists are boastful, telling of great forces which are coming. Altogether, it is stirring times just now. Lieuten Colonel Matthews is nearly one hundred miles south of us with half our regiment, and is not strong enough to risk returning to us. With Colonels Tyler and Smith, he will fortify near Gauley Bridge on [the] Kanawha. . . .

Sincerely,

R. B. Hayes.

S. Birchard

CAMP TOMPKINS, NEAR GAULEY BRIDGE,
October 17, 1861.

Dearest:—. . . My office is pleasantly located in a romantic valley on the premises of Colonel Tompkins of the Rebel army. His mansion is an elegant modern house, and by some strange good luck it has been occupied by his family and escaped uninjured while hundreds of humbler homes have been ruined. Mrs. Tompkins had kept on the good side of our leaders, and has thus far kept the property safe. . . .

We have had the finest of fall weather for several (it seems many) days. The glorious mountains all around us are of every hue, changing to a deeper red and brown as the frosts cut the foliage. I talk so much of the scenery, you will suspect me to be daft. In fact I never have enjoyed nature so much. Being in the open air a great part of each day and surrounded by magnificent scenery, I do get heady I suspect on the subject. I have told you many a time that we were camped in the prettiest place you ever saw. I must here repeat it. The scenery on New River and around the junction of Gauley and New River where they form the Kanawha, is finer than any mere mountain and river views we saw last summer. The music and sights belonging to the camps of ten thousand men add to the effect. . . .

Affectionately,

R. B. Hayes.

Mrs. Hayes.

CAMP UNION, FAYETTEVILLE, Virginia,

November 25, 1861.

Dear MOTHER:—. . . This is a rugged mountain region, with large rushing rivers of pure clear water (we drink it at Cincinnati polluted by the Olentangy and Scioto) and full of the grandest scenery I have ever beheld. I rode yesterday over Cotton Hill and along New River a distance of thirty miles. I was alone most of the day, and could enjoy scenes made still wilder by the wintry storm.

We do not yet hear of any murders by bushwhackers in this part of Virginia, and can go where we choose without apprehension of danger. We meet very few men. The poor women excite our sympathy constantly. A great share of the calamities of war fall on the women. I see women unused to hard labor gathering corn to keep starvation from the door. I am now in command of the post here, and a large part of my time is occupied in hearing tales of distress and trying to soften the ills the armies have brought into this country. Fortunately a very small amount of salt, sugar, coffee, rice, and bacon goes a great ways where all these things are luxuries no longer procurable in the ordinary way. We try to pay for the mischief we do in destroying corn, hay, etc., etc., in this way. . . .

Affectionately,

R. B. Hayes.

CAMP UNION, FAYETTEVILLE, VIRGINIA, . . .

Thursday, January 2, 1862. . . .

Nobody in this army thinks of giving up to Rebels their fugitive slaves. Union men might perhaps be differently dealt with—

probably would be. If no doubt of their loyalty, I suppose they would again get their slaves. The man who repudiates all obligations under the Constitution and laws of the United States is to be treated as having forfeited those rights which depend solely on the laws and Constitution. I don't want to see Congress meddling with the slavery question. Time and the progress of events are solving all the questions arising out of slavery in a way consistent with eternal principles of justice. Slavery is getting death-blows. As an "institution," it perishes in this war. It will take years to get rid of its debris, but the "sacred" is gone. . . .

Wednesday, January 8.—. . . Rode with Adjutant Avery and two dragoons to Raleigh, twenty-four miles. . . .

Tuesday, January 14, 1862.—. . . Spent the afternoon looking over a trunk full of letters, deeds, documents, etc., belonging to General Alfred Beckley. They were buried in the graveyard near General Beckley's at Raleigh. Some letters of moment showing the early and earnest part taken by Colonel Tompkins in the Rebellion. The general Union and conservative feeling of General Beckley shown in letters carefully perserved in his letterbook. Two letters to Major Anderson, full of patriotism, love of Union and of the Stars and Stripes—replies written, one the day after Major Anderson went into Sumter, the other much later. His, General Beckley's, desire was really for the Union. He was of West Point education. Out of deference to popular sentiment he qualified his Unionism by saying, "Virginia would stay in the Union as long as she could consistently with honor."

General Beckley's note from "J. C. Calhoun, Secretary of War," informing him of his appointment as a cadet at West Point, and many other mementos, carefully preserved, were in the trunk. Title papers and evidence relating to a vast tract of land, formerly owned by Gideon Granger and now by Francis Granger and brother, were also in it. All except a few letters as to the Rebellion were undisturbed.

Wednesday, January 22, 1862.—. . . Three prisoners brought down last night. . . . Another prisoner, a son of General Beckley, aged about sixteen. Why he was taken I don't understand. He carried dispatches when the militia was out under his father, but seems intelligent and well-disposed. Disliking to see one so young packed into a crowded guardhouse (thinking of Birch and Webb, too), I took him to my own quarters and shared my bed with him last night. He talked in his sleep incoherently, otherwise a good bedfellow. . . .

CHARLESTON, CAMP ELK, July 2, 1864.

Dearest:—. . . Back again to this point last night. Camped opposite the lower end of Camp White on the broad level bottom in the angle between Elk and Kanawha. My headquarters on one of the pretty wooded hills near Judge [George W.] Summers'. . . .

You wrote one thoughtless sentence, complaining of Lincoln for failing to protect our unfortunate prisoners by retaliation. All a mistake, darling. All such things should be avoided as much as possible. We have done too much rather than too little. General Hunter turned Mrs. Governor Letcher and daughters out of their home at Lexington and on ten minutes' notice burned the beautiful place in retaliation for some bushwhackers' burning out Governor Pierpont [of loyal Virginia]. And I am glad to say that General Crook's division officers and men were all disgusted with it. . . .

You use the phrase "brutal Rebels." Don't be cheated in that way. There are enough "brutal Rebels" no doubt, but we have brutal officers and men too, I have had men brutally treated by our own officers on this raid. And there are plenty of humane Rebels. I have seen a good deal of it on this trip. War is a cruel business and there is brutality in it on all sides, but it is very idle to get up anxiety on account of any supposed peculiar cruelty on the part of Rebels. Keepers of prisons in Cincinnati, as well as in Danville, are hard-hearted and cruel. . . .

Affectionately,

R.

Mrs. Hayes.

—Charles Richard Williams, ed., *Diary and Letters of Rutherford Birchard Hayes*, II, 48-49, 68-69, 116-18, 146-47, 173-74, 182, 187, 193, 478-79. By permission of the Ohio Historical Society, The Ohio State Museum, Columbus 10, Ohio.

125. Those Who Served

Because of enlistments of West Virginia residents in other states, enlistment of non-residents in West Virginia units, service in independent organizations, and loss of muster rolls, the number of West Virginians in the armed forces of the United States and of the Confederacy can only be approximated. West Virginia counties contributed twenty-six regiments to the Union cause, including 212 "Colored Troops." The adjutant general of West Virginia reported that of the 31,884 which the State supplied of all arms for Union service to April 30, 1865, "only two hundred and fifty-seven men have been drafted. . . . and only five hundred and seventy-three substitutes have been furnished, . . ." Union death casualties numbered 3,224, including 820 killed in action, 108 killed accidentally, and 2,296 who died of wounds or disease.

Students of the subject have estimated the number of West Virginia Confederates at from seven thousand to ten thousand. The famous "Stonewall Brigade" numbered twelve companies of West Virginians, the Thirty-first and Thirty-sixth Virginia regiments mustered nine and six companies of West Virginians, respectively, while the Twenty-second Virginia regiment was composed entirely of West Virginians. Reports of the adjutant general of West Virginia tend to show that West Virginia supplied in excess of nine thousand men to the Confederate armed forces, although partisans of the Confederacy have claimed a greater number.

The first table below shows Union quotas and credits of men to April 30, 1865; the second lists the bounties paid by counties to volunteers mustered into the United States service. In the third extract the authors challenge the accuracy of these tables and contend that West Virginia supplied the greater number to the Confederacy.

The State of West Virginia in account with the United States

Dr.		Cr.	
1861 To quota, calls of 1861	8,497	1861 By men furnished under calls of 1861	12,686
1862 " " July 2d	4,650	1862 By men furnished under calls of July 2	3,888
1862 To quota, calls for 300,000 nine months' militia, reduced to three years standard	1,162	1863 Credits by enlistments from May 26th, to December 31st	3,281
1864 To quota, under call of February 1st, for 500,000 men	5,127	1864 Credits by enlistments from January 1st, to January 31st	131
1864 By quota, under call of Mar. 14, for 200,000 men	2,051	1864 Enlistments and re-enlistments from February 1st, to August 1st	4,712
1864 By quota, under call of July 19th, for 500,000 men	5,928	1864 By men furnished from Aug. 1st, to Dec. 31st	1,956
1864 By quota, under call of Dec. 19th, for 300,000 men	4,431	1865 By credits from Jan. 1st, to Aug. 31st.	2,509
		Total credits to Aug. 31, 1865	29,163
		Deficiency	2,683
	31,846	Total	31,846

Bounties for United States Volunteers

County	Total Amount levied and paid	Remarks
Barbour	$ 46,684.91	— — — —
Brooke	85,155.14	— — — —
Doddridge	71,355.00	— — — —
Gilmer	3,698.71	— — — —
Jackson	14,000.00	— — — —
Kanawha	9,400.00	— — — —
Lewis	28,575.20	$1,400 of this amount appropri-
Monongalia	154,425.00	ated for relief of soldiers' fam-
Marion	103,075.00	ilies.
Pleasants	37,900.00	— — — —
Ritchie	30,270.00	— — — —
Tyler	16,330.00	— — — —
Wirt	27,975.00	— — — —
Mason	40,110.00	— — — —
Harrison	258,438.04	— — — —
Ohio	334,959.00	— — — —
Preston	135,700.00	— — — —
Upshur	55,843.00	— — — —
Wetzel	65,478.42	$500 of this amount appropriated
Hancock	60,830.00	for soldiers' families.
Marshall	181,325.65	$1,500 of this amount appropri-
Putnam	12,630.00	ated for soldiers' families.
Wood	187,791.00	$8,000 of this amount appropri-
Cabell	3,600.00	ated for soldiers' families.
Total	$1,965,549.07	

Note.—There are several counties from which no statements have been received, and the total amount levied and paid is probably over two millions of dollars.

—*Annual Report of the Adjutant General of the State of West Virginia, 1865, pp. 398, 401.*

According to the reports of the Adjutant-General, the state of West Virginia was credited with furnishing to the Union army, from first to last, a total of 31,884 men. Several entire regiments which are credited to West Virginia, were recruited in Ohio or elsewhere, and officered by Ohio men. During the last two years of the war, when large bounties were paid for enlistments to complete the quota of troops called for, the volunteers came almost entirely from abroad, and when substitutes were secured to take the places of conscripted men, these substitutes were for the most part obtained in Northern cities or were newly-arrived immigrants from abroad. It is now impossible to obtain any accurate figures as to the number of soldiers furnished to the Southern armies by the counties composing West

Virginia. The muster-rolls have been lost or destroyed, and it is not known that any record even approaching completeness is now in existence. Recruiting was active in many of the counties at the beginning of the war; but when the Federal armies advanced in 1861, of course enlistment in the Confederate army ceased at all points within the Federal line, though it went on with increased activity and thoroughness in the counties not under Federal control, and it can scarcely be doubted that the total number of West Virginians who served at one time or another in the Confederate army exceeded by several thousands the number who espoused the Union cause.—O. S. Long and W. L. Wilson, "Reconstruction in West Virginia," *Why the Solid South,* edited by Hilary A. Herbert, p. 259.

XI. The Ordeal of Reconstruction, 1865-1872

126. A Trip to Charles Town in 1865

No West Virginia county played a more significant role in the Civil War than Jefferson County. John Brown had been captured, tried, and executed there. Indeed as Charleston, South Carolina, became the symbol of secession, Harpers Ferry and Charles Town, Virginia, became symbols of slavery.

Jefferson and Berkeley counties, moreover, formed a strategic area in the conduct of offensive and defensive military operations. While providing a natural gateway to Maryland and Pennsylvania, these counties conversely opened a door to the "granary of the Confederacy"—the Shenandoah Valley. Through this area ran the main line of the Baltimore and Ohio Railroad, the Winchester and Potomac Railroad, and the Valley Turnpike, each the side of a triangle with military bases at Harpers Ferry, Winchester, and Martinsburg. However bound to the Valley by geographical location and economic interests, the inhabitants of these counties, especially Jefferson, were joined to eastern Virginia by social and cultural ties. Jefferson County contained 3,960 slaves at the beginning of the war and supplied approximately 1,600 men for the Confederate army.

Small wonder that Jefferson County was West Virginia's conquered province. An observer who traveled from Harpers Ferry to Charles Town late in the summer of 1865 described prostrate Jefferson still in the ashes.

At the end of a long hour's ride we arrived at Charlestown, chiefly interesting to me as the place of John Brown's martyrdom. We alighted from the train on the edge of boundless unfenced fields, into whose melancholy solitudes the desolate streets emptied themselves—rivers to that ocean of weeds. The town resembled to my eye some unprotected female sitting sorrowful on the wayside, in tattered and faded apparel, with unkempt tresses fallen negligently about features which might once have been attractive.

On the steps of a boarding-house I found an acquaintance whose countenance gleamed with pleasure "at sight," as he said, "of a single loyal face in that nest of secession." He had been two or three days in the place, waiting for luggage which had been miscarried.

"They are all Rebels here,—all Rebels!" he exclaimed, as he took his cane and walked with me. "They are a pitiably poverty-stricken set; there is no money in the place, and scarcely anything to eat. We have for breakfast salt-fish, fried potatoes, and treason. Fried potatoes, treason, and salt-fish for dinner. At supper the fare is slightly varied, and we have treason, salt-fish, fried potatoes, and a little more treason. My landlady's daughter is Southern fire incarnate; and she illustrates Southern politeness by abusing Northern people and the government from morning till night, for my especial edification. Sometimes I venture to answer her, when she flies at me, figuratively speaking, like a cat. The women are not the only out-spoken Rebels, although they are the worst. The men don't hesitate to declare their sentiments, in season and out of season." My friend concluded with this figure: "The war-feeling here is like a burning bush with a wet blanket wrapped around it. Looked at from the outside, the fire seems quenched. But just peep under the blanket, and there it is, all alive and eating, eating in. The wet blanket is the present government policy; and every act of conciliation shown the Rebels is just letting in so much air to feed the fire."

A short walk up into the centre of the town took us to the scene of John Brown's trial. It was a consolation to see that the jail had been laid to ashes, and that the court-house, where that mockery of justice was performed, was a ruin abandoned to rats and toads. Four massive white brick pillars, still standing, supported a riddled roof, through which God's blue sky and gracious sunshine smiled. The main portion of the building had been literally torn to pieces. In the floorless hall of justice rank weeds were growing. Names of Union soldiers were scrawled along the walls. No torch had been applied to the wood-work, but the work of destruction had been performed by the hands of hilarious soldier-boys ripping up floors and pulling down laths and joists to the tune of "John Brown,"—the swelling melody of the song, and the accompaniment of crashing partitions, reminding the citizens, who thought to have destroyed the old hero, that his soul was marching on. . . .

As we were taking comfort, . . . the townspeople passed on the sidewalk, "daughters and sons of beauty," for they were mostly a fine-looking, spirited class; one of whom, at a question which I put to him, stopped quite willingly and talked with us. I have seldom see a handsomer young face, a steadier eye, or more decided poise and aplomb; neither have I ever seen the outward garment of courtesy so plumply filled out with the spirit of arrogance. His brief replies, spoken with a pleasant countenance, yet with short, sharp, downward inflections, were like pistol-shots. Very evidently the death of John Brown, and the war that came swooping down in the old man's path to avenge him, and to accomplish the work wherein he failed, were not pleasing subjects to this young southern blood. And no wonder. His coat had an empty sleeve. . . .—J. T. Trowbridge, *The South: A Tour of Its Battlefields and Ruined Cities, a Journey Through the Desolated States, and Talks with the People,* pp. 70-72.

127. The Test Oath and Proscription Amendment

Although spared the excesses of the carpetbag governments, the people of West Virginia nevertheless underwent a severe reconstruction ordeal. In 1863 the Legislature enacted war measures which required loyalty oaths of officials and voters and confiscated all property belonging to Confederates. On February 25, 1865, it enacted a comprehensive test-oath law designed to deny the ballot to returning Confederates and voters who were unwilling to reaffirm their loyalty when challenged at the polls. Finally, on March 1, 1865, the Legislature adopted a constitutional amendment which, after it had been published in the several counties and readopted by the succeeding Legislature, was submitted to the voters on May 24, 1866. Ratified by a majority of 7,236, this amendment disfranchised and decitizenized

*all persons who had supported the Confederacy; it thus estab-
lished a legal basis for the Radical Republican reconstruction
policy.*

No PERSON WHO, since the first day of June, 1861, has given or
shall give voluntary aid or assistance to the rebellion against the
United States, shall be a citizen of this state, or be allowed to
vote at any election held therein, unless he has volunteered into
the military or naval service of the United States, and has been
or shall be honorably discharged therefrom.—*Acts of the Legislature of West Virginia at Its Fourth Session,* 1866, pp. 135-36.

128. The Continuing Strife

*Former Confederates showed their resentment of the pro-
scriptive laws in many ways varying from intimidation of public
officials to violence. They boycotted businesses, churches, and
social gatherings; some migrated. The following excerpts have
been taken from Governor Arthur I. Boreman's messages to the
Legislature and from a joint article written by a Union and a
Confederate Democrat. They throw much light on political, social, and economic conditions in West Virginia during the reconstruction period.*

PERMANENT CIVIL ORGANIZATION has been restored throughout
our own State, except in five or six counties on the extreme eastern border. These have been partially organized, and would
have been entirely so, had my efforts to that end been seconded
as they should. But I regret to be compelled to state that many
of the intelligent and leading participants in the Rebellion, instead of counselling observance of the law, have pursued a
course of conduct that has prevented complete organization in
the five or six counties mentioned. These parties either became
candidates themselves, or induced others who, like themselves,
had committed acts of disloyalty, to become candidates for office, at the election in October last; and in a number of cases
these ineligible parties were elected. They cannot take the oath
of office prescribed by existing law, and as a consequence, these

offices are not filled by persons elected by the people, but their functions, are performed, as far as it is practicable to have them performed at all, by appointees. . . . —Annual Message of the Governor, January 16, 1866, *Journal of the House of Delegates,* p. 8.

While the condition of the State as a whole is very gratifying, I am compelled to repeat, what I said to your predecessors a year ago, that in some localities, chiefly in four or five counties bordering on the States of Virginia and Kentucky, a spirit of insubordination still continues to be manifested. . . . The judge of the ninth circuit has received anonymous letters threatening his life if he persists in holding his courts; and while he was holding a term of his court in the town of Lewisburg, Greenbrier county, during the last Fall, these malcontents held a public meeting in the town, in which they resolved to mob the judge and the prosecuting attorney of his court, and were only induced to desist from executing their purpose by the interposition of more considerate friends. . . . Another instance of utter disregard of the laws is that in one or two counties, as I am informed, persons who aided and abetted the rebellion are performing the duties of county and township offices, and this, of course, without taking the oaths required by law; and yet they are not indicted by the grand juries—in some cases probably from sympathy of the jurors with the rebellion, and in other cases through intimidation.

In this aspect of affairs it became apparent that the laws could not be enforced by the civil authorities and that military aid was necessary for that purpose; and on application to General Grant, a small detachment of United States troops has been stationed at Union, in Monroe County, . . .

The leading spirits amongst those that are defying the laws and disturbing the good order of society are men of superior intelligence,—some of them learned in the law,—and are therefore the more culpable.—*Annual Message of the Governor,* January 15, 1867, pp. 3-4.

Order has reigned during the year throughout the greater part of the State. In two or three localities, however, the peace has been disturbed, the laws have been set at naught and the officers resisted, and, indeed, forcibly driven away from the performance of their duties.

During the war, and since, there has been a band of armed rebels in the counties of Wayne and Logan, led by a fellow known and notorious as "Captain Bill Smith," murdering, robbing and plundering the people of that region. . . . During last winter, this band, several times, robbed peaceable citizens and committed other depredations in Wayne county, and near the first of March, by force and violence, they put the officers of the county in fear and drove them away from the performance of their duties at the court house, the latter feeling themselves unsafe in resuming their offices without protection; and again, this band took possession of the jail, overpowered the jailor, put him under restraint, and released one of their associates, who was confined therein on a criminal charge. . . . Under these circumstances, and upon the urgent application of officers and other good citizens of the counties interested, I asked the proper authorities of the United States for a small body of troops, and a company was sent into Wayne county early in the spring—a detachment of them being afterwards stationed at Logan Court House. . . . In Logan county there had been no taxes collected since the war, except a few hundred dollars in a small portion of the county. In other portions of the county, there were many that had returned from the rebel army, bringing their arms with them, who denied the authority of the State Government, and utterly refused to pay taxes for its support, or for the support of the county organization under it, and threatened to resist with arms, and to the death, if the collection of taxes should be attempted. . . .

In another section of the State—in the three adjoining counties of Randolph, Tucker and Barbour—there have been very decided manifestations of opposition to the execution of the registry law during the year. . . . I therefore called on the proper authorities for a few United States troops for the emergency, and they were promptly furnished, and stationed at Philippi. After their arrival the execution of the law proceeded without interruption. They remained until after the election, when, on my suggestion, they were ordered away.—*Sixth Annual Message of Governor Boreman, of West Virginia,* January 21, 1868, pp. 3-5.

. . . I am happy to be able to say that the laws are now being executed in every portion of the State, and that there is more of peace and harmony within its borders than at any previous period since its organization. As was anticipated, however, by the good and true men of the State, the eradication of the spirit of insubordination, engendered by the late rebellion, has proven to be a work of time; . . .

On Tuesday, the 6th of October [1868], I was informed by written communication, received from the Board of Registration of Marion county, and by the representations of other citizens of the county in person, that on the preceding day the Board had attempted to hold the regular session prescribed by law for the purpose of disposing of the cases of such persons, claiming to be voters, as might come before them; that they were met at the Court House by a large number of men, who were much excited, and a majority of whom were armed; that several persons claiming to be a committee representing this riotous assemblage, laid down certain rules for the government of the Board in the business before them and demanded that they adopt the same, and stated that if this was done the committee would see that the Board were not disturbed, but if the rules thus prescribed were not adopted, the Board would be left subject to the violence of the mob. Under these circumstances, and against their convictions as to the legality, as well as the propriety of the demands thus made, the Board unwillingly assented to the terms proposed, and proceeded to try and decide one of the cases before them; the decision was not satisfactory, however, and was immediately followed by the hootings and jeers of the crowd, and by such threats and demonstrations of violence towards the Board that they could proceed no further, and were compelled to adjourn until the next day. The rioters then held a meeting in front of the Court House, when inflammatory speeches were made, and a resolution adopted to return the next day. On Tuesday the numbers as well as the violence of this assemblage increased, and the Board were not allowed to transact any business on that day. The same thing occurred again on Wednesday. . . . I therefore went to Washington, applied for and obtained, a company of United States troops, who remained at Fairmont until after the Presidential election. . . .

While this company of troops were stationed at Fairmont, Lieutenant Halloran, the officer in command, reported to me that several boxes of United States guns had been brought into Marion county on private account, and that he had captured one box and found it to contain twenty-three guns, with bayonets, accoutrements and ammunition. . . . It is difficult to divine for what purpose these arms were imported into our State at this time. If intended for ordinary sporting purposes, why the bayonets and accoutrements used only in war? Yet there are certainly no considerable number of people in our midst who would now be guilty of the madness and folly of armed resistance to the constituted authorities. I make no recommendation on the subject, but present the facts as having transpired in the State within the year.—Annual Message of the Governor, January 19, 1869, *Journal of the Senate*, pp. 7-9.

The condition of the ex-Confederate soldier in West Virginia during the five years which immediately followed the end of the war, was, therefore, reduced to this: He was denied citizenship in the place of his birth; he could not hold office; he could not vote; he could not practice law; he could not sit as a juror; he could not teach school; he could not sue in the courts; he could not make defense to suits brought against him in his absence, and at least one of the circuit judges held that he could not qualify as an executor or administrator, and hence when he died he must commit to a Republican neighbor for distribution, whatever estate he had been able to save from the rapacity of those who had sued him for offenses for which he was not guilty.

. . . The courts went hand in hand with the Legislature; whatever one did the other pronounced good. There is not a single instance during all the period between 1863 and 1870 in which an act or a section of an act, passed by the Legislature, was pronounced unconstitutional by the Supreme Court of Appeals. . . . One circuit judge was impeached and removed from office because he had appointed an ex-Confederate to be the temporary sheriff of one of the counties in his circuit; another was impeached and removed because he had permitted three distinguished lawyers to practice in his courts without taking the Attorney's test-oath. . . .

The decision by the Supreme Court of the United States in "The Prize Cases," at December term, 1862 . . . was generally understood by the members of the legal profession as conceding to the armies of the Confederate States, "belligerent rights." This construction was amply sustained by many subsequent decisions of the Supreme Court, in which reference was made to the cases mentioned. . . . It was a concession made necessary by the dictates of humanity and civilization in view of the magnitude of the war and its long duration. Under the doctrine of "belligerent rights," neither of the combatants can afterwards be held liable, either civilly or criminally, for any act done "in accordance with the usages of civilized warfare." But the decisions of the Supreme Court in this regard were nullified in West Virginia. . . . —O. S. Long and W. L. Wilson, "Reconstruction in West Virginia," *Why the Solid South*, pp. 272-73.

129. Peter G. Van Winkle Defends President Andrew Johnson

One of the West Virginia state-makers attained national renown for his political courage. Peter G. Van Winkle (1808-1872) had come from New York to Parkersburg in 1835, studied law in the office of General John J. Jackson, and practiced as an associate of Jackson until he formed his own partnership. Successful from the beginning as a lawyer, Van Winkle matched his performance at the bar in his business enterprises which included the building of the Northwestern Virginia Railroad from Grafton to Parkersburg (1853-1857). But Van Winkle made his greatest contributions to government. He served as a delegate to the Virginia Constitutional Convention in 1850-51, the Second Wheeling Convention, and the first West Virginia Constitutional Convention where, as chairman of the Committee on Fundamental and General Provisions, he influenced decisions on important issues such as boundary, education, and internal im-

provements. Van Winkle was sitting as a member of the first West Virginia House of Delegates when, on August 4, 1863, the Legislature elected him along with Waitman T. Willey to a Senate seat.

Senator Van Winkle opposed repeal of the Fugitive Slave Act in 1864 but supported the adoption of the Thirteenth Amendment a year later. He voted against the adoption of the Fourteenth Amendment because he opposed citizenship for the freedmen and Federal rule in the seceded states in peacetime. A conservative Whig turned Republican, Van Winkle never became a Radical, although he supported some Radical measures in Congress. In the Senate he served as a member of the Finance Committee and as chairman of the Committee on Pensions.

In 1868 Peter G. Van Winkle ignored tacit instructions of the West Virginia legislature and courageously joined six Republican and twelve Democratic senators to defend President Andrew Johnson against impeachment charges. Alphabetically the last of the recusant seven Republicans on roll call, Van Winkle's vote was crucial and decisive. Like his Republican colleagues who voted "Not Guilty" on that momentous occasion, he "looked into his political grave"; for surely he would have failed of re-election had he been a candidate in 1869.

The passages below include resolutions of instruction adopted by the West Virginia legislature, a sample of Republican editorial comment, and the resolutions of censure voted by the West Virginia senate.

SENATE JOINT RESOLUTION No. 11, "Relating to the impeachment of the President of the United States." . . .

Resolved by the Legislature of West Virginia, That Andrew Johnson, President of the United States, in the attempted removal of the Secretary of War, and the designation of the Adjutant General to perform the duties of the office *ad interim,* the Senate being in session, has been guilty of a wilful and flagrant violation of law, and in the opinion of the Legislature of West Virginia, ought to be impeached for high crimes and misdemeanors.

Resolved, That the Governor be authorized to tender Congress the assistance of West Virginia, in sustaining the authority and enforcing the laws of the United States.—*Journal of the West Virginia Senate*, February 24, 1868, p. 141.

To all his other offences Mr. Van Winkle has added the blackest ingratitude. It was the party upholding the great Cause which he now stabs like an assassin, that gave West Virginia leave to place two men on the floor of the United States Senate; and the spokesman of that party who plead for us then and there was Benjamin F. Wade. Now our loyal Representatives at Washington are overwhelmed with the reproaches of the Republicans in both Houses, whose confidence in West Virginia loyalty is almost destroyed. But for these men five years ago, West Virginia would be to-day but an outlying province of ruined old Virginia, governed like her by the sword. Yet Van Winkle had scarcely warmed his seat in the Senate before he began to show his antipathy to their principles and his hatred to the men who alone have ever befriended us. But the crowning act of treachery and malignity was reserved for this crisis, chosen by him and his coadjutors with a belief that the life of the organization they sought to destroy might be taken at a single blow. . . .

It seems impossible for a man with the sense of honor which we have hitherto attributed to him could have done what he has done. We confess, we have been somewhat mistaken in the man. When appealed to by our Representatives not to join our enemies in declaring Johnson blameless, they were reminded of his "oath", which like Shylock he had registered in heaven. . . .

Mr. Van Winkle's responsibility in this matter is one we would not care to shoulder. His single vote decided. Had he been able to elevate himself to the level of a statesman and declare what Johnson himself confesses and what is notorious to the whole world, Andrew Johnson would now be a private citizen and the country would be tranquil and hopeful. . . .

In the hands of Mr. Van Winkle's constituents (though he may not be aware of their existence) we leave him. . . . When they have done with him, we shall be willing to consign him to the same tomb of disgraceful oblivion as will hide the venerable but not lamented Grimes, there to slumber like his illustrious ancestor, till some future age when such qualities as honor, fidelity and gratitude shall no more be known among men save only in the traditions of the past.—Wheeling *Intelligencer,* May 18, 1868.

Resolved by the Legislature of West Virginia, That in the trial of Andrew Johnson, President of the United States, before the Senate, upon the Articles of Impeachment exhibited against him by the House of Representatives, according to the published evidence there adduced, the said Andrew Johnson was, in our opinion, proved guilty of the high crimes and misdemeanors as in said articles charged; that we believe his conviction thereof would have been a vindication of law and justice, and of great and enduring advantage to the nation; and that it is to be deplored that a Senator from West Virginia should have felt constrained to vote said Andrew Johnson innocent, thereby securing his acquittal.—*Journal of the West Virginia Senate, Extraordinary Session,* June 11, 1868, p. 18.

130. The Liberal Republican Movement

The ratification and implementation by statute of the proscriptive amendment of 1866 effectively disfranchised between ten and twenty thousand West Virginia citizens and denied them the right to practice law, sit on juries, sue in the courts, and teach in the public schools. Laws which made a dead letter of President Lincoln's amnesty proclamations and which corrupt officers shaped to personal and party ends drove Republicans by the hundreds into opposition ranks. When Horace Greeley advised West Virginia Republicans to amnesty the former Confederates, moderate Republican leaders began a movement to obtain repeal of the amendment and proscriptive laws. In September, 1869, Archibald W. Campbell circulated an "Address to the Republican Voters of Ohio County," signed by 138 fellow Republicans, which urged a relaxation of Radical Republican policy, and Governor William E. Stevenson, though he had won election in 1868 as a Radical Republican, recommended general amnesty for all former Confederates.

Following the Greeley letter below are extracts from Campbell's "Address" and the first annual legislative message of Governor Stevenson.

NEW YORK, NOVEMBER 18, 1868.

I have yours of the 18th. Its leading positions have long been understood and appreciated in this quarter. Now hear *me*.

Every year one thousand of your rebels die, and one thousand (or more) of their sons become of age. You can't disfranchise THEM. You have now five thousand majority. Six years at farthest will convert this into a rebel majority of one thousand. Then the rebels will be enfranchised in spite of you, and the Blacks will be left under foot—and you under-estimate these at two thousand.

Go your own way, and see if the rebels don't have you under foot in *less* than six years.

I speak from a wide experience when I tell you that your house is built on the sand. It cannot stand. Every year will see the passions of the war cool, and the demand for amnesty strengthened. *Now* you can amnesty the rebels. Soon the question will be, Shall they amnesty *you*? Look at Kentucky and Maryland and read your certain fate in theirs.—Wheeling *Intelligencer*, May 21, 1869.

TO THE REPUBLICAN VOTERS OF OHIO COUNTY:

We believe that the test oaths that were adopted in this State during, and at the close of the war, were, in the main, necessary, if not absolutely indispensable. They protected the weak and exposed counties against the proscription and aggression that must have followed a return of the disloyal element to power and influence. And, in addition, they have served well throughout the whole State, as a part of the great moral lesson taught by the war. . . . And therefore, no rigor, or semblance of persecution, is excusable after the public safety is reasonably assured. And as regards the safety of our loyal people at this time, even in the most exposed counties, our information impresses us with the belief that we can afford to inaugurate the necessary steps for discontinuing everything known as far as legislation.

. . . We do not advocate an instant abrogation of the disfranchising clause in our Constitution, for that is impossible, but we do favor prompt steps by our next Legislature towards putting it in process of repeal—a process, by the way, that will consume upwards of two years from next winter. And, in the meantime, we shall hope to see the next Legislature take early opportunity to do away with the test oaths now resting upon Lawyers, Suitors, and School Teachers. . . . And as for the voters' oath, we presume by the time it can be legally dispensed with under the repeal process alluded to, there will be few disinterested citizens in our midst, however bitter their remembrances of the war, who will really regret its discontinuance. . . .

Hence, in conclusion, every consideration that can appeal to us from the better instincts of our human nature in favor of that mercy toward the erring which we all need, down to the best interests of our mere party organization, prompt us to lay before our Republican brethren of Ohio county these views, and to ask them to unite with us in giving them effect in the canvass this fall.—Archibald W. Campbell Papers, West Virginia Collection, West Virginia University Library.

The subject of removing legal disabilities placed upon persons within the State, who gave voluntary aid to the rebellion, has been for some time agitating the public mind; . . .

These restrictive measures were adopted during a time of great public peril; they were prompted by that instinct of self-preservation which impels every community to shield itself from present or impending danger. . . .

. . . I am gratified to be able to state that in most of the counties, where, during and after the war, the Federal and State authorities were resisted, good order now prevails, and the laws are respected and obeyed. I regret that in a few of these counties there still lingers among some of the people a remnant of that turbulent spirit so fruitful of violence and anarchy during the war. There is strong reason to believe that the spirit of lawlessness would soon disappear, were not the worst passions of the thoughtless and reckless frequently appealed to by men of influence to subserve merely selfish and partizan purposes; for the people of no State are better disposed or more law-abiding than our own.

It is not a just policy to continue in our midst a class deprived of the privileges of citizenship, unless the public welfare clearly demands it; nor is it a wise policy to confer or restore these privileges where there is good reason to apprehend they would be used to the injury of the State or the subversion of its laws. . . .

There seems to be a very general conviction in the minds of the people that the acts imposing what are known as the attorneys' and teachers' test oaths should be repealed. Numbers of persons engaged in these professions have already been relieved from their operation. In view of this fact, and the remoteness of the circumstances which at first require the passage of these laws, their continuance in the case of remaining individuals seems to be inexpedient. I therefore recommend their repeal. There are numbers of citizens in whose judgment I have great confidence, who believe that the time has not yet come for the repeal of what is known as the suitors' test oath; still I think the wisdom of its further continuance on the statute book is questionable; it is comparatively inoperative, and besides, it would seem that the necessity for it has, in great measure, passed away.

Upon the question of amending the Constitution so as to restore the privileges of citizenship to those now disfranchised, there is much difference of opinion; the only differences, however, as a general thing, are to the mode and time of restoration, as there are but a few who desire disfranchisement to be perpetual. . . .—*First Annual Message of Governor Stevenson,* pp. 15-16.

131. The Flick Amendment

Although proscription carried the germ of its own destruction, it was reaction to congressional policy that sounded the knell of Radical reconstruction in West Virginia. Republicans who had accepted the Fourteenth Amendment as a necessity to guarantee Negro residents civil rights bolted to the Democrats when the

Legislature ratified the Fifteenth Amendment. Alarmed when the trek to the Democratic Party became general in the state election of 1869, a group of moderate Republicans united with Democrats in the Legislature to propose an amendment to the constitution that repealed the controversial disqualifying amendment of 1866. Introduced in the House of Delegates by W. H. H. Flick and passed by both houses in 1870, it received the concurrence of the next Legislature and was ratified on May 26, 1871, by a vote of 23,546 to 6,323. The amendment enfranchised Negroes and restored political and civil rights to the former Confederates.

Below are passages from Governor William E. Stevenson's message to the Legislature recommending adoption of the Flick amendment, and the text of the amendment.

THE MALE CITIZENS OF THE STATE shall be entitled to vote at all elections held within the election districts in which they respectively reside; but no person who is a minor, or of unsound mind, or a pauper, or who is under conviction of treason, felony or bribery in an election, or who has not been a resident of the State for one year, and of the county in which he offers to vote for thirty days next preceding such offer, shall be permitted to vote while such disability continues.—*Journal of the West Virginia House of Delegates, 1870, pp. 68-69.*

The conviction has become very general among our citizens, that we are remote enough from the scenes of strife which belonged to our civil war, and have sufficiently outgrown the bitterness which for a considerable time survived it, to justify us in removing all political disabilities from this class of our citizens. It is not to be denied that there are still to be found in the State a considerable number of persons who continue to cherish a feeling of hatred toward the government of the union, and to manifest a spirit of intolerance to its friends—a spirit which developed itself during our recent political contest in several cowardly attempts to assassinate leading citizens of the State. This class, however, is made up chiefly of persons who during our civil troubles professed devotion to the federal government, and those who gave aid to the rebellion, indirectly, and always at a safe distance from scenes of actual conflict and danger. With few exceptions, those who were in the armies of the confederacy are law abiding citizens.

This state of facts seems to demand favorable and immediate action upon the proposed amendment. Another reason for speedy action is found in the fact that the more dishonest and unscrupulous of those who aided in the war against the government, are already, in consequence of gross perversions of law, exercising the right to vote, while the more candid and conscientious steadily decline to do so, until the privilege is conferred upon them in a legitimate way under the Constitution and laws of the State. In this the persons composing the latter class, have shown a principle of honor which we should not fail to recognize; and certainly no stronger reason than their conduct, could be urged to show that if political rights be restored to them, they will not be used to the detriment of the State, or for the subversion of its laws.—*Second Annual Message of Governor Stevenson of West Virginia,* January 17, 1871, pp. 21-22.

132. Virginia Sues to Recover Berkeley and Jefferson Counties

Of the seven Virginia counties east of the Alleghenies which the convention of 1861-62 had authorized to join the State of West Virginia, only three ratified the constitution at the elections held April 3, 1862. Morgan County voters approved the constitution at elections held on May 5, 1862. When convinced that no part of the Baltimore and Ohio Railroad should remain on Virginia soil, the reorganized General Assembly at Wheeling passed acts in January and February, 1863, which provided that polls should be opened in Berkeley and Jefferson counties on the fourth Thursday of May, 1863, to ascertain the wishes of the voters on the question of joining West Virginia. Berkeley County favored annexation by a vote of 645 for, to 7 against, and Jefferson by a vote of 248 to 2. These elections were held under the protection of Union soldiers three weeks before Lee's Confed-

erate army swept down the Valley in the Gettysburg campaign. The reorganized Virginia government, sitting at Alexandria, certified the results to the West Virginia legislature, which passed acts on August 5, 1863, and November 2, 1863, incorporating Berkeley and Jefferson into West Virginia. Finally, on March 10, 1866, a joint resolution of the Thirty-Ninth Congress approved these transfers.

After the Civil War Virginia tried to reunite the old state and the new. When this movement failed, she brought suit in the United States Supreme Court in 1867 to recover Berkeley and Jefferson counties. Meanwhile, on December 8, 1865, Virginia had repealed both her act of May 13, 1862, consenting to the formation of West Virginia and the acts of January and February, 1863, authorizing Berkeley and Jefferson counties to vote on their inclusion in West Virginia. Virginia argued that because she had withdrawn her consent the congressional joint resolution of March 10, 1866, which approved the transfer of Berkeley and Jefferson counties was null and void. Moreover, Virginia charged the coercion of voters and insisted that only a minority had participated in the elections. She also had the support of many residents who resented their summary inclusion in the war-born State of West Virginia. So piqued, for example, were the people of Jefferson by their alienation from Virginia that newspapers at the county seat carried "Charlestown, Virginia" at their mastheads.

West Virginia claimed that the admission of the state to the Union was a political question and thus outside the jurisdiction of the court. But the court took jurisdiction on the ground that it was essentially a boundary dispute and in its decision, handed down in 1871, not only denied Virginia's claim to Berkeley and Jefferson counties but also affirmed tacitly the constitutionality of the formation of West Virginia.

MR. JUSTICE MILLER DELIVERED the opinion of the court. . . . This [Second Wheeling] convention passed an ordinance, August 20, 1861, calling a convention of delegates from certain designated counties of the State of Virginia to form a constitution for a new State to be called Kanawha. . . .

The convention authorized by this ordinance assembled in Wheeling, November 26, 1861. It does not appear that either

Berkeley or Jefferson was represented, but it framed a constitution which, after naming the counties composing the new State in the first section of the first article, provided, by the second section, that if a majority of the votes cast at an election to be held for that purpose in the district composed of the counties of Berkeley, Jefferson, and Frederick, should be in favor of adopting the constitution, they should form a part of the State of West Virginia. . . . A distinct section also declares, in general terms, that additional territory may be admitted into and become part of the State with the consent of the legislature. . . .

Next in order of this legislative history is the act of the Virginia legislature of May 13, 1862, passed shortly after the vote above mentioned had been taken. This act gives the consent of the State of Virginia to the formation of the State of West Virginia out of certain counties named under the provisions set forth in its constitution, and by its second section it is declared that the consent of the legislature of Virginia is also given that the counties of Berkeley, Jefferson, and Frederick, shall be included in said State "*whenever* the voters of said counties shall ratify and assent to said constitution, at an election held for that purpose, at such time and under such regulations as the commissioners named in the said schedule may prescribe." . . .

The State of Virginia, in the ordinance which originated the formation of the new State, recognized something peculiar in the condition of these two counties, and some others. It gave them the option of sending delegates to the constitutional convention, and gave that convention the option to receive them. For some reason not developed in the legislative history of the matter these counties took no action on the subject. The convention, willing to accept them, and hoping they might still express their wish to come in, made provision in the new constitution that they might do so, and for their place in the legislative bodies, and in the judicial system, and inserted a general proposition for accession of territory to the new State. The State of Virginia, in expressing her satisfaction with the new State and its constitution, and her consent to its formation, by a special section, refers again to the counties of Berkeley, Jefferson, and Frederick, and enacts that whenever they shall, by a majority vote, assent to the constitution of the new State, they may become part thereof; and the legislature sends this statute to Congress with a request that it will admit the new State into the Union. . . .

It seems to us that here was an agreement between the old State and the new that these counties should become part of the latter, subject to that condition alone. Up to this time no vote had been taken in these counties; probably none could be taken under any but a hostile government. At all events, the bill alleges that none was taken on the proposition of May, 1862, of the Virginia legislature. If an agreement means the mutual consent of the parties to a given proposition, this was an agreement between these States for the transfer of these counties on the condition named. The condition was one which could be ascertained or carried out at any time; and this was clearly the idea of Virginia when she declared that *whenever* the voters of said counties should ratify and consent to the constitution they should become part of the State; and her subsequent legislation making special provision for taking the vote on this subject, as shown by the acts of January 31st and February 4th, 1863, is in perfect accord with this idea, and shows her good faith in carrying into effect the agreement.

2. But did Congress consent to this agreement?

Unless it can be shown that the consent of Congress, under that clause of the Constitution which forbids agreements between States without it, can only be given in the form of an express and formal statement of every proposition of the agreement, and of its consent thereto, we must hold that the consent of that body was given to this agreement. . . .

It is, therefore, an inference clear and satisfactory that Congress by that statute, intended to consent to the admission of the State with the contingent boundaries provided for in its constitution and in the statute of Virginia, which prayed for its admission on those terms, and that in so doing it necessarily consented to the agreement of those States on that subject.

There was then a valid agreement of those States consented to by Congress, which agreement made the accession of these counties dependent on the result of a popular vote in favor of that proposition.

3. But the Commonwealth of Virginia insists that no such vote was ever given; and we must inquire whether the facts alleged in the bill are such as to require an issue to be made on that question by the answer of the defendant.

The bill alleges the failure of the counties to take any action under the act of May, 1862, and that on the 31st of January and the 4th of February thereafter the two other acts we have mentioned were passed to enable such vote to be taken. These statutes provide very minutely for the taking of this vote under the authority of the State of Virginia; and, among other things, it is enacted that the governor shall ascertain the result, and, if he shall be of opinion that said vote has been opened and held and the result ascertained and certified pursuant to law, he shall certify that result under the seal of the State to the governor of West Virginia; and if a majority of the votes given at the polls were in favor of the proposition, then the counties became part of said State. . . .

These statutes were in no way essential to evidence the consent of Virginia to the original agreement, but were intended by her legislature to provide the means of ascertaining the wishes of the voters of these counties, that being the condition of the agreement on which the transfer of the counties depended.

The State thus showed her good faith to that agreement, and undertook in her own way and by her own officers to ascertain the fact in question.

. . . The vote was taken under these statutes, and certified to the governor. He was of opinion that the result was in favor of the transfer. He certified this fact under the seal of the State to the State of West Virginia, and the legislature of that State immediately assumed jurisdiction over the two counties, provided for their admission, and they have been a part of that State ever since.

Do the allegations of the bill authorize us to go behind all this and inquire as to what took place at this voting? To inquire how many votes were actually cast? How many of the men who had once been voters in these counties were then in the rebel army? Or had been there and were thus disfranchised? For all these and many more embarrassing questions must arise if the defendant is required to take issue on the allegations of the bill on this subject.

These allegations are indefinite and vague in this regard. It is charged that no fair vote was taken; but no act of unfairness is alleged. That no opportunity was afforded for a fair vote. That the governor was misled and deceived by the fraud of those who made him believe so. This is the substance of what is alleged. No one is charged specifically with the fraud. No particular act of fraud is stated. The governor is impliedly said to have acted in good faith. No charge of any kind of moral or legal wrong is made against the defendant, the State of West Virginia.

But, waiving these defects in the bill, we are of opinion that the action of the governor is conclusive of the vote as between the States of Virginia and West Virginia. . . . In a matter where that action was to be the foundation on which another sovereign State was to act—a matter which involved the delicate question of permanent boundary between the States and jurisdiction over a large population—a matter in which she took into her own hands the ascertainment of the fact on which these important propositions were by contract made to depend, she must be bound by what she had done. She can have no right, years after all this has been settled, to come into a court of chancery to charge that her own conduct has been a wrong and a fraud; that her own subordinate agents have misled her governors, and that her solemn act transferring these counties shall be set aside, against the will of the State of West Virginia, and without consulting the wishes of the people of those counties. . . . —Virginia v. West Virginia, 11 Wallace, 53-63, 1870.

133. The Constitution of 1872

Although the proposed Flick amendment provided for the restoration of the franchise to the former Confederates, the Democratic legislature of 1871, without waiting for the referendum on the amendment, repealed the proscriptive laws and submitted a proposal for a constitutional convention, which the voters adopted on August 24, 1871, by a vote of 30,220 to 27,638. At the October elections in 1871, the voters chose seventy-eight delegates to the convention, only a dozen of whom were Republicans. Democrats objected particularly to the township system of local government, voting by ballot, and omissions in the bill of rights. They argued that the Constitution of 1863 had been adopted as a wartime measure and ratified without the consent of the whole people.

The Convention assembled at Charleston on January 16, 1872, and organized with Samuel Price of Greenbrier County, a former lieutenant governor of Confederate Virginia, as presiding officer. The new constitution, which the Convention drafted in 84 days, closed the door to proscription and reformed state and local governments in the Virginia tradition. One of its provisions restored the magisterial district with a modified county court system, another gave the option to voters of selecting an open or a secret ballot. The new instrument contained an elaborate bill of rights affirming "the equality of man, the sovereignty of the people, the inalienable right of the majority and the repugnance of test oaths to the principles of free government." While reorganizing the legislative, executive, and judicial branches of state government to conform closely to the provisions of the Virginia constitution of 1851, the framers made martial law unconstitutional, prohibited political test oaths, denied the Legislature power to enact a registration law for voters, and guaranteed former Confederates against civil and criminal action for wartime deeds. The constitution was submitted to the voters on August 22, 1872, and ratified by a majority of 4,567 in a total vote of 80,121.

Whatever its merits as an instrument of government, the Constitution of 1872 wrote the epitaph of Radical reconstruction in West Virginia. The following passages are typical of its provisions.

THE PROVISIONS OF THE CONSTITUTION of the United States, and of this State, are operative alike in a period of war as in time of peace, and any departure therefrom, or violation thereof, under the plea of necessity, or any other plea, is subversive of good government, and tends to anarchy and despotism.—Article I, Sec. 3.

Political tests, requiring persons, as a pre-requisite to the enjoyment of their civil and political rights, to purge themselves by their own oaths, of past alleged offences, are repugnant to the principles of free Government, and are cruel and oppressive.

No religious or political test oath shall be required as a pre-re-quisite or qualification to vote, serve as a juror, sue, plead, appeal, or pursue any profession or employment. Nor shall any person be deprived by law, of any right or privilege, because of any act done prior to the passage of such law.—Article III, Sec. 11.

No citizen shall ever be denied or refused the right or privilege of voting at an election, because his name is not, or has not been registered, or listed, as a qualified voter.—Article IV, Sec. 12.

No citizen of this State who aided or participated in the late war between the government of the United States and a part of the people thereof, on either side, shall be liable in any proceeding, civil or criminal; nor shall his property be seized or sold under final process issued upon judgments or decrees heretofore rendered, or otherwise, because of any act done according to the usages of civilized warfare, in the prosecution of said war. . . .

The Legislature shall provide, by general law, for giving full force and effect to this section by due process of law.—Article VIII, Sec. 35.

134. J. H. Diss Debar's Promotional Campaign

Joseph H. Diss Debar, author of the state motto and designer of the state seals, was West Virginia's first good-will ambassador and salesman. As Commissioner of Immigration from 1864 to 1871, he promoted an advertising campaign in the United States and abroad designed to interest the capitalist and settler in the opportunities provided by the State's natural resources and geographical location. He was instrumental in establishing the Swiss colony of Helvetia in Randolph County.

For all his pains Diss Debar received scant public support. Without salary over long periods and with meager expense funds, he wrote personal letters, contributed articles to newspapers, issued pamphlets in several European languages, and finally in

1870 published at his own expense the classic WEST VIRGINIA HAND-BOOK AND IMMIGRANT'S GUIDE. *When refused an appropriation by the Legislature, Diss Debar paid out of his own pocket for a display of West Virginia products at the Paris Exposition in 1867.*

Democratic Governor John J. Jacob ignored Diss Debar's unexcelled qualifications and removed him from office in 1871, despite supporting recommendations from leaders in both political parties. The following passages throw light on West Virginia and its people as Diss Debar described them and reveal his plans to attract refugees of the Franco-Prussian War to West Virginia.

THE GENUINE RURAL WEST VIRGINIAN is not much addicted to precipitous motion, rarely loses his temper or self-possession, and beyond the acquisition of the necessaries of life, limited by almost Spartan frugality, is disposed to leave the improvement of things around him to time and chance. This unprogressive disposition is the more striking, as his native intellect and sagacity are extraordinary and susceptible of high development under proper direction or the stimulus of personal ambition. Perhaps nowhere on the continent are there such treasures of natural power buried under the rust of indolence and prejudice, and at the same time such a display of urbanity and hospitality prompted by native tact and geniality. The political differences, private feuds and various changes consequent upon the late civil strife, may have left their mark upon the traditional virtues of West Virginians, yet enough survives of these to suggest a favorable contrast with popular manners in States North and West of us. Very unlike the proverbial Jonathan, the West Virginian seldom inquires into his neighbors business with indelicate curiosity, and no matter how strong or antagonistic his convictions, never intrudes them upon strangers in aggressive or controversial discourse.

Yet, to presume from these amiable traits upon an unlimited dose of meekness in the West Virginia mountaineer would be a serious mistake. His self-esteem is not by far the least prominent of his characteristics, and insults, even more than injuries, are quickly resented. The history of the late war teems with feats of West Virginia valor; both armies counted her sons by thousands, and among them not a few distinguished leaders, and heroes of the rank and file. On many a memorable field, schoolmates, friends, relatives, nay, brothers, met face to face under the deadly fire, always true to their cause and worthy of each others steel.

Nor is the geniality of the West Virginian permitted to temper his acuteness in matters of business, when business there is. While he seldom steps out of a leisurely walk in the pursuit of wordly lucre, he watches his personal interests with an eye that kindles up never more brightly behind its drowsy lashes, than when a chance for a *trade* or a speculation comes within reach. Then quickly his dormant faculties are aroused and concentrated upon the point—vital to his fame no less than to his purse—how to get the best of the bargain; and whether the object of barter be a horse or a saddle, an ox or a gun, a house or a farm, the principle "your eyes *is* your market" is strictly kept in view and a bargain once struck is seldom rued, except for a consideration. Many a cunning speculator whose laurels were conquered in Wall Street or in more northern latitudes, after plying his arts among our homespun population, recrossed the Alleghanies a wiser and a *lighter* man.—*The West Virginia Hand-Book and Immigrant's Guide*, pp. 33-36.

I herewith have the honor to enclose two documents giving the details of a plan for the attraction of immigration, which I had submitted to the Legislature at the last session, but was not acted upon by the proper Committees, because no hope was entertained of securing a sufficient appropriation to carry it out.

The appropriation to carry out the immigration bill introduced by Hon. Lewis Baker of the Senate should have been $5000. Despairing to obtain this sum, the friends of the bill reduced the amount to $2500, from which another $1000 was striken off on the final vote. So that The Board of Immigration has only $1500 to pay the Commissioner and all expenses for the current year. . . .

With the scant appropriation of $1500, it is out of question to carry out the plan I submitted to the Legislature, but with judgment and economy much may be done at least to keep the inducements of our State before the world. Whether I am permitted to retain the office or not, I respectfully beg leave to submit my views in regard to the most judicious application of that fund

5,000 pamphlets of 8-to 10 pages, English	$	150.-
3,000 " " " German	"	90.-
2,000 " " " French	"	60.-
400 copies of W. Va. Handbook, paper bd.	"	300.-
One trip to other States to appoint correspondents for distribution of printed informn.	"	100.-
Postages, stationery, advertising, and contingencies	"	200.-
Salary and office rent of Commr.	"	600.-
		$1500

... I need scarcely say that until Charleston is placed in more direct communication with the seaports and Northern States, the office of the Commr. to be of practical service, should be located at some point of the Balt. & O. R. R.. I was induced by Gov. Boreman to remove from my home in Doddridge Cy, to Parkersburg, which is accessible both by river and rail, and cannot be excelled in the State for convenience in my business.

Having lately placed the inducements of W. Va. to manufacturing enterprises before the Chambers of Commerce of Strasbourg, & Mulhouse in Alsace* and of Metz in Lorraine, with a view of securing a portion of the valuable population, skill and capital about to emigrate from those provinces, I am of opinion, that a formal invitation from the Executive, or The Board of Immigration, confirming my representation of our resources would be of great weight with the people there at present. I have no doubt but that other States will not neglect so rare an opportunity to parade their inducements, and I shall therefore take the liberty to submit to you by tomorrows mail, the form of a document for the purpose indicated.—J. H. Diss Debar to Governor John J. Jacob, March 6, 1871, John J. Jacob Papers, West Virginia Collection, West Virginia University Library.

*My native province.

XII. The Bourbon Years, 1871-1897

135. Tax Exemptions and Fiscal Policy, 1863-1883

West Virginia tax receipts fell short of revenue needs during the early years of statehood. Not only did the Legislature exempt certain agricultural and industrial products from assessment but State and local governments failed to bring certain railroads under the general tax laws. The Baltimore and Ohio challenged the right of taxing authorities to levy upon its property on the ground that the railroad was exempt from taxation under provisions of its charter and an act of the Legislature, passed December 3, 1863. While defending its claims in the courts, the railroad company carried its fight to the West Virginia legislature, where leaders in both political parties supported measures providing for low levies on property of the company or exemption of the road from taxation altogether. Finally on March 4, 1869, the Legislature adopted a joint resolution which authorized the State Board of Public Works and county supervisors to compromise taxes assessed against the Baltimore and Ohio up to December 31, 1868. The company withdrew the two cases it had appealed to the United States Supreme Court but for a decade frustrated the efforts of State and local governments to tax much of its property.

The State found the Achilles' heel of the tax-exempt interests when Governor Henry Mason Mathews challenged the legality of a provision of the charter granted by the Legislature to the Covington and Ohio Railroad, March 1, 1866, which exempted that company from State and local taxes until the annual net profits of the corporation amounted to ten per cent of the capital invested. Soon renamed the Chesapeake and Ohio and opened to Huntington in 1873, that company successfully resisted State and local taxation until 1879, when the Legislature passed an act which brought it under the general assessment and tax laws.

Thus when the Chesapeake and Ohio Railway Company obtained an injunction against the assessment and taxation of its properties, Auditor Joseph S. Miller carried the issue to the

State Supreme Court of Appeals which, on April 22, 1882, handed down a decision that ended most tax exemptions claimed by the railroads as well as those enjoyed by farmers and others under a section of statutes passed in 1863, 1875, and 1881, which exempted from assessment certain farm products and articles of manufacture. As a result, in April, 1883, after the Legislature had refused to repeal the act of 1881, Auditor Miller, acting at the request of Governor Jacob B. Jackson, issued an order to county assessors directing them to disregard the statutory exemptions and list for taxation all property not plainly exempted from levy by the constitution.

The following documents and extracts throw a flood of light upon West Virginia's early fiscal problems.

[No. 19] Joint Resolution creating a board to settle with the Baltimore and Ohio Railroad Company for back taxes.

1. The board of public works, consisting of the governor, auditor, and treasurer of this State, is hereby constituted a board or committee, with full power to adjust, compromise and settle, on fair, equitable and liberal terms, all State and school taxes assessed against the Baltimore and Ohio Railroad Company and Parkersburg branch thereof, up to December thirty-first, eighteen hundred and sixty-eight, and upon payment into the State treasury of the amount agreed between said board and said company, the said company shall be discharged from all liability for the same.

2. The board of supervisors of each county through which the Baltimore and Ohio Railroad and Parkersburg branch runs, are hereby authorized and empowered to compromise and settle, on fair and liberal terms, all taxes assessed against said company by any of the said counties and townships.

ADOPTED, March 4, 1869—*Acts of the Legislature of West Virginia,* p. 113.

PROPERTY EXEMPT FROM TAXATION

43. All property, real or personal, described in this section, and to the extent herein limited, shall be exempt from taxation, that is to say: . . .

Agricultural productions grown directly from the soil, and the products and increase in number of livestock produced within this State during the year preceding the first day of February, and remaining unsold on that day in the possession of the original owner or his agent;

The produce during the same time of mines, salt wells, and oil wells within this State, remaining unsold in the hands of the producer or his agent, on the first day of February; And all manufactured articles and products of mechanical skill and labor, produced in this State during the same time, and remaining unsold on the first day of February in the hands of the producer or his agent.—*Acts of the Legislature of West Virginia,* 1875, pp. 93-94.

JOHNSON, PRESIDENT . . .

The provision in question is section 1 of Article VIII of the Constitution of 1863. It is as follows: "Taxation shall be equal and uniform throughout the State; and all property, both real and personal, shall be taxed in proportion to its value, to be ascertained as directed by law. No one species of property, from which a tax may be collected, shall be taxed higher than any other species of property of equal value; but property used for educational, literary, scientific, religious or charitable purposes, and public property may by law be exempted from taxation." . . .

No authority, to which we have been cited, or which we have found, sustains the constitutionality of so much of the seventh section of the act of March 1, 1866, as exempts the property therein mentioned from taxation. Can there be any doubt, that the said act to this extent is in violation of the Constitution of 1863? The section of the Constitution we have been considering declares, first, that "taxation shall be equal and uniform throughout the state." This is very strong language and, to say the least of it, would prevent inequality and want of uniformity in taxing the subjects, which the Legislature might declare should be taxed. . . .

Much respect as we have for the Legislature, a co-ordinate branch of the government, we must pay greater respect to the sovereign will of the people expressed in the Constitution, which they have adopted for their own government. And where the court sees, that the Legislature has plainly violated that instrument, it is the highest duty of the court, plainly required by the written Constitution, which it is its sworn duty to support, to pronounce such act of the Legislature unconstitutional.—Chesapeake and Ohio R. Co. v. J. S. Miller, Auditor, 19 W. Va., 423-37, 1882.

136. The Great Railway Strike of 1877

Henry Mason Mathews (1834-1884) was the first of the line of West Virginia Democratic governors called the "Virginia Dynasty." Born at Frankford, Greenbrier County, educated at the Lewisburg Academy and the University of Virginia, he studied law at Lexington, practiced at Lewisburg, and taught in Allegheny College at Blue Sulphur Springs. Mathews served in the Confederate army during the Civil War and rose to the rank of major. When elected to the West Virginia senate in 1865, that body refused to seat him because of his Confederate service. After the restoration of political and civil rights to former Confederates, he sat as a member of the constitutional convention of 1872 and served as attorney general of West Virginia from 1873 to 1877. His term as governor (1877-1881) marked the transition in West Virginia from depression to upturn in the West Virginia economy.

Nevertheless Governor Mathews faced many problems growing out of the depression of the 1870's. When the Baltimore and Ohio Railroad company reduced wages of non-salaried employees in the summer of 1877, members of the locomotive firemen and engineer unions at Martinsburg left their jobs and precipitated a strike which spread to other trunk lines. Governor Mathews promptly called out the few companies of militia fit for duty, only to find many of the men sympathetic with the strikers. He then appealed to President Hayes for troops which promptly restored order and suppressed the strike at Martinsburg.

Governor Mathews recounted the events of those July days in a message to the West Virginia legislature.

DURING THE NIGHT OF THE 16TH OF JULY, 1877, I was informed that the engineers and firemen of the Baltimore and Ohio Railroad Company had become dissatisfied with the wages offered them, and had ceased to work; that a large mob had assembled at Martinsburg, where there were many trains loaded with freight, some of which consisted of live stock and perishable goods, and that they would not permit the trains to be moved—threatening violence to persons and destruction to property. I was applied to for aid to enable the civil authorities to execute the laws, and was also informed that rioters, when arrested, were immediately rescued by the mob. I at once telegraphed to Colonel C. J. Faulkner, Jr., *Aide-de-Camp*, and requested him to inform me as to the trouble, and his reply confirmed the information which I had already received.

Colonel Faulkner had a short time before organized a volunteer company, which had been armed and equipped, and I instructed him to aid, with his company, the civil authorities to preserve the peace, to execute the laws, and to protect from interference and violence those who were willing to work in moving trains or otherwise.

He endeavored promptly to carry out these instructions. The next morning, as a train was moving out from the depot, one of the rioters attempted to stop it by displacing a switch. The switch was being adjusted by one of the volunteers, when he was fired upon and wounded by one of the rioters. The fire was returned and a rioter mortally wounded. This was the only conflict which occurred in this State during the period of the disturbances. Immediately after this occurrence, Colonel Faulkner advised me that his force was too small to cope with the mob, who seemed to be sustained by the sympathy of the citizens, and that if troops were to be used, they should be sent from some other point; that many members of his company were railroad employees, in sympathy with the rioters, and could not be relied upon. There were then but two other companies in the State—one at Wheeling, commanded by Captain (now Colonel) W. W. Miller, the other at Moorefield, commanded by Captain J. Chipley. I ordered Captain Miller to proceed at once, with his company, to Martinsburg, and report to the civil authorities, and gave him instructions similar to those which had been given to Colonel Faulkner. . . .

Having brought into the service all of the State troops, and the civil authorities having confessed that with the aid of this force it was still impossible to execute the laws, the condition of affairs was such that either the riot would continue or the Federal Government must be applied to for a sufficient force. Under these circumstances I telegraphed to the President of the United States and asked for such a force, and in a short time was informed by the Secretary of War, that two hundred and fifty soldiers would be furnished. They were sent to Martinsburg and arrived there the morning of the 19th. The presence of these troops had a salutary effect. The rioters were dispersed and arrests were then made by the civil authorities, supported by Captain Miller's company....

It was deemed advisable to retain the troops, both State and Federal, for several weeks, at Martinsburg, Sir John's Run, Keyser, Piedmont and Grafton, as for some time there was considerable excitement along the Baltimore and Ohio railroad, and especially at these points were there indications of the existence of a spirit of lawlessness.... —Message of Governor Henry Mason Mathews, *Journal of the House of Delegates*, 1879, pp. 32-33.

137. The Floating Capital

The location of the State capital became a subject of political and sectional controversy soon after the Civil War when Governor Arthur I. Boreman requested the Legislature to designate a permanent capital site. But the law-makers took no action until 1869, when they adopted a resolution declaring that failure to locate the capital had created great dissatisfaction among the people, deterred enterprise, and rendered West Virginians "an unsettled people in the estimation of the public." It was therefore no surprise that the Legislature promptly named Charleston as the capital city, effective April 1, 1870.

Although Charleston residents provided a capitol building with accessory accommodations and the Chesapeake and Ohio Railroad reached the city in 1872, the Legislature, after political logrolling, passed an act in 1875 which again established the seat of government at Wheeling. The selection of a permanent location for the offices of state government remained a topic of "earnest discussion" until February 1877, when the Legislature

voted to submit the choice of site to the voters who would cast
ballots at an election to be held August 7, 1877, for one of three
cities—Charleston, Clarksburg, and Martinsburg. When the cer-
tified election returns showed that Charleston had received a
majority of the votes cast, Governor Henry M. Mathews issued
a proclamation declaring that city the permanent capital of the
State, effective May 1, 1885.

The table below shows how voters cast their ballots by coun-
ties at the election held August 7, 1877.

Counties	Clarks-burg	Mart-ins-burg	Char-les-ton	Counties	Clarks-burg	Mart-ins-burg	Char-les-ton
Barbour	1,415	4	4	Mineral	561	160	155
Berkeley	48	3,569	1	Monongalia	1,188	4	626
Boone	____	____	960	Monroe	8	7	1,404
Braxton	293	11	951	Morgan	40	573	5
Brooke	656	40	34	Nicholas	15	____	965
Cabell	6	____	1,832	Ohio	2,165	1,193	218
Calhoun	160	2	587	Pendleton	189	146	280
Clay	____	____	479	Pleasants	446	8	93
Doddridge	1,587	2	39	Pocahontas	259	____	241
Fayette	____	____	1,760	Preston	1,798	32	42
Gilmer	653	1	225	Putnam	5	____	1,654
Grant	310	87	116	Raleigh	2	____	1,034
Greenbrier	5	____	1,902	Randolph	859	2	31
Hampshire	160	149	573	Ritchie	1,572	2	145
Hancock	414	8	95	Roane	2	____	1,995
Hardy	226	187	594	Summers	3	1	1,410
Harrison	3,875	____	13	Taylor	1,086	172	141
Jackson	68	1	2,169	Tucker	363	1	6
Jefferson	41	1,340	328	Tyler*	____	____	____
Kanawha	42	2	6,140	Upshur	843	60	163
Lewis	1,426	29	261	Wayne	2	1	2,011
Lincoln	____	____	1,167	Webster	79	____	362
Logan	1	1	885	Wetzel	1,226	2	51
McDowell	____	____	308	Wirt	238	24	612
Marion	2,431	12	140	Wood	1,253	186	1,302
Marshall	1,473	23	206	Wyoming	2	____	566
Mason	18	3	3,004				
Mercer	____	____	1,017	Totals	29,942	8,046	41,243

*No return

—*Second Biennial Report of the Department of Archives and*
History, 1908, p. 312.

138. Archibald W. Campbell: Republican Profile

As editor of the only anti-slavery daily newspaper in Virginia before the Civil War, Archibald W. Campbell displayed great political and personal courage. Campbell won a badge of courage in the Republican National Convention at Chicago in 1880 when he and two other West Virginia delegates opposed a resolution introduced by Senator Roscoe Conkling, of New York, designed to commit the Convention to the support of the nominee in advance. After Senator Conkling had offered a resolution to expel the dissenting West Virginians, Campbell delivered a heroic speech which not only caused Conkling to withdraw the resolution but opened the way for the nomination of James A. Garfield for President.

MR. CAMPBELL, of West Virginia. *Mr. President:* Before the resolution is put to this Convention, I desire to make a few remarks. There are three gentlemen from West Virginia, good and true Republicans, who have voted in the negative. I came to the City of Chicago, when a young man, from the State of Virginia, after having submitted for twenty years to contumely and to violence in that State for my Republican principles,—and if it has come to this, that in this City of Chicago, a delegate from that State to a Republican Convention cannot have a free expression of his opinion, I for one am willing to withdraw from this Convention. Mr. President, I have been a Republican in the State of Virginia from my youth. For twenty-three years I have published a Republican newspaper in that State. I have supported every Presidential Republican nominee in that time. I expect to support the nominee of this Convention. But, sir, as a Republican, I imbibed my principles from the great statesman from New York, William H. Seward, with whom I had an early acquaintance by virtue of my having gone to school with him near the City of Utica, from which the gentleman from New York [Mr. Conkling] now hails. I was a Republican then, and I made the acquaintance of that distinguished gentleman. I came home, and in my youth I became a newspaper editor. From that day to this—from the John Brown raid on Harper's Ferry all through the troubles of the last twenty-five years—I have consistently and always supported our State and National Republican nominees. But, Mr. President, I feel, as a Republican, that there is a principle in this question, and I will never come into any Convention and agree beforehand that whatever may be done by that Convention shall have my endorsement. Sir, as a free man, whom God made free, I always intend to carry my sovereignty under my own hat. [Applause.] I never intend that any body of men shall take it from me. I do not, Mr. President, make my living by politics; I make it by my labor as a newspaper editor; and I am not afraid to go home and say that I stood up here in this Convention and expressed my honest opinion, as I was not afraid to stand up in the State of West Virginia, when but 2,500 men were found to vote for Abraham Lincoln, though, I am glad to say, that that party has risen to-day to 45,000 votes under the training that we received, and from the early inspiration of Republican principles. I am not afraid, sir, to go home and face those men as I have faced them always.—*Proceedings of the Republican National Convention, Held at Chicago, Illinois,* June 2-8, 1880, pp. 36-37.

139. Resources and Advantages of West Virginia, 1880-1900

Although the State withheld financial support after 1879, the campaign to advertise West Virginia resources and opportunities launched by J. H. Diss Debar moved ahead, as West Virginia officials and business leaders endeavored to attract capital and labor to the State. Messages, speeches, books, pamphlets, articles, editorials and letters advertised the climate, natural resources, cheap lands, transportation and market facilities, low taxes, and other inducements offered by the Mountain State. The following extracts are typical.

RARE COMBINATION OF BEAUTIFUL VALLEY and lordly mountain, railroad and deep river, forest and mineral, and golden laden grain fields.

Not alone is the eye attracted by the glistening steel of the great trunk lines, but West Virginia energy and pluck is driving the locomotive up the lesser valleys, opening up new avenues of commerce, and carrying, like the trickling rivulets, each its drop to the great arteries of trade. . . .

What is the conclusion of the whole matter? The State is filled with coal and timber and oil, and has vast quantities of iron ore. It is an axiom of political economy that the coal, iron and heavier products will attract the lighter products, cotton, wheat and wool and each of their products and manufactures. The hand of Providence has placed us at the gateway of the rich Mississippi valley, with which we are connected by river and rail, and to which region we are nearer than any other good coal and coke producing State. We lie contiguous to the great ore producing regions of the lakes; they must have and are now taking all of the coal and coke that we can produce. We are less than twenty-four hours travel of the manufactories of New York, Philadelphia and the east. The State is not alone confined to the west and the east and our own southern country, but the great wharves at Norfolk and Newport News have been constructed primarily to send abroad by steam and sail, West Virginia's coal and coke. . . .

With no drouths nor cyclones, with a climate that the workman can labor outside twelve months in the year, with cheap lands, with coal inexhaustible in extent and perfect in quality, with no racial question nor sectional feeling, with the markets at our doors, with timber and iron and oils, with a liberty-loving and conservative people, with a hearty welcome to the intelligent stranger who will come among us, West Virginia is confidently marching onward to commercial greatness and power.—*Address of Governor William A. MacCorkle at the World's Columbian Exposition, Chicago, on "West Virginia Day," August 23, 1893,* pp. 6, 11-12.

Then again, the impression is abroad that West Virginia is a far-off southern state. Is this correct? . . . The position of the state in the Union makes it easy of access from all the great business centers. No state in the Union is so well situated in respect to an outlet for its products, and no other state enjoys the exceptional advantages of having for its market both the east and west. About one-half of its coal, coke, lumber and other products go east to the Atlantic seaboard, while the other half go west and is distributed in the great Mississippi valley. West Virginia coal and coke are shipped daily to Chicago. . . . According to its area, West Virginia is the richest state in the Union in natural resources. Its future is assured, and it is destined to be both populous and prosperous.—*Speech of Hon. Stephen B. Elkins of West Virginia, Delivered on West Virginia State Day at the Columbian Exposition, Chicago, August 23, 1893, pp. 1-3.*

Native labor is largely used in these mines, that of the young white men raised in the vicinity. The superintendent informed us that it was abundant, and in his opinion as good as any the world could furnish. As an evidence of its character and thrift we may mention that two of these young men have received in cash, at the end of each month, of the last 18 never less than $100 apiece, as wages for mining coal by the ton, and that in the mean time they have bought and paid some $2,000 for a farm and have nearly another $1,000 in cash on hand.—We desire to call the attention of our strong young men, who are so frequently drifting westward to "take their chances," to the sure and good rewards that honest labor can now find in healthy occupations, at the rapidly developing mines and iron works of our Virginia states. The world nowhere offers better inducements for the industrious, all things considered, than are now offered here.— "Hawks-nest Coal Co., (limited)," *The Virginias*, II, (April, 1881), 52.

The Gauley river with its several large tributaries drains a valley which covers nearly 5,000 square miles; its length is about 110 miles, much less than that of the Elk, which is a long slender stream, but it occupies a much broader valley and has twice the volume of water of the Elk. . . . Above a point 15 miles from its mouth no timber has been touched except by the few settlers. In the lower part of the valley of the Gauley, for 15 or more miles the timber is chiefly oak, poplar, walnut, etc. The Gauley and its large affluents, the Cherry, Cranberry and Williams rivers, all head back in the forests of black spruce, which sometimes take entire possession of the mountain tops; a little lower, yet often mingled with the spruce, hemlocks and black cherry abound. On Cherry river the cherry trees so predominate over all others as to have given their name to the stream. Here are trees often 4 feet in diameter. The region intermediate between the lower and the upper districts of the Gauley thus described, contains much beech, sugar maple and black cherry. . . .—"The Forests of West Virginia," *The Virginias*, VI, (February, 1885), 31-32.

140. Johnson N. Camden Defends Standard Oil

Born in Lewis County, Johnson Newlon Camden (1828-1908) received his early education in subscription schools, attended the United States Military Academy and became in turn a surveyor, lawyer, prosecuting attorney, bank clerk, merchant, and land speculator. He was a pioneer oil producer in the Little Kanawha field on the eve of the Civil War and during that conflict "attended to his own business." He established the First National Bank of Parkersburg in 1863, and two years later a successful oil refining plant. Unsuccessful as Democratic candidate for governor of West Virginia in 1868 and 1872, Camden served as United States Senator from 1881 to 1887, and from 1893 to 1895. In the meantime he acquired coal and timber lands, built railroads, erected band mills, and opened mines. In 1875 he transferred ownership of his refinery to the Standard Oil Company and became John D. Rockefeller's chief lieutenant in West Virginia.

On September 28, 1878, a joint investigating committee of the West Virginia legislature held a meeting in Parkersburg and heard the testimony of shippers who regularly employed the facilities of the Baltimore and Ohio Railroad. Johnson N. Camden, president of the Camden Consolidated Oil Company, was one of the witnesses called. At that time the open through rate for seaboard shipments on the Baltimore and Ohio for refined oil was $1.75 per barrel; Camden's company however received *secret rebates totaling $1.08 1/2, making the actual cost of shipment 66 1/2 cents per barrel. On lubricating oil it shipped on a through rate of $1.12 1/2 per barrel but received a rebate of 50 cents, making the actual rate 66 1/2 cents. Camden went willingly before the committee but curtly refused to answer important questions.*

The extract below has been taken from Camden's testimony before the joint legislative committee, appointed to investigate freight rates on the Baltimore and Ohio Railroad in West Virginia.

J. N. CAMDEN,

President of the Camden Consolidated Oil Company appeared before the Committee and after being duly sworn deposes as follows:

By Chairman D. D. Johnson.

1. Q.—What is the rate of freight that you pay upon oil transported for your Company by the Baltimore & Ohio Company from this place to Baltimore?

A.—$1.75 per barrel, is, I believe, the tariff rate of the Baltimore & Ohio Railroad.

2. Q.—Does the Baltimore & Ohio Company grant your Company any further rebate, in the rate of freights? If so, what is it?

A.—The arrangements between the Baltimore and Ohio Railroad Company and ourselves, affects our private interests, and it might be to our disadvantage to answer that question, which at present I decline to answer.

And further deponent sayeth not.—*Testimony before Joint Committee of Legislature of West Virginia Appointed to Enquire into the Charges for Freight and Travel of the Baltimore and Ohio Railroad,* p. 34, 1879.

141. A Protest Against Absentee Ownership, 1884

While public officials and businessmen endeavored to attract investment capital to West Virginia, others considered unrestrained development of the State's natural resources by outsiders inimical to the public interest. Although a voice in the wilderness, the following excerpt from the second report of the

State Tax Commission in 1884 correctly prophesied the fate of West Virginia resources and disclosed with remarkable clarity the collusion existing between corporate interests and political parties in West Virginia.

Shall Our Wealth Pass to Strangers?

The wealth of this State is immense; the development of this wealth will earn vast private fortunes far beyond the dreams even of a modern Croesus; the question is, whether this vast wealth shall belong to persons who live here and who are permanently identified with the future of West Virginia, or whether it shall pass into the hands of persons who do not live here and who care nothing for our State except to pocket the treasures which lie buried in our hills?

If the people of West Virginia can be roused to an appreciation of the situation we ourselves will gather this harvest now ripe on the lands inherited from our ancestors; on the other hand if the people are not roused to an understanding of the situation in less than ten years this vast wealth will have passed from our present population into the hands of non-residents, and West Virginia will be almost like Ireland and her history will be like that of Poland.

It is Difficult to Arrest Public Attention.

But there is another feature of the situation in West Virginia. The men who are stimulated by a private interest frequently become the managers of politics and public business is often shaped to advance their money-making schemes. The influence of these managers of politics, stimulated as they are by hopes of pecuniary gain, cannot be exaggerated. . . . The representatives of vast private interests are always present at the Legislature to advance the schemes of their employers, which schemes are often ruinous to the State and would not be tolerated for an instant if the facts were published. The representatives of these large private interests are always persistent to misrepresent the motives of and to malign every man who speaks one word or promulgates one fact to enlighten his neighbors; while on the other hand the newspapers generally find it profitable to suppress the truth and to publish what is false. The result is, that the best talent in the State is either intimidated or else excluded from the public service and the most important business of government is, to a large extent, conducted by men unacquainted with the situation and unprepared to apply the remedy.—J. M. Mason, E. A. Bennett, and Joseph Bell, *West Virginia Tax Commission, Second Report, State Development,* November 22, 1884, pp. 3, 7-8.

142. Railroad Discrimination Against the Short Haul

After completion of the Baltimore and Ohio Railroad to the Ohio River in 1853 that company consistently charged higher rates on goods shipped from stations east of the Ohio to Baltimore than on like consignments to the same destination from competitive points on the river and farther west. The Chesapeake and Ohio discriminated against West Virginia shippers in like manner. So burdensome was this differential in the mid-1880's that West Virginia shippers complained for good reason that they "would be better off 500 miles west." Clearly this Peter-to-Paul policy of the trunk line railroads retarded economic development and deprived West Virginia of inherent geographical advantages. Small wonder that the local industrialist joined the aggrieved farmer in demanding relief. Governor E. Willis Wilson urged prompt legislative action in messages to the Legislature, and United States Senator Johnson N. Camden, then expanding coal and lumber operations in interior West Virginia, argued successfully for an explicit prohibition against the short-haul discrimination in the Interstate Commerce Act of 1887.

Mr. Camden. . . . But, Mr. President, the evils of this kind of discrimination complained of are not confined by any means to the long hauls from the West. . . . Take, for instance, competitive points along the Ohio River—where low rates prevail by reason of competition—and the non-competitive points 50 and

100, or even 200 miles nearer the market, the same products going in the same direction are often charged 50 per cent more, and sometimes double the amount of the longer haul from the Ohio River or beyond it.

. . . It is a notorious fact that men engaged in agricultural and stock-raising pursuits in West Virginia and other States near the Eastern markets, who ship their products from points one-half to three-fourths nearer the markets, will be met in the same markets with the same kind of products shipped two or three times the distance, coming by their own doors at greatly less rates, often as much as one-half less. . . .

. . . I challenge any satisfactory reason for it. If we are in earnest about passing a bill that will reach the greatest evils of discrimination let us meet the question fairly and squarely. —*Congressional Record*, April 16, 1886, p. 3554.

On information from various reliable sources, the following charges will indicate to some extent, the gross and glaring injustice that has been practiced against this State:

Grain, per cwt. from St. Louis, Mo., to Atlantic Seaboard $	08
Grain, per cwt. from Hinton, W. Va., to Atlantic Seaboard	20
Coal per ton from Cumberland, Md., to Baltimore, Md.	1 00
Coal per ton from Cumberland, Md. to Harper's Ferry, W. Va.	2 10
Cattle, per car, from St. Louis, Mo., to Atlantic Seaboard	26 00
Cattle, per car, from Chicago, to Atlantic Seaboard	35 00
Cattle, per car, from Clarksburg, W. Va., to Atlantic Seaboard	65 00
Cattle, per car, from Cabell Co., W. Va., to Atlantic Seaboard	70 00
Cattle, per car, from East of Charleston, W. Va., to Atlantic Seaboard	75 00
Cattle, per car, from Summers Co., W. Va., to Atlantic Seaboard	80 00
. . . Passenger fare from Washington to Charleston, W. Va.	$12 00
. . . to Cincinnati, more than 250 miles farther . . .	11 00

A gentleman in the eastern part of this State had six or eight horses to be shipped from Cincinnati to Keyser, W. Va. He found the charges to be:

From Cincinnati to Keyser_____$96 00

From Cincinnati to Baltimore, over 200 miles farther____78 00

In another case, a gentleman of Harper's Ferry had shipped to that point from Chicago, a car load of oats. The charges were:

From Chicago to Harper's Ferry_____$120 00

From Chicago to Baltimore, but little more than 70
    miles farther_____ 50 00

A few years ago the Harper's Ferry water power was purchased from the United States, by a Mr. Savory and others, with the intention of erecting a pulp and paper manufactory, that would give employment to hundreds of people. The work was at once commenced, but, ascertaining from Baltimore and Ohio Railroad officials that the freight rates from Baltimore, Philadelphia and New York, to Cincinnati and other points, would be less than from Harper's Ferry to the same points, and even from Harper's Ferry to Baltimore, the enterprise had to be abandoned, to await the mercy and condescension of the railroad masters of trade and commerce.—Special Message of Governor E. Willis Wilson, April 20, 1887, *Journal of the House of Delegates of the State of West Virginia, Extra Session*, pp. 11-12.

143. A Liberal Democrat in The Statehouse

Of the six Democrats who occupied the governor's chair from 1871 to 1897, only Emanuel Willis Wilson (1844-1905) bore the stamp of liberal and reformer. Born at Harpers Ferry, he obtained a public-school and business-college education, read law and began practice at Charles Town in 1869. While representing Jefferson County in the West Virginia house of delegates from 1871 to 1873, he won election to the State senate and gained distinction in that body when he successfully filibustered against a bill designed to transfer public franchise rights of the Kanawha River to a private corporation. After moving to

Charleston in 1876 he entered the House of Delegates from Kanawha County and became speaker of that body. An untiring orator, Governor Wilson bore the nickname "Windy" or "East Wind" Wilson.

Wilson entered the Democratic state convention in 1884 with strong popular support and won the nomination for governor, despite the opposition of the Democratic state organization and dissaffected Bourbon leaders. Wilson triumphed over his Republican opponent Edwin Maxwell in the general election and served beyond his elected term until settlement in 1890 of the Goff-Fleming gubernatorial contest.

Governor Wilson promoted measures to improve working conditions in industry, to prevent the pollution of streams, to regulate railroads, and to revise the election laws. On his recommendation the Legislature forbade the issuance of railroad passes to public officials and strengthened the corrupt practices act but refused to enact a registration law. Wilson also recommended the adoption of the Australian ballot system without success in 1889; two years later, however, the Legislature passed an Australian ballot law upon the recommendation of his successor, Governor Aretus Brooks Fleming.

The following extracts from Wilson's messages to the Legislature indicate his views on the subjects of the railroad pass evil, political corruption, and election reform.

THE PRACTICE OF RAILROAD COMPANIES issuing to public officers, free passes over their roads, is another abuse to which I call your attention. That this is done with an improper motive is so transparent as to admit of no question. . . . it can not be a matter of surprise that a feeling of distrust prevades the public mind, when the public servant, whether Legislative, Judiciary, or Executive, holds the laws of his country in one hand and a railroad pass in the other. . . .

I most earnestly recommend the enactment of law to prohibit the delivery of such passes to any and every officer within this State; and that the penalties be sufficient to put an end to the abuse. . . .

Bribery at elections, by our laws, is a punishable crime; yet it is no violation of the law to use the very means to secure nominations for public office, that would constitute bribery at an election. . . . The use of money to secure individual support and advocacy, and the delivery of railroad passes to delegates to political conventions favoring the nomination to public office of such candidates as railroad officials may desire nominated are the common methods now practiced. The use of railroad passes for such purpose in this State, has become so open and notorious as to be thrust upon the attention of every observing man. . . . The manifest purpose of such methods is to control by corruption; crush intellectual and moral worth; deter public utterance for the public good; deprive the State of its best talent for public service; stifle public sentiment and thwart the public will. . . . I recommend that these dangerous and abominable abuses be declared felonious crimes.—Message of Governor E. Willis Wilson, January 12, 1887, *Journal of the House of Delegates,* 1887, pp. 29-30.

. . . Throughout the country, for months last past, the very atmosphere has been laden with the cry of fraud. Reproach has been cast upon our own State as never before by illegal, fraudulent and corrupt voting in almost every county within its borders. This is so palpable, that "he who runs may read." The capitations of 1884 were 133,522, and the entire vote, after the most active political campaign ever made in the State, 137,587. The capitations for 1888 were 147,408, and the entire vote was 159,440. The difference in the capitations and the vote, in 1884, was 4,065; in 1888, it is 12,032. This shows an increase of votes in four years of 21,853, which, if legitimate, would indicate a population of 900,000, and an increase in four years of much more than 100,000. It is certain that no such increase has taken place.

. . . I recommend that a registration law be enacted, and that our election laws be amended so that bribery and fraudulent voting may be prevented and the purity of the ballot-box preserved.—Message of Governor E. Willis Wilson, January 9, 1889, *Journal of the House of Delegates of the State of West Virginia,* p. 100.

The States of Massachusetts, Connecticut, Indiana, Michigan, Missouri, Illinois, Kentucky, Tennessee and Montana, have adopted, in various forms, what is known as the Australian system. Under these laws, elections have been held in Massachusetts, Connecticut and Montana, and they have been found far in advance of the old system. The crystalization of public opinion in favor of the Australian system, indicates that it will be generally adopted throughout the United States.

Knowing by experience, the difficulty of preparing a bill of considerable magnitude, during the limited time of a legislative session, as an aid to the Legislature, if it be concluded to adopt this system, I have drafted a bill in harmony with the constitutional organization of the State, which is attached hereto, and which I present as a part hereof. Having confidence that it will secure the absolute independence of the voter by enabling him to prepare and deposit his ballot without possible interference, and that it will secure fairer and purer elections in this State, I recommend that it be adopted.—Message of Governor E. Willis Wilson, January 15, 1890, *Journal of the House of Delegates of the State of West Virginia, Extra Session*, p. 19.

144. Conditions in an Early Mining Town

With the coming of the Norfolk and Western Railroad to West Virginia, mining towns sprang up along its main line and branches from Bluefield to Williamson, and the N. & W. became a synonym for coal. The coal industry transformed the thinly populated mountainous counties into populous industrial districts, as local inhabitants joined European immigrants and migrants from surrounding states. There rural isolation gave way to community living which bore a close resemblance to that of a Far-Western mining town. In the excerpt below a Welsh immigrant describes conditions in a McDowell County coal mining town in 1895.

YOU WILL I AM SURE BE SURPRISED to find I am in the wilds of West Virginia; well, I came down here in the middle of June last and I like to be here very much and I am getting on all right. . . .

Our mines are situated in the Elkhorn about 18 miles up from Pocahontas, the latter place being about 650 [sic] miles from Norfolk on the Atlantic coast. The only railway communication for this coalfield is the Norfolk and Western Railroad.

We are on what is called the Pocahontas Flat Top Coalfield which comprises a very large area. The major part of this coalfield belongs to a company called the Flat Top Coal Land Association, who own something like two hundred thousand acres and upwards. . . .

Now let me tell you something about the people we have in this country.

. . . Before I came here I was told the niggars were a most treacherous devilish lot of people to deal with and the only way to manage them was to knock them down with anything at hand, at any slight offense on their part. . . .

I started from Wilkes-Barre on a Monday and . . . got into Pocahontas at noon on Wednesday. . . . Being beastly tired of the train, I got into a large dining saloon. Presently two niggar young women came to me: they were about eighteen years old and they had delightfully melodious sweet voices and spoke in most guarded and beautiful English. "By jove," says I to myself, "if all the niggars are like these girls, I am jolly glad I came down here." Talking about modest and respectful behavior, why every other place I have ever been to both at home and America, were not in it. I came in contact with several of them, men this time, while waiting at Poco and found them all extremely well behaved and enlightened people. I am extremely fond of them and have not had the slightest trouble with them since I have been here. And I would rather manage five hundred of them than half a dozen of the white people of this country. In dealing with a niggar, you have to be very firm with them and insist upon having your instructions carried out to the letter. I treat them very respectfully and show them that I respect their race and they appreciate that more than words can tell, for most white people treat them otherwise, which is the greatest mistake. . . .

. . . The white man of this state and adjoining states is about the most contemptible person on the face of God's earth. He is unbearably ignorant and does not know it. He has generally been brought up on the mountains, hog fashion, and when they come to the mines and earn a lot of money, they swell out and don't know themselves. He is a small ferrety-eyed fellow, with hollow lanky cheeks, a thin pointed nose with about seventeen hairs on his chin and thirteen hairs on his upper lip, which he insultingly calls a mustache. That is the best description I can give you of the native white man of the South.

These detestable cranks seem to think that the poor niggar was made to receive their insults and brutality; so when they meet at those saloons where they sell poison for whiskey and vitriol for brandy, those fearful rows begin.

The white men start by clubbing the niggar on the head with a revolver, for everybody is obliged to carry his shooting iron here, and then business is busy and the shooting becomes general, everyone firing away regardless of object, friend or foe. It is nothing unusual here to find four or five fellows shot dead, and it is quite unusual if this is not the case on pay nights which, thank God, only comes but once a month. . . . It is forbidden by law to carry concealed firearms in the state, but in the face of it everybody carries one and indeed would not be safe to go without one.—John R. Williams, Algoma, McDowell County, West Virginia to William Thomas, Abedare, Wales, November 10, 1895, in *The Welsh in America*, edited by Alan Conway, pp. 204-10. By permission of the University of Minnesota Press.

145. The Beginning of Rural Free Delivery

On October 1, 1896, postal riders were dispatched from Charles Town, Uvilla, and Halltown, in Jefferson County, West Virginia, bearing the first letters delivered by government at rural gateposts in America. During Benjamin Harrison's administration Postmaster General John Wanamaker had favored the extension of the letter carrier service to rural areas, and the National Farmers' Congress and the National Grange had urged an appropriation by Congress. But Congress responded grudg-

ingly until midway in President Grover Cleveland's second term when it finally provided a sum considered adequate for the experiment.

Both President Cleveland and Postmaster General William C. Bissell argued stoutly against Rural Free Delivery; but Bissell's successor, William L. Wilson of West Virginia, who believed that the project would enable him to consolidate postoffices, eliminate star routes, reduce the number of postal employees, and extend the civil service, decided to launch it on an experimental basis. And Wilson's decision to conduct the experiment in Jefferson County was no mere act of favoritism, for his native Jefferson was a richly endowed agricultural community, topographically representative, and geographically convenient to Washington. Before Wilson left office on March 4, 1897, the service had been put on trial in some thirty states.

The first passage which follows is taken from an editorial which prophesied failure of the experiment, the second from Wilson's special report on Rural Free Delivery to the House of Representatives.

CONGRESS AT ITS LAST SESSION appropriated forty thousand dollars to try the experiment of rural postal delivery, and an officer of the department has been here looking after necessary arrangements to introduce free rural delivery in Charles Town District. Six hundred dollars is the amount appropriated. It will take at least three, and most likely four carriers and horses, at the yearly compensation of $200 each, the carriers to give $1,000 bond, ride about 20 miles each day and board themselves and horses. The experiment is a holy fizzle to commence with. No man who could give the bond will likely undertake it.—*The Farmers' Advocate*, Charles Town, W. Va., September 19, 1896.

. . . This test has been made in communities widely differing in geographical location, in the physical features of the country, and in the density and occupation of populations, and it is believed that it has been made at as low a cost for compensation of carriers as it is possible to secure. It is, of course, impossible, after so brief a test, to estimate with accuracy the cost of a free rural-delivery service for the entire country. . . . It may be said, however, that with the permanent extension of such service to the entire country or to large areas of country, it would be possible to effect some saving by the abolition of small post-offices and the discontinuance of some star routes, which would result in a net decrease of expense. It is also fair to presume that there would be some increase of revenue as the natural result of extending the mail facilities of the people. On the other hand, it is probable from past experiences, as, for instance, from the large increase in the compensation of letter carriers since the establishment of the free-delivery system, that with a wide extension of the free rural-delivery system there would come an increase in the cost of the service by increase in the compensation of the carriers.—Postmaster General William L. Wilson to Speaker of the House of Representatives, March 1, 1897, 54th Congress, 2d Session, *House Documents*, Vol. 58, No. 324, pp. 1-2.

XIII. The Progressive Era

146. Establishment of the West Virginia Geological and Economic Survey

After Governor Arthur I. Boreman and some of his successors had failed to persuade the West Virginia legislature to create an agency for the collection, study and publication of information pertaining to the geological and economic resources of the State, the law-making body finally passed an act on February 26, 1897, providing for the establishment of the West Virginia Geological and Economic Survey. The geological formations of West Virginia had attracted the attention of John Howard and John Peter Salley during their expedition down the Kanawha in 1742; George Washington emphasized the geological features of Trans-Allegheny Virginia in his diaries and letters during his journey to the Ohio in 1770, and Thomas Jefferson included reports on his observations of the natural features of western Virginia in NOTES ON THE STATE OF VIRGINIA. *The first systematic study of geologic phenomena, however, began in West Virginia in the 1830's under the direction of William Barton Rogers, the State geologist of Virginia, who conducted surveys of physical features and mineral resources in many western Virginia counties.*

Governor George W. Atkinson promptly appointed Dr. Israel C. White (1848-1927) as superintendent of the survey and head geologist. A specialist in coal, oil, and natural gas, Dr. White served as State geologist until his death. Under the leadership of Dr. White and his successors, particularly Dr. Paul H. Price who has headed the organization since 1934, the West Virginia Geological and Economic Survey has made a monumental contribution to the scientific and economic development of the State. Both Dr. White and Dr. Price have led the fight against waste and for wise use of West Virginia's natural resources. The first passage below has been taken from Dr. White's address at the White House Conference of Governors, held May 13-15, 1908, the second from Dr. Price's annual report in 1963.

SUPPOSE THAT IT WERE POSSIBLE for some Nero inspired by a mania of incendiarism, to apply a consuming torch to every bed of coal that crops to the surface from the Atlantic to the Pacific, and that the entire coal supply of the Union was threatened with destruction within a very few years, what do you think would happen? Would our State Legislatures sit undisturbed panoplied by such a carnival of fire? Would the Governors of thirty states remain silent while the demon of flame was ravaging the coal resources of the Republic? Certainly not; there would be a united effort by the Governors and Legislatures of all the states of the Union to stay the progress of such a direful conflagration; even the sacred constitutional barriers wisely erected between State and Federal authority would melt away in the presence of such an awful calamity, and the mighty arm of the Nation would be invoked to help end the common peril to every interest. And yet this imaginary case is an *actual one* with the best and purest fuel of the country, equal probably in quantity and value for heat, light and power to all of our coal resources. . . . In my own state of West Virginia, only eight years ago, not less than five hundred million cubic feet of this precious gas was daily escaping into the air from two counties alone, practically all of which was easily preventable, by a moderate expenditure for additional casing. When it is remembered that one thousand cubic feet of natural gas weighs 48 pounds, and that 6,000 cubic feet of it would yield a 42-gallon barrel of oil when condensed, so that a well flowing 6,000,000 feet of gas is pouring into the air daily the equivalent of 1,000 barrels of oil, what would our petroleum kings think if they could see this river of oil (for the equivalent of a billion feet of gas is more than 160,000 barrels of petroleum, and of practically the same chemical composition as benzine, or gasoline) rushing unhindered to the sea? . . . And yet because natural gas is invisible, and its waste is not so apparent to the eye as a stream of oil, or a burning coal mine, the agents of these oil magnates have not only permitted this destruction of the nation's fuel resources to continue, but they have prevented by every means in their power the enactment of any legislation to stop this frightful loss of the best and purest fuel that nature has given to man. . . .

For ten long years your speaker has appealed in his official capacity as state geologist to the legislature of West Virginia to put some check upon this frightful waste of our state's most valuable resource. Three patriotic Governors, including our present able executive, Governor Dawson, have in every biennial message besought the legislative branch to end this criminal destruction by appropriate legislation, but some unseen power greater than Governors or Legislatures has so far thwarted and palsied every effort to save to the state and the nation this priceless heritage of fuel, so that although five successive legislatures have attempted to deal with the question in biennial sessions not an effective line has yet been added to the statutes, and at this very hour not less than 250,000,000 cubic feet of gas, and possibly more than double that quantity is daily being wasted in this one state alone, 80 per cent of which is easily and cheaply preventable.

Why should a few oil producers in their insane haste to get rich quickly, or add to fortunes already swollen beyond safety to the Republic, be permitted thus to despoil the entire country of its choicest fuel?

But surely if men have thus permitted the loss of our gaseous fuels, often because they could neither see the substance nor realize the extent of what they were doing, certainly they would not be so wasteful of the solid fuels, the coal beds, something they can readily perceive and handle and weigh. The record here is also one to make every citizen of our nation feel distressed and humiliated, for of the total quantity of coal we have produced since mining for commercial purposes began, amounting to about five billion tons, at least an equal amount, and possibly more, has been left in abondoned mines, and irretrievably lost. . . .—*Address of Dr. I. C. White at the White House Conference on the Conservation of Natural Resources,* May 13, 1908, pp. 8-9, 10-11, 13-14.

The best development of our natural resources, and likewiso their conservation, is dependent upon knowledge of what these resources are, how they can best be recovered, and for what they can be used. The more abundant the resources are, the greater is our opportunity for better living conditions and the opportunity for employment, in diverse occupations. To determine what these resources are, where they are located and their physical and chemical properties is a primary Survey responsibility. To get this information to the industrial producer, the teacher, the planner, the conservationist and the general public in reports, maps, and lectures in ways that each will understand, is an important additional responsibility. . . .

A State which develops its mineral resources most wisely will attain the highest rewards. Our State has neither in the past nor are we at present utilizing our natural resources wisely to our greatest long-range advantage. We have ravaged our forests, depleted our soils, polluted our streams, and produced our valuable mineral fuels most wastefully. . . .

Our chief research activities continue to emphasize our interest in the fossil fuels. Continued interest in the further development of gas and oil by industry requires the attention of several members of our staff. . . .

Strong interest continues in locating additional industrial minerals including salt, metals, limestone, silica, and clays. Of continued great importance are our water resources. Our interest here lies especially in establishing the presence of large volumes of ground and water supplies and the curtailment of pollution of surface streams. . . .

West Virginia continues to lead in the production of bituminous coal, and a comfortable 100 billion ton reserve insures a steady supply of the resource for many years to come. Production declines of the past several years are gradually being reversed, and increased consumption of coal, especially by utilities, points to a brighter future for both the industry and our State.—Dr. Paul H. Price, *Annual Report*, 1963, pp. 1-3, 8.

147. Reforming the Tax Laws

Both the West Virginia constitution of 1863 and the constitution of 1872 perpetuated features of Virginia fiscal policy. For example, both constitutions prohibited a state debt. Moreover, for more than half a century the chief sources of revenue were limited to capitations, licenses, fees and property taxes. To make matters worse, State and local governments unblushingly pur-

sued a policy of low taxes, while assessors in many counties flouted the constitutional requirement of equality and uniformity of assessments and neglected to list certain taxable properties altogether.

In 1883 the Legislature created a tax commission which denounced both the existing tax system and tax policy, but it failed to submit a plan of revision. The Legislature imposed a corporation charter tax in 1885, and an inheritance tax in 1887, but these laws yielded little revenue. Reluctant to tax business, the law-makers refused in 1897 to act upon the proposal of a joint legislative committee to submit a constitutional amendment empowering the State to levy upon intangible property.

But the Legislature took an important step toward reform in 1901 when it authorized the appointment of a commission to study the tax structure. The law-makers took no action upon the recommendations of the commission at the regular session of 1903 but when called into special session by Governor Albert B. White in the summer of 1904 the Legislature created the office of State Tax Commissioner, required county assessors to assess all property at its true and actual value, increased the tax on corporation charters, inheritances and transfers, fixed maximum levies, and directed the Board of Public Works to assess public utilities.

These reforms marked a significant advance in West Virginia finances but left many sources of revenue untouched. Governors William M. O. Dawson and William E. Glasscock courageously recommended further broadening of the tax base. The passages below have been taken from their messages to the Legislature.

THE MATTER OF REVENUE, like the poor, you will always have with you. It has always been so in West Virginia, especially as you are inhibited by the constitution from creating debt, and we must therefore pay as we go, which is difficult for a young and fast-growing State. Almost no cities, nor other states, nor other governments, have been able to keep out of debt. Usually those that have grown and developed most have the largest debts. Doubtless the experience of the mother state, with her big debt in 1861, and so little to show for it, induced the people in both our constitutions to prohibit a state debt. Hence, our problem of meeting the financial wants of the state is a peculiarly difficult one.

. . . A luxury of one generation becomes a necessity to the next. To enlarge our capitol building, to build new institutions and to enlarge and equip properly with land, water and other desirable things the existing ones; to build good roads; to protect our forests and our water sources; to care efficiently for the public health; and to do many other desirable things, would require several millions of dollars more than we can hope to raise by taxation. If the money should be wisely spent, it would pay us to borrow it, for these desirable things are permanent improvements, and coming generations would have use of them and should pay part of the cost of them. So, there is no hope that we shall be able in the future to rid ourselves of the ever-increasing problem of revenue. Especially is this true because of the unwisdom of our forefathers, who gave away, not only the soil of our State, but all the vast mineral wealth that underlies it. There are those who believe that the land should no more have passed into private ownership than should air, water, the navigable streams, and the seas. However that may be, there was no necessity to give away the minerals under the soil. The pioneer cared for the soil only—the mineral wealth under it had no value to him—had no value to anyone in pioneer days. Virginia, when she freely granted the lands that comprise the soil of our State, could easily have reserved the minerals. If she had, what a heritage it would be! The royalty from our coal, oil, gas, limestone, and the like—with such an income there would be no problem of revenue, no taxes; our only problem would be how to expend it wisely. But these great natural resources, of untold value, the gift of God, and existing independently of the wit, wisdom or work of man, have become the subject of individual ownership, and it can not be changed now. But certainly it is good reason to insist that these resources, placed here for the benefit of all, shall pay the last farthing of just taxes, and that they shall no longer escape their full share of the public burdens. And is it not also good reason to stop giving more of them away? When the state finds vacant or "unappropriated" land, or when land is forfeited to the state for non-payment of taxes, or for want of heirs, or for other cause, why sell it? Why not keep it, especially as the price the state receives at sales is usually merely nominal? Let us turn about, and undo as far as we can the unwisdom of our fathers, and recover the soil and that above it and that below, whenever circumstances afford opportunity. . . .

The statistics of our mining department show that we are removing our coal at the rate of six thousand acres a year, and this rate will increase. It is the best and the cheapest mined coal that is being removed now. That our resources in oil and gas, and especially the latter, will be exhausted in a comparatively short time, we have every reason to believe. These three natural resources are our principal ones; in them consists very largely the wealth of the state. When once gone they cannot be renewed. It is the kind of wealth, therefore, that the more we produce of it the more of it we destroy. Another important phase of this matter for West Virginia is, that so little of the wealth produced by the exploitation of our coal, oil, and gas remains in the state. It is believed that from eighty to ninety per cent of the net profits resulting from the production of coal, gas, and oil go outside of the state, and only a small percentage remains in the state in the form of property upon which taxes may be collected for the support of the state and its development. As said before, there is every reason why these resources should pay a full just share of the public burdens. . . . It has been a fight all along the line to get upon the books of this property what is now upon them. In the financial statement above in this message you will see what the mining industry is costing the state. . . . It is a burning disgrace that we enact laws which put on the tax books the full value of the property of widows and orphans and let go untaxed these resources which are the property largely of the rich. . . .

The arrogance practiced by some of these interests as regards the taxation of their property, and the evasions resorted to cheat the state out of what rightly is due it, are reprehensible to the last degree. It developed in a recent suit, brought by a gas concern to overthrow the assessment of its property by the Board of Public Works, that this concern had organized two corporations, one in West Virginia and one in the other state to which it piped and marketed its gas, the wells being in West Virginia. It takes out of the state several billions of cubic feet every year. The West Virginia corporation delivered the gas to the state line where it was nominally sold to the foreign corporation, which delivered it to the consumer. The West Virginia corporation had a merely nominal capital, and, according to the report of the concern, very little property. Now, this having two corporations was a sham, and it was pretended, without blushing, before the court, that this gas from West Virginia, piped into the state line, was worth there to the other corporation, which nominally bought it, about six cents per thousand cubic feet, and that all the taxes this West Virginia corporation should pay would be on its property valued at the price of old junk. Every dollar of profit made from this enterprise had its situs in other states and not a penny of property arising from these profits is situated in West Virginia; hence it is that the state is being milked of its resources largely for the benefit of persons who prefer to live somewhere else and use the money thus made to support and develop other states than West Virginia.—Message of Governor William M. O. Dawson to the West Virginia Legislature, January 13, 1909, *Journal of the Senate* Appendix A, pp. 3-4, 20-24.

Gas is one of our most valuable natural resources and for the past twenty years and more our State has been producing vast quantities of this, the best and purest fuel with which nature has endowed us, and from which we have been receiving but very little return. The value of this fuel consumed inside and outside of the State and wasted is almost beyond computation. . . . From the best information I can obtain the annual production of gas in this State is now between 120,000,000,000 and 130,000,000,000 cubic feet. . . . Would it not be wise and just and right to remove the State tax and in lieu thereof raise the revenue which has heretofore been derived by direct taxation from a subject that is not only well able to pay it, but in justice and equity owes it to the State? It is my idea that the revenue derived from this source should be largely, if not altogether, expended for the benefit of our free schools and the maintenance and improvement of our public highways. . . . A tax of one-half cent on each thousand cubic feet of gas produced in this State would be a mere bagatelle to those who have to pay it, but would mean an enormous benefit to the subject of education and the improvement of our highways. We can maintain our State Government on the moneys we now receive, but we cannot discharge our obligations to the people of the State if we fail to conserve properly our natural resources, or fail to require every interest to bear its just share of the burden of taxation.—Message of Governor William E. Glasscock to the West Virginia Legislature, January 30, 1911, *Journal of the House of Delegates*, Appendix A, pp. 16-20.

148. Establishment of a Department of Archives and History, 1905

Despite the efforts of dedicated leaders, West Virginians failed to sustain the West Virginia Historical Society (1869-1889) and the short-lived Trans-Allegheny Historical Society (1901-1902), each established by men who earnestly desired that the State's history should be "rescued, collected and preserved in systematic, durable form." However, when Virgil A. Lewis in 1890 organized the West Virginia Historical and Antiquarian Society for the purpose of collecting the archives, artifacts, and publications pertaining to West Virginia, the Legislature supported the venture by an appropriation which enabled the society to maintain a repository in Charleston and publish a historical magazine. Finally convinced that it was not the province of private historical societies to collect and preserve archives for government, members of the society began a movement at the turn of the century for the creation of a department of state government which would be charged with the responsibility of collecting and preserving the historical materials of the State.

Governor George W. Atkinson and his successor Governor Albert B. White sensed the need for immediate action and both supported the movement in messages to the Legislature which passed an act on February 18, 1905, establishing a State Bureau of Archives and History and authorizing the transfer to the bureau of property held in trust for the State by the West Virginia Historical and Antiquarian Society.

The selections which follow have been taken from the message of Governor George W. Atkinson to the Legislature in 1901, from the act passed February 18, 1905, and from the last report of Virgil A. Lewis (1848-1912), the first State Historian and Archivist.

I FIND OUR PUBLIC RECORDS AND DOCUMENTS in the archives of the State in a very incomplete and unsatisfactory condition. . . . I can find no official records relating to the "Restored Government of Virginia." I have also made diligent effort to secure the journals of the Legislatures from 1861 to 1864, and have not been able to find them. . . . I find no Inaugural Address of any Governor of the State printed in any bound volume of the State's doings, not even my own. . . .

It is painfully evident that our public records are woefully incomplete, and some action should be taken by your honorable body, without unnecessary delay, to hunt out and print, in enduring form, all of these missing records in order that the State's archives may be perfected and completed. I beg, in view of these unfortunate conditions, to suggest that a Historical Commission be designated by your Honorable Body to perform, at least, two important duties: 1. To have all of the public records, papers and documents, from 1861 to the present, or at least to a point to where the records are found complete, and a supply sufficient to meet all reasonable demands, collected, edited and classified, and printed in a series. 2. To devise and adopt a systematic plan for the publication and preservation of all of our State archives in the future.—Message of Governor George W. Atkinson to the West Virginia Legislature, January 9, 1901, *Journal of the House of Delegates*, pp. 52-54.

Be it enacted by the Legislature of West Virginia:

Section 1. There shall be established a state bureau of archives and history in which shall be collected for permanent preservation, so far as it can now be done, all valuable papers and documents relating to the settlement of the state; to the period of the reorganized government of Virginia and to the erection and formation of West Virginia out of the territory of the mother state, with biographical matter pertaining to the men who were prominent then, together with all missing public records, state papers, documents of the legislature, executive and judicial departments, and the reports of all state officials, boards of regents and directors of state institutions, educational, charitable, penal and otherwise, from the twentieth of June, eighteen hundred and sixty-three, to which the annual additions shall be added as produced. In this bureau there shall be devised and adopted a systematic plan for the preservation and classification of all the state archives of the past, present, and future. In the said bureau there shall also be collected books, pamphlets, papers, and other works of history, biography, and kindred subjects as are usually found in such collections, together with the works of West Virginia authors and such others as will properly illustrate the bibliography of the state. In connection with the collections in said bureau, there may be a museum illustrative of history, science, the social conditions and life of the people of our country, past and present.—*Acts of the West Virginia Legislature,* 1905, pp. 466-67.

There is needed in the Department a young man of literary taste strongly developed; a reader of books; a lover of books; a "bookworm," as it were; one who will read deeply and become absorbed in all that pertains to the State and its people; one not only willing, but anxious to acquire a knowledge, not only of the titles of books, but a knowledge of their contents, of their subject matter—who, in short, will read systematically, and will acquire not only a knowledge of literature, history, biography, science, etc., but of the Public Documents and State Papers of the Federal Government, of the various State Governments, but especially of those of his own state and those of Virginia, of which State this Virginia was so long a part. . . .

This means one who is willing to become a trained historian and skilled archivist. Such an one, only, can be what he should be as an assistant to those making research and investigation in a collection such as this. Such an one must be willing to give his best efforts, and devote his whole life to the work. In doing this, he can do nothing else, but need not fear, for, should his own State not want his service, the Nation, and the other states of the Union will want him in their archives and library work. —Virgil A. Lewis, *Third Biennial Report of the Department of Archives and History,* pp. xxxv-vi.

149. Establishment of a State Department of Mines

Throughout its early history coal mining was the most hazardous of West Virginia occupations. Because of recurring accidents in the coal industry, the West Virginia legislature prescribed safety regulations and provided for mine inspection in various acts passed during the 1880's and 1890's. In 1907 it established a State Department of Mines, but not in time to prevent the appalling Monongah explosion in Marion County on December 6, 1907, which snuffed out the lives of 361 men.

Safety measures have greatly reduced the probability of mine disasters in West Virginia, but have failed to prevent their recurrence altogether. The table below shows the loss of life sustained in major West Virginia coal mine disasters since 1900.

COAL MINE DISASTERS IN WEST VIRGINIA IN WHICH TEN OR MORE MEN WERE KILLED

Date	Name of Mine	Location	Men Killed
1900 March 6	Red Ash	Red Ash	46
1900 Nov. 2	Berryburg	Berryburg	15
1901 May 15	Chatham	Farmington	10
1902 Sept. 15	Algoma No. 7	Algoma	17
1905 March 19	Rush Run & Red Ash	Red Ash	24
1906 Jan. 4	Coaldale	Coaldale	22
1906 Jan. 18	Detroit	Detroit	18
1906 Feb. 8	Parral	Parral	23
1906 March 22	Century No. 1	Century	23
1907 Jan. 26	Lorentz	Penco	12
1907 Jan. 29	Stuart	Stuart	85
1907 Feb. 4	Thomas No. 25	Thomas	25
1907 May 1	Whipple	Scarbro	46
1907 Dec. 6	Monongah Nos. 6 & 8	Monongah	361
1908 Dec. 29	Lick Branch	Switchback	50
1909 Jan. 12	Lick Branch	Switchback	67
1909 March 31	Echo	Buery	16

1910 Dec. 31	Lick Fork	Thacker	10
1911 April 24	Ott No. 20	Elk Garden	23
1911 Nov. 18	Bottom Creek	Vivian	18
1912 March 26	Jed	Jed	80
1914 April 28	Eccles Nos. 5 & 6	Eccles	183
1915 Feb. 6	Carlisle	Carlisle	22
1915 March 2	Layland No. 3	Layland	112
1915 March 30	Boomer No. 2	Boomer	23
1916 March 28	King	Kimball	10
1916 Oct. 19	Jamison No. 7	Barracksville	10
1917 Dec. 15	Yukon No. 1	Yukon	18
1918 May 20	Villa	Charleston	13
1923 March 2	Arista	Arista	10
1923 Nov. 6	Glen Rogers	Beckley	27
1924 March 28	Yukon No. 2	Yukon	24
1924 April 28	Benwood	Benwood	119
1925 March 17	Barrackville	Barrackville	33
1926 Jan. 14	Jamison No. 8	Farmington	19
1926 March 8	Crab Orchard No. 5	Eccles	19
1927 April 30	Federal No. 3	Everettville	97
1928 May 22	No. 1	Yukon	17
1929 Jan. 26	Kingston No. 5	Kingston	14
1930 March 26	Yukon	Arnettsville	12
1936 Sept. 2	Hutchinson Coal	MacBeth	10
1937 March 11	Hutchinson Coal	MacBeth	18
1940 Jan. 10	Pond Creek Poca Co. No. 1 Mine	Bartley	91
1942 May 12	Christopher No. 3	Osage	56
1942 July 9	Pursglove No. 2	Pursglove	20
1943 Jan. 8	Pursglove No. 15	Pursglove	13
1943 Nov. 6	Nellis No. 3	Nellis	11
1944 March 25	Katherine No. 4	Lumberport	16
1946 Jan. 15	Havaco No. 9	Havaco	15
1951 Jan. 18	Kermit	Kermit	11
1951 Oct. 15	Bunker	Cassville	10
1951 Oct. 31	United No. 1	Wevaco	12
1954 Nov. 13	No. 9	Farmington	16
1957 Feb. 4	Poca Fuel Co. No. 35	Bishop	37
1957 Dec. 27	Poca Fuel Co. No. 31	Amonate	11
1958 Oct. 27	Pocahontas Fuel Co. No. 35 Mine	Bishop	22
1958 Oct. 28	Oglebay Norton Coal Burton Mine	Summersville	14
1960 March 8	Island Creek Coal Co. No. 22 Mine	Holden	18

—*Annual Report of Department of Mines*, 1961, pp. 133-34.

150. The Failure of the Conservation Movement

The conservation of the State's natural resources became the concern of a few West Virginians at the turn of the century when spirited citizens and officials took steps to halt destruction and waste in the extractive industries. For a generation West Virginians had been writing the most shameful chapter in their history, as avarice and greed took reckless toll of the timber, coal, oil and gas. In 1902 the State Tax Commission recommended the enactment of laws to prevent forest fires and promote reforestation, and State Geologist I. C. White emphasized the great waste of the fuel resources in an address delivered at the White House Conference of Governors, May 13, 1908 (see No. 146 above). Governors Albert B. White, William M. O. Dawson, and William E. Glasscock emphasized the urgency of conservation legislation, and in 1908 Governor Dawson appointed a commission soon after his return from the White House Conference of Governors on conservation. But despite graphic disclosures and recommendations by officials and experts, West Virginia refused to join the current national movement led by President Theodore Roosevelt, and the conservation commission ceased to function after submitting a single report.

The passages below have been taken from the report of the first conservation commission and Governor Dawson's legislative message in 1909.

A MATTER OF VITAL IMPORTANCE is that of the saving of our natural resources—our coal, natural gas, forests, and soil. . . . Suffice it to say that the facts show an alarming state of affairs in regard to the exhaustion of our coal, gas and timber, and of damage to our tillable soil and to our rivers by the destruction of our forests. A lumber famine in the near future seems certain. Millions of feet of our natural gas, the best and most valuable of all fuels, is yearly lost by escaping from abandoned wells and from oil wells in use, while the waste of this precious fuel in the use of wasteful methods of consumption is also very great. . . .

That something might be done—at least a beginning made—I appointed a commission consisting of Mr. Hu Maxwell, of the Forestry Division of the United States Department of Agriculture, Mr. James H. Stewart, Chief of the Experiment Station of the West Virginia University, and Mr. Neil Robinson, the well-known coal expert. . . . Their report has been printed and is before you. It recommends that the Legislature enact three statutes: First, a forest law; second, a law to check waste of natural gas; third, to lessen the waste of by-products in the manufacture of coke. The forest law provides for a state forester, with all constables as ex officio fire marshals; authorizes the acquiring and setting apart of lands by the state for the purpose of forestry; and provides a way to co-operate with private timber owners in the management of their holdings. The remission of a portion of the tax on cut-over lands is impossible under the constitution (another argument for classification of taxable objects) but the Commission recommends that steps be taken toward that end. The proposed natural gas act requires the plugging of abandoned wells, and the saving of the gas from active oil wells. The proposed coke measure sets a time five years in the future after which the construction of by-product ovens only will be permitted. The report recommends that the state co-operate in all practical ways with the Federal Government for the protection of forests and the improvement of navigable streams in West Virginia, and suggests the advisibility of furnishing, at the state's expense, free sites and rights of way for locks, dams, roads, and storage reservoirs. Although beyond the Commission's power to point out particular and practical ways of using the immense quantity of low-grade coal taken from mines and at present unsalable, and of utilizing the power that might be developed from the rivers, yet it recommends that every possible means of accomplishing that result be employed. These resources are now wasted, but they have a positive value of millions of dollars annually. The commission appreciates the necessity of laying a broad foundation for development along that line, and as a means to that end it recommended the establishment of a high class technical school, in connection with the State University, for educating electrical, mechanical, hydraulic, and mining engineers, with special instruction concerning the state's resources and the lines along which development should go. An experimental irrigation farm is recommended to test whether the artificial watering of some of the West Virginia valleys would be profitable; also an experimental farm in each congressional district, for the study of soils and all matters relating to scientific farming under the climatic and other conditions existing in West Virginia. Recommendation was made that an investigation be undertaken to determine whether it is practicable to dispose of sewage from towns and factories of the state without discharging it into the running streams. The want of complete and reliable data concerning the state's resources and business affairs led the Commission to recommend that the state make use of a better method of collecting and publishing statistics.—Message of Governor William M. O. Dawson to the West Virginia Legislature, January 13, 1909, *Journal of the Senate,* Appendix A, pp. 25-28.

Why was it [waste of natural gas] permitted? Simply because it was nobody's business to stop it, and it was somebody's business not to stop it. The waste was principally due to oil operators who let the gas escape, because it would cost something to plug the wells. Fifteen hundred million dollars worth of the best fuel in the world (at 10 cents a thousand cubic feet) has been lost forever in West Virginia because it was nobody's business to save it.

Whose gas was it? The oil operators perhaps supposed it was theirs, because they held the leases, but it was not theirs. They might have used it, but had no right to squander it. The public has rights in matters like that. The natural resources do not belong to individuals or companies, except to a limited extent. Their right to use does not carry with it license to destroy. The heritage that has been squandered—fifteen hundred dollars for every man, woman, and child in West Virginia—belonged to the people of this generation and those which are to follow. . . .

The waste of natural gas continues. It is probably not so great as formerly because the supply in the earth seems to be diminishing. The better price and greater demand for it also has something to do with saving it. But the waste is still enormous, from unplugged wells, from wells from which both oil ond gas flow, from leaky pipes, and otherwise. The total waste of gas in West Virginia has now fallen to probably the equivalent of 10,000 tons of coal a day. . . .

A country's natural scenery may have a good deal more than an asthetic value. It may be worth money, and from a business standpoint its care and improvement is frequently of great importance. . . .

West Virginia has not, up to the present time, done much with its scenery except to mar it, mutilate it, and burn it up. Except in the case of mineral springs, practically nothing has been done in this State to make scenery attractive or to bring it to the attention of the outside world. West Virginia may never rival Switzerland, but it can equal Maine. The summer climate is glorious among its high mountains and elevated valleys. A series of summer hotels from 3,000 to 4,400 feet above the sea might stretch across the State, following the Alleghany and parallel ranges of mountains. . . .

A good many things must be done before West Virginia will take its due rank as a resort for tourists, healthseekers, and sight seers. It must first protect its woods and make them attractive. It must clean its streams and stock them with fish, and make and enforce civilized laws for protection of the fish. It must stop the senseless slaughter of birds and game. It must build roads that can be traveled with speed and safety by modern vehicles. In building these roads the value of scenery must be considered in regions where scenery is attractive.—*Report of the West Virginia Conservation Commission*, 1908, pp. 15, 38-39.

151. The Maryland Boundary Dispute

The Maryland-Virginia boundary line again became an issue in 1781 when Maryland granted land west of Fort Cumberland to her veterans and employed Francis Deakins to lay out lots. These tracts were located east of a meridian line 37 miles long which Deakins established in 1788 between the Fairfax Stone and the Mason and Dixon Line. Although Maryland eventually accepted the Fairfax Stone as the beginning point of her western boundary, in 1859 she surveyed a meridian line which termi-

nated at the Pennsylvania boundary about three-fourths of a mile west of the Deakins Line. The new line, commonly called the Michler Line, reopened the boundary question and became the basis of the later controversy with West Virginia. The boundary in dispute separated Preston County, West Virginia, and Garrett County, Maryland, from the headwaters of the Potomac to the Pennsylvania line. Although West Virginia was willing to yield her jurisdiction over the narrow strip if Maryland would validate all grants, patents, and titles previously made by Virginia, Maryland refused. In a suit brought before the United States Supreme Court in 1891, Maryland revived her demand that the meridian should begin at Potomac Spring and injected her old claim to the South Branch as the main stream. West Virginia filed a cross bill claiming the north bank of the Potomac River as her boundary. The case dragged on until 1910, when the Supreme Court sustained West Virginia's claims on the western boundary but denied her jurisdiction over the Potomac River beyond the low water mark of the south bank. The extract below has been taken from the Supreme Court decision.

MR. JUSTICE DAY . . . This record leaves no doubt as to the truth of the statement contained in the report of the committee of the Maryland Historical Society, that the Deakins line, before the passage of the act under which the Michler line was run, had long been recognized as a boundary and served as such. Even after the Michler line was run and marked the testimony shows that the people generally adhered to the old line as the true boundary line. There are numerous Virginia grants and private deeds of land given in the record, which call for this old Maryland line as the boundary.

The testimony shows that the people living along the Deakins line worked and improved the roads on the Virginia side, as a general rule, up to this line. Correspondingly, Maryland worked the roads on the other side of this line. On the west of the line the people paid taxes on their lands in Preston County, West Virginia. They voted in that county, and with rare exceptions regarded themselves as citizens of West Virginia. As a general rule, the schools established there were West Virginia schools. The allegiance of nearly all these people has been given to West Virginia. . . .

And the fact remains that after the Deakins survey in 1788 the people living along the line generally regarded that line as the boundary line between the States at bar. In the acts of the legislatures of the two States, to which we have already referred, resulting in the survey and running of the Michler line, it is evident from the language used that the purpose was not to establish a new line, but to retrace the old one, and we are strongly inclined to believe that had this been done at that time the controversy would have been settled. . . .

We think, for the reasons which we have undertaken to state, that the decree in this case should provide for the appointment of commissioners whose duty it shall be to run and permanently mark the old Deakins line, beginning at a point where the north and south line from the Fairfax Stone crosses the Potomac River and running thence northerly along said line to the Pennsylvania border.

As to the contention made by West Virginia in her cross bill, that she is entitled to the Potomac River to the north bank thereof, we think that claim is disposed of by the case of *Morris* v. *United States,* 174 U. S. 196, already referred to. In that case, among other things, there was a controversy between the heirs of James H. Marshall and the heirs of John Marshall as to the ownership of the bed of the Potomac River from shore to shore, including therein certain reclaimed lands. Claims of the one set of heirs were based upon the charter of Lord Baltimore of June, 1632, and that of the others upon the grant of King James II to Lord Culpeper, afterwards owned by Fairfax, to which we have already referred. . . .

A decree should be entered settling the rights of the States to the western boundary, and fixing the same, as we have hereinbefore indicated, to be run and established along the old line known as the Deakins or old state line; and commissioners should be appointed to locate and establish said line as near as may be. The cross bill of the State of West Virginia should be dismissed in so far as it asks for a decree fixing the north bank of the Potomac River as her boundary. Maryland *v.* West Virginia, 217 U. S., 1-47, 1910.

152. The Virginia Debt Controversy

The ordinance adopted by the Second Wheeling Convention on August 20, 1861, and ratified by the voters on October 24, 1861, provided for the assumption by the proposed State of Kanawha of a just proportion of the public debt of Virginia prior to January 1, 1861, and the West Virginia constitution of 1863 declared that the State would pay an equitable portion of the Virginia debt as of the same date. Immediately after the Civil War both Virginia and West Virginia tried to settle the debt question, but negotiations were interrupted in 1867 when Virginia sued West Virginia for the recovery of Jefferson and Berkeley counties. Virginia took the debt matter into her own hands in 1871, when the General Assembly determined the amount of the Virginia public debt in 1861, passed an act refunding it, and allocated one-third of the amount as the portion justly belonging to West Virginia. Virginia issued bonds for West Virginia's share, which were marketed as "West Virginia Certificates."

Although the West Virginia constitution of 1872 did not mention the debt specifically, it authorized the Legislature to pay any previous state indebtedness. Meanwhile, in 1871, a West Virginia commission found that West Virginia owed Virginia only $953,360.23, after deductions, while in 1873 a committee of the West Virginia legislature headed by Jonathan M. Bennett, who had served as auditor of Virginia at Richmond during the Civil War, reported after an extended investigation that Virginia owed West Virginia $525,000.

As the debt controversy dragged on, holders of the "West Virginia Certificates" grew impatient and demanded help from Virginia in making collection. When West Virginia refused to honor the certificates, Virginia sued in the United States Supreme Court.

The Court recognized the existence of a debt and appointed a master to determine what amount West Virginia should pay. In March, 1911, the Court awarded Virginia $7,182,507.46, but in a later decision allowed credit claims which reduced the principal to $4,215,622.28. But with interest charges from 1861 to 1919, West Virginia's obligation to Virginia amounted to

$14,562,867.16. The State made a cash payment of $1,062,867.16 and issued bonds for the remainder, which it redeemed in full in 1939. Below is an extract from the historic decision of 1911 written by Associate Justice Oliver Wendell Holmes.

THIS IS A BILL brought by the Commonwealth of Virginia to have the State of West Virginia's proportion of the public debt of Virginia as it stood before 1861 ascertained and satisfied. . . .

The amount of the debt January 1, 1861, that we have to apportion no longer is in dispute. The master's finding was accepted by West Virginia and at the argument we understood Virginia not to press her exception that it should be enlarged by a disputed item. It was $33,897,073.82, the sum being represented mainly by interest-bearing bonds. . . .

The liability of West Virginia is a deep-seated equity, not discharged by changes in the form of the debt, nor split up by the unilateral attempt of Virginia to apportion specific parts to the two States. . . .

It remains true then, notwithstanding all the transactions between the old Commonwealth and her bondholders, that West Virginia must bear her equitable proportion of the whole debt. With a qualification which we shall mention in a moment, we are of opinion that the nearest approach to justice that we can make is to adopt a ratio determined by the master's estimated valuation of the real and personal property of the two States on the date of the separation, June 20, 1863. A ratio determined by population or land area would throw a larger share on West Virginia, but the relative resources of the debtor populations are generally recognized, we think, as affording a proper measure. It seems to us plain that slaves should be excluded from the valuation. The master's figures without them are, for Virginia $300,887,367.74, and for West Virginia $92,416,021.65. These figures are criticised by Virginia, but we see no sufficient reason for going behind them, or ground for thinking that we can get nearer to justice in any other way. . . . Taking .235 as representing the proportion of West Virginia we have $7,182,507.46 as her share of the principal debt.

. . . There are many elements to be taken into account on the one side and on the other. The circumstances of the asserted de-

fault and the conditions surrounding the failure earlier to procure a determination of the principal sum payable, including the
question of laches as to either party, would require to be considered. A long time has elapsed. Wherever the responsibility
for the delay might ultimately be placed, or however it might
be shared, it would be a severe result to capitalize charges for
half a century—such a thing hardly could happen in a private
case analogous to this. Statutes of limitation, if nothing else,
would be likely to interpose a bar. As this is no ordinary commercial suit, but, as we have said, a quasi-international difference referred to this court in reliance upon the honor and constitutional obligations of the States concerned rather than upon
ordinary remedies, we think it best at this stage to go no farther,
but to await the effect of a conference between the parties,
which, whatever the outcome, must take place. If the cause
should be pressed contentiously to the end, it would be referred
to a master to go over the figures that we have given provision-
ally, and to make such calculations as might become necessary.
But this case is one that calls for forbearance upon both sides.
Great States have a temper superior to that of private litigants,
and it is to be hoped that enough has been decided for patriotism, the fraternity of the Union, and mutual consideration to
bring it to an end.—Virginia v. West Virginia, 220 U.S., 1-36,
1911.

153. The Temperance and Prohibition Movement

*Western Virginians played a prominent part in the work of
the Virginia Temperance Society, organized in 1826, and gave
enthusiastic support to the Sons of Temperance which exerted
a strong influence in the western counties before the Civil War.
The Sons of Temperance, the Independent Order of Good Templars, and the Grand Lodge of the World attempted to launch
a prohibition movement in West Virginia after the war but
found the public apathetic. However, the dry forces mustered
new strength when the West Virginia branch of the Women's*

Christian Temperance Union, organized in 1883, joined the Protestant Churches and the Prohibition Party in a demand for a state-wide referendum on the liquor issue. Although the voters defeated the proposed prohibition amendment by a decisive majority in 1888, the dry forces obtained the enactment of a statute requiring the teaching of physiology and hygiene in the public schools with emphasis on the ill effects of alcohol and narcotics on the human body.

The temperance movement again attained the proportions of a crusade in West Virginia soon after the organization of a branch of the Anti-Saloon League in 1896. The rural population generally supported the cause of prohibition, as well as others who noted the debaucheries of the saloon and the unsavory role which the liquor interests played in politics. Thus when the Legislature submitted a prohibition amendment at the November election in 1912, approximately 72 per cent of the population lived in counties where liquor was not sold.

The dry forces presented a solid front behind leaders of the Anti-Saloon League, the Women's Christian Temperance Union, the evangelical Protestant Churches, and the Prohibition Party. Their opponents organized the Taxpayers' Protective Association and urged the need of the revenue derived from licenses. The wets also questioned the right of the State to confiscate summarily the property of citizens. Of significance in the campaign was a stratagem which William E. "Pussyfoot" Johnson, press secretary of the Committee on Temperance of the Presbyterian Church of the United States, allegedly employed to minimize the influence of opposition newspapers. Posing as "C. L. Treavitt" of Washington, D. C., Johnson sent a letter to some two hundred West Virginia editors offering each a substantial sum "for the privilege of laying arguments against prohibition before your readers." The wet forces promptly denied authorship but not before sixty acceptances of the offer had been received.

In a total of 235,000 votes cast, the voters ratified the constitutional amendment by a majority of 92,000 and in 1913 the Legislature passed a stringent enforcement act, known as the Yost law, which became effective July 1, 1914. This statute remained in force until 1934, when the voters repealed the pro-

hibition amendment and the Legislature a year later gave to the State monopolistic control of all liquor sales. Below are excerpts from the statutes of 1887, 1913, and 1935.

Be it enacted by the Legislature of West Virginia:

1. That the nature of alcoholic drinks and narcotics, and special instruction as to their effects upon the human system, in connection with the several divisions of the subject of physiology and hygiene, shall be included in the branches of study taught in the common or public schools, and shall be taught as thoroughly and in the same manner, as other like required branches are in said schools, to all pupils in all said schools throughout the State. . . .

3. No certificate shall be granted to any person to teach in the public schools of the State, after the first of January, anno domini eighteen hundred and eighty-nine, who has not passed a satisfactory examination in physiology and hygiene, with special reference to the nature and the effects of alcoholic drinks and narcotics upon the human system.—*Acts of the Legislature of West Virginia,* 1887, pp. 5-6.

Be it enacted by the Legislature of West Virginia:

Sec. 3. Except as hereinafter provided, if any person acting for himself, or by, for or through another shall manufacture or sell or keep, store, offer or expose for sale; or solicit or receive orders for any liquors, or absinthe or any drink compounded with absinthe, he shall be deemed guilty of a misdemeanor for the first offense hereunder, and upon conviction thereof shall be fined not less than one hundred dollars nor more than five hundred dollars, and imprisoned in the county jail not less than two nor more than six months; and upon conviction of the same person for the second offense under this act, he shall be guilty of a felony and be confined in the penitentiary not less than one nor more than five years; . . . and any person, except a common carrier, who shall act as the agent or employe of such manufacturer or such seller, or person so keeping, storing, offering or exposing for sale said liquors, or act as the agent or employe of the purchaser of such liquors, shall be deemed guilty of such manufacturing or selling, keeping, storing, offering or exposing for sale, as the case may be; . . . *Acts of the Legislature of West Virginia,* 1913, pp. 96-97.

Be it enacted by the Legislature of West Virginia:

Article I, Section 1. The purpose of this chapter is to give effect to the mandate of the people expressed in the repeal of the state prohibition amendment; and to assure the greatest degree of personal freedom that is consistent with the health, safety and good morals of the people of the state. To these ends the police power of the state is pledged to the sound control and the temperate use of alcoholic liquors. . . .

Sec. 3. Subject · to the provisions of this chapter, alcoholic liquors, in this state:

(1) Shall be sold only in sealed packages.

(2) Shall not be sold for consumption on the premises where sold.

(3) Shall be manufactured only by persons licensed under the provisions of this chapter.

(4) Shall not be consumed or sold for consumption in a public place.

Sec. 4. Alcoholic liquors shall be sold at wholesale and retail in this state only by or through the West Virginia Liquor Control Commission, or its retail agencies. . . .

Article III, Section 1. The sale of alcoholic liquors at wholesale and retail in this state shall be a state monopoly. Alcoholic liquors shall be sold at retail only through the state stores and the agencies of the West Virginia Liquor Control Commission.

The commission may sell such liquors at wholesale to persons licensed to purchase at wholesale as provided in this chapter.

Sec. 2. The commission shall establish state stores and agencies at places throughout the state so as to serve adequately and reasonably the demand for the sale at retail of alcoholic liquors, subject only to the limitations imposed by article five of this chapter. It may discontinue a store or agency when in its opinion it is advisable to do so.—*Acts of the West Virginia Legislature,* 1935, pp. 12, 18.

154. The Paint Creek-Cabin Creek Strike, 1912-1913

In 1890, following the organization of the United Mine Workers of America as an affiliate of the American Federation of Labor, the union established District 17 with temporary headquarters at Wheeling and began organizing the West Virginia miners. The United Mine Workers proceeded to the task only to meet determined resistance from the West Virginia operators, who used both legal and extra-legal means to thwart the union movement. When in 1907 the operators of the Central Competitive Field agreed in a conference with union leaders at Indianapolis to extend financial aid, the United Mine Workers renewed the contest and were preparing to carry their campaign into the New River field when they met counter-resistance south of the Kanawha. On April 1, 1912, after the operators in the Paint Creek region refused to renew the union contract, miners there were joined by those on nearby Cabin Creek in a strike which focused the eyes of the nation on West Virginia. On September 2, 1912 Governor William E. Glasscock proclaimed martial law which he suspended in October but restored a month later and employed intermittently during the remainder of his term. The strike ended on April 8, 1913, after Governor Henry D. Hatfield persuaded the opposing parties to compromise their differences.

The use of martial law where the civil courts remained open aroused heated discussion and resulted in two important test cases in the State Supreme Court of Appeals. The strike also became the special concern of a United States Senate Sub-Committee on Education and Labor, which investigated conditions in the Paint Creek-Cabin Creek fields in June, 1913.

The following documents and excerpts throw a flood of light on social and economic conditions in the strike-bound area.

BRO. WORKERS, GREETINGS:

Our fellow Miners and Workers on Paint creek are fighting for living conditions and against the "Guard System" maintained by the Coal Operators of this State.

The Workers on Cabin Creek have suffered from these conditions for years. Now is the time to throw off the yoke of bondage and strike for freedom. Will freemen submit to being driven and hounded by armed thugs? Exert your rights as free born American citizens. Organize yourselves for mutual protection and to protect your wives and babies.

As a committee from the Miners of Cabin Creek, we ask you to lay down your tools and come out with the balance of the workers.

It depends on you whether or not these conditions shall continue. Be a man and strike for your rights. Only cowards will submit to the wrongs we have suffered.

This is a duty we owe ourselves as men; this is a duty we owe our wives and babies as husbands and fathers; this is a duty we owe our brother workers on Paint Creek, who are battling bravely for justice and right. DARE WE SHRINK THESE DUTIES AND STILL CALL OURSELVES MEN?

Men and Workers, we ask you in the name of the outraged women and murdered miners of Paint Creek to lay down your tools and join your striking brothers, Tuesday, August 6th, and meet in Mass Meeting at Eskdale on that Date.

Committee of Cabin Creek Miners.

—*Documents from Hearings before the Committee on Education and Labor, 1913,* National Archives.

GOVERNOR GLASSCOCK'S SECOND PROCLAMATION OF MARTIAL LAW, NOVEMBER 15, 1912

Whereas, great public danger to life and property has for some time past and now exists, and numerous homicides have been committed, and unlawful assemblages of armed persons have congregated and resist the enforcement of the laws; and

Whereas, the civil authorities have been and are now powerless to enforce the laws of the State in the territory hereinafter described, and the Sheriff of the County of Kanawha has made demand upon the Governor for military aid, and in pursuance of said demand, and the laws in such cases made and provided, such aid has been rendered said sheriff; and . . .

Whereas, on the 14th of November, 1912, a large body of armed men, whose names are unknown, fired hundreds of shots at and into a passenger train operated by the Chesapeake & Ohio Railway Company on what is commonly called its Cabin Creek branch, in which said train there were a number of people; and

Whereas, a number of men have recently been beaten up and injured without any apparent cause therefor, all of which constitutes breaches of the peace, tumult, riots, unlawful assemblage, resistance of law and insurrection, which cannot be effectually prevented or suppressed by the Sheriff of Kanawha County, or by the ordinary posse comitatus and peace officers, and all of which endangers the peace and safety of the people of said district and obstruct the execution of the laws; and

Whereas, said sheriff commanded the said persons unlawfully assembled to disperse and retire peacefully to their respective abodes and business; and

Whereas, such persons unlawfully assembled refused to disperse and retire to their respective abodes and business, but remained in armed resistance to the enforcement of the law by the civil officers, and peace, order and quiet have not been restored, and tumult, riot and insurrection exists in the territory hereinafter described; now

THEREFORE, I, William E. Glasscock, Governor of the State of West Virginia, and as such Governor *ex officio* Commander-in-Chief of the Military forces of the State, in view of the foregoing, and in order to execute the laws, and to protect the public peace, lives and property of quiet and ordinary citizens, by virtue of the Constitution and laws of the State, do hereby declare and proclaim a state of war to exist in the District of Cabin Creek, in the County of Kanawha, and State of West Virginia, . . .

And I do hereby further declare and proclaim that said territory is and shall remain under martial law until the necessity therefor ceases to exist.—William E. Glasscock Papers, West Virginia Collection, West Virginia University Library.

STATE SUPREME COURT OF APPEALS UPHOLDS MARTIAL LAW

[JUDGE GEORGE POFFENBARGER:]

To say there cannot be a trial by a military commission under martial rule is a contradiction of authority everywhere. . . .

Though a military commission is a military court, its jurisdiction is not confined to military persons. It extends to citizens as well as soldiers. That citizens may be brought within the exercise of their power is revealed by the reason for their constitution. Courts-martial do not extend to citizens. As, in the exercise of military government, it often becomes necessary to rule, govern and punish citizens and the powers of courts-martial established by law, not by the will of the commander, do not reach such cases, a military commission to deal with citizens in the war area, is necessary. . . .—*Ex Parte Jones,* 71 W. Va., 567-625, 1913.

JUDGE IRA E. ROBINSON'S TWO DISSENTING OPINIONS

The offenses of Nance and Mays were *cognizable* by a civil court. That is, they were capable of being tried in the proper criminal court of Kanawha county, by a jury, upon presentment and indictment by a grand jury. The disturbance did not make it impossible to give them the constitutional course of trial. . . . The only excuse for their not being tried there is that the Governor ordered otherwise. Thus the Governor alone made the necessity. Under the circumstances, in any considerate view, their trials and sentences were not by due process of law, and were grossly illegal and void.

There were no courts, other than those of justices, within the actual theater of the disturbances on Cabin Creek that could be rendered inoperative by the riotous condition there. The criminal court that pertained to that part and to the whole of the county was far from the seat of riot and wholly unaffected in its powers for regular and orderly presentment and trial. Even as to offenses cognizable only by justices, there was power and opportunity to bring offenders from that region to trial before justices in undisturbed districts of the county. But it does not even appear that the disturbances in the district rendered it impossible, by the aid of the militia there present, for the courts of justices of the peace there to mete out justice according to the civil law. The war must put the ordinary courts out of business, *out of reach,* before military courts can ever take their place. . . . The state courts were more accessible than the state prison. This principle, that accessibility to the ordinary civil courts excludes resort to martial law, is established by the decision in the Milligan case in no uncertain language. We need no greater precedent. . . .—Nance and Mays v. Brown, 71 *W. Va.*, 519-67, 1912.

. . . The State can not be preserved by a suspension of constitutional rights. Nothing will kill it quicker. . . .

A clash between mine owners and miners can not be considered public war, and the participants dealt with as enemies of the State. . . . Because of warfare between themselves and violations of the law in relation thereto, has neither side any constitutional rights which the State is bound to respect? Nothing in the record justifies the conclusion that either the mine owners and their guards on the one hand, or the miners on the other, have lost their allegiance to the State by the unfortunate clash between them or by any other act. Neither faction has made war against the State. Each time the militia has been sent to the district, all has remained quiet. . . . Yet the majority opinion deals with the citizens of the district as rebels. It deals with a part of Kanawha county as enemy country. In this it can not be sustained by reason or authority. *Cabin Creek District has not seceded!* . . .

Is it not a spectacle for the notice of a people who rest their liberties on our form of constitutional government that in one of the States of the Union a section thereof is given to an independent military rule, which admits no power of the civil courts to enter, and which claims cognizance as against all found therein of every imaginable accusation from mere words spoken to perjury, rape or murder? . . .

The persistency with which a military rule heretofore unknown has been sanctioned, has demanded this second protest on my part. Unfortunate indeed is the generation that forgetteth the memories of its fathers.—*Ex Parte* Jones, 71 *W. Va.*, 567-625, 1913.

REPORT OF THE SENATE SUB-COMMITTEE ON EDUCATION AND LABOR, 1914

[Senator Claude A. Swanson:]

The conditions existing in this district for many months were most deplorable. The hostility became so intense, the conflict so fierce, that there existed in this district for some time well-armed forces fighting for supremacy. Separate camps, organized, armed, and guarded, were established. There was much violence and some murders. Pitched battles were fought by the contending parties. Law and order disappeared, and life was insecure for both sides. Operation and business practically ceased. . . .

Among the contributing causes may be enumerated the following:

The failure of the operators in the Paint Creek district to renew their expiring contract with the United Mine Workers; the determination of the coal operators under no circumstances to recognize the miners as an organization or union and the equal determination of the miners to organize and form a union, a right as they claim guaranteed to them without discrimination by the laws of West Virginia; the employment by the operators of mine guards, many of whom were aggressive and arbitrary; mine guards in the employment of the operators acting as deputy sheriffs and clothed with the authority of law; the failure of the civil authorities to attempt even to preserve peace and order at the beginning of violence and permitting things to drift from bad to worse without vigorous interference and assertion of authority; discontent among the miners occasioned by no opportunity to purchase homes; no cemeteries except upon the company's grounds; post offices located in the company's stores; private roads only to the schools and stores; the disposition of the coal operators to keep strict espionage of all strangers who entered the district and to exercise their right of private ownership of this large district and to exclude from it all persons objectionable to them.

[SENATOR JAMES E. MARTINE:]

God has blessed West Virginia with a prolific hand; a topography grand to contemplate; a wealth unparalleled in coal, iron and oil—her hills fairly groan with undeveloped resources, and all of these at the very threshold of the great marts of trade and commerce of our country. Here, above all sections, should peace, plenty, and happiness reign supreme. On the contrary, your committee found disorder, riot, bitterness, and bloodshed in their stead.

In no spirit of malice or hatred, but with a view that the country, through knowledge of the true conditions, may right the wrong, I charge that the hiring of armed bodies of men by private mine owners and other corporations and the use of steel armored trains, machine guns and bloodhounds on defenseless men, women, and children is but a little way from barbarism. . . .

Asked what is my solution of this and similar unhappy conditions, I would state: A millionaire owner of a great section of the State of West Virginia calmly admitted on the witness stand that so long as he got his per ton lease he never inquired further. Our duty under the premises: Coal, under our civilization is a necessity. This great commodity can not be increased a fraction of a pound, yet our population is multiplying by leaps and bounds each year, thereby increasing the demands for this article. We must have warmth for our bodies and fuel with which to cook our foods. With this condition existing and, with avarice as the dominating characteristic in man, I, at the risk of criticism by my many friends and countrymen, unhesitatingly say that Government ownership of the mines is the only hope or solution for those who may come after us. . . .

[SENATOR WILLIAM S. KENYON:]

. . . It is well to inquire as to the reasons for such deplorable conditions. Many things appear on the surface which might be deemed causes, but they are only surface indications of a deeper trouble. A reading of the record will lead one to the belief that there were many causes for the conditions existing.

Among them might be related the employment of mine guards, high prices charged the miners at company stores, mine guards acting as deputy sheriffs, post offices located in company stores, private roads to the schools and stores, no opportunity to purchase homes, cemeteries upon company grounds, attempts to unionize the miners, alien ownership of large tracts of land—in one instance 21,000 acres. . . . The basic cause is the private ownership of great public necessities, such as coal; this coupled with human greed, incident to such ownership, has brought about the deplorable and un-American conditions in the West Virginia coal fields under investigation.

Bishop Donahue was asked the question as to what was the fundamental trouble. He answered that the causes were deep rooted and very obscure to a man unless he thinks, and thinks, and thinks, and traces the roots down into their primary causes. Quoting from the bishop:

I should say if I were asked to put it very briefly that it is human greed on both sides.

It is a little difficult to realize how there can be much human greed on the side of a man who is supporting a family and working day by day in the mines at ordinary living wages, but there is greed on the part of the owners of the property, and there always will be such greed. There are apparently more labor troubles in mining properties than in any other line of business, and all of these troubles are leading more or less to the dissipation of the coal of the country.

If the Government should take over the coal properties of the country, in some manner, of course, to be provided by law, whereby reasonable compensation would be made therefor, and itself lease these coal properties, maintaining a strict governmental regulation over the same, the question of labor troubles in relation thereto would doubtless be solved. . . .—*Senate Reports*, 63rd Congress, 2d Session, 1913-1914. Report No. 321, pp. 5, 18-19, 20-21.

155. Mother Jones – "Angel of the Miners"

Of the labor leaders who went to West Virginia to organize the miners, the most colorful was Mary Harris Jones (1830-1930), the "angel of the miners." Born at Cork, Ireland, Mary Jones, nee Harris, moved to Canada with her parents in 1835, attended school in Toronto, taught in a convent at Monroe, Michigan, and operated a dressmaking shop in Chicago. In 1861 she resumed teaching in Memphis and there met her husband, a member of the Iron Moulders' Union. It was there, too, that her husband and four children died of yellow fever in 1867.

Mary Jones returned to Chicago only to meet further disaster in 1871, when the "Great Fire" destroyed her home and dressmaking establishment. Without employment and homeless, she became a member of the Knights of Labor and dedicated her life to improvement of working conditions in industry. For half a century she carried the banner for organized labor where the battle raged hottest. Clarence Darrow called her the Wendell Phillips of the labor movement.

Mother Jones became an organizer for the United Mine Workers in 1891 and went to West Virginia in that capacity eleven years later. She played a leading part in the first efforts to organize the Fairmont, Kanawha, New River and Pocahontas fields as well as a picturesque role in the Paint Creek-Cabin Creek strike of 1912-1913. For her defiance of martial law on Cabin Creek in 1912 she was sentenced by a military commission to serve twenty years in the Moundsville penitentiary only to receive a pardon from Governor Hatfield. In 1921 she returned to the Kanawha Valley to assist the miners but failed to dissuade them from their fateful "March on Logan."

Mother Jones was a forceful, effective public speaker. She spoke vigorously and courageously, frequently punctuating her sentences with a mild profanity. She also possessed a ready wit and a sharp sense of the dramatic, which combined with feminity and advanced age, made her invaluable as a union organizer. In the excerpts below Mother Jones relates her first experiences as a union organizer in West Virginia and describes conditions as she found them in the Paint Creek-Cabin Creek region ten years later.

In June of 1902 I was holding a meeting of the bituminous miners of Clarksburg, West Virginia. I was talking on the strike question, for what else among miners should one be talking of? Nine organizers sat under a tree near by. A United States marshal notified them to tell me that I was under arrest. . . .

That night several of the organizers and myself were taken to Parkersburg, a distance of eighty-four miles. . . .

We were taken to the Federal court for trial. We had violated something they called an injunction. Whatever the bosses did not want the miners to do they got out an injunction against doing it. The company put a woman on the stand. She testified that I had told the miners to go into the mines and throw out the scabs. She was a poor skinny woman with scared eyes and she wore her best dress, as if she were in church. I looked at the miserable slave of the coal company and I felt sorry for her: sorry that there was a creature so low who would perjure herself for a handful of coppers.

I was put on the stand and the judge asked me if I gave that advice to the miners, told them to use violence.

"You know, sir," said I, "that it would be suicidal for me to make such a statement in public. I am more careful than that. You've been on the bench forty years, have you not, judge?"

"Yes, I have that," said he.

"And in forty years you learn to discern between a lie and the truth, judge?"

The prosecuting attorney jumped to his feet and shaking his finger at me, he said "Your honor, there is the most dangerous woman in the country today. She called your honor a scab. But I will recommend mercy of the court if she will consent to leave the state and never return."

"I didn't come into the court asking mercy," I said, "but I came here looking for justice. And I will not leave this state so long as there is a single little child that asks me to stay and fight the battle for bread." . . .

One morning when I was west, working for the Southern Pacific machinists, I read in the paper that the Paint Creek Coal Company would not settle with their men and had driven them out into the mountains. I knew that Paint Creek country. I had helped the miners organize that district in 1904 and now the battle had to be fought all over again.

I cancelled all my speaking dates in California, tied up all my possessions in a black shawl—I like traveling light—and went immediately to West Virginia.

. . . It had started on the other side of the Kanawha hills in a frightful district called "Russia,"—Cabin Creek. Here the miners had been peons for years, kept in slavery by the guns of the coal company, and by the system of paying in script so that a miner never had any money should he wish to leave the district. He was cheated of his wages when his coal was weighed, cheated in the company store where he was forced to purchase his food, charged an exorbitant rent for his kennel in which he lived and bred, docked for school tax and burial tax and physician and for "protection," which meant the gunmen who shot him back into the mines if he rebelled or so much as murmured against his outrageous exploitation. No one was allowed in the Cabin Creek district without explaining his reason for being there to the gunmen who patrolled the roads, all of which belonged to the coal company. The miners finally struck—it was a strike of desperation.

The strike of Cabin Creek spread to Paint Creek, where the operators decided to throw their fate in with the operators of Cabin Creek. Immediately all civil and constitutional rights were suspended. The miners were told to quit their houses, and told at the point of a gun. They established a tent colony in Holly Grove and Mossy. But they were not safe here from the assaults of the gunmen, recruited in the big cities from the bums and criminals.

To protect their women and children, who were being shot with poisoned bullets, whose houses were entered and rough-housed, the miners armed themselves as did the early settlers against the attacks of wild Indians. . . .

The train stopped at Paint Creek Junction and I got off. There were a lot of gunmen, armed to the teeth, lolling about. Everything was still and no one would know of the bloody war that was raging in those silent hills, except for the sight of those guns and the strange, terrified look on everyone's face. . . .

I went up to the miners' camp in Holly Grove where all through the winter, through snow and ice and blizzard, men and women and little children had shuddered in canvas tents that America might be a better country to live in. I listened to their stories. I talked to Mrs. Sevilla whose unborn child had been kicked dead by gunmen while her husband was out looking for work. I talked to widows, whose husbands had been shot by the gunmen; with children whose frightened faces talked more effectively than their baby tongues. I learned how the scabs had been recruited in the cities, locked in boxcars, and delivered to the mines like so much pork. . . .

I traveled up and down the Creek, holding meetings, rousing the tired spirits of the miners. I got three thousand armed miners to march over the hills secretly to Charleston, where we read a declaration of war to Governor Glasscock who, scared as a rabbit, met us on the steps of the state house. We gave him just twenty-four hours to get rid of the gunmen, promising him that hell would break loose if he didn't. He did. He sent the state militia in, who at least were responsible to society and not the operators alone. . . .

The struggle went on with increasing bitterness. The militia disarmed both gunmen and miners but they were of course, on the side of the grand dukes of the region. They forbade all meetings. They suspended every civil right. They became despotic. They arrested scores of miners, tried them in military court, without jury, sentenced them to ten, fifteen years in the Moundsville prison.—*Autobiography of Mother Jones,* edited by Mary Field Parton, pp. 49-52, 148-52, 160.

156. West Virginia in World War I

In the First World War, 323,383 West Virginians registered for military duty, and 45,648 were inducted into the armed forces under the Selective Service Act of May 18, 1917. The West Virginia National Guard mustered an additional two thousand men, and approximately thirteen thousand West Virginians volunteered either into United States combat forces or for service in Allied units. One hundred seventy-seven West Virginia women served in the Army Nurse Corps. West Virginians served in almost every combat unit and in every sector of the European front. Of the sixty thousand who entered the armed forces of the United States, 26,677 went overseas, 517 were killed in action, almost three thousand received battle wounds, 194 died of wounds, 51 were captured, and 1047 died of disease and other causes—making a total of approximately five thousand casualties or one twelfth of the whole number in the service during the war.

Meanwhile West Virginians at home "went over the top" in fund drives and drives to conserve food and fuel, to mobilize manpower, and to sharpen the fighting edge. The extracts which follow throw light on West Virginia's part in the war.

DESPITE BAD COMMUNICATION with many interior counties, West Virginia was among the first to complete and report the result of the first registration. Its per capita cost was among the lowest of the States and out of the class of registrants of June 5th (1918) it developed a higher percentage of fighting men than any state in the Union, 64.7 per cent, North Dakota coming next with 58.7 per cent, while Connecticut fell to 28.4 per cent. Among my priceless possessions is a chart showing the standing of the several States, presented to me personally by General Crowder, on which he autographed the following:

"Presented to the Governor of West Virginia with the congratulations and compliments of E. H. Crowder, Provost Marshal General." . . .

The state's record in the various war-work activities is one of which its citizens may very well be proud. As the second coal-producing State in the Union—furnishing the smokeless coals used on our war ships as well as by-product coals, so essential in the manufacture of munitions and explosives—a tremendous task was imposed upon the operators and mine workers alike. Despite the loss of man power the coal production was well maintained. The supply of fuel, coal, oil, gasoline, and natural gas which West Virginia contributed, has been a mighty factor in the prosecution of the War.

The State and its citizens have likewise met the calls upon them for funds—not only in the several Liberty Loan campaigns, over-subscribing their allotment each time—but for all other purposes also.

In the first Red Cross drive the State was allotted $500,000 and subscribed $580,000. In the second drive its allotment was $700,000 and it subscribed $1,276,000. In the first Y. M. C. A. drive the allotment was $30,000 while $35,825.19 was subscribed. In the second Y. M. C. A. campaign the allotment was $250,000 with subscriptions of $317,000. With an allotment of $30,000 for the Salvation Army War Fund, $33,770.34 was subscribed. The Liberty Loan allotments and subscriptions are given elsewhere in detail and show gratifying results, especially in the fourth campaign which came just at a time when the epidemic of Spanish influenza was sweeping over the State, which prevented public meetings and proved a great hardship.—Governor John J. Cornwell's Report, *West Virginia Legislative Hand Book and Manual, 1918,* pp. 777-78.

THE LIBERTY LOAN CAMPAIGNS

	Quota	Subscriptions	Number Subscribers
First Liberty Loan	15,172,000	16,048,800	— — — —
Second Liberty Loan	28,823,200	36,043,050	70,431
Third Liberty Loan	21,770,300	31,913,250	156,033
Fourth Liberty Loan	45,748,200	55,988,900	212,717
Victory Liberty Loan	32,160,850	33,135,600	79,683

—*West Virginia Legislative Hand Book, 1919,* pp. 572-79.

XIV. Between World Wars

157. The Hitchman Case, 1917

Following the so-called "Indianapolis Agreement" between the operators of the Central Competitive Field and the United Mine Workers of America, the Hitchman Coal and Coke Company of Benwood, Marshall County, an affiliate of the Hanna Coal Company of Cleveland, Ohio, obtained an injunction in the United States District Court for West Virginia restraining President John Mitchell and others of the United Mine Workers of America from interfering with the operations of its mines. The miners' union contested the issue through the Supreme Court of the United States, which in December, 1917, handed down a decision upholding the injunction and declaring that the Hitchman Coal and Coke Company had a legal right to operate its mines under its own rules and regulations. The opinion legalized the use of the "yellow dog" contract.

But the Hitchman opinion, like the Dred Scott decision, was soon nullified by events. For in April, 1918, when President Woodrow Wilson authorized the War Labor Policy Board to enforce an industrial code many of the West Virginia operators, except those of the smokeless field in the southern counties and in Clay County waived their rights under the Hitchman decision during the emergency and submitted to unionization of their mines. Thus when the war ended the rank and file of union miners joined their leaders not only to consolidate the gains of the war period but also to unionize that citadel of resistance—the southern West Virginia smokeless field. The futile struggle which went on there between union miners and anti-union coal operators from 1919 to 1922 featured violence on a scale not witnessed in West Virginia since the Civil War. Although successful in gaining a foothold in Mingo County, union organizers made no headway at all in Logan and McDowell counties and it was not until the 1930's, when the depression paralyzed the coal industry that operators and miners alike accepted unionization with blessings of the New Deal.

The passages below include an excerpt from the Hitchman decision, Governor Ephraim F. Morgan's first proclamation of martial law in Mingo County, and an extract from the decision of the State Supreme Court of Appeals which invalidated martail law in Mingo County.

MR. JUSTICE PITNEY . . .

That the plaintiff was acting within its lawful rights in employing its men only upon terms of continuing non-membership in the United Mine Workers of America is not open to question. Plaintiff's repeated costly experiences of strikes and other interferences while attempting to "run union" were a sufficient explanation of its resolve to run "non-union," if any were needed. . . . Whatever may be the advantages of "collective bargaining," it is not bargaining at all, in any sense, unless it is voluntary on both sides. The same liberty which enables men to form unions, and through the union to enter into agreement with employers willing to agree, entitles other men to remain independent of the union and other employers to agree with them to employ no man who owes any allegiance or obligation to the union. . . .

Plaintiff, having in the exercise of its undoubted rights established a working agreement between it and its employees, with the free assent of the latter, is entitled to be protected in the enjoyment of the resulting status, as in any other legal right. That the employment was "at will," and terminable by either party at any time, is of no consequence. . . .

Another fundamental error in defendants' position consists in the assumption that all measures that may be resorted to are lawful if they are "peaceable"—that is, if they stop short of physical violence, or coercion through fear of it. In our opinion, any violation of plaintiff's legal rights contrived by defendants for the purpose of inflicting damage, or having that as its necessary effect, is as plainly inhibited by the law as if it involved a breach of the peace.

. . .Having become convinced by three costly strikes, occurring within a period of as many years, of the futility of attempting to operate under a closed-shop agreement with the Union, it established the mine on a non-union basis, with the unanimous approval of its employees—in fact upon their suggestion—and under a mutual agreement, assented to by every employee, that plaintiff would continue to run its mine non-union and would not recognize the United Mine Workers of America; that if any man wanted to become a member of that Union he was at liberty to do so, but he could not be a member and remain in plaintiff's employ. . . . —Hitchman Coal and Coke Company *v.* Mitchell Individually, *et al.,* 245 *U. S.,* 229-74, 1917.

GOVERNOR MORGAN'S FIRST PROCLAMATION OF MARTIAL LAW, MAY 19, 1921

Whereas, A state of war, insurrection and riot is, and has been for sometime in existence in the County of Mingo, and State of West Virginia; and,

Whereas, large bodies of armed men have assembled in the mountains of Mingo County and fired into and shot up public and other buildings and fired into passenger trains while passing over the Norfolk and Western railway in said county; and,

Whereas, many lives and much property have been destroyed as a result thereof, and riot and bloodshed is still rampant and pending and,

Whereas, the Judge of the Circuit Court, the Sheriff and Prosecuting Attorney of said county have declared their inability to put down or control such insurrection and riot and have been, and are now, powerless to enforce the laws of the State within said Mingo County, and have called upon me as Governor of the State of West Virginia and as such Governor ex-officio Commander-in-Chief of the military forces of the State; and,

Whereas, there is necessity therefor:

THEREFORE, I Ephraim F. Morgan, Governor of the State of West Virginia, and as such Governor ex-officio Commander-in Chief of the military forces of the State, in view of the foregoing, and in order to execute the laws and to protect the public peace, lives and property of quiet, orderly citizens, by virtue of the Constitution of the State of West Virginia, do hereby declare and proclaim a state of war, insurrection and riot to exist in the said County of Mingo, State of West Virginia.

And I do hereby further declare and proclaim that said territory is, and shall remain, under martial law until the necessity therefor ceases to exist and my further order; PROVIDED, however, that the civil courts of said Mingo County shall continue to have jurisdiction of, and try, all crimes, misdemeanors and offenses against the civil law.

The following rules and orders are hereby promulgated and declared to be in force and effect and as controlling the civil population of said Mingo County until further orders:

1. No person or persons shall compose or take part in, or encourage, aid, abet or assist any riot, rout, tumult, mob or lawless combination or assemblage, or encourage, aid, abet or assist in the violation of any of the civil laws of the State of West Virginia.

2. No public assemblages or meetings will be permitted in any city, town or village, or in any enclosure or open air place within the county, except by special authority.

3. All processions and parades, except by special authority, are prohibited, as well as demonstrations against the authorities and officers.

4. No persons, except the constituted municipal, state and federal authorities, militia, troops, police and other officers of the law, are permitted to carry or have arms or weapons of any character or description, or equipment, explosives, ammunition or munitions of war in their possession, or at any place, except at their own homes or places of business.

5. All military and other officers shall have the right of way in any street or highway through which they may pass.

6. Any person or persons entering or remaining in said Mingo County for the purposes of interfering in any manner whatever with the rights of citizens or property of said Mingo County shall be arrested, detained and imprisoned.

7. All persons are admonished to observe and carefully and rigidly comply with the civil laws of the State of West Virginia and with the letter and spirit of this proclamation and these rules and orders; and any person or persons violating the same in said Mingo County shall be arrested, disarmed, detained and imprisoned.

8. Any person or persons, except the constituted municipal, state and federal authorities, militia, troops, police and other

officers of the law, carrying or in possession of arms, or weapons of any character or description, or equipment, explosives, ammunition or munitions of war, at any place other than at their homes or places of business, shall be arrested, disarmed, detained and imprisoned.

9. No publication, either newspaper, pamphlet, hand-bill, or otherwise, reflecting in any way upon the United States or the State of West Virginia or their officers, or tending to influence the public mind against the United States or the State of West Virginia or their officers, may be published, distributed, displayed or circulated in said Mingo County, and the publication, distribution, displaying or circulation of any such publication above specified is prohibited, and any person or persons violating this paragraph shall be arrested, detained and imprisoned. . . . —Morgan Papers, West Virginia Collection, West Virginia University Library.

[JUDGE POFFENBARGER:]

The substitution of military, for the civil law, in any community, is an extreme measure. Socially, economically and politically, it is deplorable and calamitous. Its sole justification is the failure of the civil law fully to operate and function, for the time being, by reason of the paralysis or overthrow of its agencies, in consequence of an insurrection, invasion or other enterprise hostile to the state and resulting in actual warfare. And then such substitution at any place within the state cannot extend beyond the limits of the theater of actual war. . . . It is perfectly manifest, that the proclamation of war did not, *ipso facto,* nor *ex proprio vigore,* inaugurate martial law in Mingo County.

The Governor's attempt to inaugurate it and put it into effect in that county, in the manner hereinbefore described, was clearly futile and inoperative. The irresistible logic of the precedents already cited and of all others bearing upon the subject is that martial law is an incident of military operations within the area of actual, not merely theoretical, warfare. . . . In other words, the Governor, being expressly authorized to conduct military operations for suppression of insurrection and in resistance of invasion, is impliedly authorized to conduct such operations in accordance with the usages and customs of war, and so has all the powers recognized as being incident to the office of commander-in-chief of any army engaged in such enterprises. . . . Administration and enforcement of martial law by civil agencies could not be brought within the terms of that section. . . . In other words, he cannot by a mere order convert the civil officers into an army and clothe them with military powers, for the purpose of suppressing an insurrection or repelling an invasion. He can raise an army only in the manner prescribed by law, and his military authority can be exerted in respect of things authorized to be done with the military forces, only by means of an army. . . . —*Ex Parte* A. D. Lavinder *et al.*, 88 W. Va., 713-21, 1921.

158. The March on Logan and the Treason Trials

Frustrated in their efforts to organize the southern West Virginia smokeless coal field and aroused by the use of martial law in Mingo County, union miners of the Kanawha Valley mobilized at Marmet near Charleston in the summer of 1921 to assist embattled miners along the Tug. On August 24, 1921, this army of approximately 3,000 men took up the line of march toward Logan, gathering recruits and supplies, and commandeering automobiles and freight trains along the way. After alerting the militia and State Police, Governor Ephraim F. Morgan appealed to President Harding, who readied troops and sent General Harry H. Bandholtz to Charleston to confer with the governor. Federal and State authorities and union officials momentarily persuaded the marchers to turn back, but they resumed the march following a clash with State Police at Sharples in Logan County.

Ignoring a proclamation by President Harding to disperse, the miners reached the watershed of the Coal and Guyandotte rivers where on August 31, 1921, they met an opposing force, said to exceed 1,200 men. For almost a week, the forces skirmished along a twenty-five mile front, with severe fighting on Blair Mountain. The Logan defenders reported three killed and forty wounded but the number of casualties suffered by the miners has never been disclosed. Hostilities ended on September 4, 1921, with the arrival of the Tenth U. S. Infantry from Fort Thomas, Kentucky, and a squadron of Martin bombers from Langley Field, Virginia.

For alleged participation in the "March on Logan," a Logan County grand jury indicted 598 persons, 54 of them for treason against the State of West Virginia. The defendants obtained a change of venue to Jefferson County, where John Brown had been tried and convicted on charges of murder and treason sixty-three years before.

The treason trial of William Blizzard, alleged field marshal of the armed marchers, began on April 21, 1922, with Judge J. M. Woods of Martinsburg on the bench. The prosecution had not only to prove that Blizzard had participated as a leader and that his acts had been seen by two witnesses, but also that he had warred against the State. The defense contended that the miners had no grievance against the State but only against an industrial autocracy which had arrogated to itself the police powers of the State.

The defense attorneys completely discredited the testimony of the two witnesses against Blizzard, and the prosecution failed to prove that he was with the marchers at the time alleged. The trial of Blizzard for murder was first moved to Berkeley Springs, Morgan County, then to Lewisburg, Greenbrier County, where it ended in a jury deadlock. He was never retried. Meanwhile the court at Charles Town convicted minor participants charged with treason, murder and conspiracy, but dropped treason charges against the union leaders. The trial of C. Frank Keeney, president of District 17 of the United Mine Workers, on charges of murder and conspiracy, was moved to Fayette County only to be dropped from the docket. The affair ended when Governor Ephraim F. Morgan commuted the sentences of the few convicted offenders, and his successor Governor Howard M. Gore extended them a full pardon.

Extracts from the treason indictment by the Logan County grand jury and the report of the Senate Committee on Education and Labor which investigated conditions in the southern West Virginia coal fields in 1921, appear below with the full text of President Harding's proclamation of August 30, 1921.

A PROCLAMATION
BY THE PRESIDENT OF THE UNITED STATES.

Whereas, the Governor of the State of West Virginia has represented that domestic violence exists in said State, which the authorities of said State are unable to suppress, and,

Whereas, it is provided in the constitution of the United States that the United States shall protect each state in this Union on application of the legislature or the executive when the legislature cannot be convened, against domestic violence, and

Whereas, by the law of the United States, in pursuance of the above, it is provided that in all cases of insurrection in any state or of obstruction to the laws thereof it shall be lawful for the President of the United States, on application of the legislature of such state or of the executive when the legislature cannot be convened, to call forth the militia of any other state or states or to employ such part of the land and naval forces of the United States as shall be judged necessary for the purpose of suppressing such insurrection and causing the laws to be duly executed and,

Whereas, the legislature of the State of West Virginia is not now in session and cannot be convened in time to meet the present emergency and the executive of said State, under section 4 of Article IV of the constitution of the United States and the laws passed in pursuance thereof, has made due application to me in the premises for such part of the military forces of the United States as may be necessary and adequate to protect the State of West Virginia and the citizens thereof against domestic violence and to enforce the due execution of the laws, and

Whereas, it is required that whenever it may be necessary in the judgment of the President to use the military forces of the United States for the purposes aforesaid, he shall forthwith by proclamation command such insurgents to disperse and retire peaceably to their respective homes within a limited time,

Now, therefore, I, Warren G. Harding, President of the United States, do hereby make proclamation and I do hereby command all persons engaged in said unlawful and insurrectionary proceedings to disperse and retire peaceably to their respective abodes on or before twelve o'clock, noon, of the first day of September, nineteen hundred twenty one, and hereafter abandon

said combinations and submit themselves to the laws and constituted authorities of said state, and I invoke the aid and co-operation of all good citizens thereof to uphold the laws and preserve
the public peace.

In Witness whereof, I have hereto set my hand and caused the
seal of the United States to be affixed.

Done at the City of Washington, this thirtieth day of August,
in the year of our Lord one thousand nine hundred and
twenty one, and of the independence of the United States
the one hundred and forty sixth.

By the President: Warren G. Harding

Charles E. Hughes, Secy of State. — Morgan Papers, West
Virginia Collection, West Virginia University Library.

INDICTMENT FOR TREASON, FEBRUARY 4, 1922

In the Circuit Court of Logan County:

The grand jurors of the State of West Virginia, in and for the
body of the County of Logan, upon their oaths present that
Frank Keeney, Fred Mooney, Scott Reese, William Ray, Dave
Ware, Eb Oakes, James Corbitt, William Blizzard, A. C. Porter,
R. F. Toney, Frank Snyder, A. D. Lavender, U. S. Cantley, C.
Vorholt, Ross Hagar, Clyde Estep, Walter Allen, Doc Munsey,
Lawrence Dwyer, James Gilmore, Henry Alford, Dewey Bailey,
Deck Tony, Thomas Ayers, Anderson Fauber, Owen Atkins, Ralph
Legg, Anthony Neff, Arthur McCormick, James Burnside, Okey
Johnson, William Petry, Isaac Scott, Sam Hensley, James Eichel-
berger, W. H. Stevens, Chap Bailey,J. A. Bailey, W. F. Carter, L.
Forman, L. C. Whitlock, J. B. Mooney, Gib Riffle, Ed. Dueser,
Clarence Plants, Chas. Elswick, W. H. Stevens, Wm. Cordel,
James Glenn, S. C. Garley, Ned Williams, W. H. Phaliah, T. J.
Garten, W. E. Craigo, of Kanawha, Boone and Raleigh Counties,
West Virginia, on the ————day of August, 1921, they the said
Frank Keeney, [et al.], being persons then and there abiding
within the State of West Virginia, and deriving protection from
the laws of said State, and then and there owing allegiance and
fidelity to the said State, and being then and there members and
citizens thereof, not regarding their duties of their said allegiance
and fidelity, but wickedly devising and intending the peace and

tranquility of the said State, to disturb and destroy on the ————
————————of August, 1921, at Marmet, Kanawha County, West
Virginia, and at the city of Charleston in said Kanawha County,
West Virginia, did then and there unlawfully, maliciously and
traitorously conspire, to levy war against the said State of West
Virginia; and to fulfill and effect the said traitorous compassings,
intentions and conspirings of them the said Frank Keeney,
[et al.], they, the . . . aforesaid, that is to say on the ————————
———— of August, 1921, and the said————————————of September,
1921, at Marmet in said Kanawha County with Mose Adkins,
[and 543 others listed in the indictment], with a great multitude
of other persons, whose names are to the jurors aforesaid and yet
unknown, to the number of from eight to ten thousand, armed
and arrayed in a warlike manner, that is to say, with machine
guns, high power rifles, military rifles, pistols and revolvers and
other warlike weapons, ammunition and supplies, as well offensive as defensive, being then and there unlawfully, maliciously
and traitorously assembled and gathered together, did falsely,
maliciously and traitorously assemble, combine, conspire and
join themselves together against the said State, and then and
there with force and arms, did wickedly, . . . and in a warlike and
hostile manner, array and dispose themselves against the said
State, and then and there on the day and dates above mentioned in pursuance of such malicious and traitorous intentions, conspirings and purposes they the said Frank Keeney [et al.], did
with the said Mose Adkins, [543 others] and the other said persons to the jurors aforesaid unknown, so as aforesaid traitorously assembled, armed and arrayed, in manner aforesaid, most
wickedly, . . . did ordain, and prepare and levy war against the
said State, contrary to their duties of the allegiance of the said
Frank Keeney, [et al.], did then and there. . . march in battle or
military array to Blair, Logan County and to other places in said
Logan County and did then and there. . . on the ———————— days
of August, 1921, and the ———————— days of September, 1921,
did engage in a series of battles with the military forces of the
State of West Virginia, and with other forces who were then and
there acting under the control and direction of the Chief Executive, the Governor of the State of West Virginia, . . . all with the
malicious, wicked and traitorous intentions . . . of destroying and

to destroy and nullify by force of arms, violence, murder and open warfare, martial law in said Mingo County and the military occupation of said county, which martial law had been duly proclaimed by the Governor of the State of West Virginia, the Honorable E. F. Morgan, on the 27 day of June, 1921, . . . and to release from imprisonment persons who had been duly and legally arrested and incarcerated in the jails of Mingo County for violation of law and violations of the martial law proclamation of the said governor of West Virginia, against the peace and dignity of the State of West Virginia.—Courtesy of William C. Blizzard.

THE [SOUTHERN] WEST VIRGINIA COAL FIELDS

The issue is plain and perfectly apparent. The operators in this particular section of West Virginia under consideration openly announce, and did before the committee, that they will not employ men belonging to the unions, for, as they say, they believe they will become agitators; and further, that they have the right, and will exercise it if they desire, to discharge a man if he belongs to the union, and in making these claims they believe themselves to be within their constitutional rights.

On the other hand, the United Mine Workers are determined to unionize these fields which are practically the only large and important coal fields in the United States not unionized.

. . . The operators claim a constitutional right to discharge a man if he belongs to a union. The workmen claim a constitutional right to join a union if they desire. How are these propositions to be harmonized?

The miners also claim that the constitutional right of free speech and free assembly has been violated.

If men are to be driven out of counties because they go there to engage in free speech and to endeavor in peaceable ways to have men join unions there is a clear violation of constitutional right.

If men belonging to unions interfere with nonunion men securing positions and by threats and violence make it impossible for nonunion men to work, there is another clear violation of constitutional rights. . . .

There have been violations of law on both sides of this controversy. There has been an arrogance upon both sides, seeming to indicate that, in the opinion of some of the leaders, the question was entirely one between the operators and the workers. Both sides have been forgetful of the great third party — the public — which has a vital interest in preserving industrial peace, especially in a region furnishing the percentage of coal that this region furnishes.

If this matter is none of Congress's business, as is intimated in some of the briefs, then this committee should not have been appointed, but the intimation is merely a confirmation of the arrogance of those who assume that the public has no interest whatsoever in these matters. If it is no business of the National Goverment, then Federal troops should not have been requested to preserve peace. . . .

They [the operators] have a right to operate their plants on a nonunion basis or on a union basis. They have the right to employ men whether they belong to a union or whether they do not. They have the right to discharge men because they belong to a union or to discharge them because they do not belong to a union. They have the right not to employ men if they do not desire to do so. They have no right to use force and violence to keep men out of a county who are there for the purpose of inducing men to join the union. They have the right to protect their property. The fundamental of protection should be, however, upon the State. It is the duty of the State to protect the properties of the operators if anyone attempts to use force and violence against them. There is no right in public policy or public morals for the operators to pay the salaries of deputy sheriffs. The State police power and private police can not work together. The State can not abdicate its function of protecting the public. . . .

The right of collective bargaining means the right to employees, when they so desire, to deal collectively with their employers. It likewise implies a limitation upon the freedom of their employers to discharge employees for membership in unions. . . .

Furthermore, the granting of this right to the workers is in the interest of sound public policy. A large industry, such as the coal industry, is vested with a public interest hardly second in importance to railroad transportation. The public therefore cannot be indifferent to the relations between employer and employee in that industry when conditions arise which threaten or interrupt the supply of one of the commodities most essential to life and industry. If direct and uncontrolled relations between operators and labor are no longer capable of maintaining peace and insuring a coal supply at a fair price, the State must intervene to the extent, if necessary, of infringing upon private rights. . . .—William S. Kenyon, "West Virginia Coal Fields," *Senate Reports*, Vol. 1, 67th Cong., 2d Sess., No. 457, pp. 4-10, 21-22.

159. West Virginia Tries to Pre-empt Natural Gas

First in the nation in the production of natural gas at the beginning of World War I, the West Virginia fields had for many years supplied consumers in other states as well as in West Virginia. Of the 265 billion cubic feet of gas produced in 1918, 227 billion cubic feet reached market through facilities of the pipeline companies—70 billion to consumers in the State and 157 billion to consumers in other states. However, when faced with the decline of output on the one hand and the increase of local demand on the other, the Legislature enacted a statute on February 10, 1919, which required pipeline companies in the State to supply West Virginia consumers with whatever gas was needed for local purposes before channeling it elsewhere. Because many Ohio and Pennsylvania consumers of natural gas depended solely upon West Virginia production, and change to any other form of fuel would entail great expense, these states brought suits to prevent West Virginia from enforcing the act. Below is an excerpt from the decision of the United States Supreme Court.

MR. JUSTICE VAN DEVANTER . . . In West Virginia the production of natural gas began as much as thirty years ago and for the last fourteen years has been greater than in any other State. The producing fields include thirty-two of her fifty-five counties. At first the gas was produced only in the course of oil operations, was regarded as a nuisance and was permitted to waste into the air. But it soon came to be regarded as valuable for heating and lighting, and the economy and convenience attending its use made it a preferred fuel. Its use within the State became relatively general, but was far less than the production, so the producers turned to neighboring States, notably Pennsylvania and Ohio, for a further market.

West Virginia sanctioned that effort. She permitted the formation under her laws of corporations for the purpose of constructing pipe lines from her gas fields into other States and carrying gas into the latter and there selling it. She also permitted corporations of other States to come into her territory for that purpose. And she extended to all these companies the use of her power of eminent domain in acquiring rights of way for their pipe lines. In no way did she then require, that consumers within her limits be preferred over consumers elsewhere. . . .

The gas carried into Pennsylvania and Ohio, respectively, and there supplied to the State and her municipal agencies for strictly public use is not negligible, but amounts to billions of cubic feet per year. It is fuel with which food is cooked and water heated for thousands of dependents in charitable and penal institutions, with which hundreds of school houses are heated and made comfortable for thousands of children, and with which municipal water works are operated in several cities, notably Cincinnati and Toledo. The heating and other appliances have been adjusted to its use and to make the changes incident to substituting other fuel would involve an expenditure in each State of a very large sum of public money. . . .

The private consumers in each State not only include most of the inhabitants of many urban communities but constitute a substantial portion of the State's population. Their health, comfort and welfare are seriously jeopardized by the threatened withdrawal of the gas from the interstate stream. This is a matter of grave public concern in which the State, as the representative of the public, has an interest apart from that of the individuals affected. It is not merely a remote or ethical interest but one which is immediate and recognized by law. . . .

. . . Of course, in the last analysis, the question is whether the enforced withdrawal for the benefit of local consumers is such an interference with interstate commerce as is forbidden to a State by the Constitution. The question is an important one; for what one State may do others may, and there are ten States from which natural gas is exported for consumption in other States. Besides, what may be done with one natural product may be done with others, and there are several States in which the earth yields products of great value which are carried into other States and there used. . . .

Natural gas is a lawful article of commerce and its transmission from one State to another for sale and consumption in the latter is interstate commerce. A state law, whether of the State where the gas is produced or that where it is to be sold, which by its necessary operation prevents, obstructs or burdens such transmission is a regulation of interstate commerce, —a prohibited interference. . . . The West Virginia act is such a law. . . . On full consideration, we reach the conclusion that the act is unconstitutional. . . . —Commonwealth of Pennsylvania *v.* State of West Virginia; State of Ohio *v.* State of West Virginia, 262 *U.S.*, 553-600, 1923.

160. State 4-H Camp at Jackson's Mill

West Virginia played a leading part in launching the 4-H Club movement. Soon after becoming state-club leader in 1911, William H. Kendrick (1882-1937), a West Virginia University Agricultural Extension specialist, adapted a four-fold program of mental, social, spiritual and physical growth to the work of boys' and girls' agricultural clubs; and in 1915 J. Versus Shipman, agricultural agent of Randolph County, conducted at Camp Good Luck on the Tygart River near Huttonsville what is commonly regarded as the first organized 4-H Camp. After World War I came expansion of the movement and demand for a state camp. Consequently, when the Monongahela West Penn Public Service Company donated to the State a five-acre tract, embracing the boyhood home of General Stonewall Jackson at Jackson's Mill in Lewis County, the West Virginia legislature in 1921 established the Jackson's Mill State 4-H Camp.

Since expanded to enclose 523 acres and supervised by the Extension Division of the West Virginia University College of Agriculture, the 4-H Camp at Jackson's Mill has become the outstanding conference camp of the State. Besides providing a meeting place for 4-H boys and girls, it serves as a point of assembly for numerous business, social, educational, cultural and religious groups as well as a convention site for institutes, cooperative associations, and professional organizations. Since 1921 West Virginia counties have erected 14 cottages which provide lodging for 375 persons. The Mount Vernon Dining Hall, completed in 1925, has a seating capacity of 350. In addition to the historic mill, the camp also contains an assembly hall, chapel, auditorium, health center, farm electrification building, vesper knoll, outdoor theatre, swimming pool, and a livestock pavilion as well as workshops, council circles, flower gardens, athletic fields and other facilities "for work and play."

The passage below was written by William H. Kendrick who became the first director of the 4-H Camp at Jackson's Mill.

WHAT IS THE 4-H IDEA?

Believing that every influence is a human influence and that personality is the largest factor in human make-up, we have bent every effort to building up personal power with a strong reserve force to back it up. The most effective use of personality is through leadership. Trained leadership is therefore the goal of our work and instruction. Leadership requires a vision of ends to be attained, therefore, we have during the past twelve years, worked out a vision that is clear enough to be seen, strong enough to draw one to it, and beautiful enough to challenge the best there is in us. This Four-H vision is the goal to be gained by all boys and girls who enter Four-H club work.

The Four-H Club vision is the simultaneous development of Head, Hand, Heart, and Health. This is the pattern set by the boy Jesus in whose image all boys and girls must grow or refuse to grow. . . . After catching any vision the most important thing for the attainer to do is to get a picture of himself doing it. Everything a boy or girl does ties up with Head, Hand, Heart, Health. Every action has its four leads to the vision. When a boy steps up to the plate to bat a ball, his *Head* decides whether to strike this one or not; his *Hand* knocks it over the fence, if skillful; his *Heart* makes him do a sacrifice hit and advance the other fellow; his *Health* gives him steam to go—"to keep on keepin' on."

All activities therefore of those boys and girls who are struggling upward to attain the Four-H vision become expressional activities of the vision. When a Four-H boy is found to have a lousy pig, it shows up that he has a lousy idea about caring for a pig. To give a boy on the farm a runty pig tends to make a runty boy of him. Therefore the method of developing personality by the exercise of leadership is one of continually struggling upward toward better things, . . .

A method of procedure has been devised that presents a challenge in the form of a goal to be attained that is within the reach of the climber, that is a part of a larger goal to be reached that draws nearer and nearer to the clear vision. These goals are called projects. The project is a go-between the actual daily work and the fullness of the vision of Four-H development. A project is divided into problems and through the learning and skill developed, lead a youngster out into a fuller Four-H development. This fuller development leads out into life in the community of "going about doing good." Whenever one starts such a life program they have the very essence of leadership which is the correct functioning of the personality in the community.—W. H. Kendrick, *The Four-H Trail*, pp. 11-12.

161. West Virginia Enacts a Gross Sales Tax

State administrations after World War I continued the efforts of their predecessors to provide additional revenue and to establish an equitable tax system. In 1919, the Legislature increased the general property tax to ten cents on each one hundred dollars of assessed value to meet the Virginia debt obligation, and, two years later to twenty cents to meet ordinary state expenses. In

1920, when the voters ratified the good roads amendment which authorized the issuance of $50,000,000 in bonds for highway construction, the rate was further augmented. In the meantime the Legislature increased the license tax on charters and inheritances. Finally in 1923 it levied a tax on gasoline.

In 1921 the Legislature imposed a tax on the gross receipts of businesses and professions when gross sales and gross annual incomes exceeded $10,000 annually. However, in 1925 it exempted from provisions of the act the gross annual income of professional persons and those engaged in the sale of real estate and personal property as an avocation. Although the extractive industries now carried the largest part of the gross sales tax burden, these interests regarded a gross sales tax superior to a corporation income tax, and generally accepted it as a satisfactory substitute for proposed depletion and severance taxes.

But the gross sales tax did not go unchallenged. In 1925 the Hope Natural Gas Company obtained from the Circuit Court of Kanawha County an injunction to prevent the collection of the tax on gas produced in West Virginia and sold in neighboring states. This company held leases on 860,750 acres of oil and gas territory in 25 West Virginia counties, and operated 3,178 gas wells which produced 23,194,711,000 cubic feet for the year ending June 30, 1925. It also purchased from other producers in the State an additional 25,456,947,000 cubic feet. Four fifths of the 48,651,658,000 cubic feet of natural gas marketed by the Hope Natural Gas Company that year went through pipelines to Ohio and Pennsylvania consumers.

The court granted the injunction on the ground that the tax imposed a burden on interstate commerce and deprived the plaintiff of rights guaranteed by the Fourteenth Amendment. The State Supreme Court of Appeals vacated the injunction and the Hope Company appealed the case to the United States Supreme Court which handed down a decision in 1927 upholding the constitutionality of the West Virginia gross sales tax. The following passage is taken from the sustaining decision of the United States Supreme Court.

MR. JUSTICE McREYNOLDS. . . . Here it has been argued that the challenged Act burdens interstate commerce and therefore conflicts with Section 8, Article I, of the federal Constitution. Also, that to enforce the Act would deprive plaintiff in error of property without due process of law and deny equal protection of the laws.

Counsel admit that without violating the commerce clause the State may lay a privilege or occupation tax upon producers of natural gas reckoned according to the value of that commodity at the well. . . . But they insist that, accepting the statute under consideration as construed by the highest court of the State, plaintiff in error will be subjected to an unlawful direct tax upon gross receipts derived from interstate commerce. This argument rests chiefly upon certain language excerpted from the opinion below. But we review the final decree and must accept the statute as authoritatively construed and applied. The plain result of the opinion and final decree is to require that the tax be computed upon the value of the gas at the well, and not otherwise. If, hereafter, executive officers disregard the approved construction and fix values upon any improper basis appropriate relief may be obtained through the courts.

The suggestion concerning deprivation of due process goes upon the assumption that the imposition is upon gross receipts from interstate commerce, in reality upon property beyond the State's jurisdiction. As already pointed out, this assumption conflicts with the definite ruling of the highest court of the State.

The claim that equal protection of the laws has been denied rests upon the assertion, first, that an unlawful tax has been imposed upon the gross proceeds from sales regardless of their place and, second, that the exemption of ten thousand dollars from gross income. . . . creates undue inequality. The true meaning of the statute and the thing actually taxed oppose the first assertion. We cannot say that the Legislature acted either arbitrarily or unreasonably by authorizing the deduction. Nothing indicates a purpose to extend different treatment to those of the same class; no actual unreasonable inequality has been shown. Plaintiff in error is permitted to deduct ten thousand dollars; the same privilege, and nothing more, is extended to all other producers.—Hope Natural Gas Company v. Hall, State Tax Commissioner, et al. 274 U. S., 284-89, 1927.

162. The Tax Limitation Amendment, 1932

Despite the enactment of new tax laws, levies on personal property and real estate rose steadily throughout the 1920's. When it became apparent that agricultural interests were paying more than their just share of taxes and that real estate bore a larger proportion of the tax burden than any other class of property, the Legislature in 1926 submitted to the voters a constitutional amendment which classified property as intangible and "all other", and set a maximum rate of fifty cents on each one hundred dollars of assessed valuation on intangible property. Because of the special treatment accorded to a single class of taxpayers and the narrow classification of two categories the West Virginia electorate rejected the measure at the ensuing November election.

Then came the demand for emergency tax relief during the depression and the deadlock on a proposed tax-limitation amendment during the regular session of the Legislature in 1931, when a Democratic house of delegates favored a broad classification of property and a Republican senate insisted upon a narrow one. However, when the Legislature met in extraordinary session in the summer of 1932, Governor William G. Conley, United States Senator Henry D. Hatfield, and the Republican candidate for governor, Thomas C. Townsend, persuaded the West Virginia senate to adopt a house measure which authorized the broad classification and fixed ceilings on tax rates for each class of property. The voters ratified the amendment at the following November election by a resounding majority.

The Tax-Limitation Amendment equalized taxes to a degree, shifted a large portion of the tax burden from tangible to intangible property holders, and thus reduced the dangers of forfeiture of real estate during the depression. It also shifted fiscal responsibility to the State government and compelled the Legislature to provide revenue from state-wide indirect and consumption taxes. By the same token it centralized the functions of government and reduced the freedom of action of local governments. Said to be among the most rigid of its kind in the United States, the Tax-

Limitation Amendment of 1932 has failed to keep pace with changing social and economic conditions. The text of the amendment appears below.

Subject to the exceptions in this section contained, taxation shall be equal and uniform throughout the State, and all property, both real and personal, shall be taxed in proportion to its value to be ascertained as directed by law. No one species of property from which a tax may be collected shall be taxed higher than any other species of property of equal value; except that the aggregate of taxes assessed in any one year upon personal property employed exclusively in agriculture, including horticulture and grazing, products of agriculture as above defined, including live stock, while owned by the producer, and money, notes, bonds, bills and accounts receivable, stocks and other similar intangible personal property shall not exceed fifty cents on each one hundred dollars of value thereon and upon all property owned, used and occupied by the owner thereof exclusively for residential purposes and upon farms occupied and cultivated by their owners or bona fide tenants, one dollar; and upon all other property situated outside of municipalities, one dollar and fifty cents; and upon all other such property situated within municipalities, two dollars; and the Legislature shall further provide by general law for increasing the maximum rates authorized to be fixed by the different levying bodies upon all classes of property by submitting the question to the voters of the taxing units affected, but no increase shall be effective unless at least sixty percent of the qualified voters shall favor such increase, and such increase shall not continue for a longer period than three years at any one time, and shall never exceed by more than fifty percent the maximum rate herein provided and prescribed by law; and the revenue derived from this source shall be apportioned by the Legislature among the levying units of the State in proportion to the levy laid in said units upon real and other personal property; but property used for educational, literary, scientific, religious or charitable purposes, all cemeteries, public property, the personal property, including live stock, employed exclusively in agriculture as above defined and the products of agriculture as so defined while owned by the producers may by law be exempted from taxation; household goods to the value of two hundred dollars shall be exempted from taxation. The Legislature shall have authority to tax privileges, franchises, and incomes of persons and corporations and to classify and graduate the tax on all incomes according to the amount thereof and to exempt from taxation incomes below a minimum to be fixed from time to time, and such revenues as may be derived from such tax may be appropriated as the Legislature may provide. After the year nineteen hundred thirty-three, the rate of the state tax upon property shall not exceed one cent upon the hundred dollars valuation, except to pay the principal and interest of bonded indebtedness of the state now existing.—West Virginia Constitution, Article X, Section 1.

163. West Virginia Establishes a Conservation Commission, 1933

The indiscriminate slaughter of wildlife caused the first West Virginia legislature to re-enact a law of Virginia to protect certain game animals, and at the request of Governor William E. Stevenson the law-makers amended the statute in 1869, so as to include certain species of birds. In 1877 the Legislature created a fish commission with authority to establish hatcheries, stock waters, construct fish ladders and remove obstructions to the passage of fish in the streams. Finally, in 1897, the law-making body prescribed heavy penalties for violations of the fish and game laws and created the Office of Fish and Game Warden. But the slaughter of game and the dynamiting and pollution of streams went ruthlessly on.

Effective wildlife conservation began in West Virginia in 1909, when the Legislature made the Office of Fish and Game Warden responsible for forest protection and prescribed license fees and a code of behavior for hunters and fishermen. As forest, game and fish warden from 1909 to 1917, Jules A. Viquesney had the support of various organizations of sportsmen, the Audubon Society, fire prevention agencies, and individuals, who cooperated in the construction of fire towers, the establishment of game refuges, and in the enforcement of the forest, game and fish laws. Yet public interest lagged, for citizens showed scant respect for laws which imposed heavy penalties upon individuals but exempted from their provisions wholesale offenders, such as the coal companies.

The conservation program entered a new phase of development in 1921, when the Legislature established a three-member game and fish commission with authority to appoint a chief game protector. Under the inspiration and leadership of A. B. Brooks (1873-1944), who served as game protector from 1921 to 1926, the West Virginia Game and Fish Commission constructed new fire towers and modernized old ones, established the first state-owned game preserve at French Creek in Upshur County, purchased the first state-owned park, Watoga, in Pocahontas County, and the first state forest, the Seneca, also in Pocahontas County. The Commission also played a role in the establishment of the Monongahela National Forest. In 1927 the Legislature created a forest and park commission, and two years later, following the destructive forest fires of 1928, it consolidated the Game and Fish Commission under the name of the West Virginia Game, Fish and Forestry Commission.

The depression proved to be a blessing in disguise for the West Virginia conservation movement. For when the United States Congress established the Civilian Conservation Corps in 1933, the Legislature established at the request of Governor Herman G. Kump the Conservation Commission of West Virginia, "to provide an organization for the protection, beautification, development, and use of lands, forests, parks, fish, game, waters, plant and animal life, and the natural scenic resources of this state, and in cooperation with the federal government and private agencies provide for the use of forest lands and other resources in projects, having for their purpose the relief of unemployment throughout the state."

Expanded to cover all phases of conservation, the West Virginia Conservation Commission, renamed the West Virginia Department of Natural Resources in 1961, has long been a model state agency. The first extract below is taken from a bulletin written by H. W. Shawhan (1891-1954), who served as director of the Conservation Commission from 1933 to 1941, the second is a passage from an address by Warden M. Lane, director of the Department of Natural Resources.

GAME AND FISH PROTECTION

AT THE PRESENT TIME the Conservation Commission employs 31 game wardens, less than one per county. Considerable improvement in the zeal and efficiency of the game warden force has been brought about within the past year, as is evidenced by 1,143 arrests and 952 convictions for various infractions of the game laws, but the degree of protection is yet inadequate and should be increased and intensified at least to the extent of 55 game wardens and five district game wardens. . . .

With the enthusiastic cooperation of some 23 sportsmen's organizations, vermin control contests have resulted in the eradication of some 169,645 predatory birds, animals and reptiles. The effect of this constructive measure is already perceptible in the increased number of quail, grouse and turkeys found by hunters during the current hunting season. The Conservation Commission desires to cooperate fully in the extension of this worthy project.

FISH PROPAGATION AND DISTRIBUTION

The number of fingerling trout and bass available for planting in streams throughout the state has been materially increased during the past year through the construction of a new trout hatchery at Marlinton and through cooperation secured from the federal fish hatcheries at White Sulphur Springs and at Lee-town. . . . However, in order to meet the increased demand for fishing, originating from within the state, and to provide adequate sport and recreation for any considerable number of visiting sportsmen from outside the state, fish propagation and distribution should be doubled. This would necessarily entail the construction of additional hatchery and nursery facilities.

GAME PROPAGATION

Our game farm at French Creek still fails to produce quantities of game for restocking purposes consistent with the operating costs thereof at the present time, but prospects are excellent for an increased output of turkeys over the production of previous years. Some 400 ring-neck pheasants were reared at the game farm, in addition to some 650 turkeys. Next year an attempt will be made to rear quail on a comparatively small scale. Fifty-six deer have been purchased from the Pisgah National Forest in North Carolina, and an order has been placed for the delivery of 25 additional deer. These deer will be stocked in closed counties only. Beaver have been sought but none procured. Approximately 100 raccoon have been secured and will be stocked in suitable locations in the early Spring. In order to build up deer and turkey population to the point where hunting demands can be met, restocking will be necessary, either with birds or animals propagated by the Commission or purchased from outside sources.

FOREST PROTECTION

In order to afford adequate standards of fire protection in the forests of the state, the degree of protection within the present protected area must be increased and other counties—Clay, Lincoln, Wayne, and parts of Ritchie and Doddridge—should be added to the protected area. Such a program requires the construction of additional fire towers, employment of additional rangers and the securing of additional cooperation involving the payment by private land owners of one cent per acre per year to the state or to one of the forest fire protective associations. . . .

The Commission will, through the cooperation of the Extension Forester, seek to encourage and to extend the use of farm woodlots to the end of producing material adjunct to farm income, and to encourage the planting of forest trees upon steep, unfertile and unused portions of farms.

STATE PARKS

The Commission now has under development upon state-owned lands four state parks, namely: Babcock State Park (Fayette County), Watoga State Park (Pocahontas County), Lost River State Park (Hardy County), and Cacapon State Park (Morgan County).

It also holds an option upon the Hawks Nest property and expects to consummate purchase. A ten-year lease has been secured upon the four hundred acres surrounding Blackwater Falls.

. . . As time goes on, it is believed that other park sites, such as Droop Mountain Battlefield, Carnifex Ferry Battlefield, and Blennerhassett Island will demand consideration by the public and by the Conservation Commission, . . .

LAND ACQUISITION

An option has been secured upon some 9,000 acres of land suitable for development and maintenance as a state forest and game preserve upon the waters of Mill Creek and the Buckhannon River in Randolph County.

An option has also been secured by the Conservation Commission upon some 8,000 acres of land located upon Twelve Pole Creek in Wayne County. . . .

An area of 25,000 acres in McDowell County is under process of acquisition by the Land Policy Section of the Agricultural Adjustment Administration, which area is proposed to be placed upon a lease basis under the supervision and administration of the Conservation Commission as a state forest and game preserve.

These state forests, along with Seneca Forest, owned and operated by the Conservation Commission, will have as their ultimate objective the reproduction of a crop of merchantable timber and during the necessarily long period of years involved in timber reproduction, will serve as game preserves and as outdoor recreational centers. . . .—H. W. Shawhan, *A Conservation Program: Needs and Requirements,* 1935, pp. 2-7.

. . . We have come a long way in the last few years in conserving our natural resources and in developing land use and wildlife management plans. But much more needs to be done and time presses us to get on with it.

. . . One-half of the population of the United States lives within a day's drive of West Virginia.

We have been building our state parks and recreational areas for a quarter-century. Our 20 state parks of more than 40,000 acres, and our nine state forests comprising some 77,000 acres are recognized by many as the best in the nation. In 1962 more than two and one-half million people visited our parks, forests and recreational areas. Twenty-five years ago the total was approximately ten per cent of that figure.

. . . In Summers and Mercer counties, adjacent to Bluestone Canyon, we propose to develop through grants and loans from the Area Redevelopment Administration a great vacation and recreation playground. The natural beauty of this canyon is unsurpassed anywhere. . . .

Other facilities proposed in the state's recreational complex and financed by the same money as Bluestone, include expansion of the Blackwater Falls State Park-Canaan Valley area, in Tucker county, and the Cass-Greenbank-Watoga vacation areas in Pocahontas county. . . .

Few people, outside of those directly concerned, realize that forests cover two-thirds of the land of West Virginia. To conserve and develop West Virginia's forests is a prime responsibility of the Department's Forestry Division. We do not take that responsibility lightly. . . .

Forest fires continue to plague us. Most of them are caused by carelessness in one form or another. The best answer to this problem seems to be the increased education efforts and stricter law enforcement.

Along with reforestation, reclaiming of lands disturbed by surface mining is an extremely vital part of our Natural Resources program.

Reclamation is a basic need. . . .

The new Surface Mining Law should help to correct some of the surface mining industry's eyesores by the inclusion of a tax of $30.00 per acre attached to each new permit issued and will go into a 'Special Reclamation Fund' to be used to reclaim areas that do not meet modern standards. . . . the major responsibilities of the Department's Division of Water Resources are to reduce and abate existing pollution of our streams, to prevent future pollution and to develop a comprehensive program for maximum use of our water resources.

Our job, in the main, is to restore the purity of our streams through control of industrial wastes. The program is primarily a cooperative one.—Warden M. Lane, "West Virginia's Natural

Resource Opportunities and Expectations," *Governors Centennial Conference on Conservation Education,* April 3, 1963, pp. 15-17.

164. The Roosevelts Come to Arthurdale

The Federal Resettlement program designed to make subsistence homesteads available to indigent families was a very modest part of the massive offensive against poverty and unemployment launched by the New Deal. West Virginia, racked by the chronic sickness of the coal industry, had three homestead projects—Arthurdale in Preston County, Tygarts Valley in Randolph County, and Red House in Putnam County—each one of which accommodated an average of 170 families. The Federal Government, in addition to providing houses and gardens, encouraged cooperative farming and dairying, craftsmanship, lumbering, and small-scale industrial enterprises.

Since Arthurdale was the pilot resettlement project in the United States, it became the focus of national attention even before the first homesteaders moved in during the summer of 1934. In removing these people from their squalid, demoralizing environment to a clean, new community, the humanitarian goal of the rehabilitation program was achieved. If Arthurdale and similar experiments did not prove to be panaceas, they did provide important lessons in social planning.

Mrs. Eleanor Roosevelt, a frequent visitor to Arthurdale, and President Franklin D. Roosevelt are the authors of the two selections which follow. Mrs. Roosevelt describes with compassion the plight of the West Virginia miners and the beginning of the rehabilitation movement. President Roosevelt in a commencement address delivered at Arthurdale, May 27, 1938, explains the political philosophy behind this social experiment.

IN THE AUTUMN [1933] I was invited by the Quakers to investigate the conditions that they were making an effort to remedy in the coal mining areas of West Virginia. My husband agreed that it would be a good thing to do, so the visit was arranged. I had not been photographed often enough then to be recognized so with one of the social workers I was able to spend a whole day going about the area near Morgantown, West Virginia, without anyone's discovering who I was or that I was even remotely connected with the government.

... There were men in that area who had been on relief for from three to five years and who had almost forgotten what it was like to have a job at which they could work for more than one or two days a week. There were children who did not know what it was to sit down at a table and eat a proper meal. . . .

This trip to the mining areas was my first contact with the work being done by the Quakers. I liked the Quaker people I met, Clarence Pickett particularly, and I liked the theory of trying to put people to work to help themselves. There was a chair factory which was equipped with some of the most remarkable makeshift machinery I had ever seen, but it taught the men to do something in addition to mining and it also bolstered their hope. The men were started on projects and taught to use their abilities to develop new skills. Those who worked on chairs made furniture for their own scantily furnished homes. The women were encouraged to revive any household arts they might once have known but which they had neglected in the drab life of the mining village.

This was only the first of many trips into the mining districts but it was the one that started the homestead idea. The University of West Virginia, in Morgantown, had already created a committee to help the miners on the Quaker agricultural project. With that committee and its experience as a nucleus, the government obtained the loan of one of the university's people, Mr. Bushrod Grimes, and established the Resettlement Administration. Louis Howe created a small advisory committee on which I, Mr. Pickett, and others served. It was all experimental work, but it was designed to get people off relief, to put them to work building their own homes and to give them enough land to start growing food.

It was hoped that business would help by starting on each of these projects an industry in which some of the people could find regular work. A few small industries were started but they were not often successful. As I said in a previous chapter, only a few of the resettlement projects had any measure of success; nevertheless I have always felt that the good they did was incalculable. Conditions were so nearly the kind that breed revolution that the men and women needed to be made to feel their government's interest and concern.

I began to hear very serious reports of conditions in Logan County, West Virginia, where for many years whole families had been living in tents because they had been evicted from company houses after a strike. All the men had been blacklisted and could not get work anywhere; they were existing on the meager allowance that the state of West Virginia provided for the unemployed.

For many years I had been sending a small contribution to this area through the Women's Trade Union League, but I had never seen what the conditions were. I began to hear that the tents were worn out, that illness was rampant and that no one had any medical care. Finally Mrs. Leonard Elmhirst and I established a clinic to take care of the children. When I told my husband of the conditions there he told me to talk to Harry Hopkins and to tell him that whatever should be done must be done, and that these families must be out of tents by Christmas. It was done; and for two years, out of my radio money and Mrs. Elmhirst's generosity, we tried to remedy among the children the effects of conditions which had existed for many years.

I came to know very well a stream near Morgantown called Scott's Run, or Bloody Run because of the violent strikes that once occurred in the mines there. Some of the company houses, perched on hills on either side of the Run, seemed scarcely fit for human habitation. In one place the Quakers had established a self-help bakery and a nursery school.

I took many, many people to see this village of Jere, West Virginia, along Scott's Run, for it was a good example of what absentee ownership could do as far as human beings were concerned. The coal mines of West Virginia are owned largely by people not living in the state. The money goes out and does not come back, leaving the state poorer in cash and in personal interest than before. Most of the people living along the Run, which flows into a broader stream below, worked no more than two or three days a week. Some of the children were subnormal, and I often wondered how any of them grew up.

The Quakers tried to improve conditions by getting the children off the floors at night. It was quite usual to find all the older children sleeping on bags or rags on the floor and the mother and father and youngest children in the only bed, which might or might not have a mattress. Sometimes there was just a blanket over the springs. The WPA mattress project helped considerably, as did the building of sanitary privies. The welfare commissioner who authorized them, Miss Alice Davis, nearly landed herself in jail because they were built on private mine-owned property and she had not known it was against the law to improve privately owned property.

However, breaking rules or even laws saved a good many lives. Every spring and every autumn in this area there had been an outbreak of typhoid fever; only after several people died would the company doctor appear and inoculate the rest of the population. No efforts were made to eliminate the cause of the disease. The Run in Jere, like all the others that ran down the gullies to the larger, main stream, was the only sewage disposal system that existed. At the bottom of the hill there was a spigot from which everyone drew water. The children played in the stream and the filth was indescribable. . . .

Where there was a company store every family always owed a bill; as they were thus kept permanently in debt, they could never move away.

After the homesteads were started, I persuaded many people to go down to visit them. On all my early visits I stayed at the home of the project superintendent, Mr. Glenn Work, who had been a mine foreman and knew the conditions under which the miners and their families lived. The homestead project started near Morgantown was called Arthurdale and took in people from all the near-by mining villages. . . .

Miss Elsie Clapp, a fine teacher and a follower of Dr. John Dewey, whom Mr. Pickett knew, was asked to come and start the school. Once before she had done a similar job of creating a community where none had existed, and she now rendered a remarkable service to Arthurdale. Later the state of West Virginia took over the school. . . .

Some of the people who went with me during these years were Mr. [Bernard] Baruch, Mrs. Henry Morgenthau, junior, Mr. and Mrs. Frederick B. Adams, Mr. and Mrs. Allee Freed, Mr. and Mrs. George T. Bye, Mrs. Henry Goddard Leach, Mr. and Mrs. Robert Deans and Major Henry S. Hooker. All of them, at one time or another, helped some specific project, but our most constant helpers were Mr. Baruch, Mrs. Morgenthau and Mr. and Mrs. Freed. After Mr. Freed's death, Mrs. Freed still maintained her interest.—Selections from pp. 126-131 of "The First Year: 1933" from *This I Remember* by Eleanor Roosevelt. Copyright 1949 by Anna Eleanor Roosevelt. Reprinted by Permission of Harper & Row, Publishers.

At last after many attempts dating back through several years, I have succeeded in coming to Arthurdale—and I can greet you as old friends because you are Mrs. Roosevelt's old friends and also because I have heard so much about you.

Much has been written all over the country about you good people, about the conditions of life in certain towns in this part of the world and about what the United States has done here at Arthurdale. The Nation has heard about Scott's Run, with its very poor conditions of life, and the Nation has heard about Arthurdale with its vastly improved conditions of life. But I think I voice the thoughts of you who live here when I say to the country over the radio that about the last thing that you would want would be to be publicized as some rare and special type of Americans.

I think you will agree with me if I put history this way:

Back in 1933 the whole Nation knew that it faced a crisis in economic conditions but the Nation did not realize that it also faced a crisis in its social conditions. If anyone were to ask me what is the outstanding contribution that has been made to American life in the past five years, I would say without hesitation that it is the awakening of the social conscience of America.

As one part, and only one part, of the effort of your government to improve social conditions, we undertook, as you remember, in dozens of places scattered over almost every part of the country, to set up, with the cooperation of the local people themselves, projects to provide better homes, a better chance to raise foodstuffs, and a better chance to make both ends meet in maintaining a reasonably decent standard of living through the passing years.

Many different types of projects were undertaken—some of them in wholly rural sections, some in cities, some in suburbs, some for industrial workers, some for miners, some, like Arthurdale, a combination of industry and farming. These projects represent something new, and because we in America had little or no experience along these lines, there were some failures. . . .

On the whole, however, the percentage of good guesses in the average of these projects has been extraordinarily high, and for this success the principal part of the credit properly should go to the individual families who, themselves, have come to live in these new communities, people like you here in Arthurdale.

The lessons that we have all learned are going to save a hundred times their cost in dollars just as fast as government or private capital—or as I hope, both of them—go on with the inevitable task of improving living conditions throughout the country and helping Americans to live as modern science has made it possible for them to live. This extra cost of pioneering ventures, such as this, represents development cost which we justifiably charge off as the inevitable cost of all progress—just as we have in the past charged off the huge government share in the development costs of the railroads, the cables, the airplanes, and the hundreds of millions of dollars in improved highways that have made the automobile possible. But what is equally important to me, the lessons learned from this first bold government venture will save human lives and human happiness as well as dollars in this march of progress that lies ahead of us. . . .

When you, today's graduates, were of grade school age we, your elders in the United States, were asleep at the switch and your government also was asleep at the switch. For many years, other nations of the world were giving serious attention to and taking definite action on many social problems while we in the United States were pushing them aside with the idea that perhaps some day we might get around to meeting them. . . .

A great many sincere people—good citizens with influence and money—have been coming to West Virginia mining towns in the past two or three years, to see the conditions under which American families lived, conditions under which, unfortunately, many American families still live. . . .

They have wanted to help at the particular spot they have seen, but the lesson that I have found it difficult to get across to them has been the fact that they have seen only one spot or two spots—tiny, single spots on the great map of the United States, a map that is covered over with hundreds and even thousands of similar spots. Un-American standards exist by no means in a few coal towns only. They exist in almost every industrial community and they exist in very many of the farming counties of the country.

Now, of course, pending the time that private capital and private enterprise will take up the burden, the money your Government is spending to encourage the Nation to live better—especially that part of the Nation which most needs it—is taxpayers' money. . . .

Taxes—and I am talking about taxes to you who are graduating today just as much as your parents for the very good reason that very soon you will be taxpayers yourselves—taxes, local and state and federal combined, are nowhere near as high in this country as they are in any other great nation that pretends to be up-to-date. If I were a business man making and hoping to continue to make good profits, I would remind myself as I paid my income tax, moderate by the standards of other nations, that the most important factor in the kind of an active economic life in which profits can be made is people—able, alert, competent, up-to-date people—people to produce and people with ability to consume. Money invested to make and keep the people of this Nation that kind of people is therefore a good business investment. . . .

In accordance with recommendations that I have made during several years past, I hope that the Congress, when the new Congress comes back next January, will undertake a broader program of improving the Federal tax system as a whole, in the light of accepted principles of fairness in American taxation, and of the necessary incentives in our economic life. . . .

Two things we can well remember.

The first is that our whole tax system, state, local and federal, can and must be greatly improved in the coming year.

The second is that we in this country are getting more practical results in the way of bettering the social conditions of the nation out of our taxes than ever before in our history. That is why it is a pretty good idea to talk taxes not only to parents of America but also to the younger generation of America.

I have been thrilled today by all I have seen. I have been made happy in meeting so many people that I have heard a lot about, by seeing them in their own homes, by seeing the splendid work that has been going on. I want to tell you, my friends of Arthurdale, that I am proud of what I have seen today and I am proud of all of you, old and young alike, who are helping so greatly to make this community an American success. — *The Public Papers and Addresses of Franklin D. Roosevelt,* VII, 355-65. Compiled and collated by Samuel I. Rosenman. Copyright 1941 by Franklin Delano Roosevelt. Reprinted by Permission of The Macmillan Company, Judge Samuel I. Rosenman and the Estate of Franklin D. Roosevelt.

165. West Virginia's Contribution to World War II

The following passages give an excellent summary of West Virginia's part in World War II. The first statement is taken from an address by Clarence W. Meadows (1904-1961), Governor of West Virginia, delivered June 20, 1945, and the second passage is from an unpublished study of the war by Dr. James G. Jones, professor of history at Glenville State College.

. . . NEARLY 200,000 OF OUR YOUNG MEN and women are in uniform. Of those at home, almost without exception every able-bodied man or woman is engaged in some effort productive of the results which must be obtained in times like these if State and Nation are to survive.

During the war years—even before the actual outbreak of hostilities when it appeared that we must arm and prepare, or face overwhelming aggression—West Virginia was called upon to support the national effort with its vast store of raw materials and with the immense productivity of its mills and factories. In no particular has the State failed to meet its wartime obligations. What men and women can do with their hands, their minds, their productive ingenuity, has been done; so that our raw materials and our manufactured products, and the products of farm and orchard, have gone directly and indirectly to support our fighting men on fighting fronts all over the world.

In the late fall and early winter of 1942 the people of our State were asked for the first time to support another vital phase of the national effort—the financing of the war. West Virginia responded affirmatively in the First War Loan, in the Second, the Third, the Fourth, Fifth and Sixth. . . .

On this West Virginia Day of 1945 we are again under pledge to accomplish a specific wartime assignment. We have been assigned extraordinary quotas in the Seventh War Loan:

34-million dollars for Series E. Bonds;

64-million dollars for all securities for individuals; and

83-million dollars as our quota for all classes of investors.

As to our over-all quota, which is attained through the combined purchases of government securities by individuals and corporations, I predict we will attain our goal within a week. . . .

We are proud of the things that West Virginians in uniform have accomplished; but it is remarkable that in the field of helping finance the war they are establishing a most unusual record. As of last Monday, the men and women from West Virginia in the armed services—army, navy, all branches—have bought in excess of $1,500,000.00 in Series E. Bonds. That's approximately one dollar out of every ten dollars invested in this security by the people of the State as a whole. That's 10 per cent of all our E Bond sales. Our men and women in uniform not only are fighting the war—they're helping pay for it, too—a striking example for those of us here at home.

West Virginia's participation in a war which now seems to be moving to a victorious conclusion has not been a passive one,

Our immense raw material resources, and our great productive strength have made our contribution to the nation's effort a tremendous one. What our men and women of mine, mill and factory—of service and supply—of science and all fields of productive and humane effort have contributed toward a winning war is a bright omen for the time when our enemies will have been crushed and peace restored. The same wealth of resources, the same capacity for work, and the same feeling for the public welfare which have marked West Virginia and West Virginians in these times of stress, will mean much for ourselves and our families in the future. Let us pray that another West Virginia Day will find our people working together not for war, but toward the bright days of peace.—Clarence W. Meadows, *State Papers and Public Addresses*, pp. 48-50.

[Military Service]

A recapitulation of the work of registration of selective service in West Virginia showed a total of 465,688 ... to September 1, 1945. . . . 151,949 were inducted . . ., while 66,716 entered the services through voluntary enlistment. . . . Of the state's total of 218,665 in the armed forces, 160,234 were in the Army, 49,090 in the Navy, 7,653 in the Marine Corps and 1,688 in the Coast Guard. The casualties suffered, other than wounded, . . . were 4,865 by the Army, 654 by the Navy, 302 by the Marine Corps, and 9 by the Coast Guard.

[Agriculture, Industry and Labor]

During World War II the state's industrial potential was greatly expanded. From the beginning of the emergency practically all of the output of the state's leading manufacturers and the production of the natural-resource industries directly or indirectly went into the defense or war effort. New war plants joined the previously established ones lately converted to war production. Substantial enlargements were made to existing plants, especially to those engaged in the production of steel, alloys, non-ferrous metals, chemicals and textiles. The mining of bituminous coal, the state's largest single industry, reached production heights never before attained, an accomplishment achieved despite a gradual loss of manpower to the armed forces and to defense plants. Agricultural pursuits assumed expanded proportions, oil and gas production continued high, timber products output was greatly increased and the lesser, yet vital, industries of the state extended their production capacities.

The labor supply came under close scrutiny and supervision during the war. . . . With Selective Service constantly drawing upon the most vigorous and mentally alert of the available manpower supply, adjustments had to be made to conform to the everchanging situation on the home front. To achieve and maintain a schedule of high production of defense and war supplies, better relations were cultivated between labor and management. Close observation was maintained to reduce the practices of "job-jumping" and undue absenteeism. Men and women who had previously retired from their professions were taken back into employment. Women and the youth of school age were called on to supplement the diminished farm labor supply. State-prison labor as well as prisoner-of-war labor came up for screening and limited utilization. Labor shortages, however, became acute in some industries, especially in agriculture, timber cutting and oilwell drilling.

[Prisoners of War]

Prisoner of war labor was used in some localities in West Virginia during the last two years of the war. A prisoner of war camp for Germans was maintained at White Sulphur Springs and another for Italian war prisoners at Camp Dawson, near Kingwood in Preston County. From these camps the prisoners were sent to side camps for employment. Prisoner of war labor was made available to those communities where it could be certified by the War Manpower Commission that there was no free labor available. Those prisoners desiring employment were classified according to their prewar civil occupations and efforts were made to place the men in the type of work of their past experience so as to get the best results from their labor. The employer was required to pay the wage prevailing in his community, the prisoner getting credit of eighty cents a day for personal expenditures while the remainder went to the government for camp maintenance. In this state POW labor was largely employed in construction and maintenance of logging railroads and skid roads, in timber work and in agriculture. Most of these prisoners performed useful service, but it was usually difficult for them to follow instructions since they did not understand English. A majority of those employed on the farms were young men around twenty years of age. The people in the areas where these prisoners worked accepted them into the community without any undue opposition.

[Military Hospitals]

Since the federal government had only one hospital, the Huntington Veterans' Administration Facility, within West Virginia, two additional ones were opened within the state during the war years. One of these, the Ashford General, was situated at White Sulphur Springs. This was the second time in the town's history that it was chosen as a military hospital site. During the Civil War the hotel standing then at White Sulphur Springs, and known as "The Old White", was used as a hospital by both the Northern and Southern armies, according to which side controlled the area. In later years, the name was changed to the Greenbrier Hotel and became a world-famous resort hotel. For a time after our entry into World War II, the Axis legation personnel stranded in this country were confined here. In 1942, the hotel was taken over by the Army and converted into a 2,200-bed wartime hospital. It became a center for vascular surgery, neurosurgery, neurology, and general medicine. The hospital was later designated a replacement pool for the training of medical officers. . . . Patients from practically every battle front were brought here for treatment and care. By November, 1945, twenty thousand patients had been given admittance to Ashford General.

The Newton D. Baker General Hospital, named in honor of a native son of West Virginia who was President Wilson's Secretary of War, was located four miles east of Martinsburg, about fifteen miles north of the Virginia state line and twelve miles south of Maryland. The installation consisted of one hundred buildings connected by corridors, with a floor space of approximately thirty acres. . . . Construction of the $5,000,000 structure started early in 1943 on an area consisting of 185 acres, and was completed and ready for occupancy in less than ten months. As at Ashford General, this hospital gave medical treatment and care to thousands of wounded soldiers and provided facilities for their rehabilitation and readjustment to civil life.

[Military Training in West Virginia]

... the West Virginia Maneuver Area ... comprised some two million acres near Elkins in five of the state's most rugged counties. Approximately half of the area was under federal government lease from private individuals. The million-acre Monongahela National Forest formed the other half of the maneuver grounds. The remarkable similarity of the region to that of the Brenner Pass in northern Italy, toward which Allied forces were driving at the time of the opening of the area in this state, suggested an ideal training ground for combat and service troops in "low mountain" warfare. Tactical problems with infantry, artillery, and signal corps units utilized the rugged terrain of Allegheny Mountain, Blackwater Canyon, and other areas. Assault climbing was taught at scenic Seneca Rocks which rise 500 to 800 feet above the little stream at its base.

At another camp in the area, combat teams of infantry and artillery learned to operate as a unit on steep, wooded mountainsides. The technique of firing artillery accurately over mountains was another of the special problems studied. To facilitate these studies the Army leased a target area of 57,000 acres, known locally as Huckleberry Plain. Here, guns as large as 105 millimeter were fired into the area from various angles and elevations. Early in the summer of 1944, the Office of Scientific Research and Development established the Bear Rock Range atop Allegheny Mountain near Petersburg for the testing of new types of explosives and firing devices. Another phase of military life occurred at Stuart Recreation Area near Elkins, where Army Evacuation Hospital Training units received intensive training over a period of several months.

All supplies were brought into the widely-separated camps at night with dimmed-out headlights. This experience of driving heavily-loaded trucks over winding, tree-canopied mountain trails under simulated battle-front conditions was designed as practical training for the quartermaster units and the truck drivers.

The facilities of this maneuver area provided for the training of 16,000 troops every eight weeks. On June 30, 1944, the area was closed down by the Army Ground Forces. During the year it was active, the area had served as the training ground for many thousands of combat and service troops.—James G. Jones, "West Virginia in World War II", West Virginia University Doctoral Dissertation, 1952, pp. i-iii, 160-62, 208-10, 385-86, 390, 399-401.

XV. Education in West Virginia

166. Test Oath Required of Teachers

A matter of grave concern to county superintendents follow-ing the Civil War was the West Virginia law requiring teachers to take the test oath imposed on government officials. Could the oath be waived as a qualification for teachers in Greenbrier County, asked its superintendent. And should the oath be required of females. Disloyalty to the Union had been so prev-alent here that not one person could take the officer's oath in some of Greenbrier's school districts. The want of "loyal men" had obliged the Board of Education to appoint "altogether rebel trustees" in one district of Nicholas County. The superintendent of Wayne County wrote that some of the townships were so "completely disloyal" that officers and teachers could not be found. The discriminatory oath, the text of which is given below, was finally abolished by the Democratic legislature of 1871.

AN ACT CONCERNING OATHS AND AFFIRMATIONS
Passed November 16, 1863

Every person elected or appointed to an office of trust, civil or military, shall, before proceeding to exercise the authority or discharge the duties of the same, take the following oath: "I, A. B., do solemnly swear that I will support the constitution of the United States and the constitution of this state; that I have never voluntarily borne arms against the United States; that I have voluntarily given no aid or comfort to persons en-gaged in armed hostility thereto, by countenancing, counselling or encouraging them in the same; that I have not sought, ac-cepted nor attempted to exercise the functions of any office whatever, under any authority in hostility to the United States; that I have not yielded a voluntary support to any pretended government, authority, power or constitution within the United

States, hostile or inimical thereto; and that I take this obligation freely, without any mental reservation or purpose of evasion."—*Acts of the Legislature of West Virginia, 1st. Sess., p. 138.*

167. Superintendent White's Report

William R. White (1820-1893), a minister of the Methodist Episcopal Church and principal of the Fairmont Male and Female Seminary, became the first Superintendent of Free Schools in West Virginia following his election by joint ballot of the Legislature on February 16, 1864. The superintendent was responsible for the general supervision of the "thorough and efficient" school system about to be established and of its county superintendents. School support came from the interest of the invested school fund, from the proceeds of all forfeitures, confiscations, and fines and from such state and local taxation as might be prescribed by general laws. The voters in each township, the local administrative unit, elected a board of three commissioners empowered to employ teachers, fix their salaries, determine the curriculum, provide school buildings and collect school revenues. Also chosen by popular election were the county superintendents whose duty it was to certify teachers, improve professional standards, secure uniformity in the textbooks used in the county, and receive reports from the township boards and relay their contents to the state superintendent.

Despite his assertion that there was nothing disheartening in the educational picture, Superintendent White had some bleak statistics to convey to the Legislature in January, 1866. There were only 133 school houses in the State whose average value, excluding those in Wheeling, was less than $63; teachers' salaries averaged $34 a month for males and $22 for females; and the average number of months taught was less than three. Only Wheeling, with eight fine schools and an average salary of $139 for male teachers and $42 for women, and an academic year of nearly nine months, had cause for pride in its educational facilities. The subjoined reports of the county superintendents told of alarming illiteracy, of school buildings whose sole equip-

ment consisted of slab seats, of ignorant, prejudiced, indifferent, and not always honest commissioners, of the rejection of township levies, and of strong opposition to the leveling principles inherent in a public school system. Selections from Superintendent White's Second Annual Report follow.

SCHOOL HOUSES

Are "few and far between." Some of the buildings called by that name are almost in ruins, others are cheerless and comfortless log structures, prisons to both teachers and pupils. In some districts this state of affairs will be changed so soon as the necessary labor and material can be procured, but in other sections want of means will postpone the needed improvements to an indefinite period. The erection of log houses has been discouraged, as it is believed that in the spring a large number of frame school houses can be built and painted, with no advance on the present cost. . . .

SALARY OF TEACHERS

The statistics show the average salary of teachers in Wheeling to be for males $139, and for females $42 per month, while the average number of months is 8.8 in the calendar year. In the other districts the average salary of males is $34, and of females $22 per month, while the average number of months taught is 2.7. . . . The salary is totally insufficient to secure the services of first-class teachers. The employment of ladies, with an increased pay, will be a step in the right direction. Normal schools and institutes are developing a kind of talent which proves the entire competency of females both to instruct and to govern. . . .

. . . The people must be educated up to that point where they shall see the great advantage of being taxed to build school houses and properly remunerate the teachers of their children.

A rigid adherence to the policy that *it is the duty as well as the interest of the State to educate the youth,* will ultimately silence all opposition. A man might as well argue that as he had no personal interest in jails, penitentiaries and sheriffs; that, as he had no children to be arrested by the one, or to undergo the discipline of the other, he should not be taxed to support them, as to offer the trite objection of having no children to educate, against his paying his share of the school revenue. He must help to build jails and school houses, to support teachers and officers of justice. . . . Especially is it the duty of the State to educate the children of the poor man. . . .

A small portion of the population oppose the system *from notions of caste*. They frown upon the system as of plebian tendency. They have a fear of the institution as being fatal to their pretensions. This fear is reasonable, and the sooner it is realized the better.

SCHOOLS FOR THE FREEDMEN

Among other subjects relevant to this report, is that of the education of colored adults, who have so long and so mercilessly been deprived of this privilege. I regret to report no schools for the children of this portion of our citizens; as the law stands, I fear they will be compelled to remain in ignorance. I commend them to the favorable notice of the Legislature.

SCHOOL APPARATUS

Our schools are nearly destitute of apparatus. Globes and maps are seldom found. The blackboard is used in a few of the schools only. Indeed, some teachers regard it as a great innovation. . . .

A SCHOOL JOURNAL

A periodical devoted to the diffusion of education, the interchange of views on pedagogy, and used as an official organ of the department of Free Schools, is regarded as a necessary auxiliary to the cause of public instruction. The visits of the "California Teacher," the "School Monthly," and the "New York Teacher," have been most welcome and instructive. It is hoped that a West Virginia journal, under the auspices of the State, may not be regarded as a premature enterprise. . . .—*Second Annual Report of the Superintendent of Free Schools of the State of West Virginia, 1866, pp. 5-15.*

168. The Normal Schools

Between 1867 and 1872, the West Virginia legislature established six teacher training institutions—the "West Virginia State Normal School" at Marshall College, and other normals at Fairmont, West Liberty, Glenville, Concord Church, and Shepherdstown. The founding of so many similar schools in such a short period of time was the result of local initiative in providing sites and buildings for the institutions and of legislative catering to sectional interests. The normals, as their critics correctly pointed out, were merely state-supported high schools offering a course of study extending only three years beyond the elementary level. Professional training was limited to classes in "Theory and Practice of Teaching" and to practice teaching in "Model" schools, the first one of which was at Fairmont Normal. Tuition costs defrayed by the State were apportioned according to county population to boys of at least fifteen years and to girls of at least thirteen. Upon graduation, these non-pay students, who had been selected by the county superintendents, had to teach for one year in the public schools of the State or refund the full amount of the tuition fees. Since course requirements were uniform, students could transfer from one normal school to another without loss of credit.

The following report of the Board of Regents of the Normal Schools, composed of the State Superintendent of Schools, the Secretary of State, the State Auditor, the State Treasurer, and one person from each of the three congressional districts, illustrates the precarious state of these schools during their infancy.

MARSHALL COLLEGE

This was the first Normal School established by the Legislature of the State, and has therefore been treated as the parent school, though there is no real difference in the charters of the respective schools as each acts independent of the other, all being subject to this Board.

Marshall College is located at Huntington, Cabell county, and under the management of Prof. A. D. Chesterman and assistants, was well attended this year, the enrollment reaching one hundred and twenty-three. A few cases of small pox occurred in the town near the school during the year, and the Principal says, from the exaggerated reports of the prevalence of the disease, many persons were prevented through fear of it, from attending school. . . . The amount paid by the State on account of tuition for Normal pupils is $1,200.50. There were no persons graduated from this school this year. The Board of Regents did not visit it at the Commencement, which occurred June 10th. We have information that some repairs are needed about the building, and we therefore recommend an appropriation of $250 for this purpose.

STATE NORMAL SCHOOL AT FAIRMONT

This school, under the management of Miss M. L. Dickey, Principal, and three assistants, was very successful and largely attended the enrollment reaching one hundred and eighty-two. . . .

Eighteen persons, three ladies and fifteen gentlemen were graduated from this school, and a diploma delivered to each at the commencement, which occurred June 16. Some repairs to the roofing of the school building are necessary, and the outside wood work needs repainting. To buy cases for the preservation of the chemical and philosophical apparatus, books and mineral collection lately donated by the alumni and students of the school, we recommend an appropriation of $200 and for repairs $200.

STATE NORMAL SCHOOL AT CONCORD

This school, under the management of Prof. James H. French, and two assistants, made rapid advancement, reaching a greater enrollment than at any former time, viz: ninety-four. . . .

The Executive Committee also report that they have supplied the normal students with text books since the school was established out of the receipts of the school, and, that as the books have now, with seven years' use, become much worn, a small appropriation is asked to replace them. The building is reported in good condition but it lacks chemical and philosophical apparatus. We recommend an appropriation of $250 for these objects.

Seventeen persons, six ladies and eleven gentlemen, were graduated from this school, and a diploma delivered to each at Commencement, which occurred July 22.

SHEPHERD COLLEGE

This is one of the State Normal Schools and is located at Shepherdstown, Jefferson county. Under the management of Prof. Joseph McMurran and an assistant it made a good showing, the enrollment reaching seventy-one. . . .

Five persons, one lady and four gentlemen, were graduated from this school and a normal diploma granted to each.

Some of the public spirited citizens of Shepherdstown and vicinity have proposed to donate for the perpetual use of this school, some valuable private collections of mineral and insect specimens, if cases for their use and preservation in the school buildings are provided. Some very interesting war relics are also offered on the same conditions. The school building at this place was built for a court house and has therefore two fire proof offices which are large and well adapted for the purpose of displaying, and at the same time insuring these valuable collections against loss if placed in them. We recommend an appropriation for the purpose of $300.00.

STATE NORMAL SCHOOL AT WEST LIBERTY

This school located at West Liberty, Ohio county, under the management of Prof. R. McPheters, made some increase in its enrollment this year, reaching forty-three. . . .

Thirteen persons, six ladies and seven gentlemen, were graduated from this school, and a normal diploma delivered to each. Some repairs are needed about the roof of the school building and also to the plastering. We recommend an appropriation of $200.00 for these purposes.

STATE NORMAL SCHOOL AT GLENVILLE

This school located at Glenville, in Gilmer county, under the management of Prof. T. M. Marshall, was in session only about four months of the year. The enrollment reached twenty-five. . . .

Of the appropriation of $100.00 made by the Legislature March 6, 1879, only $20.00 have been expended. The remainder now in the hands of the treasurer of the Executive Committee was ordered expended on some much needed repairs.

The deed to this Board for the school property at Glenville, is not of record in the clerk's office of Gilmer county. The grantor claims to have delivered a deed to the chairman of the Executive Committee, who says he mailed it to Charleston (the then Capitol) to the President of this Board. It has not been found, and probably was never received. We have directed a new deed to be executed.

RECAPITULATION.

	En'll.	Graduates.
Marshall College	123	
Fairmont Normal School	182	18
Concord Normal School	94	17
Shepherd College	71	5
West Liberty Normal School	43	13
Glenville Normal School	25	2
Total	538	55

RECEIPTS.

	From State	Other Sources	Total
Marshall College	$1,200.50		$1,200.50
Fairmont Normal School	2,000.00	$ 514.58	2,514.58
Concord Normal School	1,253.00	194.00	1,447.00
Shepherd College	1,246.00	656.00	1,902.00
West Liberty Normal School	773.50	257.00	1,030.50
Glenville Normal School	259.00	37.00	296.00
Totals	$6,732.00	$1,658.58	$8,390.58

DISBURSEMENTS.

	Incidental Expenses	Teachers	Balance
Marshall College _____ _____		$1,200.50	_____
Fairmont Normal School _____$	285.59	2,200.00	$ 28.99
Concord Normal School _____	57.00	1,345.65	*44.35
Shepherd College _____	79.03	1,822.97	_____
West Liberty Normal School ___	96.62	920.50	13.38
Glenville Normal School _____	25.00	271.00	_____
Totals _____$	543.24	$ 7,760.62	$ 86.72

Portions of the salaries of a number of the teachers in the Normal Schools for the year ending June 1880, are yet unpaid on account of the failure of the Legislature of 1879 to make the usual appropriation for that year. The Board of Regents did not commit the State in terms of a contract to pay the teachers anything from the treasury for their services that year, but the Regents did say to the teachers that there was but little doubt that the Legislature would make appropriations for the schools as before. The teachers thereupon undertook and carried on the schools during that year, thus saving the Board the mortification of closing them, which would have cut off, not only the constantly increasing supply of well trained teachers, but have effectually barred the way to the young men and women of limited means in different parts of the State who desire to pursue a higher course of study than that offered in our common schools. They can afford to pay the tuition fees if they can board at home and attend school, but cannot afford to go from home, paying both tuition and board. The teachers were willing to work under these discouraging circumstances, with the certainty of but a small compensation from the tuitions for the year, and the hope, that six months after the work was done it would be paid for. At the regular session of the Legislature the matter was not acted upon. Though the State is not technically bound to pay the balance of these salaries, yet it would be injustice not to do so. We recommend therefore that the matter be brought to the attention of the Legislature, and the net balances ascertained to be due paid.

IMPROVEMENTS.

We propose to adjust the course of study in the Academic or Pay Department of each of these schools so as to fit the course prescribed in the West Virginia University, thus making more practical these already efficient feeders to the University.

As the standard of scholarship among those seeking admission to normal departments of these schools, is much higher on an average now than at any former time, the standard of admission may be raised, giving less time to the branches of academic knowledge than heretofore, (because the pupils admitted are further advanced,) and more time than heretofore to the Art of Teaching and the theory of education, thus gradually realizing the ideal Normal School.—*Report of the Board of Regents of the State Normal Schools, 1881, pp. 1-7.*

169. West Virginia University

The Agricultural College of West Virginia was established in 1867 to enable the new state to obtain the Federal subsidization provided by the Morrill Act of 1862 for encouraging instruction in agriculture, technology, and military tactics. The location of the school at Morgantown was not without understandable opposition, but northern political domination and the generosity of the trustees of Monongalia and Woodburn Academies in offering to the State the properties of these schools valued at $51,000, won the day for the community on the Monongahela. The first president of West Virginia University—the name of the College was changed by act of the Legislature on December 4, 1868—was the Reverend Alexander Martin, a staunch Methodist, a graduate of Allegheny College, and an experienced teacher. In its infancy West Virginia University had a preparatory department whose enrollment was larger than that of all the collegiate departments—literary, scientific, agricultural, and military—combined. Inadequate appropriations, no private en-

dowment, partisanship, and conflicting educational philosophies plagued the institution for some years. And despite the example set by western universities, it did not become coeducational until 1889. When William L. Wilson became president of West Virginia University in 1882, the institution still had only a few buildings, little equipment, a handful of students, and a restless faculty. The first one of the following selections shows the rigid regulations which once governed both faculty and students. The second one, written by Wilson in 1882, is a challenging plea for developing the "Morgantown school," as the University was frequently designated, into a true university.

Of the Faculty

3. The Faculty have authority to make all orders and regulations necessary to the performance of their duties. They have the general control and direction of the studies pursued in the University. They have cognizance of all offences committed by undergraduates, and it is their special duty, *individually* and collectively, to enforce the observance of all the laws and regulations for maintaining discipline and promoting order, virtue, piety and good learning in the Institution.

7. An exemplary diligence in study and in the communication of knowledge and performance of every moral and religious duty, is required of the Faculty and teachers. They shall, unless excused, attend all the public exercises of the University during the week and on the Sabbath.

12. No member of the Faculty shall connect himself, or continue connected with any secret college fraternity, whether now in existence, or which may be formed hereafter; and all the members of the Faculty are required to exert their influence for the suppression of all such secret associations.

13. The Faculty shall enact a system of government and administration, not inconsistent with these laws, which shall be uniform in all the departments, so far as it is practicable. They have adequate power for all ordinary cases of order and discipline. The rank of the President shall be first; Vice President, second; and that of the Professors shall be severally as their seniority in office.

Examinations

1. Each student, at the close of the term, shall stand a public written examination upon all the studies which he has pursued during that term. No student shall be excused for non-attendance on such examinations, except upon presentation of a reason which may be considered valid by the Faculty. . . .

Grades and Honors

1. Students shall receive from each Professor, marks of merit or demerit for their attendance, punctuality, propriety of conduct, diligence and attainments, according to the following scale:

2. The highest mark attainable shall be 10, the lowest 0. A good lesson shall be marked 8, and numbers higher than 8 shall be used only to note special excellence.

8. Any student failing to attain for his average of conduct for a year a number equal to, or exceeding, six, shall be suspended for one year, unless restored by special action of the Faculty.

Orations and Addresses

1. Declamations and exercises in Oratory shall be had every week, at such time and place as the Faculty may direct. These shall be assigned to students in rotation; . . .

4. All original orations by Undergraduates to be pronounced in the presence of the University, or of the public, shall be submitted to the President for correction or approval at least ten days before delivery.

5. Nothing indecent, immoral or disrespectful to the government of the University, shall at any time be delivered on the public stage, under penalty of such censure as the Faculty, or the Executive Committee, by their reference, shall judge proper.

6. No person shall be invited to address the Societies, or the students of the University, upon anniversaries, or other occasions, whose name has not first been submitted to the Faculty and received their approval.

Religious Worship and Instruction

1. Prayer and reading of the Scriptures shall be had with the members of the University at the beginning of the exercises of each day of the week; on which services, and also on some approved public worship, all are expected to attend punctually and with due reverence.

2. Every student is required on Sabbath, to abstain from all behavior inconsistent with that sacred day.

3. Any student shall be allowed to attend on Sabbath, the public service of any denomination of Christians having a place of worship in Morgantown, on his application to the President in writing, if of legal age, or if a minor, on the application of his parent or guardian, stating that such worship is that in which he has been educated, or which from conscientious motives he is desirous of attending.

Rates of Tuition

1. The charges for tuition shall be, in the Preparatory Department, five dollars per term; and for the different departments in the University proper, eight dollars per term.

Miscellaneous

3. Indecent and profane language, rude and boisterous conduct, tippling, frequenting taverns, inns, beer-houses, and visiting places of mere idle amusement and resort of bad company, gambling, betting, games of chance, smoking tobacco within the University enclosure, or carrying concealed firearms or other deadly weapons, and every species of vulgar and immoral conduct, are absolutely forbidden, and will subject the offender to punishment. —Rules and Regulations of West Virginia University, 1878, pp. 3-17.

I AM SURE every intelligent citizen of the State must earnestly desire to see our chief State school successful and prosperous, a seminary of high grade, affording to our young men the same means of and opportunities for thorough education, classical, scientific and professional, that are enjoyed by the youths of other States.

And when we recall the lack of such institutions in this State, —there being as I believe but one other college in its limits,— and reflect that if we depend upon the colleges of other sections to educate our young men, an inconsiderable number will attain the benefits of liberal culture, and we shall altogether miss that sentiment of State pride, which is so great and honorable an element of strength in other States, but which for many reasons, chiefly inherent in her physical structure, has, as yet, but a weak development in West Virginia, we see how strongly our necessities, our duties, and our pride are involved in this matter. . . .

Massive buildings, ornamental grounds, great libraries and laboratories, and other expensive apparatus of instruction, have but limited educational value apart from the living teachers, able, earnest and enthusiastic. If we do not aim to possess the former as yet, we can with moderate additional outlay provide the latter, and having them, we may be sure that our young men will lack neither the substance nor the power of real education, nor suffer in contrast with those of other States in the competitions of public or private life. . . .

But to secure and to hold such instructors, dwelling houses must be provided for them. . . . Morgantown does not supply the accommodations. Its houses are generally occupied by their owners, and few are for rent. My own acceptance of the presidency threw upon me the unexpected necessity of a severance from my family, and this severance would probably continue did I expect to remain another year. Other professors who have been here for years are without homes, and subjected to much uneasiness and uncertainty in this particular. This should be remedied by the immediate erection of a dozen or more inexpensive cottages, which might be arranged in a semi-circle about the present buildings, with fine effect. They would give attractiveness and stability to the teachers' position, and relieve from dependence on the local accommodations, which, in a State institution, is of obvious necessity.

There is also need for some dormitories. Students now seek rooms among the families of the town. . . . I do not advise any special change in this practice, but there should be some dormitories, if for no other reason to prevent the unavoidable loitering about the halls, in the intervals of lectures, by students who board at a distance from the University, and especially for the use of those who wish to reduce their expenses to a minimum by messing together. . . .

In the past few years a constant stream of benefactions has poured into the treasuries of other schools, and although no rivulet has yet reached the West Virginia University, the time cannot be distant when it, too, must share in this liberality. I had hoped that some of the very needs above indicated, especially the Library Building and the Cottages, might be provided by patriotic citizens, anxious to connect their names with the growth and history of their State's highest institution of learning. While admitting her present poverty, the State can justly look forward to the day not very remote when her resources are to make her surpassingly rich. It may be that today she is, in many sections but "a rough wild land whose crops are men;" but in the next generation her mineral stores, her wealth of timber and her agricultural riches will be coined by intelligence and enterprise into current money. And in the proportion that her University has contributed to this result, by equipping her young men with the knowledge and skill and power necessary for this development, will it ensure their success and receive the grateful return of generous benefaction and ever expanding endowment.

. . . It is neither economy nor wisdom to spend as much as we do, without the slight increase, which would make that expenditure so much more productive. Supply these deficiencies and we shall have a good school for the present, and a foundation on which a great State seminary may, in time, be erected. We have by solemn legal enactment declared it a University. Necessity and duty alike require that we should maintain it as such. On no other condition can we honestly urge our young men to attend it, or to prefer its advantages to those of like institutions elsewhere. No school, and least of all a State school, can, in my opinion, without dangerous approach to crime, hold out any promises to young men which it is not able to fulfill with the most exacting good faith.

If our Legislators and men of wealth could see the young men now gathered here, and who are but a few, compared with those who would, under better conditions, come from all parts of the State, there would be no hesitation in the supply of all present necessities. No where else in the country will small expenditures produce so large results.—President William L. Wilson to Colonel D. D. Johnson, December 23, 1882, *Biennial Report of the Board of Regents of the West Virginia University for the Years 1881-1882*, pp. 28-31.

170. Alexander L. Wade, a Graduating System for Country Schools

A decade after its establishment, the West Virginia school system was still in dire need of improvement from every important standpoint. The average monthly salary for white teachers was $35.70 for males and $29.55 for females; for Negro teachers it was $31.90 and $30.30, respectively. Of the 2,830 school buildings, 1,209 were of log and only eighty-one of brick or stone. The state had two high schools—one each in Kanawha and Berkeley counties, eighty-five graded schools, and 2,936 common schools whose doors were open for an average of 4.12 months.

The suspiciously low number of rejections of applications for teaching certificates obtained through examinations indicates that partisan or personal considerations, rather than proper qualifications, governed the selection of teaching personnel. While the law prescribed a uniform elementary course of study consisting of spelling, reading, penmanship, arithmetic, English grammar, history, geography, and "such other branches as the Board of Education [might] direct," in many schools the curriculum was at the mercy of teachers, parents, or even pupils.

In order to stimulate the dismal academic environment through adequate supervision and to bring about uniformity of standards Alexander L. Wade (1832-1904) devised his graduating system for country schools which received national acclaim in educational circles of this country. In 1874 Wade began to organize graduating classes in Monongalia County, where he was su-

perintendent of schools from 1875 to 1879, and two years later the first common school diplomas as advocated by his plan were awarded.

A GRADUATING SYSTEM FOR COUNTRY SCHOOLS . . .

The graduating system for country schools is simply taking the primary branches as a course of study for graduation, and making application of all the plans and appliances of the best academies and colleges to the common schools of the country.

The time in which each advanced pupil agrees to complete this course of study is announced.

Public examinations of graduating classes are held annually, at points agreed upon, in each county, and diplomas are granted to those who satisfactorily complete the course of study.

An alumni association, holding annual meetings for the mutual improvement of those who have graduated, is organized in every township or magisterial district.

A catalogue, containing a clear statement of the work of each school, is published annually in every county. . . .

This system may be introduced into the schools of a State or a county, and it can be tested even in a township or district, or in a single school. . . .

Orthography, Reading, Writing, Arithmetic, Geography, English Grammar, and *History* are the branches required by most of the States to be taught in the common schools of the country.

The propriety of readjusting the common-school course of studies and making the course uniform in all the States is worthy of the consideration of the nation's best educators. Until this be done, it is duty of teachers and school officers to see that pupils pursue the course of study prescribed by the law of the State in which they live. . . .

. . . We have been depending for success upon methods, rather than upon motives. . . . No one who begins the world poor will ever, by the work of his hands or his head, have a home of his own, unless he be led by motives to work for this end; and no one will become a scholar, unless he shall first make up his mind to be a scholar.

The graduating system is simply applying to the educational work certain rules or laws of business, which are founded on common-sense. An agreement to complete a certain amount of work in a given time for a specified sum is a rule regulating labor in the best business establishments on the globe, and is found to work equally well in the employment of men, women, or children. . . .

The unanimous verdict of all who have studied our system of popular instruction is, that the want of uniformity in the course of studies, or rather the want of any uniform plan for inducing pupils to take up and *complete* a course, is the lame limb in our educational work, which has caused so much limping all over the land. This universal lameness in our educational body is the legitimate result of our school management. . . .

I would not have you lose sight of the fact, heretofore presented, that the defective work of our country schools is not in the main the fault of our teachers, but that it is the legitimate result of the absence of a uniform system of incentives and aims. The graduating system for country schools carries with it wherever it goes this uniform system of incentives and aims, and embraces all the leading features of the laws of business.

God has wisely implanted in all of us a desire to see our names and the names of our kindred and friends mentioned in connection with honorable positions. This desire is not peculiar to any particular period in life, but is as clearly seen in childhood and youth as in maturity. . . .

The graduating system for country schools seizes upon this universal law of human nature and turns it to account. . . .— Alexander L. Wade, *A Graduating System For Country Schools,* pp. 9-15.

171. Up From Slavery — Negro Education in West Virginia

Booker T. Washington (c.1859-1915), the great Negro educator and founder of Tuskegee Normal and Industrial Institute, came to Kanawha County, West Virginia, shortly after the Civil War. Born into slavery on a plantation in Franklin County, Virginia, young Booker Taliaferro received his first education at

Malden, the center of the thriving salt industry in the Kanawha Valley. In 1872 he went to Hampton Institute where he was befriended by General Samuel C. Armstrong, the founder of this famous school for Negroes. On his graduation from Hampton in 1875, Washington returned to Malden to teach in a public school for Negroes. Eager to share his knowledge with his neighbors, he also taught an evening class for adults and two Sunday school classes, gave private instruction, and established a small reading room and a debating society for Negroes. As Washington put it, "I taught any one who wanted to learn anything that I could teach him." His first wife, Fannie N. Smith, a graduate of Hampton Institute, was a resident of Malden. It was here that Washington first saw the Ku Klux Klan foment violence in the course of which many persons were injured, including his former employer and patron, General Lewis Ruffner, who had attempted to defend the Negroes. In 1899, after Washington had won international fame and had been awarded an honorary degree from Harvard University, the citizens of West Virginia invited him "to share the hospitality" of the state capital. Members of both races attended the subsequent receptions at the Charleston Opera House and at the State House.

Although Booker T. Washington was, alike with others of his race, humiliated and discriminated against he remained singularly free of bitterness and hatred, and always remembered with profound gratitude and affection the white people who had been his friends. His respect for himself and for humanity, his emphasis on the dignity of labor, his tireless and practical approach to the solution of the race problem have won for him a very special distinction as a social leader.

. . . FINALLY WE REACHED our destination—a little town called Malden, which is about five miles from Charleston, the present capital of the state.

At that time salt-mining was the great industry in that part of West Virginia, and the little town of Malden was right in the midst of the salt-furnaces. My stepfather had already secured a job at a salt-furnace, and he had also secured a little cabin for us to live in. Our new house was no better than the one we had left on the old plantation in Virginia. In fact, in one respect it was worse. Notwithstanding the poor condition of our plantation cabin, we were at all times sure of pure air. Our new home was in the midst of a cluster of cabins crowded closely together, and as there were no sanitary regulations, the filth about the cabins was often intolerable. Some of our neighbours were coloured people, and some were the poorest and most ignorant and degraded white people. . . . Though I was a mere child, my stepfather put me and my brother at work in one of the furnaces. Often I began work as early as four o'clock in the morning.

The first thing I ever learned in the way of book knowledge was while working in this salt-furnace. Each salt-packer had his barrels marked with a certain number. The number allotted to my stepfather was "18." At the close of the day's work the boss of the packers would come around and put "18" on each of our barrels, and I soon learned to recognize that figure wherever I saw it, and after a while got to the point where I could make that figure, though I knew nothing about any other figures or letters.

From the time that I can remember having any thoughts about anything, I recall that I had an intense longing to learn to read. I determined, when quite a small child, that, if I accomplished nothing else in life, I would in some way get enough education to enable me to read common books and newspapers. Soon after we got settled in some manner in our new cabin in West Virginia, I induced my mother to get hold of a book for me. How or where she got it I do not know, but in some way she procured an old copy of Webster's "blue-back" spelling-book, which contained the alphabet, followed by such meaningless words as "ab," "ba," "ca," "da." I began at once to devour this book, and I think that it was the first one I ever had in my hands. . . . In all my efforts to learn to read my mother shared fully my ambition, and sympathized with me and aided me in every way that she could. . . . If I have done anything in life worth attention, I feel sure that I inherited the disposition from my mother. . . .

About this time the question of having some kind of a school opened for the coloured children in the village began to be discussed by members of the race. . . . As yet no free schools had been started for coloured people in that section, hence each family agreed to pay a certain amount per month, with the understanding that the teacher was to "board 'round"—that is, spend a day with each family. This was not bad for the teacher, for each family tried to provide the very best on the day the teacher was to be its guest. I recall that I looked forward with an anxious appetite to the "teacher's day" at our little cabin. . . .

The opening of the school in the Kanawha Valley, however, brought to me one of the keenest disappointments that I ever experienced. I had been working in a salt-furnace for several months, and my stepfather had discovered that I had a financial value, and so, when the school opened, he decided that he could not spare me from my work. This decision seemed to cloud my every ambition. The disappointment was made all the more severe by reason of the fact that my place of work was where I could see the happy children passing to and from school, mornings and afternoons. Despite this disappointment, however, I determined that I would learn something, anyway. I applied myself with greater earnestness than ever to the mastering of what was in the "blue-back" speller.

. . . After a while I succeeded in making arrangements with the teacher to give me some lessons at night after the day's work was done. These night lessons were so welcome that I think I learned more at night than the other children did during the day. . . . But my boyish heart was still set upon going to the day-school, and I let no opportunity slip to push my case. Finally I won, and was permitted to go to the school in the day for a few months, with the understanding that I was to rise early in the morning and work in the furnace till nine o'clock, and return immediately after school closed in the afternoon for at least two more hours of work.

The schoolhouse was some distance from the furnace, and as I had to work till nine o'clock, and the school opened at nine, I found myself in a difficulty. School would always be begun before I reached it, and sometimes my class had recited. To get around this difficulty I yielded to a temptation. . . . There was a large clock in a little office in the furnace. This clock, of course, all the hundred or more workmen depended upon to regulate their hours of beginning and ending the day's work. I got the idea that the way for me to reach school on time was to move the clock hands from half-past eight up to the nine o'clock mark. This I found myself doing morning after morning, till the furnace "boss" discovered that something was wrong, and locked the clock in a case. . . .

The time that I was permitted to attend school during the day was short, and my attendance was irregular. It was not long before I had to stop attending day-school altogether, and devote all of my time again to work. I resorted to the night-school again. In fact, the greater part of the education I secured in my boyhood was gathered through the night-school after my day's work was done. . . . There was never a time in my youth, no matter how dark and discouraging the days might be, when one resolve did not continually remain with me, and that was a determination to secure an education at any cost. . . .

. . . After hearing of the Hampton Institute, I continued to work for a few months longer in the coal-mine. While at work there, I heard of a vacant position in the household of General Lewis Ruffner, the owner of the salt-furnace and coal-mine. Mrs. Viola Ruffner, the wife of General Ruffner, was a "Yankee" woman from Vermont. . . . I was hired at a salary of $5 per month.

I had heard so much about Mrs. Ruffner's severity that I was almost afraid to see her, and trembled when I went into her presence. I had not lived with her many weeks, however, before I began to understand her. I soon began to learn that, first of all, she wanted everything kept clean about her, that she wanted things done promptly and systematically, and that at the bottom of everything she wanted absolute honesty and frankness. Nothing must be sloven or slipshod; every door, every fence, must be kept in repair.

I cannot now recall how long I lived with Mrs. Ruffner before going to Hampton, but I think it must have been a year and a half. At any rate, I here repeat what I have said more than once before, that the lessons that I learned in the home of Mrs. Ruffner were as valuable to me as any education I have ever gotten anywhere since. . . .

From fearing Mrs. Ruffner I soon learned to look upon her as one of my best friends. When she found that she could trust me she did so implicitly. During the one or two winters that I was with her she gave me an opportunity to go to school for an hour in the day during a portion of the winter months, but most of my studying was done at night, sometimes alone, sometimes under some one whom I could hire to teach me. Mrs. Ruffner always encouraged and sympathized with me in all my efforts to get an education. It was while living with her that I began to get together my first library. I secured a dry-goods box, knocked out one side of it, put some shelves in it, and began putting into it every kind of book that I could get my hands upon, and called it my "library."

Notwithstanding my success at Mrs. Ruffner's I did not give up the idea of going to the Hampton Institute. In the fall of 1872 I determined to make an effort to get there, although, as I have stated, I had no definite idea of the direction in which Hampton was, or what it would cost to go there. . . .—Booker T. Washington, *Up From Slavery: An Autobiography,* pp. 24-45.

172. Progress in Education — Acts of 1939 and 1941

The West Virginia Education Association has been the perennial, undaunted champion of teachers' rights and welfare. Through aggressive leadership and the virtually unanimous support of the teaching profession, the Association has realized many of its important objectives—a minimum nine months' term, teacher tenure and retirement, and free textbooks. The teacher retirement act of 1939 left much to be desired, however, since it affected only elementary and high school teachers, contained no provision for disability retirement under the age of sixty-two, and was not retroactive. An improved retirement act was passed in 1941. The authors of the following selections—Richard E. Hyde, F. Ray Power, H. Cliff Hamilton—have all made important contributions to West Virginia education.

IN RETIREMENT LEGISLATION a matter of primary concern is membership, or "coverage". The following classes of employees are eligible for membership: in the public schools and state supported colleges including the state university members of the administrative, research, extension, library, and instructional staff, and any person regularly employed for instructional service; the state superintendent of schools, all employees of the department of education and the state board of education who perform services of an educational nature; the secretary of the retirement board; and county school attendance directors holding West Virginia teachers' certificates.

Former teachers who completed thirty or more years of service before the effective date of this act are eligible for retirement and pension payments, beginning with the month of July. Obviously many teachers now receiving county pensions, will qualify for state pensions; however, any county or any state college may supplement such state pensions, and persons now receiving pensions from college or county may continue to do so. All persons retired under the provisions of the act of 1939 will receive payments under the new act, beginning in July.

Teachers employed after the act goes into effect are members of the system, this being one of the conditions of their employment. . . .

Beginning with the school year 1941-42 in July, each member is required to contribute monthly to his individual account four percent of that part of his salary which does not exceed two thousand five hundred dollars. . . . The amount to match the teacher's payment is transferred from the appropriation of the retirement system, and deposited in the employer's accumulation fund. . . .

Members of the retirement board are the trustees of all the funds of the system. Investments will be made only in bonds of the United States Government and bonds of the state of West Virginia, or one of its subdivisions such as a county, school district or municipality. When a governmental subdivision issues bonds, it must offer to sell to the retirement board before advertising; however, the board of public works accepts or rejects the offer.

Pensions will be granted through a computation in which experience prior to the effective date of the act is one of the two deciding factors. Each member must file with the retirement board a statement of his length of service for which he claims prior service credit. . . . Persons who become teachers after the effective date of the act are not eligible for prior service credits.

When members withdraw from service for causes other than death or retirement, upon request they are paid their own accumulated contributions with interest; at death, such payments are made to the member's estate or to a person nominated by the member by written notice filed with the retirement board. . . . —Richard E. Hyde, "Teacher Retirement Legislation," *West Virginia School Journal,* LXIX, April, 1941, 6-8.

The act of the Legislature providing for the nomination and election of a five member county board of education without reference to party affiliation is a law which was recommended by the State Education Association and the State Department of Education for a number of years. It was placed on the statute books at this time because of the sincere and courageous efforts of Governor Neely. The new statute incorporates the major provisions which the Association and the Department recommended and goes considerably further in setting up eligibility requirements for board members. It provides for the following: 1. Nomination and election of a five member board without reference to political affiliation; 2. a term of six years with no more than two members retiring at any one time; 3. nomination and election at time of general election on ballots which eliminate party designation; 4. membership on board ceases if member accepts a position as a teacher, holds membership in a party executive committee or becomes a candidate for or is appointed to any public office; 5. member not eligible for nomination or appointment to office other than to succeed himself until membership on board is terminated. . . . —F. Ray Power, "Non-Partisan School Boards," *West Virginia School Journal,* LXIX, April, 1941, 10.

A free textbook law enacted at the recent session of the legislature sets forth a systematic plan for the gradual introduction of free textbooks as funds are made available. Major provisions of the act include the following:

1. Every county is given authority to provide free textbooks for pupils enrolled in the public schools.

2. Establishment of a county free textbook account to receive state textbook funds, and to which balances in the textbook aid account as of June 30 are to be transferred. The county may supplement the free textbook account.

3. Establishment of an order of preference to be observed in the expenditure of money from the free textbook account. The preference order is:

(1) Needy children, grades one to eight inclusive.

(2) Other children, irrespective of need, grades one to eight inclusive as funds permit from year to year after caring for needy children. . . .

5. The term "textbooks" as used in the act refers to textbooks adopted by the state board of education for use in the elementary schools. . . . —H. Cliff Hamilton, "A New Free Textbook Law," *West Virginia School Journal*, LXIX, April, 1941, 11.

173. West Virginia State Board of Education et al v. Barnette et al.

In 1941 the West Virginia legislature passed an act which required all schools in the State to conduct courses in history and government for the purpose of teaching the ideals, principles, and spirit of Americanism, and directed the State Board of Education to prescribe the courses. On January 9, 1942, the Board adopted a resolution which ordered that the salute to the flag become a regular part of school activities and that all teachers and pupils be required to participate in the exercise. Citizens, Parent-Teachers' Associations, Boy and Girl Scout organizations, the Red Cross, and the Federation of Women's Clubs objected to the salute as being like Hitler's and won some concessions, but no concession was made to Jehovah's Witnesses who objected to the salute on religious grounds. When children of that faith were expelled from school and their parents and guardians made liable to fines and imprisonment under the compulsory attendance laws, members of Jehovah's Witnesses obtained a writ in the United States District Court which restrained the West Virginia State Board of Education from enforcing the statute and regulations. The State Board appealed and the United States Supreme Court handed down its decision on June 14, 1943, declaring the West Virginia law as applied by the State Board of Education unconstitutional. Below are appropriate paragraphs of the text of the resolution adopted by the State Board of Education and an extract from the majority opinion of the Supreme Court—a truly classic defense of religious liberty.

THE WEST VIRGINIA Board of Education does hereby recognize and order that the commonly accepted salute to the flag of the United States—the right hand is placed upon the breast and the following pledge repeated in unison: 'I pledge allegiance to the flag of the United States of America and to the Republic for which it stands; one Nation, indivisible, with liberty and justice for all'—now become a regular part of the program of activities in the public schools, supported in whole or in part by public funds, and that all teachers as defined by law in West Virginia and pupils in such schools shall be required to participate in the salute honoring the Nation represented by the flag; provided, however, that refusal to salute the flag be regarded as an act of insubordination, and shall be dealt with accordingly.—*Report of the West Virginia Board of Education for Biennial Period, 1940-42, pp. 12-13.*

MR. JUSTICE JACKSON . . .

. . . It is such conflicts which most frequently require intervention of the State to determine where the rights of one end and those of another begin. But the refusal of these persons to participate in the ceremony does not interfere with or deny rights of others to do so. Nor is there any question in this case that their behavior is peaceable and orderly. The sole conflict is between authority and rights of the individual. The State asserts power to condition access to public education on making a prescribed sign and profession and at the same time to coerce attendance by punishing both parent and child. . . .

Here . . . we are dealing with a compulsion of students to declare a belief. They are not merely made acquainted with the flag salute so that they may be informed as to what it is or even what it means. The issue here is whether this slow and easily neglected route to aroused loyalties constitutionally may be short-cut by substituting a compulsory salute and slogan. . . .

There is no doubt that, in connection with the pledges, the flag salute is a form of utterance. Symbolism is a primitive but effective way of communicating ideas. The use of an emblem or flag to symbolize some system, idea, institution, or personality, is a short cut from mind to mind. Causes and nations, political parties, lodges and ecclesiastical groups seek to knit the loyalty of their followings to a flag or banner, a color or design. The State announces rank, function, and authority through crowns and maces, uniforms and black robes; the church speaks through the Cross, the Crucifix, the altar and shrine, and clerical raiment. Symbols of State often convey political ideas just as religious symbols come to convey theological ones. Associated with many of these symbols are appropriate gestures of acceptance or respect: a salute, a bowed or bared head, a bended knee. A person gets from a symbol the meaning he puts into it, and what is one man's comfort and inspiration is another's jest and scorn.

. . . Here it is the State that employs a flag as a symbol of adherence to government as presently organized. It requires the individual to communicate by word and sign his acceptance of the political ideas it thus bespeaks. Objection to this form of communication when coerced is an old one, well known to the framers of the Bill of Rights.

. . . It is now a commonplace that censorship or suppression of expression of opinion is tolerated by our Constitution only when the expression presents a clear and present danger of action of a kind the State is empowered to prevent and punish. . . . But here the power of compulsion is invoked without any allegation that remaining passive during a flag salute ritual creates a clear and present danger that would justify an effort even to muffle expression. To sustain the compulsory flag salute we are required to say that a Bill of Rights which guards the individual's right to speak his own mind, left it open to public authorities to compel him to utter what is not in his mind....

Struggles to coerce uniformity of sentiment in support of some end thought essential to their time and country have been waged by many good as well as by evil men.... As first and moderate methods to attain unity have failed, those bent on its accomplishment must resort to an ever-increasing severity. As governmental pressure toward unity becomes greater, so strife becomes more bitter as to whose unity it shall be. Probably no deeper division of our people could proceed from any provocation than from finding it necessary to choose what doctrine and whose program public educational officials shall compel youth to unite in embracing. Ultimate futility of such attempts to compel coherence is the lesson of every such effort from the Roman drive to stamp out Christianity as a disturber of its pagan unity, the Inquisition, as a means to religious and dynastic unity, the Siberian exiles as a means to Russian unity, down to the fast failing efforts of our present totalitarian enemies. Those who begin coercive elimination of dissent soon find themselves exterminating dissenters. Compulsory unification of opinion achieves only the unanimity of the graveyard.

... We set up government by consent of the governed, and the Bill of Rights denies those in power any legal opportunity to coerce that consent. Authority here is to be controlled by public opinion, not public opinion by authority.

... To believe that patriotism will not flourish if patriotic ceremonies are voluntary and spontaneous instead of a compulsory routine is to make an unflattering estimate of the appeal of our institutions to free minds. We can have intellectual individualism and the rich cultural diversities that we owe to exceptional minds only at the price of occasional eccentricity and abnormal attitudes. When they are so harmless to others or to the State as those we deal with here, the price is not too great. But freedom to differ is not limited to things that do not matter much. That would be a mere shadow of freedom. The test of its substance is the right to differ as to things that touch the heart of the existing order.

If there is any fixed star in our constitutional constellation, it is that no official, high or petty, can prescribe what shall be orthodox in politics, nationalism, religion, or other matters of opinion or force citizens to confess by word or act their faith therein. If there are any circumstances which permit an exception, they do not now occur to us. . . .—West Virginia State Board of Education *et al v.* Barnette *et al,* 319 *U. S.,* 624-42, 1942.

174. The Strayer Survey

The Strayer Survey was undertaken to implement the Senate Concurrent Resolution of February 26, 1945, providing for an interim committee to make a comprehensive study of the educational system of West Virginia including the institutions of higher learning. The committee, composed of the President of the Senate and the Speaker of the House and their eight appointees, was empowered to employ such advisory assistants as it might need for the proper execution of its duties. The committee obtained the services of George D. Strayer, Professor Emeritus of Education at Teachers College, Columbia University, to survey the areas of public education specified in the above resolution. Assisting Professor Strayer in the field work for the survey were a staff of specialists in education and an advisory committee of fifteen representative citizens of the State. The survey, which was begun on July 1 and completed on December 10, 1945, gives an accurate picture of West Virginia education at the mid-point of the twentieth century. Not all of the recommendations contained in the report have been adopted. And some of the defects pointed out, such as low salaries for teachers, unrealistic property assessments, inadequate facilities for vocational education, school transportation difficulties, and lack of institutional coordination in higher education continue to exist or have only been partially corrected.

By the end of 1932, the depression had taken a staggering toll of the economic life of West Virginia. Prices of mine, farm and factory products had collapsed, bankruptcies were epidemic, wages had sadly decreased, and unemployment was rampant. Valuations of property for purposes of taxation were greatly reduced, but notwithstanding these reductions, tax delinquencies were common. Since the schools were then almost entirely depending on the property tax for support, decreasing tax valuations and increasing tax delinquencies had a devastating effect on their efficiency. Hundreds of school employees went unpaid, school terms were shortened, and scores of schools closed.

In the fall of 1932 the people of the State adopted an amendment to the Constitution classifying property for purposes of taxation and limiting the rate of taxation on each class of property. Although the amendment provided that the proposed limit could be exceeded by vote of the people, provided "at least 60 per cent of the qualified voters shall favor such increase," schools were still seriously handicapped for lack of funds.

When the Legislature met early in 1933, it was faced with the task of dividing limited revenues among different agencies of government, including the schools. To make up an anticipated deficit of approximately $10,000,000 in the revenues of the schools, two chief measures were passed. The first appropriated $10,500,000 of the state funds for aid to schools. The second, aimed at economy, abolished all school districts inside the counties and made the county the sole unit for the administration of schools. . . .

The county unit has been accompanied by many improvements in the schools of West Virginia.

Pupils in the rural schools of West Virginia generally receive, under the county unit plan, better transportation; better health services; better courses of study, textbooks, and educational supplies; and better teachers and educational leadership. . . .

On the financial side, tax rates have been equalized within the county, and many economies in purchasing and management of supplies and equipment have been made. . . .

The first duty of the county board of education is to choose a professionally competent superintendent of schools.

The board of education should take seriously the task of finding the best man available for the superintendency. The search should be state-wide, and it may well be extended to neighboring states. . . .

The quality of education in any county depends largely upon the freedom of the board of education from political pressures. . . .

No law will guarantee a board of education which is free from political pressure, nor will it guarantee a board whose members are able to withstand political pressures. . . . (1) The members of the board should be elected for a relatively long term; (2) they should be elected on a separate non-partisan ballot; (3) the election should be held at some time other than at the time of the general election—preferably, at the time of the primary election; (4) candidates for election to the board and members of the board should not hold any other public office, elective or appointive; (5) no member of the board should vote in any case where a near relative has been nominated for appointment or is a party to a contract with the board of education. . . .

Vocational education should be extended to West Virginia's new industries. . . .

Long term programs should be worked out in cooperation with such industries as the pulp and paper industry, the glass industry, the iron and steel industry, the alloy steel industry, the petroleum industry, the natural gas industry, the pottery and dinner ware industry, the synthetic rubber industry, and the chemical industries. Such programs should include consideration of the training of the junior technicians in each industry, mass production machine and equipment set-up men and adjusters, and mass production operatives, as well as skilled tradesmen in the plant maintenance crews. . . .

Local financial support is inadequate.

Analysis of the support structure indicates that the outstanding weaknesses of the structure of public education in West Virginia are found in the local aspects—in the low levels of local support and the small degree of local popular control. . . .

Additional local revenue may be obtained through the assessment of property at actual value.

... The rates of assessment in counties on the average vary from 30 per cent to 84 per cent. The average rate of assessment is somewhere near 50 per cent. In the average county, therefore, the assessment of property at full value would double the amount that would be raised by present rates of taxation. In some counties it would treble the amount; in others it would increase it by only a fourth; but on the average it would double it. This step alone would increase the potential, non-voting revenue for education approximately $12,000,000, with a possible additional $10,000,000 if the maximum Constitutional rates were used. . . .

The State has created a number and variety of higher institutions beyond the apparent disposition of the State to provide adequate support and development.

... There exists no carefully drawn, state-wide pattern of higher education into which each institution may be economically fitted.

Until the State is prepared to take certain drastic and courageous actions for the clear definition and progressive coordination of the functions of each and all of its present institutions, there is but little chance for the development of a system of higher education designed to accomplish the things essential for the economic, cultural, and civic welfare of the State. . . .

A higher percentage of West Virginia's population should be enrolled in its colleges. . . .

In 1939-40, 50.8 per cent of the 17-year old young people in the United States were graduated from high school; in West Virginia in the same year only 40 per cent of the young people of this age finished high school. . . . In 1940 West Virginia had only 11.73 per cent of its young people of college age (18-21) in school although 13.31 per cent of all the young people of college age in the United States were enrolled in educational institutions.

West Virginia has the job of up-grading its teachers.

In West Virginia, as in other states, permission to teach in the public schools has been granted initially to undertrained young people on a temporary basis and their continuance made dependent upon securing further training in summer school, through extension work, or through resumption of college attendance for a longer period. This highly desirable up-grading is of course, a responsibility of the colleges. . . .

GENERAL SCOPE OF THE PROGRAM
OF TRANSPORTATION

Of the more than 500,000 children and youth of school age living in West Virginia, representative samplings indicate that approximately 55 per cent of the children live within two miles of a graded rural or other elementary school, and 32 per cent of the youth live within two miles of an approved secondary school. It is the principal purpose of the school transportation system of West Virginia to insure that the remaining 45 per cent of children of elementary school age, and the 68 per cent of youth of high school age are given adequate educational opportunities. . . .

Transportation brings a long day for some pupils.

Educational leadership can find much to challenge its thinking, in the observation that over 63,600 children must leave their homes before 8 A. M. in order to reach schools which frequently begin class sessions at 9 A. M. Over 18,000 children must leave home before 7:30 A. M. every morning, every school day of the year. Over 3,000 children must leave home before 7 A. M. every morning. It is literally true that these youngsters have no free daylight hours from one week-end to the next.

At the opposite end of the school day, 25,300 pupils do not get home until after 5 P. M., and 812 of them arrive home after 6 P. M. Worse even than this, 174 children in the State arrive home after 6:30 P. M.

If we look only at the 63,600 children who must leave home before 8 A. M., it is apparent that almost one-half of the 130,000 pupils enrolled and transported must spend two hours each day enroute to and from school. If we look at the entire picture, it is apparent that much needs to be done to provide adequate facilities for many children. . . .—George D. Strayer, *A Report of a Survey of Public Education in ... West Virginia,* pp. 20-23, 76, 93-97, 117-18, 130-31, 290-91.

175. Location of the West Virginia Medical School

When the West Virginia legislature established a four-year School of Medicine, Dentistry and Nursing in 1951, it left the choice of a site to the governor who was required to designate a location for the school on or before July 1, 1951. After consultation with medical educators throughout the country and study of conflicting factors, Governor Okey L. Patteson (1898-) decided to locate the institution on the campus of West Virginia University at Morgantown. The following passage has been taken from an address delivered by Governor Patteson on the day following announcement of his choice of site for the West Virginia Medical School.

. . . WHEN THE FIGHT DEVELOPED over the site for the school in the 1949 Legislature, I must admit that I had heard so much about the importance of placing the school in a large metropolitan area, that I, too, decided Morgantown could not accommodate a medical school. However, when the dispute began in the 1951 Legislature, I realized that I knew nothing whatsoever about the actual requirements for a medical school, and that I had no right to think one place was better than another for its location. Therefore, when this decision was literally "dumped in my lap" by the 50th Legislature, I was able to study the problem with an entirely open mind and without prejudice. However, I frankly admit that I was most surprised to learn of the many advantages of a university site as compared with the advantages of a metropolitan area some distance from the university. It is my sincere hope that you will study my report, especially with reference to the opinions of the experts, and the experience of medical schools in other States. Most certainly, any person has a perfect right to differ with me, and I knew when I assumed this great responsibility that I could not please everyone, but some-one had to be the "goat" in order that West Virginia could have a medical school. . . .

I am humbly grateful to many who have advised me only to-day that they had been wholeheartedly for Charleston (or Hunt-ington) and that they felt I had made a terrible mistake when I announced my decision, but that after reading my report, they are now in favor of the University site and feel as I do—that I acted for the best interest of the medical school and the entire State.

I am especially pleased with the sportsmanlike attitude of the press, radio and the citizens of southern West Virginia in this matter, because I know it will do much to dispel the unfair, an-tagonistic sectional feeling which apparently exists between northern and southern West Virginia. . . . Petty bickering and jealousy only tend to make us a divided people. . . . After all, we are West Virginians whether we live in the northern, eastern, southern or western part of this State. So, let's put aside this childish unchristianlike hatred of various sections, and all unite in the common cause of making a great State ever greater and better!—Governor Okey L. Patteson, *State Papers and Public Addresses*, pp. 374-76.

176. Integration in West Virginia

William W. Trent (1876-1960) teacher, administrator, and former president of Broaddus, now Alderson-Broaddus College, was elected State Superintendent of Free Schools on the Demo-cratic ticket for six consecutive four-year terms. His long tenure, 1933-1957, which broke all records for that office, made his name almost synonymous with public education in West Virginia and enabled him to participate in some of the major educational changes in the State, notably, the introduction of the county unit, of teacher tenure and retirement, and of school integration. Despite the repeated recommendations of the State Educational Association that the state superintendent be appointed by the State Board of Education, it was not until 1958, during the in-cumbency of his Republican successor, R. Virgil Rohrbough, that the office became appointive by constitutional amendment. Trent's account of the effect of the historic Supreme Court decision of May, 1954, does credit to both Trent and West Virginia.

IN THE MID-TWENTIES, West Virginia University admitted Negro students to extension classes offered formerly for white students only. In the days of the county institutes for teachers, as far back as I can recall, Negroes and white teachers attended, with Negroes sitting in a separate part of the room. For some twelve years prior to the declaration of the Unites States Supreme Court outlawing segregation, May 17, 1954, educational conferences held by the State Department of Education were integrated for meals and sessions, and for a number of years prior, four private colleges—Alderson-Broaddus, Davis and Elkins, Bethany, and West Virginia Wesleyan—accepted Negro students. . . .

Because the school people of the State expected word from me, I prepared a letter of instructions and suggestions and requested approval or disapproval from Attorney General John Fox. . . .

In compliance with an opinion of the Attorney General of the State, the West Virginia Board of Governors, controlling West Virginia University and Potomac State School of the University; and the West Virginia Board of Education, controlling the colleges formerly maintained separately for Negro and white students, ordered that the University and all colleges within the State should, after that date—June 9, 1954—admit "any qualified student." By Novembr 1954, all colleges in the State, except one, formerly maintained for white students, had enrolled Negro students. No Negro applications had been made to Glenville State College—the one not having Negro students. . . .

With the opening of the school year 1954-55, twenty-nine of the fifty-five counties desegregated in part or in full; ten counties had no Negro pupils; and sixteen counties postponed action. . . .

In October 1954, the West Virginia Education Association for white teachers and the West Virginia State Teachers' Association for Negro Teachers, by a resolution, adopted unanimously by both organizations, united under the name of the West Virginia Education Association in which organization teachers of both races have equal rights and equal opportunities. . . .

In keeping with an act of the legislature of 1955, the school for the Deaf and Blind at Institute did not reopen in the fall of 1955. The children had been transferred to the West Virginia Schools for the Deaf and Blind at Romney which, by this action, became an integrated school. . . .

At the end of the year 1955-56, only five counties had not taken steps toward integration: Berkeley, Grant, Hampshire, Hardy, and Jefferson. In some, if not all of these counties, Negroes had asked that action be postponed. Their schools were good and teachers feared losing employment. In the counties integrating within the year, forty-eight fewer Negroes had been employed. . . .

Statistics gathered by the State Department of Education in October and November 1956, revealed that the number of Negroes (not including Kanawha County) teaching in integrated schools was 141; that the number of Negroes employed was 33 fewer than for the previous year; and that 22 counties had completed integration, 21 had partially integrated, 3 had taken no action, and 9 had no Negro pupils. Within the two years following, Berkeley, Hampshire, and Jefferson counties began desegregation. The action of these counties in beginning desegregation (the last to begin) gave the State credit for having complied with the declaration of the United States Supreme Court.
—William W. Trent, *Mountaineer Education*, pp. 134-43.

177. The Claude Worthington Benedum Foundation – Will of Michael L. Benedum

West Virginia has had its share of men of great wealth—coal and oil barons, chiefly—who gave their names to the dingy little communities which they created and who climaxed their spectacular business careers by entering politics. Absorbed as they were with their own material advancement, they demonstrated little concern for the general welfare of the state and the promotion of its culture. There were exceptions, of course, a notable one of whom was Michael L. Benedum (1869-1959), the "Great Wildcatter," born at Bridgeport, Harrison County. Benedum's successful search for oil took him to near and far corners of the world—from West Virginia to other states, and beyond the United States to Canada, Latin America, the Philippines, and eastern Europe. With the fortune which he amassed, he organized in December, 1944, the Claude Worthington Benedum Foundation, named in honor of his only son who died at Camp Meade, October 18, 1918. Established as a non-profit corporation under the laws of Pennsylvania, the Foundation was created exclusively "for religious, charitable, scientific, literary, or educational purposes or for the prevention of cruelty to children or animals. . . ."

Benedum philanthropy has given to Bridgeport a beautiful Methodist church and to West Virginia Wesleyan College one of the finest student centers in West Virginia. It has provided financial aid to hundreds of college students and research incentives to teaching personnel. It has subsidized various educational institutions, especially private and denominational colleges, such as Morris Harvey, Alderson-Broaddus, and Salem. It has, in short, supplied a long-felt need in this State for educational and religious endowments. That Michael Benedum had a very special affection for West Virginia may be seen in the codicil to his will which is given below.

THE DISPOSITION OF A NOT INCONSIDERABLE ESTATE is never an easy assignment. It has been a thorny and laborious problem for me because, recognizing my frailty and inadequacy, I have not been able to lose sight of the awesome responsibility involved.

If I could have looked upon my material goods as personal property, belonging to me alone, my task would have been immeasurably lighter. But I have never regarded my possessions in that light. Providence gives no fee simple title to such possessions. As I have seen it, all of the elements of the earth belong to the Creator of all things, and He has, as a part of the Divine Purpose, distributed them unevenly among His children, holding each relatively accountable for their wise use and disposition.

I have always felt that I have been only a trustee for such material wealth as Providence has placed in my hands. This trusteeship has weighed heavily upon me. In carrying out this final responsibility of my stewardship, I have sought to utilize such wisdom and understanding of equity as the Creator has given me. No one with any regard for his responsibility to his God and his fellow man should do less. No one can do more.

I will not attempt to deny that in certain provisions of this Last Will and Testament, I have been swayed to some extent by the tender sentiment that I have for the land of my birth and by my affection for those who are nearer and dearer to me than life itself. While I may seem to have been generous to these loved ones who are the blood of my blood, I know from experience that I am in reality merely passing a responsibility to them.

The book is not closed. The responsibility is merely lessened and divided. It is none the less fearful. I hope that these loved ones of mine will bear with me in this last word of counsel, as I again remind them of the obligation that goes with their material heritage. I have unlimited confidence that they will be faithful to this trust. . . .

Throughout my adult life, day by day and year by year, I have been instilled with the conviction that wealth cannot be measured in terms of money, stocks, bonds, broad acres or by ownership of mine and mill. These cannot bear testimony of the staple of real excellence of man or woman. Those who use a material yardstick to appraise their wealth and foolishly imagine themselves to be rich are objects of pity. In their ignorance and misanthropic isolation, they suffer from shrinkage of the soul.

All of us aspire to a higher and better life beyond this, but I feel that the individual who seeks to climb the ladder alone will never find the way to Paradise. Only those who sustain the faltering ones on the rungs above and extend a helping hand to the less fortunate on the rungs below, can approach the end with the strength of sublime faith and confidence. . . .

While I am conscious that my love for the land that gave me birth has been an influence in guiding the disposition of my estate, there are other practical reasons why I have favored my native state of West Virginia. It is not that I am unmindful or unappreciative of my adopted home of Pennsylvania, but rather that I have sought to appraise and balance the needs of each and the available potential for supplying those needs.

I cannot close my eyes to the realistic consideration that Pittsburgh and Pennsylvania abound in riches, having a citizenship in which men of great wealth are more common than rare. West Virginia is in a less fortunate position. There can be no question but that its needs are much greater than those of my adopted home. Consequently, in making specific provisions for West Virginia institutions, I have done so in good conscience, with a sense of equity and with recognition of a responsibility to distribute my estate in a way that will bring the greatest good to the greatest number. This decision was not made lightly or impetuously.

Conscious that in this Codicil to my Last Will and Testament, I am figuratively speaking from the grave, and that the great book of my account with the Creator has been closed beyond change or amendment, I submit my soul to His tender mercy, and my memory to the generosity and compassion of my fellow man.—"Portrait of Michael Late Benedum," *The Pioneer*, XV, No. 8, pp. 30-31.

XVI. Recent Years

178. The Little Report

When William Casey Marland (1918-1965) became governor of West Virginia in 1953, he faced many state-wide problems growing out of a declining economy. As economic conditions worsened Governor Marland contracted in 1954 with Arthur D. Little, Inc., of Cambridge, Massachusetts, to survey opportunities for further industrial expansion. He next created the Governor's Committee on Industrial Development to advise him and to carry out the recommendations of the Little Report. Governor Marland also gave generous support to the program of the West Virginia Industrial and Publicity Commission in publicizing the industrial advantages of the State.

Below is the gist of the findings of the Little Report.

IMBALANCE IN THE INDUSTRIAL STRUCTURE, coupled with a lack of substantial employment opportunities, have been West Virginia's major problems; until industrial development through diversification and growth of the industrial base occurs, these problems will remain.

An imbalanced structure means dependence on one or a few major industries. One automatically thinks of the dominance of coal in West Virginia's history. While coal has played a significant role, manufacturing is actually the greatest contributor to the state's income and employment. Within the manufacturing category, however, dependence on three primary industries—iron and steel, stone-clay-glass, and chemicals—adds to this imbalance. Any economic disturbance in any of these industries has an important effect on the state's economy, and therefore on its population. The recent disturbance within the coal industry, caused by loss of markets, led to substantial unemployment. Though coal is regaining its markets or creating new ones, and though unemployment has decreased, the problem still exists—too much concentration on too few industries.

The second problem, lack of employment opportunities, is directly related to the first. A balanced industrial base generally means that new opportunities absorb unemployment in other fields or keep the unemployment figure in balance. As one industry grows and uses more labor, another may suffer some recessionary tendencies and employ fewer; the net result is a fairly stable unemployment rate.

In spite of a natural increase of population, outmigration, heavily weighted with young men and women of working age, emphasizes the need for industrial development.

Though inadequately balanced, the present state of industrialization in West Virginia provides a sound base for further development. Raw materials are abundant, and primary manufactured products for further processing are available in or near the state. The existence of primary industries with the advantages offered by certain natural resources is a positive factor in the attraction of new industries, and the expansion of existing ones.

A host of factors affect industrial development: availability of labor at reasonable rates; proximity to markets; power; taxes; transportation; and other factors too numerous to exhaust in a report. Some important factors in West Virginia are:

1. *Labor.* In spite of a "reported" bad labor climate, the record indicates that in manufacturing, West Virginia has often had a lower incidence of work stoppages than the average for the nation; the supply is adequate, and there are many surplus areas. The wage rates are generally lower than the national average. Existing industries report no training problems, as education and dexterity of workers compare favorably with those of workers in competing regions.

2. *Markets.* West Virginia's position with respect to many major consumer and industrial markets of the Northeast, Middle West, and the growing Southern markets is unique. Four of the five major wholesale and retail markets are within 500 miles.

3. *Transportation.* Road, air, water, and railroad services are sufficient to fulfill demands by existing industry. Since trucking is so widely used, the road development program must continue and be improved; air and rail service will improve as industry grows. Water transportation is once again in vogue,

so that West Virginia's many navigable rivers represent a positive asset for those industries utilizing low-cost, bulk-freight shipments.

4. Taxes. West Virginia occupies a "middle" position on taxes; a comprehensive tax study will be needed before positive assessment can be made. Taxes are fair and reasonable; the tax burden is below that of the United States as a whole. The only major tax on manufacturing is a nominal .39 per cent on gross income.

5. Raw Materials. Coal, limestone, natural gas, salt brine, petroleum, and sand and gravel are found in abundance. Iron ore and other basic raw materials are found in or near the state's borders. Lumber, especially hardwood, can serve as a base for further expansion in industries using it as a raw material.

6. Electric Power. Power rates are favorable for large users; for small and medium consumers, rates are competitive with those in adjacent regions. There is ample coal to support considerable expansion in power production.

7. Water Resources. Additional water-consuming industries can be supported. A limiting factor is the availability of sites; more data on industrial sites must be made available to determine proper development. Data on ground water supplies and further study of pollution problems and control are also needed.

8. Other Locational Factors. Climate is moderate and generally a neutral factor. Topography presents some communications problems, which are being gradually overcome. Construction costs are average to low. Educational facilities and recreational services, though presently judged adequate, need to be continuously improved.

In what we term "a screening of industrial opportunities," these factors were evaluated, with selected criteria applied to specific industries. At the conclusion of the screening four industries received priority rating: chemicals, woodworking, metal fabricating, and apparel. These were further studied to determine the precise nature of each opportunity. These industries are to be promoted as the first step to achieving a well-balanced economy. . . . Arthur D. Little, Inc., "Survey of Industrial Development," *Report to State of West Virginia,* July 29, 1955, pp. 2-4.

179. Public Welfare in West Virginia

The following extract from the legislative message of Governor William C. Marland in 1955 summarizes the activities of the State Department of Public Assistance, since renamed the Department of Public Welfare.

DUE TO THE ECONOMIC CONDITIONS in our major industry [coal], the Department of Public Assistance has been faced with a considerable problem in meeting an increased demand. In the past two years, however, public assistance has been paid and other services furnished to more than fifty thousand cases monthly.

In the Department's Division of Crippled Children, more than six thousand two hundred cases have been attended. One of the highlights of the last year was the employment of a Thoracic and Cardiovascular Surgeon for the operable congenital heart cases. West Virginia is one of the few states in the country providing such treatment on its regular crippled children's program. You can well understand the importance of this when you realize that during these past two years seventy-five children, who would have been invalids and charges of the State for their lifetime, have been restored to unrestricted activity.

In the Division of Commodity Distribution, I am sure that many of you from the coal mining regions are aware of the immense job performed in the distribution of surplus commodities. The total program, including the school lunches, institutions, welfare, disaster relief, et cetera, totalled 44,731 bags of commodities such as beans, potatoes; 407,513 cases of canned commodities and 1,449,931 pounds of such things as dried milk, cheese and butter.

Much has been done in the field of blindness prevention and child welfare. You may be interested to know that the effect of West Virginia's Child Welfare program is reflected in the field of juvenile delinquency, in that the national increase for this biennium has been approximately 13 per cent, while in West Virginia during this same period, the increase has been only 5 per cent.

From the standpoint of the aged, dependent and crippled children, the totally disabled and others who are unable to provide for themselves as are their fellow citizens who are more fortunate, this Department has been a large factor in alleviating what would have been untold suffering and misery for those people. — *State Papers and Public Addresses of William C. Marland*, pp. 95-96.

180. In Appreciation of Art

The Huntington Galleries, Inc., was established in 1947, and the Daywood Art Gallery, Inc., at Lewisburg, in 1950. Both owe their existence to private generosity and civic pride and both are located in towns which possess superior cultural facilities.

The seat of the Huntington Galleries is a handsome modern structure situated on one of the hills which surround the city. The Galleries' permanent exhibits include: rare oriental prayer rugs; silver made by the greatest English craftsmen; one of the finest collections of fire arms in this country; paintings by American and foreign artists; exquisite porcelains, bronzes, and other valuable and beautiful objects. The gallery is also used for exhibitions of work of regional artists and of art on loan.

Established by Mrs. Ruth Woods Dayton, the Daywood Gallery is a charming example of early American architecture especially suitable to its locale. The gallery contains the paintings and prints collected by Arthur S. Dayton, a prominent Charleston attorney who organized the first Charleston Art Association, which has expanded into the Allied Artists of West Virginia. Among the painters and graphic artists represented in the Daywood Gallery are Robert Henri, George Inness, John H. Twachtman, Childe Hassam, Charles W. Hawthorne, Winslow Homer, Sir Francis Seymour Haden, James McNeill Whistler, Murihead Bone, Joseph Pennell, George Bellows, and Rembrandt Van Ryn.

The high purpose which inspired the establishment of the Huntington Galleries is evidenced in the following brief selection.

BASED UPON GIFTS, already committed, Huntington Galleries, Inc., a non-stock West Virginia Corporation, is dedicated to the service of the present and future citizenship of Huntington and the tri-state.

The corporation is the beneficiary under the will of the late Rufus Switzer and will receive in perpetuity an annuity estimated to total $20,000.00 annually for maintenance of a staff, building and grounds.

Fifty acres ot land, admirably suited to the housing of Huntington Galleries, Inc., have been deeded in fee simple to the Galleries. . . .

With the land given and maintenance guaranteed in perpetuity, the objects and purposes of Huntington Galleries, Inc., are:

1. *To Own, Operate and Manage an Arboretum.* Many of the trees, flowers and shrubs native to West Virginia are already grown on the site. Other plantings will be made so that school children may study, under trained direction, the flora of our mountain state.

2. *To Own and Operate a Bird Sanctuary.* Under nature's own conditions, bird life will be protected so that propagation of species may be encouraged. Ample opportunities will be afforded both adults and children for observation and study.

3. *To Own, Operate and Conduct an Historical Museum* for all kinds of historic objects and data connected with West Virginia, particularly with Huntington, Cabell and Wayne Counties, and including the entire West Virginia, Kentucky and Ohio areas.

4. *To Construct a Fireproof Building* to house a *Gallery* in which there will be spacious rooms for the study of arts and crafts by the children of Huntington and the tri-state and for the proper display of their work. In the same building there will also be housed an *Art Gallery* for the collection of paintings, etchings, bronzes, porcelains and other art objects.—*Prospectus* —The Huntington Galleries, Inc.

181. Coal Production and Coal Reserves

West Virginia has been termed "the coal bin of the United States." Since 1900 coal mining has been the State's basic industry and since 1931 West Virginia has led all other states in bituminous coal production. In 1870 West Virginia mines produced 600,000 tons but with the opening of new trunk line railroads across the State and the construction of branch and connecting lines, bituminous coal mining became West Virginia's most important extractive industry.

By 1912 West Virginia collieries produced approximately 67,-000,000 tons, 90 per cent of which was marketed outside the State. The West Virginia coal industry gained further momentum during World War I and in 1928 temporarily took first place in the nation. The State attained its peak year in 1947 when the West Virginia fields produced 173,653,816 tons. However, the substitution of residual oil and water power for coal uses, the consolidation of mining companies, exhaustion of bonanza seams, deeper mines, higher labor costs, and rate differentials against West Virginia shippers, combined to reduce output. Nevertheless, West Virginia continued to lead the nation in bituminous coal production after 1931, and in 1962 mined some 40,000,000 tons more than its closest competitor, Pennsylvania.

West Virginia mined 6,724,481,264 short tons of bituminous coal from 1863 to 1963, inclusive. The following table shows the estimated recoverable tonnage by counties based on studies made by the West Virginia Geological and Economic Survey.

	Short Tons
Barbour	1,673,323,000
Berkeley	
Boone	4,693,539,000
Braxton	1,152,787,000
Brooke	102,223,000
Cabell	26,500,000
Calhoun	150,610,000

Clay	1,900,846,000
Doddridge	671,587,000
Fayette	2,004,848,000
Gilmer	501,598,000
Grant	574,734,000
Greenbrier	665,966,000
Hancock	246,773,000
Harrison	711,487,000
Kanawha	3,102,358,000
Lewis	1,378,577,000
Lincoln	1,058,207,000
Logan	4,052,697,000
Marion	1,687,921,000
Marshall	2,159,486,000
Mason	257,076,000
McDowell	2,046,644,000
Mercer	120,603,000
Mineral	373,728,000
Mingo	3,535,836,000
Monongalia	1,528,109,000
Nicholas	3,625,947,000
Ohio	372,492,000
Pleasants	
Pocahontas	300,595,000
Preston	1,008,953,000
Putnam	238,280,000
Raleigh	1,992,630,000
Randolph	2,454,312,000
Roane	404,861,000
Summers	10,994,000
Taylor	617,631,000
Tucker	189,612,000
Tyler	568,879,000
Upshur	1,748,309,000
Wayne	875,935,000
Webster	3,747,783,000
Wetzel	1,660,868,000
Wirt	13,381,000

Wyoming _____ 2,823,116,000
Small Mines _____ 50,000,000
                                          ─────────────
                                          58,982,451,000

—West Virginia Blue Book, 1963, p. 912.

182. The Population Decline

At the time of admission to statehood in 1863 West Virginia had an estimated population of 400,000; in 1870 West Virginia residents numbered 442,014, most of whom lived along navigable rivers, the turnpikes, and the Baltimore and Ohio Railroad. Until 1880, when industrialization began to attract European immigrants and workers from neighboring states, the population increase was largely native-born. West Virginia gained in population until 1950, when the census reported a total population of 2,005,552. From 1940 to 1950, however, the State gained only 103,578 or 5.4 per cent, while the population increase in the United States was 14.5 per cent. The numerical increase during that decade was the smallest in West Virginia since 1870, and the rate of increase the smallest in the history of the State. West Virginia owed its lag in population growth during the 1940's mainly to the migration of workers, a movement that gained momentum during the 1950's, when automation of the coal mines, depression in the coal market, and exhaustion of natural resources each took a toll of existing jobs and new-job opportunities. Thus in 1960 the population of the State totaled 1,860,-421, which represented a net loss of 145,131 or 7.2 per cent during the decade of the 1950's.

The following passage contains an analysis of population trends in West Virginia in recent years.

THE GROWTH OF LARGE URBAN POPULATIONS in the industrial and commercial centers of this country has for years depended upon a steady migration of people from the predominantly rural and agricultural states, where the birth rate has typically been highest. West Virginia has always been one of these latter states, though the proportion of its labor force that emigrated has always been lower than in many other such states, at least until recently, due largely to the presence of expanding employment opportunities in coal mining.

In 1950, West Virginia's population of just over 2 million made it the 29th state by size of population. Today, the most important single fact about this population is that it is no longer growing. Indeed, from 1950 to 1954 the state is estimated to have lost nearly 3 percent of its population, the largest percentage loss of any state in the nation for this period. This fact takes on special significance when it is remembered that between 1900 and 1940, population increased in West Virginia at a faster rate than in the United States as a whole. . . . However, this trend came to an end in the decade between 1940 and 1950, when West Virginia's population continued to grow, but at a rate 9 percent slower than the national average. The rapid growth of war industries in areas adjacent to West Virginia and the slump in coal mining at the end of the decade largely explained this marked slowing down. The continuing fall in mining output and employment since 1950, with resulting secondary unemployment, has led to emigration. This emigration has changed the earlier slowing down in the growth of population into a net decline.

✿   ✿   ✿   ✿   ✿

The decline in the rate of population increase after 1940 and the beginning of an actual net population decrease after 1950 have occurred despite high birth rates and low death rates. This can only mean that fewer people are moving into West Virginia than into other states and that more of the state's own population is moving out—i.e., net emigration is increasing.

. . . Since 1920 West Virginia has lost population to other states at a rapidly increasing rate. From 1920 to 1930 the net loss amounted to 41,000; from 1930 to 1940 it more than doubled to 96,000; and from 1940 to 1950 the loss tripled, rising to 297,000. The estimated fall in the state's total population since 1950 (the first decline in its history) indicates the continuing importance of net emigration at a high rate.

Who is leaving the state? A special study by West Virginia University noted that the emigrants were predominantly young white men and women; that the number of male emigrants was slightly larger than the number of female, though the latter group was important; and that among these people there were many university graduates and World War II veterans. There is nothing surprising in this finding; these are the groups one would expect to emigrate in search of better opportunities in economically healthy areas—the young and more highly educated people at the beginning of their adult lives. These are also the people the state badly needs for its future growth.—Arthur D. Little, Inc., *Report to the State of West Virginia*, July 29, 1955, pp. 6, 8.

183. The Primary That Made a President: West Virginia 1960

On February 6, 1960, at the early hour of 12:30 A. M., Senator John F. Kennedy arrived at Kanawha Airport, Charleston. From there he went immediately to the office of West Virginia's chief election official, Secretary of State Joe F. Burdett, to file a Certificate of Announcement of his candidacy for the nomination for President of the United States. Since this was the last day for filing for the West Virginia primary which was to be held on May 10, Secretary Burdett had kept his office open to accommodate the Senator from Massachusetts. The necessary papers were signed at 1:22 A. M. and within the hour Kennedy was on his way to Bismarck, North Dakota. Two days before, February 4, Senator Hubert H. Humphrey of Minnesota had filed, through an aide, a similar certificate and like Kennedy, had paid the filing fee of one thousand dollars.

During his flying pre-dawn visit, Senator Kennedy told newsmen who were waiting for him at the State House that he had not intended to enter the West Virginia primary because the West Virginia delegates to the national convention are not obligated to support the winning candidate in the primary. But, he continued, "when Senator Humphrey issued me a challenge I was delighted to oblige." Kennedy said that he regarded West Virginia as one of the key testing grounds of the 1960 presiden-

tial campaign. "It is an important bellwether," he prophetically observed. "What happens to me in the West Virginia primary could tell really whether I'm going to be nominated."

Senator Kennedy predicted that West Virginia's sagging economy would be the leading domestic issue of the primary. "I think the most serious problem is the decline of the income level of this state," he said. "The coal industry has declined just as the textile industry has in my own state of Massachusetts, and the depressed areas haven't been able to make a comeback." As a corrective, he strongly advocated legislation providing for "research into coal," for "making more effective use of our food services," and for "minimum standards of unemployment compensation."

The vigorous and colorful campaign which the two presidential aspirants waged in West Virginia directed national attention to the State's serious economic plight. Senator Kennedy's decisive victory in this politically unpredictable and predominantly Protestant state undoubtedly helped to make him President.

ON JULY 9, 1960, "Flagship West Virginia" landed at Los Angeles. Its passengers included United States Senator John F. Kennedy. He considered it a happy omen that he had arrived on the American Airlines' plane named for the state which had made him the favored candidate for the Democratic presidential nomination. As Arthur Edson of the Associated Press, who had covered the West Virginia presidential primary that spring, wrote after the Democrats at Los Angeles had made their decision:

"If our political disputes are ever remembered as our battle-fields are now, West Virginia will become a national shrine. For it was in West Virginia's beautiful mountains, in its thriving cities, in its impoverished coal fields that the decisive battle was fought that gave Senator John F. Kennedy the Democratic presidential nomination. Everyone, including the Kennedy forces, now seems to agree this was the turning point."

The 43-year-old Massachusetts millionaire, who would become the 35th President after the closest election since 1888, had been forced to take the most dangerous route to his party's nomination—the state presidential primaries. Only through decisive victories on the vote-getting trail could he hope to convince his fellow Democrats at their national convention that his Roman Catholicism would not bring them defeat in November.

Predominantly Protestant West Virginia, where Kennedy knocked United States Senator Hubert H. Humphrey of Minnesota from the race, presented the impressive proof which party leaders could not ignore. After the West Virginia primary, hesitant leaders in such key states as Michigan, New York and Pennsylvania became convinced that Kennedy was their man. They gave him the votes he needed to win the nomination on the first ballot.

The religious issue was not buried in the West Virginia hills. But the avalanche of Protestant votes for Catholic Kennedy, which surprised most journalists and their readers across the country, did submerge it at the convention. A Protestant state, with a snugly fitting Bible Belt, made it possible for the first Roman Catholic to be elected President.—Harry W. Ernst, *The Primary That Made A President: West Virginia 1960,* p. 1. Copyright by Rutgers, The State University, 1962.

PRIMARY ELECTION RETURNS, 1960: DEMOCRATS

	Hubert H. Humphrey Waverly, Minn.	John F. Kennedy Boston, Mass.
Barbour	1,303	2,043
Berkeley	2,216	2,850
Boone	3,585	4,559
Braxton	1,704	2,380
Brooke	2,526	4,658
Cabell	9,524	8,392
Calhoun	900	1,137
Clay	1,182	1,337
Doddridge	378	524
Fayette	6,179	11,410
Gilmer	1,119	1,152
Grant	257	335
Greenbrier	2,828	5,295
Hampshire	1,468	1,117

Hancock	3,227	6,965
Hardy	955	1,511
Harrison	7,583	11,803
Jackson	1,107	1,620
Jefferson	1,467	2,367
Kanawha	22,232	24,005
Lewis	1,427	1,940
Lincoln	2,177	1,764
Logan	6,454	8,446
Marion	6,004	9,957
Marshall	1,946	4,598
Mason	1,546	1,890
Mercer	5,174	11,292
Mineral	1,251	1,561
Mingo	4,260	5,996
Monongalia	3,362	7,826
Monroe	764	1,323
Morgan	590	570
McDowell	2,708	14,336
Nicholas	2,458	3,109
Ohio	2,755	9,987
Pendleton	664	1,024
Pleasants	479	802
Pocahontas	706	1,524
Preston	877	1,746
Putnam	2,431	2,010
Raleigh	6,261	13,085
Randolph	3,475	3,706
Ritchie	486	812
Roane	776	1,468
Summers	2,231	2,597
Taylor	989	1,587
Tucker	853	987
Tyler	408	644
Upshur	766	1,185
Wayne	4,664	4,694
Webster	1,268	2,222
Wetzel	2,052	2,419

Wirt	385	404
Wood	6,011	6,939
Wyoming	1,789	6,600
Total	152,187	236,510

—*Official Returns of the Primary Election Held May 10, 1960,* p. 6.

184. West Virginia Establishes a Department of Commerce, 1961

The need of a co-ordinated development program prompted the Legislature in 1961 to abolish the sixteen-year old Industrial and Publicity Commission and the Economic Development Agency, established in 1959, and create the State Department of Commerce, which has intensified the campaign to advertise the State's industrial advantages and scenic beauty.

The following is an excerpt from the First Annual Report of Director Hulett C. Smith.

SOME 34 NEW INDUSTRIAL PLANTS have located in 27 West Virginia cities and towns during the past 10 months. . . . These have provided 4,300 new jobs and over $19 million in new payrolls. Over $17 million is being spent by new plant builders for materials, construction, laborers, taxes and the like to help West Virginia grow.

In the same 10-month period, 27 industrial firms sent representatives to 27 West Virginia communities to investigate them as potential locations for new industrial plants. During the same time, 24 cities and towns in other parts of the country were visited by members of the Industrial Development Division staff who made 59 calls on representatives of industrial firms to solicit and stimulate their interests in locating new operations in West Virginia.

Some 23 municipalities and seven counties, representing planning program costs totaling $634,000, launched development activities. More than half of these projects were approved by the federal government during the fiscal year.

The Emergency Employment Program and the Aid to Dependent Children Program employed a total of over 16,000 men in the state during the first year of operation under the administration of the department. During the latter months of the program, the average monthly employment figure was 12,000 persons. Under the combined program, the department initiated programs with the following organizations: (1) nine state agencies with facilities in all counties; (2) county courts in 22 counties; (3) county boards of education in 45 counties; and, municipal projects in 118 cities.

In the areas of increasing West Virginia's share of the federal procurement dollar and attracting and assisting new industries to locate in the state, Governor Barron's Liaison Office in Washington, D. C. brought more than 3,000 jobs and $42 million to the Mountain State in the first year of its operation.

For the first time, the glass industry in the state formed a unified front to finance and produce a brochure and conduct tours aimed at attracting tourists to visit such hand-blown glass-producing operations.

Community enterprise, cooperation and willingness to establish new tourist information centers was displayed at an unparalleled rate. At the start of the fiscal year, July 1, 1961, West Virginia had only one Tourist Information Center. By June 30, 1962, it had eight such centers operating with at least five more scheduled to go into operation by July 1, 1963.

The Planning and Research Division reported that 42 of the 50 counties in the state designated as redevelopment areas by the Area Redevelopment Administration submitted Overall Economic Development Programs for review and 30 of these were approved in the first year of the department's operation.

Private investment in new tourist accommodation facilities reached an all-time high of over $12 million in the 12-month period ending June 30, 1962.

An unprecedented number of communities launched intensive advertising and promotion programs, including publication of a record number of brochures.

The state's hard-hit coal mining areas found a "new lease on life" by developing tourist attractions around existing, new and abandoned coal mining operations.

West Virginia's first comprehensive travel survey—a study designed to lead to the state's first master plan of development for tourist attractions—was launched June 1, 1962 as a joint venture with the West Virginia University Center for Resource Development.

The federal government displayed its interest in developing West Virginia as an outdoor recreation reservoir and center for the eastern half of the nation by approving such projects as a $25,000 grant for a development study for the spacious a n d beautiful New River Gorge area of the state.

The Disaster Recovery Agency—under the supervision of the department—submitted to the federal Office of Emergency Planning 17 state project applications covering claims total-ing $1,452,163.85 in the seven-county area centered in Kanawha County, resulting from the disastrous flash floods of July, 1961. The OEP officially approved 15 applications covering claims of $1,192,182.65. Advance funds of $977,154.77 were received in the 12-month period. Of this, advance funds of $871,071.11 were dis-bursed to various applicants during the period.—*Annual Report, West Virginia Department of Commerce, 1961-62*, p. 4.

185. Railroad Mergers

In 1850 there were 97 miles of railroad in present West Vir-ginia; in 1963 there were 3,630 miles. The first trunk line con-structed across the State following the Civil War was the Chesa-peake and Ohio whose last spike was driven near Hawk's Nest, January 29, 1873. To celebrate the long-desired connection of the James and the Ohio via the Kanawha Valley, water from the eastern river was poured into the Ohio at Huntington, and from the western river into the James at Richmond. A decade later, the Norfolk and Western Railway entered West Virginia. By the 1890's this road was hauling coal from the rich Pocahontas fields and bringing prosperity to the burgeoning towns along its route.

*The Virginian Railroad was designed by its owner, Henry H.
Rogers, to take the maximum advantage of grades. Completed
in 1909, it connected Deep Water, a point on the Chesapeake
and Ohio, with Norfolk. In recent years, despite increasing competition from other means of transportation and despite the fact
that coal, the hauling of which has been a chief source of revenue, is no longer the dominant fuel, these railroads have maintained better-than-average earnings. Through consolidation they
hope to prevent ruinous competition and provide more efficient
service at reduced operating costs. The Norfolk and Western
and the Virginian merged in 1959. In January, 1963, the Interstate Commerce Commission cleared the way for a merger between the Chesapeake and Ohio and the venerable Baltimore
and Ohio which, unlike its younger prospective partner, was in
a precarious financial condition. The following selections give
an account of these railway combinations.*

WASHINGTON, Oct. 13 (AP)—The Interstate Commerce
Commission today approved a merger of the Norfolk & Western
Railroad and the Virginian Railway Company. It was the first
merger of two independent major railroads approved by the
I. C. C. in modern times.

The merged line will be a 2,746-mile system running through
the Pocahontas soft coal region in Virginia and West Virginia
to Norfolk, Va. In addition, it will extend westward to Cincinnati and Columbus, Ohio, and will operate branches through
Hagerstown, Md., Bristol, Va., Winston-Salem, N. C., and Dur-
ham, N. C.

In its report, the I. C. C. said:

"Merger of the Norfolk & Western and Virginian will plainly
result in a larger, stronger company, better able to meet the
challenges faced by the railroad industry and better able to
attract and hold competent management personnel."

The Norfolk and Western first applied to the I. C. C. to acquire control of the Virginian by lease thirty-four years ago.
That application was denied. The present unification plan was
proposed early last year.

The merger will combine two of the nation's major soft coal
hauling roads. Norfolk and Western now operates 2,138 miles

of road in six states and the Virginian 608 miles in two states. The Virginian no longer carries passengers.

938 Million in Assets

The combined road will have assets of $938,000,000. Under the agreement, the Virginian will be merged into the Norfolk and Western. A plan for exchange of stock will entitle a holder of 100 Virginian shares to fifty-five shares of the Norfolk and Western. . . .

In applying for approval of the merger, the two roads said their proposal was "part of a general and inevitable movement in the railroad industry toward greater efficiency and economy in railroad operations." They said the merger was necessary for survival.—New York *Times*, October 14, 1959.

The Chesapeake & Ohio Railway's plan for acquiring control of the Baltimore & Ohio Railroad was first discussed by executives of the two systems in January of 1958. It was not until March of 1960, however, that a tentative agreement finally was reached between Howard Simpson, then president of the B. & O., and Walter Tuohy, president of the C. & O.

When the C. & O. on June 14, 1960, formally filed its control plans with the Interstate Commerce Commission, it did so with the "hearty and enthusiastic" support of B. & O.'s management as well as C. & O.'s own board of directors. Stockholders of both carriers overwhelmingly approved the affiliation plans at special meetings during 1960, despite the strenuous opposition of the New York Central Railroad.

The Central fought vigorously for two years to effect a three-way merger of the Central, the C. & O. and the B. & O. Its efforts were unsuccessful, as was a subsequent bid that it made to share control of the B. & O. with the C. & O. Finally last January when Central and the Pennsylvania Railroad filed for the Commission's approval of a merger plan, the Central simultaneously withdrew an application it had filed earlier with the commission to be included in any affiliation of the C. & O. with the B. & O.

An Ambitious Plan

The C. & O.'s acquisition of control of the B. & O. is one of the most ambitious control plans in modern railroad history. Not since the late 1920's, when the Van Sweringen brothers of Cleveland set out to weld a coast-to-coast transportation empire has the commission given its approval for any railroad to acquire control of another system of the magnitude of the B. & O.

The B. & O., founded in 1831, is the nation's oldest railroad. Like the C. & O., which is a successor corporation to the Chesapeake & Ohio Canal Co. founded by George Washington, it is one of the four main trunk lines operating between the Midwest and the Atlantic ocean. The other two are the Central and the Pennsylvania. . . .

The greatest opportunity afforded by C. & O.-B. & O. affiliation lies in the coordinated operation of the two systems. Yards and terminals will be unified, enabling the two roads to do more business with fewer facilities. The greatest field for such savings will be in Chicago, where it is estimated that through coordination of facilities the two lines can realize operating savings of about $2,000,000 a year.

Almost as large savings are expected to be realized from unified operation at Toledo, with somewhat lesser savings available from similar coordination efforts at Portsmouth, Ohio, and Huntington, W. Va. From consolidated operations alone the two roads expect to realize annual savings of more than $13,000,000. —New York *Times,* January 2, 1963.

186. West Virginia a "Paradoxical State"

Roul Tunley has referred to West Virginia as a "paradoxical state" and a staff writer of BROADCASTING *observed that "All West Virginia's divided in two parts." The first of the following passages is taken from Tunley's article in* THE SATURDAY EVENING POST, *February 6, 1960, the second from a special report on the Ohio Valley, issued by* BROADCASTING, *March 18, 1963.*

. . . IT WOULD BE EASY for any outsider to get the impression that West Virginia is all poverty, ignorance and hopelessness. Or that it is not only sick but ready for the *coup de grâce*. But after spending several weeks there recently and covering 2,500 miles of its roller-coaster roads that took me to almost every corner of the state, I have come away convinced that West Virginia is far from moribund. It is merely suffering from an acute case of schizophrenia.

Take Charleston, for example, the brighter side of the state's split personality. This bustling city of more than 100,000 is studded with modern industry. Gleaming new offices and factories adorn its river front, and bank deposits are at an all-time high. Its airport, ingeniously and expensively embossed on three mountains by lopping off the tops and filling in the valleys, is busy all day long bringing prosperous people to and from the city.

But then consider what's going on just across the hills. Not very many miles away is a county where 41 per cent of the people—most of whom have exhausted their unemployment benefits—are being kept alive by handouts of surplus Government food. . . .

Even coal, that staple of industry which has been the backbone of the state's economy for so long, has developed a schizoid nature. Although West Virginia is still the nation's biggest producer of soft coal, it has remained so only at the cost of a gigantic, state-wide headache. In the last ten years, mechanization of the mines, carried out with the approval of both the operators and the union, has toppled the working force from 117,000 to less than 40,000 men. Scores of ghost towns have sprung up like mushrooms across the state, and thousands of men, especially those over forty, have no further prospects of re-employment in the industry.

And yet more coal is being produced and sold than ever before. Furthermore, those who produce it are receiving the highest wages of any industrial workers in the country—approximately twenty-five dollars a day. Incredible as it seems, some miners are actually working overtime!

. . . Another problem that cannot be solved by individual enterprise is taxation. At the moment West Virginia is forty-seventh among the states in per-capita income from taxes. To a certain extent this is because in past years the state's resources were largely owned and exploited by outsiders, who were interested in keeping taxes as low as possible. It is also generally admitted that, in the past at least, these men controlled the legislatures which passed the tax laws. In short, the citizens allowed others to carry away coal, timber and natural-gas resources without plowing any of the profits back.—Roul Tunley, "The Strange Case of West Virginia," *The Saturday Evening Post,* 232 (February 6, 1960), 19-21, 64-66. Courtesy of Roul Tunley and The Curtis Publishing Company.

. . . From a Wheeling eminence, the Ohio shore a mile away offers an enigma in economic images. Except for the barge-dotted water strip, southeastern Ohio and western West Virginia are part of a common economy. Yet West Virginia bears the unjustified and unrealistic stigma of poverty and Ohio doesn't, mainly due to effects of the 1950-60 automation of the coal industry. . . .

The greatest story never told, a factual account of West Virginia's industrial structure, has long been lost in a media morass.

For three decades the positive side of West Virginia's economy has waited while the miseries of the state's displaced miners have been spread over the printed page and dramatized in broadcasts.

Few newsmen have followed up their tales of miners' travails by trekking up and down the Ohio and Kanawha Valleys to inspect the growth of a new and expanding industrial complex. They bypass the affirmative economic story, focusing instead on the pathos of poor hill folk as though West Virginia had a monopoly on unemployment and poverty.

. . . Any look at West Virginia's economy must divide the state into two parts: 1, the populous industrial strips along the Ohio and Kanawha Rivers; 2, the mountainous center and south, plus the farming areas of the east.

. . . The western half of West Virginia includes markets starting with a north-south line that includes Morgantown, Fairmont, Clarksburg and Charleston. The area moves from Charleston north-westward down the Kanawha River to the Ohio River and Point Pleasant. To the north are Parkersburg, Moundsville, Wheeling and Weirton. Huntington lies near the Kentucky border.

Lining the rivers, or a short distance inland, are multi-million dollar chemical, steel, aluminum, power-generating and petro-chemical plants that comprise an all-star lineup of American industry. . . .

Blessed with unmatched natural resources and a central location near major markets, West Virginia's industrial complex looks forward to more extensive processing of the chemicals, alloys, and other basic products for American factories. Much of its aluminum goes by barge, rail or highway to outside factories.

Plastics production fans out to finishing plants making consumer goods. There are many plants turning out bottles, fancy glass, toothpaste tubes and other containers yet the major output is in the basic industry category. West Virginians are aware of this and are planning for fabricating plants. . . .

With some of the nation's most beautiful landscape, West Virginia is building up its recreational facilities and accommodations to attract tourists. Their expenditure last year is believed to have been at least $325 million.

. . . Besides the almost limitless water reserves, West Virginia has these natural bounties to offer industry:

COAL—Reserves estimated at 50 billion tons. Production averages 110 million tons a year and is likely to increase. Employment dropped from 132,000 jobs in 1948 to 41,000 in a decade-and-a-half as automation entered the industry but the decline in employment has stopped. Value of production (at the mine) is around $600 million yearly (recent peak was $854 million in 1947). No. 1 coal-producing state.

GAS—Production is up 13% for the last decade, totaling 220 billion cubic feet a year from 13,000 producing wells. Fields are in the western half of the state. Reserves are 1.8 trillion cubic feet.

SALT—Extensive brine and rock salt-beds form the chemistry industry's building-block material. Production is around 900,000 tons. Reserves are 8 trillion tons.

OIL—Production exceeds 3 million barrels a year; much of it is of Pennsylvania crude quality, commanding a premium price.

... That's a quick look at a state suffering from image troubles caused by newsmen who miss the real story of what's been happening in the West Virginia hills.—"A Special Report: Ohio River Links Vast Industrial Area," *Broadcasting*, March 18, 1963, pp. 88, 92-94. By permission.

187. The Forum of the Future

The approaching one hundredth anniversary of West Virginia statehood received legislative attention on February 1, 1955, with the adoption of a house concurrent resolution, introduced by Delegate William E. Chilton, which provided for the creation of a centennial commission. Charles Hodel became chairman of the commission and Carl R. Sullivan its executive director. Co-operating with the commission were numerous organizations and literally thousands of public spirited citizens who saw in the celebration a very special opportunity to improve the public image of their state and to express their pride in its history and confidence in its future. The commission arranged for a variety of activities—parades, exhibits, selection of a centennial queen, pageants, a science camp at the Green Bank Observatory, promotion of historical writing, and a Forum of the Future which was held at Charleston on April 25, 1963. The distinguished panelists on the Forum were Lyndon B. Johnson, Vice President of the United States, James E. Allen, President of the University of the State of New York and Commissioner of Education, Gilbert Seldes, Dean of the Annenberg School of Communications of the University of Pennsylvania, and Paul L. Davies, Chairman of the FMC Corporation. Richard L. Harkness, noted NBC commentator, acted as moderator. Excerpts from two of the addresses are given below.

IN 1910, THERE WERE ONLY 12 fully accredited high schools in the State—by 1925, there were 233. Faced with the crushing conditions of a great depression, the State had the courage to adopt in 1933 a County Unit system which was not only more efficient administratively, but which gave greater reality to the ideal of equal educational opportunity for all.

In higher education there was in the years from 1910-1955 an increase in total college enrollment from 800 to almost 16,000. Normal schools were changed to colleges. Both publicly and privately supported institutions were engaged in expansion of plant and program. West Virginia University, considered the capstone of the system, added new schools and departments, and leading the advance, served to give strength to the State's total educational effort. ...

Now in 1963, there are 446,000 pupils in the public elementary and secondary schools, housed in nearly 2,900 buildings, taught by 17,300 teachers, supported by a budget of approximately $125 million dollars. In higher education, full-time enrollments total nearly 26,000 in all colleges and universities, public and private, nearly twice the number enrolled ten years ago. ...

Montani semper liberi—Mountaineers are always free—expresses the spirit that from the beginning inspired the makers of laws in this State to have as their aim and creation of that pattern of state government which would best preserve and enhance their cherished freedom.

How wise then, the early and the continuing emphasis on education. In an address in 1911 at the inauguration of Thomas Hodges as President of West Virginia University, President William Howard Taft declared that "education, of course, is the basis of all free governments. Unless there is general education sufficient to form an intelligent public opinion, it makes no difference how highly educated a number of people may be, the cause of government must suffer."

Let it be resolved then at this Forum of the Future that the cause of government, which is in the long run welfare of the people, shall not suffer here in West Virginia, nor in the entire United States from a neglect of education. Let there be a determination that all those things which need to be done to improve education will be done to the end that the individual may be fulfilled and that his fulfillment in turn will make possible the fulfillment of all mankind.—"The Individual, the State and the Future in Education," Address of Dr. James E. Allen.

While we cannot prophesy far into the future what future generations will want the role of government to be, I believe we can expect—and predict—continuation of these principal directions of public policy and governmental responsibility.

What will be the meaning for West Virginia?

The Mountain State, one hundred years ago, elected to cast its lot with the Union. That decision then is symbolic for today. The future of West Virginia is inseparable from the future of the Union as a whole. Yet, in saying this, I realize that West Virginians may justifiably ask if this is so of the future, why has it not been so of the present and the immediate past.

In times of virtually universal American prosperity and growth, West Virginia has not shared equally in the national advance. The number of jobs has dwindled. Farm income has declined for your forty-three thousand farms. The number of businesses has decreased to twenty-five thousand. Income per capita has fallen to less than eighty per cent of the national average.

In this regard, I was interested to find—to my surprise—that despite these trends, there are twice as many persons in West Virginia owning and holding stocks on the New York Stock Exchange than in my own State of Texas.

The experiences of recent years might justify West Virginians adopting the philosophy of Mr. Dooley, who said: "Anyhow, there is always one ray of light ahead—we're sure to have hard times."

While such a philosophy might seem justified, at this start of West Virginia's centennial observance, we neither accept such an attitude nor believe it. On the contrary, we view the future from an exactly opposite perspective. As a nation, we accept as our responsibility the proposition that Americans of every State must be sure of good times ahead.

The fate which has befallen West Virginia in recent years was not determined within the borders of your State. It was determined by events and forces in other States, in the entire Nation, and even in the world.

Developments in our own Southwest and in the distant Middle East—developments as near as the coal markets of the Mid-Atlantic and as far as the common market of Europe—had their consequences and effect upon the enterprise, the jobs, the homes and, finally, even the food on the plates of West Virginians.

The people of the United States have, through the policies of their government, made a commitment to the individual and his well being. In the lesson of West Virginia, we have learned that government cannot meet this commitment merely by being ready to write a check. Government must perform more than the role of an automated charity.

In this inter-dependent world, good times for the individual American can only be assured as individual human beings throughout the world enjoy better times for themselves.

West Virginia's per capita income is, as I have mentioned, below the average for all States. But at the level of about $1,800 annually, the income of West Virginians compares as the wealth of millionaires to the income of most of the earth's population. . . .

One of the lessons we have learned in West Virginia applies also to the world. We have learned that America cannot assure better times for the world merely through the use of our check book.

Vastly more is required of responsible government than that it be a check-writing machine. The standards of government—whether its relative size be large or small—demand able and courageous performance in the four realms I have mentioned: exploration, expansion, education and conservation.

In the next one hundred years, government's role in these areas will be active and important. The objective of all that is done will be to improve life for the individual here on earth. . . .

In the first years after World War II, we in America permitted and even encouraged our government—at all levels—to limit its role to the service of the present. The consequences have been many. West Virginia is case Example No. 1. We know now —better than we have known before—that government must fill the role of serving the future or else its burden becomes oppressive and the opportunities of the people decline.

In these next one hundred years, government must assume a much more vigorous role in the level-headed pursuit of peace.

Government must open wider the door of choice for individuals.

Government must help the people to marshall to the fullest their resources of earth and spirit.

The role of government must in this next century be more than ever the role of faithful servant faithfully serving the future. We must measure its performance less by its costs than by its accomplishments in supporting the greater liberty of all the people.—"The Role of Government," Address of Vice President Lyndon B. Johnson.

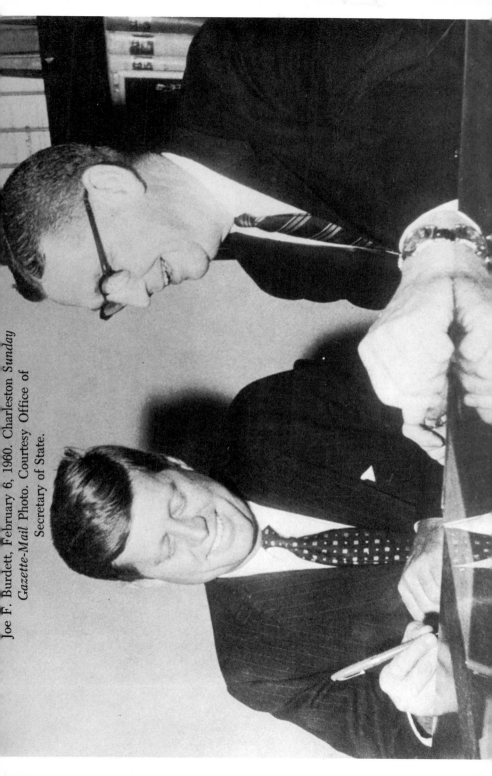

Joe F. Burdett, February 6, 1960. Charleston *Sunday Gazette-Mail* Photo. Courtesy Office of Secretary of State.

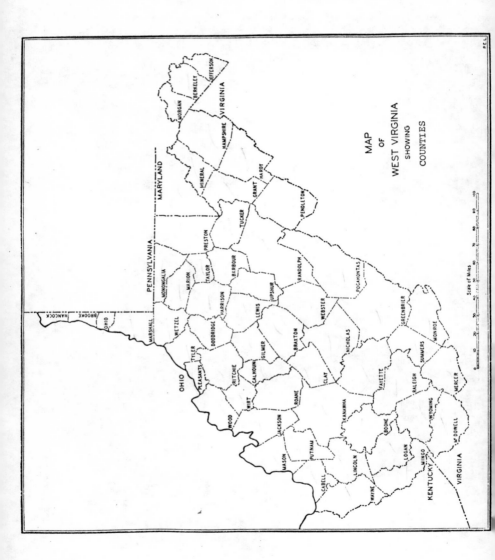

MAP
OF
WEST VIRGINIA
SHOWING
COUNTIES

Index

A

Absentee ownership, 483-85
Address of The Convention to The People of Northwestern Virginia, 295-96
Alabama Row, 232. *See* White Sulphur Springs
Alderson, John, 172
Alderson-Broaddus College, 618, 621
Alexander, Andrew, 197
Alexandria County, 310
Algoma, 492
Alleghenies, 95, 124, 196, 404, 422
"Allegheny," 337
"Allen, Major E. J.," 392-95. *See* Allan Pinkerton
Allen, James E., 650-52
Allied Artists, 621
American Federation of Labor, 522
American Philosophical Society, 142
American Revolution, 106, 107, 110, 145
Amherst, Jeffrey, 56
Ancora, Pietro, 276
Andrews, Robert, 145
Anglican Church, 24
Antietam, battle, 415
Anti-Saloon League, 519
Appalachian Mountains, 13, 15, 135
Arbitrary arrests, 389-92
Arbuckle, Matthew, 96, 100, 103
Arlington, Lord, 6
Armstrong, Samuel C., 601
Army Nurse Corps, 533
Arthurdale, 564-73
Asbury, Francis, 173; journal of, 175-82; 183, 227
Ashby, Benjamin, 80
Ashby Cavalry, 422
Ashford General Hospital, 577-78
Assessments, 612, 614-15
Atkinson, George W., 497, 505-506
Audubon Society, 560

"Augusta," 337
Augusta County, 18, 22, 23, 26, 40; casualty list, 51-56. *See* Preston's Register
Augusta Court House, 41
Australian ballot, 488-90
Averell, William W., 426

B

Babcock State Park, 563
Back Creek, 415
Bailey, Edward, 173
Baker, Lewis, 466
Baker's Bottom, 80
Baltimore, 147, 148, 205, 206, 299, 485
Baltimore, Lord, 17, 515
Baltimore and Ohio Railroad, opening, 217-21; 255, 269; dilemma of, 299-300; 325; makes a panhandle, 343-45; 384, 395, 397, 401, 403, 404, 405-407, 412, 415-16, 422, 426, 441, 457, 467, 471-73, 474-76; rebating, 482-83; 485-87, 644, 645-46
Bandholtz, Harry H., 544
Banks, Nathaniel P., 412
Baptist Church, 172, 175, 185-87
Barbour County, 446
Barker, Jer., 77
Barron, William W., 642
Baruch, Bernard, 570
Bascom, Henry B., 173
Bates, Edward, letter, 331-33; 358-59, 369
Bath, 130-33, 136, 137, 138, 141, 178, 181, 227. *See* Berkeley Springs, Warm Springs
Battelle, Gordon, on naming state, 340; plea for free state, 341-43
Batts, Thomas, 6
Batts and Fallam, expedition, 5-11
Baylor, Robert W., 272
Bear Garden, 42
Beckham, Fontaine, 271, 273
Beckley, 418
Beckley, Alfred, 432
Bedford, Pa., 147
Bell, John, 285-86

Bellaire, 397
Benedum, Michael L., 620-23
Benedum Foundation. *See* Claude Worthington Benedum Foundation
Bennett, Jonathan M., 516
Benwood, 395, 398
Berkeley, William, 6, 10
Berkeley County, 16, 108, 130, 136, 145, 173, 262, 288, 344, 441, 457-62, 516, 598, 620
Berkeley Springs, 130-33, 141, 175-76, 181, 227-29, 276, 412, 545. *See* Bath, Warm Springs
Berlin, George W., 289
Bernard, John, 156-58. *See* Blennerhassett Island
Bethany College, incorporation, 168-71; 262, 365, 619
Beverly, 398, 402, 403, 404, 417, 422, 424
Big Birch, 424
Big Sandy River, 42
Big Sandy Valley, 153, 197
Big Sewell Mountain, 223, 224, 426
Bingham, John A., on West Virginia statehood, 353, 356-57, 376
Birchard, S., 429-30
Bissell, William C., 493
Blackwater Canyon, 578
Blackwater Falls, 565
Blair, Montgomery, on West Virginia statehood, 362-64
Blair Mountain, 544
Bland, Edward, 6
Blennerhassett, Harman, 156, 157
Blennerhassett, Margaret, 156, 157
Blennerhassett Island, 156-58, 564. *See* John Bernard
Blizzard, William, 545
Blue Ridge, 6, 23, 26, 237, 251, 343
Bluefield, 490
Bluestone Canyon, 565
Board of Public Works, 501
Boerly, Thomas, 271, 273
Bonnecamps, Father, journal, 25
Boone, Daniel, 153-54
Boreman, Arthur I., 310; address, 310-11, 378; inaugural, 379-82; 444-48, 467, 476, 497
Boston, 79, 147, 148, 150
Botetourt County, 70, 205
Boundary, Committee on, 337
Bounties, wolf, 22-25
Bouquet, Henry, 57, 82
Bower, The, 145. *See* Leetown
Braddock, Edward, 40

Braddock's Road, 137, 139
Brady, Samuel, 220
Braxton County, 197
Breckenridge, James, 197
Breckenridge, John C., 285-86
Bridgeport, 621
Brockenbrough, John W., 265, 266
Brodhead, Daniel, 96, 108
Brook, Robert, 17
Brooke County, 115, 168, 238
Brooks, A. B., 561
Brooks, Elisha, 197
Brosse, Paul de, 25
Brown, James H., on naming State, 338-39; on compensated emancipation, 374-75
Brown, John, raid, 269-81; indictment, 270-74; address, 274-75; execution, 275-81; 441, 442, 545
Browning, Orville H., 358
Buchanan, James, 389
Buckhannon, 403, 417-18, 424
Bulltown, 197, 424
Burdett, Joe F., 637
Burke's Garden, 42
Burning Springs, Kanawha County, 123
Burning Springs, Wirt County, 420-21
Burr, Aaron, 157
Bushy Run, battle, 57

C

Cabell County, 197, 632
Cabin Creek, 522-29, 531-32
Cabin Creek-Paint Creek Strike, 522-32
Cabinet, President Lincoln's on West Virginia statehood, 358-64, 369
Cacapon State Park, 563
Caldwell, Elbert H., on compensated emancipation, 374, 375
Calhoun, John C., 432
Calhoun County, 262
Camden, Gideon D., 253
Camden, Johnson N., testimony on B & O rebating, 482-83; on short-haul discrimination, 485-86
Camden, Byrne and Company, 421
Camp Charlotte, 71, 80, 87
Camp Dawson, 576
Camp Dennison, 397
Camp Elk, 433
Camp Good Luck, 553
Camp Meetings, 183-84
Camp Tompkins, 430
Camp Union (Fayetteville), 431

Camp Union (Lewisburg), 70, 71

Campbell, Alexander, 168, 169, 237; address, 241-44; on fugitive-slave law, 262-65; 365

Campbell, Archibald W., 299-300; on West Virginia statehood, 364-67; letter to President Lincoln, 366-68; 452-54; Republican profile, 478-79

Campbell, Dr. A. W., 365

Campbell, William, 108

Campbell's Creek, 197

Canaan Valley, 565

Caperton, Allen T., 290, 292

Capon River, 47

Carlile, John S., 253, 293, 295, 304, 307; addresses, 308-309; 321-323; on West Virginia Bill, 350, 352-53, 376

Carnifex Ferry, battle, 408-12; 428

Carnifex Ferry Battlefield Park, 564

Carolina Row, 232. See White Sulphur Springs

Carter, Robert, 173. See Nomini Hall

Caruthers, William, 197

Celeron de Blainville, expedition of, 24-26. See leaden plates

Centennial Commission, 650-54

Central Competitive Field, 522, 539

Chambers, David, 156

Chambersburg, 416

Charles I, 17

Charles II, 10

Charles City County, 6

Charles Town, 207; John Brown at, 270-81; description, 441-43; 458, 492-94

Charleston, 153, 162, 173, 246, 252, 290, 393, 407, 416, 418, 425, 433, 463, 476-77, 505, 532, 544, 637, 650

Charleston Art Association, 631

Chase, Salmon P., 359

Cheat River, 137, 138, 140, 401

Cherokee Indians, 42, 63, 89, 101

Chesapeake Bay, 191, 412, 415

Chesapeake and Ohio Canal, 205

Chesapeake and Ohio Railroad, 471-73, 476-77, 485-87, 643-46

Chesapeake and Ohio R. Co. v. J. S. Miller, auditor, 471-73

Child Welfare, 630

Chilton, William E., III, 650

Chronicles of Border Warfare, 109. See Alexander Scott Withers

Cincinnati, 221, 397, 401

Civil War, enlistments, 434-37; casualties, 434; bounties, 436

Civilian Conservation Corps, 561

Clapp, Elsie, 569

Clark, George Rogers, 110

Clark, Jacob, 111

Clarksburg, 179, 221, 222, 252, 295, 401, 403, 418, 477, 530

Clarksburg Convention, 295-96

Clarksburg Southern Rights Convention, 297-98

Clarksburg Western Virginia Guard, 295

Claude Worthington Benedum Foundation, 620-21

Clay, Cassius M., 365

Clay County, 539

Claypole, John, 109

Clemens, Sherrard, 265-69, 376. See Clemens-Wise duel

Clemens-Wise duel, 265-69

Cleveland, Grover, 493

Climate, 629

Clinch River, 42

Cloyd's Mountain, battle, 417

Coal mine disasters, 508-509

Coal production, 633

Coal reserves, 633-35

Coal River, 544

Coalburg, 290

Colston, Rawleigh, 17

College of Agriculture, 554

"Columbia," 337

Committee of Correspondence, 78

Committee on Industrial Development, 627

Committees of Safety, 87

Commodity distribution, 630

Common schools, 161-68. See free schools

Concord Normal, 588

Confederacy, 369, 379, 395, 407, 420, 434

Confederate Army, 415

Confederate States of America, provisional government, 317

Confederates, 405, 412, 415, 422, 443-45, 462

Conkling, Roscoe, 478-79

Conley, William G., 558

Connolly, John, 63, 68, 87, 107

Conservation Commission, 560-65

Conservation movement, 510-13

Constitution of 1851, 261

Constitution of 1863, ratified 345, 345 n.; 463, 500, 516

Constitution of 1872, 462-64, 500

Constitutional Convention of 1829-30, 237-46

Constitutional Convention of 1850-51, 251-53
Constitutional Convention of 1861-63, 341, 343, 373
Constitutional Union Party, 285-86, 326
Continental Army, 106, 109
Continental Congress, First, 78, 96
Continental Congress, Second, 90, 94, 95, 123, 143
Convention of 1788, 145
Conway, Martin F., on West Virginia statehood, 354-55
Cook, John E., 272
Copeland, John, 271, 272, 273
Coppoc, Edwin, 271, 272, 273
Corbley, John, 172
Cornstalk, 63, 88, 89, 92; murder of, 96-99; 102
Cornwallis, General, 108
Cornwell, John J., 534-35
Corricks Ford, battle, 404
Cotton Hill, 420
County board of education, 607, 613-14
County unit, 613
Covington and Ohio Railroad, 471
Cox, Jacob D., 407, 408, 418, 428, 429
Craik, James, 135, 136
Crawford, William, 135, 139
Cresap, Michael, 76, 77, 82
Cresap, Thomas, 27
Crimes, 129-30
Crippled children, 630
Crockett, Walter, 108
Croghan, George, 68
Crook, George A., 417, 426, 429, 433
Crowder, E. H., 534
Crozet, Claudius, 204-206
Culpeper, Thomas Lord, 16, 515
Cumberland, Md., 218
Cumberland Road, 212. See National Road
Custom House, Wheeling, 331, 325, 337

D

Darrow, Clarence, 530
Dartmouth, Lord, 80
Davies, Paul L., 650
Davis, Alice, 569
Davis, John J., 376
Davis and Elkins College, 619
Dawson, William M. O., 501-504, 510-12
Day, Mr. Justice, 514-15
Dayton, Arthur S., 631
Dayton, Ruth Woods, 631

Daywood Art Gallery, Inc., 631
Deaf and blind schools, 620
Deakins, Francis, 513
Deakins Line, 513-15
Declaration of Independence, 95
Declaration of the People of Virginia, 319-21
Deepwater, 644
Delaware River, 143, 144
Delawares, 68, 87, 90, 101
Democratic Party, 285-86, 350, 358, 369, 376
Democrats, 462
Department of Archives and History, 505-508
Department of Commerce, 641
Department of Mines, 508-509
Department of Natural Resources, 561
Department of Public Assistance, 630
Department of Public Welfare, 630
Department of the Ohio, 392, 395
Detroit, 107
Dinwiddie, Robert, 35, 40
Disciples of Christ, 168
Diss Debar, Joseph H., 383; designs state seal, 383-85; commissioner of immigration, 464-67, 479
Doddridge, Joseph, 110, 115. See Notes on the Settlement and Indian Wars
Doddridge, Philip, 237; address, 238-41
Doddridge County, 383
Donnally, Andrew, 103
Dorsey, Dennis B., Jr., address, 312-14
Droop Mountain Battlefield, 564
Douglas, Stephen A., 285-86, 316
Dunkers Bottom, 140, 141
Dunmore, Lord, 63; proclamation, 67; letter, 69-70; 71, 76, 78, 80; report, 80-84; 87, 92, 110
Dunmore's War, 63, 69-84

E

Early, Jubal A., 426
Eastern Panhandle, 207, 343-45
Economic Development Agency, 641
Edson, Arthur, 638
Education in western Virginia, 161-68
Edwards, William H., 290-93
Election of 1860, 285-86
Electric power, 629
Elinipsies, 98

Elk River, 100, 123
Elkhorn, 491
Elkins, Stephen B., 480-81
Ellet, Charles, Jr., 213; proposes Meadow River reservoir, 223-27. *See* Meadow River reservoir
Ellicott, Andrew, 145
Elliott, Matthew, 107
Emancipation, 373-76
Emigration, 628, 636-37
England, 3
Enochs, Henry, 41
Enquirer, The Richmond, 265
"Eternal Centre," 421
Euphrates River, 15. *See* Shenandoah River
Ewing, John, 144
Ex Parte Jones, 524-26
Ex Parte A. D. Lavinder *et al*, 543-44
Excise Act of 1791, 154

F

Fairfax, Thomas Lord, 16, 17, 131
Fairfax County, 310
Fairfax Line, 16-18
Fairfax Stone, 18, 513
Fairmont, 424, 448
Fairmont coal field, 530
Fairmont Normal, 587-88
Fallam, Robert, 6
Farnsworth, Daniel D. T., 322, 331; on Jenkins' raid, 417-18
Faulkner, Charles J., 17, 253; on civil liberties, 389-92
Faulkner, Charles J., Jr., 475
Fauquier, Francis, 56; proclamation, 62
Fayette County Court, resolutions by, 407-408
Fayetteville, 407, 418, 420, 428
Federal Resettlement Administration, 566
Flat Top Coal Land Association, 491
Fleming, Aretus Brooks, 488
Fleming, William, letter, 56-58; journal, 70-76; 90, 99, 102
Flick, W. H. H., 456
Flick Amendment, 455-57, 462
Florida, 58
Floyd, John B., 301, 408, 411-12, 416
Field, Jno., 74
Fifteenth Amendment, 456
Finance, 261
Fincastle County, 87
First West Virginia Infantry, 398
First Wheeling Convention, 301; resolutions of, 304-307; 308-10

Fish and Game Warden, 560
Fithian, Philip Vickers, journal, 172-75
Fitzhugh, H., 420
Forbes, John, 56
Fontaine, John, 11
Fort Ashby, 47, 176
Fort Beech Bottom, 96
Fort Blair, 87, 96. *See* Fort Randolph
Fort Cumberland, 49, 137, 513
Fort Detroit, 90
Fort Dunmore, 87. *See* Fort Pitt
Fort Duquesne, 42, 56. *See* Fort Pitt
Fort Edward, 47
Fort Enoch, 47
Fort Fincastle, 110. *See* Wheeling, Fort Henry
Fort Frederick, 42
Fort Gower, 70
Fort Gower Address and Resolutions, 78-80
Fort Grave Creek, 96
Fort Henry, 5, 6, 11. *See* Petersburg, Va.
Fort Henry, 96; second siege, 109-12. *See* Wheeling, Fort Fincastle
Fort La Fayette, 389-90
Fort Le Boeuf, 42
Fort Maidstone, 42
Fort Necessity, 35
Fort Pitt, 56, 57, 63, 68, 107, 135. *See* Fort Duquesne, Fort Dunmore
Fort Randolph, 96, 100, 102, 103. *See* Fort Blair
Fort Stanwix, treaty, 63, 94
Fort Sumter, 404
Fort Thomas, 545
Fort Warren, 389
Forum of the Future, 650-54
Fourteenth Amendment, 458, 556
Fox, John, 619
France, 35
Franco-Prussian War, refugees, 465-67
Franklin, benjamin, 94
Franklin Society, 247
Frederick County, 22, 23, 40, 48, 344
Fredericksburg, battle, 369
Free schools, 161-68. *See* common schools
Free textbooks, 605-606
Fremont, John C., 365
French Creek, 561
French and Indian War, 51, 56, 106

Fugitive Slave Law, 262, 450

G

Gaines, Herbert P., 162, 163
Galissoniere, Marquis de la, 25
Game, Fish and Forest Commission, 561
Garfield, James A., 478
Garnett, Robert S., 401, 403-404
Garrard, John, 172
Garrett, John W., 415
Garrett County, Md., 574
Gates, Horatio, 141
Gauley Bridge, 407, 408, 418, 426, 428, 430
Gauley Bridge and Weston Turnpike, 408
Gauley Mountain, 72, 407
Gauley River, 193, 195, 224, 408-12, 430; timber resources, 481-82
George I, 14, 15
George III, 58, 79
Germanna, 12
Germantown, battle, 145
Gettysburg, battle, 416
Gettysburg campaign, 458
General Assembly, Virginia, 22-25, 95, 130-31, 133-35, 191, 237, 252, 286, 316, 323; reorganized, 345, 457
Gibson, John, 76-77
Gibson, John T., 272
Giles County, 6
Giles, Fayette and Kanawha Turnpike, 204
Gist, Christopher, second journey, 26-32
Girty, Simon, 107
Glasscock, William E., 501, 504-505, 522-24, 554
Glenville, 417
Glenville Normal, 589-90
Glenville State College, 619
Goff, Nathan, 488
Golden Horseshoe, Order of, 12
Gore, Howard M., 545
Grafton, 221, 395, 397-98, 401, 449
Grand Lodge of the World, 518
Grand Ohio Company, 94
Granger, Francis, 432
Granger, Gideon, 432
Grant County, 16, 620
Great Britain, 94
Great Kanawha Valley, 422
Great Meadows, 35. See Fort Necessity
Great Railway Strike, 474-76

"Great Skedaddle," 425-28. See Hunter's retreat
Greeley, Horace, letter, 452-55
"Green Bottom," 416
Green, Shields, 271, 272, 273
Greenbank Observatory, 650
Greenbrier Circuit, 173
Greenbrier County, 96, 100, 103, 106, 108, 172, 181, 228, 262, 292, 445, 583
Greenbrier Hotel, 577
Greenbrier River, 191, 192, 193, 196, 407
Greenbrier Valley, 181
Greenland, 424
Greensburg, Pa., 147
Greenway Court, 16
Grenadier Squaw, 102, 103. See Nonhelema
Grigsby, Benjamin, 172
Grimes, Bushrod, 567
Gross Sales Tax, 555-57
Guyandot Circuit, 173
Guyandotte, 393, 402, 407
Guyandotte River, 417, 544
Guyandotte Valley, 153

H

Hall, John, 97
Hall's Rifle Works, 207, 269
Halltown, 492
Hamilton, H. Cliff, 605, 607-608
Hammond, Allen C., 288
Hammond, Philip, 103, 104, 105
Hampshire County, 16, 18, 22, 40, 47, 108, 136, 262, 310, 344, 620
Hampton Institute, 601
Hancock, Md., 412
Hancock County, 262
Hand, Edward, 96, 97, 99, 107
Hanna Coal Company, 539
Hard Labor, treaty, 63
Harding, Warren G., 544; proclamation, 545-47
Hardy County, 16, 18, 262, 310, 344, 620
Harkness, Richard L., 650
Harman, A. W., 423
Harpers Ferry, national arsenal, 207-209; 269, 405; described, 412-15; 415, 441, 487. See John Brown, Nathaniel Hawthorne
Harper's New Monthly Magazine, 276, 277
Harrison County, 253, 295, 297, 621
Hatfield, Henry D., 522, 530, 558
Hawks Nest, 418, 564, 643

Hawthorne, Nathaniel, on Harpers Ferry, 412-15
Hayes, Lucy Webb, 429-33
Hayes, Rutherford B., 428-33, 474
Haymond, Alpheus F., 289
Helvetia, 464
Henry, Patrick, letter, 99-102; 110, 145
Higgins, John, 107
Higher education, 612, 615
Hitchman Coal and Coke Co. v. John Mitchell, et al, 539-44
Hite, Joist, 16
Hite et al v. Fairfax et al, 16
Hitt, Daniel, 183, 184
Hockhocking River, 70
Hodel, Charles, 650
Hogg, Peter, 51
Holliday's Cove, 110
Holly Grove, 532
Holmes, Oliver Wendell, 517-18
Hope Natural Gas Company v. Hall, State Tax Commissioner, 556-57
House of Burgesses, 78
House of Delegates, 95, 237, 252
Howard, John, expedition, 26, 497. See John Peter Salley
Howe, Louis, 567
Hubbard, Chester D., 307; address, 315; 379
Huckleberry Plain, 578
Hughes, Charles Evans, 547
Humphrey, Hubert H., 637-39
Hunter, David, 17, 425-28, 433
Hunter's retreat, 425-28. See "Great Skedaddle"
Huntington, 631-32, 643
Huntington Galleries, Inc., 631
Hutchins, Thomas, 145
Huttonsville, 317, 428, 553
Hyde, Richard E., 605-607

I

Imboden, John D., 422; report, 424-25
Indiana Company, 94
Indianapolis Agreement, 522, 539
Industrial development, 628
Industrial and Publicity Commission, 641
Industries, 629
Ingles Ferry, 42
Integration, 618-20
Interstate Commerce Act, 485
Interstate Commerce Commission, 644-46
Iroquois Indians, 24. See Six Nations
Irvine, William, 96, 111

Irving, Charles, 266, 267, 268

J

Jackson, Jacob B., 472
Jackson, John J., 301
Jackson, John J., 304, 376, 449
Jackson, Mr. Justice, 609
Jackson. Thomas J. (Stonewall), 405-407; valley campaign, 415; 554
Jackson, William L., 425
Jackson's Mill, 553-55. See State 4-H Camp
Jacob, John J., 465-67
James I, 3
James River, 10, 14, 191, 205, 206
James River and Kanawha Company, 217, 223, 286
James River and Kanawha Turnpike, 426
Jamestown, 3
Jefferson, Peter, 17
Jefferson, Thomas, 76, 108, 123, 497. See Notes on the State of Virginia
Jefferson Academy, 115
Jefferson College, 275
Jefferson County, 16, 145, 161, 173, 262, 270, 310, 344, 441-43, 457-62, 492-94, 516, 620
Jehovah's Witnesses, 608-609
Jenkins, Albert G., 416-18; raid, 417-18
Jere, 568-69
Johnson, Andrew, 378, 449-52
Johnson, D. D., 483
Johnson, Joseph, 219, 253, 297
Johnson, Lyndon B., 650, 652-54
Johnson, William, 94
Johnson, William E., "Pussyfoot," 519
Jones, Hugh, 15
Jones, James G., 573, 575-79
Jones, Mary Harris, 529-33. See Mother Jones
Jones, Mother, 529-33. See Mary Harris Jones
Jones, William E., 422; report, 423-24
Jones-Imboden Raid, 422-25
Jumonville, Joseph Coulon de, 35

K

Kagi, John, 272
Kanawha Airport, 637
Kanawha coal field, 530
Kanawha County, 153; education in, 161-67; 181, 252, 262, 598, 600

Kanawha County Circuit Court, 556
Kanawha Falls, 194, 195
Kanawha River, 69, 87, 94, 123, 135, 148, 191, 193, 196, 205, 206, 223, 426, 497
Kanawha Salt Industry, 197-204; trust agreement, 198-204
Kanawha, State of, 331; ordinance establishing, 333-36; 337, 516
Kanawha Valley, 26, 103, 153, 197, 246, 290, 393, 395, 402; secessionist sentiment, 407-408; 416, 417, 418, 530, 544, 643
Keeney, C. Frank, 545, 547
Kelley, Benjamin F., 310, 398
Kendrick, William H., 553-55
Kennedy, John F., 637-41
Kentucky, 94, 153
Kenyon, William S., 528-29, 549-51
Keslers Cross Lanes, battle, 408
Kingwood *Chronicle*, 293
Knights of Labor, 530
Ku Klux Klan, 601
Kump, Herman G., 561

L

Labor, 628
Labor in mines, 481
Lake Erie, 395
Lamb, Daniel, on naming State, 339
Lander, Frederick W., 412
Lane, Warden H., 562, 564-66
Langley Field, 545
Latham, George R., 307
Latrobe, Benjamin H., 219
Laurel Hill, 94, 140, 401, 402, 403, 404
Laurel Mountain, 223, 224
Laws, 123-29
Leaden plates, 24-26. *See* Celoron de Blainville
Leadsville, 404
Lederer, John, 6
Lee, Henry, 154
Lee, Robert E., 270; on battle of Philippi, 397-400; 402, 408, 415, 422, 457-58
Lee, Wilson, 173
Leetown, 145. *See* The Bower
Legislature, 443, 465, 471-73, 501, 505, 555-56, 558-59
Leigh, Benjamin W., 237
Letcher, John, 266, 286, 287; proclamation, 316-318; 426
Letcher, Mrs. John, 433
Lewis, Andrew, 26, 41, 42, 57,

69-70, 71, 90. *See* Sandy Creek expedition
Lewis, Charles, 26, 69, 71, 74
Lewis, John, 26
Lewis, Pryce, 393-95
Lewis, Thomas, journal of, 16-22
Lewis, Virgil A., 505, 507-508
Lewis, William, 26, 197
Lewis County, 197
Lewisburg, 70, 103, 104, 172, 252, 418, 426, 445, 545, 631
Lewisburg Academy, 246
Lexington, Va., 247, 426, 433
Liberal Republican movement, 452-55
Liberty Loans, 534-35
Lightburn, Joseph A. J., 418
Lincoln, Abraham, 285, 286, 287, 292, 316; on West Virginia statehood, 358, 364, 369-71; statehood proclamation, 376-77; 392, 402, 404, 452
Linsly Institute, 378-79
Literary Fund, 161; disbursements of, 167-68
Little, Arthur D., Inc., 627
Little Kanawha, 94, 137, 139, 420, 423
Little Levels, 182
Little Report, 627
Lochaber, treaty, 63
Logan, Chief, speech, 76-78; 80
Logan County, 44, 539, 544
Logan Court House, 446
Logstons, 141
London, 6
London Company, 3
Loring, William W., 417; invasion, 418-20; proclamation, 419-20
Lost River State Park, 563
Loudoun, Earl, 42
Louis XV, 25
Lowe, Governor, Md., 219
Loyal Company, 26-27
Loyalism, 107, 108
Lumber, 481
Lynch, Charles, 108
Lynchburg, 425, 426, 429

M

MacCorkle, William A., 479-80
Madison, James, 237
Madison College, Pa., 347
Malden, 197, 247, 601-602
Manufacturing, 627
Marbois, Francois, 123
March on Logan, 530, 544-45; President's proclamation, 545-47; treason indictment, 547-49. *See* treason trials

Marietta, 152, 397
Marion County, 447-48, 508
Markets, 628
Marland, William Casey, 627, 630
Marmet, 544
Marshall, James H., 515
Marshall, James M., 17
Marshall, John, 17, 191-97, 237, 515
Marshall College, 587-88
Martial law, 541-44
Martin, Alexander, 592
Martin v. Hunters Lessee, 16
Martine, James E., 527-28
Martinsburg, 155, 173, 176, 207, 275, 405-407, 415, 426, 441, 474-76, 477
Maryland, 18, 513
Maryland v. West Virginia, 513-15
Mason, James M., 347
Mason-Dixon Line, 143, 144, 316, 513
Massachusetts, 87
Mathews, Henry Mason, 471, 474-76, 477
Matthews, Stanley, 430
Maxwell, Edwin, 488
Maxwell, Hu, 511
May, John, journal, 147-53
McClellan, George B., 310, 391-92; proclamations, 395-98, 401-402, 404-405; 407, 408
McCue, John, 172
McCulloch's Path, 140
McDowell, James, 197
McDowell County, 262, 288, 490, 539
McElhenny, John, 172, 246
McIntosh, Lachlan, 96
McKee, Alexander, 68, 107
McLure House, 218, 379
McReynolds, Mr. Justice, 556-57
Meadow Bluff, 426
Meadow River, 224, 411
Meadow River reservoir, 223-27. See Charles Ellet, Jr.
Meadows, Clarence W., 573-75
Mercer, John, 47
Mercer Academy, 162, 246
Methodist Church, 172-75, 175-82. See Francis Asbury
MGloughlin, John, 110
Michler Line, 513
Military grants, 106
Millennial Harbinger, 263
Miller, Joseph S., 471-73
Mineral County, 16, 47
Mingo County, 539, 541-44
Mingoes, 63, 87, 90
Mitchell, John, 539

Monocacy Junction, 415
Monongah explosion, 508-509
Monongahela, 94
Monongahela National Forest, 561, 578
Monongahela River, 136, 137, 422
Monongahela Valley, 154, 173
Monongahela West Penn Public Service Company, 553-54
Monongalia Academy, 592
Monongalia County, 598
Monroe, James, 237
Monroe County, 262, 417, 445
Montgomery County, 108
Morgan, Charles S., 237; address, 244-45
Morgan, Daniel, 136
Morgan, Ephraim F., 539, 541-43, 544, 545, 549
Morgan, George, 94
Morgan, Morgan, 22
Morgan, Zackquill, 139
Morgan County, 16, 42, 130, 344, 457
Morgantown, 139, 141, 154, 180, 181, 182
Morrill Act of 1862, 592
Morris, Lewis, 90
Morris, Thomas A., 403
Morris Harvey College, 621
Morse, Samuel F. B., 276
Morton, Jeremiah, 291, 292
Moss, John, 304
Mossy, 532
Moundsville, 530, 533
Mountaineer, description, 465-66. See West Virginian

N
Nance and Mays v. Brown, 525-26
National Farmers' Congress, 492
National Grange, 492
National Road, 212. See Cumberland Road
Natural gas pre-emption, 551-53
Negroes, 456
Negro Schools, 586, 601-605
Nelson, Mayor, Wheeling, 219-20
New England, 147
New Market, 425
New Orleans, 26, 198
New River, 6, 193, 205, 206, 407, 408, 426, 430
New River coal field, 522, 530
New River Gorge, 643
"New Virginia," 337
Newton D. Baker General Hospital, 577-78
Nicholas County, 583

Nomini Hall, 173. *See* Robert Carter
Nonhelema, 102, 103. *See* Grenadier Squaw
Norfolk and Western Railroad, 490-91, 643-44
Normal Schools, 587-92
North Branch of Potomac, 18
North Mountain, 50
Northern Neck, 16, 17
Northern Panhandle, 143, 207
Northwestern Turnpike, 204, 404
Northwestern Virginia, 395, 397, 404, 407, 422. *See* Trans-Allegheny
Northwestern Virginia Railroad, 221-23, 397-98, 408, 449
Notes on the Settlement and Indian Wars, 115. *See* Joseph Doddridge
Notes on the State of Virginia, 76, 123. *See* Thomas Jefferson

O

Ohio, 70, 71, 78, 80, 395, 404, 417, 556
Ohio, Department of the, 392, 395
Ohio *v.* West Virginia, 551-53
Ohio Company, 26-27, 30
Ohio County, 155, 161, 452-54
Ohio River, 24, 25, 27, 69, 70, 87, 94, 135, 147, 148, 191, 205, 206, 213, 214, 215, 223, 301, 395, 397, 404, 405, 412, 415, 426, 485, 497
Ohio Stage Company, 214
Ohio University, 253
Ohio Valley, 35, 110, 143, 156, 646
Oil, 420-22, 423
Oiltown, 423-24
Old Rehoboth Church, 173, 181
Old Stone Church, 172. *See* Lewisburg
Old Town, 138
Orange County, 22, 23
Order of Good Templars, 518
Ordinance of Secession, 295, 304, 308, 310; ratification, 316-17, 326, 347
Osburne, Josiah, 172
Ottawa Indians, 90

P

Paint Creek, 291, 522-29, 532
Paint Creek-Cabin Creek Strike, 522-29
Paradise Row, 232. *See* White Sulphur Springs
Paris, Treaty of, 1763, 56

Parker, Granville, 337
Parkersburg, 221, 222, 395, 398, 403, 426, 449
Parsons, 404. *See* Corricks Ford
Patrick, Spicer, 290, 291
Patterson's Creek, 47
Patteson, Okey L., 617-18
Patton, George S., 393-95
Patton, James, 51
Paxton, James W., 307
Pendleton County, 18, 344
Pennsylvania, 80, 83, 84, 87, 94, 143, 144, 154, 213, 395, 416, 551-53, 556
Pennsylvania *v.* West Virginia, 551-53
Petersburg, 5. *See* Fort Henry, Va.
Philadelphia, 78, 79, 110, 123, 148, 150
Philippi, 310; battle, 397-400; 401, 402, 403
"Philippi Races," 398
Pickett, Clarence, 567, 569
Piedmont, 215, 252, 425
Pierpont, Francis H., 276, 304, 307; inaugural, 325-27; convenes assembly, 345; 347, 364, 365, 366; letter to Lincoln, 368; 376, 379, 402-403, 417, 433
Pinkerton, Allan, spies on General Wise, 392-95. *See* "Major E. J. Allen"
Pitney, Mr. Justice, 540-41
Pittsburgh, 69, 87; conference at, 90-93; 96, 147, 148, 213, 395
Plymouth Company, 3
Pocahontas coal field, 491-92, 530, 643
Pocahontas County, 561
Poffenbarger, George, 524-25, 543-44
Point Pleasant, 69, 70, 71; battle, 73-75; 153, 402, 407, 418
Point of Rocks, 415
Pontiac's War, 56-58, 145
Pope, John, 417, 429
Population, 635-37
"Porte Crayon," 275-81, 405-407. *See* David Hunter Strother
Porterfield, George A., 397-400
"Potomac," 337
Potomac Company, 141
Potomac River, 17, 136, 138, 141, 191, 206, 269, 344, 405, 515
Potomac Spring, 514
Potomac State School, 619
Power, F. Ray, 605, 607
Presbyterian Church, 172-75
Preston, William, journal, 41-47; 51, 69, 88, 100, 102, 108

Preston County, 18, 384, 514
Preston's Register, 51-56. *See* Augusta County
Price, Paul H., 497, 499-500
Price, Samuel, 463
Primary election, 1960, 637-41
Princeton, 429
Privy Council, 17
Proclamation of 1763, 58, 62, 63
Prohibition movement, 518-21
Prohibition Party, 519
Proscriptive amendment, 443-44, 452
Protestant churches, 518
Pryor, John, 103, 104
Pryor, Roger A., 268

Q
Quarrier, A. W., 167
Quebec, 58
Quinn, Luke, 271, 273

R
Radical reconstruction, 463
Radical Republicans, 350, 369, 378, 444, 450, 452-54
Railroad discrimination, 485-87
Railroad mergers, 643-46
Railways, extension of, 221-22
Raleigh Courthouse, 417, 432. *See* Beckley
Raleigh Tavern, 78
Randolph, Peyton, 96
Randolph County, 18, 446, 464, 553
Rapidan Valley, 12
Rappahannock River, 13
Rathbone, John V., 420-21
Rathbone, William P., 420-21
Ravenswood, 402, 407, 417
Raw materials, 629
Red Cross, 534
Red House, Md., 404
Red House, 566
Red Stone Circuit, 173
Red Sulphur Springs, 228-31
Redhawk, 98
Redstone, Pa., 147
Reorganized government, 422
Reorganization ordinance, 323-25
Republican National Convention, 1860, 365; 1880, 478-79
Republican Party, 285-86
Rich Mountain, 401, 402, 403; battle, 404, 408
Richmond, 288
Richmond Academy, 204
Ripley, 417
Ritchie, A. F., 331
Rittenhouse, David, 145

Rives, William C., 291
Roanoke River, 8, 206
Roanoke Valley, 6
Robinson, Ira E., 525-26
Robinson, John, 47
Robinson, Neil, 511
Rockefeller, John D., 482
Rogers, David, 95
Rogers, Henry H., 644
Rogers, William Barton, 497
Rohrbough, R. Virgil, 618
Romney, 412
Roosevelt, Eleanor, 566-70
Roosevelt, Franklin D., 566, 570-73
Rosecrans, William S., 403, 408-11, 428
Rowlesburg, 401, 403
Ruffner, David, 167, 197, 246
Ruffner, Henry, 246
Ruffner, Joseph, 197
Ruffner, Lewis, 292, 601
Ruffner, Viola, 604
Ruffner Pamphlet, 246-51, 316
Rural Free Delivery, 492-94
Rumseian Society, 142
Rumsey, James, 137, 141, 142, 143
Rush, Benjamin, 115
Russell, William, letter, 87-90

S
Saint Clara, 383. *See* Joseph H. Diss Debar
Saint George, 404
Saint Louis, 221
Salem College, 621
Salley, John Peter, expedition, 26, 497. *See* John Howard
Salt industry, 197-204
Salt Sulphur Springs, 417
Salvation Army War Fund, 534
Sandy Creek expedition, 41-47. *See* Andrew Lewis
Saturday Evening Post, 546-48
School buildings, 584-85, 598
School curriculum, 598-99
School for Deaf and Blind, 620
School journal, 586
School transportation, 612, 616
Scott's Run, 568, 569, 570
Secession convention, 287, 288-93, 326, 347
Secession ordinance, 286-88; vote on, 288-90; 293
Secessionist sentiment, 407-408
Second Wheeling Convention, 310-15; declaration of, 319-21; 322; adopts reorganization ordinance, 323-25; 331; establishes State of Kanawha, 333-36; 516

Segar, Joseph E., 353
Seldes, Gilbert, 650
Semple, Robert, 172
Senate Bill No. 365, 349. See West Virginia
Seneca Indians, 90
Seneca Rocks, 578
Seneca State Forest, 561, 564
Seventh Ohio Infantry, 408
Seward, William H., on West Virginia statehood, 359-61; 369, 377
Sharples, 544
Shawhan, Hubbard W., 561-64
Shawnee Indians, 42, 63; answer Virginians, 68; 80, 87, 90, 99, 101
Shephard, Hayward, 271, 273
Shepherd College, 589
Shepherdstown, 141, 207
Shenandoah River, 269
Shenandoah Valley, 11, 12, 412, 425, 429, 441. See Valley of Virginia
Sheridan, Philip, 429
Shipman, J. Versus, 553
Shippensburg, Pa., 147
Sigel, Franz, 425
Simpson, Gilbert, 135
Simpson, Howard, 645
Simpson Creek Baptist Church, 185-87
Sinsel, Harmon, on naming State, 337
Six Nations, 63, 94. See Iroquois
Smallpox, act to regulate inoculation, 133-35
Smith, Benjamin, 253
Smith, Benjamin H., 378
Smith, "Captain Bill," 446
Smith, Devereux, letter, 63-68
Smith, Fannie N., 601
Smith, Hulett C., 641-43
Sons of Temperance, 518
South Branch River, 18, 422, 515
South Branch Valley, 110, 172, 173, 404
Southern Rights Convention, 297-98
Spencer, 417
Spotswood, Alexander, 11, 12
Spotswood Expedition, 11
Springs of Virginia, 227-33
Standard Oil Company, 482
Stanton, Edwin M., 301, 359, 369
Stark, William B., 426-28
State Board of Public Works, 471
State 4-H Camp, 553-55. See Jackson's Mill

State Police, 544
State seal and motto, 383-85
State Tax Commission, 510
State Tax Commissioner, 501
Statute of Religious Freedom, 172
Staunton, 22, 26, 422, 426
Staunton and Parkersburg Turnpike, 204, 403
Stephen, Adam, 51, 57, 90; address, 145-47
Stephens, Aaron C., 271
Steubenville, 214
Stevenson, William E., 453-55, 456-57, 560
Stewart, James H., 511
Stonewall Brigade, 434
Story, Joseph, 16
Strayer, George D., 612
Strayer Survey, 612-16
Strother, David Hunter, 275-81, 405-407. See Porte Crayon
Stuart, Chapman J., on naming State, 340
Stuart, John, 96, 103
Stuart recreation area, 578
Sullivan, Carl R., 650
Sullivan, Daniel, 111
Summers, George W., address, 251-61; 290, 291, 292, 433
Summers, Lewis, 206, 237, 253
Summersville, 408, 418, 424
Sumner, Charles, 350
Surphlitt, Robert, 107
Sutton, James, 172
Sutton, 424
Swan, James, 383
Swann, Thomas, 219, 220, 221
Swanson, Claude A., 526-27
Swearingen, Thomas, 137
Sweeney, Andrew J., proclamations, 293-94
Sweet Springs, 426
Switzer, Rufus, 632

T
Tarr, Campbell, 304, 307
Tate, W. M., 425
Tax Commission, 484-85, 501
Tax exemptions, 471-73
Tax Limitation Amendment, 558-60, 613
Tax reform, 500-505
Taxation, 261, 629
Taxpayers' Protective Association, 519
Teacher certification, 598
Teacher retirement, 605-606
Teacher tenure, 605

Teachers' salaries, 584-86, 598, 612
Teay's Valley, 246
Tenth U. S. Infantry, 545
Test oath, 443, 583
Thirteenth Amendment, 450
Thirty-First Confederate Infantry, 434
Thirty-Fourth Massachusetts Infantry, 426
Thirty-Ninth Congress, 458
Thirty-Sixth Confederate Infantry, 434
Tichenell, Moses, 374-76
Tidd, Charles, 272
Tidewater, 191, 215, 252
Todd, John, 70
Tompkins, C. C., 430, 432
Topography, 629
Tories, 87, 107
Townsend, Thomas C., 558
Trans-Allegheny, 162; public improvements, 215-17; 395, 497. See Northwestern Virginia
Trans-Allegheny Historical Society, 505
Transportation, 628
Transylvania University, 173
Treason trials, 544-49. See March on Logan
Trent, William, 35
Trent, William W., 618-19
Tucker County, 446
Tunley, Roul, article by, 646-48
Tuohy, Walter, 645
Turner, George W., 271, 273
Tuskegee Normal and Industrial Institute, 600
Twelve Pole Valley, 153
Twenty-Second Virginia Infantry, 393, 434
Twenty-Third Ohio Infantry, 428
Tygart River, 408
Tygart Valley, 179
Tygart Valley resettlement project, 566
Tyler, Erastus B., 408, 430
Tyler, John, 237, 291

U
Unemployment, 627-28
United Mine Workers of America, 522, 530, 539, 549
Union, 445
United States Congress, 213, 369, 492-94
United States Constitution, 94, 145
United States District Court, 539
United States House of Representatives, debates W. Va. statehood, 353-57; 371, 493-94
United States Senate, Committee on Education and Labor, Report (1913), 522, 526-29; (1922), 545, 549-51
United States State Department, 389
United States Supreme Court, 16-17, 213, 458-62, 471, 514-15, 516-18, 539-41, 551-53, 556-57, 609-12, 619
United States War Department, 389
University of Virginia, 161
Uvilla, 492

V
Valley of Virginia, 26, 215, 252, 342, 343. See Shenandoah Valley
Valley Turnpike, 441
Van Buren, Martin, 233
Vandalia, 94, 95
Van Devanter, Mr. Justice, 551-53
Van Meter, Garret, letter, 107-109
Van Meter, Isaac, 178
Van Winkle, Peter G., 221; on naming state, 339-40; 376, 378; on Johnson impeachment, 449-52
Viquesney, Jules A., 560
Virginia, Second Charter of, 3-5
Virginia Central Railroad, 426
Virginia Court of Appeals, 17
Virginia Debt, 516-18, 555
Virginia Dynasty, 474
Virginia Gazette, 79
Virginia Military Institute, 204, 426
Virginia ordinance of secession, 286-88; delegate vote on, 288-90; 295, 304, 308, 310; ratification, 316-17; 326, 347
Virginia Senate, 237, 252
Virginia Temperance Society, 518
Virginia - Pennsylvania boundary dispute, 143-45
Virginia and Tennessee Railroad, 416, 429
Virginia v. West Virginia (1867-71), 457-62; (1906-1911), 516-18
Virginian Railroad, 644-45
Vocational Education, 612, 614

W
Wade, Alexander L., 598
Wade, Benjamin, 349, 451

Walker, John, 90
Walker, Thomas, 27, 90
Waller, John, 183
Wanamaker, John, 492
War Labor Policy Board, 539
Warm Springs, 130-33, 136, 227-29. *See* Bath, Berkeley Springs
Washington, Booker T., 600-605
Washington, Bushrod, 138
Washington, George, 35, 40, 41, 42; proposes frontier defense, 47-50; 101, 130, 141; journey, 1784, 135-41; 154, 227
Washington, Lewis W., 269-72
Washington, Samuel, 131
Washington College, 246
Washington County, Pa., 115, 145
Washington, D. C., 429, 493
Washington Hall, 304
Water resources, 629
Watoga State Park, 561, 563
Wayne County, 446, 582, 632
Webster County, 262
Welles, Gideon, 359
Wellsburg, 115, 207
West, James G., 331
West Augusta, District of, 63, 87, 95
West Liberty, 155
West Liberty Normal, 589
West Point, 204
West Union, 383
West Virginia, naming of, 337-43; statehood application, 347-49; statehood bill (*See* Senate Bill No. 365), 353-57, 359, 364-71; statehood law, 371-73; proclamation, 376-77; seal, coat of arms, motto, 383-85
West Virginia capital site, vote on, 476-77
West Virginia certificates, 516
West Virginia Conservation Commission, 510-13
West Virginia Education Association, 605, 619-20
West Virginia Geological and Economic Survey, 497-500, 633
West Virginia Handbook and Immigrants Guide, 465-67. *See* Joseph H. Diss Debar
West Virginia Historical Society, 505
West Virginia Historical and Antiquarian Society, 505
West Virginia Industrial and Publicity Commission, 627
West Virginia Maneuver Area, 578-79
West Virginia National Guard, 533

West Virginia resources and advantages, 479-82
West Virginia School of Medicine, Dentistry and Nursing, 617-18
West Virginia State Board of Education, 12
West Virginia State Board of Education *v.* Barnette *et al*, 608-609
West Virginia Supreme Court of Appeals, 472-73, 543-44, 556
West Virginia University, 553, 554; rules and regulations, 593-95; W. L. Wilson on, 595-99; 643
West Virginia Wesleyan College, 619, 621
West Virginia in World War I, 533-35
West Virginian, description, 465-66. *See* Mountaineer
Western counties, formation of, 22-25
Western Virginia, education in, 161-68
Westmoreland County, Pa., 63, 87
Weston, 417, 422, 424, 428, 429
Westsylvania, 94, 95
Wharton, Samuel, 94
Wheat, James S., 307
Wheeling, 96, 110, 111, 137, 147, 148, 173, 207; described, 209-12; 213, 217, 223; Mayor Sweeney's proclamations, 293-94; 299, 301, 310, 317, 373; 395, 398, 402, 422, 476, 522
Wheeling Bridge, 213-15
Wheeling Convention, First, 347
Wheeling Convention, Second, 310-15; declaration of, 319-21; 322; adopts reorganization ordinance, 323-25; 331; establishes State of Kanawha, 333-36; 516
Wheeling *Intelligencer*, 365
Whiskey Rebellion, 154-56
White, Albert B., 501, 505, 510
White, Israel C., at White House Conference on Conservation, 497-99, 510
White, William R., 584
White Eyes, 68
White House Conference of Governors, 497-99, 510
White Sulphur Springs, 227-28, 231-33, 291, 292, 576-77
Willey, Waitman T., 253, 304; address, 309; on naming State, 339; on B & O R.R., 344-45; presents statehood application,

347-49; on West Virginia Bill, 351-52; 376, 450
Willey Amendment, 341, 350-51, 371, 373; ratified, 376
Williamsburg, 12, 27, 78, 99, 490
Will's Creek, 26, 32
Wilson, Andrew, 307
Wilson, E. Willis, 485-90
Wilson, James, 90
Wilson, William L., 493, 593
Winchester, 22, 47, 69, 227, 441
Winchester and Potomac Railroad, 441
Winslow, Benjamin, 17
Wirt, William, 157
Wirt County, 420-21
Wise, Henry A., 265, 270, 277, 291, 292, 392-94, 407, 408, 416
Wise, O. Jennings, 265-69. *See* Clemens-Wise duel
Withers, Alexander Scott, 109. *See Chronicles of Border Warfare*
Woman's Christian Temperance Union, 518-19
Wood, Abraham, 5, 6, 7, 10
Wood, James, 90
Wood, Thomas, 11

Woodburn Academy, 592
Woods, Archibald, 156
Woods, A. P., 294
Woods, J. M., 545
Woods, Thomas, 6, 7
Woodward, S. H., 307
Work, Glenn, 569
World War I, 533-35
World War II, 573-79
Wyandot Indians, 90

Y

Yellow Creek, 76, 80
Yost law, 519-21
Yohiogany (Youghiogheny) River, 137
Young, John Russell, 421-22
Young Men's Christian Association, 534

Z

Zane, Ebenezer, report of, 109-12
Zane, Elizabeth, exploit of, 109-12
Zane, Jonathan, 110
Zane, Silas, 110
Zane, William, 110
Zanesville, 214